Greg Perry

Visual Basic® 6 in 21 Days

SAMS

A Division of Macmillan Computer Publishing
201 West 103rd St., Indianapolis, Indiana, 46290 USA

Sams Teach Yourself Visual Basic® 6 in 21 Days

Copyright © 1998 by Sams

International Standard Book Number: 0-672-31310-3

Library of Congress Catalog Card Number: 98-84132

Printed in the United States of America

First Printing: September 1998

02 01 00 8

Trademarks

All terms mentioned in this book that are known to be trademarks or service marks have been appropriately capitalized. Sams cannot attest to the accuracy of this information. Use of a term in this book should not be regarded as affecting the validity of any trademark or service mark.

Windows is a registered trademark of Microsoft Corporation.

Visual Basic is a registered trademark of Microsoft Corporation.

Warning and Disclaimer

Every effort has been made to make this book as complete and as accurate as possible, but no warranty or fitness is implied. The information provided is on an "as is" basis.

Executive Editor
Chris Denny

Acquisitions Editor
Sharon Cox

Development Editor
Tony Amico

Managing Editor
Jodi Jensen

Project Editor
Maureen A. McDaniel

Copy Editors
Bart Reed
Heather Stith

Indexer
Charlotte Clapp

Technical Editor
Bob Wasserman

Software Development Specialist
John Warriner

Team Coordinator
Carol Ackerman

Production
Mike Henry
Linda Knose
Tim Osborn
Staci Somers
Mark Walchle

Overview

Contents

APPENDIXES

About the Author

GREG PERRY is a speaker and writer on both the programming and the application sides of computing. He is known for his skills at bringing advanced computer topics down to the novice's level. Perry has been a programmer and trainer since the early 1980s. He received his first degree in computer science and a master's degree in corporate finance. Perry is the author or co-author of more than 50 books, including *Sams Teach Yourself Windows 95 in 24 Hours*, *Absolute Beginner's Guide to Programming*, *Sams Teach Yourself Office 97 in 24 Hours*, *Absolute Beginner's Guide to C*, and *Moving from C to C++*. He also writes about rental-property management and loves to travel.

Dedication

To Scott and Gail Kinney, who demonstrate the definition of friendship and blessings in all they do.

Acknowledgments

My thanks go to Sharon Cox, Tony Amico, and the entire staff of Joe Wikert's group who continue to produce only the best programming books on the market. Joe was with me on my first programming book years ago and I appreciate this one just as much as the first. Sharon Cox goes to bat for me more than an Acquisitions Editor should and I want Sharon to know how grateful that I am. In addition, if this book is good, it's more due to Tony's eagle-eye guidance than anything I've done as an author.

Among the Sams editors and staff who produced this book, I want to send special thanks to the following people who made this book a success: Jodi Jensen, Maureen McDaniel, Bart Reed, Charlotte Clapp. Special thanks go to the technical editor, Bob Wasserman.

I just couldn't write a book for Sams Publishing without mentioning Dean Miller and Richard Swadley. In every book I've written for Sams, they have had a direct influence, some way, in my motivation and gratefulness for being part of the most outstanding programming book publisher in the business.

My lovely and gracious bride stands by my side day and night. Thank you once again. You, precious Jayne, are everything that matters to me on earth. The best parents in the world, Glen and Bettye Perry, continue to encourage and support me in every way. I am who I am because of both of them and I thank them for all that they've done for me.

Tell Us What You Think!

As the reader of this book, *you* are our most important critic and commentator. We value your opinion and want to know what we're doing right, what we could do better, what areas you'd like to see us publish in, and any other words of wisdom you're willing to pass our way.

As the Executive Editor for the Visual Basic Programming team at Macmillan Computer Publishing, I welcome your comments. You can fax, e-mail, or write me directly to let me know what you did or didn't like about this book—as well as what we can do to make our books stronger.

Please note that I cannot help you with technical problems related to the topic of this book, and that due to the high volume of mail I receive, I might not be able to reply to every message.

When you write, please be sure to include this book's title and author as well as your name and phone or fax number. I will carefully review your comments and share them with the author and editors who worked on the book.

Fax:	317-817-7070
E-mail:	`vb@mcp.com`
Mail:	Executive Editor Visual Basic Programming Macmillan Computer Publishing 201 West 103rd Street Indianapolis, IN 46290 USA

Introduction

For the next 21 days, you will learn how to write Windows programs using Visual Basic. You will also have fun along the way! Visual Basic is an enjoyable language due to its visual environment. Much of building a Windows program in Visual Basic requires dragging and dropping graphic objects onto the screen from a toolbox which houses those objects. Your Windows program appears before your eyes as you add the objects. Visual Basic is one of the first programming languages to incorporate a true *WYSIWYG* (*What You See Is What You Get*) environment. The program that you build looks like the program your users see when they run the program from Windows.

If you've never written a program before, you will successfully learn to program with Visual Basic after you are through with the next 21-day sessions. Each one-hour lesson covers Visual Basic, from start to finish, in a tutorial style that includes questions and answers, exercises, and bonus projects that show specific Visual Basic commands and features in use.

This 21-day tutorial teaches both theory and applies that theory in an easy-to-understand hands-on format. You begin creating your very first Visual Basic program in the first day's lesson! The goal of teaching Visual Basic to a newcomer at times is challenging due to today's broad range of computing skills. Some move to Visual Basic after programming in more advanced (and more tedious) programming languages such as C++. Others come to Visual Basic with only a QBasic background. QBasic is a language supplied with PCs for years, but QBasic offers only a slow, text-based MS-DOS programming environment. Despite its archaic text-based mode, the QBasic language provides a wonderful introduction to Visual Basic because Visual Basic's programming language is an extension of QBasic. Some people want to program but have never programmed in any other language before, so not only is Visual Basic brand new but so is the nature of programming.

Visual Basic is much more than just a programming language. The programming language forms the background of all that takes place in a running Visual Basic program. Nevertheless, the language is a secondary consideration to the user interface. A Windows program offers a high degree of user interaction using the graphical elements that form the objects on the window the user sees. If the user interface is not correct, users will not like the program. The programmer will get more support phone calls. The users will be hesitant to upgrade to future program enhancements.

Therefore, the user interface is stressed throughout these 21 days so that you know exactly how to define the best interface for your users. Only after you build a usable interface should you then go to work on the program's mechanics that make the program do the job you designed it to do.

In today's fast-changing world, program maintenance is more critical than ever before. Companies change, industries consolidate, spin-offs happen. The computer programs of today must be fluid and maintainable so that programmers can quickly change the program to meet the needs of a changing environment in which the programs are used. This tutorial stresses the importance of proper program design, coding, testing, and maintenance every step of the way. A program is written once but updates many times, and you can ease the burden of program maintenance by following a few general guidelines when you write your program.

This 21-day tutorial strikes a balance between usability and theory, always showing you what you need and not wasting your time with the tiny fragments of Visual Basic that the typical programmer may never have to know. Importance is placed on building good programmers who can build good programs that are clear, concise, documented, and simple to maintain.

In addition, these 21 days provide ample time to study Visual Basic in depth without getting bogged down in the minor issues that don't concern the typical Visual Basic programmer. At the same time, you will learn about many aspects of Visual Basic. The following is only a partial collection of the topics that this 21-day tutorial covers:

- Building a useful user interface
- Using the Application Wizard to generate a program shell instantly
- Writing Visual Basic code in clear constructs to make the code run smoothly
- Understanding the most common tools used in the Visual Basic environment
- Mastering the art of getting the errors out of a Visual Basic program
- Incorporated database technology into your Visual Basic programs
- Embedding Internet access in the heart of your programs to put your users online to the Web
- Providing external ActiveX controls so that Visual Basic can use tools from other languages and Windows applications
- Using Visual Basic's ability to create brand new ActiveX controls so that you can increase Visual Basic's programmability and the tools that your users interact with by making your own interface objects

- Accessing the online help engine in Visual Basic so that the programs that you write are accessible to your users and offer the help services that your users require
- Creating graphics to add pizzazz to the screens that you design
- Using common dialog boxes so that your users can access the typical features they expect in a Windows application
- Putting toolbars and coolbars in your programs so that your users have one-button access to the common commands and tasks they require
- Mastering the art of programming the Windows API routines so that you can implement Windows features not normally found inside Visual Basic
- Improving the enjoyment of the programs that you write by adding multimedia sound and graphics to your Windows programs

Are you ready to make the move to Visual Basic? If you are, you will be pleased to have this copy of *Sams Teach Yourself Visual Basic 6 in 21 Days*. From the first day to the last, you will improve your Visual Basic skill set so that you can write virtually any Visual Basic program that you require.

WEEK 1

At a Glance

This week begins a rewarding experience for you. You will learn how to use Visual Basic to create your own computer programs! This first week introduces you to the preliminaries of Visual Basic by showing you how to maneuver within the Visual Basic environment, how to create the visual elements of a Windows program, and how to master the fundamentals of the Visual Basic programming language.

Where You're Going

Despite this first week's introductory nature, you will be working with Visual Basic in a hands-on mode starting in Day 1, "Welcome to Visual Basic." In the opening lesson you create a working Visual Basic application that looks and acts like other Windows programs you've used. Each succeeding lesson builds from there showing you how to add new elements to your programs and how to make them more powerful. At the end of each day, you'll find a series of questions and exercises that help focus your attention on the most important parts of the day's lesson so that you can review trouble areas and practice additional hands-on program development.

Programming requires more than just a knowledge of a language. As you progress through this week and the two weeks that follow, you will understand the importance of writing clear, well-documented programs. The environments in which people use computer programs change and so must the programs. By following a few good programming practices from the beginning, you create programs that will be easier to adapt for future updates.

Visual Basic creates Windows programs. In this first week, you learn a little about virtually every element of Visual Basic programming. You'll learn how to place objects on a Windows screen, create and respond to pull-down menus, and manage the interaction between your program and its user. You'll begin to master the heart of Visual Basic: the programming language that ties everything together.

Visual Basic programming is one of the most enjoyable ways to program. Much of creating a Visual Basic program requires placing graphic objects on the screen and setting attributes for those objects that determine how the objects are to look and behave. Visual Basic is truly the only programming language today that beginning programmers can learn easily. In addition, Visual Basic allows advanced programmers to create powerful Windows applications.

Set your sights high! If you've never programmed before, or if you've never programmed in Visual Basic, you'll enjoy what Visual Basic can do for you and you'll be surprised what you can do with Visual Basic.

WEEK 1

DAY 1

Welcome to Visual Basic

Visual Basic 6 is Microsoft's latest and greatest version of the Visual Basic programming language. Although writing programs can be a tedious chore at times, Visual Basic reduces the effort required on your part and makes programming enjoyable. Visual Basic makes many aspects of programming as simple as dragging graphic objects onto the screen with your mouse.

Today begins your 21-day Visual Basic tutorial. Before today ends, you will have created your very first Visual Basic application. In the next three weeks, you will master Visual Basic 6, and you will be able to develop applications that do work you need done.

Today, you learn the following:

- Visual Basic's history
- The programming design and authoring process
- How Visual Basic's visual interface makes programming easy and fun
- The Application wizard
- Why event-driven programming is so important to a Windows environment

Visual Basic's Background

By understanding the background of Visual Basic, you'll gain insight into Visual Basic 6 and you'll be better equipped to use Visual Basic. Microsoft based Visual Basic on a *programming language* written for beginners called *BASIC*. BASIC has been around for more than 35 years in one form or another. The original language designers wanted to develop a programming language that beginners could use. With BASIC, new programmers could become proficient right away. Other programming languages of the day, such as COBOL, FORTRAN, and Assembler, required much more study than BASIC before one could use them effectively.

NEW TERM *BASIC* stands for *Beginner's All-purpose Symbolic Instruction Code*. That's some abbreviation!

NEW TERM A *programming language* is a set of commands and command options, called *arguments*, that you use to give instructions to the computer. Computers cannot (yet) understand human languages because people deal well with ambiguous commands, and a computer cannot understand such ambiguity. A programming language must be more precise than a spoken language.

Programming languages are easier to learn than foreign languages. Computer languages often have fewer than 300 commands, and many of those commands are words you already understand, such as `Open` and `Next`.

Although the BASIC language was designed for beginners, a BASIC *program* was still rather cryptic and required study. Listing 1.1 shows a program written in BASIC. The program's goal is to print the mathematical squares for the numbers 1 through 10. Although you can probably guess at many of the program's logic and commands, the program is certainly not the clearest piece of literature in the world and requires that you understand BASIC before you can fully comprehend the reason for all of its elements.

NEW TERM *Programs* are often comprised of several files that interact with one another, so you'll often see the term *application* used as a synonym for all of a *program*'s files. The program, or application written in a programming language, is a set of instructions that directs the computer.

LISTING 1.1. EARLY BASIC PROGRAMS HAD LINE NUMBERS AND WERE SOMEWHAT CRYPTIC.

```
10 REM This program computes and prints the first ten squares
20 CLS
30 PRINT "Squares from 1 to 10"
40 PRINT "Value", "Squared"
50 FOR N = 1 TO 10
60   PRINT N, (N*N)
70 NEXT N
80 PRINT
90 END
```

Do	Don't
	DON'T fret over all this talk about squaring numbers from 1 to 10. Don't like math? No problem! Visual Basic will do all the math you need done.

If you were to run the BASIC program, here is the output you would see:

OUTPUT

```
Squares from 1 to 10
Value          Squared
1              1
2              4
3              9
4              16
5              25
6              36
7              49
8              64
9              81
10             100
```

Notice that BASIC is strictly a text-based language. Both its program and output are textual and do not produce the graphical, windowed output that today's programs produce.

Microsoft did not create Visual Basic directly from the original BASIC language. Although the BASIC language evolved through several stages over its 35-plus year history, it kept its original structure in most of its incarnations. When Microsoft decided to use BASIC as its primary programming language supplied with the original MS-DOS operating system, however, it honed the BASIC language and added functionality to

BASIC by creating several incarnations of BASIC with names such as MBASIC (for Microsoft BASIC), GWBASIC (for, some say, Gee-Whiz BASIC), BASICA (for BASIC Advanced), QuickBASIC, and QBasic (which is still supplied on Windows operating system CD-ROMs).

Throughout BASIC's evolution, the BASIC language kept its simple nature while gaining powerful new commands along the way. The text-based nature of languages such as QBasic helps new programmers get up to speed more quickly than many nontext languages such as Visual C++ do. To maintain this ease of use, Microsoft wanted to keep all its BASIC language versions *interpreted* in nature as opposed to *compiled*. A programmer can execute a program based on an interpreted language immediately and see results and errors instantly. Such feedback is critical for beginners who need a quick response when learning how to program. Compiled languages, although they run faster and are better suited for commercial program development environments, require much more effort to work with.

New Term An *interpreted* language, such as BASIC, lets you run programs *as you write them*. Interpreted languages make good learning platforms because of their quick feedback. A *compiled language* requires extra steps, called *compilation* and *linking*, before the programmer can run the program. The compiled program resides in the computer's own native language and not in the programming language that the programmer originally used.

As Windows became more popular, Microsoft realized that the text-based QBasic would not work as a windowed programming language. Microsoft developed Visual Basic, a language based on BASIC but one much more suited to today's windowed environments. Whereas QBasic and all other BASIC incarnations were text-based, Visual Basic is graphical. Although a Visual Basic program might contain *code* that looks somewhat like the program in Listing 1.1, the majority of a Visual Basic program consists of graphical elements that have little resemblance to the text-based code in Listing 1.1. Figure 1.1 shows a Visual Basic screen that contains many pieces from a Visual Basic program.

New Term *Code* is another name for a program's set of instructions.

Note

> Well before you finish the book, you'll understand every item inside Figure 1.1. Although the screen looks busy and overwhelming, Visual Basic is simple to understand.

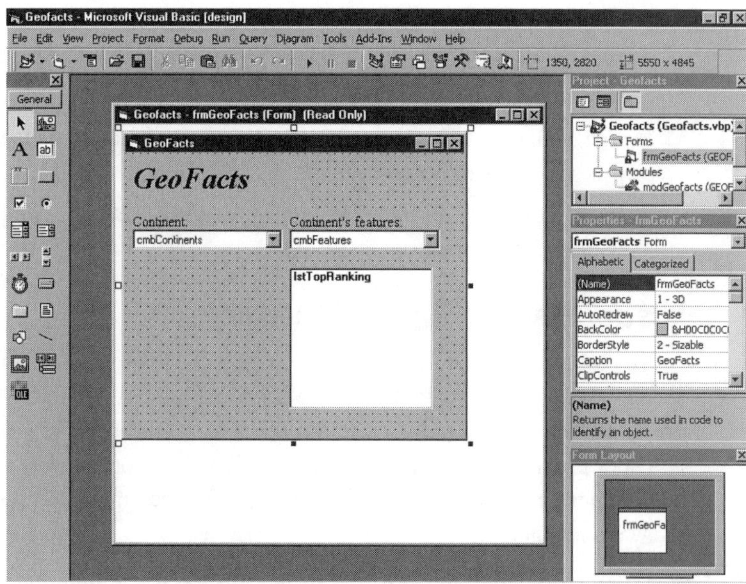

FIGURE 1.1

The Visual Basic programming screen can look busy, but it is simple to use.

In addition to being graphical and simple to use, Visual Basic has become one of today's most popular languages because it is both interpreted and compiled! You can test a Visual Basic program that you write by running the program interpretively until you get all the *bugs* out. Once you eliminate the bugs and thoroughly test your program, you then can compile the program into a fast and secure (nobody can easily modify the program) executable program that you can distribute to others to use. By making the compilation process a simple menu option, Visual Basic handles the more difficult compilation steps (including something cryptic called *link editing*) that other languages used to require you to go through.

NEW TERM A *bug* is a program error. If a program that you write does not work properly, you will need to *debug* the program by removing all the bugs.

About the time Microsoft released the first version of Visual Basic, many people were predicting the demise of the BASIC language (and its offshoots such as QBasic). These naysayers thought any language based on BASIC could not be used for serious programs because they never thought of BASIC as a serious language. Languages such as C, C++, and Pascal were all the rage because of their compilation abilities and also because their programming structures lent themselves more to a Windows environment. With Visual Basic, Microsoft taught the programming community these and other lessons:

- A BASIC-like language can be both simple to understand and powerful.
- With the right interface, a BASIC-like language works well for a Windows environment.
- Visual Basic can be both an interpreted and a compiled language depending on the programmer's requirements.
- Instead of being obsolete, a language based on BASIC can become one of the most widely used languages in the world.

Visual Basic's Visual Nature

As you saw in Figure 1.1, Visual Basic 6 is more than just a programming language. The secret to Visual Basic is in its name: *visual*. With today's Windows operating systems, a program must be able to interact with the screen, keyboard, mouse, and printer graphically. Older programming languages, such as BASIC, worked well in a text-only computing environment, but such languages do not support the graphical interface needed for today's computers.

You won't even learn much of the Visual Basic programming language in the first week of this tutorial because much of the Visual Basic programming process requires interacting with the Visual Basic visual environment and requires very little of the programming language details to make working programs. Only when you need to write more advanced programs will you need to learn more of the Visual Basic language than just the handful of commands you learn in your first few days.

> **Note**
>
> It's not just the underlying BASIC language that makes Visual Basic simple to learn and use. Much of a program's development consists of dragging and dropping (with your mouse) elements onto the Visual Basic screen when you create a program. Instead of writing a series of complicated input and output statements to interact with *users*, you will drag controls, such as text boxes and command buttons, onto the screen; Visual Basic takes care of making the controls operate properly when the user runs the program.

NEW TERM A *user* is a person who uses a program. You, the programmer who writes programs, are also a user because you use programs that you and others write. The Visual Basic programming system is nothing more than a program that you use to create other programs.

Visual Basic comes in several varieties including the following:

- **Visual Basic Enterprise Edition:** Created for team programming environments and client/server computing where applications distribute processing and data among several computers.
- **Visual Basic Professional Edition:** Geared toward professional programmers who want to get the most from the Visual Basic programming environment. This edition includes a full set of tools and wizards that help you package and distribute applications. This 21-day tutorial assumes that you use the Professional Edition as most Visual Basic programmers do. Nevertheless, if you use one of the other editions, the majority of this book also applies to you because this tutorial does not focus on the Professional Edition-only tools as much as it presents a well-rounded introduction to the Visual Basic programming environment and language.
- **Visual Basic Learning Edition:** The essentials with the standard complement of programming tools and everything one needs to get started programming. A multimedia CD-ROM called *Learn VB Now* comes with the package as well as a full set of Microsoft Developer Network documentation so that you will have the help that you require to learn and use Visual Basic.

Note

A special edition of Visual Basic comes with a package called *Visual Studio*. Visual Studio is a programming environment that supports several Microsoft languages including Visual Basic, Visual C++, and Visual J++. When you use Visual Basic, you use the same environment that users of these other languages also use. Therefore, if you move to another programming language, you will not have to master a new set of menus and dialog boxes.

Why Write Programs?

Many computer users will never need to learn computer programming. Some people buy all their programs from the store or from mail-order outlets and never need more specialized programs. Rarely, however, will you be able to find exactly the program you need for a particular task, especially if you use a computer to help you in your business or scientific research. In addition, you might think of a new game concept that you want to turn into a hot-selling computer game so that you can retire early in the Cayman Islands. If you want a specific application but cannot find what you need on the store shelves, or if you want to write new programs for a living, you'll need to design and write those programs using a programming language such as Visual Basic.

Remember that you cannot just tell a computer what to do and expect it to work for you. A computer must have a detailed list of instructions because the computer is a dumb machine that does nothing on its own. You give your computer those instructions in the form of a program. A Visual Basic program consists of program code (similar to that in Listing 1.1) and visual elements that define the screen and the Windows controls that the program's user interacts with when the user runs the program.

Tip

When you learn Visual Basic, you also learn how to automate common application programs such as those you find in Microsoft Office. Microsoft Office is comprised of several programs that work together, such as a word processor, worksheet, and database program. Microsoft Office also contains the complete Visual Basic 6 programming language with which you can automate Microsoft Office applications. (Microsoft Office 95, the edition that preceded Microsoft Office 97, contain *Visual Basic for Applications* (*VBA*), which is similar but not fully compatible to Visual Basic version 6.) For example, you can automate your accounting month-end procedures by writing a program that consolidates your month-end Excel worksheets. The Visual Basic that comes with applications is not the full Visual Basic development system you get with Visual Basic 6, but it does contain the complete language so that you can fully control the applications.

The Programming Process

Over time you'll find your own way of writing programs that works best for you. Nevertheless, you'll generally follow these standard set of steps when creating your Visual Basic programs:

1. Decide what your application is to do by creating an overall design.
2. Create the visual portion of your application (the screens and menus that your users will interact with).
3. Add Visual Basic programming language code to tie the visual elements together and to automate the program.
4. Test your application to locate and remove any bugs you find.
5. Compile your tested application and distribute the compiled application to your users.

Do	Don't
DO test your application to rid it of bugs and then distribute your application program to others. Despite the virtual impossibility of eliminating all bugs, do test, test, and test again trying all possibilities in the program to help ensure that you've found as many bugs as you can before you compile and distribute your program.	**DON'T** be surprised if a user locates another bug (or several of them). The most thorough testing never guarantees that all bugs are gone. The more that your program does, the more likely a bug will raise its ugly head some day when you and your users least expect it.

By waiting until you've thoroughly tested your Visual Basic application program before you compile the program, you help speed up the testing process. When you test your program interactively, you can locate and correct bugs that you find more easily and quickly. Visual Basic includes a special helper system called a *debugger* that you can use to help you locate bugs that appear during testing. You'll learn in Day 21, "Distributing Your Applications," how to use the debugger.

New Term A *debugger* is an interactive monitoring system that you can turn on and off inside Visual Basic that helps you locate statements that contain bugs. For example, if you run a program you've written and the program computes an amount incorrectly, the debugger can help you quickly find the statement in the program that contains the bug.

Before Visual Basic, writing a program was more tedious for several reasons. In a text-based environment, you would have to design on paper all the screens that the user would see. You would then take that paper to the users to see if you were designing exactly what they wanted. If you were designing a program for mass distribution, such as a game or a general-purpose business application, you would still write down all the screens, create complicated data flows to and from the various screens, design the disk files needed by the program, and basically plan every detail before you ever went to the keyboard.

Visual Basic's visual nature encourages you to go to the keyboard much earlier in the programming process. Instead of using paper, you'll design screens with Visual Basic's tools. Figure 1.2 contains one such screen. No code is required to produce a screen such as this one; all you need to do is drag the various controls onto the *Form window*.

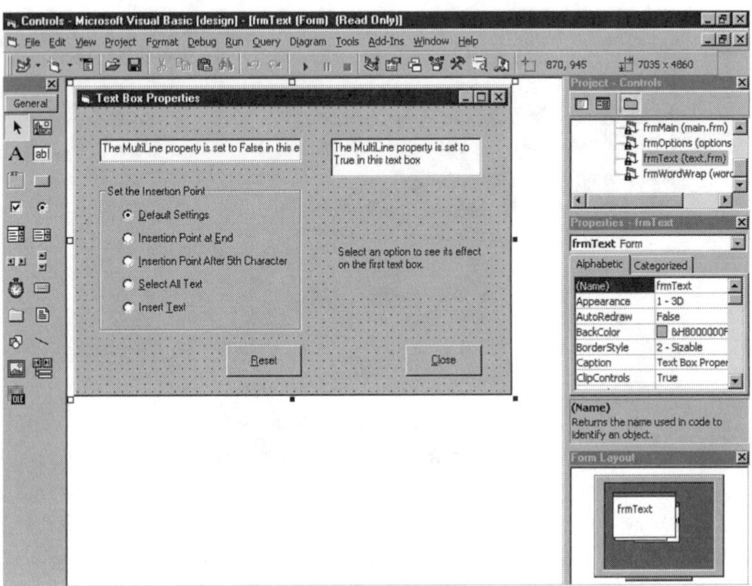

FIGURE 1.2.
Visual Basic enables you to design and create screens as you create your program.

NEW TERM The *Form window*, also called a *form*, comprises the background of a Visual Basic program's screen and contains elements such as command buttons and scrollbars. Programs may require one or more form windows depending on the nature and complexity of the program.

Even before you add code, you can test your program screens (each form is the basis for a screen) because Visual Basic enables you to run your program interactively after you create at least one form. You can make sure that your screens look good, and you can show your *prototype* to users who have requested the program to ensure that they like what you are creating. Making changes in this prototype pre-coding stage is much easier than making changes after you add the code. Visual Basic's prototyping capability is one way Visual Basic helps you create programs quickly and accurately.

NEW TERM A *prototype* is a test program that contains virtually no functionality but does contain some or all of the screens that the final program is to contain. You and your program's ultimate users can test the prototype to see whether you are including all of the needed screen elements.

Once you create your program, test your program, compile your program, and distribute your program to your users, you still can make changes to the program. Doing so, however, is tedious and requires that you re-distribute all the application's files once again to the user. Nevertheless, the earlier you locate problems, the simpler those problems are to repair.

Understanding Program Maintenance

Bugs are not the only reason that you will work on a program after you think you're completely done with it. *Program maintenance* is necessary because requirements change, companies change, and laws change. You must also change the programs you write so that they remain viable programs; you will need to update your program periodically to reflect changes that impact the program. In addition, users will think of new things that they want the program to do.

New Term *Program maintenance* is the term used for the updating of a program after the program is put into use. This update may be a result of a user's request or a change in the way the program needs to operate.

It is said that a program is written once and modified many times. The more program maintenance you perform, the more likely that your program will be up-to-date and in use. You may want to release new versions of your program so that users can, with a different version number on the opening screen that you place there, keep track of the latest version installed on their system.

Document your programs so that other programmers will understand your code if they must make changes to it later.

As you learn more about the Visual Basic programming language, you'll learn how to write code that is clear, and you'll learn how to create *documentation* for your program. The more *remarks* you put in your program and the clearer you write program code instead of using tedious, complicated, tricky program statements, the easier it will be for you and others to track errors and maintain the program later.

New Term *Documentation* is comprised of descriptions of the program. You can place documentation inside the program itself so that when you (or someone else) later make a change to the program, you'll read what sections of the program are for without having to figure out what the code's purpose is. Internal Visual Basic program descriptions are called *remarks*.

Add program remarks as you write your program because it is at that time that you understand the program the best. If you wait until after you complete an application, as many programmers do, your application might never be properly documented because other projects can take over your time, and the documentation is often pushed aside once a project is completed.

In addition, you may want to write external documentation with screen shots of the program's different screens and descriptions of what the user must do to start, use, and terminate the program. The better your user's documentation is, the more likely your user will master your program and want to use more programs that you write.

Creating Your First Program

If you are familiar with several other Windows products, such as Microsoft Publisher, you've see *wizards* that work with you, helping you create the documents you require. Visual Basic also supports wizard technology to help you create programs. When you write a Visual Basic program, you have a choice to create an application from scratch or use a wizard to create an application's shell or general structure. After the wizard creates the application's shell, you can fill in the details.

New Term A *wizard* presents step-by-step questions and prompts that you respond to. As you respond, the wizard generates an application that matches the criteria you specify. Visual Basic offers several wizards, but the one you'll use most frequently is called the *Application wizard.*

It's sometimes difficult to tell whether you should create an application shell with the Application wizard and then fill in details for your particular situation or create an application from scratch. Some people, if they've created another application already that is similar to the one they need, make a copy of the first one and make changes to the copy to create the new application. Over time, you'll learn to decide which is best for your needs in different situations.

To help you get started, this section guides you through the creation of your very first application. You'll see how easy the Application wizard is to use for an application's shell. Although the resulting application will not do much (it's only a shell after all), you will see how much Visual Basic can automatically create when you use the Application wizard. By tomorrow's lesson, you will be ready to learn how to create an application from scratch without the Application wizard.

Note

> Perhaps surprisingly, you'll probably create more applications from scratch instead of using the Application wizard, or you'll make a copy of a similar application and modify the copy when making a new program. Although the Application wizard creates a fully-functioning program skeleton, you'll develop your own style of programming over time, and you'll probably find it easier to modify a copy of an existing application than first creating a skeleton and adding to it. Your preferred style will come with time, so just sit back and enjoy learning Visual Basic. Try things, don't be afraid to mess up, and expect some errors every time you write a program. Programming is creation, and you'll find that Visual Basic makes creating fun.

As soon as you start Visual Basic, the Application wizard is there to help. The New Project dialog box, shown in Figure 1.3, appears when you start Visual Basic from the Windows Start menu. The tabs on the New Project dialog box offer these choices:

- **New** lets you create new applications by using various wizards or starting from scratch.
- **Existing** lets you select and open an existing Visual Basic *project*.
- **Recent** displays a list of Visual Basic projects you've recently opened or created.

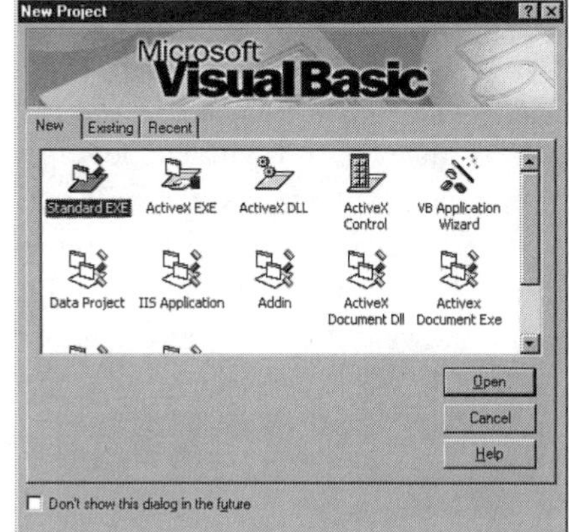

FIGURE 1.3.
You can select the Application wizard from the New Project dialog box.

Note

If you cancel the New Project dialog box, and then later want to start the Application wizard, select File, New Project to display the New Project dialog box once again. This New Project dialog box will not contain the Recent and Existing tabbed pages, however, because you are specifying from your menu choice that you want to create a new project.

NEW TERM A *project* is a collection of files that make up your application. A single application might consist of several files, and the project is the collection of those files. One or more of the files might contain code, one or more of the files might contain descriptions of screens inside their respective form windows, and one or more of the files might contain advanced programming information that your program will use to communicate with other programs and modules inside the operating system.

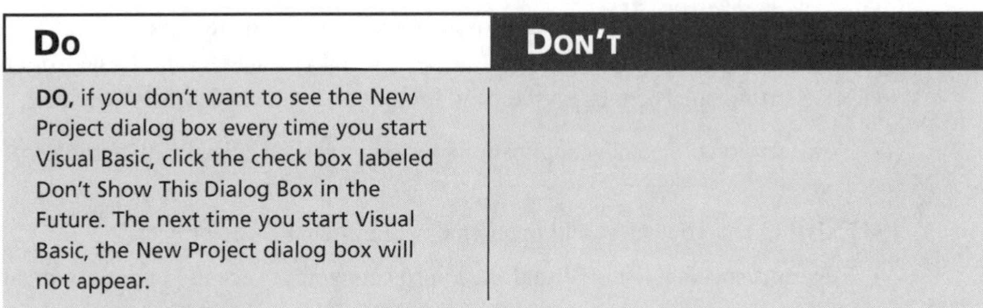

Do	Don't
DO, if you don't want to see the New Project dialog box every time you start Visual Basic, click the check box labeled Don't Show This Dialog Box in the Future. The next time you start Visual Basic, the New Project dialog box will not appear.	

When you select the icon labeled VB Application Wizard on the New tab, the wizard begins its work. The first screen that the wizard displays is an introductory title screen that explains the wizard is about to begin. (In addition, the screen lets you load another profile that defines options, but you won't need extra profile options for this book.) As with most wizards, when you finish reading and selecting from one wizard screen, you click the Next button to display the next screen that the wizard has to offer. Figure 1.4 shows the next wizard screen from which you must select an interface type.

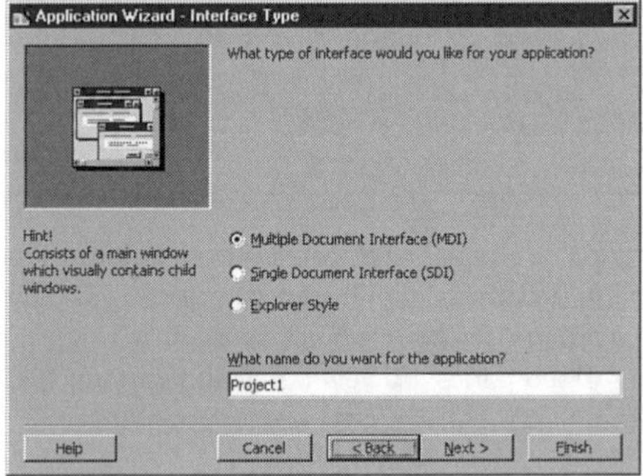

FIGURE 1.4.
The interface type determines how your application will process multiple windows.

Here are the options from which you can select:

- **Multiple Document Interface (MDI)** allows your application to contain multiple document windows. In effect, this interface lets you work with several sets of data in multiple windows within your program. Each document window is called a *child window*.
- **Single Document Interface (SDI)** limits your application to one open document window at a time. Most applications that you write will probably be SDI applications.

- **Explorer Style** lets your application take on a Windows Explorer-like interface with topic summaries in the left window and details for a selected topic in the right pane.

You can click any of the three options to read a description and see a thumbnail sketch of a sample program window. Many of your applications will contain the single document interface because many applications require only a single window with data that is open at any one time. For this first example, select the Single Document Interface option.

The wizard screen also lets you name your project. The default name, Project1, leaves a lot to be desired, so change the project name to *FirstApp* (no spaces are allowed), and click Next to display the next wizard window shown in Figure 1.5.

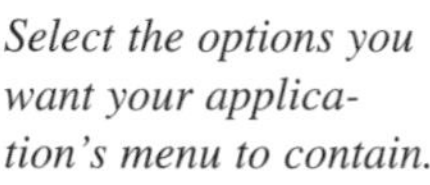

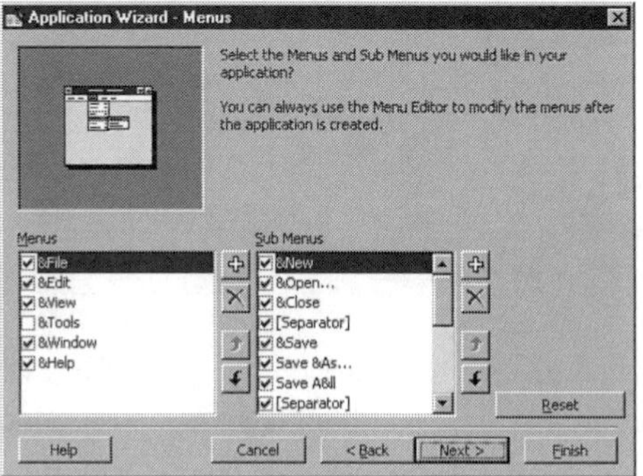

FIGURE 1.5.
Select the options you want your application's menu to contain.

The Application wizard adds the menu options that you select to your application menu. The options are common Windows options found on most Windows programs. The menus will be the typical Windows drop-down type. You can select the menu bar options (such as File, Edit, and so on) as well as submenu options, such as New, Open, and Close. The ampersand (&) next to a letter in a menu name indicates the underscored accelerator key letter; in other words, &New indicates that New (notice the underscore) appears on the menu and that the user can select the option by pressing Alt+N. If you want to place an actual ampersand in the name, use two; for example, typing `A&&B` produces A&B. For this application, leave all the options as they are (keeping the File, Edit, View, Window, and Help options checked) and click Next to continue with the wizard.

Note

> After the Application wizard finishes creating your application, the menu options will operate as expected. For example, the File menu will appear when you select Alt+F or click the File menu.

The next wizard screen, shown in Figure 1.6, lets you select the toolbar buttons that your application will have. As you can see, the Application wizard does a lot of work for you. By creating an initial toolbar, the wizard takes care of a lot of tedium that you would otherwise have to handle. The left window pane indicates the available toolbar buttons and the right window pane lists the buttons (and separator spaces between buttons) on your application's toolbar. As with the menu options in the previous screen, click Next to accept all the default toolbar settings.

FIGURE 1.6.

The Application wizard saves you time by creating an initial toolbar.

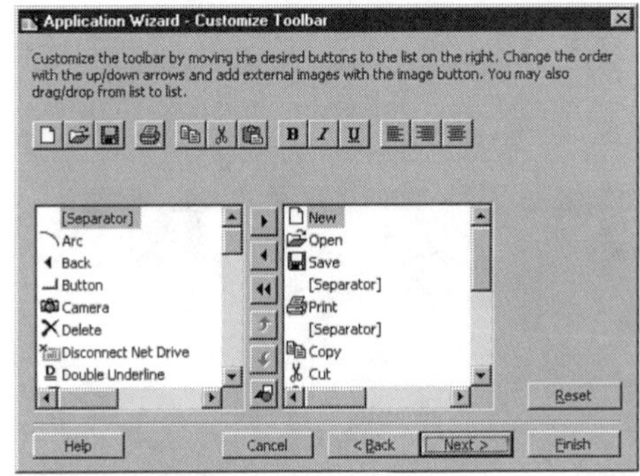

The next wizard screen to appear is the Resource screen from which you can elect to use resources in your program, such as multilanguage text files. Simple programs often do not require external resources. For this example, keep the option labeled No checked and click the Next button to continue.

The next wizard screen is the Internet Connectivity screen from which you can add an Internet interface to your program if you want one. If you were to select Yes from this window (please *don't* select Yes here), the Application wizard would add a complete Internet browser to your application that would operate much like Internet Explorer. Without any programming on your part, your application's user can access the Internet. When the user enters an Internet address (also known as an *URL* [pronounced "earl"] for *Uniform Resource Locator*), such as `http://www.mcp.com`, the browser displays that Web page in the application's browser window, first logging on, if needed, using the PC's default Internet service. You can enter a default startup page address that initially displays when the user starts the browser.

Caution

> If you add the browser to your application, you are assuming that your user has Internet access. If not, an error will result when the user attempts to use the browser.

This first application requires no Internet access, so click Next without changing any of the default options to display the next wizard screen. The screen gives you the option of adding one of these standard screens to your application:

- **Splash screen** is an opening title screen that appears when your application first begins.
- **Login dialog** is a dialog box that asks for the user's ID and password as a part of application security that you can add.
- **Options dialog** is a tabbed blank dialog box from which your users can specify attributes that you set up for the application.
- **About box** is a dialog box that appears when your users select Help, About from the application menu.

For this application, click the option labeled About Box.

> The button labeled Form Templates lets you select from several *form templates* located in the Visual Basic Templates folder. Visual Basic installs the templates you select into your application. The templates include an add-in template that lets you add a form from your own library, an ODBC Log In form that lets your users connect to advanced database access, and a Tip of the Day that displays a random tip when your user starts the application.

NEW TERM A *form template* is a model of a form that you can customize. Form templates are forms with similar properties that might appear in several different applications.

The After selecting the About Box standard form, click Next to bypass the database wizard screen that lets you add external database files to your application. You can click the button labeled Finish to instruct Visual Basic to complete your initial application.

Note

> The View Report button displays a summary of the project you have designed, and details the changes you can add and other wizards that you can run to add functionality to your new project.

Congratulations! You've just created your first application without knowing much about Visual Basic and without knowing *any* of the Visual Basic programming language! After a few gyrations on the screen, Visual Basic displays a dialog box letting you know that your application is complete. When you click OK, the dialog box disappears, and you can run your application.

> After loading an application from disk or creating one, run or execute that application to see it work just as your users will eventually do after you've tested and compiled the applications you write. Visual Basic is a lot like a kitchen. You are the cook, and your application is the recipe. Change the application (the recipe), and the resulting program (the meal) turns out to be different. The programming stage can take quite a while if your application is complex even if you use the Application wizard to generate an initial program. As you create the program, you won't see the program do work until you run it.

Run the program (the program runs interactively by default) by selecting Run, Start. You'll see from the menu option that F5 is a shortcut key for running the application as well. Figure 1.7 shows the window that appears.

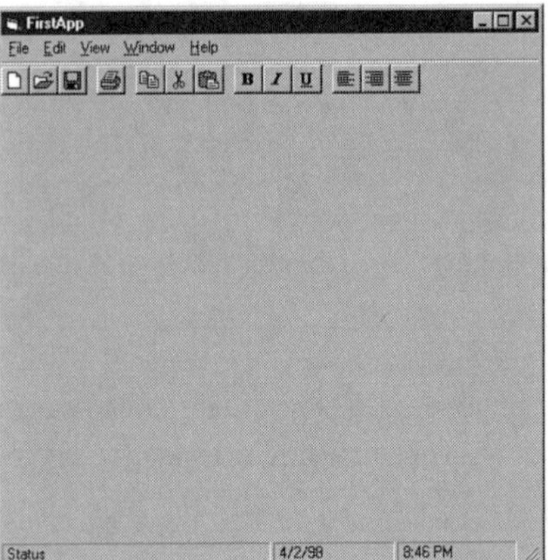

FIGURE 1.7.
Your first application is complete!

With the Application wizard, you created a fully working program (albeit only a simple shell that only does a little) just by answering the wizard's screen prompts. You have created an application that does the following:

- A standard program window appears that you can resize and move. The name of the project, FirstApp, appears in the window's toolbar.
- A status bar displays the date and time. You can turn on and off the status bar from the View menu.
- A working menu appears with four options. Only the Help, About menu option does work (try it), but the usual menu options, such as File, Open (produces a file locating dialog box) and Edit, Cut, are all there ready for you to insert active code

behind them. The About dialog box follows the standard Windows convention of displaying system information when you click its System Info button.

Tip

The System Information screen displays a complete summary of the user's operating system and hardware. This summary appears after Visual Basic executes a System Info program that searches the user's computer for specific hardware and system information. (You can call the System Info program from locations other than the About box.) Such a summary can some in handy when your users call you with problems about applications you write. You can ask the user to display the system information summary to verify that the user is using the proper operating system and hardware that your program requires. In addition, the System Info window is useful for checking available resources such as disk space and memory to ensure that your PC is running with enough resources.

- A standard toolbar appears that you can add functionality to and turn on and off from the View menu.

The application does little, yet it is complete and ready for you to fill in the blanks. You can easily change and add to the application, its menus, and its windows. The application is only a shell of things to come, yet the Application wizard generated a complete project that takes care of much tedious work that you might otherwise have to add by hand if you created the application from scratch. You'll find in tomorrow's lesson that you can create working projects quite easily, but the Application wizard adds basic functionality that applications often require.

To quit the running application, select File, Exit. Answer No to the prompts when Visual Basic asks if you want to save the project. You don't need to save the application shell because you can easily generate this project again by running the Application wizard once again.

Event-Driven Programming

Figure 1.8 shows a window from a Windows program. The window contains several kinds of Windows controls such as command buttons, check boxes, and a scrollbar. These controls are just a sample of the many Windows controls available for you within the Visual Basic programming environment to add to the programs that you write.

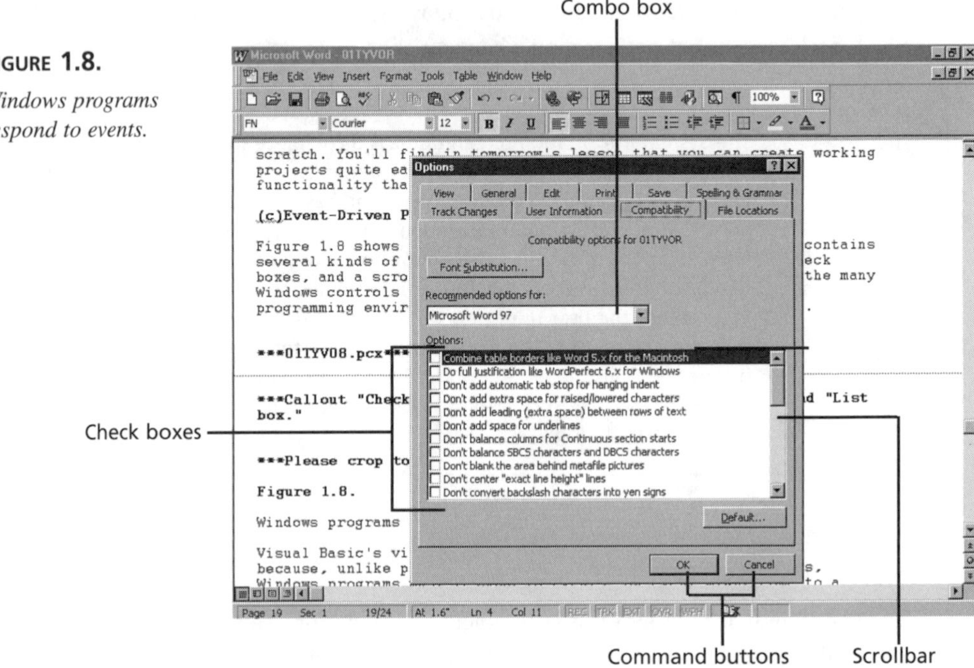

FIGURE 1.8.

Windows programs respond to events.

Visual Basic's visual nature requires these kinds of controls because, unlike programs written in older text-based languages, Windows programs must respond to *events*. An event might come to a program from any of these controls, as well as from internal activities such as the PC's clock. Events come in random order. For example, the user of Figure 1.8's window might click a command button or check one or more check boxes, or open the drop-down list box. The user might perform several of these events in a different order each time the user runs the program. You must use *event-driven programming* techniques to respond properly to the user's actions and other activities that trigger events.

NEW TERM An *event* is an activity that occurs during a program's execution, such as a mouse click or a keystroke. *Event-driven programming* applies to programming that responds to Windows events.

> Not only must your program handle random events, but if more than one Windows program is running at once, each program needs to analyze and respond to events.

As Figure 1.9 shows, Windows handles a few events but passes most to the programs currently running. Windows is a multitasking operating system so more than one program can run simultaneously. Your program must handle any and all events appropriate at the time the events occur and ignore all the others. For example, if your program needs to display a warning message at a preset time interval, your program will have to check the timer event to see whether the correct time span has passed since the last warning. If another program running at the same time did not require the timer, that program would ignore all timing events that Windows sends to it.

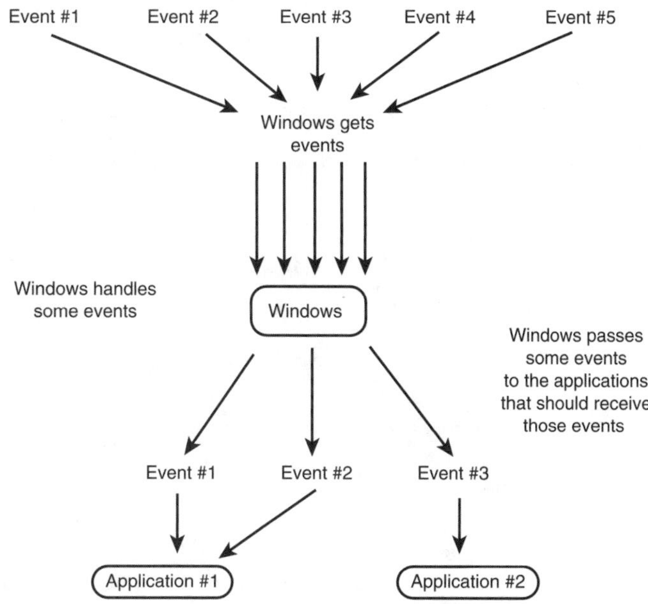

FIGURE 1.9.
Your programs must respond to some events and ignore others.

A Visual Basic program consists of the visual interface that makes up the windows and controls that the user sees and interacts with. In addition, programming code connects everything together. Each control is both automated and set up to respond to the programming code. For example, a command button will visually show a click action when the user clicks the button with the mouse when running the program. You have to do nothing more than place the button on the form (the program's window) for the button to operate. (As with all command buttons, you can trigger a command button with the Enter key as well as the mouse.) Other aspects of the command button, however, are under your control, such as the name or picture that resides on the button, the size of the button, the color of the button, and so on. These are *properties* that you can change, although Visual Basic assigns default values. Properties distinguish one command button from others.

New Term A *property* helps to differentiate a control from other controls because the property shows appearance and behavior of a control. Properties have values, such as colors, text labels, size, and location on the form. When you place a control on a form, you assign properties that make that control somehow unique from the other controls.

Figure 1.10 shows a window with several command buttons. If all of these buttons appeared in a program with no code behind them to modify the way they respond, you could click any of them and they would all respond the same way, depressing inward with the click and triggering a click Windows event. Despite these similarities, however, each button looks differently because its text caption, size, location, color, and text font property values are different from the other buttons.

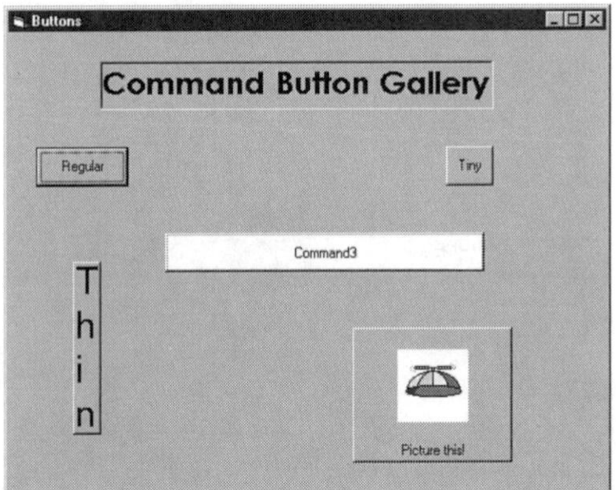

Figure 1.10.
Multiple controls look different if they have different property values.

Once you place controls on a form and assign their individual property values, you are ready to write programming code that responds to events. The same control can trigger several different kinds of events. For example, a command button may generate a single-click or a double-click event depending on what the user does. The code that you write for the program determines which of those events your program ignores or handles in some way.

> **Tip** If you write code for a particular event, your program will respond to that event when it occurs during the program's execution. If, however, you don't write code for a particular event, and that event happens, your program will ignore that event when Windows sends it to your program.

Your programming code behind the forms looks and acts, not like one long listing of text, but like several small sections of code with each section written to respond to one of the form's control events. Each of those sections sits around doing nothing until its event occurs; at that time, the program immediately starts executing that event's code. For example, if the right-click of an *object*, such as a particular command button, is to produce a warning beep and message, you must write the code to produce the beep and message. The executing program runs that code if and only if the user right-clicks over the button.

NEW TERM An *object* is an element from a Visual Basic program, such as a control, form, or code module that holds programming statements.

How do all these details work together? The answer to that will take, oh, about 20 more days. Tomorrow's lesson begins to show you how to specify control properties and how to respond to those controls when you create your very first Visual Basic program from scratch without the help of the Application wizard. Theory alone is not enough—you need to get your hands on the keyboard and begin placing controls, setting control property values, and writing code that responds to events.

Summary

You are well on your way to mastering Visual Basic. Today, you learned the background needed for programming. By understanding the programming process, you are better equipped to begin using Visual Basic, one of the most advanced programming environments available today.

Today's lesson explained how you design and write programs. Visual Basic has changed the way programmers design programs because the Visual Basic environment makes it easy to prototype your program's design and then turn that prototype into a finished application. Programming often requires several review and edit steps. Programs rarely work perfectly the first time you write them, but as you saw today, Visual Basic's interactive environment takes care of much of your work so that you can keep errors to a minimum.

The Application wizard will generate a program shell that you then can add details to so that the program becomes a separate, working application that performs its needed job. Those details consist of adding controls, setting property values, and writing code to make the program interact and respond to the controls properly. The rest of your 21-day tutorial will show you how to fill in those details to make working programs.

Q&A

Q Do I always follow the programming process steps (design, create visual elements, and so on) for all Visual Basic programs I write, or just for the small ones?

A The larger the program, the more you'll need to adhere to the program development procedure. Programs get complex quickly as you add more and more features to their requirements. One feature may affect other features, so the more you plan, the less you'll have to redo and correct later. Fortunately, the Visual Basic environment makes program changes rather simple in many cases, even changes that involve major structural design changes. Of course, if you start with an Application wizard's shell, the design of your program is your second step. As you learn how to write programs throughout this book, you'll learn more about proper program design and creation.

Q Does the Application wizard generate program code?

A The Application wizard does generate some code but not much. The purpose of program statements is to make the program perform a specific function, such as computing accounting figures or processing customer billing. It's your job as the programmer to specify the code.

Workshop

The Workshop provides quiz questions to help you solidify your understanding on the material covered and exercises to provide you with experience in using what you've learned. You should understand the quiz and exercise answers before continuing to the next chapter. Appendix A, "Answers to Exercises," provides the answers.

Quiz

1. What language did Microsoft use as the basis for Visual Basic?
2. Why is Visual Basic suitable for both beginners and advanced programmers?
3. Which is more important to newcomers to Visual Basic: the programming language or the visual interface?
4. What's the difference between a form window and the application window?
5. What do the terms *bug* and *debug* mean?
6. Which runs faster: a program written in an interpreted language or a program written in a compiled language?
7. Which is easier to debug: a program written in an interpreted language or one written in a compiled language?
8. What is the difference between a splash screen and a Tip of the Day screen?
9. What's the difference between a control and a control property value?
10. True/False. Controls hold code that makes them respond to the user's input.

Exercise

Use the Application wizard to create an application that includes an Internet browser window and a splash screen in addition to the other options you selected today when you created your first project. Run the application to see how the Internet access works. If you don't have Internet access, you will get an error when you open the browser window, but create the project anyway for the practice.

Week 1

Day 2

Working with Visual Basic

Now that you've seen how easy the Application wizard is to use, you are ready to take the plunge and create a program from scratch. Although creating a program without the Application wizard is not difficult, you need to understand Visual Basic's environment a little more before you write your first application. Today's lesson explains how to maneuver within the Visual Basic environment so that you then will be ready to create an application from scratch without the Application wizard.

Today, you learn the following:

- The parts of the Visual Basic environment
- About placing controls on a form
- How to save your project and its associated files
- The Properties window's features
- How to access the Code window

Understanding the Visual Basic Environment

Throughout the rest of your 21-day tutorial, you will be building and studying programs within Visual Basic's environment. The sooner you acquaint yourself with Visual Basic's environment, which mainly requires understanding the purpose of Visual Basic's windows, the sooner you will master Visual Basic programming. Figure 2.1 shows the Visual Basic screen with several of its common elements labeled.

FIGURE 2.1.

You should understand how Visual Basic's components work for you.

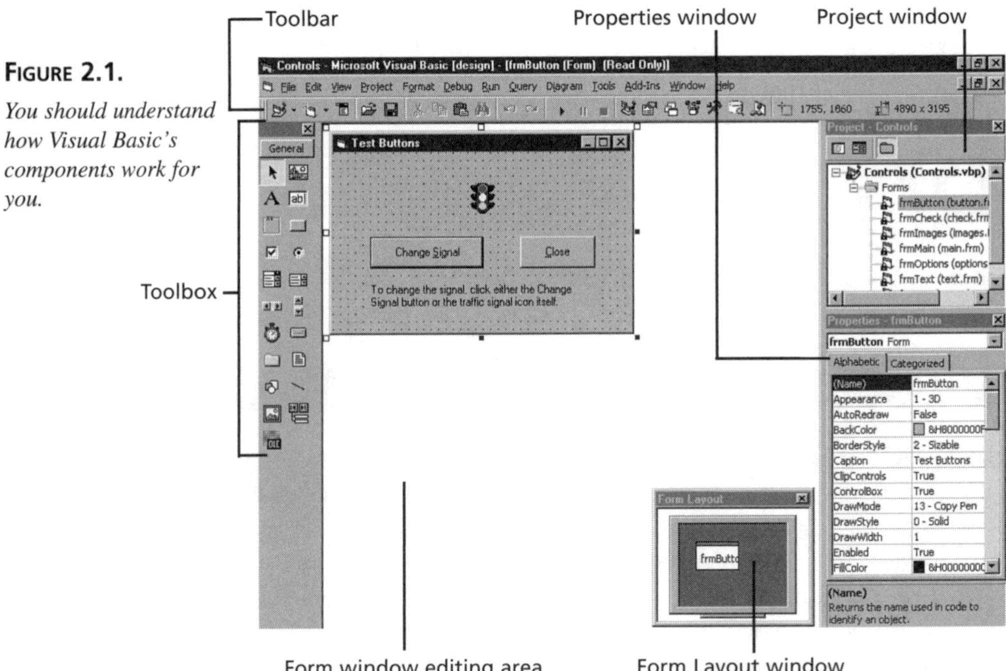

The New Project Window

As you saw in yesterday's lesson, the New Project window appears when you first start Visual Basic or when you select File, New Project. Throughout this 21-day tutorial, you'll begin most new applications from the New Project window.

If you don't create an application shell with the VB Application wizard, as you did in yesterday's lesson, you'll more than likely create a standalone program by selecting the *Standard EXE* icon. The icon is named to represent the resulting application's filename extension (.exe for executable) if you compile the application you create. Even if you will not be compiling your application right away, the Standard EXE icon is the one you'll choose most of the time while learning Visual Basic.

A *standard EXE* application is an application that you can compile or run interpretively.

You'll see several New Project window icons labeled with *ActiveX*. ActiveX is the name given to controls that you can create. These controls have the filename extension .OCX, and you can add them to the Visual Basic environment so they reside on your Toolbox window. You can write applications that become new controls and then add those controls to the Visual Basic environment for future program development. ActiveX is a rather comprehensive term that also applies to other areas of computing.

Remember that Visual Basic is nothing more than a Windows program (albeit a comprehensive program) that helps you create new Windows programs. The Visual Basic environment's toolbars, menus, dialog boxes, and windows all work just as they do in other Windows programs, so the mechanics of working in Visual Basic should not be a problem for you.

The Toolbar

The Visual Basic toolbar that you see beneath the menu bar changes as you use Visual Basic. Visual Basic has a total of four toolbars:

- **Debug.** This toolbar appears when you use the interactive debugging tools to trace and correct problems.
- **Edit.** This toolbar aids your editing of Visual Basic code.
- **Form Editor.** This toolbar helps you adjust objects on forms.
- **Standard.** This toolbar is the default toolbar that appears beneath the menu bar.

You can display and hide these toolbars from the View, Toolbars menu. Each toolbar shows multiple buttons that offer one-button shortcuts so you don't have to traverse menu items to access common operations. As you use Visual Basic, you'll run across several buttons that are helpful to you, and you'll never use others. This tutorial will point out many toolbar buttons that help speed your program development, but it will not serve as a complete reference to every toolbar button because not all buttons will necessarily help speed your program development time.

Do	Don't
DO rest your mouse cursor over a button that you don't recognize to see a pop-up ScreenTip message telling you what the button is for.	**DON'T** try to memorize all the buttons on all the toolbars.

You can dock and undock any toolbar. That is, you can drag a toolbar from its location under the menu bar to form a floating toolbar. Therefore, you can place a toolbar close to the item to which it applies so that the buttons are where you need them. You can then dock the toolbar by dragging it back under the menu bar so that it stays in the fixed toolbar area.

The Toolbox

The Toolbox window differs from the toolbar. The Toolbox window, typically called the toolbox, is a collection of tools that act as a repository of controls you can place on a form. You will learn how to add and remove tools from the toolbox as you move through this 21-day tutorial. Figure 2.2 shows the most common collection of toolbox tools that you'll see.

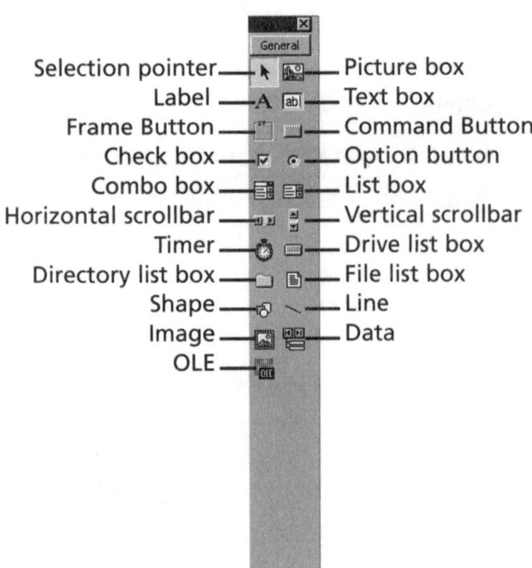

Figure 2.2.
The toolbox holds tools, or controls, that you can place on your application's form window.

Fill this in to get your Iomega Rewards Coupon!

Receipt(s), original UPC(s) and completed form must be included for you to be eligible for your coupon.

SAMPLE UPC

7 42709 31308 0

Name: ______________________________

Address: ______________________________

City: ______________ State/Province: ______________ Zip Code/Postal Code: ______________

Phone: ______________ E-Mail: ______________

I have read and understand the terms and conditions below.

Signature: ______________________________

If you have questions about the status of your savings request and the 8 weeks allowed for delivery have passed, please call 1-800-510-2586.

Terms and Conditions: Iomega Rewards Program. Buy Iomega® product(s) totaling $199-$298 (excluding tax) and receive a Coupon by mail good for $35 off of your next Iomega product purchase of $35 or more from the participating reseller. Buy Iomega product(s) totaling $299 or more (excluding tax) and receive a Coupon by mail good for $50 off of your next Iomega product purchase of $50 or more from the participating reseller. Products totaling the qualifying amount must be purchased at the same time. Coupons redeemable only at the participating reseller where initial purchase of Iomega product(s) was made. Not valid with any other Iomega offer. Offer subject to the following terms and conditions. 1. Store receipt/invoice for each Coupon requested must be dated between February 4, 2001 and March 17, 2001. No purchase orders accepted. 2. Offer does not apply to remanufactured products or products purchased for resale. 3. Each request must include completed original or photocopy of request form, original UPC label(s) printed on the carton(s) of qualifying product(s) for each Coupon requested (no photocopies), and original or photocopy of store receipt/invoice showing qualifying purchase amount for Iomega product(s) purchased, and must be received by 04/17/01. **The qualifying purchase amount for each Coupon requested must be shown on a single store receipt or invoice.** Keep copies of request materials. All materials submitted become Iomega property and will not be returned. 4. Offer limited to maximum of ten Coupons per name or address. Requests from groups or post office boxes will not be honored. 5. Offer good in US (50 states & DC) and Canada only. Coupons remitted in US dollars in US. Coupons remitted in Canadian dollars in Canada. Qualifying purchase levels refer to dollar value in currency of country where purchase is made. 6. If terms and conditions not met, Coupon will not be sent. Void where taxed, prohibited, or restricted by law. 7. Proof of mailing does not constitute proof of delivery. Iomega not responsible for lost, late, illegible, stolen, or incomplete requests, or postage-due, damaged, or separated mail. Incomplete or illegible submissions will be returned. 8. Iomega employees, agencies, distributors, or resellers ineligible. 9. Altered request materials invalid. Iomega reserves right to request additional information about a Coupon request and to refuse to honor requests if Iomega is not satisfied that these terms and conditions have been met, or if Iomega suspects a submission is fraudulent. Fraudulent submission of requests could result in federal prosecution under US Mail Fraud Statutes (18 USC, Sections 1341 & 1342). 10. Coupons will be mailed to address on request form. It is customer's responsibility to provide for mail forwarding in event of address change. Allow 8 weeks for processing and delivery of Coupon. If Coupon not received within 8 weeks, customer must notify Iomega by calling number printed on request form not later than 06/15/01 or all rights hereunder will expire. 11. Any obligation of Iomega under this Offer, and any Coupon issued pursuant hereto, will expire and be null and void if Coupon is not redeemed through the participating reseller within 45 days of its date of issue. 12. Iomega reserves right to rescind or change Offer at any time.

The toolbox does not run out of tools! When your application requires more than one command button, you will get all those buttons from the Toolbox window's Command button tool. In effect, these toolbox buttons generate tools on your form when you need them, as you'll see in today's last section when you create a new application from scratch.

The Form Window

Most of your work goes on inside the Form window. You'll design all your application's forms, which are the background windows that your users see, in the central editing area where the Form window appears. You can resize the Form window to make the windows you create in your applications as large or small as needed. (Scrollbars appear to let you scroll the Form window if you need to see parts of the forms that run off the screen or underneath other Visual Basic windows.)

Keep in mind that an application may contain multiple forms; you can display one or more of those forms in their own Form window editing areas, as shown in Figure 2.3. The active form is the form with the highlighted title bar in its window. Activate a form by clicking anywhere within the window or on the title bar.

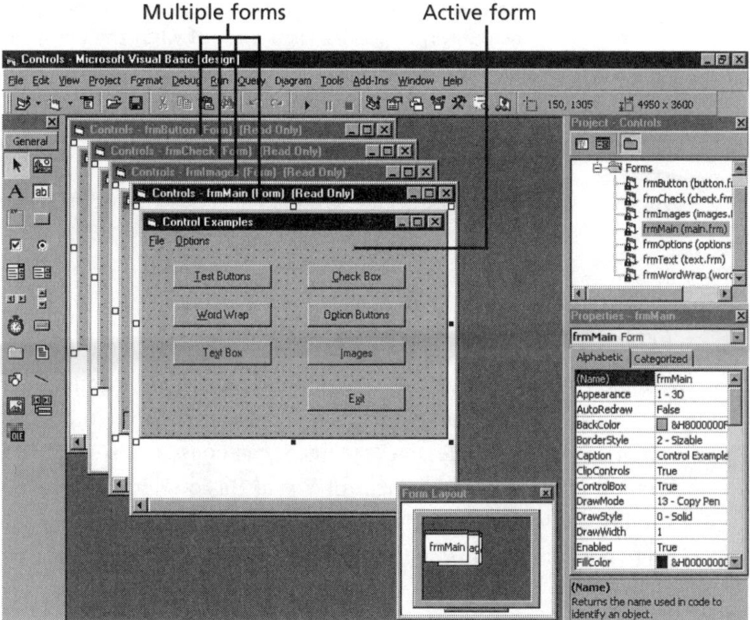

FIGURE 2.3.

Edit one or more of your application's forms in the Form window editing area.

The Form Layout Window

The Form Layout window is an interesting little window connected closely to the Form window, because the Form Layout window shows you a preview of the Form window's location. If one or more forms appear in your Form window, thumbnail sketches of those forms will also appear in the Form Layout window. The window shows you where each of the forms will appear on the screen when your user runs the application and, through using the program, views the various forms.

Not only does the Form Layout window show you where a form will appear relative to the sides of your screen when you run the program, but you can also move the initial location of a form (where the form will appear when the user runs the program) just by dragging the form in the Form Layout window to a different location. Therefore, if you want a form to appear in the center of the screen, move the form in the Form Layout window to the center, and Visual Basic will place the form there when the user runs your program.

Note

> After you learn enough of the Visual Basic programming language, you will be able to write the code to place any form at any exact screen position. You can even instruct Visual Basic to center the form on the screen as soon as the form appears, regardless of what the Form Layout window shows during the program's development.

> Many Visual Basic programmers close the Form Layout window to make room for more of the other windows inside the development environment.

The Project Window

Use the Project window to manage your application's components. As Figure 2.4 shows, the Project window can get busy. A Windows program, more accurately called an application as yesterday's lesson explained, can consist of several files. Before you compile a Windows program, the number of Visual Basic-related files can get even more numerous. The Project window enables you to manage all those components and bring the component you want to work with to the editing area where you can work on it.

FIGURE 2.4.
The Project window holds your project's components.

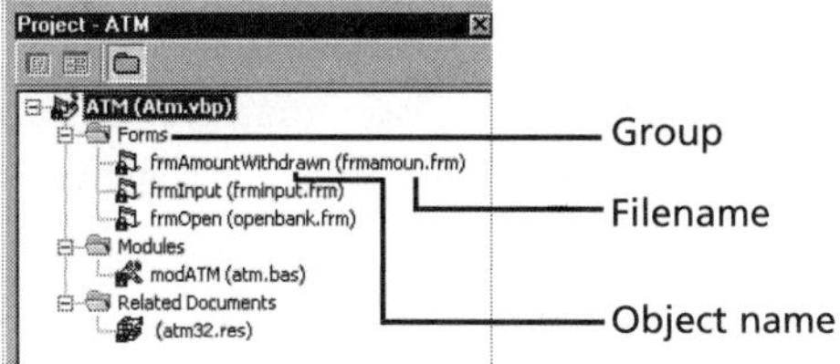

The Project window is also called the Project Explorer because of its Windows Explorer-like interface that lets you expand and shrink object groups.

The Project window lists its components in a tree-structured listing. Related objects appear together. You can expand or shrink the details by clicking the plus or minus signs that appear next to object groups. For example, if you click the plus sign next to the object labeled `Forms`, a list of the current project's forms will appear. When you double-click a form, that form's Form window appears in the Form window editing area.

Each item in the Project window has both a project name and a filename. In Visual Basic, you can assign names to objects, such as forms and modules. Each of the Project window's items is stored on your disk in a separate file. The filename, which differs from the project name for the same item (project names, unlike filenames, have no extension for example), appears in parentheses next to the Project window item. Therefore, you can tell from the Project window every filename and every project name for all your project's files, and you can activate any object's window by clicking that object inside the Project window.

Notice that the Project window contains a toolbar with three buttons. The Code Window button displays the Code window for a selected object so that you can write and change code related to the object. (The Code window did not appear earlier in Figure 2.1 but will appear in this lesson's final section when you add code to an application.) The View Object button displays the object window for a selected item. Many objects have both a Code window and an object window associated with them. Each form, for instance, has a code module and a Form window associated with it. Therefore, the Code Window button and the View Object buttons let you quickly switch between an item's code and its visual elements. The Toggle Folders button groups and ungroups the Project window's items in an Explorer-like interface.

The following kinds of objects can appear in the Project window:

- **Projects.** An application might consist of multiple projects, as can occur when you create ActiveX controls. Projects always have the filename extension .VBP.
- **Forms.** The Project window displays a list of your project's forms. Form files always have the filename extension .FRM.
- **Modules.** Your project's modules hold general and reusable routines comprised of Visual Basic programming statements. You can use the same module in several programs due to its general nature. Modules always have the filename extension .BAS.
- **Class modules.** Class modules are special code modules that define objects you've designed for a project. Class module files always have the filename extension .CLS.
- **User controls.** User controls are ActiveX controls you've added to the project. ActiveX control files always have the filename extension .OCX.
- **User documents.** User documents are document objects that describe parts of your project. User document files always have the filename extension .DOB.
- **Property pages.** Property pages (such as those found inside tabbed dialog boxes) that appear in the project file describe a particular control. Property page files always have the filename extension .PAG.

Other items can sometimes appear in the Project window, such as resources and other documents you add to your project.

For the majority of your Visual Basic application development, especially the first 21 days that comprise this tutorial, you'll be working with forms and code modules only.

The Properties Window

A form can hold many controls. As you add controls to a form, you can select a control by clicking the control. When you select a control, the Properties window changes to list every property related to that control. As you'll see in today's final section, when you add a control to a Visual Basic application, Visual Basic sets the control's initial property values. When you display the Properties window for a control, you can modify its property values.

Figure 2.5 shows a Properties window listing some of the properties for a Label control. Notice that the name, type, and description in the Property window reflect the selected control. To assign a value to a property, select the property and type a new value. Sometimes a drop-down list box will appear when you can select one of an established set of values for that property.

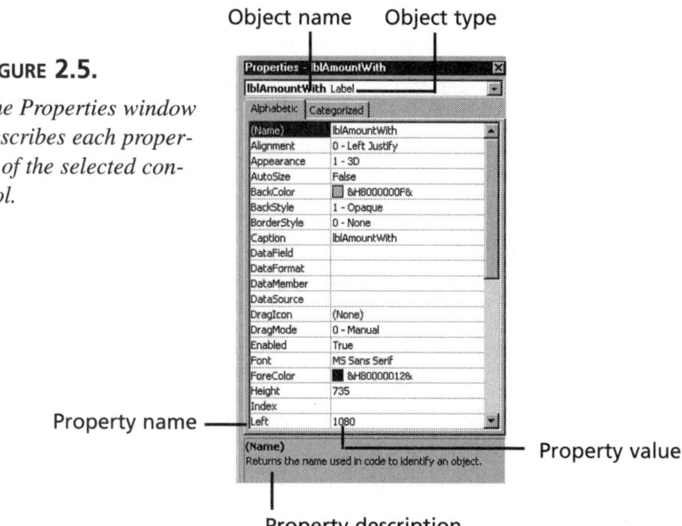

FIGURE 2.5.

The Properties window describes each property of the selected control.

Each property has a name so you can work with a particular property, and each property has a value that either you or Visual Basic assigns. For example, Visual Basic always names the first command button you add to a project `Command1`. Therefore, the `Name` property for the first command button holds the value `Command1`. You'll almost certainly want to rename the command button to something more meaningful to help document the application. You might name a command button that triggers a report `cmdReportPrint`, for example.

Do preface each object name you assign with a three-letter prefix that describes the object. Then when you later look at the list of objects, you not only know the object's name but also its type (command button, text box, form, or whatever). Table 2.1 lists common prefixes used for Visual Basic object names. Refer to Table 2.1 throughout these 21 days when you assign names to Visual Basic objects. When your project contains numerous controls, these names help you decipher the purpose and type of the controls.

TABLE 2.1. PREFACE OBJECT NAMES WITH ONE OF THESE ABBREVIATIONS.

Prefix	*Object type*
`cbo`	Combo box
`chk`	Check box
`cmd`	Command button
`dir`	Directory list box
`drv`	Drive list box
`fil`	File list box
`fra`	Frame
`frm`	Form
`grd`	Grid
`hsb`	Horizontal scrollbar
`img`	Image
`lbl`	Label
`lin`	Line
`lst`	List box
`mnu`	Menu
`mod`	Module
`ole`	OLE
`opt`	Option button
`pic`	Picture box
`res`	Resource
`shp`	Shape
`tmr`	Timer
`txt`	Text box
`typ`	User-defined data type
`vsb`	Vertical scrollbar

Do	Don't
DO use lowercase letters for the object's prefix when you assign Visual Basic names to the objects.	**DON'T** use the prefix when you assign filenames to objects.

Tip

Remember that you can move, resize, and close any Visual Basic window. At times, you'll want to see more or less of a window to make room for a different window.

Getting Help

Visual Basic contains a wide assortment of online tools that give you help when you need help. Before you create an application in today's final section, you should learn how to access the various help options so that you can learn more about a procedure when you need the help.

Receiving Local Help

Most of the time, the Visual Basic environment gives you all the help you need without you going anywhere else (other than this book, of course!). The first option on the Help menu, Contents, produces an HTML-based Windows help screen shown in Figure 2.6. The left window pane lists several online books you can open and read, and the right pane is a guided tour through several help topics by a Dr. Gui. (*GUI* is an abbreviation for the term *graphical user interface*, by the way.)

Note

Visual Basic's Help system is based on Books Online, a help reference database found in older Microsoft products. You'll need the MSDN CD-ROMs to access much of the online help.

New Term *MSDN* stands for *Microsoft Developer's Network* and is an abbreviation for a series of online articles, CD-ROMs, and newsletters that Microsoft has produced in the past few years for programmers. Visual Basic's help is now a part of the MSDN material. The online screens for MSDN are available only through a subscription service plan. You can subscribe to the online MSDN area by clicking the Help, Contents screen's MSDN Online hyperlink.

Caution

Your help may differ slightly depending on the date of your Visual Basic 6 software publication. Microsoft sometimes changes help screens from early editions of products.

FIGURE 2.6.

Visual Basic's online help gets you through trouble spots.

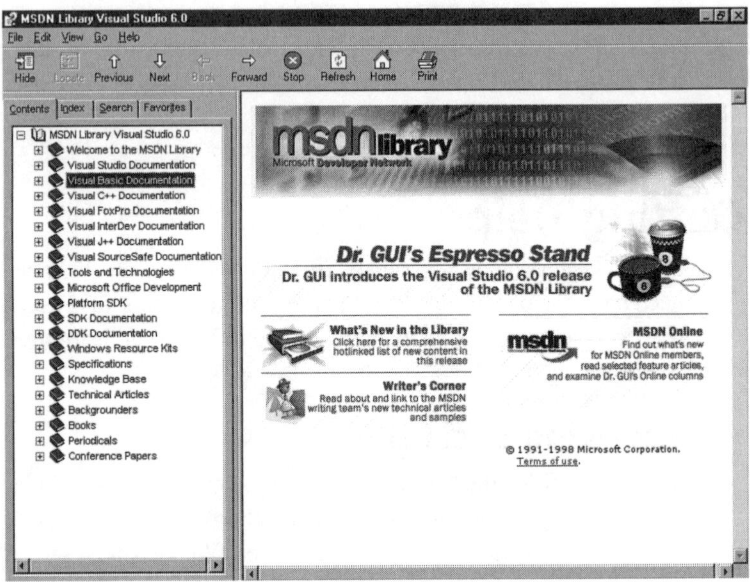

The Help dialog box offers online and immediate help in the following forms:

- **Contents.** This option offers help organized by books, such as "Visual Basic Documentation" and "Tools and Technologies."
- **Index.** This option enables you to look for help from a collection of indexed words from the Contents help references.
- **Search.** This option enables you to search within articles for specific text.
- **Favorites.** With this option, you can store useful help topics that you've collected.

Ever wonder why a large development system such as Visual Basic comes without thick, bulky manuals? Visual Basic *does* come with many manuals, but they are online as the MSDN help system. You click to "open" one of the books in the left pane and move to a chapter and page. The page appears in the right pane of the help window.

The help screens appear in their own window, separate from the Visual Basic window. Therefore, you can keep both open at once, switching between a reference and Visual Basic by pressing Alt+Tab or by clicking the appropriate Windows taskbar button.

The Help system offers references on Visual Basic, database connections, ActiveX programming, and other programming issues that you'll often use to get quick answers you need for programming problems you may encounter. Think of the Help system as a complete set of expensive reference books that, if they were bound and came as separate books with Visual Basic, would increase the cost of your software considerably and be far less simple to search when you needed help on specific topics.

Another entry on the Help menu, About Microsoft Visual Basic, produces a routine About dialog box that shows your Visual Basic version number, serial number, and registered name. In addition, when you click the System Info button, the dialog box shown in Figure 2.7 appears after the program performs a check of your system. The system information contains both software and hardware information.

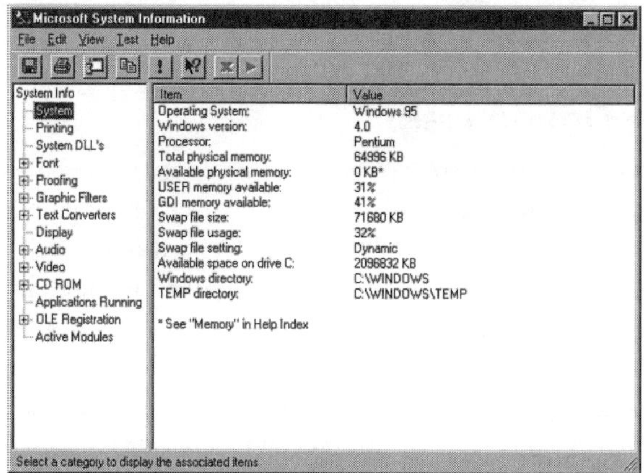

FIGURE 2.7.

The System Info button performs an important check of your system.

In Day 20, "Providing Help," you learn how to add online help to the applications that you write.

Getting Technical Support

When you select Help, Technical Support, a dialog box opens to let you know how to contact Microsoft's technical support staff for more personal help. The online help and the Books Online may not be able to answer your specific question. For example, if

Visual Basic behaves a certain way that appears to be a bug in the system itself, you may have to resort to Microsoft for help. (For such problems, though, always try to reinstall Visual Basic to see whether that fixes the problem before consulting the technical support. That's the advice they would probably give you, so save some time and reinstall before you call.)

You might wonder why you need help with contacting technical support. After all, don't you just need a toll-free phone number and the hours of operation? Microsoft offers several levels of technical support, from free to a metered service and annual subscriptions. The help guide provides a summary of the options available to you. In addition, Microsoft has technical support offices all over the world. If you live outside the United States, you'll want to contact the office closest to you.

Getting Online Help

When you select Help, Microsoft on the Web, Visual Basic offers a wide selection of online support options from which you can choose. (They all require Internet access.) When you select Online Support, Microsoft's Visual Basic Web page appears. This page is a good place to check frequently even if you don't require online help. You'll find a rich set of update information, bug corrections, tips, workarounds, sample code, and updated links to related sites. Other options from the Web menu option are links to the Microsoft home page, a Web search engine, and even a feedback link to Microsoft so that you can give Microsoft advice and comments about Visual Basic.

Check the Frequently Asked Questions site to find a list of answers to many common questions from Visual Basic developers.

Getting Used to the Screen

Before your first day was over, you created a complete, working Visual Basic application. More accurately, you created an application with the help of the Visual Basic Application wizard, which did all the work. You're about to improve on that achievement by creating an entire application from scratch.

You now understand the Visual Basic environment better than before, and you know how to get help with Visual Basic when you need it. Before you follow the next section's steps to create a new application, take a moment to load an existing application from one of the samples that come with Visual Basic. You then can familiarize yourself with the windows that appear. The following steps help guide you:

1. Start Visual Basic.
2. Insert the MSDN CD 1 into your CD-ROM drive.
3. Click the Existing tab and maneuver to the Samples folder from the Open Project dialog box.
4. Double-click the icon labeled Controls to open the project named Controls.

Tip

> You may not see the .VBP filename extension on the Controls project in the Open Project dialog box depending on your Windows Explorer option settings. Regardless of whether you display filename extensions in Windows dialog boxes, you can distinguish file types from the icon at the left of the files. The Open Project window displays only project files (unless you change the selection in the Files of Type drop-down list box), and the icon next to the Controls project is the icon that represents all Visual Basic project files.

5. After you open the Controls project, you may get a dialog box asking if you want to add the project to something called *SourceSafe*. Always respond No to this prompt throughout the book. As a follow-up, Visual Basic will offer two more SourceSafe-related dialog boxes; click OK to close each of them.

New Term *SourceSafe* is a Visual Studio tool (available for all the Visual Studio languages) with which you can keep track of versions of your *source programs*.

New Term The *source program* is the code and the visual screens that comprise any application you write. You won't distribute the source program because that is what you make changes to. You'll distribute a compiled application.

6. After you open the Controls project, your Visual Basic screen will not look all that more interesting. The Controls application does not start because you only loaded the project from the disk. To run the project's application (interpretively), select Run, Start to see the program run as shown in Figure 2.8.

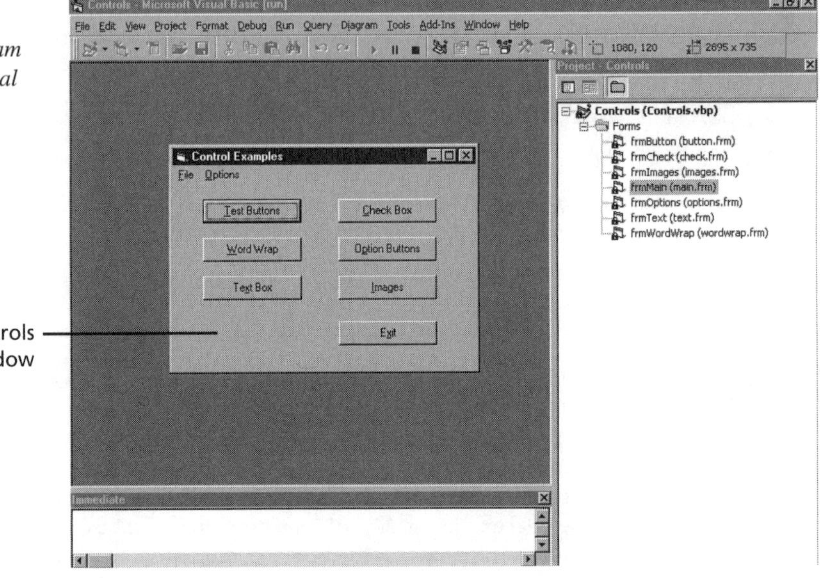

FIGURE 2.8.
The Controls program runs within the Visual Basic environment.

> **Note**
> When you run an application interpretively, the program's windows stay within the active Visual Basic environment so that you can stop the program and change it or examine areas for problems. When you compile a Visual Basic program, you run the program from Windows and outside of Visual Basic's environment.

Do	Don't
DO press F5 or click the Start toolbar button to run a program.	**DON'T** select Run, Start from the menu.

7. The Controls program demonstrates several Windows controls available on the Visual Basic toolbox. Click a button, and then test the resulting control options that appear.
8. After trying several program options, click the Exit button to stop the program's execution and close the program window. You'll be back in the Visual Basic environment. At this point, the Controls application is still loaded in the environment, but the Controls application is not running. You can now study some of the Visual Basic windows.

9. Look at the Project window. Notice that the Controls program consists of forms only. Although some code does exist (click the Project window's View Code button to see a Code window, and then click the View Object window once again to return to the list of forms), the code resides in the seven form files that accompany the project.
10. Double-click a form name within the Project window to see that form appear in the Form window editing area. The form will look somewhat like it did when you ran the program. Look at the Form Layout window (select View, Form Layout Window if you do not see the Form Layout window) to see where the form will appear on the screen when you run the program.
11. Drag the small thumbnail form in the Form Layout window to a different location. If you were to rerun the program, the initial form window would appear in the location where you dragged the thumbnail sketch.
12. Take a look at the Properties window, which shows the selected control's property values. Keep in mind that the Properties window shows property values for only a single, selected control in the Form window. In Figure 2.9, the Properties window shows properties for the option button that is selected (enclosed in eight sizing handles).

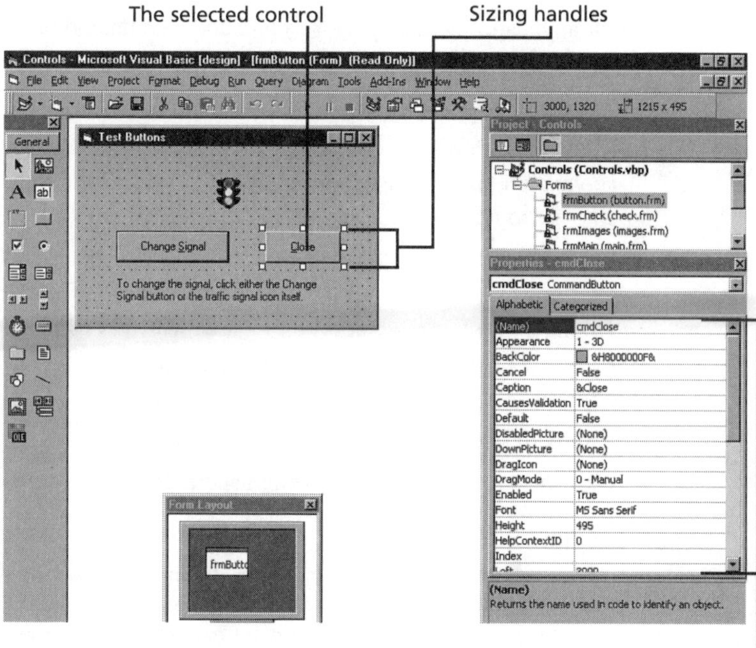

FIGURE 2.9.

The Properties window displays property values for a selected control.

13. Scroll through the property values to see the properties for the selected control.
14. Click another control on the form and look at the updated Properties window. When you select a control by clicking on it, sizing handles appear around the control, and the Properties window updates to reflect the newly selected control's properties.

Leave the project open as you move to the next section. Also, close the Edit and Form Editor toolbars if they appear on your screen because you won't need them in the next section. Now that you've gotten better acquainted with Visual Basic's environment, you are ready to fill that environment with your own creation.

Creating an Application from Scratch

This section concludes today's lesson by walking you through the creation of an application. You won't understand everything that takes place in the next few minutes, but walk through the example anyway because doing so prepares you to learn more. This first application is simple, but it illustrates how Visual Basic makes it easy to create programs. The rest of this 21-day session will explain the details of what this overview shows you.

Setting Up the Form

This first application will display a picture and a command button. The program changes the picture when you click the command button. Follow these steps to create this simple application:

1. Select File, New Project to display the New Project dialog box. If you still have an application open from an earlier section, Visual Basic may ask if you want to save changes to that application. Answer No to save any changes.
2. Select the Standard EXE icon. Your Visual Basic environment will hold only a single form named `Form1` (as the title bar shows). The form appears on the background of the Form window editing area which is white.
3. Click the Maximize window button to expand the Form window editing area (the white background, *not* the gray form itself) to its maximum size. This action gives you room to expand the form.
4. Drag the form's lower-right sizing handle down and to the right. As you drag the

Note

> Sizing handles appear around the form because the form is the only object inside the Form window editing area. Notice that the Properties window displays properties about the form. Forms, just as other objects, have property values you can set.

form, notice the width and height measurements at the right of the toolbar as they change. Size the form so that it measures about 7,400 by 5,200 *twips*. This step produces a small background for your program. Figure 2.10 shows your screen. (Your Form Layout window may appear beneath your Properties window.)

A *twip* is a screen measurement. You can think of a twip as a dot on your screen, but dif-

FIGURE 2.10.

When you resize the Form window, you are resizing your application's program window.

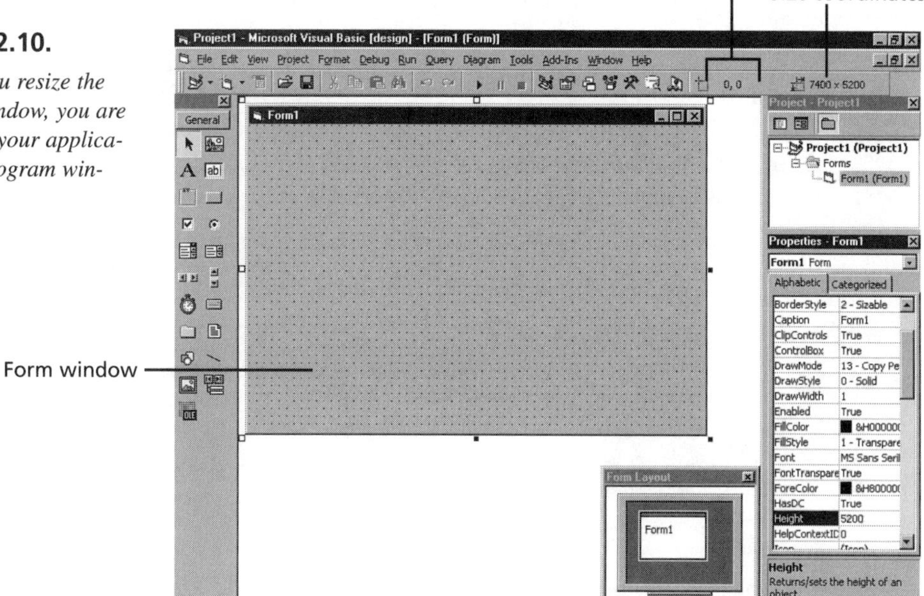

NEW TERM ferent screens and video cards provide different resolutions and, hence, a different number of dots. A twip is a resolution-independent measurement value for an imaginary small screen dot (smaller than the highest resolutions allow). Therefore, when you size a form to 7,400 twips, the form will not require 7,400 actual screen dots (called *pixels*).

5. Select View, Form Layout Window to display the window and center the thumbnail

Tip

> As you locate and size form windows, pay attention to the form-location coordinates and the size coordinates at the right of the toolbar. These values always appear in pairs. The first value in the form-location pair represents the number of twips from the left edge of the screen where the window begins. The second value represents the number of twips from the top edge of the screen where the window will appear. The second pair of

values, the size coordinates, represents the number of twips wide and high the window consumes. The form properties for the form-location coordinates are named `Left` and `Top` to represent the number of twips from the left and top of the screen. The form properties for the size coordinates are named `Width` and `Height` and represent the width and height of the Form window. Visual Basic automatically updates these values in the Properties window when you move and resize the form in the Form window editing area.

screen inside the Form Layout window so that your application window will be centered on the screen when the program starts. Although the Form window itself will not change, the form-location coordinates will reflect the new position.

6. Close the Form Layout window to give you more room for the other windows.

The *grid* is the dot pattern that comprises the Form window's background. You can adjust

The dots that appear inside the Form window make up the *grid*. You can turn on and off the grid by selecting Tools, Options, clicking the General page, and checking or unchecking the Show Grid option. The grid will not appear when you run the application; it appears solely to help you place and size controls on the form.

NEW TERM the grid's dot density from the Tools, Options dialog box.

7. Assign a better name than `Form1` to the form. To do so, you'll see how to work with the Properties window. A property called `(Name)` (enclosed in parentheses to keep the name at the top of the alphabetical property list) holds the selected form's name. (In the future, this tutorial will omit the parentheses from around the `Name` property.) Scroll the Properties window up until you see the `Name` value if you cannot see it, and notice that the `Name` value is currently assigned `Form1`.
8. Click the form's `Name` property and type `frmMyFirst` for the form name. As you type the name, the name appears to the right of the property called `Name` as well as Visual Basic's title bar.
9. Change the form's title bar from its original value to Happy Application by select-

Tip

> You'll change and assign all properties inside the Properties window the same way you just changed the form's name. Scroll to the property, click the property, and enter (or select for those properties with drop-down list boxes) a new property value.

ing the `Caption` property and typing `Happy Application`. The `Caption` property determines what appears in the form's title bar when the user runs the program. The new name appears in both the Properties window and the form's title bar.

10. Before continuing, save the form to disk for safety. Select File, Save Project. The Save Project option saves every file inside your project (your project currently holds only a single form file) as well as a project description file with the filename extension .VBP. Visual Basic asks first for the filename you want to assign to your form. Visual Basic uses the form's `Name` property as the default filename. If you accept that default name, as you should now do, Visual Basic also adds the extension .FRM to the form's filename. (If your project contained more forms or modules or other objects stored in files, Visual Basic would ask you to name the remaining items as well.) Visual Basic then asks for a project name for the project description file. Name the project `HappyApp` before saving the project. Answer No if Visual Basic asks to add the project to the SourceSafe library.

> The project description file is what you load when you want to work on your application in the future. When you load such a project description file, Visual Basic loads all files associated with that project, and their names appear in the Project window.

Adding the Details

Now that the application's background is complete, you are ready to add the details by putting controls on the form. Adding controls to a form typically involves one or more of these steps:

1. Select the control from the toolbox.
2. Place the control in its proper location.
3. Size the control.

4. Set the control's properties.
5. Activate the control with Visual Basic code if needed.

In the steps that follow, you'll quickly learn how to select controls from the toolbox and place those controls on the form. Generally, you'll do these steps in one of two ways:

- Double-click the control's icon on the toolbox. Visual Basic then places that control in the center of the form. You then can drag the control to its proper location and size the control by dragging the control's sizing handles in or out.
- Click the control's icon on the toolbox and move the resulting crosshair mouse cursor to the form when the control is to go. Click and hold your mouse button where the control is to go. As you drag the mouse, Visual Basic draws the control's outline on your form. When you've drawn the control at its proper location and size, release the mouse button to place the control in its proper location.

The following steps spruce up the application you began in the previous section:

1. Double-click the label control so that Visual Basic places the label in the center of your form. The label control contains the letter *A*, as you saw in the previous section "The Toolbar." (Remember that ToolTips pop up to let you know what a toolbox icon is for.) The label is now the selected tool on your Form window editing area so the sizing handles appear around the label. In addition, the Properties window changes to show the label's properties, and the toolbar's location and size coordinate pairs now reflect the label's measurements.

   A label displays text on a form. This new label will hold a title banner for your application.
2. Drag the label up the form until it rests approximately 1,320 twips from the left edge of the form window and 120 twips from the top of the form. The toolbar's location coordinates will let you know the location.

Unless you change the Align Controls to Grid option located on the General tab of the Tools, Options dialog box, Visual Basic automatically aligns all controls to the closest grid point on your form, ensuring that your controls align with each other properly.

3. Double-click the toolbox's command button control to place a command button in the center of your form.
4. Locate the toolbox's image control and click the control's icon once instead of double-clicking to place the control as you did with the label. Move your mouse to

the Form window and draw the image control, trying to first anchor the image at 2,520 twips from the form's left edge and 2,880 from the form's top edge. Size the image at approximately 2,175 twips wide and 1,825 twips high. As you size the image, drag the image's sizing handles slowly so that Visual Basic's ScreenTips pop up showing you the coordinates of the image. When the coordinates appear at their proper size, release your mouse button to place the image at that size. Figure 2.11 shows your screen at this point. The image control will display a graphic image when you run the program. A twip is $^1/_{1440th}$ of an inch.

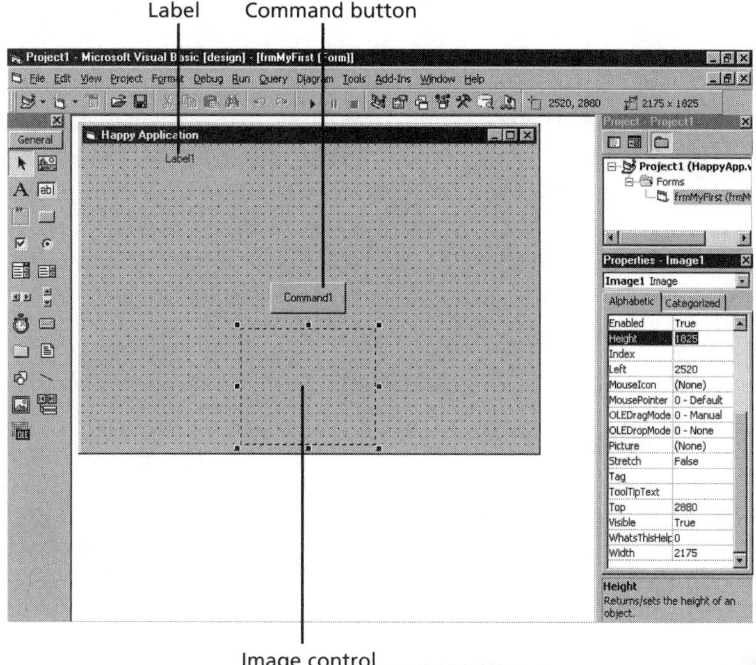

FIGURE 2.11.
Your application is taking shape.

Tip

Although you can place the image control at approximately the same location and size described here, you can match these location and size twip measurements exactly by filling in the following properties with the measurement values described in the previous step: `Left`: 2520, `Top`: 2880, `Width`: 2175, and `Height`: 1825. When property values are specified in the future, this kind of notation will be used. You now know to click the property name and then type the property value to assign new values to properties.

Location twip coordinates and size twip coordinates are always specified in pairs. Often, you'll see such coordinate pairs specified inside parentheses, as in a location value of `(2520, 2880)`.

5. Now that you're more familiar with setting property values for controls, even though you may not understand many of the properties yet, you are now equipped to set additional properties for the form and controls to finalize the look of the application. After you set appropriate property values, you will then add code to connect the controls and to make them work together.

   Table 2.2 contains a list of property values that you now need to set for the form and the three controls. Remember that you must select the form or specific control before you can change property values for that form or control. To select the form, click anywhere inside the form or title bar but not over any of the controls. The Properties window will change to display the form's properties. Click either the label, command button, or image to select the control, and then you can change one of that control's properties by clicking the property name and typing the new value.

At first, setting a control's font information is confusing. When you select the `Font` property for a control, an ellipsis appears after the property value. The ellipsis indicates that you can set more than one value for the `Font` property, and clicking the ellipsis displays a Font dialog box such as the one shown in Figure 2.12. After setting the Font dialog box values and clicking OK, several property values related to the font used on the control's caption will change to reflect your new values.

FIGURE 2.12.

The Font dialog box enables you to set multiple property values for the `Font` *property.*

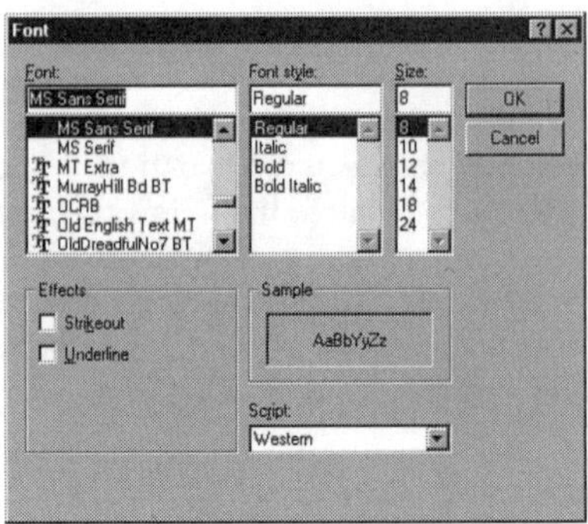

TABLE 2.2. ASSIGN THE FOLLOWING PROPERTY VALUES TO THE APPLICATION'S FORM AND CONTROLS.

Control	*Property*	*Property value*
Form	`Max Button`	`False` (open the drop-down list box to see values)
Label	`Alignment`	`Center` (open the drop-down list box to see values)
Label	`Name`	`lblHappy`
Label	`Caption`	`Have a happy day!`
Label	`Font`	`Courier New`
Label	`Font style`	`Bold`
Label	`Size`	`36`
Label	`Left`	`1320`
Label	`Height`	`1695`
Label	`Top`	`120`
Label	`Width`	`4695`
Image	`Name`	`imgHappy`
Image	`Stretch`	`True`
Command button	`Name`	`cmdHappy`
Command button	`Caption`	`Click Here`

While writing your application, you can run the application to see what you've done so far. For example, if you now pressed F5 to run the application, Visual Basic would analyze your program and display an active program window with a command button that you can click. Nothing happens when you click the command button except that the command button shows the click. In addition, nothing appears where you placed the image control, but the next section will fix both of those minor problems. To exit the program, click the program window's Close window button. You'll learn how to add more graceful exit capabilities in tomorrow's lesson.

Finalizing with Code

Adding Visual Basic programming statements will turn your creation into a working, although simple, application. The following process may seem like magic because you'll be adding code that looks somewhat cryptic in a Code window that will pop up unexpectedly. Follow the next few steps to add the code, and subsequent days will fill in the details about what you are doing:

1. Double-click the form somewhere on the grid inside the Form window. The form disappears, and a Code window appears with the following lines at the top:

```
Private Sub Form_Load()

End Sub
```

These lines are two of the four lines needed for code required by the form. The Code window works like a miniature word processor in which you can add, delete, and change statements that appear in your program code.

All code appears in *procedures*, and all procedures require beginning and ending lines of code that define the procedure's start and stop locations. Visual Basic automatically adds the first and final line of many procedures as it has done here.

NEW TERM A *procedure* is a section of Visual Basic programming code that holds Visual Basic programming statements and that performs a specific task, such as the centering of a Form window.

2. You can now type the following lines. Press the spacebar three times before each line so it appears slightly to the right of the start and end lines. Visual Basic programmers often indent the body of procedures to make it easy to locate the procedure's beginning and ending in a list of multiple procedures. This code ensures that your application window appears in the center of the screen no matter what screen resolution you run the program in:

```
frmMyFirst.Left = (Screen.Width - frmMyFirst.Width) / 2
frmMyFirst.Top = (Screen.Height - frmMyFirst.Height) / 2
```

After you type just a little of the first line, Visual Basic displays an Auto List Members drop-down list box as shown in Figure 2.13. When Visual Basic senses that you are about to specify a control's property value, Visual Basic offers this drop-down list box of property choices for that control, so you can select a property instead of typing the full property name. After you select a property and press the spacebar, Visual Basic fills in the property, and you can continue with the rest of the line.

3. Click the Project window's View Object button to return to the Form window.
4. Double-click the command button to once again open the Code window. Your previous code will be there, and a new set of beginning and ending statements will appear for a new procedure related to the command button. Press the spacebar three times and type the following line between the two that are there:

```
imgHappy.Picture = LoadPicture("\Program Files\Microsoft Visual
Studio\Common\Graphics\Bitmaps\Assorted\Happy.bmp")
```

As soon as you type the `LoadPicture`'s opening parenthesis, Visual Basic offers a pop-up help similar to the Auto List Members drop-down list box you saw a couple of steps ago. Some Visual Basic statements, especially those with parentheses such as the ones you see in this statement, require that you type one or more values. Visual Basic pops up the format of these required values, so you'll know how many to enter. You'll learn more about why these values are required as you learn more about the language. Visual Basic is a large language, so this help from Visual Basic comes in handy.

2

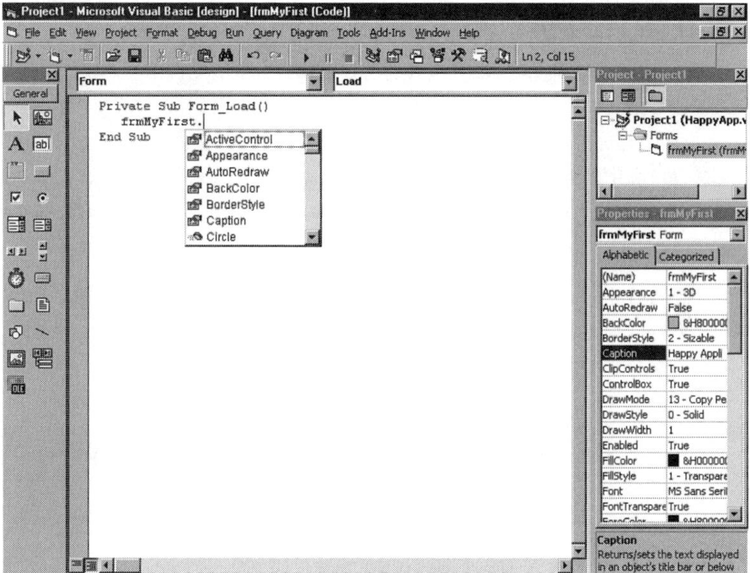

FIGURE 2.13.
Visual Basic helps speed up your entry of code.

5. Run your program and click the command button. An image like that shown in Figure 2.14 appears. You have successfully completed your new application without resorting to the Application wizard. You've created an application that displays a picture when you click the command button. The application contains code, and its controls all have property values that you've set.
6. Click the Close window button to terminate the program. Be sure to save your project before you exit Visual Basic.

FIGURE 2.14.
Your application produces a graphic image from the click of your mouse.

Summary

Today's lesson described the Visual Basic environment because you can become an effective Visual Basic programmer only with an understanding of the various windows and interface. Visual Basic supplies several levels of help, including Online Help, Web support, and personal technical support offered in a variety of ways. If the Visual Basic interface or language poses a problem too big for you to figure out alone, help is close at hand.

To create an application, you must create a new project, add controls to the Form window, set properties for the form and controls, and activate the controls with code. The project you created in today's lesson should have been surprisingly simple to produce, especially given the little bit of code required (three lines).

Tomorrow's lesson answers a few questions you may have about controls and their properties.

Q&A

Q How large should my application's Form window be?

A Your application determines how large your Form window should be, as well as how many forms the application will need. For simple programs, one form is plenty, but the size of that form depends on the number of controls you place on the form and the nature of the program.

Today's lesson could have created a project with a fully maximized form, but with only three controls, there would have been too much empty space on the form.

Q What did the code in today's lesson do?

A The code was necessary for today's application to work properly. The line with the `LoadPicture` keyword is critical because it loads the picture when the user clicks the command button. The other two lines, the ones you added when you double-clicked inside the Form window to open the Code window, center the form within the screen coordinates of whatever screen size displays the program.

Q If the code centered the Form window, did I have to use the Form Layout window to center the form?

A No matter where you placed the form in the Form Layout window, the two lines you typed in the form's procedure will center the form when the program begins.

The Form Layout window is a rough guide to give you an idea where the Form window will appear when the form loads. For completely accurate control, especially if you are unsure of the size of the screen on which your program will run, you need to position the form with code in the Code window.

Workshop

The Workshop provides quiz questions to help you solidify your understanding of the material covered and exercises to provide you with experience in using what you've learned. You should understand the quiz and exercise answers before continuing to the next chapter. Answers are provided in Appendix A, "Answers to Exercises."

Quiz

1. What is the difference between the toolbox and the toolbar?
2. What is the name of the subscription-based online service Microsoft offers for programmers?
3. True/False. The Form window holds one form at a time.
4. What happens when you click a toolbox control?
5. What happens when you double-click a toolbox control?
6. True/False. You set control properties from the Toolbox window.
7. How does Visual Basic determine which control properties appear in the Properties window?
8. What does an ellipsis indicate on a Properties window value?
9. What is the name of the property that specifies the command button's title?
10. Why should you change the control names from their default values?

Exercise

Load the application you created today so that you can modify it. Add color to the application by making the form's background blue. In addition, place an extra command button, labeled `Exit`, on the form and add an appropriate `Name` caption for the control. Add the following line inside the new procedure that appears in the Code window, which is related to the command button:

```
End
```

Run the application and click the Exit button to see a more graceful exit than you previously had in the application.

WEEK 1

DAY 3

Managing Controls

Now that you've created two applications, one with the Application wizard and one from scratch without the help of the wizard, it's time to begin studying how Visual Basic works. The previous two days' worth of hands-on sessions showed you how easy it is to create programs and helped give you a feel for the Visual Basic environment. Starting today, you'll begin to understand how the components of a Visual Basic program go together, especially how the controls and properties work together.

Today, you learn the following:

- Common control properties
- Why controls come with so many properties
- About the more common tools on the Toolbox window
- How accelerator keys help speed data entry
- How focus helps users select controls
- How event procedures work

Studying Controls

The toolbox holds the collection of controls that you use in your applications. The toolbox does not hold a limited number of each tool; in other words, you can double-click the Label control as many times as you like as you create your forms; Visual Basic sends a new label to the target form each time.

The collection of controls (also called tools) on the toolbox varies depending on your application's requirements. For much of this 21-day tutorial, the toolbox will hold the same set of tools you saw in yesterday's lesson. These tools are the standard controls loaded when you create a new application.

A control is not available to your program until that control appears in the toolbox. Therefore, you cannot, for example, add an Internet browsing control to your form until you add the Internet browsing control to your toolbox. If you use the Application Wizard, the wizard will add controls to the toolbox when needed to generate your project.

When a lesson in this book requires a control not found on the standard toolbox, the lesson will explain how you can add that control to your toolbox.

As Figure 3.1 shows, your toolbox can get quite complicated when it fills up with too many controls. Such a large toolbox can take away from your other windows' space. You can drag the Toolbox window's title bar to another location if you want to use the left edge of your screen to view your form. In addition, you can resize the Toolbox window for more or less room.

Do	Don't
	DON'T make the Toolbox so small that tools get hidden from view. No scrollbars appear if you size the Toolbox window so small that some controls are no longer visible. To use the controls that are outside the window's boundaries in this case, you have to expand the Toolbox window until the hidden tools appear once again.

FIGURE 3.1.
The Toolbox window should be a manageable size.

NEW TERM Visual Basic purists apply more strict names to the sets of controls available. The controls that first appear in the Toolbox window are called the *intrinsic controls*. The ActiveX controls, with the .OCX extension, are external controls you can add to the Toolbox window. *Insertable controls* are controls made from external applications, such as Microsoft Excel.

Many of the controls require similar properties. Table 3.1 lists some common properties that most controls support. You can probably see why so many of Table 3.1's properties exist for multiple controls. All controls have a screen location (indicated by the `Left` and `Top` properties) and a size (indicated by the `Width` and `Height` properties), and most have foreground and background colors as well as font properties, if the controls display text.

TABLE 3.1. COMMON PROPERTIES FOR SEVERAL VISUAL BASIC CONTROLS.

Property	*Description*
`Alignment`	Determines whether text on the control, such as a label or command button, is left-justified, centered, or right-justified on the control.
`BackColor`	Specifies the color of the control's background, which you select from a palette of colors when you open the property's drop-down list box of colors.
`BorderStyle`	Determines whether the control has a border around it.
`Caption`	Lists the text displayed on the control.

continues

3

TABLE 3.1. CONTINUED

Property	*Description*
`Enabled`	Set by a drop-down list box, this property is either `True` if you want the control to respond to the user or `False` if you want the control not to respond to the user. This property is useful for turning on and off controls when they are and are not available during a program's execution.
`Font`	Displays a Font dialog box from which you can set various font properties, such as size and style, for a control's text.
`ForeColor`	Specifies the color of the control's foreground, which you select from a palette of colors when you open the property's drop-down list box of colors.
`Height`	Specifies the number of twips high the control is.
`Left`	Indicates the starting twip from the left edge of the form where the control appears. For a form, the `Left` property specifies the number of twips from the left edge of the screen.
`MousePointer`	Determines the shape of the mouse cursor when the user moves the mouse over the control at runtime.
`Name`	Specifies the name of the control. As you saw in yesterday's lesson, the Properties window displays the `Name` property in parentheses so that it appears first in the list of properties.
`ToolTipText`	Holds the text that appears when the user rests the mouse cursor over the control at runtime (similar to ScreenTips).
`Top`	Is the starting twip from the top edge of the form where the control appears. For a form, the `Top` property describes the number of twips from the top edge of the screen.
`Visible`	Set by a drop-down list box, this property is `True` if you want the control to be visible on the form or `False` if you want the control to be hidden from view.
`Width`	Specifies the number of twips wide that the control is.

Remember that all controls have all their property values set before you ever change a value. As soon as you place a control, Visual Basic uses a set of predetermined property values (the most common values) for the controls. In addition, Visual Basic assigns default names and captions to the controls, although you'll surely want to change these properties. Many of the default values work well in many cases. You won't change all of a control's property values from its default set.

You already know that you can set the properties for a control when you write the application, but you can also set and change property values with Visual Basic code during the application's execution. For example, the `Enabled` property is often changed during the execution of a program if a particular control is temporarily unavailable to the user. You may, for example, disable a command button that produces a report until the user has specified the contents of the report.

Caution

Not all properties for all controls appear in the Properties window. Properties that you can set only with Visual Basic code do not appear in the Properties window.

Tip

Some control properties, such as the `Alignment` property values, may look strange because their drop-down list boxes display numbers to the left of their values. For example, the `Alignment` property can take on one of these three values: `0-Left Justify`, `1-Right Justify`, and `2-Center`. You can use your mouse to select these values from the list without worrying about the numbers in them, but you can also, after opening the drop-down list box for a property, type the number that corresponds to the value you want to quickly set that value. The numbers also come in handy when you assign property values to controls with Visual Basic code. You can assign the numeric value instead of having to type the entire value, such as `0-Left Justify`. The numbers provide shortcuts when you write code, as you'll see in future lessons.

The following sections describe the most useful standard toolbox controls. You'll learn about several important properties associated with those controls. Today, you will not learn about all the toolbox's controls, just those that you'll work with over the first few days of Visual Basic programming.

You don't need an in-depth reference on all the properties for all the controls because some of the properties are rarely used. Most Visual Basic programmers don't even know all of the properties available for a control. Generally, if you need to make a control appear a certain way, a property probably exists to accomplish that. By taking a brief tour of the controls and their properties in the following sections, you'll better understand the purpose for the controls, and you'll have a better idea of which properties are available.

Tip

Some programmers prefer to view properties in the Property window grouped by category. To group properties this way, click the Properties window's Categorized tab, as Figure 3.2 shows.

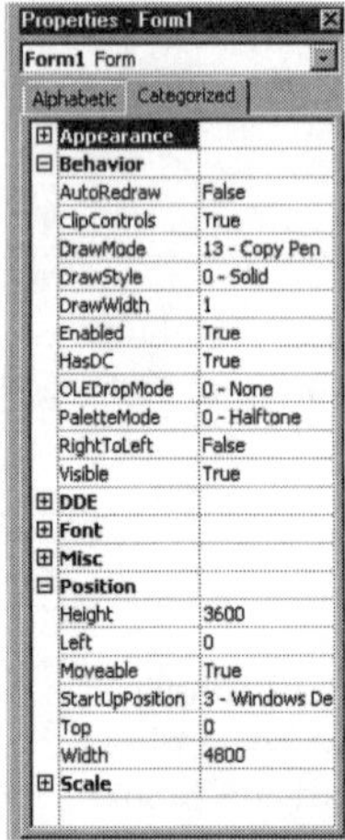

FIGURE 3.2.

You can categorize properties to more quickly locate properties you need.

The Form's Properties

Many form properties correspond with other control properties that you learned about in Table 3.1. The form, however, is unique in that it does not reside on a form, but appears on the user's window. That is why the form's `Left`, `Top`, `Width`, and `Height` properties all correspond to the edge of the screen and not to a Form window.

These form properties are important as well:

- **`BorderStyle`.** This property determines how the Form window responds to the user's efforts to resize it. Some values you may need are `0-None`, which offers a form without any edge or title bar, `1-Fixed Single`, which offers a nonsizable window (the user can close the window but not resize, minimize, or maximize the window), and `2-Sizable` (the default), which offers a regular sizable window with maximize and minimize buttons.
- **`ControlBox`.** This property's value of `True` or `False` determines whether the form's *Control menu* appears.

NEW TERM A *Control menu* is the menu that appears when you click a window's icon in the upper-left corner of the window. The Control menu enables you to move, size, minimize, maximize, and close a window.

- **`Icon`.** This property specifies an icon filename for the Windows taskbar icon that appears when the user minimizes the form.

- **`MaxButton`.** This property determines whether the form contains an active Maximize window button.
- **`MinButton`.** This property determines whether the form contains an active Minimize window button. (If you set both the `MaxButton` and `MinButton` properties to `False`, neither appears on the form.)
- **`Movable`.** This property determines if the user can move the form or if the form is to remain in its displayed location.
- **`ShowInTaskbar`.** This property's `True` or `False` value determines whether the open form appears on the user's Windows taskbar.
- **`StartUpPosition`.** This property provides a quick way to specify the starting position of the form on the screen. One of the most useful values is `2-CenterScreen` that centers the form on the user's screen when the form first appears.
- **`WindowState`.** This property determines the size (normal, maximized, or minimized) of the form (useful for starting a minimized form).

The Pointer Tool

The pointer tool is the only toolbox item that is *not* a control. About the only use for the pointer tool is to eliminate the crosshair mouse cursor that appears when you select any of the other controls in the Toolbox window.

The Label Control

The label control displays text. Although your user cannot alter the text that appears on a label, you can, at runtime, change the label's text through code. (See Day 5's lesson for details.) Programmers often use labels for titles, prompts, and descriptions. For example, when you want the user to enter a value into another control, such as a text box, you place a label next to that data-entry location on the form describing the value you want the user to enter. Without the label, the users would not know what you needed them to enter.

Two properties, `AutoSize` and `WordWrap`, affect the way you display text on a label. If you set `AutoSize` to a `True` value, the label automatically expands horizontally across the form to display all the text you've assigned to the `Caption` property. If you set `WordWrap` to `True`, Visual Basic keeps the label's width but expands the label vertically to display as many lines as needed to show the full caption. Figure 3.3 shows three versions of a label with the same `Caption` property but with a different combination of `AutoSize` and `WordWrap` properties, so you can study the effect of the two properties.

Surprisingly, for `WordWrap` to work, you must also set `AutoSize` to `True`. Visual Basic needs to be able to expand the label at least partially horizontally if a single word in the caption is larger than the label's width.

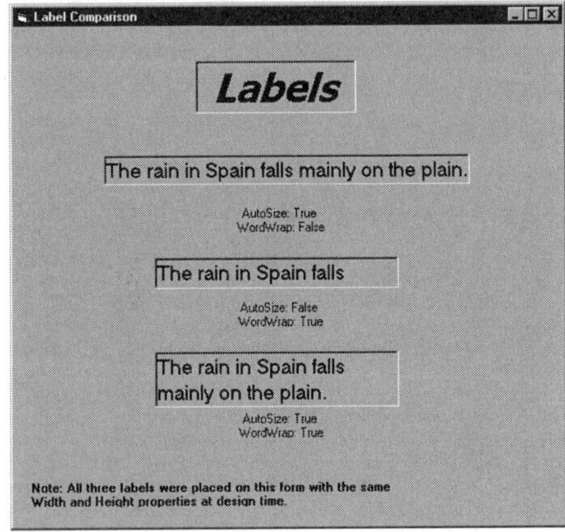

FIGURE 3.3.

The `AutoSize` and `WordWrap` properties affect the way a label displays its caption.

The Text Box Control

Use a text box control when you want the user to type something, such as an answer to a prompt, when you want to collect values, such as name and address information. Often, a default value is helpful for your users, and your Visual Basic program can supply an initial value. For example, if you are asking the user to enter a date, you might place today's date in the text box so that the user can accept the date without having to enter it.

Text boxes don't make for good yes/no, true/false answers. In other words, if you must ask your user to select between two values or answer a yes or no question, other controls—such as an option button or list box control that you'll learn about on Days 5 and 6—are better to use.

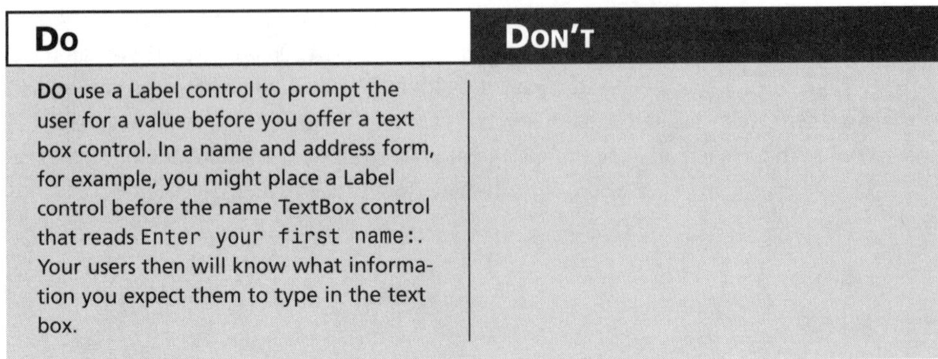

Do	Don't
DO use a Label control to prompt the user for a value before you offer a text box control. In a name and address form, for example, you might place a Label control before the name TextBox control that reads `Enter your first name:`. Your users then will know what information you expect them to type in the text box.	

NEW TERM Programmers must distinguish between *designtime* and *runtime*. Designtime is the time when you write and maintain an application. Runtime is when you or a user runs an application. When you place a value in a text box's `Text` property at designtime, you are placing the default value that the user will see at runtime. At runtime, the user then can change the text box's value to a different value by typing over or editing your default value.

When placing text boxes on forms, you'll find the following text box properties useful:

- **`Alignment`.** This property determines how the text aligns inside a text box whose `MultiLine` property is set to `True`. The `Alignment` property has no meaning for single-line text boxes.
- **`Locked`.** This property determines whether the user can enter a value or change the default value of the text box. If `True`, the user cannot change the text box value until the program, at runtime, assigns a `False` value to this property.
- **`MaxLength`.** This property specifies the maximum number of characters that the text box will accept. A value of `0` indicates that the user can enter a value of any length.
- **`MultiLine`.** If `True`, the property specifies that the text box can hold more than a single line of text. A vertical scrollbar will appear if the user enters more text than will fit on a single line, unless you've disallowed scrollbars with the `ScrollBars` property. The `Alignment` property, whose default value is `0-Left Justify`, determines how the multiple lines of text align.
- **`PasswordChar`.** This property designates a character, such as an asterisk, that will appear in place of the characters the user types into the text box. In other words, if the user is entering a secret code, only asterisks will appear on the screen as the user types the code instead of the code's value so that nobody looking over the user's shoulder can read the code. Although the asterisks appear, the text box receives the actual value that the user types.
- **`ScrollBars`.** This property determines if and how many scrollbars will appear on the text box. A value of `0-None` keeps scrollbars from appearing. `1-Horizontal` allows only horizontal scrollbars. `2-Vertical` allows only vertical scrollbars. `3-Both` allows both horizontal and vertical scrollbars.

You must set the `MultiLine` property to `True` before vertical scrollbars can appear in a text box.

- **`Text`.** This property specifies the initial text (the default value) that appears in the text box.

A special cursor comes into play with text boxes and forms. Your user enters and edits text using the *text cursor*. Clicking a text box's text places the text cursor at that point so that the user can add, change, or delete text from within the text box.

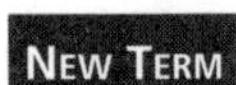

The *text cursor*, also called the *caret* or the *insertion point*, is a vertical bar used for entering and editing text in controls such as text boxes.

Load and run the sample application called Controls from your MSDN's Samples folder. Select the text box option to practice using text boxes. Figure 3.4 shows the screen that appears. You will be able to practice working with single-line and multiline text boxes as well as with the text cursor and scrollbars. The Controls application even shows that you can select text within a text box and copy, cut, and paste text to and from text boxes using standard Windows operations.

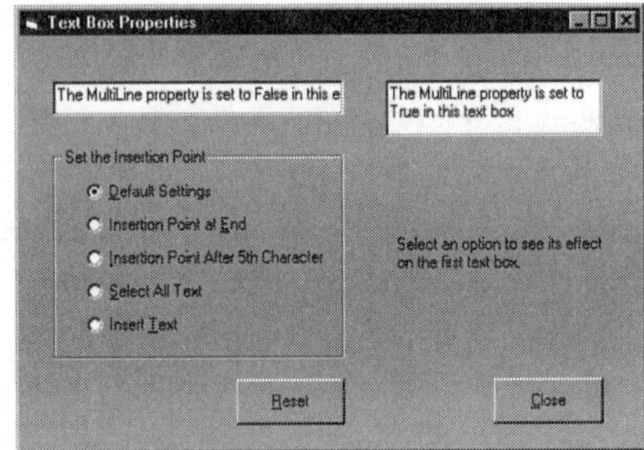

FIGURE 3.4.

The sample Controls application lets you work with several styles of text boxes.

The Command Button Control

Almost every application's form contains a command button. With the click of a command button, the user can indicate that an answer is ready, a printer has paper, or that it's time to terminate the program. As you saw in yesterday's lesson, Visual Basic takes care of showing that the command button is pressed when the user clicks it.

NEW TERM

An *accelerator key* is a key that, when combined with the Alt key, triggers a response. For example, menu bar options all have accelerator keys, such as Alt+F for the File menu option. The underlined letter in a menu bar option name or on a command button's label indicates the accelerator key for that object.

Tip

> Command buttons aren't just for mouse clicks! You can add an *accelerator key* to a command button's label so that the user can select the command button by pressing the appropriate key combination, such as Alt+R. The `Caption` property determines a command button's accelerator key. In addition to an accelerator key, the user can select a command button by pressing Enter if the command button is the selected control (see the section called "Control Focus" for more information) or if the `Default` property is `True`. In some cases, you may want the user to be able to trigger a command button by pressing the Esc key, such as when a command button offers an exit from a program and the `Cancel` property handles Esc.

The following properties are useful for command button programming:

- **`Cancel`.** This property determines how the command button responds to the Esc key. If `True`, the user can trigger (simulate a click) the command button by pressing Esc. Only one command button on a form can have a `Cancel` value of `True`. If you set more than one command button's `Cancel` property to `True`, Visual Basic resets all but the last one to `False`.
- **`Caption`.** This property specifies the text that appears on the command button. If you precede a letter with an ampersand (&), Visual Basic makes that letter the accelerator key. A `Caption` of `E&xit` produces a command button such as the one you see in Figure 3.5. The user can trigger this command button by clicking the button or by pressing Alt+X.

FIGURE 3.5.
A control's `Caption` property that contains an ampersand before a letter determines the accelerator key for that control.

- **`Default`.** This property determines how the command button responds to the Enter key. If `True`, the user can trigger (simulate a click) the command button by pressing Enter unless the user moves the control focus (see the next section) to another control first. Only one command button on a form can have a `Default` value of `True`. If you set more than one command button's `Default` property to `True`, Visual Basic resets all but the last one to `False`. The command button with a `Default` value of `True` is always the selected command button when a form first appears.

- **`Picture.`** This property specifies a graphic image that appears on the command button in place of a caption. The `Style` property must be set to `1-Graphical` before a picture will appear.
- **`Style.`** This property determines whether a command button displays a text caption (if set to `0-Standard`) or a picture (if set to `1-Graphical`).

Do	Don't
DO choose different accelerator keys for your controls.	**DON'T** use the same accelerator key for more than one control. If two or more controls have the same accelerator key, Visual Basic will select only the first one in the *focus order* (see the next section) for the accelerator key, and your user will not be able to select any of the other controls with that accelerator key.

The Image Control

A brief mention of the image control is in order here because you placed an image on the application you created in yesterday's program. The image control is one of two controls (the picture box is the other) that display graphic images. The image properties determine the file used for the image and whether the image control resizes to fit the file or the file resizes to fill the image control's size. You'll learn all about the image and picture box controls in Day 14's lesson, "Introducing VB Graphics and Multimedia."

Although many more controls exist, you'll learn about the others as you progress through these 21 days. The next section describes how the user can use the keyboard to trigger any control on the form.

Control Focus

Only one control on a form can have the *focus* at any one time. The first control with the focus is determined by the order in which you placed the controls on the form or, more accurately, the order determined by the `TabIndex` property of each control on your form. Not every control can receive focus. Only those controls the user can interact with can receive the focus. For example, a label control cannot receive the focus because the user cannot interact with label controls.

NEW TERM The *focus*, or *control focus*, is the currently selected control. Visual Basic indicates the control with the focus by highlighting the control.

For a moment, study Figure 3.6. Notice that the center command button has the focus because it's highlighted by a dashed box. Visual Basic typically displays the control with the focus with just such a dashed box. In the figure, if the user pressed Enter, the center command button would trigger because that's the command button with the focus. The user could also press Tab or Shift+Tab to move the focus to another control. If the user pressed Tab, the third command button would receive the focus, so then if the user pressed Enter, the third command button would be the one to respond.

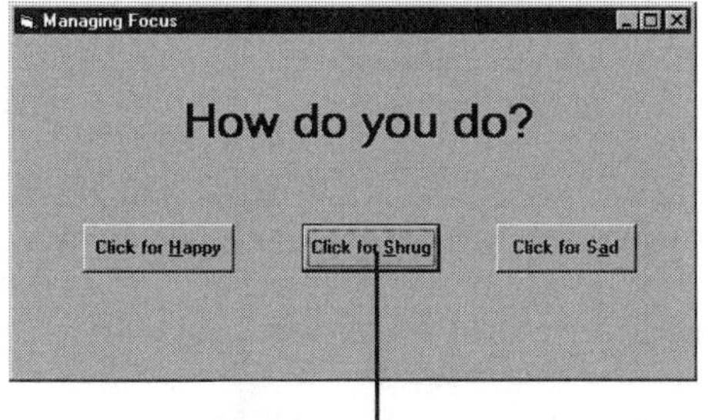

FIGURE 3.6.
The highlighted control has the focus, but the user can move the focus to a different control before pressing Enter.

Note

> Notice that the third command button's accelerator key is Alt+A, not Alt+S. The center command button already used the Alt+S accelerator key with a `Caption` property value of `Click for Shrug`, so the programmer had to select a different and unique accelerator key for the third command button.

Tip

> Remember that if a control contains a `Default` value of `True`, that control will be the one with the focus when the user first sees the form. Of course, the user can always move the focus to a different control.

All controls have a `TabIndex` property. As you place controls on a form, Visual Basic automatically sets the `TabIndex` property to 0, 1, and so on, placing a unique and sequential number in each control's `TabIndex` property. Even controls that the user does not normally interact with, such as labels, have `TabIndex` properties. The `TabIndex` property determines the focus order.

You will not always place controls on a form in the correct `TabIndex` order. Sometimes you'll add a control between two others. You may need to change the `TabIndex` order to match the focus order you desire. For example, you may want the focus to move down the form in columns as the user presses Tab, or you may want the focus to move across the controls in rows as the user presses Tab. The order you want the focus to move is determined solely by the values in the controls' `TabIndex` properties.

If the next control that gets the focus—indicated by the `TabIndex` property—is a label, Visual Basic sends the focus to the next control in sequence. Knowing this, you can offer your user an accelerator key for a text box that you could otherwise not offer. Consider the form in Figure 3.7. The `First Name:` label has a `TabIndex` one greater than the text box that follows. No matter which control has the focus, if the user presses Alt+F, Visual Basic sends the focus to the label, which immediately sends the focus down the line to the text box because labels cannot normally accept the focus. When you place text boxes with description labels on a form, consider adding accelerator keys to the labels that identify the text boxes so that your users will have quick access to any text box they want to enter or change. Of course, you must make sure that each matching pair of label and text box controls has consecutive `TabIndex` values.

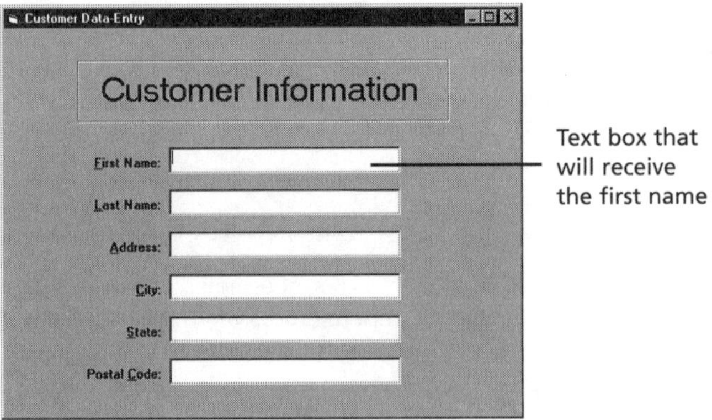

FIGURE 3.7. *The user can press Alt+F to enter the first name in the text box.*

Event Procedures

Event procedures sometimes challenge beginning Visual Basic programmers, but the concept of an event procedure is very simple. When the user presses a command button or enters text into a text box, something has to happen that tells the application the user has just made a move. You saw in yesterday's lesson that Windows receives events from all kinds of sources. Most events come directly from the user at the keyboard and mouse running applications within Windows.

When Windows recognizes that the user triggered an event and that the event is not a system event, such as a Windows Start button click, but an event directly needed by an application, Windows passes that the event to the application. If you've written an event procedure to respond to that exact event, your application will respond to the event. If you haven't written an event procedure, the event goes unhandled.

All kinds of events can occur, such as a click, a double-click, or a keystroke. In addition, multiple controls on your form can receive the same kinds of events. For example, both a command button and a text box can receive a `Click` event, because the user can click the mouse over either control. Therefore, you must not only write an event procedure for a particular event, but you must also specify which control that event belongs to.

Note

> The concept of writing event procedures for all events you want to handle and for each control is vital to your understanding of Visual Basic. How many click-related event procedures must you write to handle three command buttons on your form? You must write three event procedures, because the user can click any of the three command buttons. If you write a `Click` procedure that is not tied to a specific control, your program cannot respond differently to the command buttons. You have to write a separate `Click` procedure for each command button. When Windows passes the `Click` event to your program, Windows also passes the control that generated the event. Only if you've written an event procedure for both that control and that event will your application be able to respond to the event.

Suppose your application displays four command buttons on the form. Here's the process that can occur:

1. When the user clicks any of the command buttons, Windows recognizes that an event just took place.
2. Windows analyzes the event and notices that the event belongs to your application.
3. Windows passes the event and control to your application.
4. If your application has an event procedure written for the control that received the event, the event procedure's code (the code that you wrote in the Code window) executes.

Code inside a control's event procedure will never execute if the control's event never takes place. This quality makes Visual Basic a very responsive system, because you'll write all kinds of event procedures that sit around until their exact event occurs. Then they take over no matter what else is being done at the time.

Common Control Events

You should familiarize yourself with common events that can occur for the controls that you know about. Both the form and its controls can receive events. Here are some common form events that can occur during an application's execution:

- **`Activate`.** This event occurs when a form gets the focus. If an application contains multiple forms, the `Activate` event occurs when the user changes to a different form by clicking on the form or by selecting the form from a menu.
- **`Click`.** This event occurs when the user clicks anywhere on the form. If the user clicks a form that's partially hidden from view because another form has the focus, both a `Click` and an `Activate` event take place.

A right-click triggers the `Click` event when the user right-clicks over a form. As you learn more about programming with the mouse, you'll learn how to determine which mouse button triggered the `Click` event.

- **`DblClick`.** This event occurs when the user double-clicks the form.
- **`Deactivate`.** This event occurs when another form gets the focus. Therefore, both the `Activate` and `Deactivate` events occur when the user selects a different form. You may choose to write event procedures for both events for each form, for only one event for one of the forms, or a combination thereof depending on the needs of your application.
- **`Initialize`.** This event occurs when the form is first generated.
- **`Load`.** This event occurs right as the form is loaded into active memory and appears on the screen.
- **`Paint`.** This event occurs when Windows must redraw the form because the user uncovered part of the form from under another object, such as an icon.
- **`Resize`.** This event occurs when the user changes the size of the form.

- **`Unload`.** This event occurs when the application removes a form from the window using code. When an application is terminated, all loaded forms are first unloaded, so you must write an `Unload` event procedure for each form if you want to perform some kind of clean-up or file-saving procedure at the end of an application's session.

The following events are common text box events:

- **`Change`.** This event occurs when the user changes the text.
- **`Click`.** This event occurs when the user clicks the text box.
- **`DblClick`.** This event occurs when the user double-clicks the text box.

Note

> Some events available for most controls, such as keyboard and mouse-control events, are handled elsewhere in this 21-day tutorial.

Most of these text box events are supported by labels as well, but the nature of labels makes them trigger the events in a slightly different manner. For example, although a label control supports a `Change` event, the user cannot change a label directly. Visual Basic code, however, can change a label, and when that happens, the `Change` event takes place.

The Image control supports the same set of events as the Label control. The Image control is a lot like a Label control except that a graphic image appears in place of text on an image.

Note

> Remember that many more events exist than you are learning about today. The events described here will be useful as you begin to probe more deeply into Visual Basic.

The command button control also supports the same set of events listed previously for text boxes. Keep the following in mind when programming command button events:

- When only a single command button resides on a form, pressing the spacebar when the command button has the focus will trigger the command button's event procedure.

- If a command button's `Cancel` property is `True`, pressing Esc triggers the `Click` event.
- Pressing the accelerator key combination can trigger a command button's `Click` event.

Not all of your application's events come from the user's actions. You can trigger events with Visual Basic code. For example, you could ask your user to press a command button when the user is ready to see a computed total. The command button's `Click` event procedure will compute and print the total. However, after a certain period of time, your code can trigger that same `Click` event for the command button. Therefore, the total eventually appears with or without the user's clicking of the command button.

Writing Event Procedures

Remember that event procedures contain Visual Basic code. The event procedures are sections of code that handle a particular control's event. One control might have several event procedures if you want to respond to several different kinds of events for that control.

Visual Basic uses an event procedure's name to determine these two things about the procedure:

- Which control will trigger the procedure
- Which event will trigger the procedure

Here is the format of all event procedure names:

```
ControlName_EventName ( )
```

The underscore separates the control name from the event name and is required. All event procedures are named this way. Therefore, an event procedure named`cmdExit_DblClick ()` executes if and only if the command button named `cmdExit`'s event named `DblClick` occurs.

You'll eventually fill some event procedure parentheses with values after you learn more about Visual Basic programming. Even if the parentheses are left blank, as they were in the application you created yesterday, the parentheses are still required. The parentheses also offer a way to distinguish event procedure names from control names, even though the parentheses are not part of the actual name.

The code inside the `cmdExit_DblClick ()` event procedure executes only if the user double-clicks the command button named `cmdExit`. If this were the only event procedure in the application, the application would ignore every other event that takes place. If the user clicked the Exit command button, for example, nothing would happen, because a click is different from a double-click.

Almost every event procedure you write while you learn Visual Basic will begin with the words `Private Sub`. The `Private` keyword is optional; if you don't specify `Private`, Visual Basic assumes that the event procedure is private.

Visual Basic supports two kinds of procedures: *functions* and *subroutines*. All event procedures will be subroutines. The body of an event procedure can be one to several hundred lines long, although it's best to keep procedures as short as possible. If you find yourself writing an extremely long procedure, consider breaking it down into multiple, smaller procedures to make maintenance easier later on. Listing 3.1 is a sample of what `cmdExit_DblClick ()` might look like if it appeared inside an application.

LISTING 3.1. AN EVENT PROCEDURE THAT OCCURS WHEN THE USER DOUBLE-CLICKS THE COMMAND BUTTON.

```
1: Private Sub cmdExit_DblClick ( )
2:    lblTitle.Caption = "New Page"
3:    intTotal = intCustNum + 1
4: End Sub
```

You'll see numbers such as those to the left of Listing 3.1's code throughout the rest of the book's listings. The numbers are not part of the program; they are for reference only as you learn to program. If the text needs to refer to a line of code, the number to the left of the line makes for an easy reference.

NEW TERM A *function* acts like a baseball pitcher because a function always sends a value, called the *return value*, to somewhere else in the program. The keyword `Function` indicates that a procedure is a function and not a subroutine. A *subroutine*, indicated by the `Sub` keyword, does not send a return value, but it does perform work through its code. Event procedures are always subroutines; you'll use functions for other kinds of work. You'll learn much more about the differences between functions and subroutines as you progress through these 21 days.

The first line of this event procedure tells much about the event procedure. From the first line, you know the procedure is private (available only to the current application module). You also know that the event procedure is a subroutine, so no value is returned anywhere. The event procedure is for the command button (indicated by the prefix `cmd`) that the developer named `cmdExit`. You know the event procedure responds only to double-clicks that occur on this command button.

The body of the event procedure is two lines long. You don't have to understand anything in the body at this time. The last line of event procedures always finalizes the procedure and lets you and Visual Basic know where the procedure is to end. (All functions end, as you can probably guess, with the `End Function` statement.)

Remember that you enter all code from the Code window. The Code window acts like a simple word processor. When you are ready to write an event procedure, you can get to the Code window in several ways. You can select the control for which you want to write an event procedure for and select View, Code, or you can click the Project window's View Code toolbar button.

An even easier way is to double-click any control or form inside the Form window editing area. Visual Basic automatically opens the Code window for that object, guesses at the kind of event you want to write (using the most common event for that particular control), and writes the event's first and last lines for you! That's what happened in yesterday's application when you double-clicked the command button. Visual Basic decided that the most common event for a command button is the `Click` event and displayed the Code window with these two lines for you:

```
Private Sub cmdHappy_Click ()

End Sub
```

Visual Basic even placed the text cursor between the two lines, so you could type the body of the event procedure! After you finish the event procedure, you can write another event procedure below that one (if you do, you are responsible for the first and last line of the event procedures that you add) or click the Project window's View Object button once again to return to the Form window.

> **Note**
>
> If Visual Basic guesses wrongly, and you want to write an event procedure for an event that differs from the one Visual Basic supplies, you can change the event name, perhaps to `cmdHappy_DblClick ()`, and complete the event.

Figure 3.8 shows a Code window that lists the code for several event procedures. The Code window not only separates procedures for you, it also supports routine Windows Copy, Cut, and Paste operations. Unlike a word processor, the Code window will not wrap lines because each statement of a Visual Basic program must reside on its own line. You can continue extra long lines down to the next line if you place an underscore at the end of the first line to let Visual Basic know that the statement continues on the next line. With the underscore, Visual Basic treats the two lines as one long continuous line; but the broken lines are easier for you to read because you can see all the code without scrolling the Code window left and right.

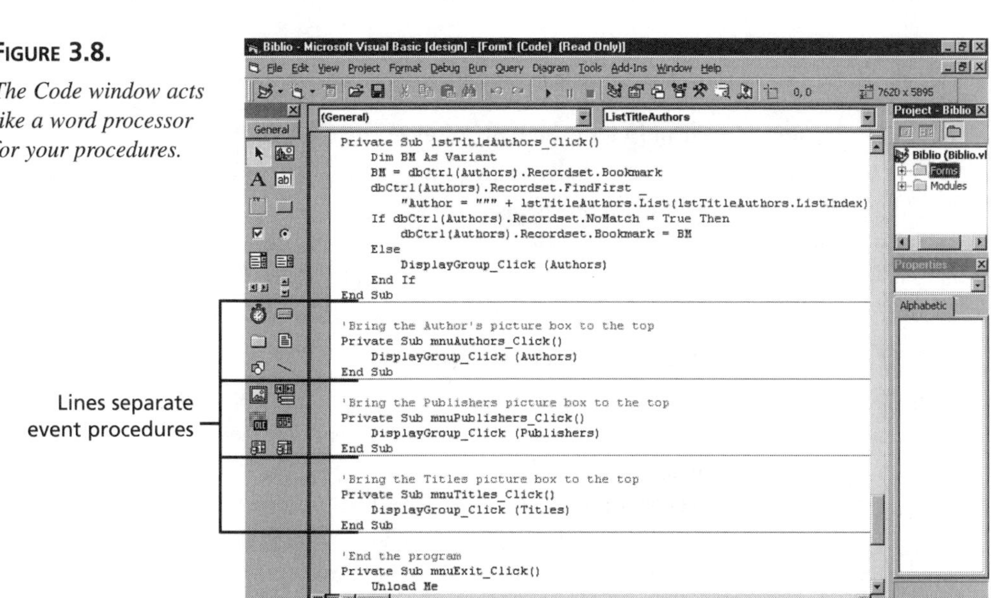

FIGURE 3.8.

The Code window acts like a word processor for your procedures.

Using Bonus Projects

You've just read through a lot of theory. Today should have answered some questions for you, but perhaps it generated additional ones. To help put things into perspective, Bonus Project 1, "Controls, Properties, and Events," appears between today's and tomorrow's lessons. You'll walk through the creation of another application from scratch so that you can put today's theory to practice. Although you won't receive as much detailed instructions as you did for yesterday's application, you don't need as much detail now that you are more familiar with the nature of Visual Basic. Throughout this 21-day tutorial, Bonus Projects will pop up between some of the chapters to reinforce your learning. Consider them homework for the next day.

Summary

Today's lesson was more theory than the first two were. You now should understand controls, properties, and events better than before. Procedures should also be less confusing, even though you've yet to learn any Visual Basic code. An event procedure must exist for each control and event that you want to respond to in your program. Without an event procedure, an event gets ignored.

Tomorrow's lesson teaches you how to add menus to your applications so that your users can more easily control the programs you write.

Q&A

Q Why do we need to indent the body of event procedures?

A Actually, you need to indent the body of *all* procedures. The indention is not required, but it helps you distinguish events from one another in long lines of code. Although the Code window does a good job of separating procedures from one another with dividing lines, you might print a program listing for study and analysis, and the indention will help keep your eyes focused on individual procedures.

Q Can I make up new names for event procedures?

A The only way to change the name of an event procedure is to first change the name of the control that triggers the procedure. Remember that the special name format of event procedures lets Visual Basic determine which controls and which events should trigger the event procedures. You'll be able to make up many of the subroutine and function procedure names you write that are not event procedures, but you are stuck using the event procedure names that correspond to the model described today.

Workshop

The Workshop provides quiz questions to help you solidify your understanding of the material covered and exercises to provide you with experience in using what you've learned. You should understand the quiz and exercise answers before continuing to the next chapter. Appendix A, "Answers to Exercises," provides the answers.

Quiz

1. What is an accelerator key?
2. True/False. Properties support multiple events.
3. Why would you assign the `Cancel` event to a command button?
4. How do you know which control contains the focus?
5. How does the user move the focus from control to control?
6. What property determines the focus order?
7. Is `LoadPicture ()` a subroutine, function, or event procedure (you may have to guess at this)?
8. True/False. Visual Basic automatically generates the first and last lines for the `Click` event procedure when you double-click a control inside the Form window editing area.
9. True/False. You can trigger a user event, such as `DblClick`, from Visual Basic code.
10. What is the purpose for the `PasswordChar` property?

Exercises

1. Write the first line for a form's `Load` event procedure. The form's name is `frmMyApp`.
2. **Bug Buster:** Why can't the following be an event procedure?

```
Private Function txtGetName_KeyDown ()
    ' Start the report
    Call ReportPrint
   lblWarning.Caption = "Get ready..."
End Function
```

3. Create an application with three multiline text boxes. Make the text boxes tall enough to display three or four lines of text. Give the first one a vertical scrollbar, the second a horizontal scrollbar, and the third one both kinds of scrollbars. In all three text boxes, supply the default text `Type here`. In addition to the text boxes, include an Exit command button, so the user can press Alt+X to terminate the program.

WEEK 1

BONUS PROJECT 1

Controls, Properties, and Events

Throughout this book's 21 sessions, you'll find Bonus Project sections scattered among them that help reinforce the material you've learned to this point. These Bonus Project sections include complete applications. You should take the time to create these applications because the practice will familiarize you with the Visual Basic environment and get you up to speed quickly as a Visual Basic programmer.

This first Bonus Project application demonstrates the text box's `PasswordChar` property. The program uses a text box property to request a password. Once the user enters a correct password, a special graphic image appears.

Experiment with the Bonus Project programs. As you learn more about Visual Basic, you can modify the Bonus Project applications to test a hypothesis you might have and to practice coding. You probably won't understand all the code you'll enter in this Bonus Project's Code window. That's okay for now, though, because you'll understand the code soon.

The password to run this application is *Sams*. Shhh... don't tell anyone.

The Visual Elements

Figure BP1.1 shows the application's Form window that you'll create. You already know how to place controls on a form, and Table BP1.1 contains all the controls and their respective property values that you need to create the application's window. To begin, follow these usual steps for creating a simple Visual Basic application:

1. Select File, New Project.
2. Select the Standard EXE icon.
3. Set the form's properties to those listed in Table BP1.1.
4. Place the remaining controls in Table BP1.1 on the form and set their properties. Leave all the default values for all the properties not listed in Table BP1.1.

You don't have to assign a control's properties as soon as you place it on the form. You can place all the controls first and then go back to set their properties.

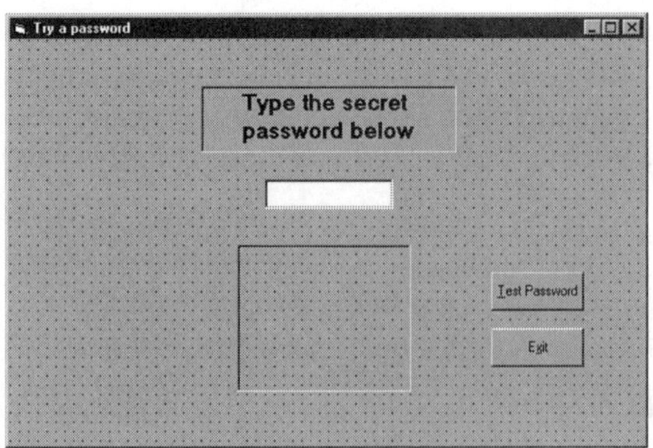

FIGURE BP1.1.
This application uses the text box control's `PasswordChar` *property.*

TABLE BP1.1. SET THESE CONTROLS AND PROPERTIES ON THE FORM.

Control Property Name	*Property Value*
Form `Name`	`frmPassword`
Form `Caption`	`Try a password`

Control Property Name	*Property Value*
Form Height	5610
Form Width	8475
Image Name	imgPassword
Image BorderStyle	1-Fixed Single
Image Height	1890
Image Left	3000
Image Stretch	True
Image Top	2640
Image Width	2295
Label Name	lblPrompt
Label BorderStyle	1-Fixed Single
Label Caption	Type the secret password below
Label Font	MS Sans Serif
Label Font Size	14
Label Font Style	Bold
Label Height	855
Label Left	2520
Label Top	600
Label Width	3375
Text box Name	txtPassword
Text box Height	375
Text box Left	3360
Text box PasswordChar	*
Text box Text	(Leave blank by clearing the default value)
Text box Top	1800
Text box Width	1695
Command button Name	cmdTest
Command button Caption	&Test Password
Command button Left	6360
Command button Top	3000
Command button #2 Name	cmdExit
Command button #2 Caption	E&xit
Command button #2 Left	6360
Command button #2 Top	3720

Adding the Code

Once you create the Form window, you're ready to enter the code. Listing BP1.1 contains the code you'll enter. Notice that two event procedures exist: `cmdExit_Click()` and `cmdTest_Click()`. Each of these event procedures responds to the `Click` event for that particular command button. When the user clicks the command button named `cmdExit`, `cmdExit_Click()` executes. When the user clicks the command button named `cmdTest`, `cmdTest_Click()` executes.

> The `Click` event is the most common event that occurs for command buttons. Therefore, you can quickly open an event procedure for each command button by letting Visual Basic complete the procedure's first and last lines. To type the small one-line body of the `cmdExit` command button's `Click` event procedure, double-click the `cmdExit` command button on the Form window and fill in the body of the procedure. To type the body of the `cmdTest` command button's `Click` event procedure, double-click the `cmdTest` command button and fill in the body of the procedure.

LISTING BP1.1. THIS CODE ACTIVATES THE PASSWORD-BASED FORM.

```
Private Sub cmdExit_Click()
   End
End Sub

Private Sub cmdTest_Click()
' This event procedure executes as soon as the
' user wants to test the entered password
   If txtPassword.Text = "Sams" Then
      ' Success!   Password matched
      Beep
      Beep        ' Now, display the picture
      imgPassword.Picture = LoadPicture("C:\Program Files\" _
        & "Microsoft Visual Studio\Common\Graphics\MetaFile\" _
        & "Business\coins.wmf")
    lblPrompt.Caption = "Show me the money!"
   Else
      lblPrompt.Caption = "Wrong password - Try Again"
      txtPassword.Text = ""    ' Erase old password
      txtPassword.SetFocus     ' Put focus on text box
   End If
End Sub
```

Analysis

Although you have yet to learn how to interpret Visual Basic programming statements, a few words about this code now would make a great introduction to the code basics you begin learning on Day 5, "Analyzing VB Data."

Lines 1 through 3 form the `cmdExit` button's `Click` event procedure. When the user clicks the `cmdExit` button, the `End` statement causes the application to terminate. The application stays on the user's screen, even if the user enters a successful password match, until the user clicks the `cmdExit` command button (or until the user closes the program window).

As you type the code, you'll notice that Visual Basic uses different colors for certain text. This syntax *coloring* is a handy tool that you can use to locate bugs early in the program-writing stage. As you program more and more, you'll recognize that Visual Basic assigns specific colors to specific kinds of text. A Visual Basic program keyword, such as a command, is always blue. An object, such as a control name and its property, is always black. Other kinds of code words are green. Therefore, if you notice that a keyword is green, you'll know immediately that you've entered something incorrectly and that you must correct the typo before Visual Basic will properly recognize the code you're writing. You can change the colors from the Tools, Options Editor Format page.

NEW TERM *Syntax* is a programming language's collection of grammar and spelling rules. If you misspell a command or forget a required punctuation character, a syntax error will occur.

Visual Basic recognizes most syntax errors as soon as you press Enter at the end of a line. Figure BP1.2 shows the dialog box that appears after a line was typed incorrectly. (The dialog box will not always describe the error as a *syntax error*; sometimes the error message is more specific and points out an incorrect command.) If you see the problem (such as the extra equal sign in this case), press OK and correct the problem. If you need more help, click the Help button, and Visual Basic will give you more information about the possible problem.

Visual Basic does not always correctly locate the problem when you type something incorrectly. Sometimes Visual Basic will not highlight the exact problem (although in Figure BP1.2, Visual Basic correctly found the problem) because it might not realize a problem exists until a few keywords after the real problem. Therefore, you may have to look back through the last line or two to locate the real problem if Visual Basic fails to highlight it.

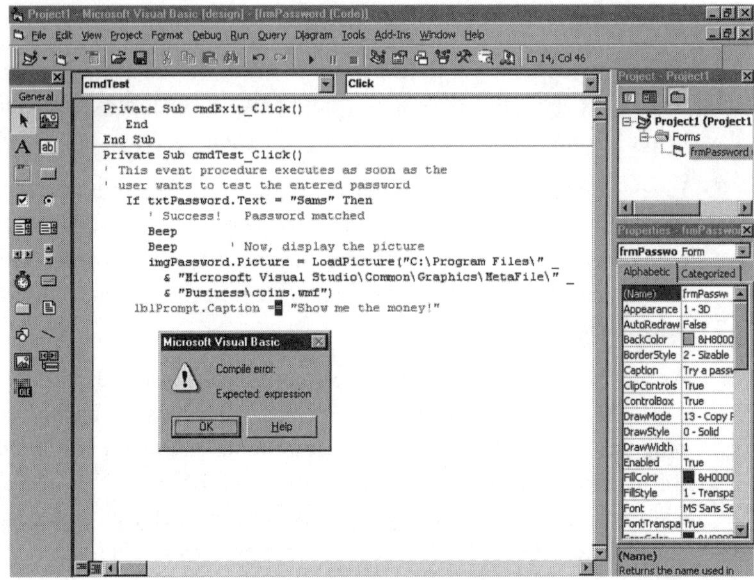

FIGURE BP1.2.
Visual Basic locates syntax errors as soon as you press Enter.

Lines 6 and 7 illustrate the primary way you'll document your Visual Basic code. You may recall from Day 1, "Welcome to Visual Basic," that documentation is important because you'll maintain your code over time, and the more descriptions you place inside the code, the more quickly you'll understand what you've written. Lines 6 and 7 are examples of *remarks*. Visual Basic completely ignores any line that begins with a single apostrophe, which indicates that a remark follows. Remember, remarks are only for people, not for computers.

NEW TERM A *remark* is a comment inside a Visual Basic program that describes the code. Sometimes, a programmer will put a remark at the top of a program with his or her name and phone number. This way, if anyone else has to modify the code later and has a question, the original program author can be contacted.

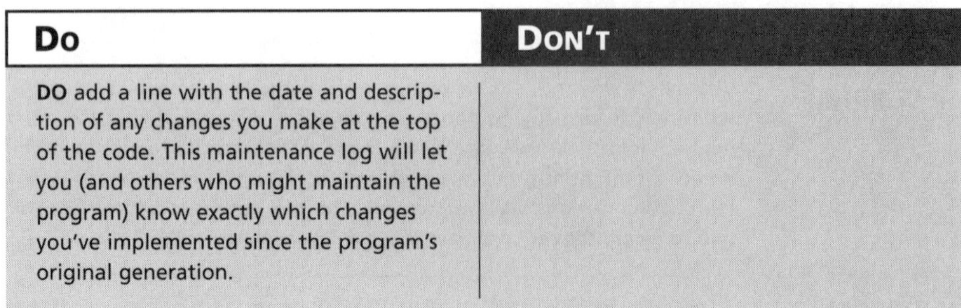

Do	Don't
DO add a line with the date and description of any changes you make at the top of the code. This maintenance log will let you (and others who might maintain the program) know exactly which changes you've implemented since the program's original generation.	

You now know part of the Visual Basic programming language! Remarks, although they are for people, are valid and important Visual Basic statements. You should scatter remarks throughout your program to describe in easy-to-understand language what the program is doing. As you can see in line 11, you can place a remark at the right of a program statement if it's a short remark. Try to fit all your Visual Basic code and remarks inside the Code window without requiring horizontal scrollbars at the bottom of the Code window. Keeping all the code in one window makes editing and debugging much simpler.

Tip

> Take advantage of Visual Basic's code-completion tools. For example, when you type `txtPassword.Text` in line 8, Visual Basic displays the properties available for the text box as soon as you type the period. Type `T` and `e` and Visual Basic scrolls to the correct property, `Text`. You can press the spacebar to continue without having to complete the final two letters because Visual Basic completes `Text` for you. Of course, this only saves you two characters, but other properties, such as `lblPrompt.Caption`, will go even quicker.

Lines 12, 13, and 14 are actually *one* single Visual Basic statement that spans three lines. The statement is long due to the long pathname required to get to the graphic. You can type the entire statement on one line, but doing so would far exceed the Code window size. Therefore, Visual Basic offers a way to continue one logical line onto two or more physical lines. When you want to break a line into an additional line, press the spacebar and type an underscore character. The underscore, being the final character on a line, tells Visual Basic that the next physical line is actually a continuation of the present one.

Caution

> The path that begins in line 12 assumes you have installed the sample images when you installed Visual Basic. If you did not, the pathname will not work. You may have to search using the Windows Find menu option for the Coins.wmf file on your Visual Basic installation CD-ROMs to locate the file. To add the graphics, insert your first Visual Basic CD-ROM in the drive and select Add/Change Options from the screen to add the graphics to your hard disk.

A special problem arises when you want to break long text enclosed in quotation marks (as is being done here). You must close the quotation marks before the space and underscore and then begin the next line with an ampersand (&) followed by another quotation mark. When you learn about text strings in Day 5's session, you'll better understand the need for the ampersand character.

> As you learn more of the Visual Basic programming language, you'll understand why some of the statements in Listing BP1.1 are indented farther to the right than others.

Here's a final thought before you quit for the day: You may be surprised that this application uses the Test Password command button. Why not let the user type the password and press Enter instead of having to click the extra command button to test the his or her password? As you'll learn in Day 7, "Advanced Keyboard and Screen Support," sensing certain keystrokes, such as Enter, would add extra code to this program. This application was kept as simple as possible because you're still early in this 21-day course.

WEEK 1

DAY 4

Creating Menus

A menu bar offers a special kind of control that lets your users select options and issue commands. Some menu options might mimic controls on your form. For example, you may want to include an Exit command button as well as a File, Exit menu option to let your users exit your application. In addition, some menu options mimic toolbar buttons that you'll supply. Other menu options might be the only way you provide access to certain areas of your program. Visual Basic makes adding menus simple.

Today, you learn the following:

- More about the Application wizard's generated menus
- What kinds of menu options are available to you
- How to create menu bars, drop-down menus, and submenus
- About menu event procedures
- How to use the Code window's Object and Procedure drop-down list boxes to enter event procedures quickly

Using the Application Wizard for Menus

You've already seen the Application wizard in action in Day 1's lesson. Figure 4.1 shows the Application wizard screen that enables you to generate a menu bar for your application. After you click the menu options and submenus you want in your applications, the Application wizard generates the appropriate menu controls and places them in the generated application.

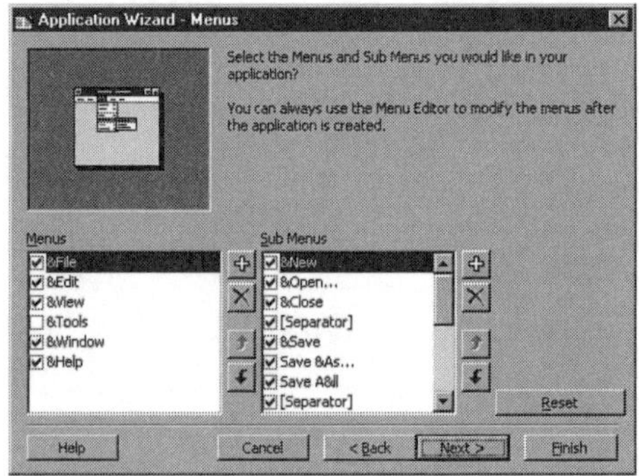

FIGURE 4.1.

The Application wizard helps you generate standard Windows menu bars and options.

> Menus are useful controls because your users already know how to use them. Users are more likely to use menu commands they understand.

If you've used many Windows programs, you'll recognize most or all of the Application wizard's menu options. Menu bar options such as File, Edit, and Window appear in many Windows programs; the corresponding submenu options that the Application wizard provides are also familiar, such as the Exit option on the File menu.

Although you'll probably never include as many menu bar options and submenus as a huge mass-distributed program such as Microsoft Word does, Word and the other top-selling Windows programs do provide good guidelines for menu design. Almost every Windows program includes a File, Exit option. Virtually every Windows application includes Edit, Cut and Edit, Copy commands. Your menus will not perfectly match other Windows applications because your application's goals will differ. Nevertheless, when you can follow general Windows menu guidelines, you should do so. Your users then will have less trouble adapting to your program. The faster your users learn your program, the more likely they will use your program and keep using subsequent editions you produce.

The Application wizard makes generating an initial menu so easy that you should strongly consider using the Application wizard to create your program's shell if you want your application to contain a complex menu. Starting in the next section, you'll see how easily you can create your own menus using the Visual Basic tools, but the Application wizard is even easier to use. All you have to do is click an option to include it in your final application. Even if you don't want a toolbar or anything else the Application wizard can provide, you may want to create an initial application with the Application wizard just to generate an application with a full menu before you add the details and special menu options that your application requires.

Do	Don't
DO check out the online MSDN help's reference book called, *The Windows Interface Guide to Software Design*. Make sure you follow the Windows standards for menus and other controls. By following the guidelines, you can be assured that your application conforms to the Windows standard and will be as familiar as possible to your users.	

Learning About Menus

You've used Windows menus many times before, including during the first three days of this course because Visual Basic includes a standard Windows menu bar. Figure 4.2 shows the Visual Basic menu with the File menu dropped down and the parts of the menu labeled. Even if you are extremely familiar with Windows programs, take a moment to study the figure's callouts so that you will know the Visual Basic names of the various menu items. The rest of today's lesson describes how to include these items on your own application's menus.

When one of your application's menu options displays a dialog box, be sure to end the option with an ellipsis as Figure 4.2 shows. When you create a menu with a submenu, Visual Basic takes care of adding the right-arrow indicator.

Some menu options produce additional menus. Figure 4.3 shows the Visual Basic View menu with a submenu coming off the Toolbars option. Notice the checked option on Figure 4.3's Toolbars submenu. The checked option indicates an option that the user turns on or off by selecting the option. The Menu Editor lets you create checked menu options as well as regular menu options.

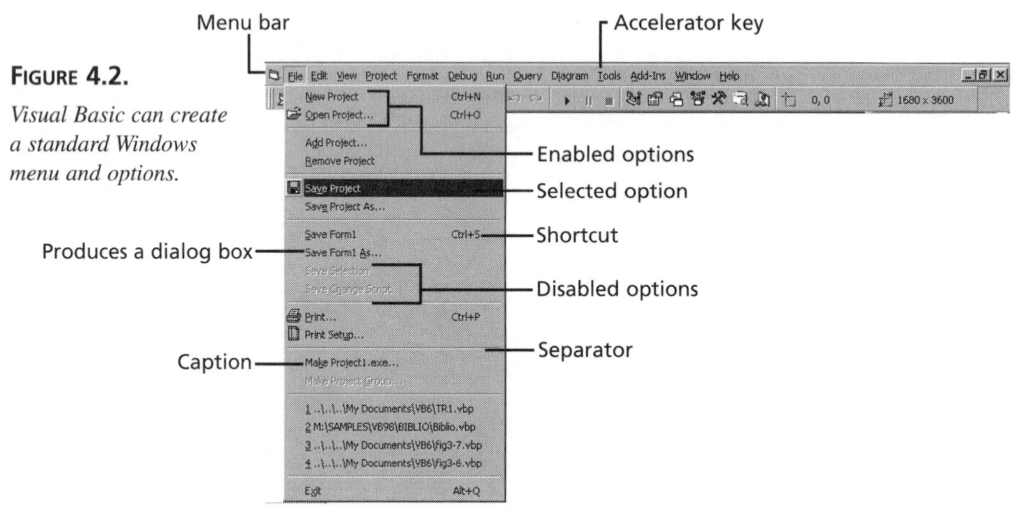

FIGURE 4.2.
Visual Basic can create a standard Windows menu and options.

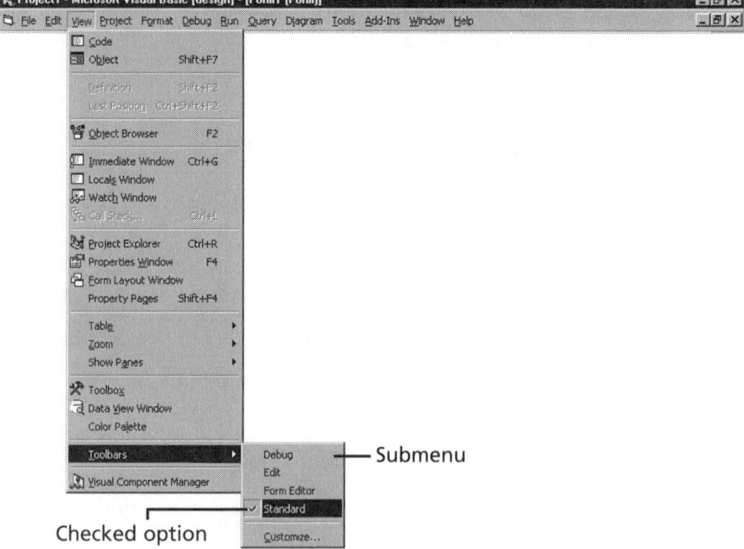

FIGURE 4.3.
Visual Basic creates submenus for you when you request them.

Introducing the Menu Editor

The Toolbox window doesn't contain any menu-creation tools. Instead, Microsoft offers a special menu tool called the *Menu Editor*, shown in Figure 4.4, that you use to create menus. From the Form window, you can press Ctrl+E (the shortcut key for Tools, Menu Editor) to display the Menu Editor.

NEW TERM The *Menu Editor* helps you design menus for your applications. In a way, the Menu Editor acts like a Properties window for the menu bar because you'll designate the names of the menu controls as well as the captions that the users see on the menus and other related information from within the Menu Editor. The Menu Editor has been around in Microsoft programming products for many years with little change during that time. The Menu Editor's longevity is a testament to its power and simplicity.

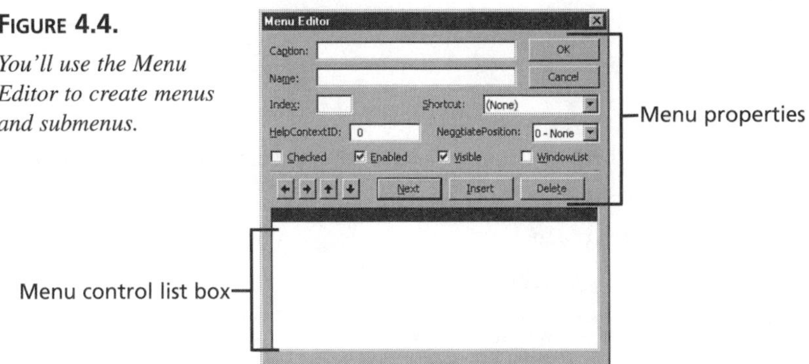

FIGURE 4.4.
You'll use the Menu Editor to create menus and submenus.

The top half of the Menu Editor, the Menu properties section, specifies the control properties for one menu option. That option can appear on the menu bar or on a submenu that pulls down from the application's menu bar. The Menu control list box adds to a tree-structured diagram of your menu bar as you build it.

Working with the Menu Editor

Perhaps the best way to learn how to build application menus with the Menu Editor is to create a simple application that includes menus. You've yet to master file-related operations and other advanced Visual Basic concepts, so this sample application's menu will not conform well to the standard Windows program menu. Nevertheless, the application does acquaint you with the steps needed to build menus, and you'll see how easy the Menu Editor is to use.

The following are the goals of the application:

- Display a label in the center of the form.
- Offer a menu option that lets the user change the label's background color.
- Offer a menu option that lets the user change the label's text.
- Offer an exit menu option that lets the user terminate the program.

As you can see, the program will be simple, but you'll gain insight into menus by creating it.

First, start a new Standard EXE application from the File, New Project menu option. Assign the form the name `frmMenu`, change the form's title bar to read Menu Application by changing the `Caption` property. Finally, resize the form to a `Height` value of 6030 and a `Width` value of 8415.

Add a label to the form with these properties:

- `Name: lblMenu`
- `Alignment: 2-Center`
- `BackColor: Red` (click the `BackColor`'s Palette tab and select the first red in the list of colors that appears)
- `BorderStyle: 1-Fixed Single`
- `Caption: Select a menu option`
- `Font Size: 24`
- `Font Style: Bold`
- `Height: 615`
- `Left: 1800`
- `Top: 2160`
- `Width: 4935`

Your PC can display from a few hundred to more than a million colors. Each color has associated with it a unique numeric color code value. Visual Basic uses the *hexadecimal numbering system* for the color values. Selecting the red color from the palette, however, is much easier than typing the red color's exact hexadecimal value, such as `&H000000FF&`.

NEW TERM A *hexadecimal numbering system*, also called *base-16*, is a counting system based on the number 16. In the normal base-10 numbering system, 10 unique digits exist, 0 through 9. In base-16, 16 unique digits exist: 0 through 9, plus the letters A, B, C, D, E, and F to represent the remaining "digits." Hexadecimal numbers are always preceded by `&H` to let Visual Basic and the programmer know the number is a base-16 number and not a normal base-10 value. You can represent a numeric value using either base-10 or base-16, but base-16 offers a more compact format for large values. With over a million color combinations available, the base-16 numbering system enables you to use fewer digits to represent each shade of color than the base-10 would allow.

Your screen should look like the one in Figure 4.5.

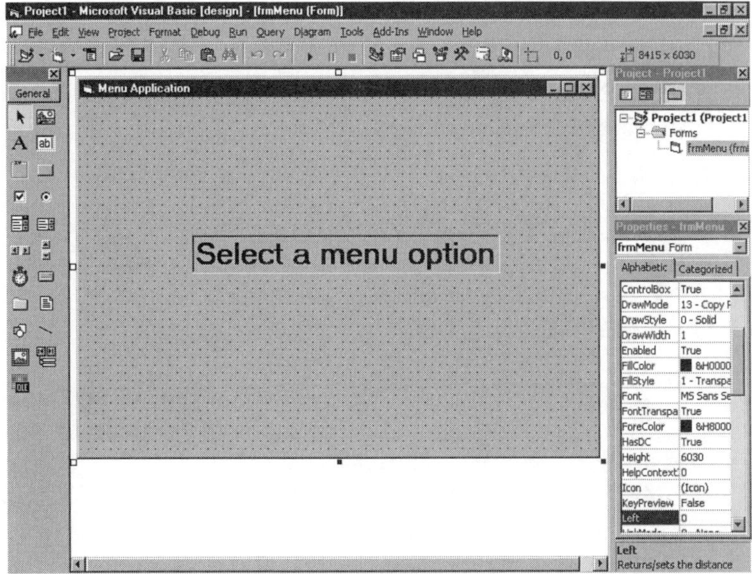

FIGURE 4.5.

You have now placed a label that you'll control with menu options.

You are ready to begin the application's menu. Click the form and press Ctrl+E to display the Menu Editor. Most of the *fields* in the Menu Editor will be blank because you must fill in values as you specify menu options.

NEW TERM A *field*, often represented by a text box, is a generic name for a location where the user or programmer types values in an application. The Menu Editor includes many fields, as do most dialog boxes, where you type values.

Here are the values that will appear on the menu bar you now create:

- File
- Color
- Message

Notice that the menu bar options all will have accelerator keys so that the user can select a menu bar option using the keyboard. When you add items to the Menu Editor, those items either appear on the application's menu bar or on a pull-down menu depending on how you specify the values. Follow these steps to add the File menu option to the application's menu bar:

1. Type `&File` for the `Caption` field. As with all other Visual Basic values, the ampersand indicates that the `F` will be the accelerator key for the menu selection. As you type the caption, Visual Basic displays the caption in the Menu control list box in the bottom half of the Menu Editor.
2. Press Tab to move to the Name field. Tab and Shift+Tab shift the focus between the Menu Editor fields.
3. Type `mnuFile` for the name of the first menu option.

Keep in mind that menu options are special controls, and like other controls, they have names.

Do	Don't
DO use a consistent naming convention for menu names. Begin all menu names with the prefix `mnu` followed by the name that appears on the menu bar. Therefore, the menu bar's File menu option is named `mnuFile`. When you create submenu options, use the related menu bar name as a prefix to the submenu name. In other words, `mnuFileExit` is a great name for the File, Exit option.	

4. Leave all the other fields alone and click the Next button to prepare for the remaining menu bar options. The Next button lets the Menu Editor know that you are through with the first option and want to enter another.
5. Type `&Color` for the next menu bar caption and type `mnuColor` for the name.
6. Click Next to add the next item.
7. Type `&Message` for the third and final menu bar caption and type `mnuMessage` for the caption. Your Menu Editor should look like the one in Figure 4.6.

FIGURE 4.6.
The first three menu bar options now exist.

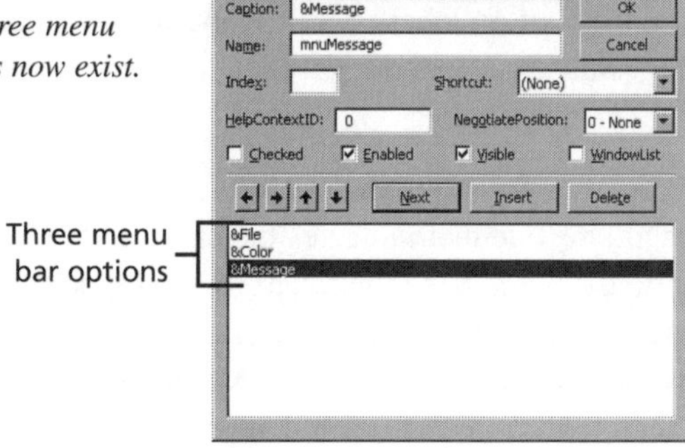

Test the Menu

You can test your menu at any point during its creation. Click the OK button to close the Menu Editor. The Form window shows your application's new menu bar. Press F5 to run your application. Because you've not yet created submenus or written event procedures, nothing happens when you select from the menu bar, but you can already see how simple adding menus can be. Click the Window Close button on the running application (or click the Visual Basic toolbar's End button) and press Ctrl+E to return to the Menu Editor.

Adding a Pull-Down Menu

You can either create pull-down menus as you build the menu bar or add the menus later. If you create the complete menu bar first, however, as you've done here, you'll have to insert the menu options in their respective locations when you are ready to add them. The Menu Editor's Insert button lets you do just that.

> **Note** The Insert button inserts a blank menu bar or menu position. Before clicking Insert, highlight the menu option that appears *after* where you want to insert an option. In other words, to add a menu option to the File menu, click to highlight `&Color` in the Menu control list box and then click Insert; Visual Basic adds a blank row between `&File` and `&Color` so that you can add a menu option to the File menu.

Somehow, Visual Basic must distinguish between a primary menu bar option and a pull-down menu option. If you inserted the Exit option after File using the same technique you used in the previous sections, Visual Basic would add the Exit option to the menu bar between File and Color and *not* as a File menu option.

After inserting a new menu position after &File, click the Menu editor's right arrow button. Visual Basic adds an ellipses after &File that indicates the current item will be a menu option and will not appear on the menu bar. Click `Caption` and type `E&xit` for the new option's caption. As you type, notice where the Menu Editor places the option: indented to the right of the other options at the bottom of the Menu control list box. The indenting shows that the item is an option from the menu that precedes it. If a menu has yet another menu coming from it, often called a submenu, you would click the right arrow twice to add two sets of ellipses before the submenu option.

Caution

Too many submenu levels can get confusing. At most, include two levels of menus—one menu that drops down from the primary menu bar and possibly one submenu coming off that.

Note

Do you know why you didn't use the E in Exit as the accelerator key? The standard Windows File, Exit option always uses the letter x for the shortcut, and you should follow the standards everywhere you can.

Type `mnuFileExit` for the name of the option. You've now completed the short File menu and its drop-down menu. You can run the program to see that selecting File now produces the drop-down menu with the Exit option. Of course, nothing happens when you select the Exit option because you've yet to write event procedure code for the menu.

Add Three Checked Options

The second menu, Color, will contain three options: Blue, Green, and Red. These colors will be mutually exclusive; the label will not be able to be all three colors at once, but only one color at a time. Such colors make perfect candidates for *checked menu options*.

New Term A *checked menu option* is a menu option that includes a check mark indicating that the option is set.

Study the drop-down Color menu shown in Figure 4.7 to see the menu you are about to create. As you can see, the check mark appears next to one menu option, and the other two options are not checked. When you create the Color menu, you will make Red the option that's first active because you are setting the label's background color to red at design time. The user will first see the red label until the user selects a different color.

FIGURE 4.7.

Only the checked menu option is active.

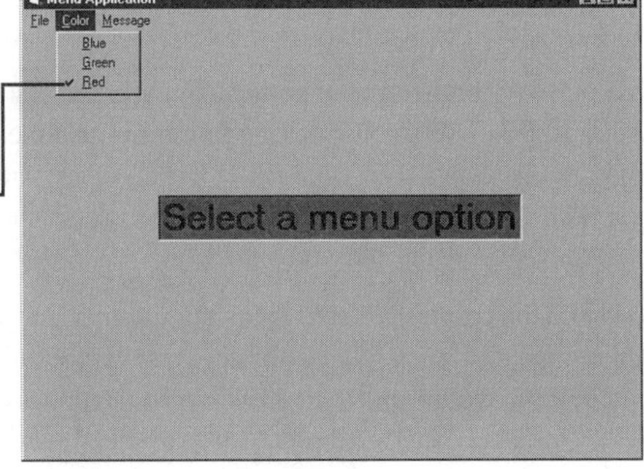

Only one color can be checked

Caution

> Actually, more than one menu option can be checked at once, but through programming the menu's event procedures properly, you can ensure that only one is checked. When the user checks a different option, the original one appears unchecked.

Then follow these steps to add the Color menu options:

1. Open the Menu Editor if you closed it in the previous section.
2. Click the &Message option in the Menu control list box to highlight that option.
3. Click the Insert button, click Right Arrow, then click Insert two more times to add three empty rows for the Color menu options.
4. Highlight the first blank row where you'll add the Blue option.
5. Type `&Blue` for the caption and `mnuColorBlue` in the Name field. When the user first runs the program, the Blue option will be unchecked to indicate that Blue is not currently selected.
6. Click Next to enter the next option.

7. Type `&Green` for the caption and `mnuColorGreen` for the name of the next option.
8. Click Next to enter the next option.
9. Type `&Red` for the caption and `mnuColorRed` for the name of the next option.
10. The Red option is to be checked when the user first starts the program. Therefore, click the Checked field to place the check mark next to Red.
11. Close the Menu Editor and run your application to test the Color menu. Your program's window should match that of Figure 4.7.

Not only can you provide checked menu options, but you can also, initially from the Menu Editor and also through Visual Basic programming statements, enable and disable menu options. Figure 4.8 shows the Visual Basic Debug menu with several enabled options and several disabled menu options. Visual Basic grays menu options that are disabled, so the user knows not even to try the option.

The Menu Editor's Enabled option lets you indicate whether you want an option enabled when you design the menu. Depending on the application, you might enable menu options as they become available and then disable some options if the user should not be allowed to select an option. Many word processors disable the Paste option on the Edit menu, for example, until the user copies something to the Windows Clipboard. Your application's menu is little more than a set of controls, and the various Menu Editor fields are all properties for the controls. Therefore, your Visual Basic code can modify the `Enabled` property for any menu item, setting it to `True` or `False` as you'll learn how to do in tomorrow's lesson, and the option will be enabled and available for the user to select or disabled and unavailable until the program once again enables the option.

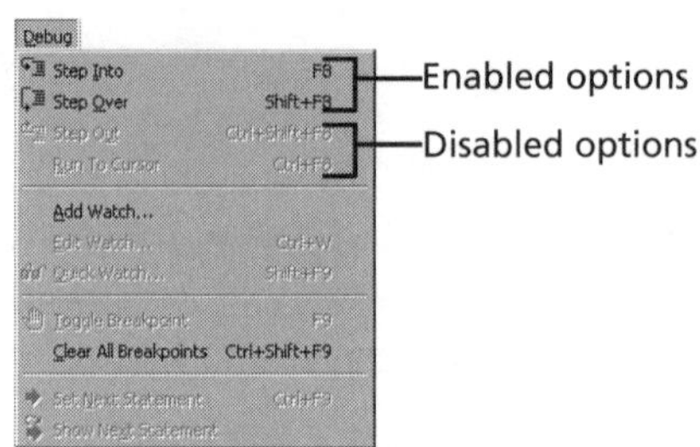

FIGURE 4.8.

The `Enabled` *property determines which menu options are enabled and disabled.*

Notice that the Debug menu, as well as most others, have shortcut keys to the right of menu options. F8 is the shortcut for Step Into, and Shift+F8 is the shortcut key for Step Over. (Accelerator keys are often called shortcut keys when referring to the keystrokes that trigger menu options, such as Ctrl+C for Edit, Copy.) If you want to add shortcut keys for some of the menu options, select the shortcut key combination you want to use from the Shortcut field's drop-down list box. Most shortcut key combinations use the Ctrl key, such as Ctrl+C.

You'll see that seven options in the Debug menu (some are disabled) have graphic icons to the left of the options. These icons indicate a corresponding toolbar button. In other words, a Debug toolbar button exists for the Debug, Step Into option, and the icon on the toolbar matches that of the menu option. The icons give users an added chance to learn which toolbar buttons mimic the various menu options. Unfortunately, Visual Basic provides no way to add an icon to the left of menu options in your application menus although some third-party controls are available that do offer this feature.

Completing the Menu's Message Submenu

The Message option will produce a drop-down menu with three options and only one checked at any one time, as to the Color menu. The checked option will be the message that currently appears in the label. Just for practice, you're going to format the Message menu differently from the normal way of doing things. The Message menu will look like the one in Figure 4.9.

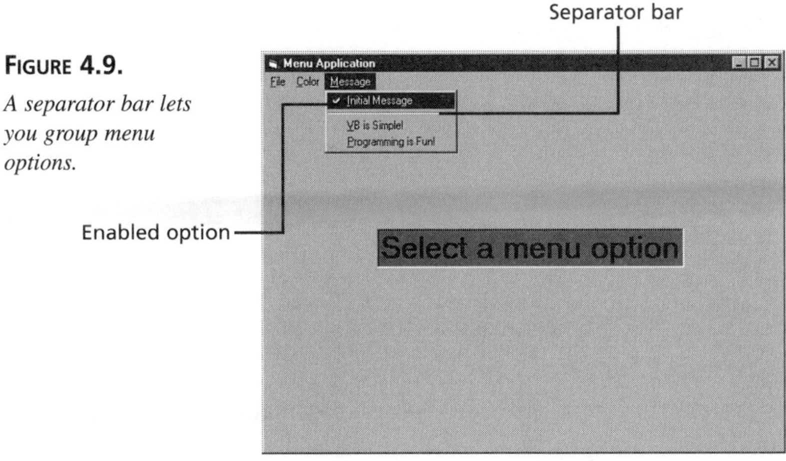

FIGURE 4.9.

A separator bar lets you group menu options.

Note that the Message menu has a separator bar. A separator bar separates some menu items from others. Your user cannot select a separator bar. As the user presses the down arrow key when a menu is displayed, the highlight moves over the separator bar to the next menu option.

Follow these steps to add the Message menu and include the separator bar on that menu:

1. Press Ctrl+E to display the Menu Editor.
2. Click the row beneath &Message in the lower half of the Menu Editor to prepare the Menu Editor to receive the next option.
3. Click the right arrow to indicate that you are about to enter a menu option that will drop down from the menu bar's Message option.
4. Type `&Initial Message` and `mnuMessageInitial` for the new option's caption and name.
5. Click the Checked field to place the check mark on the first option when the program begins.
6. Click Next to prepare for the next menu item. Notice that Visual Basic indents the next item automatically because the previous item was indented. (If you do not want an item indented, but you want to make it a menu bar item, click the left arrow to remove the ellipses. The up and down arrows let you move an item up or down the menu tree to other options.)
7. Type a single hyphen (-) for the caption of the next menu item. All separator bars have this caption. When Visual Basic encounters the hyphen for a menu caption, Visual Basic turns that hyphen into a separator bar.
8. Type `mnuMessageSep1` for the separator bar's name. Separator bars are objects and, as such, require unique names. You could name subsequent separator bars on the Message drop-down menu `mnuMessageSep2`, `mnuMessageSep3`, and so on.

Separator bars cannot be checked, disabled, or have shortcut keys.

9. Click Next to prepare for the next menu option.
10. Type `&VB is Simple!` for the caption and `mnuMessageSimple` for the name and click Next.
11. Type `&Programming is Fun!` for the caption and `mnuMessageProgramming` for the name of the next option.

Your Menu Editor window should look like the one in Figure 4.10. Close the Menu Editor and run your program to see the menu. You are almost done. The only thing left to do is add the code that activates the menu.

FIGURE 4.10.
Your menu is now finished.

> The Application wizard lets you add separator bars to the program it generates. Select the option labeled `[Separator]` when you want to add a separator to a wizard-generated program.

4

Finalize the Menu with Code

You must now add the procedure event code for the menu you just created that will make the menu do work. As with the previous days' lessons, don't worry about the details of the code at this point. For now, concentrate on getting the big picture. A menu and its options are just controls that produce events at runtime. Your users will interact with your application's menu. Each time the user selects from a menu, that selection generates a `Click` event. That menu option's `Click` event procedure then executes.

You should now know, after yesterday's lesson, that the menu option named `mnuFileExit` would require a `Click` event procedure named `mnuFileExit_Click ()`. The procedures for the other menu options are named accordingly. Listing 4.1 contains the complete code listing required for the application. You can enter the code in several ways:

- You can enter the code one procedure at a time. From the Form window, select the menu option you want to add code for. Visual Basic will open the Code window and display the wrapper lines of that option's `Click` event procedure for you. You then can fill in the body of the code. Close the Code window and click the next menu option to enter its code body until you've completed the code.

NEW TERM *Wrapper lines*, or *wrappers*, are a procedure's first and last line. You learned the requirements of an event procedure's wrapper line format in yesterday's lesson, but you did not know at the time that the lines were called wrappers.

- After entering the first event procedure using the method just described, you can select the next menu option from the Code window itself. Toward the top of the Code window are two drop-down list boxes labeled Object and Procedure. Figure 4.11 shows an open Object list. Select the next menu option for which you want to write a procedure from the Object list, and Visual Basic places the wrapper lines for that event procedure in the Code window beneath the previous event procedure. You can then complete the procedure's body. Continue adding event procedures until you've added all of them for the menu options.

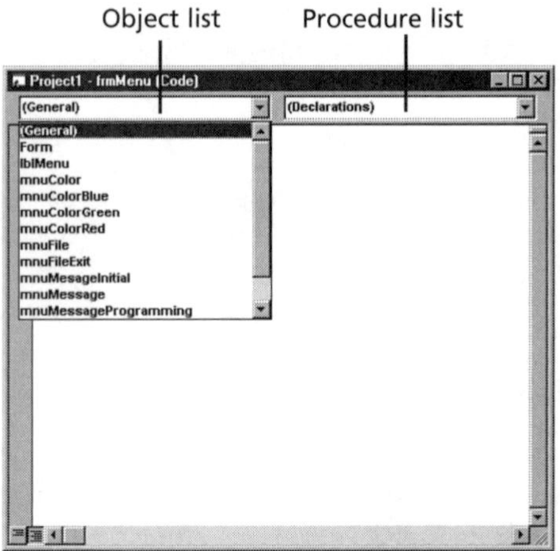

FIGURE 4.11.
You can request another pair of wrapper lines from inside the Code window.

Note

> In this application, every object other than the label is a menu control. Menu controls only support the `Click` event, so `Click` is the only event you'll see in the controls' Procedure drop-down list box. You can add an event procedure for other kinds of events using the Code window's drop-down list boxes when you work with controls that support additional events. For example, if you selected this application's label control from the Code window's Object list box and then opened the Procedure list box, you would see several event names listed because the label control supports several kinds of events.

- You can open the Code window and type the code from beginning to end. This method takes extra time, however, because you must type the wrapper lines yourself.

The Code window's Object and Procedure drop-down list boxes are useful for locating code you've already entered but want to edit or view. For example, if an application contained multiple event procedures for several kinds of controls, and you wanted to locate a specific command button's double-click event procedure, display the Code window and select the command button from the Object drop-down list box. Then select DblClick from the Procedure drop-down list box, and Visual Basic locates and displays the code for that event procedure in the Code window.

LISTING 4.1. THE MENU CODE CONTROLS THE LABEL'S COLOR AND CONTENTS.

```
Private Sub mnuColorBlue_Click()
' Color the label Blue and check the Blue
'    menu option. Make sure both the Red
'    and Green options are unchecked
   lblMenu.BackColor = vbBlue
   mnuColorBlue.Checked = True
   mnuColorGreen.Checked = False
   mnuColorRed.Checked = False
End Sub

Private Sub mnuColorGreen_Click()
' Color the label Green and check the Green
'    menu option. Make sure both the Blue
'    and Red options are unchecked
   lblMenu.BackColor = vbGreen
   mnuColorBlue.Checked = False
   mnuColorGreen.Checked = True
   mnuColorRed.Checked = False
End Sub

Private Sub mnuColorRed_Click()
' Color the label Red and check the Red
'    menu option. Make sure both the Blue
'    and Green options are unchecked
   lblMenu.BackColor = vbRed
   mnuColorBlue.Checked = Fasle
   mnuColorGreen.Checked = False
   mnuColorRed.Checked = True
End Sub
```

continues

LISTING 4.1. CONTINUED

```

Private Sub mnuFileExit_Click()
' Terminate the program
   End
End Sub

Private Sub mnuMessageInitial_Click()
' Change the label's message to the original
'    message and check the proper menu option.
'    Make sure the other options are unchecked
   lblMenu.Caption = "Select a menu option"
   mnuMessageInitial.Checked = True
   mnuMessageProgramming.Checked = False
   mnuMessageSimple.Checked = False
End Sub

Private Sub mnuMessageProgramming_Click()
' Change the label's message to a replacement
'    message and check the proper menu option.
'    Make sure the other options are unchecked
   lblMenu.Caption = "Programing is fun!"
   mnuMessageInitial.Checked = False
   mnuMessageProgramming.Checked = True
   mnuMessageSimple.Checked = False
End Sub

Private Sub mnuMessageSimple_Click()
' Change the label's message to a replacement
'    message and check the proper menu option.
'    Make sure the other options are unchecked
   lblMenu.Caption = "VB is Simple!"
   mnuMessageInitial.Checked = False
   mnuMessageProgramming.Checked = False
   mnuMessageSimple.Checked = True
End Sub
```

Again, don't worry about the code's details, but do make sure you understand how event procedures work before going further. Starting tomorrow, you will begin to learn the details of the Visual Basic language, so understanding how the language supports event procedures now will help you tomorrow when you tackle the code specifics.

Run the program and test it. Select the Color and Message menu options several times to ensure that the check mark moves accurately as you select options and that the label updates accordingly. You can change the colors before or after you change the label's text.

Summary

Today's lesson taught you how to work with Visual Basic menus. The Menu Editor operates like a special Properties window that lets you easily set menu control values. The Menu Editor lets you manage the checked and visible properties of menu options and also lets you specify shortcut keys for the various options.

Tomorrow's lesson dives into the specifics of the Visual Basic programming language. You'll learn how Visual Basic recognizes and stores data, and you'll learn how to assign property values at runtime with the code that you write.

Q&A

Q Why don't menu bar selections generate `Click` events?

A Actually, they do *unless* a drop-down menu appears on the menu bar option. If no drop-down menu appears from a menu bar, the menu bar option will generate a `Click` event when the user selects the menu bar option. If a menu appears, however, the menu takes priority over the `Click` event, and the drop-down menu will appear instead of a `Click` event being generated.

Workshop

The Workshop provides quiz questions to help you solidify your understanding of the material covered and exercises to provide you with experience in using what you've learned. You should understand the quiz and exercise answers before continuing to the next chapter. Answers are provided in Appendix A, "Answers to Exercises."

Quiz

1. What do you call the dialog box that helps in your creation of menus?
2. True/False. Menu options are controls.
3. Which event do all menu options support?
4. What is the term *shortcut key* usually reserved for?
5. How do shortcut keys relate to menu usage?
6. What events do menu options generate if the user uses a shortcut key to access the menu options?
7. True/False. The Menu Editor helps you design your menus and create `Click` event procedure code for the menu options.

8. What's the purpose of the Checked menu option?
9. True/False. More than one menu option can be checked at once.
10. In Listing 4.1, what are lines such as 57, 58, and 59 used for?

Exercises

1. Describe the difference between entering a menu bar option and a drop-down menu option within the Menu Editor.
2. **Bug Buster:** Manuel the menu master is having trouble with his menus because the check mark does not go away from a menu option when the user selects a different checked option. Can you give Manuel some general advice? (You don't have to write any code yet.)

   Add shortcut keys to every menu option in the menu application that you created today. Make sure that no two menu options have the same shortcut keys.

DAY 5

Analyzing VB Data

Today's lesson begins your foray into Visual Basic programming using the Visual Basic programming language. Instead of working with graphical objects such as command buttons, you'll type text into the Code window to give your applications the brains they need to make things happen. You'll begin first by looking at Visual Basic data, and tomorrow you'll learn how to manipulate that data using commands and controls on the form.

Today, you learn the following:

- More about the Code window
- The kinds of data you can declare
- How to distinguish between data types
- The data storage requirements of Visual Basic data
- How to declare and assign values to variables
- Why Visual Basic uses an order of operators when calculating

A Few Preliminaries

When you're working with code, you need to know a few preliminary details. You need to understand more fully just how code fits in with an application's forms and controls. To begin, remember that the Project window lets you manage your applications and view all the files associated with your application. Although you write event procedures inside the Code window, event procedures don't require their own files. They stay with their respective controls. Therefore, your projects to this point have included only one form, and that form holds controls and the event procedures related to those controls. As you'll see, a form can hold code that is not specifically event procedure code but is more general purpose also.

Some projects hold other kinds of code as well. You have learned that all code appears in procedures and that Visual Basic supports both subroutine and function procedures. Event procedures fall into the subroutine category, but as you progress through these 21 days, you'll learn how to write function procedures as well. If a procedure is not an event procedure for a particular control, that code can appear inside a separate code *module*. The Project window lists the module if one appears in the project.

NEW TERM A *module* is a file that holds procedure code. The file that holds the form and its code is technically called the *Form module,* so you've already worked with modules.

If a project contains several forms, the project contains several Form modules because each form's controls must respond to events; therefore, each form has its own set of code in the Form module. One of the first points to consider when you're adding multiple forms to a project is which form will be the first form to appear on the screen when the user starts the application. The first form you create is the default startup form, but you can designate another startup form by selecting Project|*<project name>*Properties from the Visual Basic menu, where *<project name>* is the name of the current project. Visual Basic then displays the Project Properties dialog box, as shown in Figure 5.1. As you progress through these lessons, you'll learn how to program Visual Basic so that a secondary form appears when needed.

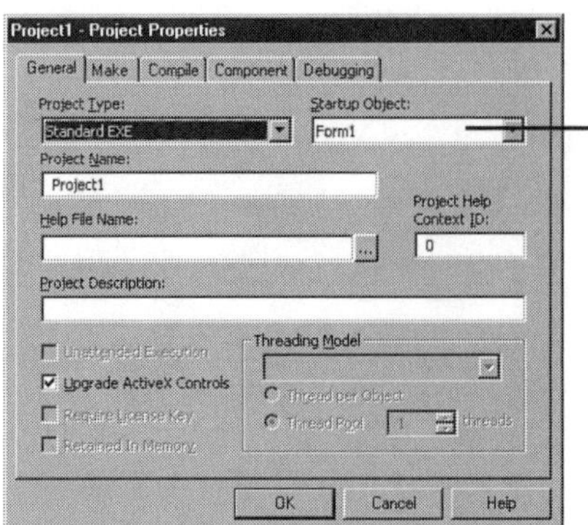

The startup form's name goes here

FIGURE 5.1.

Designate the startup form from the Project Properties dialog box.

Working Inside the Code Window

Now that event procedures are familiar to you, you'll work with event procedures over the next few days to learn the fundamentals of the Visual Basic programming language. Before starting on the language specifics, however, you need to understand that Form modules hold not only event procedures but also a *declarations section* as well. Each module that holds code also holds a declarations area.

NEW TERM A *declarations section* reserves space for and names data areas used throughout the rest of the module. You don't have to declare controls in the declarations section, but you often must declare other Visual Basic data storage areas in the declarations section.

The declarations section always appears at the top of every module that contains code. Therefore, the declarations section appears before any event procedures in a form module. Any time you type code before a module's first event procedure, that code is considered to be general purpose and not linked to a specific control. For the early part of your Visual Basic programming, you'll declare data in this area, so you'll treat the whole area as a data declaration section. Later, you'll also write general-purpose procedures in this area.

Study the Code window in Figure 5.2 to help put all this information into perspective. The details aren't important at this point, but the general concept is. The selected text makes up the declarations section starting with the first statement, which reads `Option Explicit`. Notice that the Code window's Object and Procedure drop-down list boxes read `(General)` and `(Declarations)`. The Code window lets you know where each line of code falls in the program's scheme through these drop-down list boxes.

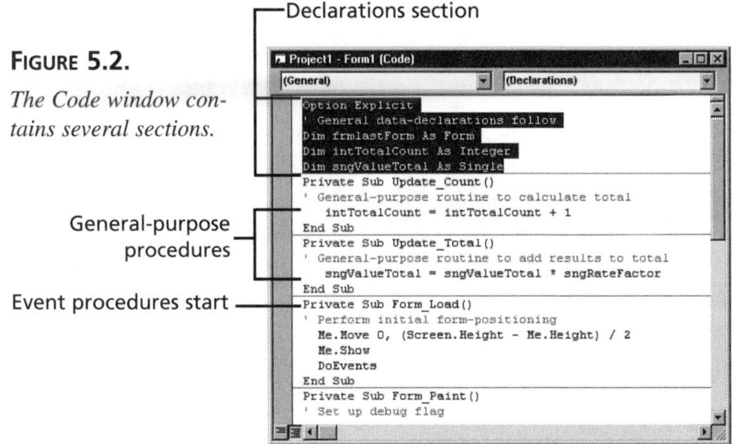

FIGURE 5.2.
The Code window contains several sections.

The next two procedures are not event procedures, and you know that fact from their names. Remember that an event procedure must contain an underscore that separates a control name from an event name. If you were to place the text cursor anywhere within the `Update_Count()` procedure, the Code window's Object drop-down list box would still read `(General)` because the code falls within the general-purpose section of the module. The Code window's `(Object)` list box, however, would read `Update_Count` because that is the name of the selected procedure, and the Code window lists the procedure name in the `(Object)` list box for all procedures that are not event procedures.

Okay, enough with the big picture, you're now ready for the nitty-gritty details.

The Data in Visual Basic

Visual Basic computing requires that you process several types of data. For example, you'll work with names, addresses, dollar amounts, large numbers, small numbers, and logical data that may be true or false (or yes or no). Visual Basic supports many data types so that it can handle all your programming needs.

Visual Basic, like most programming languages, gets picky about its data, so you must go along with Visual Basic's data requirements. Visual Basic requires that, before you work with a data value, you tell Visual Basic exactly what type of data the value is. Therefore, the place to begin learning Visual Basic programming is to learn about the data types. Visual Basic supports 12 data types.

Numeric Data

Generally, all numeric data falls into these two categories:

- **Integers**. Whole numbers without decimal points such as 614, 0, –934, and 3,918,938. Integers represent ages, counts, year numbers, and other whole number values.
- **Decimals**. Numbers with decimal points that can represent fractional values such as 8.709, 0.005, and –402.35534. Decimals (sometimes called *floating-point numbers*) represent temperatures, dollar amounts, and interest rates. All decimals require decimal points even if the fractional portion to the right of the decimal point is zero.

NEW TERM These sample numeric values are called *literals* or sometimes *constants* because they never change. The value 614 is always 614. In the later section "Working with Variables," you'll see how to declare data that can change.

Integers and decimals are stored differently inside Visual Basic, and Visual Basic treats them differently even though people don't always treat them differently. For example, –8 is not the same as –8.00 to Visual Basic.

Some data types consume a lot of memory and are inefficient, whereas others consume less memory and compute more quickly. You cannot tell by looking at a number how much memory it consumes. The number 29,999 requires the same number of memory locations as the number 701.

As you learn about the data types that Visual Basic supports, you'll also see how much memory each data type requires. Although memory requirements are less important now than they used to be, you, as a programmer, will want your program to run as efficiently as possible. Therefore, if you have the choice of using two or more data types for a value, use the data type that consumes the least amount of memory.

Table 5.1 describes each of the seven numeric data types that Visual Basic supports, the storage requirements of each data type, and the range that each data type covers. Use the storage requirements and ranges to determine the data type you want to use when you declare data. For example, if you need to represent negative numbers, you cannot use the `Byte` data type. If you need a way to hold people's ages, however, the `Byte` data type would be the most efficient and best data type to use.

NEW TERM A *byte* is one storage location in a PC's memory.

TABLE 5.1. VISUAL BASIC SUPPORTS SEVEN NUMERIC DATA TYPES.

Type	*Storage*	*Range*
`Byte`	1 byte	0 to 255
`Integer`	2 bytes	–32,768 to 32,767

continues

TABLE 5.1. CONTINUED

Type	*Storage*	*Range*
`Long`	4 bytes	–2,147,483,648 to 2,147,483,647
`Single`	4 bytes	–3.402823E+38 to –1.401298E-45 for negative values; 1.401298E-45 to 3.402823E+38 for positive values
`Double`	8 bytes	–1.79769313486232E+308 to –4.94065645841247E-324 for negative values; 4.94065645841247E-324 to 1.79769313486232E+308 for positive values
`Currency`	8 bytes	–922,337,203,685,477.5808 to 922,337,203,685,477.5807 (the extra precision ensures that monetary calculations are kept accurate to two decimal places)
`Decimal`	12 bytes	+/–79,228,162,514,264,337,593,543,950,335 if you use no decimal; +/–7.9228162514264337593543950335 with up to 28 decimal places (the `Decimal` data type is not fully supported in Visual Basic yet but remains for compatibility with future versions)

Some of the data values in Table 5.1 are expressed in *scientific notation*.

NEW TERM *Scientific notation* is a shortcut method for approximately representing extremely large or extremely small decimal values. The *E* means *exponent* (stored as a single-precision, `Single`, data type), and high-precision scientific notation numbers use a *D* for *double-precision exponent* (stored as a `Double` data type). Lowercase *e* and *d* are allowed as well. To convert a value from scientific notation to its numeric equivalent, multiply the number to the left of the E or D by 10 raised to the number on the right. If the scientific number contains a negative sign after the E or D, divide the number to the left of the E or D by 10 raised to the number on the right. For example, 5.83E+5 is 5.83 times 10 to the 5th power, or 5.83 times 100,000, or 583,000 stored as a single-precision value. Although the scientific notation is not shorter in this case than writing 584,000, the scientific notation would be much shorter for 5.83E+125 (which translates to 583 followed by 123 zeros). The number –3.2D-6 represents –3.2 divided by 1,000,000 or –.0000032 stored as in a `Double` memory location.

The issue of data types may still seem unimportant because you've yet to learn about data storage areas, but you will shortly in the section called "Working with Variables." When you type the literal value –8.3 in a program, you don't have to specify that the literal is the `Single` data type. You must be concerned, however, with the type of the location that will hold that literal value. You cannot store –8.3 in an integer location and expect Visual Basic to represent the value properly.

Sometimes when you use a literal, you'll want to guarantee that Visual Basic uses a specific data type for that literal. For example, suppose that you are going to use –8.3 in a calculation that requires high-precision mathematics combined with values that are `Double`. If Visual Basic assumes the –8.3 is a `Single` data type, the calculation may not be carried out to as many decimal places as needed in some cases. Therefore, you can add a data-type suffix character to literals to ensure that Visual Basic treats the literal as a specific data type. Table 5.2 lists these data-type suffix characters. If you type `-8.3#` in the calculation, therefore, Visual Basic knows that you want the –8.3 treated from the beginning as a double-precision number with the highest decimal accuracy possible.

TABLE 5.2. VISUAL BASIC SUFFIX CHARACTERS FOR LITERALS.

Suffix	*Data Type Represented*
`&`	`Long`
`!`	`Single`
`#`	`Double`
`@`	`Currency`

Caution

The E and the D in scientific notation values represent `Single` and `Double` data types, so no suffix character is needed for scientific notation values that you type because the scientific notation itself declares the literal's type.

Visual Basic respects the Windows International settings you've specified for your PC. Therefore, if you've set up to use your PC for a European country, for example, you use the comma in place of a decimal point.

The good news is that, despite this section's heavy theory, you don't have to worry too much about data types when you're working with literal values. If you need to assign a number to a control's property, just do so. Only in special cases, such as high-precision scientific and mathematical work do you need to concern yourself with whether a literal is single or double precision. One of the most important things to watch for is that you don't embed special characters inside a number. For example, don't put commas inside a long numeric literal unless your Windows International settings are set to a country that uses a comma in place of a decimal point for fractional values.

The Remaining Data Types

The nonnumeric data types are easier to understand than some of the higher-precision numeric data types if you are not mathematically inclined. One of the reasons that BASIC and its incarnations have remained on the scene, despite the proliferation of "more powerful languages" over the years, is the result of BASIC's text-handling power. BASIC, and therefore Visual Basic, far surpasses virtually every other language available when it comes to processing text *strings*.

A *string* is a series of zero or more characters. Although a string may hold numeric digits, a string is never used in calculations but only holds characters. You use strings for names, addresses, codes, Social Security numbers, and other data values that you do not need to compute with. Use the numeric data types only when you need to compute or hold strict numeric information such as monetary amounts.

In addition to string data, Visual Basic supports other kinds of data such as dates and *Boolean* data. Table 5.3 lists the nonnumeric data types that Visual Basic supports.

TABLE 5.3. VISUAL BASIC SUPPORTS SEVERAL NONNUMERIC DATA TYPES.

Data Type	*Storage*	*Range*
`String` (fixed length)	Length of string	1 to about 65,400 characters
`String` (variable)	Length + 10 bytes	0 to 2 billion characters
`Date`	8 bytes	January 1, 100 to December 31, 9999
`Boolean`	2 bytes	`True` or `False`
`Object`	4 bytes	Any embedded object
`Variant` (numeric)	16 bytes	Any value as large as `Double`
`Variant` (text)	Length plus 22 bytes	Same as variable-length `String`

NEW TERM *Boolean* data, named after the mathematician George Boole, represents data that can take only two values. These values are usually represented as true or false although they can also be treated as yes or no values.

Always enclose string literals in quotation marks. Strings can contain any characters; all the following are valid string literals:

```
"Oh me, oh my"
"543-00-0234"
"1020 S. Yale Avenue"
""
```

Anything between two quotation marks is a string, even the *null string* at the end of the list.

NEW TERM A *null string*, sometimes called a *zero-length string*, is zero bytes in length and is sometimes used to initialize string data to a value of nothing. The special Visual Basic value called `Null` also represents null strings. Visual Basic also supports a special string value called an *empty string*, represented by the `Empty` keyword. Empty strings represent strings that are similar to null strings but hold a slightly different interpretation; a control property that contains the `Empty` keyword is assumed not to have been initialized with any value yet, not even a null string.

The distinction between fixed-length strings and variable-length strings will become more critical as you learn more about Visual Basic data storage methods.

When you type a date or time literal, enclose the date or time value between two pound signs (#). Visual Basic allows for virtually any kind of date and time format. The dates and times can follow whatever international setting you've assigned to your PC. All the following are valid date and time literals:

```
#July 4, 1776#
#7:11 pm#
#19:11:22#
#1-2-2003#
#5-Dec-99#
```

The `Boolean` data type is useful for setting values to a control property that takes only a `True` or `False` value such as an `Enabled` property value.

The `Variant` data type can hold any kind of data except fixed-length strings. You employ variant data for different uses, especially when a data storage area is to hold different kinds of data. A variant storage area can act as a temporary storage location for any data type that you will later place elsewhere in a more specific data-typed area.

Perhaps you've heard of the year 2000 problem, also known as the *Y2K bug*. For many years, programmers used two-digit years in code to save the space needed to carry the full year. These kinds of programs may have problems when the two-digit year moves from 99 to 00. Visual Basic is year-2000 compliant which means that the internal date representations take the next millennium into account. Therefore, at midnight on December 31, 1999, your Visual Basic programs should have no trouble moving to the next year.

Nevertheless, some Visual Basic programmers resort to fancy time- and spacing-saving tricks, so not all Visual Basic code will necessarily work. As a newcomer to Visual Basic programming, keep focued on the Y2K problem and always work with the full year in your programs. You should have no problems when the year 2000 finally hits.

Working with Variables

Variables hold values that can change. A variable's value can change because a variable is nothing more than a storage area, not unlike a box, that can hold one value at a time. When you store a different value in a variable, the original value is replaced. The literal value `54` never changes, but if you were to store `54` inside a variable, the variable would hold the `54` until you stored a different value in the variable, and then the variable would hold something else.

NEW TERM A *variable* is a temporary named storage area inside your program's memory that holds data. Variables hold intermediate calculations and values that you assign to and load from controls on the form.

You are responsible for naming all variables in your code. Two different variables cannot have the same name within the same procedure because Visual Basic cannot distinguish between them. Unlike control properties that are already named, variables don't have names until you give them names. Before you can use a variable, you must declare the variable by telling Visual Basic the name and data type that the variable is to hold. Variables can hold data only from the data type you've defined the variable to hold. A variable declared as `Byte` cannot hold a string value. (The exception to this rule is a variable declared as a `Variant` data type.)

Declaring Variables

The `Dim` statement declares variables by assigning them a name and data type. Before you can use a variable, you must first declare that variable with a `Dim` statement. You can relax this rule a bit, but doing so can make for sloppy programming that produces errors at times. Visual Basic's Tools, Options menu produces a dialog box. When you select the Editor tab, you can check the Require Variable Declaration option to ensure that Visual Basic requires the initial declaration. The declarations section of your code also includes a statement, by default, that looks like this:

```
Option Explicit
```

This statement tells Visual Basic that the rest of the code in this module is to declare all variables before they are used. Thereafter, if you misspell a variable name in the middle of your program, Visual Basic will catch the error. If you do not require explicit declaration before you use a variable, Visual Basic treats the misspelled variable as an uninitialized variable and uses a bad value when the variable appears inside calculations.

> If you don't require explicit variable declarations, Visual Basic assumes that an undeclared variable is of the `Variant` data type.

Here is the format of the `Dim` statement that you use to declare variables:

```
Dim VarName As DataType
```

`VarName` is the name you assign to the variable, and *`DataType`* is one of the data types listed in Tables 5.1 and 5.3. If you declare variables inside a procedure (event procedures or nonevent procedures), you declare them immediately after the opening wrapper line. The variable is then available to that procedure and only to that procedure. No other procedure knows about the variable, which keeps the variable local to the procedure. If you declare a variable in a module's declarations section, every procedure in that module has access to the variable. The variable is then said to be *global to the module,* but no other module in the application has access to the variables. You can even make some variables global to an entire project, but the more local you make your variables, the less likely you will attempt to use the same variable for two different purposes.

Note

> Two variables can have the same name and still be different variables as long as they are declared locally within different procedures. In addition, two procedures can share a variable that is local to only one of the procedures. You'll learn about how to share local variables on Day 8, "The Nature of VB Programs."

You make up variable names, so you should know the rules for naming them. When naming variables, you must

- Begin all variables with an alphabetic letter.
- Use letters or numbers in the name.
- Keep the name from 1 to 255 characters in length (so don't make up 256-character names).
- Use a limited set of special characters in the name. To be safe, use only the underscore character (_) in the name. When you stick to letters, numbers, and the underscore, you don't have to worry about forgetting which special characters are and are not allowed. Especially, don't embed spaces in a variable name.

The following are not hard and fast rules but good general rules of thumb to follow when naming your variables:

- Preface variable names with a prefix that describes the variable's data type. This way, you don't have to keep referring to the declarations section of a long program to locate the variable's data type, and you are less likely to store an incorrect data-typed value in the variable. Table 5.4 lists common variable-name prefixes you can use.

You can store some values of one data type into variables declared for a different type if the data types are compatible in type and size. For example, you can store a byte data value in an integer variable because the `Integer` data type accepts a larger range of integer numbers than the `Byte` data type.

- Use names that are meaningful, such as `curHighTotal` instead of something ambiguous such as `a` or `curX1`. The names help document the code.
- Use a combination of uppercase and lowercase letters to separate parts of variable names. (This tutorial uses only letters and numbers in variable names although many programmers prefer to use the underscore to separate parts of a name, such as `curHigh_Sales`.) A combination of uppercase and lowercase is called *camel notation* due to its hump-like nature (that is, `aCamelHump`).

TABLE 5.4. VARIABLE NAME PREFIXES THAT DESCRIBE THE VARIABLE'S DATA TYPE.

Prefix	*Data Type*	*Example*
bln	Boolean	blnButtonEnabled
byt	Byte	bytLength
cur	Currency	curSales98
dte	Date	dteOverdue
dbl	Double	dblScientificAmt
int	Integer	intYear1998
lng	Long	lngWeatherDistance
obj	Object	objWorksheetAcct99
sng	Single	sngSales1stQte
str	String	strFirstName
vnt	Variant	vntValue

Here are some possible variable declarations using `Dim`:

```
Dim intTotal As Integer
Dim curSales99 As Currency
Dim dteFinal As Date
Dim strName As String
Dim blnIsChecked As Boolean
```

Name your variables of the `Boolean` data type like a question that can be answered as yes or no (or true or false), as done here with `blnIsChecked`.

5

You can also combine variable declarations in one `Dim` statement, separated with a comma, but you must use the `As` *`DataType`* clause for each variable, as in the following:

```
Dim intTotal As Integer, curSales99 As Currency
```

If you don't specify the `As` *`DataType`* clause, Visual Basic declares the variable as a `Variant` data type. Therefore, the following statements are equivalent:

```
Dim vntControlVal As Variant
Dim vntControlVal
```

When you declare variant variables, always specify `As Variant` to clarify your intentions with the variable.

Declaring Strings

Strings pose an extra problem when you declare them because the `String` data type works for two kinds of strings: variable length and fixed length. The most common string data type is the variable-length string; such string variables are the easiest to declare because they follow the same `Dim` statement format as the other data types. The following statements declare two variable-length string variables:

```
Dim strCityName As String
Dim strStateName As String
```

Both `strCityName` and `strStateName` can hold strings of any length. If you first store `"Indianapolis"` in `strCityName`, you can later store `"Tulsa"` in that same name and the variable adjusts to the new string length. Most of the time you'll work with variable-length strings; however, this book does not describe fixed-length strings too much unless the length is vital, as is sometimes the case when working with disk files. In addition, you may want to limit the number of characters that appear in a label or some other control by assigning only fixed-length strings to them.

The quotation marks are not stored as part of the string but serve only to delimit the string in a string literal.

Here is the format of the `Dim` statement that you must use to declare fixed-length strings:

```
Dim VarName As String * Length
```

The `* Length` option tells Visual Basic that the `Dim` statement declares a fixed-length string that will never hold more characters than *`Length`* specifies. The following declaration declares a variable that will hold at most five characters:

```
Dim strZipcode As String * 5
```

If you attempt to store more characters than a fixed-length string variable allows, Visual Basic stores only the fixed number of characters and discards the rest. Such bugs are often difficult to trace.

Using Variable Storage

After you declare a variable, you can store data in the variable. Using the *assignment statement* is the easiest way to store values in variables. Here is the format of the assignment statement:

```
ItemName = Expression
```

ItemName can be a declared variable, and is for most of today's lesson, but *ItemName* can also be a control property value. *Expression* can be any of the following:

- A mathematical expression
- A literal
- A variable
- A logical or string expression
- A control's property value (control properties are `Variant`, but Visual Basic converts them to a data type when you store them in variables)
- A mathematical, logical, or string expression that contains a combination of literals, variables, and control property values

The concept of an expression may seem daunting at this point, but an expression can be virtually anything that becomes a value. All the following are valid assignment statements:

```
curSales = 5712.75
strFirstName = "Terry"
blnPassedTest = True
blnIsEnabled = lblTitle.Enabled
dblValue = 45.1
intCount = intNumber
dteOld = #4-1-92#
sngOld97Total = sngNew98Total - 1000.00
```

You can easily see how the assignment works from the first assignment here. The value `5712.75` is stored in the variable named `curSales`. You can add a data-type suffix after a literal, as done in the fifth assignment, to keep both sides of the assignment the same data type. In this case, however, `45.1` is smaller than a `Double` data type, so Visual Basic would automatically make the conversion if you omitted the suffix. Assign variables declared with the `Boolean` data type either `True` or `False`, or a property value that contains either `True` or `False`. Notice that the last assignment includes a minus sign. You'll learn how to write mathematical expressions in the next section.

5

Note

Visual Basic still supports an older assignment statement format that starts the assignment with the `Let` keyword. The following two statements do exactly the same thing:

```
Let intCount = 1
```

```
intCount = 1
```

Throughout the first four lessons, you learned that you can store control property values through Visual Basic code. You use the assignment statement to do just that. The following statement changes the value shown on the form's label named `lblTitle`:

```
lblTitle.Caption = "The task is completed"
```

All controls have default properties that are the properties Visual Basic assumes you are assigning to if you don't specify a property name. The default property for label controls is the `Caption` property, so the following assignment is equivalent to the preceding one:

```
lblTitle = "The task is completed"
```

Although assigning to controls' default properties requires less typing, the more explicit you make your code, the more self-documenting the code will be and the more clear the code will be to readers. Always type the property you are assigning to even if that property happens to be the default property. When you later maintain the code, the statement will be less ambiguous.

The moment a statement assigns a value to a control, that control is updated on the form. Therefore, the new title appears immediately as soon as this assignment to the title is made. The user will instantly see the new title on the screen.

Visual Basic's Operators

Visual Basic supports numerous mathematical and string *operators*. Table 5.5 lists the most common operators. You use these operators in expressions when calculating and working with data.

Operators manipulate data by combining or computing results. Most operators are symbols, but some, such as `Mod`, look more like Visual Basic commands.

TABLE 5.5. THESE COMMON OPERATORS PERFORM CALCULATIONS AND MANIPULATE DATA.

Operator	*Meaning*	*Example*	*Result*
^	Exponentiation	2 ^ 3	8
*	Multiplication	2 * 3	6
/	Division	6 / 2	3
+	Addition	2 + 3	5
-	Subtraction	6 - 3	3

Operator	*Meaning*	*Example*	*Result*
/Mod	Modulus	11 Mod 3	2
/\	Integer division	11 \ 3	3
+ or &	String concatenation	"Hi," & "There"	"Hi,There"

The exponentiation raises a number to a power. Therefore, 2 ^ 3 is the same as 2 raised to the 3rd power, or 2 times 2 times 2, which equals 8. You can raise fractional values to a power, and you can raise values to a negative power to compute the root of the number if you need an *n*th root. The multiplication and division operators work as you would expect. The expression 10 / 3 results in the approximate value 3.3333, and 10 * 3 results in a value of 30.

The `Mod` operator returns the remainder from an integer division. Only integer values can appear on each side of `Mod`; if you include a different data type, Visual Basic attempts to convert and round the data to an integer before proceeding with the modulus. For example, 11 Mod 3 returns a 2 simply because 11 divided by 3 is 3 with a remainder of 2. The integer division operator, \ (notice that the backslash and not the forward slash denotes division), returns the whole number value of a division and discards any remainder. Therefore, 11 \ 3 is 3 because 11 / 3 is 3 with a remainder of 2. (Using the normal division operator, 11 / 3 would compute a fractional value, such as 3.666.)

The plus sign (+) is an overloaded operator because it performs two operations depending on the data you place on either side of it. When you place two string values on either side of the plus sign, or on either side of the ampersand, `&`, Visual Basic *concatenates* the strings and treats the concatenated string as a single string. Visual Basic adds nothing between the concatenated strings, so if you want a space between them, you have to concatenate a space between them specifically.

5

NEW TERM An *overloaded operator* is an operator that performs more than one operation depending on the context in which you use it.

Concatenation is the merging together of two or more strings into one longer string.

The following assignment concatenates the values from two labels into a single string variable, putting a space between them:

```
strCompleteName = lblFirst.Caption & " " & lblLast.Caption
```

To avoid possible confusion with the addition operator when you maintain your code, use the ampersand only when you are concatenating strings.

Analyzing the Order of Operators

Visual Basic performs math in a strict predefined order, which is illustrated in Table 5.6. Exponentiation is performed first, and then multiplication and division are performed before any addition and subtraction in an expression unless parentheses override that order.

TABLE 5.6. VISUAL BASIC FOLLOWS AN ORDER OF OPERATORS WHEN COMPUTING RESULTS.

Order	*Operators*	*Example*	*Result*
1	Parentheses ()	`(2 + 3) * 7`	35
2	^	`2 ^ 3 + 1`	9
3	*, /, \, `Mod`	`2 + 3 * 7`	23
4	+, -	`10 - 4 * 2 + 1`	3

Unless parentheses override the default order, Visual Basic always calculates the intermediate results of any multiplication and division in an expression before the addition and subtraction. Exponentiation has an even higher priority.

If multiplication and division both appear in the same expression, Visual Basic performs them from left to right unless parentheses override that order. Therefore, the following expression produces a result of 15 because Visual Basic first divides 10 by 2 to get 5 and then multiplies the 5 by 3 to get 15. In the same way, addition and subtraction compute in their left-to-right order if they appear in an expression without other operators or parentheses changing their behavior.

```
10 / 2 * 3
```

If you embed one set of parentheses within another, Visual Basic computes the innermost set first. Therefore, Visual Basic computes the (8 – 3) before anything else in the following expression:

```
(10 + 2 - (8 - 3)) + 1
```

Summary

Today's lesson introduced you to preliminary details of Visual Basic code. First, you learned how the declarations section fits into the overall Visual Basic application, and then you studied the specifics of code starting with data types.

Visual Basic supports several kinds of data, as you learned today. You must not only understand how to distinguish between two or more data types but also how to declare the various data types that you want to work with. You'll use variables for intermediate storage as a program runs, but before you use a variable, you must properly declare that variable and name it. After you declare a variable, you might then use the Visual Basic math operators to calculate results and store those results in the variables that you've defined.

Tomorrow's lesson takes you to the next step of Visual Basic programming by showing another set of operators with which you can compare data. After you tackle the operators, you then will learn new programming statements and controls that work with those operators.

Q&A

Q Why does Visual Basic not compute all operators from left to right?

A Visual Basic follows a standard and historical algebraic operator hierarchy. Don't blame Visual Basic; blame the mathematicians! Seriously, the order of operators keeps ambiguity from your code by defining a preset order that is always followed. Actually, you don't have to rely on the order of operators because you can dictate all order by using extra parentheses, even where they are not needed. For example, the following assignment would store the same result with or without the parentheses, but the parentheses might be clearer because they eliminate all possible ambiguity:

```
intValue = (8 * 9) + intResult
```

Q Why are local variables better than global variables?

A You'll gain more insight into the local versus global discussion as you learn more about Visual Basic programming. The rule of thumb is that local is always better than global with few exceptions. Generally, a procedure should work on a need-to-know basis. It should have access only to variables that it needs and not to any others. Such separation helps eliminate nasty and hard-to-find bugs that can appear if all variables are global.

Perhaps already you realize that controls are global to the entire project. Any procedure may need to modify or read a control's property value so that a form's controls are available to all code within a project.

Workshop

The Workshop provides quiz questions to help you solidify your understanding of the material covered and exercises to provide you with experience in using what you've learned. Try to understand the quiz and exercise answers before continuing to the next day's lesson. Answers are provided in Appendix A, "Answers to Exercises."

Quiz

1. What kind of code goes in the declarations section of a program?
2. What can you do if two or more procedures need access to another procedure's local variable?
3. True/False. A literal's value never changes.
4. True/False. A variable's value never changes.
5. Why does Visual Basic support two kinds of division operators?
6. What is an overloaded operator?
7. Which operator is preferred for concatenating string expressions?
8. Which data type holds any other data type?
9. True/False. The variable prefixes are required in variable names.
10. What two ways can you use to ensure that Visual Basic doesn't allow for undeclared variables?

Exercises

1. What do you think Visual Basic will do with the following variable declaration statement?

   ```
   Dim intCnt As Integer, abc, curSales As Currency
   ```

2. **Bug Buster:** Sally is having difficulty calculating a correct average using the following expression. Can you help her?

   ```
   sngAvg = sngGrade1 + sngGrade2 + sngGrade3 / 3
   ```

3. What is the result of each of the following formulas?

   a. 1 + 2 * 4 / 2

   b. (1 + 2) * 4 / 2

   c. 1 + 2 * (4 / 2)

   d. 9 \ 2 + 1

   e. (1 + (10 – (2 + 2)))

4. Write assignment statements that convert each of the following formulas to their Visual Basic equivalents:

   a.
   $$a = \frac{3+3}{4+4}$$

   b.
   $$x = (a - b) * (a - 2)^2$$

   c.
   $$f = \frac{a^{1/2}}{b^{1/2}}$$

5. The program from the first Bonus Project, “Controls, Properties, and Events,” included the following procedure:

```
1:  Private Sub cmdTest_Click()
2:  ' This event procedure executes as soon as the
3:  ' user wants to test the entered password
4:     If txtPassword.Text = "Sams" Then
        ' Success!   Password matched
5:        Beep
6:        Beep        ' Now, display the picture
7:        imgPassword.Picture = LoadPicture("C:\Program Files\" _
8:          & "Microsoft Visual Studio\Common\Graphics\MetaFile\" _
9:          & "Business\coins.wmf")
    lblPrompt.Caption = "Show me the money!"
10:    Else
11:       lblPrompt.Caption = "Wrong password - Try Again"
12:       txtPassword.Text = ""      ' Erase old password
13:       txtPassword.SetFocus       ' Put focus on text box
14:    End If
15: End Sub
```

   Study this procedure to see how the assignments are made. More importantly, can you now see why long statements that you continue with an ending underscore, such as lines 7, 8, and 9, must include ampersands when you break string literals?

WEEK 1

BONUS PROJECT 2

Variables and Expressions

This Bonus Project's code demonstrates variable declarations, assignment statements, and expressions. Now that you've mastered the basics of form design using some of the controls, you need to tackle the details of code and learn how to activate an application's controls with Visual Basic programming statements. The place to start is with data.

The simple code in Listing BP2.1 demonstrates the concepts you learned about in Day 5's lesson ("Analyzing VB Data"). No visual Form window is described here so that you can concentrate on the code. If you want to create a Form window to test the code, you can do so by designing a form that contains three labels named `lblGrossPay`, `lblTaxes`, and `lblNetPay`. Add a command button named `cmdCalcPay` to trigger the code. You only need to create a simple form, such as the one shown in Figure BP2.1. After performing some calculations, the code will place the payroll results in the three labels.

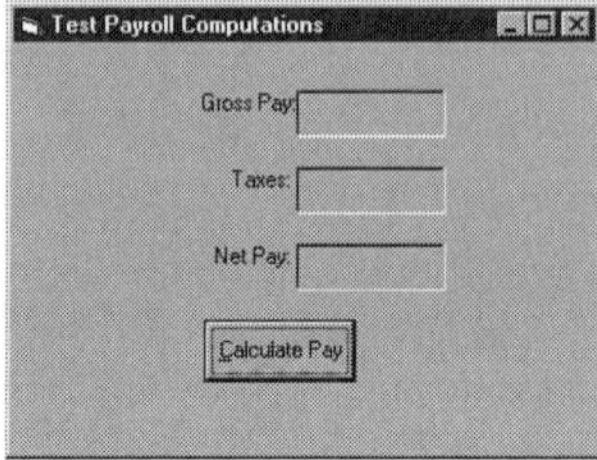

FIGURE BP2.1.
You can create a simple form to test this code.

LISTING BP2.1. THIS CODE DEMONSTRATES VARIABLES AND ASSIGNMENT STATEMENTS.

```
1:  Private Sub cmdCalcPay_Click()
2:  ' Computes three payroll variables
3:     Dim intHoursWorked As Integer
4:     Dim sngRate As Single, sngTaxRate As Single
5:     Dim curTaxes As Currency, curGrossPay As Currency
6:     Dim curNetPay As Currency
7:
8:     ' Initialize the variables
9:     ' (Normally, data such as this would
10:    '  come from the user or from a file)
11:    intHoursWorked = 40      ' Total hours worked
12:    sngRate = 7.8            ' Pay per hour
13:    sngTaxRate = 0.42        ' Tax rate percentage
14:
15:    ' Calculate the amounts
16:    curGrossPay = intHoursWorked * sngRate
17:    curTaxes = sngTaxRate * curGrossPay
18:    curNetPay = curGrossPay - curTaxes
19:
20:    ' Display results in appropriate labels
21:    lblGrossPay.Caption = curGrossPay
22:    lblTaxes.Caption = curTaxes
23:    lblNetPay.Caption = curNetPay
24: End Sub
```

Analysis

Lines 1 and 24 are the wrapper lines for the command button's event procedure. Lines such as 2 and 8 help document the code for ease of maintenance. Lines 3 through 6 declare several variables. Three of the variables are of the `Currency` data type.

Lines 11, 12, and 13 assign data values to three variables. Normally, payroll data might come from the user entering the values from the keyboard or perhaps from a data file; however, because you have yet to master keyboard and file input, the assignment statements work well for this short example. Notice also that when a literal is assigned to an integer variable in line 11, no decimal point is used; however, a decimal does appear in the assigned values for the two single-precision variables in lines 12 and 13.

Lines 16, 17, and 18 perform the payroll calculations. The order of operators does not come into play in any of the expressions because they are short. You'll see that data types are mixed in the expressions, but all the data is compatible with each other.

Finally, lines 21, 22, and 23 assign variable values to the label controls. As soon as each assignment is made, the corresponding form updates the labels with the computed and assigned values.

Caution

> An assignment statement copies an expression on the right side of the equal sign to the data holder (such as a variable or control) on the left side of the equal sign. The assignment is not a move operation. After line 21 executes, for example, the variable `curGrossPay` still holds its value, but that value also now appears in the label's caption as well.

DAY 6

Controlling Programs

Today's lesson continues to teach you about Visual Basic operators, but the operators you'll study today compute no mathematical results. Today you'll learn about the conditional and logical operators that perform data comparisons. In addition, you'll learn some control statements so that you can write programs that repeat sections of code as many times as needed and that test various data conditions.

Today, you learn the following:

- Conditional operators that you can use to test data
- The logical operators and how they enable you to combine conditional operators
- About the `If` statement
- When to use a loop
- The difference between the four kinds of `Do` loop formats
- How the `For` and `Do` loops compare

Conditional Operators

Consider the scenario in which you are writing an accounts payable application. The application totals owed amounts for each vendor that you do business with and prints the checks to the vendors. What if you did no business with one of the vendors within that past pay cycle? Do you want the program to print a check made out for $0.00? Certainly not. Until now, all program code within a procedure that you've seen has executed one statement after another. By using conditional operators and related statements that you'll learn today, you can write a program so that it changes its order of statement execution if the data requires such a change. Therefore, the application can print checks only to those vendors to whom you owe money.

Table 6.1 lists several new Visual Basic operators. None of these operators perform math as did the ones in yesterday's lesson. Instead, these *conditional operators* compare data. These conditional operators make your Visual Basic programs somewhat smarter. By comparing data and analyzing results, your Visual Basic program can decide an appropriate course of action based on data alone. By writing programs with conditional operators and statements, you let Visual Basic decide, at runtime, which statements to execute in a program.

NEW TERM The *conditional operators* let you compare one Visual Basic data value to another. Through the conditional operators, you can learn if a value is less than, equal to, or greater than another.

TABLE 6.1. VISUAL BASIC SUPPORTS SIX CONDITIONAL OPERATORS.

Operator	*Description*	*Example*	*Result*
=	Equal to	`7 = 2`	False
>	Greater than	`6 > 3`	True
<	Less than	`5 < 11`	True
>=	Greater than or equal to	`23 >= 23`	True
<=	Less than or equal to	`4 <= 21`	True
<>	Not equal to	`3 <> 3`	False

Notice that Table 6.1 has a result column. What is the result of 6 > 3? Is 6 greater than 3? Yes, so the result of that conditional expression is true. As you know from yesterday's lesson, Visual Basic supports the `Boolean` data type that accepts a true or false value. The Visual Basic programming language supports the keywords `True` and `False`, so you can use them inside code to assign values to Boolean variables and to control properties that accept `True` and `False`.

Note

> From Table 6.1, you can see another operator that is overloaded in addition to the plus sign that you learned about yesterday. The equal sign is used in assignment statements to assign expressions to variables and controls. The equal sign is also used for equality comparisons. Visual Basic distinguishes between the two operations from the context in which the equal sign appears in your code.

Before you see these operators inside Visual Basic code, make sure that you understand how they work. The expression `23 >= 23` is true because 23 is greater than *or equal to* 23. Study the result column in Table 6.1 to make sure you understand how the values compare.

Literals aren't the only values that can appear on each side of a conditional operator. You can place literals, expressions, variables, controls, and combinations of all of them around conditional operators. Visual Basic works with many kinds of data, and your programs have to test to see how data compares before determining the best code to execute.

A special case occurs if a value on one side or the other of a conditional contains the `Null` value. Visual Basic returns neither `True` nor `False` but `Null` for the conditional's result. You have to be on the lookout for the `Null` value if you suspect such a value is possible in one of the values you are comparing. In these cases, you look for three possible results: `True`, `False`, or `Null`. Because such results get confusing, Visual Basic contains tools called *internal functions* that can help you detect `Null` values; you'll learn about them on Day 8, "The Nature of VB Programs." Along these same lines, the conditional operators assume that an `Empty` value (meaning that a control or variable has yet to be initialized with any value, as you read in yesterday's lesson) is the same as zero, or a null string if you are comparing strings.

You use the conditional operators to compare strings just as you do for numeric values. Generally, string comparisons follow these rules of thumb:

- Uppercase letters are less than lowercase letters, so "ST. JOHN" comes before "St. John."
- Letters compare in alphabetical order, so "A" is less than "B" and the name "Walter" is greater than (comes before) "Williams."
- Numbers are less than letters, so "3" is less than "Three."

If these general rules of thumb seem confusing, you can be assured that Visual Basic compares most string data in the same order that you find names listed in your phone book. Being able to compare string data lets your program alphabetize names, test passwords, and analyze information.

Visual Basic supports a special statement in the declarations section of a module that reads as follows:

```
Option Compare Text
```

If this statement appears in a module's declarations section, possibly along with the `Option Explicit` statement you learned yesterday, uppercase and lowercase letters compare equally. If you do not want a case-sensitive comparison, you can include the `Option Compare Text` statement in your module, but generally, you won't want to compare uppercase and lowercase letters equally because you would then be unable to alphabetize properly in most situations.

Visual Basic follows the *ASCII table* order when comparing strings unless the `Option Compare Text` statement appears in the module.

NEW TERM An *ASCII table* (pronounced *ask-ee*) is a list of all 256 characters available on the PC along with a corresponding and unique number assigned to each character. The letter *A* has an ASCII value of 65, *B* has 66, and so on. If you search for *ASCII codes* in Visual Basic's help index, the ASCII table appears on your monitor, as shown in Figure 6.1. In addition to the online help that's always available, Appendix C contains an ASCII table.

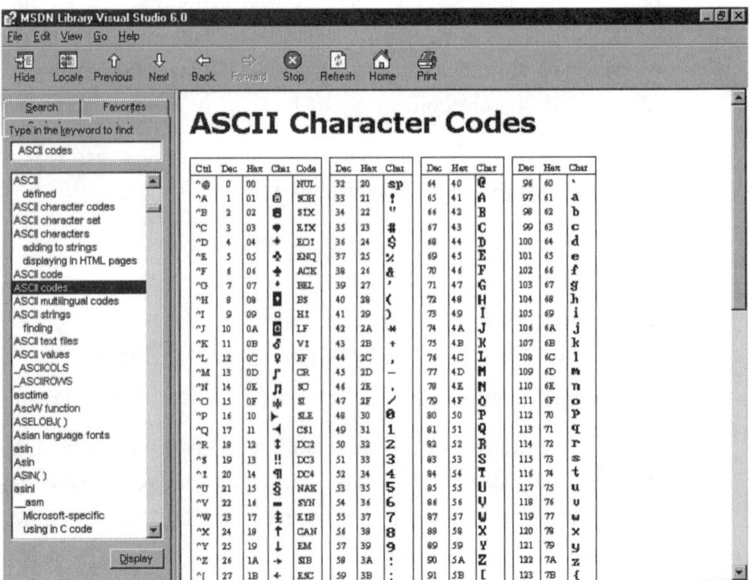

FIGURE 6.1.
Visual Basic follows the order of the ASCII table when comparing string data.

Consider the following string comparisons:

```
"abcdef" > "ABCDEF"
"Yes!" < "Yes?"
"Computers are fun!" = "Computers are fun!"
"PC" <> "pc"
"Books, Books, Books" >= "Books, Books"
```

Each string comparison you see here returns a `True` result.

Visual Basic supports another conditional operator, `Like`, which compares values based on a wildcard match. Perhaps you've used the `*` and `?` wildcard characters when working with files. `*` stands for zero or more characters, and `?` stands for only one character. In addition, `Like` uses a third wildcard character, `#`, to stand for a numeric digit. A few examples should help explain `Like` quickly. Consider these conditional expressions that use `Like` and that all return the value `True`:

```
"Sams Publishing" Like "Sa*"
"Qtr???" Like "QtrOne"
"Data##" Like Data98"
"X" Like "[XYZ]"
```

The last example shows a special kind of `Like` expression. If the character is like any character inside brackets, a `True` result is produced. The brackets offer a way to test for one of a few characters. All the following compare true when you use `Like` against a string value of "`Code[12345]Red": "Code1Red", "Code2Red", "Code3Red", "Code4Red"`, and `"Code5Red"`.

In real-world Visual Basic programming, you'll compare variables and controls, and the data in them can change as the program executes. These examples compare literals against literals only to show you how the operators work.

The equality conditional operator would return false for these expressions because = does not recognize wildcard characters.

6

Conditional Data

Always compare two values whose data types are compatible. For example, you can compare one number of any numeric data type against another to see which is larger. You can compare strings against each other and Booleans against each other. Don't try to compare a string and a number, however, because the results are usually wrong.

Strings, Booleans, currency values, dates, times, and the integer data types (`Byte`, `Integer`, and `Long`) compare against each other well for equality. Never try to compare two single- or double-precision values against each other for equality, as in `sngSales = sngGoal`. Due to the way Visual Basic stores precision data, two equal single-precision values may compare as unequal because of rounding that Visual Basic performs to such values internally. If you want to test for two equal precision variables, you have to subtract them and test the size of the difference to see whether they are approximately equal. Such coding is tedious, so avoid it if you can.

Visual Basic handles the `Variant` data type nicely when you make a conditional comparison because you'll often compare a control's value, such as a text box's `Text` value, to a variable or to a literal. Control properties generally compare as if they were variant data. If the variant variable or control holds characters that correspond to a number, such as `234.56`, and you compare that variant value to a numeric variable, Visual Basic makes a numeric comparison by temporarily converting that variant value to a number. If, however, you compare a variant variable or control to a string, Visual Basic temporarily turns that value into a string to make a true character-by-character, ASCII-based string comparison. Therefore, Visual Basic takes care of some ugly details that would otherwise be difficult to handle when one side of a comparison is the `Variant` data type.

Visual Basic issues a nasty runtime error if you compare a variant value to a numeric value and the variant's value does not properly translate into a number. Be sure that you know your data. Visual Basic offers help for testing of data types in some internal functions that you'll read all about in Day 8's lesson.

Combining Conditional Operators with Logical Operators

Technically, the six conditional operators offer enough power to test for any condition, but you can greatly enhance their flexibility by combining the conditional operators with Visual Basic's *logical operators*. Table 6.2 lists the logical operators.

NEW TERM The *logical operators* let you combine two or more sets of conditional comparisons. Like the `Mod` operator, the logical operators use keywords instead of symbols.

TABLE 6.2. VISUAL BASIC SUPPORTS THREE LOGICAL OPERATORS.

Operator	*Description*	*Example*	*Result*
`And`	Both sides must be true	`(2 < 3) And (4 < 5)`	True
`Or`	One side or other must be true	`(2 < 3 ) Or (6 < 7)`	True
`Xor`	One side or other must be true but *not both*	`(2 < 3) Xor (7 > 4)`	False
`Not`	Negates truth	`Not (3 = 3)`	False

Programmers use `And` and `Or` much more often than the other two logical operators. The `Xor` operator helps you distinguish between mutually exclusive options. If more than one option is true in a mutually exclusive situation, such as a user selecting multiple months for a date of birth, `Xor` lets you know that more than one option was selected (or that none were) due to a false `Xor` result. Finally, the `Not` negates true and false expressions, although using `Not` too much can confuse code because you have to swap the logic when writing and debugging code that uses `Not`. Don't overdo the use of `Not`.

Consider the following expression that combines conditional operators with the `And` logical operators:

```
(curSales < curMinSales) And (intYrsEmp > 10)
```

If the current sales are less than the minimum required and the number of years employed is more than 10 (see how meaningful variable names help document code?), the entire expression is true. Although you could test both of these conditions separately without combining them, the `And` lets you do so in one expression.

Caution

Don't combine too many conditional expressions with logical operators, or your code will become more confusing. Break up extra-complex expressions such as the following:

```
(a > 6) And (b < 1) Or Not(1 = c) Xor (d = 4)
```

6

The order of operators affects the placement and execution of conditional and logical operators. Consider the following expression:

```
curSales * sngCommission > curHighSales / 10
```

Which operation does Visual Basic perform first? Does Visual Basic compare `sngCommission` to `curHighSales` and then multiply the answer by `curSales` and divide that by 10? That order of operation makes no sense because the greater than operator returns a True or False result, and performing math on such a result makes no sense.

Table 6.3 shows a more complete order of operators than the one shown in yesterday's lesson. Table 6.3 shows how the conditional and logical operators work in conjunction with mathematical operators when they all appear in the same expression.

TABLE 6.3. THE COMPLETE ORDER OF OPERATORS TABLE INCLUDES CONDITIONAL AND LOGICAL OPERATORS.

Order	*Operators*
1	Parentheses
2	^
3	*, /, \, Mod
4	+, -
5	Conditional operators including Like
6	Not logical operator
7	And
8	Or
9	Xor

Just to make sure that your programs are as clear as possible, add parentheses around expressions to reduce ambiguity with their order of operation. The preceding expression would then clearly read like this:

```
(curSales * sngCommission) > (curHighSales / 10)
```

The If Statement Uses Conditional Operators

One of the most popular commands in the Visual Basic language is If. The If command is part of an overall multiline statement called the *If statement*, whose format is this:

```
If conditional Then
   Block of one or more Visual Basic statements
End If
```

The *conditional* is any expression that returns a `True` or `False` result. Therefore, the *conditional* might be a Boolean variable, a control that equates to a `True` or `False` value, or a longer expression that includes conditional and possibly one or more logical operators.

Note

Visual Basic still supports the old BASIC-like `If` statement that appeared all on one line. Its format is

```
If conditional Then Visual Basic statement
```

`If` statements almost always trigger more than one statement, so the multiline `If` makes more sense and is more in use today. Even if the `If` is to trigger a single statement and the one-line `If` would work, use a multiline `If` to make adding to the `If` easier in the future.

Do	Don't
DO indent the body of an `If` statement so that you can, at a glance, tell when an `If` statement begins and ends. All multiline `If` statements have a matching set of `End If` statements somewhere later in the program. The `End If` always goes with the most recent `If` no matter how you indent the code.	

People use `If`-like statements every day. Consider the following:

```
If I go to work early, then I will finish early.
If I clean my room and empty the trash, then I can play baseball.
```

In other words, people use exactly the same `If` statement format as Visual Basic does. The `If` statement works this way: If and only if the *Condition* is true does the code body of the `If` execute. Read the two previous real-world `If`-like statements again. If and only if you go to work early will you finish early. If you don't go to work early, well, you won't finish early. The second statement says that both conditions must be true: If you clean your room *and* empty the trash will you play baseball.

Consider the Visual Basic `If` statement in Listing 6.1.

LISTING 6.1. COMPARE DATA USING `If`.

```
1:  If (curSales > curSalesGoal) Then
2:     ' The salesperson beat the goal
3:     curSalaryBonus = 1000.00
4:     lblSalesNote.Caption = "You beat the goal!"
5:     lblSalesNote.BackColor = Red
6:     lblSalesNote.FontBold = True
7:  End If
8:  ' Rest of program code continues here
```

If the value in `curSales` is greater than the value in `curSalesGoal`, the four statements (not counting the remark) in lines 3 through 6 execute. If the value is not greater (even if it's equal), lines 3 through 6 do not execute. Either way, the program continues, starting at line 8 after the `If` does whatever job it's supposed to do. Do you see that the data drives the `If` statement? Do you see that the program is making a decision at *runtime*? That decision is whether to execute certain parts of the code, namely the code inside the body of the `If`.

The parentheses around the condition are not required in an `If` statement, but they do help pinpoint the expression to make the `If` clearer.

Completing the `If` with `Else`

The preceding sections described one form of `If`, but programmers often use the expanded form that takes the following format:

```
If conditional Then
   Block of one or more Visual Basic statements
Else
   Block of one or more Visual Basic statements
End If
```

As with all multiline statements, the indention of the body is suggested for clarity but not required. The first `If` format offered code that executed if the condition was true but did not offer code that executed if the condition was false. The `Else` does just that. The `If...Else` statement provides two bodies of code: one that executes if the condition is true and the other that executes if the condition is false. No matter what the condition is, the rest of the program continues after the `If...Else` test finishes.

Bonus Project 1, "Controls, Properties, and Events," contained an `If...Else` to test a password field. Listing 6.2 contains that `If...Else`.

LISTING 6.2. `If` TESTS A PASSWORD FOR A MATCH.

```
1:  If txtPassword.Text = "Sams" Then
2:     ' Success!   Password matched
3:    Beep
4:    Beep        ' Now, display the picture
5:    imgPassword.Picture = LoadPicture("C:\Program Files\" _
6:      & "Microsoft Visual Studio\Common\Graphics\MetaFile\" _
7:      & "Business\coins.wmf")
8:    lblPrompt.Caption = "Show me the money!"
9: Else
10:   lblPrompt.Caption = "Wrong password - Try Again"
11:   txtPassword.Text = ""     ' Erase old password
12:   txtPassword.SetFocus      ' Put focus on text box
13: End If
```

Line 1 performs a test to see whether the text box control contains the correct password. If so, the body of code right after the `If`, starting in line 2, executes. The `Beep` statement rings the PC's speaker so that, if the password matches, lines 3 and 4 make the PC do a double-beep. The image then gets the picture in the continued lines 5, 6, and 7, and the label's caption changes to reflect the correct password. After the `If` is over, the program executes starting on the line that follows the `End If` statement. If, however, the condition is not true and the password does not match, the body of the `Else` keyword executes, and lines 10, 11, and 12 inform the user that the password did not match.

You can embed one `If` within another as Listing 6.3 shows.

LISTING 6.3. NESTED `If` STATEMENTS ADD POWER TO DATA COMPARISONS.

```
If (curSales > 10000.00) Then
   If (intHrsWorked > 40) Then
      curBonus = 750.00
   Else
      curBonus = 500.00
   End If
   Else lblBonus.Caption = "Good work!"
End If
```

When you embed `If...Else` statements like this, each `Else` and `End If` always goes with the most recent `If`. The further indention of each embedded `If` body helps show where one `If` begins and another one ends.

An Early Exit

Sometimes, depending on the data, you may want to terminate an event or other kind of procedure early. You can combine the `If` and `Exit` statement to do just that.

The `Exit` statement has the following format:

```
Exit Sub ¦ Function ¦ Do ¦ For
```

The vertical bars between the keywords indicate that only one of those keywords can follow `Exit`; the one you use depends on what you want to exit from. To exit from an event procedure, which is a subroutine as you learned in Day 4, "Creating Menus," you use the `Exit Sub` statement. To exit from a function procedure, you use the `Exit Function`. The `Exit Do` and `Exit For` statements will become clear before today's lesson is finished.

Listing 6.4 terminates the event procedure in line 3 if the `If` statement's condition is true.

LISTING 6.4. USE AN `Exit Sub` TO TERMINATE A PROCEDURE EARLY.

```
1:  Private Sub cmdCalc ()
2:     If (txtSales.Text < 5000.00) Then
3:       Exit Sub    ' Terminate procedure
4:     Else
5:       ' If the bonus is at least $5,000...
6:       ' perform the next statement that
7:       ' displays the sales as a percentage
8:       ' of the sales
9:       lblBonus.Caption = txtSales.Text * .05
10:    End If
11: End Sub
```

Nesting `If...Else` Statements

If you embed one `If...Else` statement inside another `If...Else` statement, you have to use the `ElseIf` to start the *nested* `If` statement. Consider the code in Listing 6.5.

LISTING 6.5. THE `ElseIf` HELPS COMBINE TWO OR MORE NESTED `If...Else` STATEMENTS.

```
If (intHours <= 40) Then
   curOverTime = 0.0
' Now test for hours between 40 and 50
' and pay time and a half
ElseIf (intHours <= 50) Then
```

```
6:         curOverTime = (intHours - 40) * 1.5 * sngRate
7:       Else
8:         ' Must pay double time over 50 and
9:         ' time and a half for the hours between
10:        ' 40 and 50
11:        curOverTime = ((intHours - 50) * 2 + (10 * 1.5)) * sngRate
12: End If
```

NEW TERM A *nested* statement is one statement that appears inside another's body.

The `ElseIf` statement in line 5 starts a new `If...Else` block of code. If the hours are not 40 hours or less in line 1, the hours must be more than 40. Therefore, line 5 tests to see if the hours are between 40 and 50 (line 5 would never execute unless the hours were at least 40). Time and a half is computed for those overtime hours. If line 5 is false, then the hours worked must be more than 50. Line 11 contains a complex expression that computes double time for all hours over 50 and time and a half for the 10 hours between 40 and 50.

Do nested `If...ElseIf...End If` statements like these get confusing and difficult to debug? Of course, they do, and this simple example illustrates just how difficult they can be. In the next section, you'll see how the `Select Case` statement offers a better alternative.

Selecting with `Select Case`

The `Select Case` statement is more suited to checking for multiple conditions. Having more than three or four embedded `If...Else` statements results in a complicated program. You get into messy logic such as "If this is true, then if this is true, then if one more thing is true, then do something, else...." Here is the `Select Case` statement's format:

```
Select Case Expression
  Case expressionMatch
     Block of one or more Visual Basic statements
  [ Case expressionMatch1
     Block of one or more Visual Basic statements]
  [ Case expressionMatch2
     Block of one or more Visual Basic statements]
      :
  [ Case expressionMatchN
     Block of one or more Visual Basic statements]
  [Case Else
     Block of one or more Visual Basic statements]
End Select
```

`Select Case` selects from one of several conditions. The number of conditions, indicated by the `[ Case` *`expressionMatch#`* `...]` body, varies depending on the number of conditions that you need to test. If none of the cases perform a match, the `Case Else` code body executes if you supply one.

Despite its foreboding format, `Select Case` is simple to use. Consider the example in Listing 6.6.

LISTING 6.6. `Select Case` **STATEMENTS COMPARE AGAINST MULTIPLE VALUES.**

```
1:  ' Test for a child's letter grade
2:  Select Case txtGrade.Text
3:    Case "A"
4:       lblAnnounce.Caption = "Perfect!"
5:    Case "B"
6:       lblAnnounce.Caption = "Great!"
7:    Case "C"
8:       lblAnnounce.Caption = "Study harder!"
9:    Case "D"
10:      lblAnnounce.Caption = "Get help!"
11:   Case "F"
12:      lblAnnounce.Caption = "Back to basics!"
13:   Case Else
14:      lblAnnounce.Caption = "Error in grade"
15: End Select
```

Note

The data type of the *`Expression`* must be the same as for each case's *`expressionMatch`*. Listing 6.6's code assumes that `txtGrade.Text` holds string letter grades; for that reason, lines 3, 5, 7, 9, and 11 all check to see whether that string value matches a string value.

If the text box named `txtGrade.Text` holds the letter *A*, line 3's `Case` body executes, and then Visual Basic skips all the remaining cases. Once that happens, the code that begins after line 13 executes. If the text box named `txtGrade.Text` holds the letter *B*, line 5's `Case` body executes, and so on. The body of a `Case` can cover several lines, although only single lines of code are shown in this example. Visual Basic knows that after a `Case` *`expressionMatch`* is made, each line in that matching `Case` body executes until the next `Case`, at which point the entire `Select Case` has done its job and the program can continue.

If, for some reason, a grade other than *A*, *B*, *C*, *D*, or *F* appears in the text box, the `Case Else` takes over and warns of the error by setting the label's value.

Visual Basic supports another form of `Select Case` that lets you specify one conditional operator for each *`expressionMatch`* using the `Is` keyword. Listing 6.7 rewrites the preceding `Select Case` to take advantage of conditional `Select Case` choices.

LISTING 6.7. YOU CAN USE CONDITIONAL `Select Case` COMPARISONS.

```
' Test for a child's numeric grade
Select Case txtGrade.Text
  Case Is >= 90
     lblAnnounce.Caption = "Perfect!"
  Case Is >= 80
     lblAnnounce.Caption = "Great!"
  Case Is >= 70
     lblAnnounce.Caption = "Study harder!"
  Case Is >= 60
     lblAnnounce.Caption = "Get help!"
  Case Is < 60
     lblAnnounce.Caption = "Back to basics!"
  Case Else
     lblAnnounce.Caption = "Error in grade"
End Select
```

Given this format and the numeric grades, each case is dependent on the numeric grade being 90 or above for the best message and below 60 for the worst message. Notice that no test has to be made for a numeric grade less than 60 because if the grade is not between 60 and 100, the grade has to be below 60. (This example assumes that the grade will fall between 0 and 100 and not be bad data to illustrate how the `Case Else` can work as one of the `Case` statement bodies.)

> **Caution**
>
> `Select Case` statements don't work for all nested comparisons. No `Select Case` format supports the inclusion of logical operators, so you cannot use `And`, `Or`, `Xor`, or `Not` for the `Select Case`'s test expression. You have to resort to a nested `If...ElseIf...End If` statement for complex nested conditions.

One final format of `Select Case` appears in the Visual Basic language; that `Select Case` allows for a range of choices using the `To` keyword. The range determines which `Case` body executes. Use the range-based `Select Case` when you can order the possibilities sequentially as shown in Listing 6.8.

LISTING 6.8. USE A RANGE FOR `Select Case` WHEN COMPARING FROM GROUPED VALUES.

```
1:  ' Test for a child's numeric grade
2:  Select Case txtGrade.Text
3:    Case 0 To 59
4:       lblAnnounce.Caption = "Back to Basics"
5:    Case 60 To 69
6:       lblAnnounce.Caption = "Get help!"
7:    Case 70 To 79
8:       lblAnnounce.Caption = "Study harder!"
9:    Case 80 To 89
10:      lblAnnounce.Caption = "Great!"
11:   Case Else
12:      lblAnnounce.Caption = "Perfect!"
13: End Select
```

Notice that the order of Listing 6.8's cases is different due to the range format being used. The first `Case` test, in line 3, checks for the lowest possible range. If the numeric grade falls between 0 and 59, the worst message appears in the label. (Integers are assumed, which could produce errors if someone enters `79.5` for a grade; but integers keep things simpler here.) Each succeeding range moves up sequentially. You can also test for string ranges as long as the lowest strings, conditionally according to the ASCII table, are tested earliest.

You can combine the various forms of `Case` expressions into a single `Select Case` statement. Here's a `Case` that uses all the formats to check for a value:

```
Case 101, 102, 201 To 205, Is > 300
```

If the expression in the `Select Case` statement is 101, 102, 201, 202, 203, 204, 205, or more than 300, the body of this `Case` executes.

Repeat Code with Loops

Visual Basic supports *loops* through a series of statements called *looping statements*. Your PC is fast. Therefore, your PC can process large amounts of information quickly, such as calculating customer payroll records. The secret to processing large amounts of data or testing a large number of values is to put such code inside looping statements and let your program process the data over and over until the data runs out.

A *loop* is a series of one of more statements that execute more than one time. The loop statement repeats until a certain predetermined condition is met.

Loops pave the way for tomorrow's lesson, which teaches you how to get input from the user without using text box controls. Some input just doesn't lend itself well to text box controls. Often, you need to ask your user questions and grab the answers when the user presses Enter. A text box is a little cumbersome for simple answers to which your program responds. (Text boxes are great for input of form information, such as name and address values and payroll amounts.)

You need to understand loops before learning about getting user input because the user does not always enter the expected answer. Suppose you ask a user how old he or she is, and you get the answer 291. The user obviously made a mistake. With a looping mechanism, you can keep asking the user that question until a reasonable answer is given. Of course, your program won't know whether the user entered his or her true age, but you can keep asking until the user enters an age that is more plausible than 291. As you can see, loops can repeat any block of code.

The `Do` Loop

Visual Basic includes a multiline statement called the `Do` loop. As with the `If` statement, `Do` loop statements come in several formats, as shown here:

```
Do While condition
   Block of one or more Visual Basic statements
Loop
```

```
Do
  Block of one or more Visual Basic statements
Loop While condition
```

```
Do Until condition
   Block of one or more Visual Basic statements
Loop
```

```
Do
  Block of one or more Visual Basic statements
Loop Until condition
```

The *`condition`* in each `Do` loop is any expression, control, or Boolean value that equates to true or false. Your choice of formats primarily depends on your preference and style. The differences between them lie in the following areas:

6

- The location of the conditional test; if the conditional test appears at the top of the loop in the `Do` statement, the loop's body may never execute. If the conditional test appears at the bottom of the loop in the `Loop` statement, the body always executes at least once because Visual Basic does not perform the test until the bottom of the loop.

- The nature of the conditional test; the `Do` loops can continue either while a condition is true or until a condition is true. In the former case, the body of the loop keeps executing as long as the condition is true and in the latter case, the loop keeps executing until the condition is met.

Figure 6.2 shows one `Do` loop and illustrates how the loop repeats. This code simply increases the value shown in a label's `Caption` property from 1 to 10 and then the loop stops repeating. In reality, the code would execute on today's PCs so quickly that the label would be a blur and you couldn't see the numbers step up from 1 to 10, but remember that the loop is important for study.

FIGURE 6.2.

A loop repeats a body of statements.

```
' Section of code to
' demonstrate Do loops
Dim inCtr As Integer
intCtr = 1      'initialize counter
Do
    lblOut.Caption = intCtr
    intCtr = intCtr + 1
Loop Until (intCtr = 10)
```

These statements repeat until the condition being tested becomes equal to True

Figure 6.2's code demonstrates a special assignment in which the same variable name appears on each side of the equal sign. When you see such an assignment, the statement is updating the value of the variable. In this case, the statement `intCtr = intCtr + 1` adds one to the variable `intCtr` each pass through the loop.

The body of Figure 6.2's code executes 10 times, and each time the code adds one to the variable named `intCtr`. This `Do` loop uses the `Do...Loop Until` format so that the loop keeps repeating until `intCtr` is equal to 10. Listing 6.9 shows an identical loop that uses the `Do While...Loop` format.

LISTING 6.9. USE ANY DO LOOP FORM THAT YOU PREFER.

```
Do While intCtr <= 10
   ' This loop does the same thing as
   ' the one in Figure 6.2
   lblOut.Caption = intCtr
   intCtr = intCtr + 1
Loop
```

Caution

> You must somehow change the loop-testing condition inside the loop's body; otherwise, the loop never ends. If you accidentally write an endless loop, your application freezes until you click Visual Basic's toolbar's End button or close the application's window. Something inside a loop's body must allow for the condition being tested to change, or the loop keeps executing.

Some loops, especially loops that perform user input, require that the body of the loop execute at least once, so that fact dictates the kind of loop you use. When you want a loop to execute at least once, you need to use a loop that tests the condition at the bottom of the loop, such as the loop shown in Listing 6.10.

Caution

> The following code examples are not complete. They use remarks in place of statements that accept user input and display error messages. Concentrate on learning how loops work now, and tomorrow's lesson will explain how to code the user's input and output.

LISTING 6.10. YOUR USER MAY REQUIRE SEVERAL TRIES BEFORE ENTERING VALID DATA.

```
1:  Dim strAns As String
2:  '
3:  ' Ask the user a yes or no question
4:  lblPrompt.Caption = "Do you want to continue (yes or no)?"
5:  '
6:  ' Get input into the string variable
7:  '  named strAns
8:  ' Check the answer and keep asking
9:  ' if the user fails to enter yes or no
10: Do While (strAns <> "Yes" And strAns <> "No")
11:   Beep    ' Warning
12:   lblError.Caption = "You need to answer yes or no")
13:    ' Get input into the string variable
14:    ' named strAns once again
15: Loop
16: ' Erase the error message
17: lblError.Caption = Null
```


Line 10 begins the `Do` loop. If the user typed `Yes` or `No` in lines 6 and 7 (remember, remarks are used here for the input), the loop warns the user with an error label in line

12. The remarked lines 13 and 14 simulate getting the user's input all over again, and line 15 sends the loop right back up to line 10 to test that input again. How many times does this loop execute? Either never (if the user types `Yes` or `No`) or as long as the user fails to type one of the two required answers.

Of course, the user's Caps Lock key may be on or off, and the user could type YES or yes or NO or no. In that case, line 10 would fail because the two strings would not match in case. You'll learn how to test strings that differ only in case in Day 8's lesson.

If you ever need to exit a loop before its normal termination, you can use the `Exit Do` statement to do so. For example, you may be processing a series of customer payments inside a loop that loops until the final customer account number is reached. If, however, a bad customer number appears, tested with an `If` statement inside the loop, you can display an error message and exit the loop with `Exit Do`.

For Loops

Visual Basic supports another kind of loop called the `For` loop. `For` loops execute a series of one or more statements a fixed number of times or until a condition is reached. The `For` loop is a multiline statement (just as the `Do` loops are) because of the `For` loop's body. Here is the format of the `For` statement:

```
For intCounter = intStart To intEnd [Step intIncrement]
  Block of one or more Visual Basic statements
Next [intCounter]
```

`intCounter` must be a numeric variable that controls the body of the loop. Visual Basic initializes the *`intCounter`* variable to the initial value in *`intStart`* before the first *iteration* of the loop. The *`intStart`* value is typically 1 but can be any numeric value (or variable or control value) that you specify. Every time the body of the loop repeats, the *`intCounter`* variable changes (increments or decrements) by the value of *`intIncrement`*. If you don't specify a `Step` value (notice that the `Step` clause is optional because it appears within brackets in the statement's format), the `For` statement assumes an *`intIncrement`* of 1.

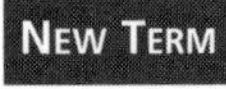

An *iteration* is one loop cycle. If a loop repeats three times, three iterations of that loop occurred.

IntEnd is a number (or variable or control value) that controls when the loop ends. When *intCounter* is greater than *intEnd*, Visual Basic does not repeat the loop but continues at the statement that follows `Next`. `Next` is Visual Basic's way of ending the loop. If *intCounter* is less than *intEnd*, Visual Basic increments *intCounter* by the value of *intIncrement*, and the body of the loop repeats again. (Notice that you don't have to repeat *intCounter* after `Next` as it's optional and serves only as a reminder to which `For` loop the `Next` statement is terminating.)

Despite this long introduction to `For`, the `For` loop in most forms is simple and does nothing more than automatically count up or down for you as the loop repeats. A `For` loop counts up if the `Step` value is positive, and a `For` loop counts down if the `Step` value is negative.

Listing 6.11's `For` loop repeats one shown earlier in Listing 6.9 as a `Do` loop. The `For` increments the label's counter variable automatically.

LISTING 6.11. USE A `For` LOOP IF YOU WANT VISUAL BASIC TO INCREMENT A COUNTING VARIABLE.

```
1:  For intCtr = 1 to 10
2:    lblOut.Caption = intCtr
3:  Next
```

Isn't that simple? This loop repeats 10 times. The first time that line 1 executes, `intCtr`, is assigned 1 (the *intStart* value). The body of the loop, line 2, executes using that value. Line 3 sends the loop to repeat again by incrementing `intCtr` by 1 (the implied `Step` value if you don't specify one) as long as `intCtr` is not more than 10 (the *intEnd* value).

The following statement is identical to line 3 in Listing 6.11 because the `Next` statement's variable is optional:

```
Next intCtr
```


Modifying the `Step` Value

Listing 6.12's `For` loop begins at 10 and increments by five until the loop variable reaches 100.

LISTING 6.12. CHANGE THE INCREMENT TO MAKE THE LOOP BEHAVE DIFFERENTLY.

```
For intCtr = 10 to 100 Step 5
  lblOut.Caption = intCtr
Next
```

Listing 6.13's `For` loop begins at 1000 and *decrements* by 100 until the loop variable reaches zero.

LISTING 6.13. A NEGATIVE `Step` VALUE COUNTS DOWN.

```
For intCtr = 1000 to 0 Step -100
  lblOut.Caption = intCtr
Next
```

You can see from these short examples how the *`intStart`*, *`intEnd`*, and *`intIncrement`* values affect the loop. (If you use a negative `Step` value, the *`intStart`* value must be more than the `intEnd` value; otherwise, the loop's body never executes.)

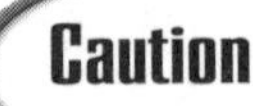

Don't confuse loops with the `If` statement. Both loops and the `If` statements rely on conditional values, but loops can repeat their bodies as many times as necessary. The `If` statement's body, however, executes at most one time.

Use the `Exit For` statement if you want to terminate a loop before its normal termination.

Nesting `For` Loops

As with all other Visual Basic statements, you can nest two or more `For` loops inside one another. Anytime your program needs to repeat a loop more than once, use a nested loop. Figure 6.3 shows an outline of a nested `For` loop. Think of the inside loop as looping "faster" than the outside loop. The inside loop iterates faster because the variable `In` goes from 1 to 10 in the inside loop before the outside loop's first iteration has completed. Because the outside loop does not repeat until the `Next Out` statement, the inside `For` loop has a chance to finish in its entirety. When the outside loop finally does iterate a second time, the inside loop starts all over again.

FIGURE 6.3.

The outside loop determines how many times the inside loop executes.

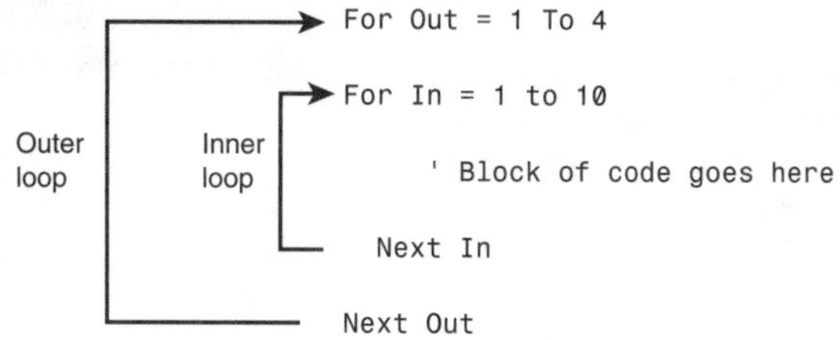


```
' Program continues when outer loop end
```

Figure 6.3's inner loop executes a total of 40 times. The outside loop iterates four times, and the inside loop executes 10 times for each of the outer loop's iterations.

Figure 6.4 shows two loops nested within an outer loop. Both loops execute completely before the outside loop finishes its first iteration. When the outside loop starts its second iteration, the two inside loops repeat all over again.

FIGURE 6.4.

Two or more loops can nest within another loop.

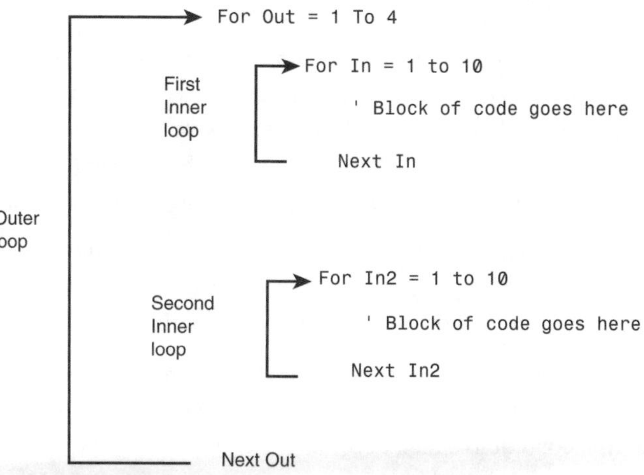


```
' Program continues when outer loop ends
```

The blocks of code inside Figure 6.4's innermost loops execute a total of 40 times each. The outside loop iterates four times, and each inner loop executes, first the top and then the bottom, in their entirety each time the outer loop iterates once again.

Do	Don't
DO match `Next` with `For` statements when you nest loops. Each `Next` must go with the most recent `For` before it in the code. Visual Basic issues an error if you write a program whose inside loop's `Next` statement appears after the outside loop's `Next` statement. If you omit the `Next` variable, Visual Basic aligns each `Next` with the most recent `For` for you, but adding the `Next` statement's variable often helps to document the loops and more clearly show where a loop begins and ends.	

Summary

Today's lesson taught you how to control your programs. By adding conditional operators to your Visual Basic language repertoire, you can now make Visual Basic analyze data and respond according to the values inside variables and controls. Using the `If` statement, you can now write a program in which Visual Basic tests a variable or control's value and decides on an appropriate course of action based on the data.

In addition to the `If` statement, Visual Basic supports the `Select Case` statement, which makes nested `If` situations much simpler to understand. `Select Case` comes in three formats, depending on how you want to compare the various conditions.

If you want sections of your code to repeat more than once, you can use one of the looping statements taught in today's lesson. The `Do` loops loop as long as a condition is met or until a condition is met, depending on the format that you use. The `For` loop continues for a certain number of iterations or until a condition is met. Unlike `Do`, the `For` loop automatically changes its controlling variables by adding or subtracting to or from the controlling variable each time the loop iterates.

Tomorrow's lesson shows you how to ask the user for input using input boxes. You will also learn how to display answers for the user with message boxes. Input and message boxes offer simple ways to interact with your user when a form's control for such input is unnecessary.

Q&A

Q Why should I avoid the `Not` operator?

A Do not use `Not` because not using `Not` makes things not as complicated as using `Not`. Get the picture? Positive statements are clearer to understand.

Consider the following expression: `Not(A <= B)`. Wouldn't such an expression be clearer if you wrote it this way: `(A > B)`? You don't have to avoid `Not` altogether because using `Not` for Boolean data types often is clear, such as the statement that begins `If Not(blnClearedScreen)`. This `If` statement says this: If the screen is not yet cleared, then do what follows the `If`. Generally, however, you can almost always reverse expressions that use `Not` to simplify them and make them easier to maintain.

Q If I can write equivalent `Do` and `For` statements, does it matter which I select when I'm programming?

A Which loop you use is up to you. The choice is not just between the `For` and `Do` loops, but between several formats of each loop. Generally, `For` loops are useful when you must count values or iterate the loop's body for a specified number of times. The `Do` loop is useful for iterating until or while a certain condition is met. If you are counting up or down, the `For` loop is easier to write and is slightly more efficient than an equivalent `Do` loop.

Workshop

The Workshop provides quiz questions to help you solidify your understanding of the material covered and exercises to provide you with experience in using what you've learned. Try to understand the quiz and exercise answers before continuing to the next day's lesson. Answers are provided in Appendix A, "Answers to Exercises."

Quiz

1. What logical operator returns a `True` result if either expression is `True`?
2. What is the difference between a conditional operator and a logical operator?
3. What is a loop?
4. Describe the following assignment statement's action:

```
intTotal = intTotal - 10
```

5. How many times does the following code execute the `Beep` statement?

```
intN = 0
Do While (intN > 0)
```

```
    intN = intN + 3
    Beep
Loop
```

6. Why should `Exit For` be part of an `If` statement instead of appearing by itself in the body of a `For` loop?
7. True/False. Both blocks of an `If...Else` might execute.
8. True/False. A `For` loop may never execute, depending on the start and ending values.
9. Why would you nest a `For` loop?
10. What is the difference between a decision statement and a looping statement?

Exercises

1. Write an `If` statement that compares three numbers for equality.
2. **Bug Buster:** Larry is not able to loop. What, if anything, is wrong with Larry's code that follows?

```
intN = 10
Do
  Beep
Loop Until (intN > 100)
```

3. True/False. The clock in a football game counts down 15 minutes to zero. It does this four times. Think through the four iterations, and describe the kind of Visual Basic equivalent statements such an event imitates.
4. Visual Basic lets you combine each `Select Case` format in a single `Select Case` statement. Therefore, you can use a regular matching `Case` combined with a conditional `Case` combined with a range `Case`. Rewrite the nested payroll example shown earlier in today's lesson as a `Select Case` that utilizes at least two kinds of `Case` bodies for the three payroll possibilities.

WEEK 1

DAY 7

Advanced Keyboard and Screen Support

Today's lesson shows you how to get the user's input and send information to the screen as output. You've already seen ways to get the user's input using text boxes, and you've already displayed information on the screen with labels. Nevertheless, controls like these don't always lend themselves well to asking the user questions and getting answers, interactively, as the program runs. Text boxes are great for forms and placeholders that hold the user's text, but sometimes a more immediate response is needed from the user. Today's lesson shows you how to get such a response with very little programming required.

Today, you learn the following:

- Internal functions
- The `MsgBox()` function
- How to handle optional function parameters
- The `InputBox()` function
- Keyboard event-handling
- About check boxes

- About option buttons
- How to combine option button groups in Frame controls

Introduction to Internal Functions

Functions are a kind of procedure, not unlike the subroutine procedures you learned about in Day 3, "Managing Controls." The difference between them is that functions, after they finish their job by executing the code in them, send a value to another part of the program. You'll learn how to write functions and how they work in detail in tomorrow's lesson.

For now, you must understand what an *internal function* is because you'll use internal functions to perform I/O throughout the rest of today's lesson. An internal function operates like a magic box that takes values you send to it and sends back, or returns, a single value to your program. Figure 7.1 shows what a function does.

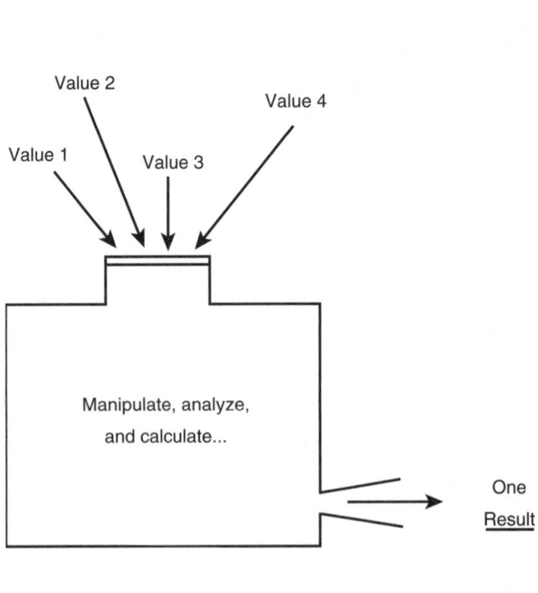

FIGURE 7.1. *Functions accept zero, one, or more values and sends back a single value.*

NEW TERM An *internal function*, sometimes called an *intrinsic function*, is a function supplied with the Visual Basic language that does a job such as a calculation or *I/O*. You must know the name of an internal function and its requirements before you can use one. Although you won't see the code in an internal function (internal functions are as much a part of the Visual Basic language as the `For` command is), you will be able to use the internal functions in your programs.

NEW TERM *I/O* stands for *input/output*. Programmers use the term *I/O* generically to refer to any form of getting input from a device (such as the keyboard) and sending output to a device (such as the screen).

You'll use functions for many things and the more you learn about them in this and especially tomorrow's lesson, the better you'll understand them. For now, keep in mind the following:

- You typically pass one or more values to a function; rarely will a function require nothing to be passed to it. These values that you pass are called *arguments*.

NEW TERM An *argument* is a value you pass to a function.

- The function name always has parentheses following it (with the rare exception of those functions that require no arguments).
- You place the function's arguments, separated by commas if you pass multiple arguments, inside the function's parentheses.

You've used an internal function already (the rest of today's lesson simply refers to *functions* rather than *internal functions*) in Day 2's lesson when you loaded an image into the Image control that you placed on the form. Here is the line of code you used, with the argument shortened somewhat to make things easier to describe:

```
imgHappy.Picture = LoadPicture("\Happy.bmp")
```

The function's name is `LoadPicture()`. (As is often done, this book keeps the empty parentheses after the function name when discussing the function so that you can distinguish between functions, variables, and control names.) This function has only one argument, a string.

> **Note**
>
> Many functions require one or more arguments but make some of the arguments optional. `LoadPicture()` requires an initial single string argument but the remaining arguments are optional.

> **Caution**
>
> You must match the argument data type and order that the function requires. For example, if a function requires two arguments, an integer followed by a string, enter those arguments in that order.

7

What does this code send `LoadPicture()`? A string with a filename. What does `LoadPicture()` return? The graphic image located at that file. This assignment that you entered in Day 2's lesson then assigns that picture to the image control's `Picture` property. Without the `LoadPicture()` function, the Image control could not display the image. An Image control requires a graphic image for the `Picture` property, not a pathname (unless you're specifying an initial picture at designtime in which you can select a path from the Properties window and Visual Basic will assign the graphic to that control).

Visual Basic has to do a lot of work for you when you use the `LoadPicture()` function. Visual Basic must analyze your argument list to make sure you've complied with the required arguments in number and data types; then Visual Basic must make sure the path you supply for the image is correct; then Visual Basic must see if you have network access rights to the file (if you are networked); and finally, Visual Basic must load the image from the file into the graphic image. Thankfully, Visual Basic supplies `LoadPicture()` so you don't have to do all this yourself through tedious code! That's the beauty of functions: they save you work. Functions let you concentrate on the important stuff (your application's specifics) and take care of routine details for you.

Note

Functions exist to work with graphics, calculate common mathematical formulas, and manipulate disk files. The functions you learn about in today's lesson are some of the easiest to work with and perhaps the best introduction to using functions. You'll study many more functions that Visual Basic provides in tomorrow's lesson.

Let the User Respond with `MsgBox()`

Now that you better understand how functions work, you can examine the `MsgBox()` function closely. `MsgBox()` is a function that produces a pop-up message box. Figure 7.2 shows a message box. As you can see, a message box displays an icon and a message along with at least one command button. The command button gives the user a chance to read the message in the message box and click the command button when done.

NEW TERM A *message box* is a small dialog box used for output during a program's execution. The user can close the message box by clicking a command button and can move the message box but the user cannot resize the message box.

The arguments that you supply to the `MsgBox()` function determine which icon the `MsgBox()` function displays, the message, and the number of command buttons. Therefore, the programmer controls exactly how the message box appears to the user. When the `MsgBox()` completes, its return value specifies which command button the user clicked. Therefore, your program will always test the `MsgBox()` function's return value if the `MsgBox()` function displayed two command buttons. The program can then use an `If` statement to determine the best course of action based on the user's command button selection.

FIGURE 7.2.

The `MsgBox()` function displays a message and lets the user respond when finished reading the message.

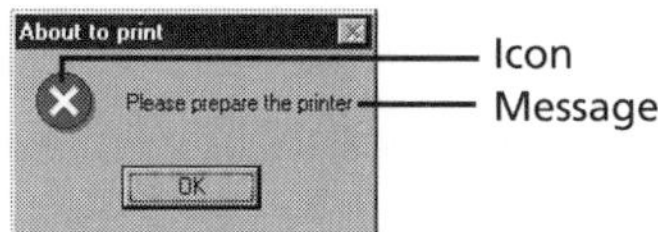

Previous versions of Visual Basic included a `MsgBox` statement. Unlike the `MsgBox()`, the `MsgBox` statement could not interpret the user's button click. The `MsgBox` statement is considered obsolete although Visual Basic 6 still supports it for backwards compatibility.

The following is the format of the `MsgBox()` function:

```
intResponse = MsgBox(strPrompt[, intStyle][, strTitle])
```

This format shows two optional arguments, *`intStyle`* and *`strTitle`*. Although the format uses italicized placeholders to show where you place literal, variable, or control arguments, the format uses variable name prefixes so you know the argument's required data types. As you can see, a `MsgBox()` function always requires a string argument, and the second and third arguments are both optional depending on how you want the message box to appear.

`intResponse` holds the function's integer return data type. The first argument is a string (or variable or control that holds a string) that displays as the message box's message. The second argument determines the style of the buttons that appear. The last argument determines the title that appears in the message box's title bar.

All message boxes display a command button. Your executing program must know when your user is finished reading the message box. The program's execution temporarily halts until the user clicks one of the message box's command buttons. As soon as the user clicks the command button, the program continues executing at the statement that follows the command button.

If you display a message string that's too long to fit on one line of a message box, Visual Basic breaks the line into two or more lines. Visual Basic breaks properly between words.

Suppose you need to wait for the user before printing a report. You could issue the following very simple message box:

```
intResponse = MsgBox("Click when you are ready for the report")
```

You would have had to declare the variable named `intResponse` somewhere in the `Declarations` section of the procedure (or possibly in the module's `Declarations` section although you already know not to declare too manyglobal variables). If you don't specify otherwise, in the second function argument that was omitted here, Visual Basic displays one command button with the word `OK` that the user can click when she or he is done viewing the message box. Given that this statement contains a `MsgBox()` function that displays only one command button, the integer assignment does not help you much—although you must do something with the function's return value so you might as well assign it to something. Figure 7.3 shows this simple message box.

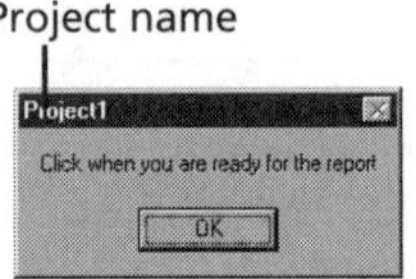

FIGURE 7.3.
All `MsgBox()` functions display a message with at least one command button.

Notice something else that Visual Basic does if you don't specify all the `MsgBox()` arguments: Visual Basic uses the project's title for the message box's title bar. Therefore, you almost always want to assign a better name to the title bar, which you can do after you learn about the first optional argument.

If you want more control of the buttons, you can use an integer value (or a variable or control) for the first optional argument to specify the style of the buttons. With only one button, the return value, although required in all cases, makes little difference. With more than one command button, the return value holds a value that corresponds to the command button clicked. You can use this information in an `If` statement or a `Select Case` to execute one of two sets of code that handles either button.

Table 7.1 lists the integer button style values you can use for the `MsgBox()` function's first optional argument.

TABLE 7.1. USE INTEGER VALUES TO DETERMINE THE BUTTONS INSIDE MESSAGE BOXES.

Value	*Named Constant*	*Description*
0	`vbOKOnly`	OK button
1	`vbOKCancel`	OK and Cancel buttons
2	`vbAbortRetryIgnore`	Abort, Retry, and Cancel buttons
3	`vbYesNoCancel`	Yes, No, and Cancel buttons
4	`vbYesNo`	Yes and No buttons
5	`vbRetryCancel`	Retry and Cancel buttons

Figure 7.4 shows the message box that appears in response to the following statement:

```
intResponse = MsgBox("Ready to print?", 1)
```

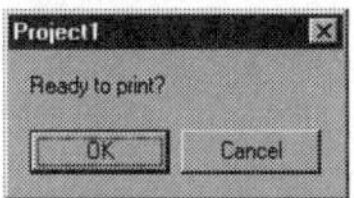

FIGURE 7.4.
The user's button selection determines what happens next.

The `1` specifies that two command buttons, the OK and Cancel buttons, appear on the message box. This combination is useful for processes that your program is about to do, such as getting ready to print, because the user can either click OK to indicate the print is ready or click Cancel to stop the printing process and return to an earlier part of the program.

Table 7.2 lists the return values that are possible from the `MsgBox()` function. Therefore, the following might be the `If` statement that handles the previous message box (with the details remarked out to simplify the `If`):

```
If (intResponse = 1) Then
    ' Code goes here that handles
    ' the OK button click
Else
    ' Code goes here that handles
    ' the Cancel click
End If
```

Of course, if the message box displayed other message buttons, the `If` statement would have to check for additional values, or possibly you would write a `Select Case` statement to handle multiple return values.

7

TABLE 7.2. TEST THESE RETURN VALUES TO DETERMINE WHICH COMMAND BUTTON THE USER CLICKED.

Value	*Named Constant*	*Description*
1	`vbOK`	The user clicked OK
2	`vbCancel`	The user clicked Cancel
3	`vbAbort`	The user clicked Abort
4	`vbRetry`	The user clicked Retry
5	`vbIgnore`	The user clicked Ignore
6	`vbYes`	The user clicked Yes
7	`vbNo`	The user clicked No

If the user presses Esc at the message box, Visual Basic responds as if the user clicked the Cancel button and returns the appropriate value.

No matter how many command buttons you display in a message box, the user can click only one button. As soon as the user clicks any of the message box's buttons, the message box disappears and the return value is filled with the clicked button's value.

Using Named Constants

Look back at Tables 7.1 and 7.2 and you'll notice the column labeled *Named Constants*. Visual Basic supports hundreds of named constants that you can use in any procedure in place of using literals in their place.

NEW TERM A *named constant* is a name that Visual Basic applies to an internal list of values. Visual Basic's named constants usually begin with the `Visual Basic` prefix. You cannot change the value of the named constants (that's why they are *constant*) as you can change the value of variables that you declare, but you can use the named constants in function argument lists and anywhere else that a literal can go.

Named constants make your programs more readable and understandable. For example, each of the following statements are identical but, in the second statement, the command button that appears is obvious:

```
intResponse = MsgBox("Ready to print?", 1)
intResponse = MsgBox("Ready to print?", vbOK)
```

When you write a program, you can use the named constants without referring to a reference manual or the online help and without memorizing all the named constants. Visual

Basic's editor pops up a list of named constants from which you can select as you type a function that can use them, such as `MsgBox()`. Later, when you maintain the program and make changes, you'll have no trouble understanding how the message box will look. If, instead of named constants, you used literal values, you would have to look up the value before you would know how to change the message box to something else.

Do	Don't
DO use named constants everywhere you can. They require no extra typing because you can select them from the Visual Basic editor's pop-up list as you enter function arguments.	

Triggering Default Buttons

The first command button on a message box is always the default command button. Visual Basic selects the first (the leftmost) command button and, if the user presses Enter without clicking a command button, the selected command button is triggered.

You can change the button that appears as the default button when the message box first appears by adding one of the values in Table 7.3 to the command button argument.

TABLE 7.3. ADD ONE OF THESE VALUES TO THE COMMAND BUTTON ARGUMENT TO SPECIFY THE INITIAL DEFAULT BUTTON.

Value	*Named Constant*	*Description*
0	vbDefaultButton1	First button is default
256	vbDefaultButton2	Second button is default
512	vbDefaultButton3	Third button is default

Despite their length, the named constants are easier to maintain than the integer literals so use the named constants as done in the next statement:

```
intResponse = MsgBox("Is the printer on?", vbYesNoCancel +
vbDefaultButton1)
```

If you are displaying a message box that controls a critical process, such as the deletion of a data file, make the Cancel button the default. If the user accidentally presses Enter, the Cancel button is triggered and the most critical process is not accidentally performed, as would be the case if you left the OK button selected.

Specifying the Icon

Adding an additional value to the second argument specifies the icon used to the left of the message inside the message box. Until now, the message box code has not specified this part of the argument in this lesson so the resulting message boxes have had no icons.

The MsgBox() function actually supports a few additional and optional arguments but they do not apply to this discussion and are rarely used for simple programs.

Table 7.4 contains the named constant values and the icons they produce.

TABLE 7.4. THESE VALUES PRODUCE AN ICON IN YOUR MESSAGE BOX.

Value	*Named Constant*	*Description*	*Icon*
16	vbCritical	Critical Message icon	
32	vbQuestion	Question mark icon	
48	vbExclamation	Warning Message	
64	vbInformation	Information Message	

The following statement produces a complete message box, building on what you've seen, that displays all the elements because all of the arguments are specified. Figure 7.5 shows the resulting message box.

```
intResponse = MsgBox("Is the printer on?", vbYesNoCancel + vbQuestion +
vbDefaultButton2, "Question Box")
```

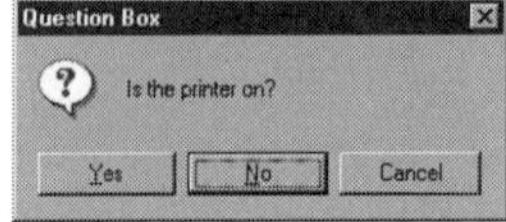

FIGURE 7.5.
The user's button selection determines what happens next.

Getting Input with InputBox()

The MsgBox() function exists to display messages to your users but gives users a way to respond with the command buttons that appear in the message boxes. The command button they click guides the next course of action. Of course, if the message is for information only, you might display the message box with the single command button so the user can close the message box when finished reading the message and the program can continue.

If you need to ask the user a question, and need a quick answer that a text box control would make too cumbersome, you can use another function that is the MsgBox() function's cousin: InputBox(). The InputBox() function displays a message box but also allows the user to enter a value that your program can respond to. This combination message box and input field is called an *input box*. Figure 7.6 shows what an input box looks like.

NEW TERM An *input box* is a message box with a field in which the user can type a value, such as a word or phrase that might answer a question you ask in the input box's title. As with a message box, the user can move or close an input box but not resize it. Unlike message boxes, you cannot control which command buttons appear in input boxes. The OK and Cancel command buttons are the only buttons that input boxes display.

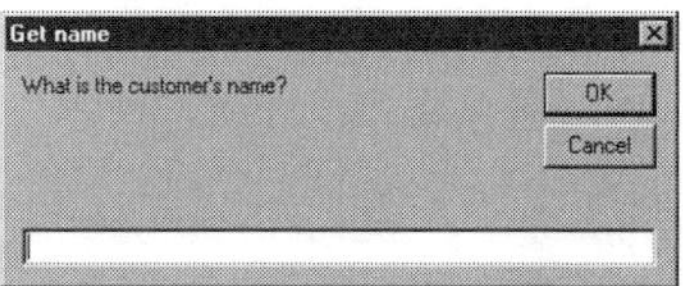

FIGURE 7.6.
The input box provides a title and a field for data entry.

Input boxes don't offer a way to supply an icon as does the MsgBox() function. Here is the format for the InputBox() function:

```
strAnswer = InputBox(strPrompt[, strTitle][, strDefault][, intXpos]
[, intYpos])
```

The InputBox() function returns a Variant data typed value that you can always interpret as a string; so you can assign the InputBox() function to a string or use it anywhere you can use a string value. (The Variant return data type allows you to assign the return value to a control property if you want to do so.) The returned string is the user's typed response at the input box. Only the first argument is required. Here are all the arguments described:

- ***strPrompt***—The message, such as the question you ask, that appears in the input box. *StrPrompt* can be as long as 1,024 characters. Always phrase the prompt as a question so the user will know how to respond to the input box.
- ***strTitle***—The text that appears in the input box window's title bar. In the absence of a title, Visual Basic uses the project name.
- ***strDefault***—A default value that appears in the input box's input field. Your user can accept your default answer, which is returned when the user closes the message box, change the answer, or type a completely new answer. Use default answers for predictable answers to which the user generally only has to press OK to accept.
- ***intXpos***, ***intYpos***—The twip coordinate where you want the input box to appear in the form window. You might want to position the input box out of the way of another form or dialog box you've displayed if the input box is asking a question about the other window. If you don't specify twip coordinates, Visual Basic places the input box in the center of the screen.

Note

A *twip* is 1/1440 of an inch and 1/567 of a centimeter.

The following statement generated the previous input box:

```
strAnswer = InputBox("What is the customer's name?", "Get name")
```

If you want to supply a default value and position the input box at an exact screen location, you do so like this:

```
strAnswer = InputBox("What is the customer's name?", "Get name", "Jane
Doe", 500, 750)
```

You must have a way to know if the user clicked the OK button (or pressed Enter to select OK because OK is the default button) or clicked Cancel. The `InputBox()` function returns a zero-length string, equal to `""` if the user clicks Cancel instead of entering a value or selecting OK to accept the default value. Therefore, your testing code might follow something like this format:

```
If (strAnswer <>"") Then
   ' Code that handles the user's input
Else
   ' Code that handles the user's Cancel click
End If
```

Remember that Visual Basic supports a special value named `Empty` that you can use in place of `""`. The `Empty` keyword makes your code clearer. You can rewrite the previous `If` like this:

```
If (strAnswer <> Empty) Then
```

Suppose a user indicates that he wants to compute totals for a specific department's data. You could, with an input box, ask the user for the department name. If the user enters the name, you would then calculate the needed totals. If, however, the user selects Cancel, the program would assume that the user changed his mind.

Handling the Keyboard

Your programs cannot handle all keyboard activity with controls and input boxes. Sometimes, you need to respond to specific keystrokes as the user types them. Windows passes special keyboard events to your applications so they can monitor the keyboard's input. These events are the `KeyPress`, `KeyDown`, and the `KeyUp` events. These events respond to combination keystrokes such as Alt+G and Shift+P, as well as individual keys. You can test for these combination keystrokes when a keyboard event occurs.

After your application receives keyboard input, the application can then modify the input or ignore the pressed key if it isn't an expected keystroke. Keystroke testing is useful for triggering a splash screen's closing, validating input, and even playing some types of games.

Keyboard-Triggered Events

The `KeyPress` event occurs when users press any key that corresponds with one of these characters:

- Uppercase and lowercase letters
- Numeric digits
- Punctuation
- Enter, Tab, and Backspace

The `KeyPress` event tests for most ASCII characters. `KeyPress` doesn't test for *all* ASCII characters (such as the horizontal tab, arrow keys, and other special control-related ASCII characters that appear between ASCII values 0 and 31), but `KeyPress` certainly does test for most ASCII characters. Use `KeyPress` to determine exactly which key users pressed. For example, `KeyPress` returns a letter A if users press that key.

The KeyPress event occurs on the downstroke. If the user holds down the key, the event occurs when the keyboard auto-repeats characters.

An event, as you know, is always associated with an object, such as a command button or the form. The KeyPress event always associates with whatever object now has the focus when users press the key. If no object has the focus, the KeyPress event associates with the form. (An exception can occur, depending on the KeyPreview property explained in the section "Prioritizing Responses" later in today's lesson.)

Caution

Don't use a keystroke event to test for a menu shortcut key. The Menu Editor supports shortcut keys for you and sets up the response automatically by triggering the menu item's Click() event procedure. If you test for keystroke events, your program cannot respond to menu selections.

The KeyPress event procedure always contains an integer argument. Therefore, if you were to write a KeyPress event for a TextBox control, the event procedure might begin and end like this:

```
Private Sub Text1_KeyPress (KeyAscii As Integer)
  '
  ' Code goes here to test and respond to keystroke
  '
End Sub
```

The KeyAscii argument is an integer that represents the ASCII code of the character the user pressed. You can use If or a Select Case statement to see whether the character is an expected keystroke.

One of the most important tasks you can perform with KeyPress is to change users' keystrokes. The KeyPress event occurs as soon as users press the key and before a control gets the keystroke. Normally, for example, a TextBox control immediately displays whatever key users pressed when the TextBox control has the focus. If, however, you write a KeyPress event procedure for a TextBox control, the KeyPress event procedure can change the key, as is done in the following code:

```
Private Sub txtTryIt_KeyPress(KeyAscii As Integer)
  ' Change any uppercase A to an uppercase B
  If KeyAscii = 65 Then    ' 65 is ASCII for A
    KeyAscii = 66          ' 66 is ASCII for B
  End If
End Sub
```

If the text box named `txtTryIt` has the focus, the text box accepts and displays any keystroke the user presses until the user presses an uppercase A with an ASCII code value of 65. The `If` statement changes the keystroke's `KeyAscii` value to a letter `B` (ASCII 66), and the TextBox control shows the `B` and not the `A` because the `KeyPress` event gets the keystroke before the text box gets the `KeyAscii` value.

Tip

> Search VB's online help for *Key Code Constants*. The online help displays named literals that you can use in keyboard testing. For example, you can test for a Backspace press by checking `KeyAscii` for `vbKeyBack`, test for an Enter press by checking for `vbKeyReturn`, and test for Tab press by checking for `vbKeyTab`. (Remember that `KeyPress` tests for only these three keys, in addition to letters, numbers, and punctuation.) Although the text box respects the other keystroke controls (such as Home and End), `KeyPress` reliably responds only to Enter, Tab, and Backspace.

Whereas `KeyPress` tests for a wide range of keystrokes, the `KeyDown` event is more specific. `KeyDown` occurs when users press a key down just as `KeyPress` does, but `KeyDown` gives you a more detailed—albeit slightly more complicated—status of your keyboard. For example, `KeyPress` returns a different ASCII value for the uppercase T and the lowercase t keypresses. `KeyDown` returns the *same* value, as well as another value called the *state* argument that describes the state of the Shift key.

Note

> The `KeyDown` event occurs whenever users press a key. Therefore, both the `KeyDown` and `KeyPress` events can occur at the same time (assuming that users press an ASCII key).

Tip

> Use `KeyPress` if you want to test for an ASCII keystroke, because `KeyPress` is simpler to program than `KeyDown`.

The following are the opening and closing statements of a `KeyDown` event procedure:

```
Private Sub txtTryIt_KeyDown(KeyCode As Integer, Shift As Integer)
  '
  ' Keyboard code handler goes here
  '
End Sub
```

7

KeyCode contains the keystroke, and the Shift argument determines the state of the control keys such as Shift, Ctrl, and Alt. The KeyCode matches the *uppercase* equivalent of the key pressed. Therefore, if users press a lowercase t, the KeyCode argument contains 84 (the ASCII value for an uppercase T).

Caution

Be careful because KeyDown's ignorance of the lowercase keys can cause confusion if you're not careful. If you receive a number keypress, you *must* check the Shift argument. If Shift indicates that users pressed Shift at the same time as the number, users actually wanted the corresponding character above the number (such as the caret [^] above the 6).

The primary advantage of KeyDown over KeyPress is that, despite KeyDown's Shift problems, you can check for virtually *any* keystroke, including the arrow keys, Home, End, and so on. Again, check online help for the key-code constants that VB uses to test these special keystrokes.

The *shift state* is the key—either Shift, Ctrl, Alt, or none—that users press with the other key. The internal binary pattern of the shift argument determines the kind of shift state. To check the shift state, you must perform an And against a number 7. (This special kind of And is called a *bitwise And*, as opposed to the more common logical And that works as a compound comparison operator.) The code in Listing 7.1 is the shell that performs the common shift state test.

LISTING 7.1. YOU CAN WRITE CODE THAT TESTS FOR THE SHIFT STATE.

```
Private Sub Text1_KeyDown(KeyCode As Integer, Shift As Integer)
  Dim intShiftState As Integer
  intShiftState = Shift And 7  ' Special bitwise And
  Select Case intShiftState
    Case 1
      ' Code for Shift combinations
    Case 2
      ' Code for Ctrl combinations
    Case 3
      ' Code for Alt combinations
    Case 4
      ' Code for Shift+Ctrl combinations
    Case 5
      ' Code for Shift+Alt combinations
    Case 6
      ' Code for Ctrl+Alt combinations
    Case 7
```

```
        ' Code for Shift+Ctrl+Alt combinations
      End Select
End Sub
```

The `KeyUp` event occurs whenever users release a pressed key. You can test for the specific key released (such as the A if the user releases half of a Shift+A keystroke) by analyzing the argument passed to `KeyUp()`. Therefore, `KeyUp` occurs after both `KeyDown` and `KeyPress` events.

The following code shows an event procedure for a text box. The code converts any lowercase letters the user types into the TextBox control to uppercase:

```
Private Sub txtTry_KeyPress(KeyAscii As Integer)
  ' Convert any lowercase letters to uppercase
  If (KeyAscii >= 97) And (KeyAscii <= 122) Then
    KeyAscii = KeyAscii - 32   ' Adjust to upper
  End If
End Sub
```

The ASCII value range for lowercase letters, as you can verify from Appendix C, "ASCII Code Table," is 97 (for a) to 122 (for z). The ASCII value difference between the uppercase letters and their lowercase counterparts is 32. Therefore, if the `KeyPress` event procedure successfully gets a lowercase letter ASCII value, the procedure subtracts 32 from the value to convert the value to its uppercase equivalent.

Caution

> Don't use the keyboard events to write your own masked edit routine. Press Ctrl+T and add the Microsoft Masked Edit Control 6.0 to the toolbox. (Day 9's lesson explains in more detail how you add tools to the Toolbox window.) The Masked Edit control lets you set up input fields, such as phone numbers with area codes and automatic parentheses and hyphens. If you were to write your own routines, you would be reinventing the wheel and wasting time that you could spend at the beach.

Sending Keystrokes from Your Program

The `SendKeys` statement sends keystrokes to your application as though the user were typing those keystrokes. `SendKeys` is useful for controlling the placement of the text cursor because you can send keystrokes such as the Home and End keys to position the text cursor in a text box or other data-entry control. Here is the syntax of `SendKeys`:

`SendKeys` *`strKeystrokes`*`[,` *`blnWait`*`]`

`strKeystrokes` is often a string literal, such as "Widgets, Inc.," if you want to type the value for users. The Boolean *`blnWait`* option is usually omitted and, if `False` (the default

if you omit *blnWait*), control returns to the executing procedure as soon as the keystrokes are sent. If *blnWait* is True, the system processes the keystrokes before the code continues, meaning that the keystroke events are active during the keystroke entry.

You must enclose the following special characters inside braces ({}) if you send them with SendKeys: caret (^), plus sign (+), percent sign (%), tilde (~), and parentheses. Therefore, to simulate typing 7 + 6, the SendKeys statement must embed the plus sign in braces, like this:

```
SendKeys "7 {+} 6"
```

Several special keystroke characters, such as the Home and function keys, require a SendKeys code and the braces. For example, to send the Home keypress to an application, you must use the {Home} literal as follows:

```
SendKeys "{Home}"
```

All these special keys have code equivalents you can use. You can look up SendKeys in online help to learn which keystroke codes are defined for the special keys.

You can't send the Print Screen keystroke to an application with SendKeys.

Prioritizing Responses

When users press a key, either the form or the control with the active focus gets the keystroke. If no control currently has the focus, the form gets the keystroke event. If, however, a control has the focus, either the control or the form gets the focus, depending on the result of the form's KeyPreview property.

If the form's KeyPreview property is True, the form receives the keystroke event. Therefore, if you had coded two event procedures named frmAcct_KeyDown() and txtEntry_KeyDown(), and if the form's KeyPreview property contains True, the frmAcct_KeyDown() event procedure executes when users press a key. If the form's KeyPreview property contains False, the txtEntry_KeyDown() control executes (assuming that the text box has the current focus).

Additional Controls

Input boxes and message boxes offer a convenient way for you to display information and get input using pop-up windows that come and go as needed. The message and input boxes are a great addition to labels and text boxes because they display output and accept user input differently from those controls.

Other controls accept input and offer the user choices that you've yet to learn. The rest of today's lesson introduces you to those other controls. By the time you finish today, you will know how to add several kinds of new controls to your Visual Basic applications.

Check Boxes

A check box offers an option for the user. A check box might appear by itself or perhaps along with several other check boxes. The check box, when clicked, displays a check mark (meaning the user has selected the check box option) and the check mark goes away when the user clicks the check box once again.

NEW TERM A *check box* is an option on a form that is checked when selected and unchecked when not selected. Use CheckBox controls when you want to offer the user two-value choices, such as whether something is true or false or possibly on or off.

Remember that a CheckBox control is either checked or not. The check box property value that determines the current state of the check box resides in the `Value` property. If the `Value` property is 1, the check box is selected and the check mark appears; but if `Value` holds 0, the check box is not selected and no check mark appears.

A single check box offers the `True` or `False` value selection as indicated by its `Value` property of 1 or 0. If you just want a yes or no answer to a prompt, don't supply two check box options but supply only one. Actually, check boxes are better suited for indicating selected options than for answering yes or no questions. Figure 7.7 shows a form with three Check-Box controls. Each of the controls might be checked or unchecked depending on the user and depending on the value the programmer stored in each check box's `Value` property at design time.

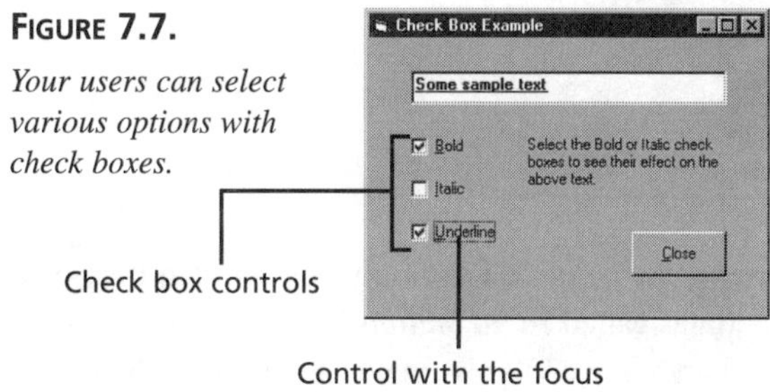

FIGURE 7.7.
Your users can select various options with check boxes.

> If you add an accelerator key to the check box's `Caption` property value, the user can check and uncheck the check box by pressing the accelerator keystroke, such as Alt+B.

Check whether or not a check box is checked with an `If` statement that takes the following format:

```
If (chkUnder.Value = 1) Then
   ' Code to handle checked conditions
Else
   ' Code to handle unchecked conditions
End If
```

Remember that your form might contain one, two, or more check boxes. Although you can, through tedious coding, ensure that one and only one check box is selected at any one time, Visual Basic supplies a better way to provide mutually-exclusive options than check boxes. You'll learn about the Option button control in the next section.

Option Buttons

Option buttons let the user select from one of several choices. Unlike check boxes, however, Visual Basic lets the user select one and only one option button at a time. Figure 7.8 shows three option buttons with only one selected. If the user clicks another, Visual Basic takes care of unselecting the first option button and selecting the one the user clicked.

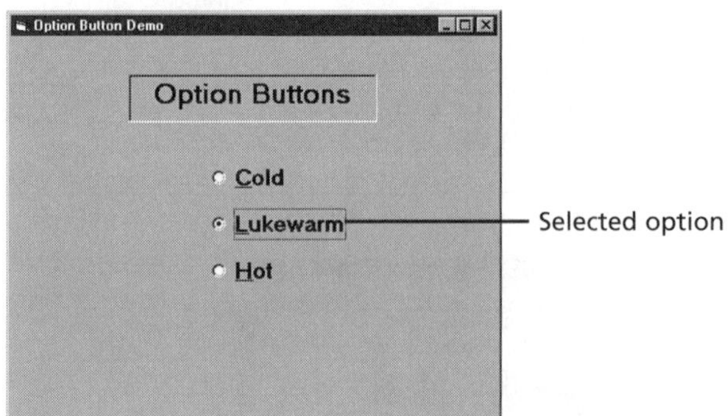

FIGURE 7.8.
Your users can select one and only one option button at a time.

NEW TERM An *option button* offers the user a choice of one and only one selected item on a form. Option buttons are sometimes called *radio buttons* because they mimic the way old car radio pushbuttons used to work. One and only one pushbutton can be pushed at once; as soon as you push in another, the first one resets by popping out.

When you place option buttons on the form, you can set the option button's Value properties all to `False` at runtime in the `Form_Load()` event procedure. The form appears with none of the option buttons selected. After the user selects an option, that option is selected until the user selects another option button. When you add accelerator keys to the option button's `Caption` property value, the user can select an option by pressing that accelerator keystroke instead of clicking the option button on the form.

Never place just one option button on a form because the user can select that option button but cannot deselect it.

Group Options with the Frame Control

Technically, the user can select more than one option button at a time as long as the two option buttons reside in separate *frames*. You can use frames to hold groups of option buttons so that the user can select one of multiple option button groups.

NEW TERM A *frame*, sometimes known as a *container control*, holds controls on a plane that differs from the form itself. Although you can only provide one set of option buttons on a form, you can provide multiple option button sets on the screen as long as one or more sets reside on one or more frames. Frames can hold more than option buttons. A frame can hold any kind of control that you want to visually group with other controls.

Figure 7.9 shows an application with two option buttons selected. Visual Basic allows this because the application contains option buttons on the form as well as set on the frame. Without the frame, only one of the five options buttons can be selected at a time.

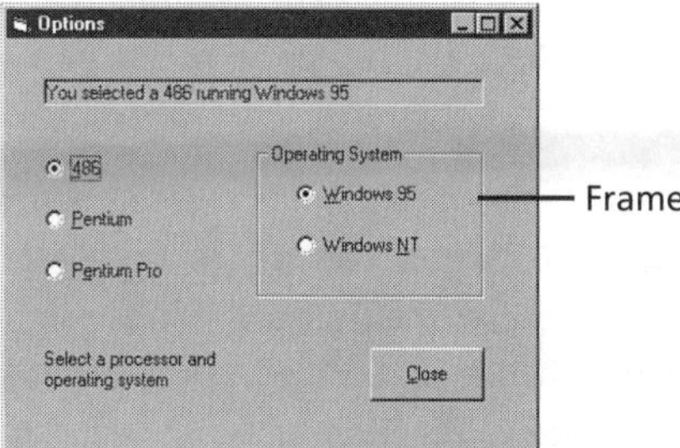

FIGURE 7.9.
If you place a group of option buttons on a frame, the user can select one from the frame as well as one from the form.

Do	Don't
DO use as many frames as you need to provide multiple option button sets on a form	

7

Frames require very little effort to add. The following properties are useful when setting frames on your applications' forms:

- **`BorderStyle`**—Either `0-None` or `1-Fixed single`. As with any property with such values, you can assign the `BorderStyle` property a 0 or 1 at runtime using Visual Basic assignment statements or you can select the proper initial value from the Properties window at design time. When you select no border, the frame is invisible and has no caption or line to differentiate the frame from the form. An unbordered frame can still group option buttons but your user will have a difficult time knowing that the options are a group separate from another group that might appear on the form.
- **`Caption`**—The text that appears at the top of the frame.
- **`Font`**—Determines the font values for the value in the `Caption` property.

The Bonus Project that appears between today's and tomorrow's lessons, "Variables and Expressions," builds a complete project that uses a frame to hold option buttons. You will learn how to place controls on the frame properly by drawing the form's Option button control on top of the frame that you place on the form. You must place option buttons on the frame in this manner for Visual Basic to recognize that the option button is no longer part of the form's group of buttons but is now part of the frame's separate group of options.

Summary

Today's lesson introduced you to internal functions. As you progress through these 21 days, you'll learn more internal functions. Visual Basic supplies these functions so that you can call the functions by name, passing them arguments, and use the return values without having to write the function's tedious code yourself to accomplish the same purpose.

The `MsgBox()` function displays messages to your users in pop-up windows. The user can respond by clicking a command button. If you are prompting the user to continue with a selected process, you will want to give the user a combination of command buttons that lets the user continue or cancel the process. Whereas the `MsgBox()` function displays messages, you'll use the `InputBox()` function to ask the user questions and get responses that you can use in your program.

Other controls, such as check boxes, option buttons, and grouped option buttons on frames, also give your users a way to inform your program. The selected controls let your program know choices the user is making.

Tomorrow's lesson teaches more about the structure of a Visual Basic application. You'll gain more insight into local and global variables. In addition, tomorrow's lesson teaches almost all the remaining internal functions that you'll ever need.

Q&A

Q Why can't an internal function return more than one value?

A An internal function is said to become its return value. In other words, an internal function works just like an expression works in that a single value is produced. Often, you'll pass an internal function a value or set of values that you want the internal function to manipulate or combine in some way. The return value is the result of that manipulation or combination. For example, the `LoadPicture()` function accepts a string argument that specifies a pathname to an image, and the return value is the actual picture at that location that you can assign to a graphic property of a control.

The nature of internal functions are such that you can use them anywhere you can use the function's return value. Therefore, instead of displaying a string literal or variable in a message box, you can use an `InputBox()` function in place of the message box's string prompt value. In this way, you nest a function within a function. The innermost function, the `InputBox()`, executes first and gets a string from the user. The `MsgBox()` function then displays that string in a message box as follows:

```
intResp = MsgBox(InputBox("What is your name?"))
```

How often will you embed an `InputBox()` function in a `MsgBox()` function? Possibly never, but this assignment statement clearly shows that an internal function, in this case the `InputBox()`'s, becomes its return value so that other code can then immediately use the return value.

Q What other internal functions are available?

A Internal functions exist that work with numbers, strings, and the other kinds data. You'll learn many of these in tomorrow's lesson, "The Nature of VB Programs."

Workshop

The Workshop provides quiz questions to help solidify your understanding on the material covered and exercises to provide you with experience in using what you've learned. Try to understand the quiz and exercise answers before continuing to the next chapter. Answers are provided in Appendix A, "Answers to Exercises."

Quiz

1. What is the difference between an *argument* and an *internal function*?
2. True/False. You can specify the default button on a message box.
3. What is an equivalent keyword for the empty string literal, `""`?
4. True/False. Tables 7.1, 7.2, and 7.3 describe three different arguments that you can use in `MsgBox()` functions.
5. What does Visual Basic use in the title bar of message and input boxes when you don't specify a title argument?
6. What's the primary difference between a check box and an option button?
7. True/False. You can display a set of option buttons on a form without any being selected.
8. Which property value determines if a check box is selected or not?
9. Which property value determines if an option button is selected or not?
10. Why is a frame sometimes necessary when placing option buttons on a form?

Exercises

1. Describe how your code can determine if the user entered an input box value (or perhaps accepted the default value you supplied) or clicked the Cancel button?
2. Write the `MsgBox()` function needed to produce the message box shown in Figure 7.10.

FIGURE 7.10.

How would you produce this message box?

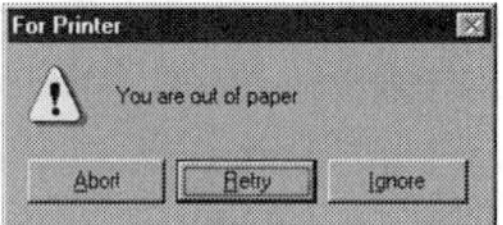

3. Write a command button event procedure that asks the user for a city, then for a state name, in two separate input boxes. Then, concatenate the names after placing a comma and space between them and display the merged city and state string in a message box.
4. Write an application with a long form that contains five option buttons that simulate radio buttons across the top of the form. Label each of the buttons with your city's top five radio stations. Create an event procedure for each option button that displays the type of music or talk that station plays. Display this information in a message box.

Week 1

Bonus Project 3

User Input and Conditional Logic

This Bonus Project's code demonstrates the use of check boxes, option buttons, and frames so that you can practice handling the user's responses using the controls you now know.

Handling so many controls and responding to them will require some Visual Basic programming, and this Bonus Project contains the most code of any you've seen so far. Here are the goals of this application:

- To display a series of check boxes for the user to select one or more countries to see their respective flags displayed next to their names.
- To display that same series of country names with option buttons so the user can select one and only one country at a time.
- To issue a message box–based error if the user fails to respond correctly to the required input.
- To add a second set of option buttons, along with the country option buttons, that determines if the selected flag displays in a small or large image box control.

In addition to teaching you about these controls, this application introduces you to a new concept: multiple forms in a single project. This application uses a total of three forms. You'll learn how to load and display the proper form when needed at runtime.

As is the case with many applications in this 21-day tutorial, this application requires the use of graphics files that come with Visual Basic. Depending on your installation choices, you might not have the Graphics folder on your disk in your Visual Basic directory. If so, you'll have to change the pathname to your CD-ROM drive and insert your first VB6 installation CD-ROM pathname in place of this application's pathname. To add the graphics, insert your first Visual Basic CD-ROM in the drive and select Add/Change Options from the screen to add the graphics to your hard disk.

Creating the Initial Form

Figure BP3.1 shows the first form you'll create.

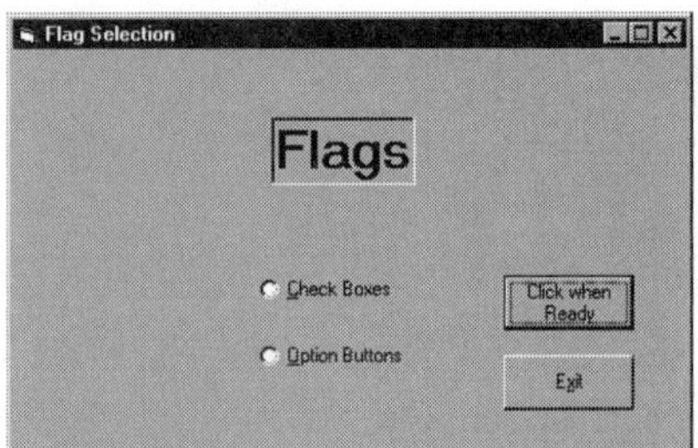

FIGURE BP3.1.
This form lets the user select the type of flag display desired.

Table BP3.1 lists the properties for the elements of the form.

TABLE BP3.1. SET THESE CONTROLS AND PROPERTIES ON THE FORM.

Control Property Name	*Property Value*
Form `Name`	`frmSelect`
Form `Caption`	`Flag Selection`
Form `Height`	`4035`
Form `Width`	`6390`
Label `Name`	`lblFlags`
Label `BorderStyle`	`1-Fixed Single`
Label `Caption`	`Flags`
Label `Font`	`MS Sans Serif`

Control Property Name	*Property Value*
Label Font Size	24
Label Font Style	Bold
Label Height	615
Label Left	2400
Label Top	600
Label Width	1335
Option button #1 Name	optCheck
Option button #1 Caption	&Check Boxes
Option button #1 Left	2280
Option button #1 Top	1920
Option button #1 Width	1575
Option button #2 Name	optOption
Option button #2 Caption	&Option Buttons
Option button #2 Left	2280
Option button #2 Top	2520
Option button #2 Width	1695
Command button #1 Name	cmdSelect
Command button #1 Caption	Click when &Ready
Command button #1 Left	4560
Command button #1 Top	2040
Command button #2 Name	cmdExit
Command button #2 Caption	E&xit
Command button #2 Left	4560
Command button #2 Top	2760

Although the code needed for this form is simple, it does introduce a new concept. The code, shown in Listing BP 3.1, demonstrates how to load a different form than the one currently onscreen.

LISTING BP3.1. GETTING THE USER'S REQUEST FROM THE OPTION BUTTON SELECTION.

```
Private Sub cmdSelect_Click()
' Perform error-checking then
' Display the proper form according to the user's selection
```

continues

LISTING BP3.1. CONTINUED

```
4:    Dim strMsg As String     ' Holds message box return value
5:    If ((optCheck.Value = False) And (optOption.Value = False)) Then
6:      strMsg = MsgBox("You need to select an option, try again", _
        vbCritical, "Error!")
7:    ElseIf (optCheck.Value = True) Then
8:           frmFlagsCheck.Show    ' Flags with Check boxes
9:        Else
10:          frmFlagsOpt.Show    ' Flags with Option buttons
11:   End If
12: End Sub
13:
14: Private Sub Form_Load()
15: ' Clear each of the option buttons
16:   optCheck.Value = False
17:   optOption.Value = False
18: End Sub
19: Private Sub cmdExit_Click()
20: ' Stop the program
21:   End
22: End Sub
```

The Startup Form's Analysis

Lines 14 through 18 determine what happens when the application first starts and the initial form loads. (The Project, Properties dialog box should show the form named `frmSelect` as the startup form.) Lines 16 and 17 set the option buttons to `False`. This forces the user to select one of them.

If the user clicks the command button without selecting an option button, line 5's compound conditional statement finds out. If both option button `Value` properties are still `False` once the user clicks the command button, line 6 displays a message box that warns the user he or she must make a selection.

If the user has selected one of the option buttons, lines 7 through 9 determine which option button is selected and show the proper form. Notice that the line actually shows the form with the command `frmFlagsCheck.Show`. Actually, this does not look like a command but rather like some kind of property value named `Show`. However, there is no property value named `Show` for forms. `Show` is a *method*, and a method is a command that is not a Visual Basic command (such as `Next`), but rather a command you apply only to a specific object. In this case, that object is the form `frmFlagsCheck`. The `Show` method displays whatever form you apply it to. Therefore, as soon as line 8 or 10 executes, the user will see the appropriate form on the screen sitting atop the selection form.

Creating the Check Box Form

Figure BP3.2 shows the next form you'll design.

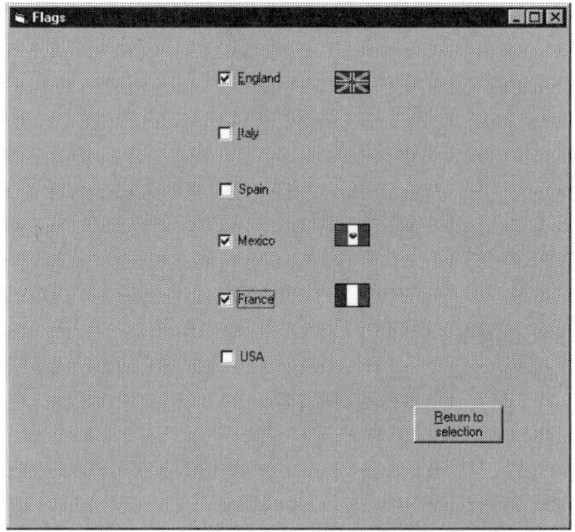

FIGURE BP3.2.
The user can display the flag from any country.

The form contains six country names, and six possible flags can appear next to the country names. You'll have to create a new form and add it to the current project. To do this, follow these steps:

1. Right-click inside the Project window.
2. Select Add, Form from the pop-up menu. Visual Basic displays a tabbed dialog box from which you can select a new form or an existing one.
3. Double-click the icon labeled Form because you're going to create a new form for this application. The form will appear on your screen inside the form editing area.

Table BP3.2 lists the properties for the elements of the form. Remember that you need to change the pathname for the images' `Picture` properties to your PC's path for those files (and possibly to your Visual Basic CD-ROM if you did not install the Graphics folder).

TABLE BP3.2. SET THESE CONTROLS AND PROPERTIES ON THE FLAG SELECTION.

Control Property Name	*Property Value*
Form `Name`	`frmFlagsCheck`
Form `Caption`	`Flags`
Form `Height`	`7035`
Form `Width`	`7710`

continues

Table BP3.2. continued

Control Property Name	*Property Value*
Check box #1 `Name`	`chkEngland`
Check box #1 `Caption`	`&England`
Check box #1 `Left`	`2835`
Check box #1 `Top`	`420`
Check box #2 `Name`	`chkItaly`
Check box #2 `Caption`	`&Italy`
Check box #2 `Height`	`495`
Check box #2 `Left`	`2835`
Check box #2 `Top`	`1155`
Check box #2 `Width`	`1215`
Check box #3 `Name`	`chkSpain`
Check box #3 `Caption`	`&Spain`
Check box #3 `Height`	`495`
Check box #3 `Left`	`2835`
Check box #3 `Top`	`1905`
Check box #3 `Width`	`1215`
Check box #4 `Name`	`chkMexico`
Check box #4 `Caption`	`&Mexico`
Check box #4 `Height`	`495`
Check box #4 `Left`	`2835`
Check box #4 `Top`	`2595`
Check box #4 `Width`	`1215`
Check box #5 `Name`	`chkFrance`
Check box #5 `Caption`	`&France`
Check box #5 `Height`	`495`
Check box #5 `Left`	`2835`
Check box #5 `Top`	`3375`
Check box #5 `Width`	`1215`
Check box #7 `Name`	`chkUSA`
Check box #7 `Caption`	`&USA`
Check box #7 `Height`	`495`
Check box #7 `Left`	`2865`

Control Property Name	*Property Value*
Check box #7 `Top`	`4140`
Check box #7 `Width`	`1215`
Image #1 `Name`	`imgEngland`
Image #1 `Height`	`480`
Image #1 `Left`	`4440`
Image #1 `Picture`	`\Program Files\Microsoft Visual Studio\Common\Graphics\Icons\Flags\Flaguk`
Image #1 `Top`	`480`
Image #1 `Visible`	`False`
Image #2 `Name`	`imgItaly`
Image #2 `Height`	`480`
Image #2 `Left`	`4440`
Image #2 `Picture`	`\Program Files\Microsoft Visual Studio\Common\Graphics\Icons\Flags\Flgitaly`
Image #2 `Top`	`1155`
Image #2 `Visible`	`False`
Image #3 `Name`	`imgSpain`
Image #3 `Height`	`480`
Image #3 `Left`	`4440`
Image #3 `Picture`	`\Program Files\Microsoft Visual Studio\Common\Graphics\Icons\Flags\Flgspain`
Image #3 `Top`	`1890`
Image #3 `Visible`	`False`
Image #4 `Name`	`imgMexico`
Image #4 `Height`	`480`
Image #4 `Left`	`4440`
Image #4 `Picture`	`\Program Files\Microsoft Visual Studio\Common\Graphics\Icons\Flags\Flgmex`
Image #4 `Top`	`2520`
Image #4 `Visible`	`False`
Image #5 `Name`	`imgFrance`
Image #5 `Height`	`480`
Image #5 `Left`	`4440`

continues

TABLE BP3.2. CONTINUED

Control Property Name	*Property Value*
Image #5 `Picture`	`\Program Files\Microsoft Visual Studio\Common\Graphics\Icons\Flags\Flgfran`
Image #5 `Top`	`3315`
Image #5 `Visible`	`False`
Image #6 `Name`	`imgUSA`
Image #6 `Height`	`480`
Image #6 `Left`	`4440`
Image #6 `Picture`	`\Program Files\Microsoft Visual Studio\Common\Graphics\Icons\Flags\Flgusa02`
Image #6 `Top`	`4080`
Image #6 `Visible`	`False`
Command button `Name`	`cmdReturn`
Command button `Caption`	`&Return to selection`
Command button `Left`	`5520`
Command button `Top`	`5040`

You now must add the code to the form. Double-click the form named `frmFlagsCheck` and add the code in Listing BP3.2. The goal of this application's form is to display a picture of a country's flag when the user clicks a check box. Therefore, you need to associate a procedure with the `Click` event for each check box.

LISTING BP3.2. DISPLAYING A FLAG WHEN THE USER CLICKS A CHECK BOX CONTROL.

```
Private Sub chkEngland_Click()
  ' Displays the flag if checked
  If chkEngland.Value = 1 Then
    imgEngland.Visible = True
  Else
    imgEngland.Visible = False
  End If
End Sub
Private Sub chkItaly_Click()
  ' Displays the flag if checked
  If chkItaly.Value = 1 Then
    imgItaly.Visible = True
  Else
    imgItaly.Visible = False
  End If
```

```
End Sub
Private Sub chkSpain_Click()
  ' Displays the flag if checked
  If chkSpain.Value = 1 Then
    imgSpain.Visible = True
  Else
    imgSpain.Visible = False
  End If
End Sub
Private Sub chkMexico_Click()
  ' Displays the flag if checked
  If chkMexico.Value = 1 Then
    imgMexico.Visible = True
  Else
    imgMexico.Visible = False
  End If
End Sub
Private Sub chkFrance_Click()
  ' Displays the flag if checked
  If chkFrance.Value = 1 Then
    imgFrance.Visible = True
  Else
    imgFrance.Visible = False
  End If
End Sub
Private Sub chkUSA_Click()
  ' Displays the flag if checked
  If chkUSA.Value = 1 Then
    imgUSA.Visible = True
  Else
    imgUSA.Visible = False
  End If
End Sub
Private Sub cmdReturn_Click()
' Return to the selection form
  frmFlagsCheck.Hide
  frmSelect.Show
End Sub
```

The Check Box Form's Analysis

The six check box event procedures are similar. You already filled in each image control's `Picture` property when you designed the form and placed the controls. Therefore, the event procedure only needs to set the `Visible` property to `True` to shows the picture. However, a problem exists: What if the user clicks the check box once again to clear the check mark? The code must turn *off* the picture's display.

Lines 43 through 46 show how the code works in each event procedure. Line 43 looks at the check box's `Value` property. If the `Value` property holds a `1`, the user clicked the box to turn on the check mark, and the code, therefore, turns on the picture's display. If `Value` holds a `0`, the user unchecked the box; therefore, the code must turn off the picture's display, as is done in line 46.

Finally, the command button's `Click` event procedure performs two tasks in lines 51 and 52. Line 51 shows a new method called the `Hide` method that hides the form you apply this method to. (`Hide` is the opposite of `Show`.) Line 51 hides the check box form, and line 52 displays the startup form once again so the user can select another option.

Creating the Option Button Form

Figure BP3.3 shows the next form you'll design. The flag may be small or large, depending on which option the user chooses.

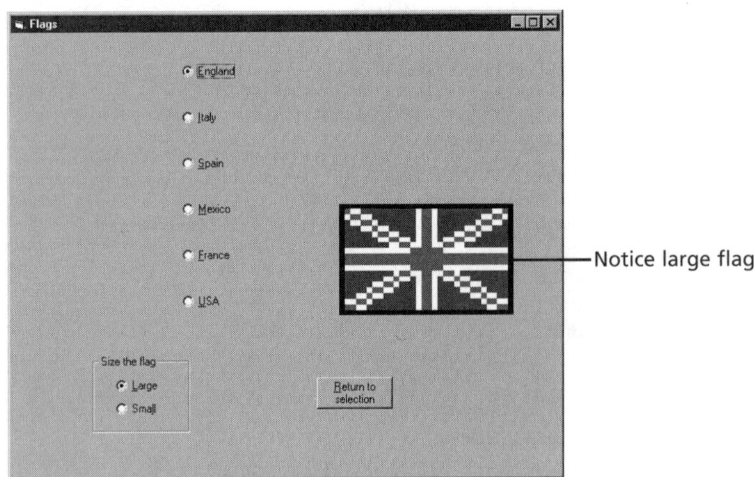

FIGURE BP3.3.
This form lets the user display one flag at a time and select the flag's display size.

The form contains six option buttons next to the six country names, and one of six possible flags can appear next to the country name. In addition, a frame holds two more option buttons that determine the size of the flag displayed.

To add option buttons to a frame control, you *must* draw the option buttons on the frame. In other words, if you double-click the option button tool and an option button appears in the center of the form, Visual Basic does *not* assume that the option button resides on the frame. Therefore, to separate a frame's option buttons from the rest on the form's option buttons, you must draw the option button by clicking the toolbar's option button control *once* and dragging the new option button on top of the form's frame. That option button, and all others you place on the frame this way, will be considered part of the frame and distinct from the other option buttons.

As before, you have to create a new form and add it to the current project. Once you add the form (the third form in the project), assign the controls and properties shown in Table BP3.3 to it.

TABLE BP3.3. OPTION BUTTONS CHANGE THE WAY THE FLAGS DISPLAY ON THE FORM.

Control Property Name	*Property Value*
Form `Name`	`frmFlagsOpt`
Form `Caption`	`Flags`
Form `Height`	`7335`
Form `Width`	`8955`
Option button #1 `Name`	`optEngland`
Option button #1 `Caption`	`&England`
Option button #1 `Height`	`495`
Option button #1 `Left`	`2760`
Option button #1 `Top`	`360`
Option button #1 `Value`	`True`
Option button #1 `Width`	`1215`
Option button #2 `Name`	`optItaly`
Option button #2 `Caption`	`&Italy`
Option button #2 `Height`	`495`
Option button #2 `Left`	`2760`
Option button #2 `Top`	`1080`
Option button #2 `Width`	`1215`
Option button #3 `Name`	`optSpain`
Option button #3 `Caption`	`&Spain`
Option button #3 `Height`	`495`
Option button #3 `Left`	`2760`

continues

TABLE BP3.3. CONTINUED

Control Property Name	*Property Value*
Option button #3 `Top`	`1800`
Option button #3 `Width`	`1215`
Option button #4 `Name`	`optMexico`
Option button #4 `Caption`	`&Mexico`
Option button #4 `Height`	`495`
Option button #4 `Left`	`2760`
Option button #4 `Top`	`2520`
Option button #4 `Width`	`1215`
Option button #5 `Name`	`optFrance`
Option button #5 `Caption`	`&France`
Option button #5 `Height`	`495`
Option button #5 `Left`	`2760`
Option button #5 `Top`	`3240`
Option button #5 `Width`	`1215`
Option button #6 `Name`	`optUSA`
Option button #6 `Caption`	`&USA`
Option button #6 `Height`	`495`
Option button #6 `Left`	`2760`
Option button #6 `Top`	`3960`
Option button #6 `Width`	`1215`
Frame `Name`	`fraSize`
Frame `Caption`	`Size the flag`
Frame `Height`	`1215`
Frame `Left`	`1320`
Frame `Top`	`5040`
Frame `Width`	`1575`
Frame option #1 `Name`	`optLarge`
Frame option #1 `Caption`	`&Large`
Frame option #1 `Height`	`255`
Frame option #1 `Left`	`360`
Frame option #1 `Top`	`360`
Frame option #1 `Width`	`1095`

Control Property Name	*Property Value*
Frame option #2 `Name`	`optSmall`
Frame option #2 `Caption`	`Sma&ll`
Frame option #2 `Height`	`255`
Frame option #2 `Left`	`360`
Frame option #2 `Top`	`720`
Frame option #2 `Width`	`1095`
Image #1 `Name`	`imgEngland`
Image #1 `Height`	`480`
Image #1 `Left`	`5280`
Image #1 `Picture`	`\Program Files\Microsoft Visual Studio\Common\Graphics\Icons\Flags\Flguk`
Image #1 `Stretch`	`True`
Image #1 `Top`	`2160`
Image #1 `Visible`	`True`
Image #2 `Name`	`imgItaly`
Image #2 `Height`	`480`
Image #2 `Left`	`5280`
Image #2 `Picture`	`\Program Files\Microsoft Visual Studio\Common\Graphics\Icons\Flags\Flgitaly`
Image #2 `Stretch`	`True`
Image #2 `Top`	`2160`
Image #2 `Visible`	`False`
Image #3 `Name`	`imgSpain`
Image #3 `Height`	`480`
Image #3 `Left`	`5280`
Image #3 `Picture`	`\Program Files\Microsoft Visual Studio\Common\Graphics\Icons\Flags\Flgspain`
Image #3 `Stretch`	`True`
Image #3 `Top`	`2160`
Image #3 `Visible`	`False`
Image #4 `Name`	`imgMexico`
Image #4 `Height`	`480`
Image #4 `Left`	`5280`

continues

TABLE BP3.3. CONTINUED

Control Property Name	Property Value
Image #4 Picture	\Program Files\Microsoft Visual Studio\Common\Graphics\Icons\Flags\Flg\Flgmex
Image #4 Stretch	True
Image #4 Top	2160
Image #4 Visible	False
Image #5 Name	imgFrance
Image #5 Height	480
Image #5 Left	5280
Image #5 Picture	\Program Files\Microsoft Visual Studio\Common\Graphics\Icons\Flags\Flgfran
Image #5 Stretch	True
Image #5 Top	2160
Image #5 Visible	False
Image #6 Name	imgUSA
Image #6 Height	480
Image #6 Left	5280
Image #6 Picture	\Program Files\Microsoft Visual Studio\Common\Graphics\Icons\Flags\Flgusa02
Image #6 Stretch	True
Image #6 Top	2160
Image #6 Visible	False
Command button Name	cmdReturn
Command button Caption	&Return to selection
Command button Height	495
Command button Left	4920
Command button Top	5400
Command button Width	1215

Listing BP3.3 contains the code for the option buttons form module. Get ready as it gets lengthy! You'll see, however, that the code is repetitive and primarily consists of six similar routines that go with each of the six option buttons.

Listing BP3.3. Add code that controls the flag's display using option buttons.

```
Private Sub optEngland_Click()
  ' Displays the flag if checked
  If optSmall.Value = True Then
     imgEngland.Height = 480
     imgEngland.Width = 480
  Else  ' Large image
     imgEngland.Height = 2800
     imgEngland.Width = 2800
  End If
  imgEngland.Visible = True
   ' Turn off display of all other flags
   imgItaly.Visible = False
   imgSpain.Visible = False
   imgMexico.Visible = False
   imgFrance.Visible = False
   imgUSA.Visible = False
 End Sub
 Private Sub optItaly_Click()
   ' Displays the flag if checked
  If optSmall.Value = True Then
      imgItaly.Height = 480
      imgItaly.Width = 480
   Else  ' Large image
      imgItaly.Height = 2800
      imgItaly.Width = 2800
   End If
   imgItaly.Visible = True
   ' Turn off display of all other flags
   imgEngland.Visible = False
  imgSpain.Visible = False
   imgMexico.Visible = False
   imgFrance.Visible = False
   imgUSA.Visible = False
 End Sub
 Private Sub optSpain_Click()
 ' Displays the flag if checked
   If optSmall.Value = True Then
      imgSpain.Height = 480
      imgSpain.Width = 480
  Else  ' Large image
      imgSpain.Height = 2800
      imgSpain.Width = 2800
   End If
   imgSpain.Visible = True
   ' Turn off display of all other flags
   imgItaly.Visible = False
   imgEngland.Visible = False
   imgMexico.Visible = False
```

continues

LISTING BP3.3. CONTINUED

```
   imgFrance.Visible = False
  imgUSA.Visible = False
End Sub
Private Sub optMexico_Click()
   ' Displays the flag if checked
   If optSmall.Value = True Then
      imgMexico.Height = 480
      imgMexico.Width = 480
   Else  ' Large image
      imgMexico.Height = 2800
      imgMexico.Width = 2800
  End If
   imgMexico.Visible = True
   ' Turn off display of all other flags
   imgItaly.Visible = False
   imgSpain.Visible = False
   imgEngland.Visible = False
   imgFrance.Visible = False
   imgUSA.Visible = False
End Sub
Private Sub optFrance_Click()
' Displays the flag if checked
   If optSmall.Value = True Then
      imgFrance.Height = 480
      imgFrance.Width = 480
   Else  ' Large image
      imgFrance.Height = 2800
      imgFrance.Width = 2800
   End If
   imgFrance.Visible = True
   ' Turn off display of all other flags
  imgItaly.Visible = False
   imgSpain.Visible = False
   imgMexico.Visible = False
   imgEngland.Visible = False
   imgUSA.Visible = False
End Sub
Private Sub optUSA_Click()
' Displays the flag if checked
   If optSmall.Value = True Then
      imgUSA.Height = 480
     imgUSA.Width = 480
   Else  ' Large image
      imgUSA.Height = 2800
      imgUSA.Width = 2800
   End If
```

```
   imgUSA.Visible = True
   ' Turn off display of all other flags
   imgItaly.Visible = False
   imgSpain.Visible = False
   imgMexico.Visible = False
   imgFrance.Visible = False
    imgEngland.Visible = False
  End Sub
  Private Sub cmdReturn_Click()
  ' Return to the selection form
    frmFlagsOpt.Hide
    frmSelect.Show
  End Sub
  Private Sub optSmall_Click()
  ' Hide all flags shown
  ' Subsequent flags will be small
     imgEngland.Visible = False
     imgItaly.Visible = False
     imgSpain.Visible = False
     imgMexico.Visible = False
     imgFrance.Visible = False
     imgUSA.Visible = False
     ' Reset option buttons
     optEngland.Value = False
     optItaly.Value = False
    optSpain.Value = False
     optMexico.Value = False
     optFrance.Value = False
     optUSA.Value = False
  End Sub
  Private Sub optLarge_Click()
  ' Hide all flags shown
  ' Subsequent flags will be large
     imgEngland.Visible = False
     imgItaly.Visible = False
    imgSpain.Visible = False
     imgMexico.Visible = False
     imgFrance.Visible = False
     imgUSA.Visible = False
     ' Reset option buttons
     optEngland.Value = False
     optItaly.Value = False
     optSpain.Value = False
     optMexico.Value = False
     optFrance.Value = False
    optUSA.Value = False
 End Sub
```

The Option Button Form's Analysis

Most of the event procedures consist of virtually the same code, except that the primary country name is different. Taking the first set (lines 1 through 17), you can see that the code first checks to see if the small or large option button is selected in line 3. If the small option button is selected, the control's `Height` and `Width` properties are set to 480 twips in lines 4 and 5. If the large option button is selected, the code sets the flag's `Height` and `Width` properties to 2800 twips.

The rest of the event procedure simply makes the selected country's flag visible by setting the `Visible` property to `True` in line 10 and turning off the display of the other flags in lines 12 through 16. Again, the subsequent six event procedures that appear in lines 17 through 102 mimic the first event procedure, except that a different country's flag is the target.

Line 103 begins a short event procedure that works just like the one in the check box form module. It hides the option button form and displays the selection form once again so the user can select a different form or quit the program.

Lines 108 and 125 both start virtually identical event procedures that turn off the visibility of all flags on the screen. Of course, only one flag is visible, but instead of looking for the one that's displayed and turning its `Visible` property to `False`, the code turns all the image controls' `Visible` properties to `False`. Although five of the six are already `False`, this code ensures that no flag will be visible.

The reason that clicking the large or small option buttons turns off the flag display is so the next flag the user clicks can appear in the large or small size. The application could be rewritten to change the size of the displayed flag, but that would have made this project even longer, and you have enough to type as it is!

Without a doubt, this application is tedious! Its code is repetitive—the same section of code is repeated twice for each of the six option buttons and check boxes. Before you finish this 21-day tutorial, you'll learn a way to streamline such code. When several similar controls appear on a form and the controls mimic each other almost identically, you'll learn to use a *control array*, which shortens the code and makes it easier to maintain.

WEEK 1

In Review

Now that you've finished your first week, you can be proud of yourself because you are on your way to becoming a full-fledged, official Visual Basic programmer!

As you now realize, Visual Basic programming involves much more than learning a programming language. In a way, the programming language itself is secondary to Visual Basic's visual programming. Much of creating a Windows application requires placing graphic elements on a form. Once you place the visual objects, you must set properties to make those properties look and behave in a certain way.

Your Week's Worth

In this week, you have mastered the following:

- **Visual Basic's history**—How Visual Basic got its roots from the BASIC language (Day 1).
- **Program maintenance**—Why clear and concise programming makes subsequent changes and bug fixes much easier (Day 1).
- **Program structure**—The visual elements, known as controls, have properties that you must set. These controls interact with the user at runtime by responding to Windows events (Day 1).
- **Application Wizard**—Visual Basic creates a program skeleton for you. You must fill in the details to customize the skeleton and hone your application (Day 1).
- **Visual Basic's environment**—Visual Basic's environment includes all the windows and toolbars you need to work within the Windows visual programming mode (Day 2).

- **Form Layout window**—Adjust the form's location on your screen by clicking and dragging with your mouse (Day 2).
- **Visual Basic Online Help**—Visual Basic offers all the online help that you'll ever need. From within Visual Basic, you can access the MSDN (assuming you install MSDN) books online and read complete reference books on the Visual Basic language and programming environment (Day 2).
- **Creating applications**—You don't have to use the Application Wizard to create applications. Instead, you can control every aspect of your program's creation by starting with a blank slate (actually, a blank Form window) and adding all the controls and code yourself (Day 2).
- **Property values**—Understanding and setting control properties is simple, especially with help from the Properties window (Day 3).
- **Label controls**—The Label control holds the text that you want to appear on your forms (Day 3).
- **Text box controls**—Let your users enter text into your application in text boxes that your provide (Day 3).
- **Command button controls**—Your users will trigger actions and indicate when they are ready by using the command buttons you place on your forms (Day 3).
- **Menus**—Windows applications that require menus use a standard menu bar with pull-down menu options that you can add to your own Visual Basic applications (Day 4).
- **The Menu Editor**—The Menu Editor is a dialog box that enables you to create menus quickly and easily (Day 4).
- **Menu response**—Menu options trigger `Click` events that are easy to program (Day 4).
- **The Code window**—Use the editing tool inside Visual Basic's Code window to create the most accurate code possible (Day 5).
- **Visual Basic data**—Numeric, string, and special kinds of data exist and Visual Basic supports all kinds (Day 5).
- **Variables**—Store temporary values and results in named storage locations called variables (Day 5).
- **Operators**—Perform math and data-manipulation with Visual Basic's extensive collection of operators (Day 5).
- **Operator hierarchy**—Visual Basic computes mathematical expressions in a predefined order (Day 5).

- **Conditional operators**—Visual Basic makes decisions, at runtime, based on data by using the conditional operators to analyze results (Day 6).
- **The selection statements**—The `If` and `Select Case` programming statements take advantage of the conditional operators and execute certain lines of code based on the data (Day 6).
- **Loops**—Visual Basic has as many or more kinds of loops available as any computer language in existence (Day 6).
- **Keyboard control**—The Toolbox window's controls are not the only way your users interact with your applications. You can take control of the keyboard (Day 7).
- **Check box controls**—When your users need to select from among several choices, check box controls enable them to select options simply by clicking the mouse (Day 7).
- **Option buttons**—Use option buttons when your users have to choose one, and only one, option from a set of options (Day 7).
- **Frame control**—By placing several frames on a form, you can group option buttons together to offer your users a more complete set of choices (Day 7).

WEEK 2

At a Glance

Congratulations on finishing your first week of Visual Basic programming! As you have seen, Visual Basic programming is fun. In addition, Visual Basic makes programming simple. Whereas programmers before Visual Basic had to write code that drew controls and made the controls respond to the user, Visual Basic programmers can leave those trivial details to Visual Basic and concentrate on the application's specific requirements. The fun has just begun because this week you spice up your applications even more.

Where You're Going

The next week continues to hone your Visual Basic skills. Over the next few days, you'll master virtually all of the Visual Basic programming language that you'll ever use. In Day 9, "The Dialog Box Control," you learn how to access the many internal functions that Visual Basic supplies so that you can get more done with less code. When you tap into Visual Basic's internal routines, you let Visual Basic handle common details such as calculations and data manipulations.

This week is not just about coding, however. You learn how to place dialog boxes inside your applications so that your users see a familiar interface when they open a file or send something to the printer. By using standard dialog boxes, your applications will be more familiar to users and they will adapt to your programs more quickly.

In your first week, you learned how to interact with the user through controls on the screen. This week teaches additional ways you can interact with the user. You learn how to trap and analyze keystrokes so that you can provide more control over the user's entered responses. In addition, you will learn how to respond to mouse clicks, double-clicks, and movements so that your programs interact with the user in every way possible. If you want to offer a drag-and-drop operation for a control, you will see in Day 10, "Adding Power with the Mouse and Controls," that Visual Basic's methods make quick work of drag-and-drop operations.

Data input is not the only skill that will improve this week. Your programs will become more flexible and usable as you add printing capabilities to your applications. You will be able to produce reports from the data that you process. On Day 14, "Introducing VB Graphics and Multimedia," you learn to liven your screens with graphics and even multimedia presentations. Visual Basic includes controls that provide the graphics and multimedia support. With these controls' properties, events, and methods, your applications will seem to come alive.

Week 2

Day 8

The Nature of VB Programs

Today's lesson shows you how to understand complex Visual Basic applications that contain multiple modules and procedures that need to share data between each other. When writing extensive applications, you must be able to share data between procedures and modules by declaring the variables appropriately and by writing procedures in such a way that other procedures can access them.

Not only will you write many procedures of your own, but you'll use Visual Basic's internal functions to perform common analysis and data-manipulation of strings, numbers, and other kinds of data. Today's lesson describes all the Visual Basic internal functions you'll need to work within most situations.

Today, you learn the following:

- Proper program structure
- How general procedures eliminate duplicate code
- About variable scope
- To set up argument lists

- Numeric functions
- Data analysis functions
- String manipulation functions
- Date and time functions

Mastering Program Structure

You already have a good idea of how Visual Basic programs operate. When the user interacts with controls, events take place. If the application contains event procedures that match the control and event combination, that event procedure executes. The Visual Basic program code is, for the most part, one long set of event procedures with a Declarations section at the beginning of the code.

Remember that each form has a set of code, located in the Form module, for the controls on that form. Therefore, when you display a form inside the Form window editing area, the code is available for that form when you click the Project window's View Code button.

It's time to turn your attention to other program content that a Visual Basic application might hold. Event procedures are not the only procedures that can appear in code. Figure 8.1 reviews the code that can appear in a Form module. In addition to declarations and event procedures, the Form module might contain *general procedures* and *class procedures*.

FIGURE 8.1.

A Form module can contain several kinds of code.

The Form Module

```
Declarations

Private Sub Gen _ Proc1 []
 ' Body of 1st general procedure
End Sub

Private Sub Gen _ Proc2 []
 ' Body of 2nd general procedure
End Sub

Private Sub Event _ Proc1 []
 ' Body of 1st event procedure
End Sub

Private Sub Event _ Proc2 []
 ' Body of 2nd event procedure
End Sub

Private Sub Class_ Proc1 []
 ' Body of 1st class procedure
End Sub
```

NEW TERM A *general procedure* is a procedure that is not linked to a control event but performs general calculations and routine processing.

NEW TERM A *class procedure* defines a special object in Visual Basic that you create. In a way, a class defines a new data type or variable that you can use.

You might recall the two drop-down list boxes in the Code window that determine the object and procedure that you are viewing in the Code window. When you select the Object drop-down list box, you'll see an entry for each control on the current form (the form whose Form module you are viewing). In addition, you'll see, at the top of the list, a special object listed as `(General)`. (The parentheses around the name indicates that the entry is not a control named General but a special section.) The general section holds both the declarations code that appears at the top of a Code window and general procedures you write.

Calling General Procedures

General procedures can be function or subroutine procedures. Why would you need a general procedure? In Bonus Project 2 ("Variables and Expressions"), the following code appeared in two event procedures (`optLarge_Click()` and `optSmall_Click()`):

```
imgEngland.Visible = False
imgItaly.Visible = False
imgSpain.Visible = False
imgMexico.Visible = False
imgFrance.Visible = False
imgUSA.Visible = False
' Reset option buttons
optEngland.Value = False
optItaly.Value = False
optSpain.Value = False
optMexico.Value = False
optFrance.Value = False
optUSA.Value = False
```

That's a lot of typing to have to repeat. Of course, you can use copy and paste commands inside the Code window to keep from typing the code twice but there's a problem with doing that. What if you must make a change to the code? If so, you must remember to make the change everywhere the code appears. Repetitive code is not just a bad thing because of extra typing but because of subsequent maintenance hassles that arise.

When you have this situation, you can place the code in its own general procedure, similar to that in the following code. Notice that you give general procedures a name.

(Procedure names follow the same rules as variable names.) In addition, a general procedure can be a function or a subroutine procedure:

```
Private Sub Clear_Flags()
' Hide all flags shown
' Subsequent flags will be small
   imgEngland.Visible = False
   imgItaly.Visible = False
   imgSpain.Visible = False
   imgMexico.Visible = False
   imgFrance.Visible = False
   imgUSA.Visible = False
   ' Reset option buttons
    optEngland.Value = False
    optItaly.Value = False
    optSpain.Value = False
    optMexico.Value = False
    optFrance.Value = False
    optUSA.Value = False
End Sub
```

When you get to the place in another procedure that needs to execute this code, you can *call* the general procedure like this:

```
Call Clear_Flags()
```

To *call* a procedure means to execute one procedure from inside another procedure.

The `Call` statement tells Visual Basic to temporarily put on hold the currently running procedure (whether it's an event procedure or general procedure does not matter) and execute the code inside the called procedure. After the called procedure is through, the calling procedure's code continues executing from the line that follows the `Call` statement.

Private and Public Procedures

Using `Call` can be a time-saver and make your programs much more maintainable because you put common code in a procedure and call that procedure from anywhere in the program when you need the code to execute. You might even write a routine in one application that you will want to use elsewhere in another application. For example, perhaps you write a report title that includes your company's name and address, and you want to place that title at the top of other reports generated in other applications.

If the procedure is located in the general section of a Form module, no other application can use that procedure without that Form module. Therefore, you can place that procedure inside a Code module. Over time, you might fill a particular reporting Code module with several routines that you will use for reporting. Then, any application that produces reports can use those procedures without your having to rewrite them for each application. All you must do is right-click over the application's Project window and select Add, Module from the pop-up menu to bring your general procedure module into whatever application that can use the code.

In a way, after you write general procedures and bring them into other applications, you build your own library of internal functions. They aren't actually internal (or, more accurately, they are not called *intrinsic functions*) because they are not part of the Visual Basic system; but you have added them to whatever applications you load the procedures into. You never have to write code again to perform those same procedures. To use them, you only need to call those procedures from the application.

Code inside a Form module can use the code inside an added Code module. All you need to do is call the procedure from the Form module code *with one exception*: You can call public procedures from outside the current module, not private procedures. Consider the following procedure declaration statement:

```
Private Sub ReportIt()
```

This procedure can only be called from the module in which it resides. If you wrote the procedure as a public procedure, by defining it as follows, *any* procedure from *any* module in that application can call the procedure:

```
Public Sub ReportIt()
```

Therefore, the general-purpose procedures that you write should all be public if you want those procedures to be callable from other modules.

Therefore, you now can understand these rules:

- A procedure declared as `Private` can be used only within its own module.
- A procedure declared as `Public` can be used by any procedure within its application.

Variable Scope

Not only can code be public or private, but variables also can also have public and private *scope*, although programmers usually refer to them as *global* and *local*. The difference is based on how available the variables are from surrounding code.

New Term A *local variable* can be used only by code to which it is visible.

New Term A *global variable* can be used by code outside its declared area.

New Term The term *scope* refers to the availability of a variable from within the application's code.

All controls are *always visible and public to all code within the application.* Controls on the form are never hidden from view.

Suppose you are a contract programmer for a local video store. You might write a general-purpose procedure that computes sales tax using your state, county, and city percentages. The code computes sales tax on the current total sale. You then decide that the sales tax computation will be rather common because you'll compute sales tax on video purchases, as well as other kinds of sales made such as soft drink purchases which are handled from a different module. Instead of putting the same calculations twice in the application, you place the sales tax calculation in a Code module file you have created for the video applications you write. The sales tax procedure will be public so that any procedure in any application that you add the module to can call it and compute sales tax.

One problem exists, however. Procedures cannot always share data. Consider the following code fragment:

```
Private Sub GetSalesTotal()
' Subroutine that adds each item's
' price text box and computes a
' total amount for the sale
  Dim curTotal As Currency
  '
  ' Rest of procedure continues here
```

The `GetSalesTotal()` procedure adds together all text boxes on a sales form and stores them in the variable named `curTotal`. You then want to use a sales tax procedure to compute the sales tax on this procedure's `curTotal` amount. You cannot do so with the tools you know so far because `curTotal` is a local variable!

Note

> Only code within a procedure can use a local variable you declare within that procedure. The variable is *visible* only within the procedure that declared it.

NEW TERM The term *visible* refers to a variable's usage. A variable is visible only to procedures that have access to that variable. For example, a local variable is visible only within the procedure that declared it, and a global variable is visible within the module in which you declare it.

You can declare `curTotal` as a variable that's global to the module, however, by pulling out the `Dim` statement from the procedure and declaring the variable in theForm module's Declarations section like this:

```
Option Explicit
' All public variable declarations go here
Dim curTotal As Currency
```

Any code within the Form module can now access the variable named `curTotal`. Has that helped you at all? The answer might surprise you. You have made the situation even *worse*. You might recall from Day 5 that local variables are almost always preferred over global variables because procedures should have access only to data they need. If you make the variable global, as you do when you declare the variable in a module's Declarations section (in the `(General)` section of the Code window), you have made that variable visible to all procedures in the module, even to many that don't need the variable, but the variable is still not visible to other modules!

Note

> With Visual Basic applications containing more than one module, the terms *local* and *global* actually do not properly define all situations. Therefore, you might more accurately define a variable as being *local* if it is visible to a procedure in which you declare it, a *module-level variable* if the variable is visible from the module in which you declare it, and *global*—or *public*—if the variable is visible from anywhere in the entire application.

To make a variable truly global to an entire project, you must use the `Public` keyword instead of `Dim` to declare the variable. Also, you must place the `Public` declaration in a module's Declarations section for the variable to be public, and hence global, to the entire application.

Two public variables can have the same name. You can declare them with `Public` in two separate modules. To ensure that you are using the proper public variable, if you ever use a public variable, qualify the variable name with the module's name. Therefore, `MyLibrary.curSales` refers specifically to a variable named `curSales` in the Code module named `MyLibrary`. If a public variable named `curSales` exists in any other module, `MyLibrary.curSales` guarantees that Visual Basic will use the correct one.

As a review of the concepts discussed so far, study Figure 8.2 to see how public, module-level, and local variables relate to one another and within applications. Each rectangular box within the two modules represents a procedure. The callouts show which variables are available to which procedures.

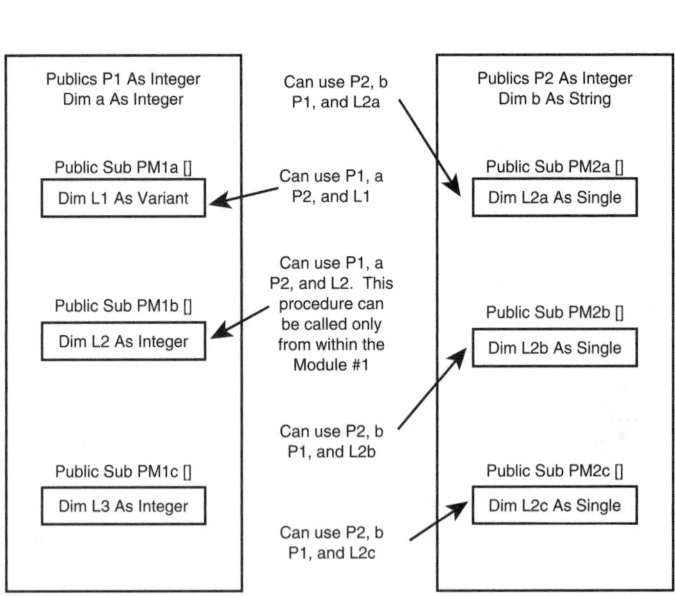

FIGURE 8.2.

A variable's scope affects which procedures can use that variable.

All this talk about public variables really saddens the die-hard programmers who want maintainable code. They have a point when they say something like, "If module-level variables are not good, then publicly declared variables available to an entire application are even worse because they are visible from all procedures within all modules within the application."

You might see the dilemma here. Except in rare cases when the same variable must be used in almost every procedure within a module, you should declare only local variables using `Dim` inside their procedures. However, other procedures often have need of those variables, especially general procedures located in outside Code modules. There must exist a means for the sharing of local data, and Visual Basic gives you the means as you'll see in the next section.

Passing Data

When two procedures need to share data values, the calling procedure can send its local variables to any called procedure. To pass the variables, you need to list the variables within the procedure's parentheses. You've already passed arguments to procedures, for example, when you used `InputBox()`. The prompt string inside the `InputBox()` parentheses was local data to the procedure that called `InputBox()`, and `InputBox()` received the data and worked with the data you passed it.

The requirement of the called procedure is that it must declare, inside the receiving parentheses, all passed arguments. A simple example will clarify everything. Listing 8.1 contains two procedures. One sends two values, a total and a discount amount, to the second procedure which computes sales tax of the total less the discount. The sales tax procedure uses the data passed to it from the first procedure and displays a message box with the total tax.

LISTING 8.1. THE FIRST PROCEDURE SENDS ARGUMENTS TO THE SECOND.

```
Private Sub GetTotal()
' This procedure collects totals from a form
' and sends the grand total and a discount
' percentage to a sales tax procedure
   Dim curTotal As Currency
   Dim sngDisc As Single    ' Special tax discount
   '
   ' Collect the totals from the form's text boxes
   curTotal = txtSale1.Text + txtSale2.Text + txtSale3.txt
   '
   ' Send the total to a sales tax procedure
   Call SalesTax(curTotal, sngDisc)
End Sub

Public Sub SalesTax(curTotal As Currency, sngRateDisc As Single)
' Compute sales tax and deduct percentage discount
  Dim curSalesTax As Currency
  Dim intMsg As Integer  ' For MsgBox()
  '
```

continues

LISTING 8.1. CONTINUED

```
20:    ' The following computes a tax based
21:    ' on 3% plus a millage of 1/2 percent
22:    curSalesTax = (curTotal * .03) + (curTotal * .005)
23:    '
24:    ' Now, deduct percentage discount
25:    curSalesTax = curSalesTax - (sngRateDisc * curTotal)
26:    '
27:    ' Display Tax
28:    intMsg = MsgBox("The sales tax is " & curSalesTax)
29:    '
30:    ' Procedures automatically return to their
31:    ' calling procedure when finished
32: End Sub
```

Note

Notice that the passed variable and the receiving argument's names do not have to match (as in `sngDisc` in line 12 and `sngRateDisc` in line 15) but the number of arguments and data types must match in both the sending and receiving argument lists. The called procedure refers to the arguments by whatever names it received them as.

The `SalesTax()` procedure might reside in a different Code module from the `GetTotal()` procedure which could reside in a Form module's general section. Line 12 calls the sales tax computing procedure that begins in line 15. Notice that the two variables passed are local to `GetTotal()` and yet `GetTotal()` makes them available to `SalesTax()` by passing the variables as arguments. The arguments are required because `SalesTax()` must receive two arguments of the data type specified.

After the two values get to `SalesTax()`, the `SalesTax()` procedure can treat them as if they were local variables to `SalesTax()`. Computations are performed with the values, and line 28 displays the computed sales tax in a message box.

Figure 8.3 shows how `GetTotal()` sends its values to `SalesTax()`.

8

FIGURE 8.3.

`GetTotal()` sends two arguments to `SalesTax()` for further computations.

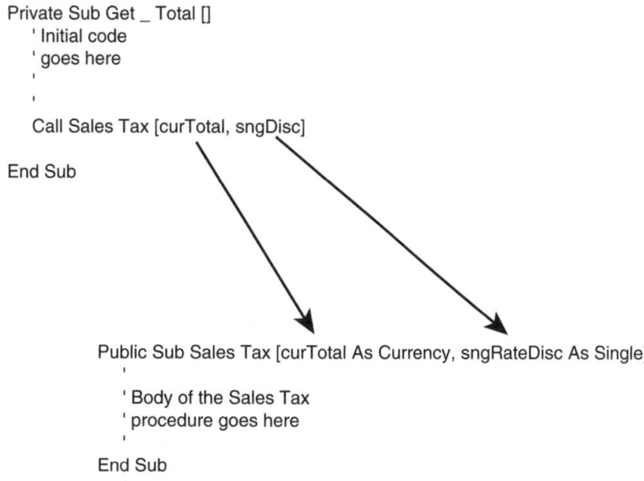

Private Sub Get _ Total []
' Initial code
' goes here
Call Sales Tax [curTotal, sngDisc]
End Sub
Public Sub Sales Tax [curTotal As Currency, sngRateDisc As Single]
' Body of the Sales Tax
' procedure goes here
End Sub

Note

Line 28 seems to mismatch data types but Visual Basic handles such a mismatch accurately. Although `MsgBox()` requires an initial string argument, and although the & operator concatenates strings, if you concatenate a string to a number (or vice versa), Visual Basic converts the number to a string to make the proper concatenation.

Do	Don't
DO use `Exit Sub` if you ever need to terminate a subroutine earlier than its normal `End Sub` statement. (`End Function` works the same for function procedures.) Always use `Exit Sub` inside an `If` or other conditional statement because you would not want the procedure to end there *every time* or the code that follows `Exit Sub` would never execute.	

Visual Basic supports a secondary way to call subroutines. You can omit both the `Call` statement and the parentheses. The following two statements are equivalent:

```
Call PrintTitle (Title)
PrintTitle Title
```

By Reference and By Value

Listing 8.1 passes its variables using a method called *by reference*, meaning that the called procedure can change the arguments in the calling procedure. If, however, you precede the arguments in the receiving function's argument list with the `ByVal` keyword, Visual Basic receives arguments *by value*, meaning that the called procedure cannot change the arguments in the calling procedure. (`ByRef` is an optional argument qualifier because all arguments are passed by reference by default.)

For example, if the `SalesTax()` procedure in Listing 8.1 modified the value in either the `curTotal` or the `sngRateDisc` argument, that same variable in `GetTotal()` would also be modified. The default method for passing arguments, by reference, means that the calling procedure's arguments are unprotected from change by the called procedure.

If line 15 in Listing 8.1 were written like the following line, however, the calling procedure `GetTotal()`'s variables are safe because nothing that `SalesTax()` can do will harm the original argument values after the program control resumes in the `GetTotal()` procedure:

```
Public Sub SalesTax(ByVal curTotal As Currency, ByVal sngRateDisc As _
Single)
```

Therefore, unless it is a procedure's goal to modify one of the arguments in the calling procedure, pass all arguments by value to help protect them. Although the called procedure can use the modified values, those values don't stay modified when control returns to the calling procedure.

> You can use the `ByVal` keyword before all, one, or some of a receiving function's argument list variables.

How Function Procedures Differ

A function differs from a subroutine, not only by its first and last statement (the *wrapper* statements) but also by the way that a function returns a single value back to the calling procedure. In the previous section, you saw code that called a subroutine procedure. Calling a function procedure differs only slightly. You call a function procedure just as you call an internal function—that is, you use the function name and arguments but you don't use the `Call` statement. The function call becomes its return value, and you use that value in an expression or statement.

A function procedure's first line, known as the *function declaration*, must follow this format:

```
Public¦Private Function FuncName([Arg As dataType][, ...]) As dataType
```

The vertical bar between `Public` and `Private` indicates that a function can be either private to its module or public to the whole application. A function does not have to have arguments, and if it does not, you can omit the parentheses, but most functions receive at least one argument. The `As dataType` clause, not found on subroutine procedures, declares the data type of the function's return value. A function can return one and only one value, and that value's data type is determined by the data type you specify for the `dataType`.

The previous `SalesTax()` procedure, if rewritten to be a function that returns the computed sales tax, might have the following declaration line:

```
Public Sub SalesTax(curTotal As Currency, sngRateDisc As Single) As _
Currency
```

As with subroutine procedures, you can pass arguments by value or by reference depending on how much protection you want to provide for the calling function's arguments.

Somewhere in the function, you *must* assign the return value to a variable that has the same name as the function name. You don't declare this variable but you can use it. Therefore, if the final statement in `SalesTax()` assigned a value to a variable named `SalesTax`, that would be the return value of the function. When the function ends, either at the `End Function` or by an `Exit Function` statement, whatever value is in the return variable is the function's return value.

The calling procedure must therefore supply a place for the return value. Generally, you assign the returned value to a variable. In a calling procedure, it's not unusual to see a statement such as the following:

```
curDailyNet = CalcNetAdj(curGrSls, sngTaxRt, curGrRate, curStrExp)
```

`CalcNetAdj()` is a function; the four values are passed to it, computed, and a variable named `CalcNetAdj` is assigned a value somewhere inside `CalcNetAdj()`. That value is assigned to this calling procedure's variable named `curDailyNet` as soon as the function ends.

The exercise section at the end of today's lesson gives you the opportunity to change Listing 8.1's `CalcTax()` procedure from a subroutine procedure to a function procedure. For study, take a moment to look at Listing 8.2 to help seal your understanding of the way functions work.

LISTING 8.2. FUNCTIONS RETURN A SINGLE VALUE BACK TO THE CALLING PROCEDURE.

```
1:  ' Calling procedure is next
2:  Private Sub CP()
3:     Dim varR As Variant     ' Local variables that help produce
4:     Dim varV As Variant     ' the function's return value
5:     Dim intI As Integer     ' Holds the return value
6:
7:     varR = 32               ' Initial values
8:     varV = 64
9:
10:    intI = RF(varR, varV)   ' Call the function and pass varR
11:                            ' and varV. intI gets return value
12:    MsgBox("After return, intI holds " & intI)
13:    MsgBox("After return, varR holds " & varR)
14:    MsgBox("After return, varV holds " & varV)
15:
16: End Sub
17: ' Receiving function is next
18: Public Function RF (varR As Variant, ByVal varV As Variant) As Integer
19: ' Received one by reference and one by value
20:    varR = 81          ' Change both arguments
21:    varV = varV + 10
22:    ' Set the return value
23:    RF = varR + varV
24: End Function
```

Line 10 passes `varR` and `varV` (32 and 64) to the function. The function immediately changes the arguments to hold 81 and 74 in lines 20 and 21. Due to the fact that `varR` was passed by reference, `varR` will now be 81 in the calling procedure (`CP()`) as well. Line 23 adds the function's arguments of 81 and 74 together and assigns the sum to the function name setting up the function's return value. When the `End Function` executes, the calling procedure's line 10's assignment completes assigning 155 to `intI`. Line 12 displays the value. Line 13 shows that `varR` was changed by the called function by displaying 81 in a message box. Line 14 displays 64 in the message box because it was protected from change by the called function.

Passing Controls as Arguments

Variables aren't the only kind of data you can pass between procedures. You can pass control values as well. You might write a procedure that works with the value of a control but you need to know which kind of control was passed. Perhaps the procedure is called from several different modules and different kinds of controls might be passed depending on the processing requirements. You can use the `If TypeOf` statement set to check for an argument's data control type.

Here's the format of the typical `If` statement that uses `TypeOf`:

```
If TypeOf object Is objectType Then
   Block of one or more Visual Basic statements
Else
   Block of one or more Visual Basic statements
End If
```

The `object` can be any *control variable* or argument and `objectType` can be any one of the following values:

```
CheckBox     Image     OptionButton     Rectangle
ComboBox     Label     OptionGroup     Shape
CommandButton     Line     PageBreak     TextBox
Graph     ListBox     PictureBox     ToggleButton
```

NEW TERM A *control variable*, sometimes known as an *object variable*, is a variable declared as a control. Not only can variables take on the data type of integers, strings, and currency amounts, but you can also declare a variable to be `Object` that can be any possible object in Visual Basic, including controls. The following variable declarations declare control variables:

```
Dim objCmdFirst As CommandButton
Dim objNameList As ListBox
Dim objPhoto As Image
```

In addition, a receiving argument list might receive a control variable like this:

```
Public Function FixControls (objIncoming As Object)
```

If a function receives an argument declared as the `Object` data type, you can test the kind of control the argument holds with code such as this:

```
If TypeOf objIncoming Is CommandButton Then
   MsgBox("You sent a command button")
ElseIf TypeOf objIncoming Is CheckBox Then
   MsgBox("You sent a check box")
ElseIf TypeOf objIncoming Is TextBox Then
   MsgBox("You sent a text box")
End If
```

Internal Functions

You've seen these three internal functions: `LoadPicture()`, `MsgBox()`, and `InputBox()`. Visual Basic supplies scores of other internal functions. In the rest of today's lesson, you'll learn the most important internal functions so that you can use them to build more powerful programs. After you complete today's lesson, you will not only know how to write your own subroutines and procedures but you'll also understand most of Visual Basic's internal functions as well. The tools you are developing today strengthen your Visual Basic programming skills considerably. Starting tomorrow, you can begin to put these new language skills to work by building more advanced applications than were possible before you mastered the Visual Basic language.

> After you finish today's lesson, you will understand about as much of the Visual Basic programming language as you'll need for a while. Although subsequent lessons teach additional commands, you've already learned the bulk of the language that you need as a beginning and intermediate programmer. That's good news because you'll think the rest of Visual Basic is a snap! Much of the next several lessons describe more controls and properties that you can use on your applications' forms.

The Numeric Functions

The simplest place to begin learning the internal functions is with the integer conversion functions. The format for the two most common appear here:

```
Int(numericValue)
Fix(numericValue)
```

The *`numericValue`* can be any numeric literal, variable, or expression, including another embedded function that returns a number. Whatever numeric data type you pass, both functions return that data type, but you can use the return value as an integer.

Do	Don't
	DON'T pass a non-numeric argument to `Int()` or `Fix()` or Visual Basic displays a runtime error when you execute your application.

Both functions appear to round their arguments down to the nearest integer. The difference lies in how they treat negative values. In the following statements, the remark shows each function's return value:

```
intAns1 = Int(6.8)     ' 6
intAns2 = Fix(6.8)     ' 6
intAns3 = Int(-6.8)    ' -7
intAns4 = Fix(-6.8)    ' -6
```

Notice that neither `Int()` nor `Fix()` rounds values up. `Int()` returns the next-lowest integer portion of its argument. Therefore, negative numbers round *down* to the next lowest negative number. `Fix()` returns the *truncated* integer portion of the argument and keeps whatever whole number portion exists in the argument.

New Term To *truncate* means to remove. `Fix()` truncates the decimal portion from its argument. A truncated 5.23 would become 5 and a truncated –5.23 would become –5.

The *absolute value* function is useful when you want to compute the differences between values such as distances and temperatures.

New Term *Absolute value* is the positive value of any number. The absolute value of 19 is 19 and the absolute value of –19 is also 19.

The `Abs()` function is the internal function that computes absolute value. Suppose you need to know how many years two employees differ in age. You can compute the absolute value of their age difference to find out as shown here:

```
intAgeDiff = Abs(intEmpAge1 - intEmpAge2)
```

No matter which employee is older, this statement ensures that the positive age difference is stored in the variable named `intAgeDiff`. Without the `Abs()` function, the calculation would produce a negative number if the first employee were younger than the second.

The `Sqr()` function returns the square root of any positive number. The remarks in the following statements describe the results of each `Sqr()` function call:

```
intVal1 = Sqr(4)      ' 2
intVal2 = Sqr(64)     ' 8
intVal3 = Sqr(4096)   ' 16
```

`Sqr()` returns the approximate square root of decimal values as well.

Visual Basic supports several advanced scientific and trigonometric functions. Here is a partial list:

- `Exp()` returns the base of a *natural logarithm* (a value known as *e* which is approximately 2.718282) raised to the power found in the argument.
- `Log()` returns the natural logarithm of the argument.
- `Atn()` returns the arctangent of its argument in radians.
- `Cos()` returns the cosine of its argument in radians.
- `Sin()` returns the sine of its argument in radians.
- `Tan()` returns the tangent of its argument in radians.

If you need to use trigonometric functions that use an argument valued in degrees and not radians, multiply the argument by (*pi* / 180). *pi* is approximately equal to 3.14159.

Data Type Functions

Visual Basic supports several functions that work with the data type of their arguments instead of the argument values:

- The data-inspecting functions `IsDate()`, `IsNull()`, and `IsNumeric()`, and `VarType()`
- The `IIf()` and `Choose()` shortcut functions
- The data type conversion functions

The Data-Inspection Functions

The data-inspection functions inspect data types and special contents of variables. Your programs work with many different kinds of data, and you sometimes don't know in advance what kind of data you have to work with. Before you make a calculation, for example, you want to make sure that the data is numeric.

Table 8.1 lists the `Is()` data inspection functions and provides a description of what they do. Each function receives one argument of the `Variant` data type.

Table 8.1. The `Is()` data-inspection functions test for variable and control contents.

Function Name	*Description*
`IsDate()`	Determines whether its argument is a date data type (or whether the data can be converted to a valid date)
`IsEmpty()`	Determines whether its argument has been initialized
`IsNull()`	Determines whether its argument holds a `Null` value
`IsNumeric()`	Determines whether its argument holds a number (or whether the data can be converted to a valid number)

Note

Each `Is...()` function accepts the `Variant` data type because they must be able to inspect any data and determine what type it is.

The code section shown in Listing 8.3 is rather simple but demonstrates what happens when you apply the `IsEmpty()` function to variables that have and haven't been initialized. You can use `IsEmpty()` to determine if the user has entered a value into a field.

Listing 8.3. Testing for empty variables.

```
' Code that tests the Is() functions
Dim var1 As Variant, var2 As Variant,
Dim var3 As Variant, var4 As Variant
Dim intMsg As Integer   ' MsgBox return
' Fill variables with sample values to test
var1 = 0         ' Zero value
var2 = Null      ' Null value
var3 = ""        ' Null string
' Call each Is() function
If IsEmpty(var1) Then
   intMsg = MsgBox("var1 is empty", vbOKOnly)
End If
If IsEmpty(var2) Then
   intMsg = MsgBox("var2 is empty", vbOKOnly)
End If
If IsEmpty(var3) Then
   intMsg = MsgBox("var3 is empty", vbOKOnly)
End If
If IsEmpty(var4) Then
   intMsg = MsgBox("var4 is empty", vbOKOnly)
End If
```

The only output from this code is a message box that displays the following:

```
var4 is empty
```

You receive this response because all the other variables have some kind of data (they've been initialized).

Use `IsNull()` to see whether a control or field on a report or form contains data. Use `IsEmpty()` just for variables.

`IsNull()`checks its argument and returns true if the argument contains a `Null` value. The value `Null` is a special value that you can assign to variables to indicate either that no data exists or that there's an error. (The way your program interprets a `Null` value depends on how you code the program.)

Caution

Given that you can assign a `Null` value to a variable (as in `varA = Null`), you might be tempted to test for a `Null` value like this:

```
If (varA = Null) Then ....
```

Be warned that such an `If` always fails. Using `IsNull()` is the only way to check for a `Null` value in a variable.

Checking for data is simple. If your Visual Basic procedure needs to know whether a form's text box named `txtHoursWorked` has data, the procedure can check it with an `If` statement, as follows:

```
If IsNull(txtHoursWorked) Then
   intMsg = MsgBox("You didn't enter hours worked!", vbOKOnly)
Else                   ' Thank them for the good hours
   intMsg = MsgBox("Thanks for entering hours worked!", vbOKOnly)
End If
```

This `If` statement checks to ensure that users typed something in the field before the program continues.

`IsNumeric()`checks its argument for a number. Any `Variant` value that can be converted to a number returns a true result in the `IsNumeric()` function and a false result otherwise. The following data types can be converted to numbers:

- Empty (converts to zero)
- Integer

- Long integer
- Single-precision
- Double-precision
- Currency
- Date (returns false always)
- String, if the string "looks" like a valid number

The following code asks users for their age by using a `Variant` variable. The program displays an error message if a user enters a non-numeric number:

```
1:  Dim varAge As Variant
2:  Dim intMsg As Integer   ' MsgBox() return
3:  varAge = InputBox("How old are you?", "Get Your Age")
4:  If IsNumeric(varAge) Then
5:     intMsg = MsgBox("Thanks!", vbOKOnly)
6:  Else
7:     intMsg = MsgBox("What are you trying to hide?", _
       vbOKOnly+vbQuestion)
8:  End If
```

Line 4 ensures that the user entered a numeric age and did not type a word or phrase for the answer.

If you need to know what data type a variable is, use the `VarType()` function. Table 8.2 lists the return values from the `VarType()` function, and `VarType()` returns no other values than the 16 listed in the table.

TABLE 8.2. `VarType()` RETURN VALUES DETERMINE DATA TYPES.

This Value Returned...	*Named Literal*	*If the Variant Contains This Data Type...*
0	`vbEmpty`	`Empty`
1	`vbNull`	`Null`
2	`vbInteger`	`Integer`
3	`vbLong`	`Long`
4	`vbSingle`	`Single`
5	`vbDouble`	`Double`
6	`vbCurrency`	`Currency`
7	`vbDate`	`Date`
8	`vbString`	`String`
9	`vbObject`	`Object`

continues

TABLE 8.2. CONTINUED

This Value Returned...	*Named Literal*	*If the Variant Contains This Data Type...*
10	`vbError`	An error value
11	`vbBoolean`	`Boolean`
12	`vbVariant`	`Variant` (for `Variant` arrays, see Day 10's lesson)
13	`vbDataObject`	A data-access object
14	`vbDecimal`	`Decimal`
17	`vbByte`	`Byte`
8192	`vbArray`	An array (VB adds 8192 to the data type to indicate an array so 8194 indicates an integer array)

The procedure in Listing 8.4 uses a`Select Case` statement to print the data type of whatever data is passed to it.

LISTING 8.4. USE `VarType()` TO DETERMINE THE DATA TYPE PASSED.

```
Private Sub PrntType(varA)   ' Variant if you don't specify otherwise
  Dim intMsg As Integer      ' MsgBox() return
  Select Case VarType(varA) ' VarType() returns an integer
    Case 0
    intMsg = MsgBox("The argument is Empty")
    Case 1
    intMsg = MsgBox("The argument is Null")
    Case 2
    intMsg = MsgBox("The argument is Integer")
    Case 3
    intMsg = MsgBox("The argument is Long")
    Case 4
    intMsg = MsgBox("The argument is Single")
    Case 5
    intMsg = MsgBox("The argument is Double")
    Case 6
    intMsg = MsgBox("The argument is Currency")
    Case 7
    intMsg = MsgBox("The argument is Date")
    Case 8
    intMsg = MsgBox("The argument is String")
    Case 9
    intMsg = MsgBox("The argument is an Object")
    Case 10
    intMsg = MsgBox("The argument is an Error")
    Case 11
```

```
        intMsg = MsgBox("The argument is Boolean")
        Case 12
        intMsg = MsgBox("The argument is a Variant array")
        Case 13
        intMsg = MsgBox("The argument is a Data Access Object")
        Case 14
        intMsg = MsgBox("The argument is Decimal")
        Case 17
        intMsg = MsgBox("The argument is Byte")
        Case Else
        intMsg = MsgBox("The argument is an Array")
      End Select
  End Sub
```

The `IIf()` and `Choose()` Shortcut Functions

A kinder, gentler `If...Else` statement equivalent exists in the form of a function that you can always substitute for single-body `If...Else` statements. The `IIf()` function works a lot like the `@If()` function in popular worksheet programs. The format for `IIf()` follows:

```
IIf(condition, TrueBody, FalseBody)
```

`IIf()` works well only for short `If...Else` statements such as the following:

```
If (curSales < 5000.00) Then
   curBonus = 0.00
Else
   curBonus = 75.00
End If
```

Each of the two bodies of this `If...Else` is a single line long so you can rewrite the `If...Else` like this using a shorter `IIf()` function and assigning the return value to `curBonus`:

```
curBonus = IIf(curSales < 5000.00, 0.00, 75.00)
```

Figure 8.4 shows how this `IIf()` operates.

Although `IIf()` is shorter than an equivalent multi-line `If...Else`, `IIf()` is not as clear as the multi-line `If...Else`. In addition, if you ever have to add to the body of either the true or false side of the `IIf()`, you have to convert the function to a multi-line `If...Else` at that time. Therefore, in most cases, you are better off using the multi-line format of the `If...Else` statement.

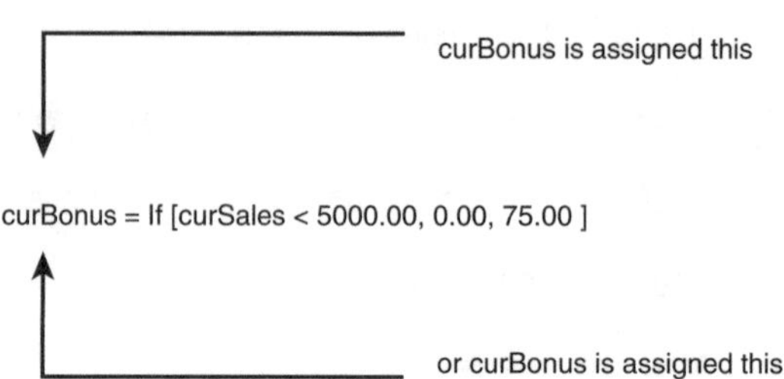
curBonus is assigned this
curBonus = If [curSales < 5000.00, 0.00, 75.00]
or curBonus is assigned this

FIGURE 8.4.
One of two values is assigned to the value at the left of `IIf()`.

You can't divide by zero (division by zero is undefined in mathematics). Therefore, the following `IIf()` function returns an average sale price or a `Null` value if division by zero results:

```
curAveSales = IIf(intQty > 0, curTotalSales / intQty, Null)
```

Visual Basic interprets zero values as false results in all situations. Knowing this, you can rewrite the preceding statement as follows:

```
curAveSales = IIf(intQty, curTotalSales / intQty, Null)
```

The `Choose()` function provides a shortcut for some `Select Case` statements. `Choose()` can have many arguments—more arguments than any other built-in function. Depending on the value of the first argument, `Choose()` returns only one of the remaining arguments. Here's the format of `Choose()`:

```
Choose(intIndexNum, expression[, expression] ...)
```

After the second argument (`expression`), you can have as many expression arguments as needed. *`intIndexNum`* must be a variable or field that equates to a number from 1 to the number of expressions in the function.

If, for example, you need to generate a small table of price codes, abbreviations, or product codes, using `Choose()` is more succinct than using an `If` or `Select Case` statement. `Choose()`, however, is more limited in scope than `If` because `Choose()` selects on an integer value only, not on a more complete comparison.

Caution

`Choose()` returns `Null` if *`intIndexNum`* isn't between 1 and the number of expressions inclusive.

8

The first argument of `Choose()` can be an expression. Therefore, you have to adjust the first argument so that it falls within the range of the number of arguments that follow. If the values possible for the index go from 0 to 4, for example, add 1 to the index so that the range goes from 1 to 5 and selects from the `Choose()` list properly.

Suppose that a form contains a Price Code label. When users enter a new product, they should also enter a price code from 1 to 5, which corresponds to the following codes:

1	Full markup
2	5% discount
3	10% discount
4	Special order
5	Mail order

The following `Choose()` function assigns to a description field the correct description based on the price code:

```
Descript = Choose(lblProdCode, "Full markup", "5% discount", "10% discount",
"Special order", "Mail order")
```

The Data Type Conversion Functions

Table 8.3 describes the data type conversion functions, denoted by their initial letter *C* (for *convert*). Each function converts its argument from one data type to another.

TABLE 8.3. THE DATA TYPE CONVERSION FUNCTIONS CONVERT ONE DATA TYPE TO ANOTHER.

Function Name	*Description*
`CBool()`	Converts its argument to the `Boolean` data type
`CByte()`	Converts its argument to the `Byte` data type
`CCur()`	Converts its argument to the `Currency` data type
`CDate()`	Converts its argument to the `Date` data type
`CDbl()`	Converts its argument to the `Double` data type
`CDec()`	Converts its argument to the `Decimal` data type
`CInt()`	Converts its argument to the `Integer` data type
`CLng()`	Converts its argument to the `Long` data type
`CSng()`	Converts its argument to the `Single` data type
`CStr()`	Converts its argument to the `String` data type
`CVar()`	Converts its argument to the `Variant` data type

You must be able to convert the argument to the target data type. You can't convert the number 123456789 to a `Byte` data type with `CByte()`, for example, because the `Byte` data type can't hold a number that large.

Unlike `Int()` and `Fix()`, `CInt()` returns the closest rounded integer to the argument. For negative numbers, `CInt()` also rounds to the closest whole integer. Look at the remarks to the right of each of the following statements to see what's stored in each variable:

```
intA1 = CInt(8.5)          ' Stores an 8 in intA1
intA2 = CInt(8.5001)       ' Stores a 9 in intA2
```

The following code converts each argument to different data types. Remember that you also can pass these functions expressions that produce numeric results so that you can control the data types of your calculated results before storing them in a field or variable:

```
curVar1 = CCur(123)        ' Converts 123 to currency data type
dblVar2 = CDbl(123)        ' Converts 123 to double-precision data type
sngVar3 = CSng(123)        ' Converts 123 to single-precision data type
varVar4 = CVar(123)        ' Converts 123 to the variant data type
```

The String-Related String Functions

The string-related functions manipulate and analyze string data. One of Visual Basic's greatest strengths over other programming languages, thanks to Visual Basic's BASIC background, is the strong support for string data.

`Len()` Determines Length

`Len()` is one of the few functions that can take either a numeric variable or a string for its argument—although you'll use `Len()` primarily for string data. `Len()` returns the number of memory bytes needed to hold its argument. Here's the format of `Len()`:

```
Len(Expression)
```

`Len()` accepts any string value (variable, literal, or expression). However, only numeric variables, not numeric literals or expressions, work as `Len()` arguments.

`Len()` returns the length (number of characters) of the string variable, string constant, or string expression inside its parentheses. The following `MsgBox()` function displays a 6 as its output:

```
intMsg = MsgBox(Len("abcdef"))
```

If the string contains `Null`, `Len()` returns a value of 0. Testing for a null string lets you test to see whether a user entered data in response to an `InputBox()` function or a control value.

Converting Strings

Several conversion functions work with string data. Table 8.4 describes each string-conversion function used in the following examples.

TABLE 8.4. THE STRING-CONVERSION FUNCTIONS CONVERT TO AND FROM THE `String` DATA TYPE.

Function Name	*Description*
`CStr()`	Changes its argument to a string
`Str()`	Converts its numeric argument to a string (actually, to a `Variant` data type that you can use as a string)
`Val()`	Converts its string argument to a number, assuming that you pass `Val()` a string-like number

`CStr()` and `Str()` convert their arguments to string values. The only difference is that `CStr()` doesn't add a leading blank before positive numbers converted to strings; `Str()` does. Listing 8.5 demonstrates the difference between `CStr()` and `Str()`.

LISTING 8.5. `Str()` ADDS A LEADING BLANK BEFORE POSITIVE NUMBERS THAT `CStr()` DOES NOT ADD.

```
Private Sub convStr ()
  Dim str1 As String, s2 As String
  Dim intMsg As Integer   ' For button clicked
  str1 = CStr(12345)
  str2 = Str(12345)
  intMsg = MsgBox("***" & str1 & "***")
  intMsg = MsgBox("***" & str2 & "***")
End Sub
```

Line 6 produces a message box that displays `***12345***`, and Line 7 displays `*** 12345***`. Notice the blank before the number that `Str()` added.

The ASCII Functions

Use `Chr()`and `Asc()` to convert strings to and from their numeric ASCII values. The ASCII table lists every possible character available on the PC and assigns a sequential number (an *ASCII code*) to each character.

By putting a number inside the `Chr()` parentheses, you can produce the character that corresponds to that number in the ASCII table. By using `Chr()`, you can generate characters for variables and controls that don't appear on your computer's keyboard but that do appear in the ASCII table.

The `Asc()` function is a mirror image of `Chr()`. Whereas `Chr()` takes a numeric argument and returns a string character, `Asc()` requires a string argument and converts that argument to its corresponding ASCII table number.

Therefore, an A is stored in `strVar` in the following assignment statement because the ASCII value of A is 65:

```
strVar = Chr(65)    ' Stores an A in aVar
```

Of course, it makes more sense to store an A directly in the `strVar` variable in the preceding example's statement. But what if you want to ask a Spanish question inside a message box? Spanish questions always begin with an upside-down question mark, and no upside-down question mark appears on your keyboard. Therefore, you can resort to using `Chr()` as follows:

```
' Chr(241) produces an n with a tilde over it
strMyQuest = Chr(164) & "Se" & Chr(169) & "or, como esta?"
intMsg = MsgBox(strMyQuest)
```

Figure 8.5 shows the message box displayed from this code.

`Asc()` returns the ASCII number of the character argument you give it. You can find the ASCII numbers by searching Visual Basic's online help. The argument must be a string of one or more. If you pass `Asc()` a string of more than one character, it returns the ASCII number of the first character in the string.

The following code demonstrates a good use for `Asc()`:

```
strAns = InputBox("Do you want to see the name")
If ((Asc(strAns) = 89) Or (Asc(strAns) = 121)) Then
   b = MsgBox("The name is " + aName)
End If
```

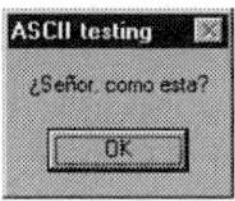

FIGURE 8.5.
Use ASCII characters to display characters not on the keyboard.

The user can answer the prompt with y, Y, Yes, or YES. The `If...Then` test works for any of those input values because 89 is the ASCII value for Y, and 121 is the ASCII value of y. `Asc()` returns the ASCII value of its string argument's first letter.

The Substring Functions

The substring functions return parts of strings. `Right()` returns characters from the right side of a string. `Right()`'s cousin, `Left()`, returns characters from the left side of a string. `Mid()` takes up where `Right()` and `Left()` fail—`Mid()` lets you pick characters from the middle of a string.

Here are the formats of the substring functions:

```
Left(stringValue, numericValue)
Right(stringValue, numericValue)
Mid(stringValue, startPosition[, length])
```

The following section of code demonstrates `Left()`:

```
strA = "abcdefg"
partSt1 = Left(strA, 1)    ' Stores a
partSt2 = Left(strA, 3)    ' Stores abc
partSt3 = Left(strA, 20)   ' Stores abcdefg
```

> **Note:** If you try to return more characters from the left of the string than exist, `Left()` returns the entire string.

`Right()` works in the same manner as `Left()`, except that it returns the rightmost characters from a string:

```
strA = "abcdefg"
partSt1 = Right(strA, 1)    ' Stores g
partSt2 = Right(strA, 3)    ' Stores efg
partSt3 = Right(strA, 20)   ' Stores abcdefg
```

`Mid()` accomplishes what `Left()` and `Right()` can't—it returns characters from the middle of a string. `Mid()` uses three arguments: a string followed by two integers. The first integer determines where `Mid()` begins stripping characters from the string (the position, starting at 1), and the second integer determines how many characters from that position to return. If you don't specify two integers, `Mid()` uses 1 as the starting position.

`Mid()` can pull any number of characters from anywhere in the string. The following example shows how the `Mid()` function works:

```
strA = "Visual Basic FORTRAN COBOL C Pascal"
lang1 = Mid(strA, 1, 12)   ' Stores Visual Basic
lang2 = Mid(strA, 14, 7)   ' Stores FORTRAN
lang3 = Mid(strA, 22, 5)   ' Stores COBOL
lang4 = Mid(strA, 28, 1)   ' Stores C
lang5 = Mid(strA, 30, 6)   ' Stores Pascal
```

If you don't specify the *`length`* argument, VB returns all the characters to the right of the starting position. If the length is longer than the rest of the string, VB ignores the *`length`* argument.

Note

`Mid()` works both as a command and a function. It works as a command when it appears on the left side of an assignment statement's equal sign; it's a function when it appears anywhere else. Following is its format:

```
Mid(string, start[, length])
```

When you use the `Mid()` statement, `Mid()` changes the contents of the string used inside the statement's parentheses. The following code initializes a string with three words and then changes the middle word with `Mid()`:

```
strSentence = "Rain in Spain"
' Change the middle word
Mid(strSentence, 6, 2) = "on"
' After the change
intMsg = MsgBox("After change: " & strSentence)
' Prints Rain on Spain
```

Converting to Uppercase and Lowercase

The `UCase()` function returns its string argument in all uppercase letters. `LCase()` returns its string argument in all lowercase letters. The following `MsgBox()` function displays `VISUAL BASIC`:

```
intMsg = MsgBox(UCase("Visual Basic"))
```

Justifying and Trimming Strings

`LTrim()` and `RTrim()` trim spaces from the beginning or end of a string. `LTrim()` returns the argument's string without any leading spaces. `RTrim()` returns the argument's string without any trailing spaces. The `Trim()` function trims leading and trailing spaces.

Here are the formats of the string-trimming functions:

```
LTrim(stringExpression)
RTrim(stringExpression)
Trim(stringExpression)
```

The following statements trim spaces from the beginning, end, or both sides of strings:

```
st1 = LTrim("      Hello")  ' Stores Hello
st2 = RTrim("Hello      ")  ' Stores Hello
st3 = Trim("   Hello    ")  ' Stores Hello
```

Without the trimming functions, the spaces are copied into the target variables as well as the word *Hello*.

`Str()` always converts positive numbers to strings with a leading blank (where the imaginary plus sign appears); therefore, you can combine `LTrim()` with `Str()` to eliminate the leading blank. The first of the following two statements stores the leading blank in `str1`. The second uses `LTrim()` to get rid of the blank before storing the string into `str2`:

```
str1 = Str(234)            ' Stores " 234"
str2 = LTrim(Str(234))     ' Stores "234"
```

The following `ReverseIt()` function includes several of the string functions described in today's lesson. This function, shown in Listing 8.6, reverses a certain number of characters within a string.

LISTING 8.6. THIS FUNCTION REVERSES A STRING BY USING THE STRING FUNCTIONS.

```
Public Function ReverseIt (strS As String, ByVal n As Integer) As _
String
' Accepts: a string and an integer indicating the number of
'          characters to reverse
' Purpose: reverses the specified number of characters in the
'          specified string
' Returns: the modified string

' Reverses the first n characters in s.

    Dim strTemp As String, intI As Integer

     If n > Len(strS) Then n = Len(strS)
     For intI = n To 1 Step -1
         strTemp = strTemp + Mid(strS, intI, 1)
     Next intI
     ReverseIt = strTemp + Right(strS, Len(strS) - n)
 End Function
```

Suppose that the `ReverseIt()` function is called with the following statement:

```
newStr = ReverseIt ("Visual Basic", 6)
```

If all goes well, the string named `newStr` will hold the characters `lausiV Basic` (the first six characters are reversed). Line 10 declares two local variables, the first of which, a string variable named `strTemp`, holds the reversed string as it's being built. The second variable, `intI`, is used in the `For` loop.

Starting with version 6, Visual Basic now includes a string function named `StrReverse()` that returns the reversed string of its single string argument. Listing 8.6, although certainly not as efficient as using `StrReverse()`, does help demonstrate the `Mid()` function.

Line 12's `If` statement ensures that the integer passed to `ReverseIt()` isn't larger than the length of the string passed. It's impossible to reverse more charactersthan exist in the string. If more characters are passed, the `If` statement ensures that the entire string is reversed by changing the length to reverse to the exact length of the string via the `Len()` function.

In line 13, the `For` loop then counts down, from the position to reverse (stored in `n`) to 1. By using the `Mid()` function in line 14, Visual Basic concatenates one character from the string, at position `n`, to the new string being built. As `n` reaches 1, the reversed characters are sent to the new string in line 14. After all the characters that need to be reversed are reversed, the rightmost portion of the passed string is concatenated as is to the reversed characters.

Special Functions

Visual Basic offers date and time functions that help you analyze and manipulate date and time values. Such functions are critical for recording exactly when a field was edited for security or verification purposes. Also, all printed reports should have the date and time (often called *date-* and *time-stamping*) printed on the report, showing exactly when the report was produced. In a stack of like reports, the date and time stamps show when the latest report was printed.

In addition to the date and time functions, Visual Basic supports a special data-formatting function that you can use to display formatted strings.

8

Working with Dates and Times

Your Windows settings determine the format of the `Date` and `Time` return values. For example, on many systems the `Date` function returns the system date in the `Variant` data type in the following format:

mm-dd-yyyy

where *mm* is a month number (from 01 to 12), *dd* is a day number (from 01 to 31), and *yyyy* is a year number (from 1980 to 2099). The `Date` requires no parentheses because `Date` is one of the few functions that accepts no arguments.

`Time` returns the system time in the `Variant` data type in the following format:

hh:*mm*:*ss*

where *hh* is the hour (from 00 to 23), *mm* is the minute (from 00 to 59), and *ss* is the second (from 00 to 59).

`Time` uses a 24-hour clock. Therefore, all hours before 1:00:00 in the afternoon equate to a.m. time values, and all times from 1:00:00 until midnight have 12 added to them so 14:30 is 2:30 in the afternoon.

`Now` combines the `Date` and `Time` functions. `Now` returns a `Variant` data type in the following format (if you were to print the `Variant` return value of `Now` in a message box, you'd see this format):

mm/*dd*/*yy* *hh*:*mm*:*ss* AM¦PM

where the placeholder letters correspond to those of the `Date` and `Time` functions, with the exception that a 12-hour clock is used and either `AM` or `PM` appears next to the time. The vertical line in the format indicates that either `AM` *or* `PM` appears, but not both at once.

The most important thing to remember about all three date and time retrieval functions is that they return date and time values that are stored internally as double-precision values (with enough precision to ensure that the date and time values are stored accurately). The best way to format date and time values is to use `Format()`, which you learn about in today's final section.

Assuming that it's exactly 9:45 in the morning, the statement

```
currentTime = Time
```

stores 9:45:00 in the variable `currentTime`. If the date is 2/23/99, the statement

```
currentDate = Date
```

stores 2/23/99 in the variable `currentDate`. The statement

```
currentDateTime = Now
```

stores 2/23/99 9:45:00 AM in the variable `currentDateTime`.

Note

When you enter date and time values, you must enclose them between pound signs such as the following:

```
#11/21/1993#
```

Because there are several date formats, just about any way you're used to specifying the date is recognized by Visual Basic. As long as you enclose the date between pound signs, you can use any of the following formats when specifying a date:

```
mm-dd-yy
mm-dd-yyyy
mm/dd/yy
mm/dd/yyyy
monthName dd, yyyy
mmm dd, yyyy (where mmm is an abbreviated month name, _
as in Dec)
dd monthName yy
dd-mmm-yy (where mmm is an abbreviated month name, as in Dec)
```

Here are some of the ways you can express the time:

```
hh
hh:mm
hh:mm:ss
```

You must use a 24-hour clock with `Time`.

Computing the Time Between Events

The `Timer` function returns the number of seconds since your computer's internal clock struck midnight. The format of `Timer` is simple:

```
Timer
```

As you can see, `Timer` is a function that accepts no arguments and is one of the rare times that you don't specify the parentheses after a function. `Timer` is perfect for timing an event. For example, you can ask users a question and determine how long it took them to answer. First, save the value of `Timer` before you ask users; then subtract that value from the value of `Timer` after they answer. The difference of the two `Timer` values is the number of seconds users took to answer. Listing 8.7 shows a procedure that does just that.

LISTING 8.7. YOU CAN TIME THE USER'S RESPONSE.

```
1:  Public Sub CompTime ()
2:  ' Procedure that times the user's response
3:    Dim intMsg As Integer   ' MsgBox() return
4:    Dim varBefore, varAfter, varTimeDiff As Variant
5:    Dim intMathAns As Integer
6:    varBefore = Timer     ' Save the time before asking
7:    intMathAns = Inputbox("What is 150 + 235?")
8:    varAfter = Timer      ' Save the time after answering
9:    ' The difference between the time values
10:   ' is how many seconds the user took to answer
11:   varTimeDiff = varAfter - varBefore
12:   intMsg = MsgBox("That took you only" + Str(varTimeDiff) & " seconds!")
13: End Sub
```

Line 6 stores the number of seconds since midnight before asking for an answer. Line 7 asks for an answer and, as soon as the user types an answer, line 8 immediately stores the number of seconds since midnight at that point. The difference, computed in line 11, determines how long the user took to answer.

`Timer` finds the number of seconds between time values, but only for those time values that fall on the same day. `DateAdd()`, `DateDiff()`, and `DatePart()` take up where `Timer` leaves off. Table 8.4 lists these three date arithmetic functions and their descriptions.

TABLE 8.4. THE DATE ARITHMETIC FUNCTIONS COMPARE DATE VALUES.

Function Name	*Description*
`DateAdd()`	Returns a new date after you add a value to a date
`DateDiff()`	Returns the difference between two dates
`DatePart()`	Returns part (an element) from a given date

All three date arithmetic functions can work with the parts of dates listed in Table 8.5. Table 8.5 contains the parts of dates these functions work with, as well as their interval values that label each part. You use the interval values inside the date arithmetic functions to get to a piece of a date or time.

TABLE 8.5. THE DATE ARITHMETIC FUNCTIONS WORK WITH THESE TIME PERIOD VALUES.

Interval Value	*Time Period*
`yyyy`	Year
`q`	Quarter
`m`	Month
`y`	Day of year
`d`	Day
`w`	Weekday (Sunday is 1, Monday is 2, and so on for `Day()`, `Month()`, `Year()`, and `DateDiff()`)
`ww`	Week
`h`	Hour
`n`	Minute (note that it's not `m`)
`s`	Second

Despite its name, `DateAdd()` works with both dates and times (as do all the date functions) because the date passed to `DateAdd()` must appear in a `Date` data type format. Here's the format of `DateAdd()`:

```
DateAdd(interval, number, oldDate)
```

The *`interval`* must be a value (in string form) from Table 8.5. The interval you specify determines what time period is added or subtracted (a second value, minute value, or whatever). The *`number`* value specifies how many of the interval values you want to add. Make *`interval`* positive if you want to add to a date; make *`interval`* negative if you want to subtract from a date. The *`oldDate`* is the date or time from which you want to work (the date or time you're adding to or subtracting from). The *`oldDate`* doesn't change. The `DateAdd()` function then returns the new date.

Suppose that you buy something today with a credit card that has a 25-day grace period. The following statement adds 25 days to today's date and stores the result in `intStarts`:

```
intStarts = DateAdd("y", 25, Now)
```

The date stored in `intStarts` is the date 25 days from today.

You can use either `"y"`, `"d"`, or `"w"` for the interval if you're adding days to a date.

Suppose that you work for a company that requires 10 years before you're vested in the retirement program. The following statement adds 10 years to your start date and stores the vested date in `vested`:

```
vested = DateAdd("yyyy", 10, hired)
```

Notice that the interval string value determines what's added to the date.

For any of the date arithmetic functions, if you don't specify a year, the current year (the year set on the system's clock) is returned.

`DateDiff()`returns the difference between two dates. Embed `DateDiff()` inside `Abs()` if you want to ensure a positive value. The difference is expressed in the interval that you specify. Here's the format of `DateDiff()`:

```
DateDiff(interval, date1, date2)
```

The following statement determines how many years an employee has worked for a company:

```
beenWith = Abs(DateDiff("yyyy", hireDate, Now))
```

`DatePart()` returns a part of a date (the part specified by the interval). With `DatePart()`, you can find what day, month, week, or hour (or whatever other interval you specify) that a date falls on. Here's the format of `DatePart()`:

```
DatePart(interval, date)
```

The following statement stores the day number that an employee started working:

```
DatePart("w", hireDate)
```

The date and time functions you've been reading about work with *serial values*. These values actually are stored as double-precision values to ensure the full storage of date and time and that accurate date arithmetic can be performed.

A *serial value* is the internal representation of a date or time, stored in a `VarType 7` (the `Date` data type) or a `Variant` data type.

The following is the format of the `DateSerial()` function:

```
DateSerial(year, month, day)
```

`year` is an integer year number (either 00 to 99 for 1900 to 1999, or a four-digit year number) or expression; *`month`* is an integer month number (1 to 12) or expression; and *`day`* is an integer day number (1 to 31) or expression. If you include an expression for

any of the integer arguments, you specify the number of years, months, or days from or since a value. To clarify the serial argument expressions, you use the following two `DateSerial()` function calls, which return the same value:

```
d = DateSerial(1998, 10, 6)
```

and

```
d = DateSerial(1988+10, 12-2, 1+5)
```

The `DateSerial()` functions ensure that your date arguments don't go out of bounds. For example, 1996 was a leap year, so February 1996 had 29 days. However, the following `DateSerial()` function call appears to produce an invalid date because February, even in leap years, can't have 30 days:

```
d = DateSerial(1996, 2, 29+1)
```

Nothing is wrong with this function call because `DateSerial()` adjusts the date evaluated so that `d` holds March 1, 1996, one day following the last day of February. The function in Listing 8.8 contains an interesting use of the `DateSerial()` function.

LISTING 8.8. THIS CODE CALCULATES THE NEXT WEEKDAY VALUE AFTER A SPECIFIED DATE.

```
Function DueDate (dteAnyDate) As Variant
' Accepts: a Date value
' Purpose: Calculates the first non-weekend day of the month
'           following the specified date
' Returns: the calculated date

    Dim varResult As Variant

    If Not IsNull(dteAnyDate) Then
        varResult = DateSerial(Year(dteAnyDate), Month(dteAnyDate) + 1, 1)
         If Weekday(varResult) = 1 Then      ' Sunday, so add one day.
             DueDate = Result + 1
         ElseIf Weekday(varResult) = 7 Then  ' Saturday, so add two days.
             DueDate = varResult + 2
         Else
             DueDate = varResult
         End If
     Else
         varResult = Null
    End If
End Function
```

When this function is called, it's passed a date value stored in the `Variant` or `VarType 7 Date` data type. As the remarks tell, the function computes the number of the first weekday (2 for Monday through 6 for Friday) of the next month (the first business day of the month following the argument).

The `DateValue()` function is similar to `DateSerial()`, except that `DateValue()` accepts a string argument, as the following format shows:

```
DateValue(stringDateExpression)
```

`stringDateExpression` must be a string that VB recognizes as a date (such as those for the `Date` statement described earlier in this section). If you ask the user to enter a date a value at a time (asking for the year, then the month, and then the day), you can use `DateValue()` to convert those values to an internal serial date. If you ask the user to enter a full date (that you capture into a string variable) such as October 19, 1999, `DateValue()` converts that string to the serial format needed for dates.

The `TimeSerial()` and `TimeValue()` functions work the same as their date counterparts. If you have three individual values for a time of day, `TimeSerial()` converts those values to an internal time format(the `Variant` or `VarType 7`). Here's the format of `TimeSerial()`:

```
TimeSerial(hour, minute, second)
```

`TimeSerial()` accepts expressions for any of its arguments and adjusts those expressions as needed, just as `DateSerial()` does.

If you have a string with a time value (maybe the user entered the time), `TimeValue()` converts that string to a time value with this format:

```
TimeValue(stringTimeExpression)
```

`Day()`, `Month()`, and `Year()` each convert their date arguments (of `Variant` or `VarType 7` data type) to a day number, month number, or year number. These three functions are simple:

```
Day(dateArgument)
Month(dateArgument)
Year(dateArgument)
```

Also, `Weekday()` returns the number of the day of the week (refer to Table 8.5) for the date argument passed to it.

Pass today's date (found with `Now`) to `Day()`, `Month()`, and `Year()` as shown here:

```
d = Day(Now)
m = Month(Now)
y = Year(Now)
```

The current date's day of month number (refer to Table 8.5), month number, and year are stored in the three variables.

The `Format()` Function

One of the most powerful and complex functions, `Format()`, returns its argument in a different format from how the argument was passed. Here's the format of the `Format()` function:

```
Format(expression, format)
```

`Format()` returns a `Variant` data type that you'll almost always use as a string. The expression can be any numeric or string expression. You can format all kinds of data—numbers, strings, dates, and times—to look differently. For example, you might want to print check amounts with commas and a dollar sign.

The format is a string variable or expression that contains one or more of the display-format characters shown in Tables 8.6 through 8.8. The table that you use depends on the kind of data (string, numeric, or date) that you want to format. The tables are long, but after looking at a few examples, you'll learn how to use the display-format characters.

TABLE 8.6. THESE CHARACTERS FORMAT STRING DISPLAYS.

Symbol	*Description*
`@`	A character appears in the output at the `@` position. If there's no character at the `@`'s position in the string, a blank appears. The `@` fills (if there are more than one) from right to left.
`&`	This character is just like `@`, except that nothing appears if no character at the `&`'s position appears in the string being printed.
!	The exclamation point forces all placeholder characters (the `@` and `&`) to fill from left to right.
<	Less-than forces all characters to lowercase.
>	Greater-than forces all characters to uppercase.

TABLE 8.7. THESE CHARACTERS FORMAT NUMERIC DISPLAYS.

Symbol	*Description*
Null string, `""`	This string displays the number without formatting.
`0`	A digit appears in the output at the `0` position if a digit appears in the number being formatted. If no digit is at the `0`'s position, a `0` appears. If not as many zeros in the number are being formatted as there are zeros in the format field, leading or trailing zeros print. If the number contains more

Symbol	Description
	numeric positions, the `0` forces all digits to the right of the decimal point to round to the display-format's pattern and all digits to the left print as is. You mostly use this display-format character to print leading or trailing zeros when you want them.
#	The pound-sign character works like `0`, except that nothing appears if the number being formatted doesn't have as many digits as the display-format has #s.
.	The period specifies how many digits (by its placement within `0` or #s) are to appear to the left and right of a decimal point.
%	The number being formatted is multiplied by 100, and the percent sign (%) is printed at its position inside the display-format string.
,	If a comma appears among `0`s or #s, the thousands are easier to read because the comma groups every three places in the number (unless the number is below 1,000). If you put two commas together, you request that the number be divided by 1,000 (to scale down the number).
`E-`, `E+`, `e-`, `e+`	The number is formatted into scientific notation if the format also contains at least one `0` or #.
:	The colon causes colons to appear between a time's hour, minute, and second values.
/	The slash ensures that slashes are printed between a date's day, month, and year values.
-, +, $, space	All these characters appear as is in their position within the formatted string.
\	Whatever character follows the backslash appears at its position in the formatted string.

TABLE 8.8. THESE CHARACTERS FORMAT DATE DISPLAYS.

Symbol	Description
`c`	Displays either the date (just like the `ddddd` symbol if only a date appears), the time (just like `ttttt` if only a time appears), or both if both values are present.
`d`	Displays the day number from 1 to 31.
`dd`	Displays the day number with a leading zero from 01 to 31.
`ddd`	Displays an abbreviated three-character day from `Sun` to `Sat`.
`dddd`	Displays the full day name from `Sunday` to `Saturday`.

continues

TABLE 8.8. CONTINUED

Symbol	*Description*
`ddddd`	Displays the date (month, day, year) according to your settings in the International section of your Control Panel's Short Date format (usually *m/d/yy*).
`dddddd`	Displays the date (month, day, year) according to your settings in the International section of your Control Panel's Long Date format (usually *mmmm dd, yyyy*).
`w, ww`	Refer to Table 8.5.
`m`	Displays the month number from `1` to `12`. The `m` also means minute if it follows an `h` or `hh`.
`mm`	Displays the month number with a leading zero from `01` to `12`. The `mm` also means minute if it follows an `h` or `hh`.
`mmm`	Displays the abbreviated month name from `Jan` to `Dec`.
`mmmm`	Displays the full month name from `January` to `December`.
`q`	Displays the quarter of the year.
`y`	Displays the year's day number from `1` to `366`.
`yy`	Displays the two-digit year from `00` to `99` (when the year 2000 hits, `yy` still returns only the 2-digit year).
`yyyy`	Displays the full year number from `1000` to `9999`.
`h, n, s`	Refer to Table 8.5.
`ttttt`	Displays the time according to your settings in the International section of your Control Panel's Time format (usually `h:nn:ss`).
`AMPM`	Uses the 12-hour clock time and displays `AM` or `PM`.
`ampm`	Uses the 12-hour clock time and displays `am` or `pm`.
`AP`	Uses the 12-hour clock time and displays `A` or `P`.
`ap`	Uses the 12-hour clock time and displays `a` or `p`.

The following statements demonstrate the string display-format characters. The remarks to the right of each statement explain that the target variable (the variable on the left of the equal sign) is receiving formatted data:

```
strS = Format("AbcDef", ">")    ' ABCDEF is assigned
strS = Format("AbcDef", "<")    ' abcdef is assigned
strS = Format("2325551212", "(@@@) @@@-@@@@")    ' (232) 555-1212
```

As the last statement shows, you can put string data into the format you prefer. If the data to be formatted, such as the phone number in the last line, is a string variable from a table's text field, the `Format()` statement works just the same.

Suppose that it's possible to leave out the area code of the phone number that you want to print. `Format()` fills from right to left, so the statement

```
strS = Format("5551212", "(@@@) @@@-@@@@")
```

stores the following in `strS`:

```
(   ) 555-1212
```

If you had included the area code, it would have printed inside the parentheses.

Only use the `!` when you want the fill to take place from the other direction (when data at the end of the string being formatted might be missing). The statement

```
strS = Format("5551212", "!(@@@) @@@-@@@@")
```

incorrectly stores the following in `strS`:

```
(555) 121-2
```

Listing 8.9 demonstrates how numeric formatting works. The remark to the right of each statement describes how the data is formatted.

LISTING 8.9. YOU CAN LEARN HOW `Format()` WORKS BY STUDYING EXAMPLES.

```
strS = Format(9146, "¦######¦")  ' ¦9146¦ is stored
strS = Format(2652.2, "00000.00") ' 02652.20 is stored
strS = Format(2652.2, "#####.##") ' 2652.2 is stored
strS = Format(2652.216, "#####.##") ' 2652.22 is stored
strS = Format(45, "+###") ' Stores a +45
strS = Format(45, "-###") ' Stores a -45
strS = Format(45, "###-") ' Stores a 45-
strS = Format(2445, "$####.##")   ' Stores a $2445.
strS = Format(2445, "$####.00")  ' Stores a $2445.00
strS = Format(2445, "00Hi00")  ' Stores 24Hi45
```

Listing 8.10 demonstrates how date and time formatting works. The remark to the right of each statement describes how the data is formatted.

LISTING 8.10. USE `Format()` TO FORMAT DATE AND TIME VALUES.

```
Dim varD As Variant
varD = Now       ' Assume the date and time is
                 ' May 21, 1999 2:30 PM
strND = Format(varD, "c") ' Stores 5/21/99 2:30:02 PM
strND = Format(varD, "w") ' Stores 6 (for Friday)
strND = Format(varD, "ww")' Stores 22
```

continues

LISTING 8.10. CONTINUED

```
strND = Format(varD, "dddd") ' Stores Friday
strND = Format(varD, "q") ' Stores 2
strND = Format(varD, "hh") ' Stores 14
strND = Format(varD, "h AM/PM") ' Stores 2 PM
strND = Format(varD, "hh AM/PM") ' Stores 02 PM
strND = Format(varD, "d-mmmm h:nn:ss") 'Stores 21-May 14:30:02
```

Summary

Today's lesson explained the overall Visual Basic program structure. When writing programs with several modules and procedures, you must keep in mind the variable scope so that procedures have access to the data they need. In most cases, a variable should be local, so you'll have to pass arguments between procedures that need access to one another's data. In writing procedures, you'll write both subroutine and function procedures. In creating these procedures, you'll create your own library of routines that you can load into other applications.

In addition to the procedures you write, Visual Basic contains an extensive collection of internal functions that analyze and manipulate numbers, strings, and other data values. The internal functions are available from any module at any time so you can use them when you want them.

Tomorrow's lesson returns to the visual nature of Visual Basic and shows you how to add standard dialog boxes to your applications.

Q&A

Q Why aren't there local and global controls?

A All controls must be available to all code and therefore, in a sense, all controls are public to all code. The controls are public because they truly are separate from code. Unless you create control variables and store the contents of a control's properties in a control variable, you never have to worry about the scope of controls.

Workshop

The Workshop provides quiz questions to help you solidify your understanding of the material covered and exercises to provide you with experience in using what you've learned. Try to understand the quiz and exercise answers before continuing to the next chapter. Answers are provided in Appendix A, "Answers to Exercises."

Quiz

1. Which variable—scope-local, module-level, or public—has the broadest scope?
2. Which variable—scope-local, module-level, or public—has the narrowest scope?
3. True/False. The keyword `ByRef` is optional.
4. How many values can a subroutine procedure return?
5. Name two functions that act as shortcuts to the `If` statement.
6. What happens if the first argument of `Choose()` is less than 1?
7. What does `Abs()` do?
8. What's stored in the variable named `strS` in each of the following statements?

   a.`strS = Format("74135", "&&&&&-&&&&")`

   b.`strS = Format(d, "h ampm")`

   c.`strS = Format(12345.67, "######.###")`
9. Without looking at an ASCII table, what does `intN` hold after the following assignment statement completes?

   `intN = Asc(Chr(192))`
10. What's the difference between the `Now` function and the `Time` function?

Exercises

1. Rewrite Listing 8.1 so that `SalesTax()` is a function procedure that returns the computed sales tax to the calling procedure. Have the calling procedure, `GetTotal()`, use a `MsgBox()` function to print the sales tax computed by `SalesTax()`.
2. Rewrite the following `If` statement as an `IIf()` function:

```
If (intTotal >1000) Then
   strTitle = "Good job!"
Else
   strTitle = "Didn't meet goal"
End If
```

3. Rewrite the following `If` statement as a `Choose()` function:

```
If (ID = 1) Then
  intBonus = 50
ElseIf (ID = 2) Then
  intBonux = 75
ElseIf (ID = 3) Then
  intBonus = 100
End If
```

4. What values are assigned in these statements?

```
intN = Int(-5.6)
intO = Fix(-5.6)
intP = CInt(-5.6)
```

WEEK 2

DAY 9

The Dialog Box Control

Today's lesson shows you how to add dialog boxes to your applications. You won't just randomly create dialog boxes, however. Instead, you'll take advantage of a special control called the Common Dialog Box control that produces six different common dialog boxes that you can use in your applications. When your user needs to select from a file list or print a report from within your Visual Basic application, the Common Dialog Box control helps you display a standard dialog box that the user will recognize.

Today, you learn the following:

- Why common dialog boxes are important for user acceptance
- How to place the Common Dialog Box control
- The Common Dialog Box control methods needed to produce dialog boxes
- Properties you assign that set up the proper dialog box options
- How to respond to a dialog box
- The `On Error Goto` statement that lets you know when the user clicks the dialog box's Cancel button

The Need for a Common Dialog Box

The more your application matches the look and feel of popular Windows applications, such as Microsoft Word, the more likely your users will adapt quickly to your application. If you write software to sell, you know the importance of user acceptance, especially when it comes to convincing the user to purchase future upgrades. If you don't write software to sell but you write programs for a company whom you work for, happy users means fewer maintenance calls and more productivity points for you.

Therefore, when you write an application that opens a file or prints to the printer, you can do one of the following:

- Mimic the style of other applications' dialog boxes that perform the same tasks
- Write your own dialog boxes hoping to improve upon the style of standard dialog boxes

Although you can probably improve upon the style of a dialog box that appears when a user selects File, Open, it is not prudent to do so. For one thing, your application will then *not* be standard! Your users will have a learning curve when they must master a dialog box to do exactly what they already know how to do in most other Windows applications. In addition, your programming requirements will be heavier because it will take you longer to write programs that don't use standard dialog boxes for common tasks.

Do	Don't
DO create standard applications that have the same menu and dialog box structure as most Windows applications.	

The reason you will take longer to create the application is because Visual Basic includes a *Common Dialog Box control* with which you can add the following dialog boxes to your applications and you don't have to design the dialog boxes yourself. These dialog boxes will look and behave exactly like the dialog boxes in standard Windows programs:

- **Color selection**—Displays a dialog box in which users can select a color from a palette of colors and even customize colors.
- **Font selection**—Displays a dialog box in which users can select font styles and sizes.

- **Open File**—Displays a dialog box that lets users select a filename to open from folders, drives, and even from network PCs.
- **Print selection**—Displays a dialog box that lets users select a printer and print settings for any Windows printer.
- **Save File**—Displays a dialog box that lets users specify a filename to save to from folders, drives, and even from network PCs.
- **WinHelp**—Starts the Windows help engine and displays an initial dialog box the user can select from to get help you've provided for your application.

The *Common Dialog Box control* is a control you can add to your applications that produce one of several standard dialog boxes with very little effort on your part.

Without the Common Dialog Box control, you can create dialog boxes that mimic the standard dialog boxes, but you are then responsible for placing all the text boxes, scroll bars, list boxes, and other dialog box elements exactly where they go on a form. Writing dialog boxes can be tedious even though they are little more than controls on forms. If you use the Common Dialog Box control, your time is better used elsewhere in the application.

The dialog boxes that the Common Dialog Box control produce are *modal*.

A *modal* dialog box is one that the user must close, by clicking OK or Cancel, before he or she can continue with any other part of the application.

Adding the Common Dialog Box Control

If you look through the controls on the toolbox, you won't find the Common Dialog Box control. Visual Basic does not place all possible controls on the toolbox because the Toolbox window would take up too much room and you just don't need all the possible controls available at all times. Nevertheless, when you want to place a dialog box in an application that matches one of the common dialog boxes, you'll have to add the Common Dialog Box control to your Toolbox window.

To add the control, perform these steps:

1. Press Ctrl+T (the shortcut keystroke for Project, Components) to display the Components dialog box shown in Figure 9.1.

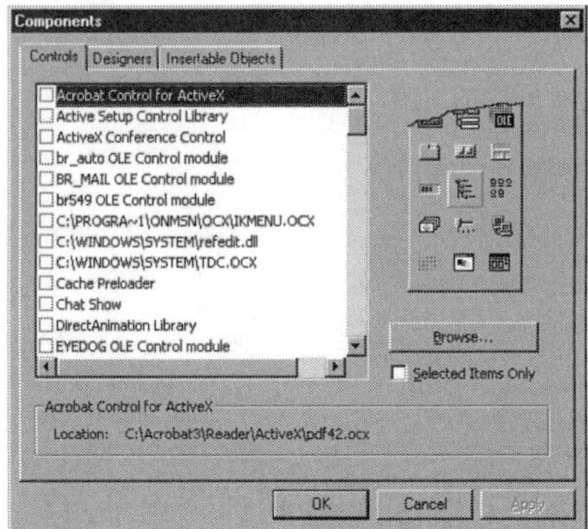

FIGURE 9.1.

The Components dialog box lists the available controls on your system that you can add to your toolbox.

2. Scroll to the control labeled *Microsoft Common Dialog Control 6.0.*
3. Select the entry and click OK. The last control in your toolbox will now be the Common Dialog Box control.

Look through the items in the Project, Components menu option for other controls you can add. These are all ActiveX controls. Most of them are named so that you recognize what the controls do from their names. For example, the Microsoft Calendar Control 8.0 is a control that lets you add calendar operations to your application, such as you might need if you were writing a personal information organizer or a time billing application. You can search through the controls' properties after you add them to see which properties are available. Check the online documentation for more help on the events and methods they support. You can find additional controls in programming magazines and on the Internet that you can add to your projects to help speed up your application development. In Day 17's lesson, you'll learn how to write your own ActiveX controls that you can add to your toolbox.

Working with the Common Dialog Box Control

Figure 9.2 shows a Common Dialog Box control placed in the center of a form. As you can see, the control doesn't look like any of the dialog boxes listed earlier. Instead, the control looks too small to be any good at all. If you try to resize the control, Visual Basic ignores your request, despite the eight sizing handles that appear around the control.

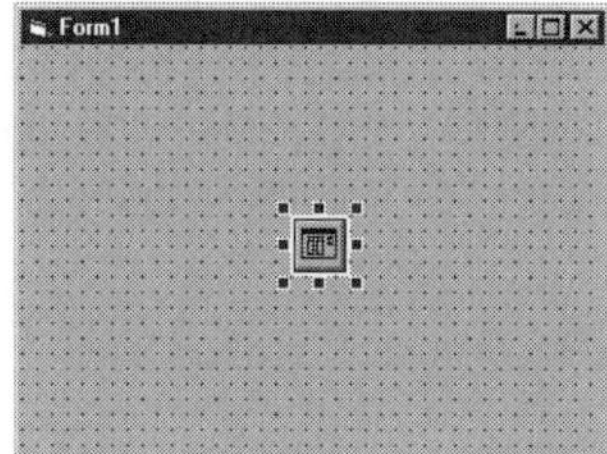

FIGURE 9.2.
The Common Dialog Box control doesn't look like much on your form.

9

When you run the program, the Common Dialog Box control takes on the appearance on one of the dialog boxes listed earlier. As a matter of fact, Visual Basic takes care of the dialog box display by putting the dialog box in the center of the screen no matter where you place the Common Dialog Box control on the form. Therefore, you can place the Common Dialog Box control out of the way from other controls so that you can concentrate on your form's regular controls and their design. Know that, when the Common Dialog Box control is finally triggered, Visual Basic takes care of placing the control in the center of the screen. Until the Common Dialog Box control is displayed, Visual Basic hides the control so it does not appear on top of other controls on your running application's form.

When your program triggers one of the Common Dialog Box control's specific dialog boxes, the appropriate dialog box appears on the screen because you'll write your Visual Basic application to display the correct dialog box.

The way you determine which form of the Common Dialog Box control displays is by setting appropriate properties and executing the correct method that prompts the control to display the dialog box. As you might recall from earlier lessons, a method is an internal procedure that you apply to a specific control. You must apply one of the following methods to the Common Dialog Box control to display a specific dialog box:

- `ShowColor` displays the Color selection dialog box.
- `ShowFont` displays the Font selection dialog box.
- `ShowHelp` displays the Windows Help dialog box.
- `ShowOpen` displays the File Open dialog box.
- `ShowPrinter` displays the Print dialog box.
- `ShowSave` displays the File Save dialog box.

Therefore, if you named a Common Dialog Box control `dbFont`, you can apply the `ShowFont` method to the control like this in code to display the Font selection dialog box after setting some initial properties:

```
dbFont.ShowFont    ' Display the Font dialog box
```

If you later need to display a File Open dialog box, you could apply the `ShowOpen` method to the `dbFont` control, perhaps in response to a File, Open menu selection, like this:

```
dbFont.ShowOpen    ' Display the File Open dialog box
```

As you can see, you only need one Common Dialog Box control to produce one or more of the dialog boxes. The method triggers the control, although you should set properties before activating any of the six dialog boxes as described in the next few sections.

Note

When you need to display more than one of the common dialog boxes in an application, you can place one Common Dialog Box control and apply the different methods to it, as shown here, or place multiple Common Dialog Box controls and use them solely for one kind of dialog box each. Although one control is easier to manage than several, you might want to place several so that you only set their property values once for each dialog box. With only one control, you have to change its properties as you change the dialog boxes that you display.

None of the dialog boxes produced by the Common Dialog Box control do any actual work other than provide selections for the user. In other words, if the user selects a font from the Font selection dialog box and then clicks OK, the screen fonts don't change. If the user selects a file from the File Open dialog box and clicks OK, that file does not then open. The goal of the Common Dialog Box control is only to provide a common interface for the common dialog boxes and set properties in response to the user's selection. You will, through Visual Basic code, have to analyze the Common Dialog Box control's property values when the user closes the dialog box and perform any action necessary.

Producing the Color Dialog Box

Due to the large numbers of colors that Windows can produce, a Color dialog box provides a simple way for your users to specify color values. For example, if you were going to let your user change the background color for a form, you would not be advised to ask the user for a color in an input box like this:

```
strAns = InputBox("What color do you want the background? ")
```

Remember that the `BackColor` property requires a hexadecimal color code (as do all the other color-related properties such as `ForeColor`). If your user typed `Red` in response to the `InputBox()`, you could *not* then assign the answer to the `BackColor` property like this:

```
frmTitle.BackColor = strAns    ' Will NOT work!
```


Not only does the Color dialog box offer a standard way for your user to select a color, but the Color dialog box also converts the user's selected color to its hexadecimal value. Therefore, after the user closes a Color selection dialog box, you can assign one of the dialog box's properties to the form's `BackColor` property to change the form's background.

To turn a Common Dialog Box control into the Color selection dialog box and display the Color selection dialog box, follow these steps:

1. Set the Common Dialog Box control's `DialogTitle` property to the title you want to appear in the Color selection's title bar, such as `Select a background color`.
2. Set the Common Dialog Box control's `Flags` property to one of Table 9.1's values. The table describes the way the Color selection dialog box first appears. If you want to set more than one of Table 9.1's flags, such as an initial color as well as providing a Help button, you can add the flag values together.
3. Trigger the Font selection dialog box's display by applying the `ShowFont` method to the Common Dialog Box control in code.

TABLE 9.1. YOU CAN COMBINE ONE OR MORE OF THESE `Flags` PROPERTY VALUES TO SET UP THE COLOR SELECTION DIALOG BOX.

Named Literal	`Flags` *Value*	*Description*
`cdlCCRGBInit`	1	Sets the initial color value
`cdlCCFullOpen`	2	Displays the entire dialog box, including the Define Custom Colors section
`cdlCCPreventFullOpen`	4	Prevents users from defining custom colors
`cdlCCHelpButton`	8	Displays a Help button in the dialog box

Suppose you want to display the Color selection box, let the user select a custom color, if desired, and provide a help button on the color selection dialog box. If you placed a Common Dialog Box control named `cdbColor` on the form, you could produce the Color selection dialog box with the following code:

```
' Set the Color Flags property.
cdbColor.Flags = cdlCCFullOpen + cdlCCHelpButton ' Display complete Color DB
' Display the Color dialog box.
cdbColor.ShowColor
```

Figure 9.3 shows the dialog box that appears.

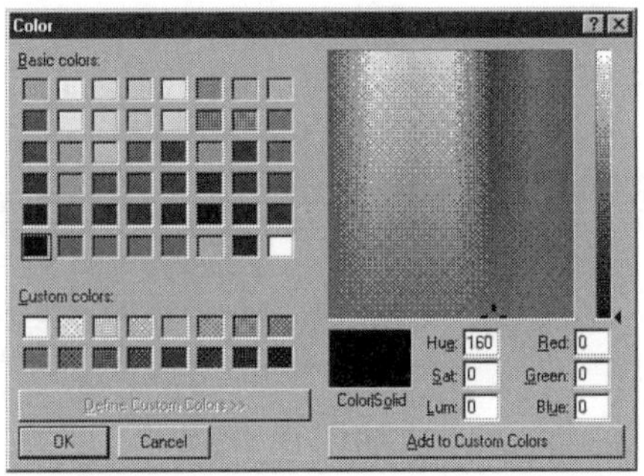

FIGURE 9.3.

The color selection dialog box appears from the ShowColor method.

If you want to limit the user to an initial smaller set of colors, requiring the user to click the Define Custom Colors button to customize colors, omit the `cdlCCFullOpen` flag value. Figure 9.4's smaller Color dialog box appears.

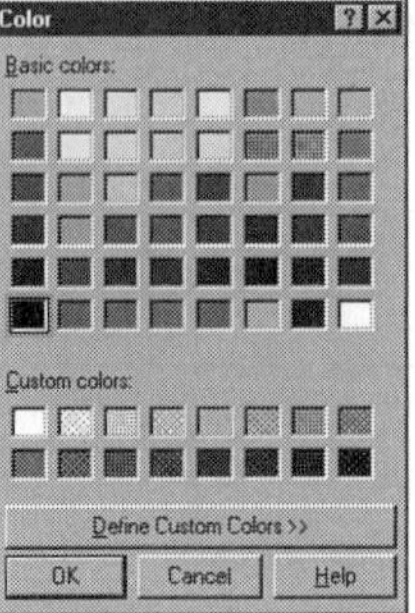

FIGURE 9.4.

You can limit the size of the Color selection dialog box that appears.

When the user closes the dialog box, the dialog box's properties are set according to the user's selection. The most important property is the `Color` property which will then hold the hexadecimal value of the color the user selected or created. You could write the following code that follows the dialog box's display:

```
' Set a form's background color
' to the Color dialog box's selected color
frmTitle.ForeColor = cdbColor.Color
```

Handling the Cancel Button

Your code needs to be able to determine if the user selected a color and clicked OK or if the user clicked the Cancel button which means that the user does not want to change any color value. Not only do you need to be able to capture the Cancel click on the Color dialog box but also on the other common dialog boxes as well.

To test to see whether users have clicked Cancel, you need to learn a new Visual Basic command—the `On Error Goto` statement. This statement jumps the program execution down to a code label if an error occurs during subsequent statements. Therefore, the statement

```
On Error Goto dbErrHandler
```

tells Visual Basic to jump to the code labeled `dbErrHandler` if an error occurs during any line that follows the `On Error Goto` statement (until the end of the procedure).

A *code label* is a label inside your Code window's code that you name using the same naming rules used for variables. A label, however, must end in a colon to distinguish it from a variable name. With the example just given, the procedure must have the following code label somewhere after the `On Error Goto` statement (generally, programmers put the error code label toward the bottom of the procedure) :

```
dbErrHandler:
```

The statements after the error-handling code label are executed if an error occurs in the procedure and an `Exit` statement can terminate the procedure early. Visual Basic triggers an error condition if users click the Cancel button and you've set the `CancelError` property to `True`. Although clicking Cancel isn't a real error, treating it like an error condition lets you write code like that in Listing 9.1 to handle it.

LISTING 9.1. YOU CAN CONTROL THE USER'S CANCEL SELECTION.

```
Private Sub mnuViewColor_Click()
  cdbColor.CancelError = True   ' Forces an error if
                                ' user clicks Cancel
  On Error Goto dbErrHandler  ' Jump if an error occurs

  ' Set the Color Flags property.
  cdbColor.Flags = cdlCCFullOpen + cdlCCHelpButton ' Display complete
Color DB
  ' Display the Color dialog box.
  cdbColor.ShowColor

```

continues

LISTING 9.1. CONTINUED

```
12:     ' Set a form's background color
13:     ' to the Color dialog box's selected color
14:     frmTitle.ForeColor = cdbColor.Color
15:     Exit Sub   ' The regular procedure is done
16:   dbErrHandler:
17:     ' The user clicked cancel so ignore
18:     ' the procedure and change no color
19:     Exit Sub
20: End Sub
```

If the user selects a color and clicks OK, line 14 assigns the selected color to the form's background. Rather than end the procedure if users click Cancel, you might choose to set default values (between lines 16 and 19) for the form's background rather than retain the current values and exit the procedure.

The error-handler in line 16 will execute if any error takes place, not just the Cancel button click. In Day 16's lesson, you learn how to check the `Err` system object to determine exactly which error occurred by the error number triggered.

Producing the Font Dialog Box

The Common Dialog Box control produces the Font dialog box that you've seen in your Windows applications. The reason that you will want to use the Font dialog box, as opposed to writing your own, is not just because the dialog box is standard. You don't know exactly which fonts your application's PC will contain. The Common Dialog Box control's Font dialog box searches the user's system for all the fonts on the computer and displays those fonts inside the Font dialog box.

Figure 9.5 shows the typical Font dialog box that appears when you apply the `ShowFont` method to the Common Dialog Box control.

As with the Color dialog box, you must set the Common Dialog Box control's `Flags` property to a certain value. The `Flags` property values differ from those of the Color dialog box because the Font dialog box is actually more complex than the Color dialog box.

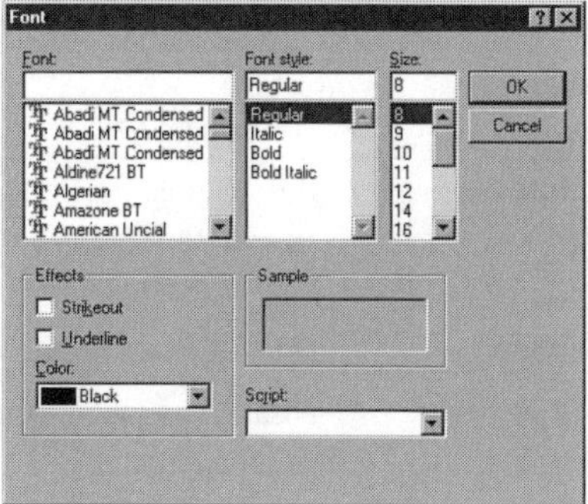

FIGURE 9.5.

Users can select a font style and size from your application's Font dialog box.

The Font dialog box's `Flags` values can get large. Therefore, Visual Basic programmers assign either named constants or hexadecimal values to the `Flags` property. Table 9.2 contains the `Flags` property values you can set. As in most areas of Visual Basic programming, program maintenance is simpler if you use the named constants because their names suggest their purpose, whereas the hexadecimal values don't document their purpose well.

TABLE 9.2. SET THESE FONT DIALOG BOX `Flags` VALUES BEFORE CALLING THE `ShowFont` METHOD.

Named Literal	`Flags` *Value*	*Description*
`cdlCFANSIOnly`	`&H400`	Ensures that the dialog box allows only fonts from the Windows character set and not a symbol-based font
`cdlCFApply`	`&H200`	Enables the dialog box's Apply button
`cdlCFBoth`	`&H3`	Lists the available printer and screen fonts in the dialog box; the `hDC` property identifies the device context associated with the printer
`cdlCFEffects`	`&H100`	Lets the dialog box enable strikethrough, underline, and color effects
`cdlCFFixedPitchOnly`	`&H4000`	Ensures that the dialog box selects only fixed-pitch fonts
`cdlCFForceFontExist`	`&H10000`	Displays an error message box if users try to select a font or style that doesn't exist
`cdlCFHelpButton`	`&H4`	Displays the dialog box's Help button

continues

TABLE 9.2. CONTINUED

Named Literal	Flags *Value*	*Description*
`cdlCFLimitSize`	`&H2000`	Ensures that the dialog box selects only font sizes within the range specified by the `Min` and `Max` properties
`cdlCFNoFaceSel`	`&H80000`	No font name is selected as the default
`cdlCFNoSimulations`	`&H1000`	Disallows graphic device interface (GDI) font simulations
`cdlCFNoSizeSel`	`&H200000`	No font size is selected as the default
`cdlCFNoStyleSel`	`&H100000`	No font style is selected as the default
`cdlCFNoVectorFonts`	`&H800`	Disallows vector-font selections
`cdlCFPrinterFonts`	`&H2`	Lists only the fonts supported by the printer, specified by the `hDC` property
`cdlCFScalableOnly`	`&H20000`	Allows only the selection of scalable fonts
`cdlCFScreenFonts`	`&H1`	Lists only the screen fonts supported by the system
`cdlCFTTOnly`	`&H40000`	Allows only the selection of TrueType fonts
`cdlCFWYSIWYG`	`&H8000`	Specifies that the dialog box allows only the selection of fonts available on the printer and onscreen (if you set this flag, you should also set `cdlCFBoth` and `cdlCFScalableOnly`)

Caution

You must at least set one of these three `Flags` property values before the Font dialog box will appear: `cdlCFScreenFonts`, `cdlCFPrinterFonts`, and `cdlCFBoth`. If you don't set one of these `Flags` values, Visual Basic issues an error message when you apply the `ShowFont` method.

Listing 9.2 shows how you can set up, show, and respond to the Font dialog box.

LISTING 9.2. DISPLAY THE FONT DIALOG BOX WHEN YOUR USERS MUST SELECT FROM A LIST OF FONT STYLES AND SIZES.

```
1:  ' Set the Font Flags property.
2:  CdbFont.Flags = cdlCFBoth Or cdlCFEffects
3:  CdbFont.ShowFont  ' Display the Font DB
4:  ' Set a label's properties to the
5:  ' user's selected font information
6:  LblMessage.Font.Name = CdbFont.FontName
7:  LblMessage.Font.Size = CdbFont.FontSize
8:  LblMessage.Font.Bold = CdbFont.FontBold
9:  LblMessage.Font.Italic = CdbFont.FontItalic
10: LblMessage.Font.Underline = CdbFont.FontUnderline
11: LblMessage.FontStrikethru = CdbFont.FontStrikethru
12: LblMessage.ForeColor = CdbFont.Color
```

Pay attention to the multipart assignments in lines 6 through 10. You've not seen two periods separating property names before now. Remember when you click the ellipses on the `Font` property inside a control's Properties window, the Font dialog box appears in which you can set several values. Therefore, a `Font` property holds much more than a single value and you must further qualify the `Font` property value that you want to set. There are several `Font` property values, each of which indicates a different kind of font style, size, color, and so on. Read such multipart names from right to left. Consider the following statement from line 8:

```
LblMessage.Font.Bold = CdbFont.FontBold
```

Line 8 tells Visual Basic to assign the dialog box's `FontBold` property (which is either `True` or `False` provided by the Font dialog box) to the `Bold` attribute of the `Font` property of the label named `lblMessage`.

Help with Setting Controls

Although you can set all the common dialog box control properties at runtime, Visual Basic provides an ingenious way to set many properties at design time.

The common dialog box control contains a property named `Custom`. When you click the ellipsis for this property setting in the Properties window, Visual Basic displays the Property Pages dialog box. (Figure 9.6 shows the dialog box's Font page.)

This Property Pages dialog box makes it easy for you to set some initial dialog box properties. Here you can review the most important properties for each style of common dialog box. For example, if you want the Font dialog box's default font to be 12-point Bold, type `12` in the FontSize text box and click to select the Bold check box.

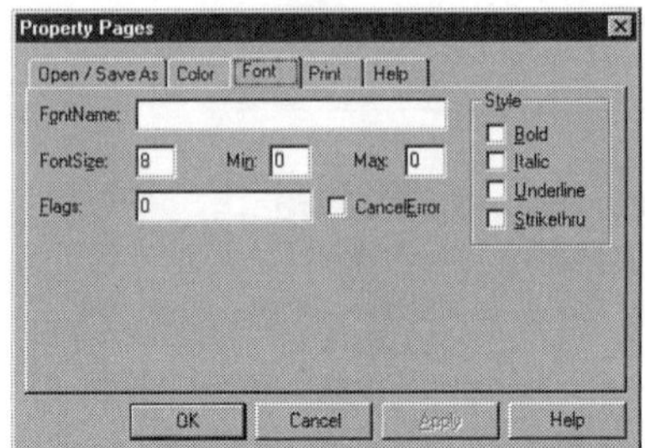

FIGURE 9.6.

You can set properties at design time from the Property Pages dialog box.

Producing File Open Dialog Boxes

Table 9.3 shows the `Flags` property values that you can assign before applying the `ShowOpen` method. The File Open dialog box, shown in Figure 9.7, offers a standard interface for your users when they must select a file to open. The dialog box handles the folder and network selections if the user wants to make any before selecting a file.

> You'll also use Table 9.3 when setting the `Flags` property value for the File Save dialog box.

TABLE 9.3. THE FILE OPEN AND SAVE DIALOG BOX'S `Flags` VALUES.

Named Literal	`Flags` *Value*	*Description*
`cdlOFNAllowMultiselect`	`&H200`	Lets the File Name list box accept multiple file selections. The `FileName` property then returns a string that contains all the selected filenames (names in the string are delimited by spaces).
`cdlOFNCreatePrompt`	`&H2000`	Prompts users to create a file that doesn't currently exist. This flag automatically sets the `cdlOFNPathMustExist` and `cdlOFNFileMustExist` flags.
`cdlOFNExplorer`	`&H80000`	Uses the Explorer-like Open a File dialog box template.
`cdlOFNExtensionDifferent`	`&H400`	Indicates that the extension of the returned filename is different from the extension specified by the `DefaultExt` property. This flag isn't set if the `DefaultExt` property contains `Null`, if the extensions match, or if the file has no extension. You can inspect this flag's value after the dialog box is closed.

Named Literal	Flags *Value*	*Description*
`cdlOFNFileMustExist`	`&H1000`	Lets users enter only names of existing files. If this flag is set and users enter an invalid filename, a warning is displayed. This flag automatically sets the `cdlOFNPathMustExist` flag.
`cdlOFNHelpButton`	`&H10`	Displays the dialog box's Help button.
`cdlOFNHideReadOnly`	`&H4`	Hides the Read Only check box.
`cdlOFNLongNames`	`&H200000`	Allows long filenames.
`cdlOFNNoChangeDir`	`&H8`	Forces the dialog box to set the current directory to what it was when the dialog box was opened.
`cdlOFNNoDereferenceLinks`	`&H100000`	Disallows dereferencing of *shell links* (also known as *shortcuts*). By default, choosing a shell link causes it to be dereferenced by the shell.
`cdlOFNNoLongNames`	`&H40000`	Disallows long filenames.
`cdlOFNNoReadOnlyReturn`	`&H8000`	Specifies that the returned file won't have the Read Only attribute set and won't be in a write-protected directory.
`cdlOFNNoValidate`	`&H100`	Allows invalid characters in the returned filename.
`cdlOFNOverwritePrompt`	`&H2`	Causes the Save As dialog box to generate a warning message box if the selected file already exists. (Users then choose whether to overwrite the existing file.)
`cdlOFNPathMustExist`	`&H800`	Lets users enter only valid paths. If this flag is set and the users enter an invalid path, a warning message is displayed.
`cdlOFNReadOnly`	`&H1`	Selects the Read Only check box when the dialog box is created. This flag also indicates the state of the Read Only check box after the dialog box is closed.
`cdlOFNShareAware`	`&H4000`	Indicates that possible sharing violation errors will be ignored.

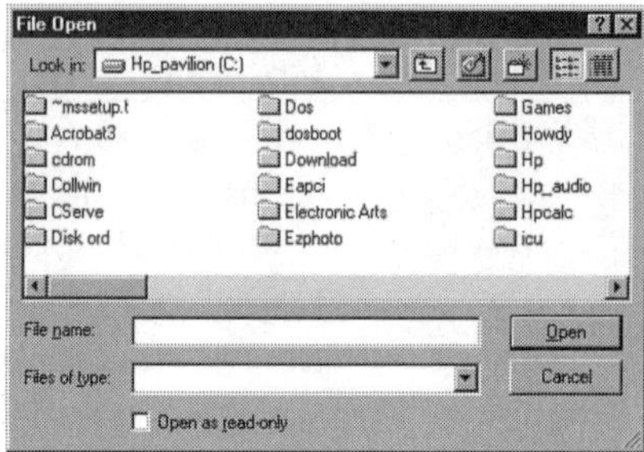

FIGURE 9.7.

The Common Dialog Box control can display the File Open dialog box.

Often, when you see a File-related dialog box such as the File Open dialog box, a filter is applied to the filename extensions so that the dialog box shows files of a certain extension only, such as all files that meet the *.doc wildcard selection. Although the user can override the default filter by entering a different filter, or by typing *.* and showing all files in the File dialog box, you can specify the initial filter if you assign the `Filter` property a value that follows this format:

```
"FilterDescrip1 ¦ extension1 ¦ FilterDescrip2 ¦ extension2 ¦ _
FilterDescrip3 ¦ extension3"
```

For example, the following statement assigns a filter that shows only Word and Excel documents when the Open dialog box appears:

```
cdbFiles.Filter = "Word Docs (*.doc)¦*.doc¦Excel Docs (*.xls)¦*.xls"
```

Don't confuse the file extensions in the description with the actual extensions in the filter. In the example, `Word Docs (*.doc)` is text to be displayed to users, and the `*.doc` following the first pipe symbol is the dialog box's first actual filtering instruction.

You can supply multiple filters by including multiple strings for the `Filter` property. If you specify more than one filter, you must set the `FilterIndex` property to the filter you want to use for the current File Open dialog box. The first filter has a `FilterIndex` of 1; this number is incremented if you supply additional filters.

The common dialog box control's `FileName` property holds the selected filename after users close the dialog box.

Producing the File Save Dialog Box

The File Save dialog box is virtually identical to the File Open dialog box except for the title and a few other options such as the command button titles. For example, if an application is a Multiple-Document Interface (MDI) application, you might allow the user to select multiple files to open from within a File Open dialog box because each data file will be able to appear in its own document window. If you were to offer a File Save dialog box, however, your user can select or enter only a single filename.

Figure 9.8 shows you that the File Save dialog box looks almost exactly like the File Open dialog box. Use Table 9.3's `Flags` property values to set up the File Save dialog box just as you did the File Open, including the filter setting procedure that you learned at the end of the previous section.

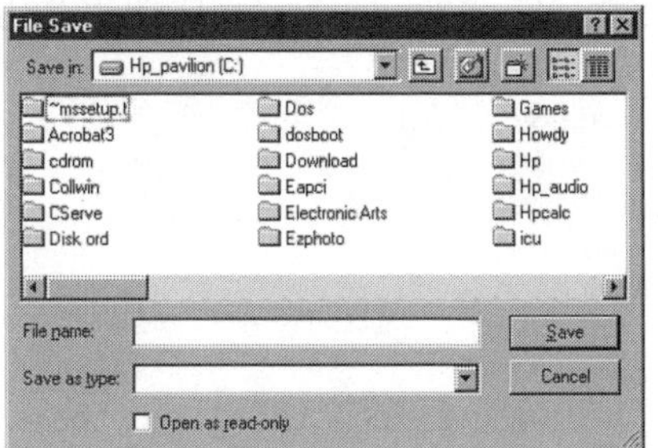

FIGURE 9.8.
The Common Dialog Box control can display the File Save dialog box.

Producing the Print Dialog Box

Figure 9.9 shows the Print dialog box that the Common Dialog Box control produces when you apply the `ShowPrinter` method to a Common Dialog Box control. Your users can select the printer type, number of copies, range of pages, and several other printing options. Each printer setup for the users' system displays a different set of Print dialog box options. When users enter the desired values, your application can use that information (taken from the Common Dialog Box control's properties) to direct the print output properly.

Your Print dialog box will vary from Figure 9.9, depending on your printer type.

FIGURE 9.9.

The Print dialog box lets users select printer options.

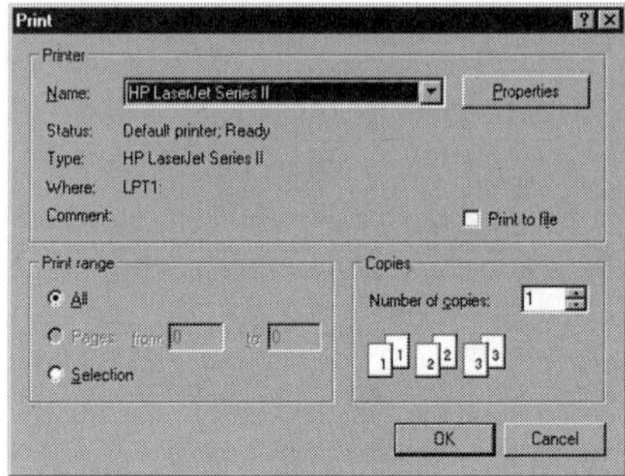

Listing 9.3 shows code that opens the Print dialog box in response to a menu selection.

LISTING 9.3. USE THE COMMON DIALOG BOX TO DIRECT THE PRINTED OUTPUT.

```
Private mnuFilePrint_Click()
   Dim intBegin As Integer, intEnd As Integer
   Dim intNumCopies As Integer, intI As Integer
   ' Assumes Cancel is set to True

   On Error Goto dbErrHandler
   ' Display the Print dialog box
   cbdPrint.ShowPrinter
   ' Get user-selected values from the dialog box
   intBegin = cbdPrint.FromPage
   intEnd = cbdPrint.ToPage
   intNumCopies = cbdPrint.Copies
   '
   ' Print as many copies as needed
   For intI = 1 To intNumCopies
     ' Put code here to send data to your printer
   Next intI
   Exit Sub

dbErrHandler:
  ' User pressed Cancel button
  Exit Sub
End Sub
```

As Listing 9.3 shows, you don't have to set any properties before displaying the Print dialog box (except perhaps for a `DialogTitle` property if you want a specific title to appear in the Print dialog box's title bar), but you can check the dialog box's return values stored in properties such as `Copies`, `FromPage`, and `ToPage` to determine how the user wants to print a report that you are about to print.

The Help Dialog Box

Day 20, "Providing Help," explains how to integrate the Windows Help dialog box, produced by the Common Dialog Box control, into your applications.

Summary

Today's lesson explained how you can set up common dialog boxes to perform standard tasks. When you must display a dialog box to open a file, for example, you'll want to use the standard dialog box so that your users will feel comfortable with your application and have less of a learning curve.

The Common Dialog Box control requires that you set some property values and then apply the correct method to the Common Dialog Box control. The Common Dialog Box control does no work except to set properties; your code must ensure, when the user closes the dialog box, that you interpret the user's selections as well as handle the potential Cancel click properly.

Tomorrow's lesson teaches you how to monitor the user's mouse movements so that your applications acquire yet another way to interact with your users. In addition, you'll learn how to program the list box-related controls that let you offer your users several choices to choose from.

Q&A

Q Why doesn't the Common Dialog Box control support other dialog boxes I see in applications, such as the View, Zoom dialog box in Word and Excel?

A The Common Dialog Box control cannot do everything or the control would be unwieldy and consume too many resources to be efficient. Nevertheless, you'll work with many dialog boxes in popular Windows programs and, although you can create any dialog box in Visual Basic using forms and controls, not every dialog box is common enough to be a Windows standard. For example, most Windows applications do not have a View, Zoom menu option even though Word and Excel do.

Q What kinds of controls can I add to my Toolbox window?

A You can add ActiveX controls to your collection of tools. These include ActiveX controls you write yourself (as described in Day 17's lesson) and those you obtain elsewhere. You'll find such controls on Microsoft's Web site as well as other places on the Internet. You'll find several good programming magazines and journals on the computer magazine racks. These often have many advertisements that offer Visual Basic controls that you can order and add to your system.

Workshop

The Workshop provides quiz questions to help you solidify your understanding of the material covered and exercises to provide you with experience in using what you've learned. Try to understand the quiz and exercise answers before continuing to the next chapter. Answers are provided in Appendix A, "Answers to Exercises."

Quiz

1. What must you do to the Toolbox window before you can place a Common Dialog Box control onto the form?
2. Name the specific dialog boxes that the Common Dialog Box control displays.
3. What purpose does the Common Dialog Box control serve?
4. Why can't you adjust the size of the Common Dialog Box control on the form?
5. True/False. The Open dialog box doesn't really open any file.
6. What role does the Filter property play in the file-related dialog boxes?
7. What does the `Flags` property do?
8. True/False. You must set a `Flags` value or Visual Basic won't display the Fonts dialog box.
9. True/False. You must set a `Flags` value or Visual Basic won't display the Print dialog box.
10. True/False. The `Show` method displays a Common Dialog Box control.

Exercises

1. Change the code in Listing 9.2 to handle the Cancel command button selection. Make sure that the code changes no properties if the user clicks Cancel.
2. Write a procedure that produces the File Open dialog box shown in Figure 9.10. Use the same `*.txt` filter shown in the figure. Add code to ignore the dialog box settings if the user clicks the Cancel button.

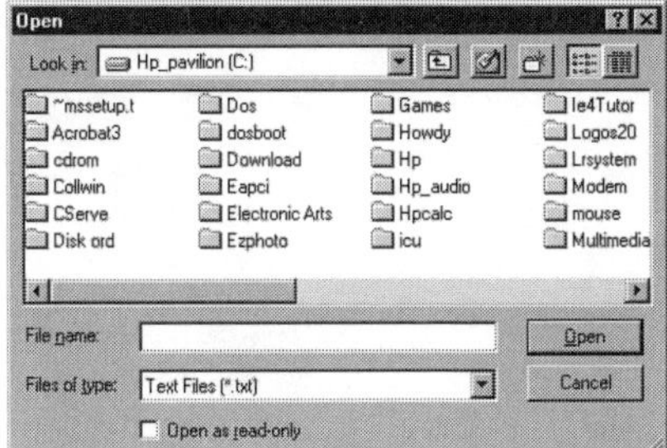

FIGURE 9.10.

Create this File Open dialog box.

WEEK 2

DAY 10

Adding Power with the Mouse and Controls

Today's lesson expands your Visual Basic knowledge by showing you how to write programs that respond to mouse movements, clicks, and drags. The use of the mouse is vital to Windows programs and, depending on your program's requirements, you'll want to add mouse support to give your users yet another way to interact with your form's controls.

The mouse discussion makes a good transition into a new set of controls that you'll learn about today—the *list controls*. You've worked with list boxes in other applications, and today's lesson teaches you how to create and manage your own application's list controls. More than one kind of list control exists, and you'll master each one today.

The list controls provide your users with lists of items from which to choose. The controls have many similarities to *variable arrays*, which you'll learn about today as well. By learning about arrays, you'll be able to make your programs more efficient when they must process large data sets.

Today, you learn the following:

- About mouse events
- How to determine which mouse button the user clicked
- How to program drag-and-drop operations
- How to use the timer control
- About list and combo box controls
- How to initialize, add to, and delete items from the list controls
- How to declare and use arrays
- About control arrays

Responding to the Mouse

One of the foundations of Windows applications is that they respond to the mouse. Windows sends mouse events to your program when the user works with the mouse while running your application. When you write your programs, you'll want it to inspect for mouse events and respond to them if necessary. If your user uses the mouse to click an option button or check box, your program doesn't need to respond to the mouse, of course, but the click will trigger an event for those controls.Visual Basic also monitors mouse events when the user drags and drops an item on the screen or copies and pastes information.

Actually, you should write your Windows programs to respond to *both* the keyboard and the mouse. The Windows standard states that all programs should be accessible from the keyboard alone, if necessary. This lets a user who prefers the keyboard or whose mouse is broken to run Windows applications. Nevertheless, some programs by their very nature do not function well without mouse support. For example, a drawing program would be quite hard to use without a mouse.

Visual Basic includes no mouse control for your toolbox window because your application responds to a mouse only through events, not control properties.

Mouse Events

You have full control over how your application responds to mouse events. A mouse event can be triggered by any of the following actions:

- Mouse movement
- A button click
- A double-click
- A right-click
- A drag-and-drop operation

Adjusting the Mouse Cursor

As the user moves the mouse, the mouse cursor, sometimes called the *mouse pointer* (due to its default arrow shape), travels across the screen to show the movement. Often, an application changes the mouse pointer during a drag-and-drop operation, or perhaps when the user moves the mouse over an object on the screen that cannot be activated by the mouse. The changed mouse pointer can show an hourglass, for example, to indicate that processing is taking place such as a sort of data.

Your application can control the mouse cursor's shape. Table 10.1 lists the possible mouse cursors you can set. To change the mouse cursor's shape when it passes over a control on your form requires that you set the control's `MousePointer` property. Almost every control you place on a form contains the `MousePointer` property, which can take any of the values shown in Table 10.1. You can set these values at runtime by assigning the named constants or at design time by selecting one of the values in a control's `MousePointer` property.

TABLE 10.1. YOU CAN CONTROL THE MOUSE POINTER'S SHAPE.

Named Constant	*Description*
`VbArrow`	Regular mouse pointer arrow
`VbCrosshair`	Crosshair
`VbIbeam`	I-beam
`VbIconPointer`	Small square within a square
`VbSizePointer`	Four-pointed arrow pointing up, down, left, and right
`VbSizeNESW`	Double-arrow pointing northeast and southwest
`VbSizeNS`	Double-arrow pointing up and down

continues

TABLE 10.1. CONTINUED

Named Constant	*Description*
`VbSizeNWSE`	Double-arrow pointing northwest and southeast
`VbSizeWE`	Double-arrow pointing left and right
`VbUpArrow`	Up arrow
`VbHourglass`	Hourglass (indicating wait)
`VbNoDrop`	Not drop (the international Not sign with a red slash through a circle)
`VbArrowHourglass`	Arrow with an hourglass
`vbArrowQuestion`	Arrow with a question mark
`vbSizeAll`	Double-pointing arrow that appears when you resize a window
`vbCustom`	The shape indicated by the `MouseIcon` property

You can make up your own mouse cursor. The cursor must be in the same 16-by-16 pixel resolution as other icons (icons have the .ICO filename extension; most drawing programs will let you create standard icons). If you want to display your own icon graphic file in place of one of the predefined mouse pointers from Table 10.1, set the `MouseIcon` property to your custom icon file and set the `MousePointer` property to `99 - Custom`. The mouse pointer will remain your custom shape until you once again change the cursor. Bonus Project 5, "Practice with the Mouse," appears before Day 11 ("Working with Forms") and explains further how to change the mouse pointer.

When the User Moves and Clicks the Mouse

Windows generates mouse movement and click events and sends them to your program. Your program might choose to ignore these events if you omit event procedures for them; however, you can place code in any events you want to respond to. Table 10.2 describes what happens at each mouse event.

TABLE 10.2. WINDOWS GENERATES THESE MOUSE EVENTS AS THE MOUSE IS USED.

Event	*Description*
`Click`	The user clicked a mouse button.
`DblClick`	The user double-clicked a mouse button.
`MouseDown`	The user pressed and held a mouse button.
`MouseMove`	The user moved the mouse.
`MouseUp`	The user released the mouse button.

All the mouse events are associated with controls. You'll find mouse events listed for almost every control (by displaying the Object drop-down list box in the Code window) as well as forms. For example, if you want to test for a mouse button click on your form named frmTest, the event procedure would be named `frmTest_Click()`.

> Some events related to mouse button clicks require that you test an event procedure argument to see which button the user clicked.Only the `MouseDown` and `MouseUp` event procedures pass arguments that specify which mouse button the user clicked.

Is a double-click a single event or two click events? That answer depends on how accurately the user performs the double-click. Windows provides click-related mouse events in the following order:

10

1. `MouseDown`
2. `MouseUp`
3. `Click`
4. `DblClick`
5. `MouseUp`

Therefore, a `MouseDown` event occurs first when the user clicks the mouse button; then a `MouseUp` occurs and then a `Click` event occurs. When a user double-clicks a mouse button, the `DblClick` and `MouseUp` events occur also. (Windows doesn't trigger a `MouseDown` event if user the double-clicks the mouse.)

The `MouseDown`, `MouseMove`, and `MouseUp` event procedures always require these four arguments:

- `intButton`. Describes the button pressed: 1 for the left button, 2 for the right button, and 4 for both buttons (or for a center button if you have a three-button mouse).
- `intShift`. Describes the shift state value by showing, through a bit comparison, whether the user pressed Alt, Ctrl, or Shift while moving or clicking the mouse.
- `sngX`. The horizontal twip value where the user clicked or moved the mouse.
- `sngY`. The vertical twip value where the user clicked or moved the mouse.

Visual Basic generates a movement event after the user moves the mouse every 10 to 15 twips, which is an extremely small portion of the window. Visual Basic doesn't generate a mouse movement event for each twip.

The following statement declares a `MouseDown` event procedure so that you can see how the arguments arrive:

```
Private Sub imgMouse_MouseDown(intButton As Integer, intShift As Integer, _
sngX As Single, sngY As Single)
```

Upon entering this procedure, `sngX` and `sngY` hold the twip coordinates of the mouse click. `intButton` contains `1`, `2`, or `4`, which describes which button was pressed. You don't always need to know which button the user pressed, but if you were to respond differently to a left-click than to a right-click, you would use the `MouseDown` event to determine the button. If the user pressed Shift, Ctrl, or Alt, and you need to know which key the user pressed in conjunction with the mouse button, you can perform a test similar to the shown in Listing 10.1.

LISTING 10.1. ANALYZING THE SHIFT VALUE TO SEE WHICH KEY THE USER PRESSED IN CONJUNCTION WITH A MOUSE EVENT.

```
1:  Private Sub imgMouse_MouseDown(intButton As Integer, intShift As _
    Integer, sngX As Single, sngY As Single)
2:    Dim intShiftState As Integer
3:    intShiftState = intShift And 7  ' Special bitwise And
4:    Select Case intShiftState
5:      Case 1
6:        ' Code for Shift combinations
7:      Case 2
8:        ' Code for Ctrl combinations
9:      Case 3
10:       ' Code for Alt combinations
11:     Case 4
12:       ' Code for Shift+Ctrl combinations
13:     Case 5
14:       ' Code for Shift+Alt combinations
15:     Case 6
16:       ' Code for Ctrl+Alt combinations
17:     Case 7
18:       ' Code for Shift+Ctrl+Alt combinations
19:     End Select
20: End Sub
```

The special `And` comparison in line 3 tests an internal bit flag value to determine which key the user pressed along with the mouse event.

Do	Don't
DO test for a keystroke and mouse click combination if your application allows for the selection of text by dragging while holding down the Ctrl key or the selection of multiple items by clicking while holding down the Ctrl key. Many controls, such as the list box control you'll learn about in today's lesson, automatically handle "Ctrl+mouse" combinations when you select values from the list; so you do not need to worry about keystrokes that occur in combination with the mouse inside list box controls.	

Bonus Project 5 that appears before Day 11's lesson demonstrates a complete application that shows how to respond to mouse clicks and movements.

Following Drag-and-Drop Operations

When your user drags one object from a form to another location, your application needs to know about it! *Drag-and-drop* is a process where the user, with the mouse, clicks an object onscreen, holds down the mouse button, and drags that object to another location onscreen. Surprisingly, programming for drag-and-drop operations is relatively simple thanks to the Windows operating system, which generates appropriate information along with drag-and-drop events that occur.

Visual Basic supports two kinds of drag-and-drop operations:

- Automatic drag-and-drop
- Manual drag-and-drop

The first method is the simplest. You trigger automatic drag-and-drop through control properties. Almost every control in the toolbox contains the property `DragMode`. This property lets the user move the control with the mouse. When the user moves the control, Visual Basic displays an outline of the control. Your job is to move the control to the place where the user releases the mouse button. Although the automatic mode shows the moving control's outline, it doesn't actually move the object.

The form's `DragDrop` event controls the placement of the drop. To set up the drag, you only need to change the control's `DragMode` property to `1 - Automatic`. The control can then be dragged and show the moving outline. The `Form_DragDrop()` event procedure takes care of the second half of the drag-and-drop operation by placing the dragged control in its new location.

Although the control's outline normally appears as the user drags the mouse, you can change the icon used as the outline by changing the `DragIcon` property to point to any icon file (such as the icon files in the \Graphics folder if you installed graphics with Visual Basic). When a user drags the control, the icon replaces the mouse pointer during the drag. After the user completes the drag, a `Form_DragDrop()` procedure can take care of moving the object to its final location. The `DragDrop` event takes care of moving the control from the first location and to the placed location. Here's the code that performs such a movement:

```
1:  Private Sub frmTitle_DragDrop(Source As Control, X As Single, Y As _
    Single)
2: ' This code receives as an argument the actual control that
3:  ' the user dragged.
4:    Source.Move X, Y  ' Move to the dropped location
5:  End Sub
```

The `Move` method in line 4 moves the control from its original location to the coordinates of the dropped location (where the user releases the mouse button).

> The `DragOver` event occurs when the user drags one control over another. If you want to change the mouse pointer over items that you don't want the user to drop another control on top of, change the mouse cursor inside the `DragOver` event procedures for those controls that don't accept dropped objects. `DragOver` receives four arguments:
>
> - The control
> - The mouse pointer's x-coordinate
> - The mouse pointer's y-coordinate
> - The state of the drag, which takes on one of three possible values: `0` (when the drag first covers the object), 1 (when the drag leaves the object), and 2 (when the control is being dragged through the object)

Manual drag-and-drop works just like automatic drag-and-drop, with these three differences:

- You must set the `DragMode` property to `0 - Manual`.

- Manual drag-and-drop lets the control respond to a `MouseDown` event before beginning the drag so that the control's original location coordinates can be recorded.
- You must add code to the `MouseDown` event procedure to invoke the drag.

The `MouseDown` event procedure can perform the special `Drag` method on the object if you want to continue the drag-and-drop process. The following code drags the image if the image control's `DragMode` property is set to `0 - Manual`:

```
Private Sub imgMouse_MouseDown(Button As Integer, Shift As Integer, X As _
Single, Y As Single)
  ' Clicked over the image
  txtMouse.Text = "Clicked over the image at " & X & ", " & Y
  imgMouse.Drag
End Sub
```


The `Drag` method turns on drag-and-drop. Without the `Drag` method, the `MouseDown()` event procedure couldn't initiate the drag-and-drop operation. Use manual drag-and-drop operations if you want to set up drag-and-drop limitations before and during the drag-and-drop process.

In Bonus Project 7, "Working with Scrollbars," that appears after Day 14's lesson, "Introducing VB Graphics and Multimedia," you'll create an application that allows you to right-click to display a pop-up menu.

List Box Controls

You're now ready to learn about the additional controls that appear in your toolbox window. Many of the controls you have yet to master require programming to make them work. You cannot just place them on a form, as you can a command button, because they require initialization, which can only be performed with code. For example, you can't fill a drop-down list box with items until runtime. Although you can initialize some controls, such as labels, you can't initialize many of the multivalue controls. The multivalue controls (such as list boxes) require some programming.

Here's a list of the different types of list boxes:

- The simple list box
- The drop-down list box
- The drop-down combo box
- The simple combo box

Simple List Boxes

The simple list box control gives your users a way to select one or more items from a list of choices. To add a simple list box to your form, use the list box control on the toolbox window.

Note

You'll initialize some list box control properties from the Properties window, such as the location, size, and color properties, but you'll generally not initialize the list box control's list of values from within the Properties window.

The preceding note states that you will *generally* not initialize the list box control's list of values from within the Properties window because Visual Basic does give you the means to initialize the list at runtime. If you open the `List` property in a list box control's Properties window, a blank scrolling list opens in which you can add values. List box controls, however, almost always store values that come from the user and other data sources. You'll only initialize small list boxes whose values do not change directly from the Properties window. The rest of today's material focuses on the most common way to initialize the list controls: using methods that build the list at runtime.

You use the `AddItem` method to add items to a list (see Listing 10.2).

LISTING 10.2. INITIALIZING THE LIST BOX IS BEST DONE IN THE `Form_Load()` EVENT PROCEDURE.

```
Private Sub Form_Load()
  ' Initialize the list control values
  lstColors.AddItem "Red"
  lstColors.AddItem "Blue"
  lstColors.AddItem "Green"
  lstColors.AddItem "Yellow"
  lstColors.AddItem "Orange"
  lstColors.AddItem "White"
End Sub
```

The `Form_Load()` event procedure is a good place to load initial list values, although more values will probably be added as the user uses the program. The `Form_Load()` event procedure ensures that the initial values, if any are known when the program first begins, load before the user sees a form that contains the list box. When you run your application, the runtime module initially loads the form (or forms, if you have multiple forms). Forms support the `Load` event, which occurs when a form loads. Through the `Load` and `Unload` Visual Basic form commands, you can specify exactly when a form is to be loaded as well as when the form should be unloaded to free up resources.

Once you add the initial items, you can use the `AddItem` method to add more items to the list box. For example, if your list box is named `lstColors`, you can specify that list box's `AddItem` method as shown in the preceding `Form_Load()` subroutine; you add an item to the list by specifying the `AddItem` method followed by the item to add. Visual Basic adds items to the list in the same order your code adds the items, unless you change the list box's `Sorted` property to `True`, in which case Visual Basic sorts the items in the list alphabetically or numerically as they are added.

Note

> You can add initial values in the Properties window's `List` property, but doing so makes maintenance more difficult. Putting the initial values in the code makes the items much easier to change in the future.

The following statement adds the color "Aqua" to the list that the `Form_Load()` event procedure sets up:

```
lstColors.AddItem "Aqua"
```

Tip

> Sometimes it's difficult to distinguish Visual Basic's commands, declarations, methods, properties, and controls. Think of a method as a request that an item makes to itself. In other words, `lstColors.AddItem "Aqua"` is saying, "Add an item named Aqua to me." As a list box, lstColors knows how to fulfill this request because Visual Basic's designers added this method to the repertoire of methods for a list box. Most controls have their own set of methods available. You can learn the names of each control's methods from documentation that comes with each control that you obtain.

Assuming that a list box control named `lstColors` appears in the center of a form that contains the previous `Form_Load()` form procedure, the list box will appear, with its color names, as shown in Figure 10.1.

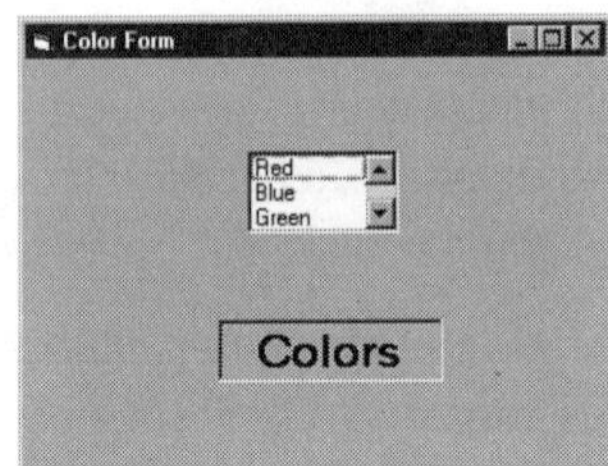

FIGURE 10.1.
The list box holds the added color values.

Unless you're initializing one or more list box values at designtime, you'll need to empty the `List` property from within the Properties window after you name the list box control you've placed on the form. Visual Basic uses the name of the list box as the first item in the list, unless you erase the list.

The list box shown in Figure 10.1 is known as a *simple list box*.

NEW TERM A *simple list box* is a list box that displays items from a list. The programmer initializes the list, and the user cannot directly add items to the list.

If needed, vertical and horizontal scrollbars appear in the list box if the height (or width) of the list box isn't sufficient to display all the items added to the list. Also, if the list box can display all the items but the application later adds more items, Visual Basic adds the scrollbars when they become needed, during the program's execution.

Users can select items from the list box. That's the purpose of a list box: to let users select from a list of choices rather type the values. When a user selects an item in the list, the following actions happen:

- The item changes color to highlight the selection.
- Visual Basic copies the selection into the list box's `Text` property. Therefore, `lstColors.Text` changes during the application's execution, depending on which item the user selects.

Text can hold one, and only one, value. To demonstrate the list box's `Text` property, consider what would happen if you added a text box named `txtColor` to the application shown in Figure 10.1. The following procedure sends the selected list box item to the text box as soon as the user selects an item in the list box (`lstColors`):

```
Private Sub lstColors_Click()
  ' Copy the selected item to the text box
  txtColor.Text = lstColors.Text
End Sub
```

When you place a text box on a form to hold a selected list box item, you should erase the text box's `Text` property in the Properties window at designtime so that nothing appears in the text box until the user selects an item. The text box's default `Font` property almost always needs to be changed because the setting is too small. In addition, you'll have to increase the size of the list box if you want to see more than two items at a time. Figure 10.2 shows the result of selecting one of the list box items and sending that selected item to the text box.

FIGURE 10.2.
The text box now holds the list box's selected item.

List box items have index values, and you distinguish each list box item from the others by its index. The index starts at zero for the first item and increases without any duplicates in the list. The list box's `ListIndex` property holds the value of the currently selected list box item. Therefore, you can determine which value is selected. Other list box methods, such as the `RemoveItem` method, uses the `ListIndex` property to remove items you want removed from the list. For example, to remove the third list box item, your program would do this:

```
lstColors.RemoveItem 2
```

As the program removes items, the index values automatically renumber. Therefore, the fourth item in a list will have the index value `3` (due to the indexes starting at `0`), but if you remove an item that comes before it, the fourth item becomes the third item and, therefore, takes on the index value `2`. If you've set the `Sorted` property to `True`, Visual Basic re-sorts the index values after each add or remove operation.

> **Tip**
>
> Once in a while, you'll want to let the user select multiple items from a list box, when appropriate. The user holds down the Ctrl key while selecting several items in the list box to specify the multiple values. Obviously, the list box's `Value` property cannot hold all the selected values, so other provisions must be made when you allow for multiple selections. Bonus Project 5, which appears before Day 11's lesson, demonstrates how you can set up a list box to allow for, and recognize, multiple user selections.

List box index values work a lot like arrays, as you'll see in the final section of today's lesson.

Users cannot directly add values to a list box. A list box gains items only when the code inside the application uses the `AddItem` method to add additional items. Users also cannot directly delete items. The code's `RemoveItem` method has to do the removal. Suppose you needed the application to remove all the items added so far to a list box. Although you could apply the `RemoveItem` method to each list box item, a `For` loop makes more sense. You can code the loop as follows (given the previous example's list box):

```
' Removes the first 5 items from the list
For intI = 0 To 5
  lstColors.RemoveItem 0
Next intI
```

When using a `For` loop, you must keep track of how many items are in the list. Because your code is what adds those items to the list, you should have no trouble keeping track of the count.

If, through programming, you give users a chance to add items to the list (by giving a data-entry text box and a command button that, when clicked, triggers the `AddItem` method), the list could grow, but you can still keep track of the count through a variable that is added to or decreased every time an item goes into or comes off the list. (The user simply cannot directly add or remove items from a simple list box.)

Although you can keep track of a counter variable every time an item goes on or off a list, you don't have to keep track of your list's items, because Visual Basic internally keeps a count of the number of items for you. The `ListCount` property keeps a running total of the number of items in the list. `ListCount` is always one greater than the highest `ListIndex`, because `ListIndex` starts at zero. Therefore, any time you want to reference the entire list box with a `For` loop, or any time you need to know the current total of list box items, you can use the `ListCount` property, as shown in this loop:

```
' Removes all the items from the list
intTotal = lstColors.ListCount  ' Save number
For intI = 1 To intTotal
  lstColors.RemoveItem 0
Next intI
```

The list box control's `Clear` method clears all items immediately without requiring a loop. Therefore, if you want to clear all the contents at once, instead of using a range (which you'd normally use for a `For` loop), you can erase the entire list by using `lstColors.Clear`.

Combo Box Controls

The combo box control comes in the following three flavors:

- The drop-down list combo box
- The simple combo box
- The drop-down combo box

New Term Whereas a simple list box appears on the form in the size you designate, the *drop-down list combo box* always takes a single line on the form until the user opens the list to display its values.

New Term The *simple combo box* looks and operates like a simple list box with an attached text box. Users can add values to a simple combo box by entering them in the control's attached text box.

New Term The *drop-down combo box* saves screen space by remaining closed, looking like a one-line list box, until the user selects the control. Then, the drop-down combo box opens to display a list of items. The user can select from the list or enter a new value. into the text box that your code can then add to the list.

All the combo box controls are similar to the list box in the way you initialize and access them from your code. Their primary differences lie in the way they appear on the screen and the way they allow your users to select and enter data.

All three types of combo boxes come from a single source: the toolbox's combo box control. When you place a combo box control on a form, you must tell Visual Basic, through the combo box's `Style` property, which combo box you want to use. The default style when you first place a combo box on a form is `0 - Dropdown Combo`. This is the simplest combo box to begin with.

Tip

Remember that the `Sorted` property automatically keeps lists sorted for you, alphabetically or numerically, even when users add new values to the list. If you don't specify `True` for the `Sorted` property, the list remains unsorted in the order that items are put into it.

The drop-down list combo box acts and works just like a list box, except that a list box commonly takes up more room on a form than a drop-down list combo box. When a user clicks the drop-down list combo box's arrow, however, the drop-down list combo box opens up to display a list of values.

Figure 10.3 shows a form with two drop-down list combo boxes that each hold the same values. Before the right combo box was pulled down, both boxes took up the same amount of space on the form. A user, by clicking the right drop-down list combo box's arrow, can open the combo box to see the entries and to select one or more values from the combo box.

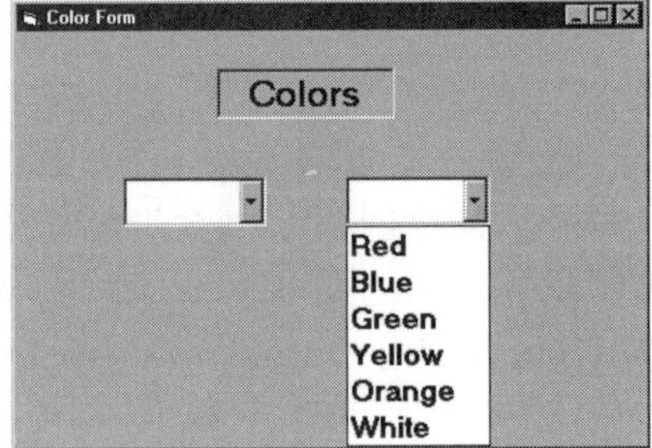

FIGURE 10.3.
A drop-down list combo box takes up only a small part of the form until a user selects it.

Use drop-down list combo boxes when you need to offer a list of choices but also need to save room on the form. As you can see from Figure 10.3, a drop-down list combo box displays no text until a user selects the control. Therefore, you need to make sure you explain to your users, via a label or a message box, exactly what the drop-down list combo box contains.

Use the `AddItem` method to add entries to the drop-down list combo box just as you did with the list box. The following code adds the six colors to the controls on Figure 10.3:

```
Private Sub Form_Load()
' Initialize both combo boxes
    cboColor1.AddItem "Red"
    cboColor1.AddItem "Blue"
    cboColor1.AddItem "Green"
    cboColor1.AddItem "Yellow"
    cboColor1.AddItem "Orange"
    cboColor1.AddItem "White"

    cboColor2.AddItem "Red"
    cboColor2.AddItem "Blue"
    cboColor2.AddItem "Green"
    cboColor2.AddItem "Yellow"
    cboColor2.AddItem "Orange"
    cboColor2.AddItem "White"
End Sub
```

The drop-down list combo box supports the same methods and properties as the list box.

The next combo box, the simple combo box, works like a list box with a text box at the top of the list. In other words, users can select from a list or enter new values in the list. When you add a combo box control to a form and set the `Style` property to `1 - Simple Combo`, Visual Basic changes the control so that you can size it the same way you'd size a list box. If you don't give the simple combo box more width and height than is needed to display its values at any time during the application's execution, the simple combo box displays scrollbars to let users scroll through the items.

Figure 10.4 shows the colors listed in a simple combo box control. Your code can load the box with names by using the `AddItem` method, and users can enter additional items. Be sure to blank out the simple combo box's `Text` property when you place the control on the form; otherwise, the control's name will appear in place of the users' data-entry space. If you specify a `Text` property at design time, the simple combo box control uses that value for the default, which users can accept or change.

FIGURE 10.4.
A user can enter a color value or select one from the list of existing colors.

The colors listed in the simple combo box in Figure 10.4 appear alphabetically due to the `Sorted` property. To ensure that the items appear alphabetically, no matter in which order they entered in the list, set the `Sorted` property to `True`.

When you place a simple combo box control on a form and set its `Style` property to `1 - Simple Combo`, you must change the control to the size in which you want it to appear. Unlike a drop-down list, the simple combo box always stays the same size.

A simple combo box doesn't add user entries automatically. You must supply code that adds the entries to the combo box when the user is allowed to add values. Although most programmers place simple combo boxes on forms to let the user select or enter a new value, if you want to add the user's value to the simple combo box list, you must provide the following code inside the simple combo box's `LostFocus()` event procedure:

```
Private Sub cboColor_LostFocus()
  cboColor2.AddItem cboColor1.Text
End Sub
```

The `LostFocus()` event procedure executes when the control loses focus, which happens when the user clicks another control or moves the focus away from the simple combo box with the Tab key. Right as the focus moves to another control, the `LostFocus()` event procedure executes and the code saves the simple combo box's value entered by user (stored in the `Text` property) into the simple combo box's list using the `AddItem` method. Figure 10.4 shows a command button because after the user enters a new color name, he or she must shift the focus to another control. Otherwise, the simple combo box won't be able to add the new entry.

The best of all list and combo controls seems to be the drop-down combo box. The drop-down combo box saves screen space by remaining closed until users select the control. Then, the drop-down combo box opens to display a list of items. Users can select from the list or enter a new value. The `Selected` and `ListCount` properties, as well as other list box properties, work for drop-down combo boxes, so your code can always determine whether the user entered a new value or selected an existing one. Unlike the drop-down list box, the drop-down combo box can be added to.

Make sure the combo box's `Style` property is set to `0 - Dropdown Combo` (the default) when you want to work with a drop-down combo box. To continue using this lesson's familiar color list example, Figure 10.5 shows the color list—except this list appears as a drop-down combo box.

FIGURE 10.5.

The user can select a value or enter a new value.

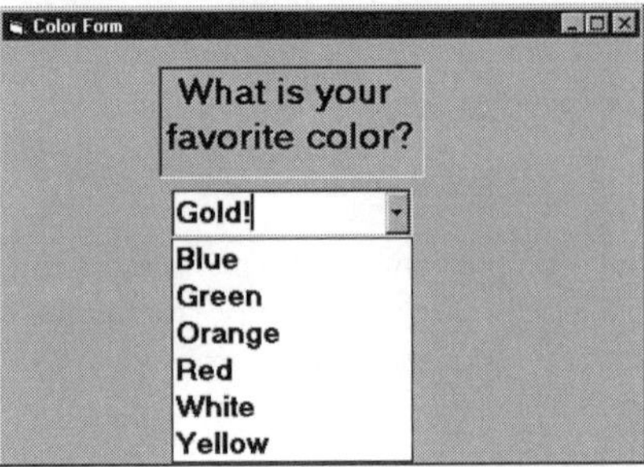

As with the simple combo box, be sure to clear the drop-down combo box's `Text` property when you place the control on the form so that nothing appears in the text box at the top of the drop-down combo box. Users can enter new values (adding those values when the focus leaves the control, as was done in the previous example) or open the drop-down combo box to display and select from the list.

The Timer Control

The timer control enables you to generate responses based on the value of the computer's internal clock. You can write code that executes after a certain amount of time passes, and you can use the timer control to perform background processing. Your computer's clock triggers a timer event 18 times a second. The clock is vital to the workings of your CPU, memory, and disk, because data must flow in an orderly and timed manner.

Note

Your PC generates a timer event 18 times a second, no matter how fast or how slow your PC is.

Visual Basic applications can respond to the clock's time events. Although the user does not generate timer events, your PC does, and Windows passes those events onto every running program. You can set up a preset interval of time after which Windows sends an event message to your application. As with all events, you can write event procedures that execute each time the timer event takes place. The bottom line is that you can write code that executes whenever a fixed amount of time passes, and you don't have to rely on the user's PC speed in any way because the time is constant.

The timer control receives the timer events and responds according to the properties you set. When you place the Visual Basic timer control on a form, you set up the time interval that determines the frequency of timer events. That time interval is one of the timer control's properties. When the interval of time passes, the timer control triggers the event procedure that you've set up to handle the timer events.

Note

You can add multiple timer controls to your application the same as you can add several instances of other controls. For example, your application can perform an event procedure every minute, every half hour, and every hour (as might be required of a time and billing application) if you place three timer controls on the application's form and set the three time intervals.

> You'll think of many uses for the timer control as you become more familiar with it. For example, you can use timer event procedures to perform background processing. Also, you can animate graphics by redrawing the graphic image every time your preset timer event occurs, such as every half a second.

The best way to place a timer control on your form is to double-click the timer control icon in the toolbox and then move the control that appears on the form out of the way of the other objects. The timer control is similar to the common dialog box control in that you cannot resize it and it doesn't appear on your form at runtime.

Figure 10.6 shows a timer control placed in the center of a new form.

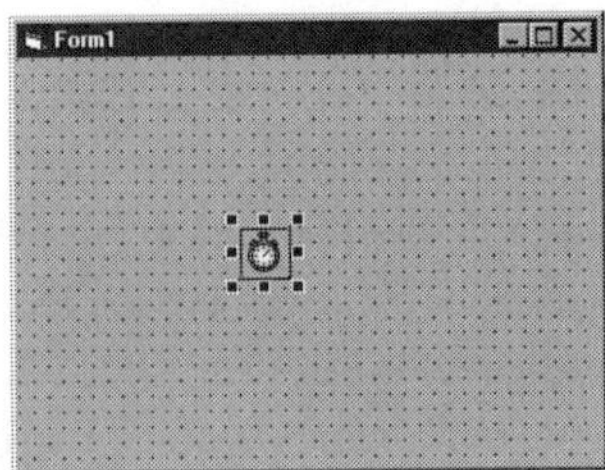

FIGURE 10.6.
You can move a timer control around on the form, but you cannot resize it.

The timer control supports very few properties. Of the six design time properties you can set, five aren't particularly unique:

- `Left` and `Top` determine the timer control's location.
- `Enabled` determines the timer's activated state.
- `Tag` holds remark information that you might want to include with the control.
- `Index` determines the control's subscript in a control array.

> If you set the timer control's `Enabled` property to `False` at designtime, the timer control won't begin responding to events until your code sets `Enabled` to `True`.

The only property critical and truly unique to the timer control is the `Interval` property. The `Interval` property determines the frequency with which you want the timer control to generate events. You enter at design time or runtime the number of milliseconds that have to pass before the timer control responds to an event. For example, if you set the `Interval` property to a value of `1000`, the timer events will occur every 1,000 milliseconds, or roughly once per second.

The timer control seems to have some drawbacks at first. The `Interval` property can hold values only from `0` to `64,767`. Therefore, you can set a time interval that spans only about 65 seconds and no more. If you need to set an event interval greater than 65 seconds, you simply can't do so. However, in the timer control's `Timer` event procedure, you can ignore events and return to the application without responding to the event until a certain amount of time passes. In other words, although the event procedure you've set up for the timer control might trigger every 60 seconds, you can place code at the top of the event procedure to return to the application and not respond to the event unless a fixed amount of time has passed (such as an hour or whatever) since the previous execution of the event procedure.

Caution

> The timer control isn't actually extremely accurate. Although the crystal inside your computer's clock is highly accurate, by the time Windows sends a timer event to your application, some accuracy is lost. Also, other events that occur can slow down the timer, such as a network access or modem update. Your computer can't do two things at once, and a timer control inside a running Visual Basic application doesn't always get high priority. Therefore, the timer control works well when time sensitivity is important to the nearest second; however, no control exists in Visual Basic that provides higher precision.

The timer control supports only a single event: the `Timer` event. Therefore, if your timer control is named `tmrClock`, you'll write only a single event procedure for the timer control: `tmrClock_Timer()`. You'll put the code inside `tmrClock_Timer()` that you want Visual Basic to execute once every time the interval passes.

For practice, you can follow these steps to create a simple application that demonstrates the timer control:

1. Create a new project and place a timer control on the form.
2. Set the timer control's `Interval` property to `1000` so that the it responds to the timer event procedure every second.
3. Name the timer `tmrTimer1` and move it to the lower-left corner of the form window.
4. Place another timer control named `tmrTimer2` on the form next to the first one. Set its `Interval` property value to `500` so that it responds to its timer event procedures every half second.
5. Add two text boxes to the form named `txtTimer1` and `txtTimer2`. Position the text boxes as shown in Figure 10.7.

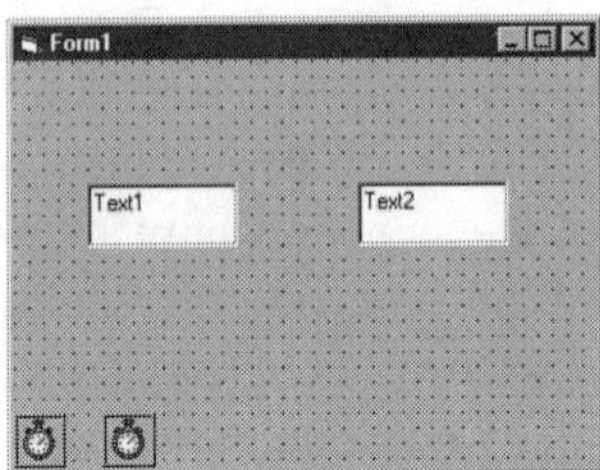

FIGURE 10.7.

The timer-based application is almost finished.

6. Type `1` for both text box controls' `Text` properties and set the text box font size to 18. Set both text box `Alignment` properties to `2 - Center` so that their text appears centered inside the boxes at runtime. Set both text box `Width` properties to `1000`.
7. Double-click the first timer to switch to the Code window and enter the following code for the `tmrTime1_Timer()` procedure (Visual Basic already types the first and last lines for you):

```
Private Sub tmrTimer1_Timer()
  ' Add one to the display
  txtTime1.Text = txtTime1.Text + 1
End Sub
```

8. Add the following code for the second timer's event procedure:

```
Private Sub tmrTimer2_Timer()
  ' Add one to the display
  txtTime2.Text = txtTime2.Text + 1
End Sub
```

   This code adds a numeric 1 to the text box values because Visual Basic stores the values with the Variant data type.
9. Add a couple labels beneath the text boxes. One should read *Slow* and the other should read *Fast*.
10. Run the application. Your form should look something like the one shown in Figure 10.8. Two things are happening: The first text box updates every second, and the second text box updates every half a second. Depending on the accuracy of the timer events, the second text box should update twice as fast as the first text box.

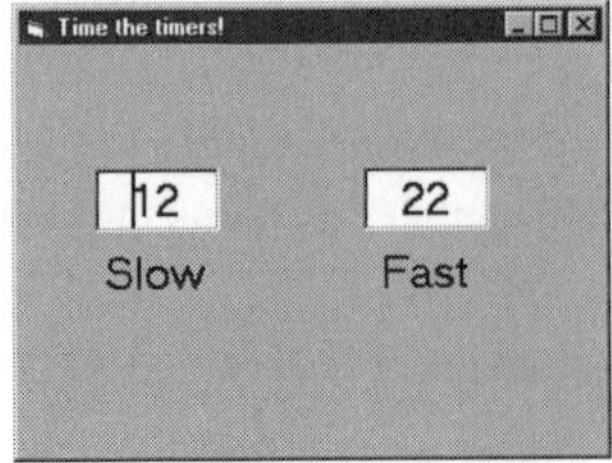

FIGURE 10.8.

The two timers update at different time intervals.

Working with Arrays

The list box controls demonstrated the use of index values. Each item in a list box has an index that begins at 0. The subsequent list box items have an index that have an index of 1, 2, 3, and so on. The list box has just one name but can have many items in the list. You distinguish the items by their index values.

The indexed items in a list box provide a good analogy for the new concept you'll learn in this section: *arrays*. Whereas a list box is a control that contains indexed items, an array is a list of variables that contains indexed items. In programming terminology, an array's *index* value is called a *subscript*.

New Term An *array* is a list of variables, all with the same data type and name. Programmers distinguish between the individual variables in the list by the list's *subscript*.

New Term A *subscript* is the numeric index value of the elements in an array.

The following variables are individual variables and are not part of an array:

```
intCount      curPay      sngLength      strDeptCode
```

If you need to store individual values in variables, such as a bonus amount for a salesperson, individual variables work well. However, if you need to store a list of similar values, you'll want to use an array.

Not all your Visual Basic data will be stored in arrays once you learn how to declare and use them. Arrays are for lists of data. You still use individual variables (such as those you've seen throughout these lessons) for loop control and user input. When you have multiple occurrences of data that you must be tracked within your application (such as fields from a table that you read into memory), an array is the perfect holder for that data.

Tip

What if you had to process 100 salespeople's bonus payment statistics and needed to find the average bonus, the maximum, the minimum, and the standard deviation between the values? One way to keep track of all 100 salespeople's bonus amounts is to declare 100 variables, all with different names, such as `curBonus1`, `curBonus2`, and so on. Think of how you would add together those bonuses! You would have to list, every time you added or compared the bonuses, 100 variable names inside a single statement. Such a situation lends itself perfectly to arrays. Instead of 100 variable

> names, you only need to declare *one* array. The array will contain the list of 100 bonuses. The array has only one name. To step through the array values, you don't need a list of 100 variable names, you only need a simple `For` loop, which steps through the subscripts from 1 to 100. Are you beginning to see how arrays will help in such situations?

To make things even clearer, here's a fragment of the code used to add 100 separate variables together if they had different names:

```
curTotal = curBonus1 + curBonus2 + curBonus3 + curBonus4 + ...
```

Here's the code that adds together 100 elements from an array:

```
For intCtr = 1 To 100
  curTotal = curTotal + curBonus(intCtr)
Next intCtr
```

You can also loop backwards through the bonuses if you want. In addition, you never have to access the array elements in order. Suppose to want to average the first and last bonuses in the array. The following statement does just that:

```
curAvgBonus = (curBonus(1) + curBonus(100)) / 2.0
```

Just from this code, you can glean the following information about arrays:

- Array subscripts go inside parentheses after the array name.
- All elements of an array have the same data type.
- You can access any array element in any order by specifying its subscript.
- The subscripts range from 1 to the total elements in the array.

Actually, that last item shows my bias toward a starting subscript of 1. Visual Basic allows a subscript of 0, but Visual Basic programmers (unlike C and C++ programmers) seem to prefer starting with the 1 subscript and ignoring the 0 subscript. In reality, all subscripts begin at 0 unless you insert the following statement in the module's Declarations section:

```
Option Base 1
```

Visual Basic offers yet another way to specify the lower range value of the subscript, as you'll see in the next section when you learn how to declare arrays.

Tip

> Some Visual Basic programmers like to use an additional variable name prefix for array names, such as `strar` as the prefix for a string array and `intar` as the prefix before the name of an array of integers.

> Visual Basic supports two kinds of arrays: static arrays and dynamic arrays. This book discusses static arrays, which are fixed in size and can't be changed at runtime. (You can change dynamic array sizes during the program's execution.) Static arrays are much more efficient and more utilized in Visual Basic programming.

In one respect, accessing an array value works like a set of boxes in a post office. The address of all the boxes is the same (they're all located in the same building), but mail is inserted into the appropriate box number.

Declaring Arrays

As with individual variables, you must tell Visual Basic that you're going to use an array by declaring the array before you use it. You use the `Public` or `Dim` statement to declare arrays just as you would use them for declaring individual variables. Your choice of statements depends on the kind of array scope you need and where you want to declare the array.

Use `Public` to declare a public array that can be used throughout the entire application (across all modules). The `Public` statement must appear in the standard module's `Declarations` section. If you use a `Dim` statement in a module's `Declarations` section, you create a module-level array that can be used throughout the module. You can declare local arrays with `Dim` at the top of any procedure.

The only difference between declaring arrays and individual variables is the introduction of subscripts in the declaration statements. Here are the respective formats of the two statements:

```
Public arName(intSub) [As dataType][, arName(intSub) [As dataType]]...
```

```
Dim arName(intSub) [As dataType][, arName(intSub) [As dataType]]...
```

Name arrays just as you would regular variables (with the exception of using the extra `ar` prefix characters if you wish). You can create an array of any data type, so *`dataType`* can be `Integer`, `Single`, or any of the data types with which you're familiar. The *`intSub`* portion of the commands describes the number of elements and how you refer to those array elements. In the preceding statement formats, `intSub` can take on the following format:

```
[intLow To] intHigh
```

This lesson teaches you how to declare *single-dimension* arrays, which are arrays with only one subscript. You can declare multidimensioned arrays, better known as *tables*, with Visual Basic as well.

Unlike other programming languages, Visual Basic offers one exception to the rule that says all elements of an array must be the same data type. Although an array *can* hold only one data type, you can declare an array to be of the Variant data type, and, if you do, the array elements can hold values of different data types because variant data can be any type of data.

The following statement declares an integer array with five elements (assume an `Option Base 1` statement appears in the Declarations section):

```
Dim intCounts(5) As Integer
```

Figure 10.9 shows what this array looks like in memory.

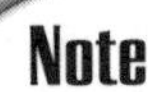

Without the `Option Base 1` statement, the `Dim` statement that declares the `intCounts` array would have declared a six-element array with the subscripts 0 through 5.

What is in `intCounts(1)` through `intCounts(5)`? You don't know and neither does the programmer. Like any other variable, the program must initialize the array elements before they are used. As long as you use the subscript, you can use array elements anywhere you use other variables, as in the following statements:

```
intNumber = intCounts(2) * intFactor / 15

txtValue.Text = intCounts(4)

intCounts(5) = 0
```

Both of the following statements are equivalent:

```
Dim intCounts(5) As Integer

Dim intCounts(1 To 5)
```

FIGURE 10.9.
The `intCounts` array has five elements with a starting subscript of 1.

You can, with the `To` clause, specify the starting and ending subscript values. Consider the following three array declarations:

```
Public varCustNumber(200 To 999) As Variant

Public strCustName(200 To 999) As String

Public curCustBalance(200 To 999) As Currency
```

The first subscript in each array is 200, and the last is 999. With this declaration, if you attempted to use `strCustName(4)`, Visual Basic would generate an error because the subscripts don't begin until 200.

The highest subscript doesn't necessarily specify the number of array elements when you use the `To` clause. These three arrays, for example, have a total of 800 elements each (subscripted from 200 to 999).

You may find that your data fits within subscript ranges that differ from the defaults (those that start at 0 or 1). The previous declarations might be good to use, for example, if you were storing customer information and your lowest customer number is 200. Therefore, it makes sense to begin the array subscripts at 200 and store the first customer at his or her array subscript number, 200.

The highest subscript that you declare should leave you ample room so that you have enough elements for the data list you want to hold.

Visual Basic includes a special built-in function called `Array()`. The `Array()` function lets you declare and initialize an array quickly.

> The `Array()` function works somewhat like the old BASIC `READ` and `DATA` statements. You can quickly initialize small arrays if you know the array data values at programming time.

A `Variant` data type can contain any other data type, including arrays. Suppose you want to store the number of days in each month (ignoring leap year) in an array named `Days`. You can declare a `Variant` variable like this:

```
Dim Days As Variant
```

You can then initialize the array in one step with the `Array()` function (rather than using a `For` loop), like this:

```
Days = Array(31, 28, 31, 30, 31, 30, 31, 31, 30, 31, 30, 31)
```

If the `Option Base 1` statement appears in the module's `Declarations` section, the first subscript of `Array()` is 1, or 0 otherwise. You can declare and initialize strings and dates as well by using the simple `Array()` function assignment to a `Variant` value.

Using Arrays

As you saw in the previous section, you may use arrays in calculations, just as you use non-array variables, as done in the following statement:

```
curFamilyDues(5) = curFamilyDues(4) * 1.5
```

To use data in an array, you have to use only the subscript of the array element you want to work with.

The best way to learn how to use subscripts is to see examples of them in use. Although the following example shows array elements being filled up by an `InputBox()` function, most programs get most of their input data from files and forms. Because arrays can store very large amounts of data, you don't want to have to type that data into the variables every time you run a program. Assignment statements don't suffice either, because they aren't good statements to use for extremely large amounts of data and interactive programs.

In Listing 10.3 is a program that declares two arrays for a neighborhood association's 35 family names and their annual dues. The program prompts for the input and then prints the data.

> If you run this program, you may want to change the number from 35 down to 5 or so to keep from having to type so much input.

LISTING 10.3. ARRAYS SIMPLIFY DATA STORAGE.

```
1:  Private Sub association ()
2:  ' Procedure to gather and print 35 names and dues
3:    Dim strFamilyName(35) As String ' Reserve the array elements
4:    Dim curFamilyDues(35) As Currency
5:    Dim intSub As Integer
6:    Dim intMsg As Integer  ' MsgBox() return
7:
8:    ' Loop getting all of the data
9:    For intSub = 1 To 35
10:     strFamilyName(intSub) = InputBox("What is the next family's name")
21:     curFamilyDues(intSub) = InputBox("What are their dues?")
22:   Next intSub
23:
24:   ' You now can display all the data
25:   ' This example uses a series of message boxes simply
26:   ' because that's what you know at this point
27:   intSub = 1 ' Initialize the first subscript
28:   Do
29:     intMsg = MsgBox("Family " & intSub & " is " & strFamilyName(intSub))
30:     intMsg = MsgBox("Their dues are " & curFamilyDues(intSub))
31:     intSub = intSub + 1
32:   Loop Until (intSub > 35)
33: End Sub
```

Notice that the program can input and print all the names and dues with simple routines. The input routine in lines 9 through 22 uses a `For` loop, and the printing routine in lines 28 through 32 uses a `Do` loop. The method you use to control the loop isn't critical. The important thing to see at this point is that you can input and print a great deal of data without having to write a lot of code. The array subscripts and loop-controlling statements make the printing possible.

This example illustrates *parallel arrays*—that is, two arrays working side by side. Each element in one array corresponds to an element in the other array. Parallel arrays work in memory like joined fields work together in tables.

The neighborhood association program is fine for an illustration, but it works only if there are exactly 35 families. What if the association grows? If it were to grow, you would have to change the program. Therefore, most programs don't have a set limit size for data, as the preceding program did. Most programmers declare more than enough array elements to handle the largest array ever needed. The program then allows users to control how many of those elements are really used.

The program in Listing 10.4 is similar to the one in Listing 10.3, except that it declares 500 elements for each array. This number reserves more than enough array elements for the association. Users then input only the actual number (from 1 to 500 maximum). The program is very flexible, allowing a variable number of members input and printed each time it's run. It does need an eventual limit, however, but that limit is reached only when there are 500 members.

Declare enough array space for your estimated needs, but don't declare more array space than you can possibly use. For every extra array element that you reserve but don't use, memory is wasted.

LISTING 10.4. YOU CAN RESERVE MORE ELEMENTS THAN YOU CURRENTLY NEED.

```
Private Sub varyNumb ()
' Procedure to gather and print names and dues
  Dim strFamilyName(500) As String    ' Reserve enough array elements
  Dim curFamilyDues(500) As Currency
  Dim intSub As Integer, intNumFam As Integer
  Dim intMsg As Integer  ' MsgBox() return
  intNumFam = 1

  ' The following loop asks for family names and dues until the
  ' user presses Enter without typing a name. Whenever a zero-length
  ' string is entered (just an Enter keypress), the Do-Loop exits
  ' early with sub holding the number input to that point.
  Do
    strFamilyName(intNumFam) = InputBox("What is next family's name?")
    If (strFamilyName(intNumFam) = "") Then Exit Do      ' Exits early
    curFamilyDues(intNumFam) = InputBox("What are their dues?")
    intNumFam = intNumFam + 1 ' Add one to the subscript variable
  Loop Until (intNumFam > 500)

 ' When the last loop finishes, intSub holds one
 ' more than the actual number input
```

```
23:   ' Displays all the input data
24:  For intSub = 1 To intNumFam - 1
25:     intMsg = MsgBox("Family" & intSub & "is " & strFamilyName(intSub))
26:     intMsg = MsgBox("Their dues are " & curFamilyDues(intSub))
27: Next intSub
28: End Sub
```

Line 15's empty Enter keypress is a good way to trigger the early exit of the loop. Just because 500 elements are reserved for each array doesn't mean that you have to use all 500 of them.

The program in Listing 10.5 shows how to access various elements from an array in random order. The program requests salary data for the last 12 months. It then waits until a user types the month he or she wants to see. That month's sales are then printed, without the surrounding months getting in the way. This is how you begin to build a search program to find requested data that's stored in arrays; store the data in an array, and then wait for a request from the users to see only specific pieces of that data.

LISTING 10.5. USE ARRAYS FOR DATA-SEARCHING CODE.

```
1:  Private Sub salary ()
2:  ' Store 12 months of salaries, and print selected ones
3:    Dim curSal(1 To 12) As Currency   ' Reserve elements for 12 salaries
4:    Dim intSub As Integer     ' Loop subscript
5:    Dim intNum As Integer     ' User's month number
6:    Dim intMsg As Integer        ' MsgBox() return
7:    Dim strAns As String
8:
9:    For intSub = 1 To 12
10:     curSal(intSub) = InputBox("What is salary for month" & Str(intSub) _
        & "?", 0.00)
11:   Next intSub
12:
13:     ' Request the month number
14:   Do
15:     intNum = InputBox("For what month (1-12) do you want a salary?")
16:     intMsg = MsgBox("The salary for month" & Str(intNum) & " is " & _
        curSal(intNum))
17:   strAns = InputBox("Do you want to see another (Y/N)?")
18:   Loop While (strAns = "Y" Or strAns = "y")
19: End Sub
```

After a user enters the 12 salaries into the array in lines 9 through 11, he or she can request any or all of them, one at a time, simply by supplying the month number (the number of the subscript).

The program in Listing 10.6 shows some of the math operations you can perform on arrays. Study the program to see how it asks for a list of temperatures and keeps asking for them until the user enters –99 to signal that there are no more temperatures. The program then computes the average temperature by adding all the temperatures and dividing by the total number of temperatures.

LISTING 10.6. LET THE USER TELL YOUR PROGRAM WHEN NO MORE DATA REMAINS TO BE ENTERED.

```
Private Sub tempAvg ()
' Prompt the user for a list of temperatures and average them
  Dim sngTemp(1 To 100) As Single ' Up to 100 temps
  Dim sngTotalTemp As Single    ' Holds totals as user enters temps
  Dim sngAvgTemp As Single
  Dim intSub As Integer         ' Subscript
  Dim intMsg As Integer         ' MsgBox() return

  ' Prompt user for each temperature
  For intSub = 1 To 100   ' Maximum limit
     sngTemp(intSub) = InputBox("What is next temperature (-99 ends)?")
     ' If user wants to stop, decrease count by 1 and exit loop
     If (sngTemp(intSub) = -99) Then
       intSub = intSub - 1   ' Adjust for early exit
       Exit For
     End If
     sngTotalTemp = sngTotalTemp + sngTemp(intSub)    ' Add to total

  Next intSub
  ' Compute average
  sngAvgTemp = sngTotalTemp / intSub
  intMsg = MsgBox("The average temperature was " & sngAvgTemp)
End Sub
```

Preparing for Control Arrays

Throughout the rest of this 21 day tutorial, you'll see the term *control array* used. A control array is nothing more than a list of controls, just as a variable array is a list of variables. The advantage to using a control array is the same as for using a variable array: You can step through several variables using a loop instead of having to name each individual control.

You now have the foundation laid for control arrays. Different topics, such as Day 16's object discussion ("Objects and Visual Basic"), will return to the concept of control arrays and show you how they fit in with that subject's discussion.

Summary

Today's lesson explained how you integrate the mouse into your Visual Basic applications. The mouse events inform your program of clicks, double-clicks, and the buttons pressed. By using the appropriate methods, you can provide drag-and-drop operations that let users drag one item, such as a control, from one part of the form to another.

Today's lesson also explained how to use the timer control to add time-sensitive processing to your applications. The timer control keeps track of the milliseconds that pass between PC clock ticks. When a certain amount of time has passed, the timer control triggers an event.

The list controls come in several varieties. You access the list controls via the toolbox window's combo box control and list box control. The difference between them can get confusing, but the examples in today's lesson showed all four combinations so that you can learn which ones work best for your particular applications.

Today's lesson concluded by springboarding from the list controls into variable arrays, which are similar in structure to the items in a control's list. A variable array holds multiple values, and you get to those values by the array's numeric subscript.

Tomorrow's lesson explores how you can manage forms from Visual Basic applications.

Q&A

Q How do I determine which list control to use?

A The list controls all work a bit differently, and you apply them with the list box control and the combo box control from the toolbox window. The list box control places a list box that the user can select from. The list retains the same width and height as when you placed the control on the form. Also, the user cannot add values to the list, and scrollbars appear, if needed, to display all the items in the list.

The combo box control is the control that, through its `Style` property, can mimic one of three kinds of list controls. The drop-down combo box remains closed to give your form more room until the user opens the box to display its items. The simple combo box offers a location for the user to enter new values in the list. The drop-down list box combines the space-saving feature of the drop-down combo box with the ability to have items added to the list.

Q Should I use one of the list boxes or arrays when I must present my users with a list of values?

A You don't choose between the list controls and arrays when you must offer your user a list of values. Perhaps you'll use both in the same application. The array can hold the data while your application collects and processes the data, and then you can use one of the list controls to display the data.

Workshop

The Workshop provides quiz questions to help you solidify your understanding on the material covered and exercises to provide you with experience in using what you've learned. Try to understand the quiz and exercise answers before continuing to the next chapter. Answers are provided in Appendix A, "Answers to Exercises."

Quiz

1. Which mouse events respond to specific mouse buttons? Which mouse events respond to *either* mouse button?
2. How can you determine the button clicked when a `MouseDown` event occurs?
3. How can you change the icon that appears during a drag operation?
4. How can you set up an event procedure to respond to a time interval greater than 65 seconds (the approximate limit for the timer control)?
5. How do you initialize a list control?
6. How does a program determine which item the user has selected?
7. Name two ways to remove all the items from a list control.
8. When using a combo box control that lets users enter new values, why must you offer at least one additional focus control on the form?
9. How can you ensure that a list control's list holds sorted values no matter how many items are added or removed from the list at runtime?
10. How many elements are reserved by the following `Dim` statement?

```
Dim varStaff(-18 To 4) As Variant
```

Exercises

1. Write a program that lists members of your family in a list box. Include enough so that the list box requires scrollbars. Keep the list sorted at all times.
2. Run the sample Visual Basic project `Listcmbo`, which comes with Visual Basic. The application provides a database containing computer book publishers. Click the option button labeled Use Standard Combo Box and then click to open the State field. Click the option button labeled Use Standard List Box and then click to open the State field again. You'll quickly see how the two kinds of lists differ.
3. Modify the application you wrote in Exercise 1 so that all three kinds of combo boxes appear on the form and display the same data. When one combo box changes (when the user enters a new value in the list), reflect that change in the other combo boxes.

BONUS PROJECT 4

Multiple List Boxes

This Bonus Project's application demonstrates how you can set up list boxes so that the user can select multiple items. In addition, studying this Bonus Project's application helps cement your knowledge of arrays. Part of any such application involves allowing multiple selections by setting the appropriate property value, as well as being able to determine if the user has selected more than one value and then picking the selected values out of the list to use elsewhere.

Multiple selections are often needed. For example, a community college entrance program might display a list box with a list of schools in your area, and users are to select one or more of the schools they attended. Perhaps, instead, a business might offer customers several products in a list and let the customer click one to buy it or, preferably, click *several* to buy a lot.

Preparing for Multiple Selections

To set up a list box control to accept multiple selections, you need to change the `MultiSelect` property. When you set this property to `1 - Simple` (as opposed to the default value, `0 - None`), users can select multiple values. If you set the `MultiSelect` property to `2 - Extended`, users can hold down the Shift key while clicking to select a range of items; also, users can hold down the Ctrl key while clicking to select disjointed items (just as you can do inside Windows Open dialog boxes).

Figure BP4.1 shows an application that contains several text boxes that display "Selected" when the corresponding city's list box item is selected, and "Not Selected" when the list box item isn't selected. The top list labeled "Destination" has its `MultiSelect` property set to `2 - Extended` to allow for the multiple selections.

FIGURE BP4.1.

Multiple selections in the list box are now possible.

The first thing you must do is add the controls to the form. Follow Table BP4.1 to do just that.

TABLE BP4.1. SET THESE CONTROLS AND PROPERTIES ON THE FORM.

Control Property Name	*Property Value*
Form `Name`	`frmDest`
Form `Caption`	`List Box Demo`
Form `Height`	`6600`
Form `Width`	`7230`
Label #1 `Name`	`lblListBoxCap`
Label #1 `Caption`	`Destination`
Label #1 `FontStyle`	`Bold`
Label #1 `FontSize`	`24`
Label #1 `Height`	`600`
Label #1 `Left`	`2190`

Control Property Name	*Property Value*
Label #1 Top	120
Label #1 Width	3060
Label #2 Name	lblChicago
Label #2 BorderStyle	Fixed Single
Label #2 Caption	Chicago
Label #2 FontStyle	Bold
Label #2 FontSize	18
Label #2 Height	495
Label #2 Left	360
Label #2 Top	1995
Label #2 Width	2655
Label #3 Name	lblWashington
Label #3 Caption	Washington
Label #3 BorderStyle	Fixed Single
Label #3 FontStyle	Bold
Label #3 FontSize	18
Label #3 Height	495
Label #3 Left	4035
Label #3 Top	1980
Label #3 Width	2655
Label #4 Name	lblDallas
Label #4 Caption	Dallas
Label #4 BorderStyle	Fixed Single
Label #4 FontStyle	Bold
Label #4 FontSize	18
Label #4 Height	495
Label #4 Left	360
Label #4 Top	3480
Label #4 Width	2655
Label #5 Name	lblHouston
Label #5 Caption	Houston
Label #5 BorderStyle	Fixed Single

continues

TABLE BP4.1. CONTINUED

Control Property Name	*Property Value*
Label #5 FontStyle	Bold
Label #5 FontSize	18
Label #5 Height	495
Label #5 Left	4035
Label #5 Top	3480
Label #5 Width	2655
Label #6 Name	lblSeattle
Label #6 Caption	Seattle
Label #6 BorderStyle	Fixed Single
Label #6 FontStyle	Bold
Label #6 FontSize	18
Label #6 Height	495
Label #6 Left	360
Label #6 Top	4920
Label #6 Width	2655
Label #7 Name	lblDayton
Label #7 Caption	Dayton
Label #7 BorderStyle	Fixed Single
Label #7 FontStyle	Bold
Label #7 FontSize	18
Label #7 Height	495
Label #7 Left	4035
Label #7 Top	4920
Label #7 Width	2655
List box Name	lstFirstList
List box Height	840
List box Left	2865
List box MultiSelect	2-Extended
List box Top	870
List box Width	1335
Text box #1 Name	txtChicago
Text box #1 FontSize	24

Text box #1 `FontStyle`	`Bold`
Text box #1 `Height`	`495`
Text box #1 `Left`	`120`
Text box #1 `Text`	`Not selected`
Text box #1 `Top`	`2520`
Text box #1 `Width`	`3105`
Text box #2 `Name`	`txtWashington`
Text box #2 `FontSize`	`24`
Text box #2 `FontStyle`	`Bold`
Text box #2 `Height`	`495`
Text box #2 `Left`	`3840`
Text box #2 `Text`	`Not selected`
Text box #2 `Top`	`2520`
Text box #2 `Width`	`3105`
Text box #3 `Name`	`txtDallas`
Text box #3 `FontSize`	`24`
Text box #3 `FontStyle`	`Bold`
Text box #3 `Height`	`495`
Text box #3 `Left`	`120`
Text box #3 `Text`	`Not selected`
Text box #3 `Top`	`3960`
Text box #3 `Width`	`3105`
Text box #4 `Name`	`txtHouston`
Text box #4 `FontSize`	`24`
Text box #4 `FontStyle`	`Bold`
Text box #4 `Height`	`495`
Text box #4 `Left`	`3840`
Text box #4 `Text`	`Not selected`
Text box #4 `Top`	`3960`
Text box #4 `Width`	`3105`
Text box #5 `Name`	`txtSeattle`
Text box #5 `FontSize`	`24`
Text box #5 `FontStyle`	`Bold`

continues

TABLE BP4.1. CONTINUED

Control Property Name	*Property Value*
Text box #5 `Left`	`120`
Text box #5 `Height`	`495`
Text box #5 `Text`	`Not selected`
Text box #5 `Top`	`5400`
Text box #5 `Width`	`3105`
Text box #6 `Name`	`txtDayton`
Text box #6 `FontSize`	`24`
Text box #6 `FontStyle`	`Bold`
Text box #6 `Height`	`495`
Text box #6 `Left`	`3720`
Text box #6 `Text`	`Not selected`
Text box #6 `Top`	`5400`
Text box #6 `Width`	`3105`

Adding the Code

Table BP4.1 did not offer blanks in the text box values because you can do that in the `Form_Load()` procedure. Listing BP4.1 shows the code that you need to enter for this project.

LISTING BP4.1. YOU MUST INITIALIZE THE LIST BOX AND CHECK FOR MORE THAN ONE SELECTED VALUE.

```
Private Sub Form_Load()
  ' Executes when the form loads
  lstFirstList.AddItem "Chicago"
  lstFirstList.AddItem "Dallas"
  lstFirstList.AddItem "Seattle"
  lstFirstList.AddItem "Washington"
  lstFirstList.AddItem "Houston"
  lstFirstList.AddItem "Dayton"
End Sub

Private Sub lstFirstList_Click()
  ' Copy the selected item to the first text box
  ' Copy the selected index to the second text box
  If lstFirstList.Selected(0) Then
```

```
15:     txtChicago.Text = "Selected"
16:   Else
17:     txtChicago.Text = "Not Selected"
18:   End If
19:
20:  If lstFirstList.Selected(1) Then
21:     txtDallas.Text = "Selected"
22:   Else
23:     txtDallas.Text = "Not Selected"
24:   End If
25:
26:   If lstFirstList.Selected(2) Then
27:     txtSeattle.Text = "Selected"
28:   Else
29:     txtSeattle.Text = "Not Selected"
30:  End If
31:
32:   If lstFirstList.Selected(3) Then
33:     txtWashington.Text = "Selected"
34:   Else
35:     txtWashington.Text = "Not Selected"
36:   End If
37:
38:   If lstFirstList.Selected(4) Then
39:     txtHouston.Text = "Selected"
40:  Else
41:     txtHouston.Text = "Not Selected"
42:   End If
43:
44:   If lstFirstList.Selected(5) Then
45:     txtDayton.Text = "Selected"
46:   Else
47:     txtDayton.Text = "Not Selected"
48:   End If
49:
50: End Sub
```

Analysis

Lines 3 through 8 simply initialize the scrolling list box. Remember that due to the list box's `MultiSelect` property value of `Extended`, the user can, at runtime, select more than one city value at the same time.

When multiple selections are possible, Visual Basic must create a special array that acts like a variable array but is comprised of properties. This property array is named `Selected` for the list controls. In this case, the array ranges from `Selected(0)` to

`Selected(5)`, because six selections appear in the list box. The array holds only Boolean data types.

The property array value is `True` or `False`, depending on the selection. When the program first executes, all the `Selected` values are `False`, because the user hasn't had a chance to select an item from the list box. As the user selects items, more values in the `Selected` array become `True`. The list box's `Click()` procedure (lines 11 through 48) updates all six text boxes every time the user selects another item.

If the user deselects an item by clicking a selected item, that item's `Selected` value goes back to `False`.

WEEK 2

BONUS PROJECT 5

Practice with the Mouse

This Bonus Project's application demonstrates how you write programs that respond to the mouse. By responding to mouse-based events and analyzing event procedure arguments, your application can determine if the user clicks, double-clicks, moves, or drags the mouse.

This Bonus Project works a bit differently than the others. First, you'll see a short example that describes how you change the icon used for the mouse. Then, the last few sections walk you through the creation of an application that responds to mouse events.

Changing the Mouse Icon

Changing the mouse pointer when you move the mouse over a control on a form is simple. Consider an extremely simple form with a command button in the center of it. Suppose you want the mouse cursor to change to a happy face when a user moves it over a command button named `cmdHappy`. From the command button's Properties window, you would click the ellipses to select an icon file from the \Graphics\Icons\Misc directory. The file named Face03.ico does a good job.

Now that you've displayed the mouse icon, change the command button's `MousePointer` property to `99 - Custom`. The customized value tells Visual Basic to check the `MouseIcon` property for the file to display if and only if the user moves the mouse over the command button. Figure BP5.1 shows the resulting happy mouse pointer.

FIGURE BP5.1.
The mouse pointer now looks happy.

If you create a small application with a command button in the center of the form, as shown in Figure BP5.1, you'll see that Visual Basic takes care of all the details involved in changing the icon when you move the mouse pointer over the command button.

Programming the Mouse

This project describes how to create a new project with an image control that displays a picture as you saw in Day 2's lesson ("Working with Visual Basic"). You'll set the value of the image's `Picture` property to the bull's-eye icon, which can be found in the \Graphics\Icons\Misc directory. Once you add a text box named `txtMouse` to the form (as explained in Table BP5.1), the text box will display the mouse status as you move and click the mouse. This project is useful for studying how mouse-related event procedures detect mouse actions.

Figure BP5.2 shows the form you'll create.

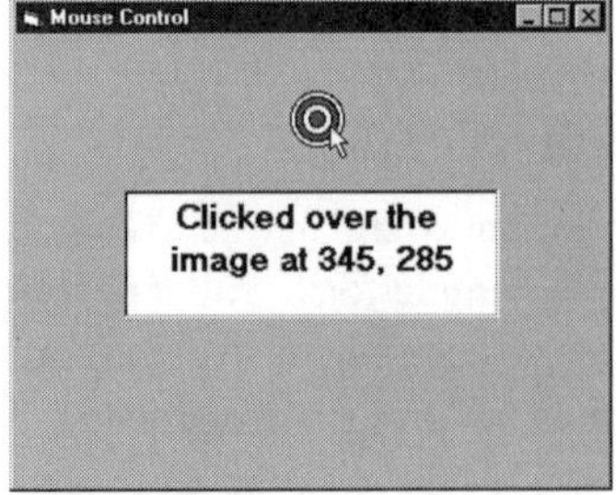

FIGURE BP5.2.
The user will click this image.

The first thing you must do is add the controls to the form. Follow Table BP5.1 to do just that.

TABLE BP5.1. SET THESE CONTROLS AND PROPERTIES ON THE FORM.

Control Property Name	*Property Value*
Form `Name`	`frmMouse`
Form `Caption`	`Mouse Control`
Form `Height`	`4230`
Form `Width`	`5265`
Text box `Name`	`txtMouse`
Text box `Alignment`	`2-Center`
Text box `FontStyle`	`Bold`
Text box `FontSize`	`14`
Text box `Height`	`1095`
Text box `Left`	`840`
Text box `MultiLine`	`True`
Text box `Text`	`Use the mouse`
Text box `Top`	`1320`
Text box `Width`	`3255`
Image `Name`	`imgMouse`
Image `Height`	`480`
Image `Left`	`2400`
Image `Picture`	`\Program Files\Microsoft Visual Studio\Common\Graphics\Icons\Misc\Bullseye`
Image `Top`	`480`

Entering the Code

BP5.1 provides the event code you need to enter for this project.

LISTING BP5.1. YOU CAN TEST FOR THE MOUSE EVENTS.

```
Private Sub Form_Click()
  txtMouse.Text = "You clicked the form"
  Beep   ' To let user know a Click event occurred
End Sub
Private Sub Form_DblClick()
  txtMouse.Text = "You double-clicked the form"
End Sub
```

continues

LISTING BP5.1. CONTINUED

```
8:
9:  Private Sub Form_MouseDown(intButton As Integer, _
    intShift As Integer, sngX As Single, sngY As Single)
10:    ' Clicked over the form
11:    txtMouse.Text = "Clicked over the form at " & sngX & ", " & sngY
12: End Sub
13: ' The arguments were ignored in the previous procedure
14:
15:  Private Sub Form_MouseMove(intButton As Integer, _
     intShift As Integer, sngX As  Single, sngY As Single)
16:    txtMouse.Text = "Moving the mouse..."
17:  End Sub
18:  ' The arguments were ignored in the previous procedure
19:
20: Private Sub imgMouse_Click()
21:   txtMouse.Text = "You clicked the image"
22: End Sub
23:
24: Private Sub imgMouse_DblClick()
25:   txtMouse.Text = "You double-clicked the image"
26: End Sub
27:
28: Private Sub imgMouse_MouseDown(intButton As Integer, intShift As _
    Integer, sngX As Single, sngY As Single)
29: '
30: ' Clicked over the image
31:   txtMouse.Text = "Clicked over the image at " & sngX & ", " & sngY
32: End Sub
33:
34: Private Sub imgMouse_MouseMove(intButton As Integer, _
    intShift As Integer, sngX As Single, sngY As Single)
35:   txtMouse.Text = "You moved over the image"
36: End Sub
```

Analysis

The various event procedures test for mouse activity. Lines 1 through 4 offer the simplest event procedure, which responds when you click anywhere on the form. The reason for the `Beep` statement is that the `Click` event will never be seen! It happens too fast and is over before you know it. The `MouseDown` event, you'll remember from Day 10 ("Adding Power with the Mouse and Controls"), occurs *before* a `Click` event if both events coexist in the code. Therefore, you'll see the `MouseDown` text appear, showing where you clicked over the form. Then, when you release the mouse button, the `Click` event text will appear very quickly and disappear. Hence, the `Beep` statement produces audible proof that the click event did eventually occur.

Note

> It's interesting to note that a double-click over the form also produces a `MouseDown` event and then a `Click` event before producing the `DblClick` event (handled by lines 9 through 12). You'll hear the beep as soon as you double-click the mouse. However, you'll first see the coordinates pass by as the `MouseDown` event changes the text to show where it occurred.

Caution

> One of the drawbacks that frustrates programmers is that a `MouseMove` event will trigger every time you click the mouse.

Lines 9 through 12 show the use of the mouse arguments from the `MouseDown` event. The `sngX` and `sngY` coordinate twip values show where you clicked the mouse. Remember that this code will execute when you left-click as well as when you right-click, because both trigger the `MouseDown` event. The procedure executes only when you click over the form, and a `Click` event will immediately follow as soon as you release the mouse.

Lines 15 through 17 handle the movement of the mouse for those times when you move the mouse over the form.

Lines 20 through 22 demonstrate what can happen when you apply the mouse to the bull's-eye icon. When you click the image, the text box updates to show that you clicked over the image and not over the form (due to the image's `Click` event procedure). However, due to the `MouseDown` event that precedes the `Click` event, you won't actually see the quick `Click`-related text that appears; if you've inserted a `Beep` statement in the `Click` event, however, you will hear the beep even though the `MouseDown` event text appears in the box.

Lines 24 through 26 demonstrate the mouse's `DblClick` event response over the image. Lines 28 through 32 demonstrate the image's `MouseDown` event that occurs, and actually takes over, before the `Click` event can proceed. Finally, lines 34 through 36 handle mouse movements over the image.

Note

> Although you could include the coordinates of a `MouseMove` event in the text box, the coordinates would change too rapidly to read.

By studying the effects of this Bonus Project, you'll know better what to expect when programming the mouse. You'll also understand how the `MouseDown` event precedes the `Click` and `DblClick` events in priority.

Implementing Automatic Drag-and-Drop

Adding drag-and-drop to the application is simple. Change the image's `DragIcon` property so that a different icon appears when you drag the mouse. Select the icon filename Clock02.ico. To implement automatic drag-and-drop, change the image's `DragMode` property to `1 - Automatic` so that Visual Basic takes care of the dragging details for you.

Now, add the following `MouseDown` event procedure:

```
Private Sub Form_DragDrop(cntSource As Control, sngX As Single, _
sngY As Single)
  Source.Move sngX, sngY   ' Drop the image
End Sub
```

The `DragDrop` event's `Source` argument is the control you're dropping onto the form, and the `sngX` and `sngY` coordinate values tell the control where the drop is occurring. The `Move` method actually moves the control (the image in this case) to the location of the drop.

Run the application and drop the bull's-eye image at different places on the form. When performing most drag-and-drop operations, you'll want to use automatic drag-and-drop so that Visual Basic handles the details of the drag.

Implementing Manual Drag-and-Drop

Manual drag-and-drop operations require that you change the `DragMode` property to `0 - Manual` and then change the `MouseDown` procedure to the following code so that the drag-and-drop takes place:

```
Private Sub imgMouse_MouseDown(intButton As Integer, _
intShift As Integer, sngX As Single, sngY As Single)
  ' Clicked over the image
  txtMouse.Text = "Clicked over the image at " & sngX & ", " & sngY
  imgMouse.Drag     ' Initiate the drag and drop
End Sub
```

The only new statement is the `imgMouse.Drag` statement. Your `MouseDown` event must initiate the drag-and-drop operation. The advantage is that you can now perform other kinds of processing in response to the `MouseDown` event, if needed, before starting the drag-and-drop operation. Without the manual drag mode, the drag would take place outside your control.

Use manual drag-and-drop when you want to perform tasks in addition to the drag-and-drop.

The `Drag` method turns on drag-and-drop. Without the `Drag` method, the `MouseDown()` event procedure couldn't initiate the drag-and-drop operation. Use manual drag-and-drop operations if you want to limit the way the drag-and-drop performs before or during the drag-and-drop process.

WEEK 2

DAY 11

Working with Forms

Today's lesson shows you how to manage and program with forms in more depth than was possible before today. You'll learn about most of the form's properties, events, and methods. One of the most helpful methods, in this lesson and when you begin printing reports, is the `Print` method, which places text directly on the form without a control. Interestingly, `Print` is a method directly based on the old BASIC language's `PRINT` command, and they both work exactly the same.

Not only will you learn how to control forms, but you'll gain more insight into the advantages and disadvantages of MDI and SDI applications, which contain multiple forms. You'll also learn how to place toolbars and coolbars on your form windows to offer users yet another way to interact with your program.

Today, you learn the following:

- Form properties, events, and methods
- Form collections
- How to send text to a form with the `Print` method
- More about MDI and SDI applications

- How to create your own form properties
- The toolbar control
- The coolbar control
- Why the image list control is so vital to toolbars and coolbars

Properties, Events, and Methods

Although you've only studied Visual Basic for 10 days, you've spent your time learning the controls and the language and are well on your way to becoming a Visual Basic programming pro! Nevertheless, one of the most important parts of a Visual Basic application, the form, has been left on the sidelines, being brought up only when a discussion of a specific form issue was needed. Today, all that changes as the form becomes the focus of today's lesson.

You already know how to use properties to change the look and behavior of forms. You can add a form caption, size the form, and control whether or not the user has form-sizing buttons available, such as the maximize and minimize buttons. In addition, you've used the `Form_Load()` event procedure to initialize list controls. This is a great place for the initialization that needs to occur before the user sees the form. (The form name is not required here because the code appears inside the Form module. The only form the code applies to is the current form, no matter what its name is.)

The `Form_Unload()` event procedure provides a place for clean-up code to execute after a form leaves the user's screen and memory. Unlike the `Form.Hide` and `Form.Show` methods, the `Form_Load()` and `Form_Unload()` event procedures perform memory management. `Form_Load()` actually loads the form into the user's memory at runtime, and `Form_Unload()` removes the form from memory at runtime. The `Show` and `Hide` methods are only aliases for the form's `Visible` property values of `True` or `False`.

Do	Don't
DO use the `Form.Hide` and `Form.Show` methods when you want to hide or display a form. Only use `Form_Load()` and `Form_Unload()` when you want to add or remove a form from the application's memory space.	

The next section, "Form Collections," describes a special use for the `Form_Unload()` event.

Often, you'll see code similar to the following inside a `Form_Load()` procedure:

```
frmAForm.Left = (Screen.Width - frmAForm.Width) / 2
frmAForm.Top = (Screen.Height - frmAForm.Height) / 2
```

This code centers the form inside the screen's coordinates. In Day 16 "Objects and Visual Basic," you'll learn about special objects that Visual Basic supports. One of those objects is the `Screen` object, which represents the user's screen. The `Screen` object changes depending on the user's screen and video card resolution. You can know the user's screen resolution at any time by accessing the `Screen` object's `Width` and `Height` properties.

One way to reduce typing is to eliminate the default object from an event procedure. Instead of typing the form name, you can rewrite the form-centering code like this:

```
Left = (Screen.Width - Width) / 2
Top = (Screen.Height - Height) / 2
```

As long as this code resides inside the form's event procedure, such as in the `Form_Load()` event procedure, you can omit the form name. Almost always, however, when you reduce typing, you increase the risk of ambiguity in your code. If you always specify all objects, even the default objects, you'll make your code clearer and easier to maintain later.

11

New Term A *default object* is the object (a form, control, or some other object) that Visual Basic uses in code if you don't provide a specific object.

Such form-centering code is useful to study because it reminds you of the form's relationship with the screen, the `Screen` object's properties, and the `Load` and `Unload` events. Nevertheless, keep in mind that the form's Properties window does include a special property named `StartUpPosition` that you can set to one of the four values, as shown in Table 11.1.

TABLE 11.1. YOU CAN SPECIFY THE INITIAL POSITION OF A FORM FROM THESE `StartUpPosition` VALUES.

Property	*Named Constant*	*Value*	*Description*
`0-Manual`	`vbStartUpManual`	0	Does not specify a starting form position
`1-CenterOwner`	`vbStartUpOwner`	1	Centers the form on the screen
`2-CenterScreen`	`vbStartUpScreen`	2	Centers the item on the screen
`3-WindowsDefault`	`vbStartUpWindowsDefault`	3	The upper-left corner of the screen

A form's events are often important to an application that uses the form. Other than the `Load` and `Unload` events, which you already understand, and the mouse-related form events that you learned yesterday, you may want to study some of the more useful form-related events that can occur. Table 11.2 lists three of these events.

TABLE 11.2. YOU CAN USE THESE FORM-RELATED EVENTS IN YOUR APPLICATIONS.

Event	*Description*
`Activate`	Occurs when the form becomes active due to the user clicking an uncovered edge of the form or switching to the application's form from another application.
`Deactivate`	Occurs when another application or form goes active.
`Resize`	Occurs when the user resizes the form or when the program uses assignments to change the form's `Height` and `Width` properties.

Tip

You can use the `Resize` property to rearrange controls on a form when the user changes the form's size. If you place the controls in a relative position to the form (using the form's size properties to place the controls), the controls stay centered when the user changes the form's size.

You may recall that the Project, Properties menu option produces the dialog box shown in Figure 11.1. This dialog box includes the Startup Object drop-down list box, where you can select one of the application's forms or a special procedure named `Main`. Some applications don't have a startup form. Such an application might be a background utility that never shows a form or, perhaps, before a form appears, a data value is checked to see exactly which form should appear. An application might also need to locate a password before displaying the startup form.

FIGURE 11.1.

Specify the startup form or procedure from the Project Properties dialog box.

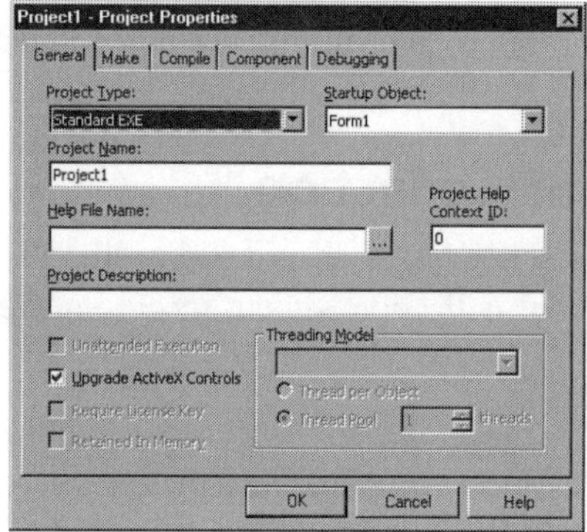

If you want code to execute before any form loads in the project, you should create a procedure called `Main()` (in the Code module's general procedure, not in a Form module) and select the `Main()` procedure from the Startup Object drop-down list in the Project Properties dialog box. The code inside `Main()` will execute before any form loads. As a matter of fact, no form ever will load unless the `Main()` procedure triggers the `Show` method for a form.

11

> **Note**
>
> You'll learn about more form-related methods when you get to the lessons in Day 13, "Printing VB Output," and Day 14, "Introducing VB Graphics and Multimedia."

Form Collections

As mentioned in the previous section, a *form* is often known as an *object*. Visual Basic supports several kinds of objects—for example, controls, forms, and objects that reside outside your application, such as an OLE object. (OLE stands for *object linking and embedding*; you learn more about objects and OLE in Days 16, "Objects and Visual Basic," and 17, "ActiveX Controls.")

All your form objects comprise the `Forms` collection, which changes as you create and remove forms within your project. The `Forms` collection contains the name of every form. Therefore, frmAboutBox might be the name of one of your forms within the `Forms` collection. A predefined object named `Form`—without the *s*—defines the currently open form. Visual Basic uses this predefined form object to handle the default object, which you don't have to specify when you issue methods without qualifying the current form's name.

A `Forms` collection is the group of forms currently defined in your application.

Accessing the `Forms` Collection

Before accessing the `Forms` collection, you should realize that Visual Basic lets you refer to all the forms within the `Forms` collection without specifying the names of the individual open forms.

For example, assume you have open three forms named `frmAcPay`, `frmAcRec`, and `frmAcReview`. The predefined object `Forms` contains these three forms. Each form is indexed, starting at zero, and you can refer to the forms by the index number instead of by name. This number, usually called the *subscript*, follows after the `Forms` collection object enclosed by parentheses. Table 11.3 shows you how you can refer to the three forms by using the subscript.

The `Forms` collection operates like a list box's values or an array's elements.

Table 11.3. Use subscripts to access objects in the `Forms` collection.

Form Name	`Forms` *Subscript Notation*
`frmAcPay`	`Forms(0)`
`frmAcRec`	`Forms(1)`
`frmAcReview`	`Forms(2)`

Visual Basic lets you specify a specific form within a collection by using yet another notation if you know the form name. Here's an example:

```
Forms![frmAcPay]
```

This example refers to the form named `frmAcPay` inside the current collection. (Unlike in statement formats, these brackets are required.) You can also use parentheses to refer to a collection's form by name, as follows:

```
Forms!("frmAcPay").
```

Using the Subscripts

You may also refer to individual controls, such as text box fields, inside your forms by a subscript number instead of by name. This way, your programs can step through all the controls in a form without having to access the fields' individual names.

Suppose you have a form named `frmStore` that contains five controls: three label fields (`lblStoreNum`, `lblStoreName`, and `lblStoreLoc`) and two list box controls (`lstStoreEmps` and `lstStoreMgrs`). Your Visual Basic procedures can refer to each control by a subscript number, starting at 0, as shown in Table 11.4. Notice that you separate the control name from the `Forms` collection with an exclamation point to get an individual control within that collection.

TABLE 11.4. YOU MAY USE SUBSCRIPTS TO REFER TO CONTROLS ON A FORM.

Control Name	`Forms` *Subscript Notation*
`lblStoreNum`	`Forms!frmStore(0)`
`lblStoreName`	`Forms!frmStore(1)`
`lblStoreLoc`	`Forms!frmStore(2)`
`lstStoreEmps`	`Forms!frmStore(3)`
`lstStoreMgrs`	`Forms!frmStore(4)`

Don't confuse the subscripts used with specific form names with those in a `Forms` collection. If `Forms` precedes the subscript, the subscript refers to a particular form or subform. If the form name appears before the subscript, as shown in Table 11.4, the subscript refers to a control on that form.

The `Count` Property

Just as controls have properties, so do collections. The `Count` property is available to you when you need to work with the `Forms` collection. The `Count` property simplifies your programming so that you don't have to know how many individual forms reside in the collection. By using `Count`, you can write generalized procedures that work on all the currently open forms. The `Count` property always contains an integer.

Note

`Count` also contains the number of controls on a form if you apply the property to a specific form name (for example, `frmAcPay.Count`, which contains the number of controls on the form named `frmAcPay`). `Count` includes hidden and visible controls.

The following code declares an integer variable, `intC`, and then stores the number of open forms in `intC`:

```
Dim intC As Integer
intC = Forms.Count      ' Save the number of open forms
```

If you want to know the number of controls on a specific form, you can use the `Count` property as well. The following code declares an integer variable, `intCC`, and stores the number of controls on a form named `frmMyForm` in `intCC`:

```
Dim intCC As Integer
intCC = frmMyForm.Count    ' Save the number of controls on the form
```

`Count` following a form name refers to the number of controls on that form. `Count` following the `Forms` collection refers to the number of forms in the project.

A `For` loop is the perfect tool for stepping through all the open forms in the current project. Always remember to start the controlling loop with a beginning value of zero, as done here, because zero is the subscript of the first form.

The following code steps through all the open forms and hides the forms:

```
For intI = 0 To Forms.Count - 1
  Forms(intI).Visible = False    ' Hide each form
Next intI
```

You may want to hide all forms when performing a system task that requires no user I/O. After your work is done, you can then repeat the loop and set each form's `Visible` property to `True`.

Visual Basic supports a special `For` loop called the `For Each` loop. It steps through a collection without requiring you to control a loop variable. Here's identical code that hides all the open forms:

```
Dim varFrmObj As Variant
For Each varFrmObj In Forms
  varFrmObj.Visible = False    ' Hide each form
Next
```

The only loop variable you need to declare for the `For Each` loop is a `Variant` variable, which holds each form name as the loop iterates through the forms in the collection. In the same manner, the following `For Each` loop's first statement sets up a loop that steps through every control on the form named `frmMyForm`, no matter how many controls are in the collection:

```
For Each varControl In frmMyForm
```

Unloading Forms

As stated earlier in the section "Properties, Events, and Methods," a special use of the `Form_Unload()` event procedure occurs when dealing with forms. The `Unload` event can be helpful for clean-up routines, such as saving all data to disk before the application ends, but sometimes the `Unload` event is critical to proper program termination.

Suppose your application contains several forms. If your application hides a form, the user will have no way of knowing that the form is still loaded. If the user closes the primary application's window, that one form is still loaded and Windows thinks the program is still executing. Therefore, the program is still partially taking up memory when the user thinks that all forms are gone.

Many Visual Basic programmers routinely add the following code to their normal application-terminating menus or command buttons (such as the File, Exit menu option):

```
For intCtr = (Forms.Count — 1) to 0 Step - 1
  Unload Forms(intCtr)   ' Unloads both hidden and shown forms
Next intCtr
```

11

Placing Text on Forms

Instead of using a label or text box control to place text on a form, you can use the `Print` method. `Print` writes text on forms directly. One of the drawbacks to `Print` is that you must write extra code to make `Print` behave the way you want it to. `Print` is not a control, so you cannot easily set properties at designtime; instead, though code, you program how the `Print` method is to behave. For example, you must write code that makes `Print` print at a certain location on the form if you need to ensure that `Print` does not overwrite other controls.

Learning `Print` now not only shows you how to send text to forms but also provides advanced instruction for sending text to the printer. As you'll learn in Day 13's lesson, `Print` is the primary method used to direct output to the printer.

You use `Print` to send text to an object. For today's lesson, that object will be your application's form. `Print` applies to forms, picture boxes, the Printer object, and the Debug object (which is a special Immediate window to which you can send test results as a program runs). However, the easiest of all objects to write to with the `Print` method is the form.

You can practice with `Print` right now without building a complete application. Open a new project and double-click the Form1 window you see the Code window. Because you've just opened the project, no objects are available to use other than Form1 and the general procedure where the `Declarations` section resides. All predefined procedures that the form can recognize are shown in a drop-down list box. Choose Click from the list and then type the code in Listing 11.1 (as always, Visual Basic adds the wrapper lines, so you only need to type the middle statements).

LISTING 11.1. THE `Print` STATEMENT WRITES DIRECTLY TO THE FORM.

```
Private Sub Form_Click()
' Demonstrates writing to the form
  Dim strString As String
  strString = "Visual Basic"
  ' Print string three times
  Form1.Print strString & " " & strString & " " strString
End Sub
```

When you run the program, the form appears, but nothing will happen until you click the form. Remember that you entered code into the `Form_Click ()` subroutine—until you click the form, nothing should happen. Click the form several times. You should see results similar to those shown in Figure 11.2.

FIGURE 11.2.
The `Print` method sends output directly to the form.

`Print` is the one of simplest methods you can use to output information from your program to the form. To print on any form in your program, you just need to reference the form name and the `Print` method, separated by a period. Here's the format of the `Print` method when you apply it to a form:

```
frmFormName.Print DataToPrint
```

`frmFormName` is the form on which you want to print, and *`DataToPrint`* is the data you want to print.You can print literals (numeric, string, and date), variable values, and controls.

Format with `Print`

You can format the `Print` method's output by including either the `Spc()` function or the `Tab()` function. Each works inside the `Print` method to add spacing to the data you're printing.

Consider Listing 11.2, which uses `Spc()` and the semicolon (`;`) to print two strings on the same line. `Spc(5)` tells the `Print` method to skip five spaces before the text string begins printing in the sixth column. If you end a `Print` statement with a semicolon, the next `Print` statement prints where the current one left off rather than printing on the next line, as would happen without the semicolon.

LISTING 11.2. YOU CAN SUPPRESS A CARRIAGE RETURN SO THAT TWO `Print` STATEMENTS WRITE ON THE SAME LINE.

```
Private Sub Form_Click ()
  Dim strString As String
  strString = "Visual Basic"
  Form1.Print "*"; Spc(5); strString;   ' Notice semicolon.
  Form1.Print Spc(2); strString
End Sub
```


The following output will appear on the form as you click it several times to trigger the code:

```
*     Visual Basic  Visual Basic
*     Visual Basic  Visual Basic
*     Visual Basic  Visual Basic
```

The code forces the `Print` method to skip five spaces before the first `Visual Basic` text appears. After two more spaces, the second `Print` statement also prints `Visual Basic`. The next time you click, you force the event procedure to execute again, repeating the process.

If you use `Tab()` instead of `Spc()`, Visual Basic moves to the column argument located inside the parentheses and prints the next data item there. `Spc()` forces the next `Print` to begin a certain number of spaces over, whereas `Tab()` forces the next `Print` to begin in a specific column. Listing 11.3 provides an example.

LISTING 11.3. CONTROLLING THE `Print` STATEMENT'S SPACING WITH THE `Tab()` AND `Spc()` FUNCTIONS.

```
1:  Private Sub Form_Click()
2:    Dim strString As String
3:    strString = "Visual Basic"
4:
5:    Form1.Print "*"; Tab(5); strString; Tab(20); strString
6:    Form1.Print "*"; Spc(5); strString; Spc(20); strString
7: End Sub
```

In line 5, `Tab()` keeps the printing in specific columns, but `Spc()` in line 6 moves the printing over by a certain number of spaces.

Here's the output from this procedure:

```
*    Visual Basic   Visual Basic
*     Visual Basic                    Visual Basic
```

You can use the `Print` method to print blank lines on a form by not specifying any data. Consider the code in Listing 11.4.

LISTING 11.4. YOU CAN USE `Print` TO PRINT BLANK LINES ON THE FORM.

```
Private Sub Form_Click()
  Dim strString As String
  Dim CurLine As Integer

  CurLine = 1
  strString = "Visual Basic"

  ' Print the line
  Form1.Print strString & " is on Line #" & CurLine

  For CurLine = 2 To 6
    Form1.Print     ' Print blank lines!
  Next CurLine

  ' Print the line now
  Form1.Print strString & " is on Line #" & CurLine
End Sub
```

The output contains five blank lines between the lines printed:

```
Visual Basic is on Line 1





Visual Basic is on Line 7
```

Lines 11 through 13 print blank lines because the `Print` method has no data after it to print.

Positioning the `Print` Method

Often, you'll need to specify exactly where on a form you want to print. Visual Basic supports several other form-related properties that you can use with `Print` to place text on a form. These properties use the current position of the text cursor, which Visual Basic moves as the `Print` method executes. Information containing the location of the cursor is stored in the `CurrentX` and `CurrentY` properties. These properties let you determine exactly where you want your output to appear.

11

Another property, `ScaleMode`, affects how `CurrentX` and `CurrentY` behave. A form can recognize several different modes, depending on the `ScaleMode` property you set. This mode refers to the scale used for drawing graphics and text on the form. Table 11.5 shows the other `ScaleMode` values you can set. Many of these are graphics related, and you'll want to use many of the `ScaleMode` values when you learn to print to the printer in Day 13.

TABLE 11.5. THE `ScaleMode` VALUES DETERMINE THE `Print` METHOD'S COORDINATES.

Named Constant	*Value*	*Scales By*
`vbUser`	0	The programmer specifies the scale used.
`vbTwips`	1	This is the default `ScaleMode` until you change it. Specifies a scale of twips.
`vbPoints`	2	One typestyle point (1/72nd of an inch).
`vbPixels`	3	The smallest dot on the object (for a screen, the screen's dot size determines the pixel size).
`vbCharacters`	4	One character size.
`vbInches`	5	One inch.
`vbMillimeters`	6	One millimeter.

continues

TABLE 11.5. CONTINUED

Named Constant	*Value*	*Scales By*
`vbCentimeters`	7	One centimeter.
`vbHimetric`	8	Instead of pixels, some programmers prefer to work in a *Himetric* measurement that is device independent so that Windows translates the coordinates to the highest possible resolution at runtime.
`vbContainerPosition`	9	The control's container (an object that holds the current object) `ScaleMode` value determines the current object's `ScaleMode` when used as a positional value.
`vbContainerSize`	10	The control's container `ScaleMode` value determines the current object's `ScaleMode` when used as a positional value.

The most common `ScaleMode` property for text is *character mode*. This means that when `CurrentX` and `CurrentY` are both set to 5, the next `Print` method will begin at column 5, row 5. The starting position of the `ScaleMode` property is the upper-left corner of the form (with the coordinates 0,0). The `Click` event procedure in Listing 11.5 uses the `ScaleMode`, `CurrentX`, and `CurrentY` properties.

LISTING 11.5. CONTROLLING THE PLACEMENT OF THE OUTPUT WITH THE `CurrentX` AND `CurrentY` PROPERTIES.

```
1:  Private Sub Form_Click()
2:    ' Set up for characters
3:    Form1.ScaleMode = VbCharacters  ' Character (4)
4:
5:    Form1.CurrentX = 20   ' Move across 20 chars
6:    Form1.CurrentY = 6    ' Move down 6 lines
7:    Form1.Print "Down and across"
8:
9:    Form1.CurrentX = 0   ' Move back to the left
10:   Form1.CurrentY = 0   ' Move back up
11:   Form1.Print "Upper left"
12: End Sub
```

Line 3 sets the `ScaleMode` value to the named constant, which indicates a character scaling. Study the output in Figure 11.3. Notice that the output of the second `Print` method appears higher on the form than the first `Print` method's output due to the coordinate placement.

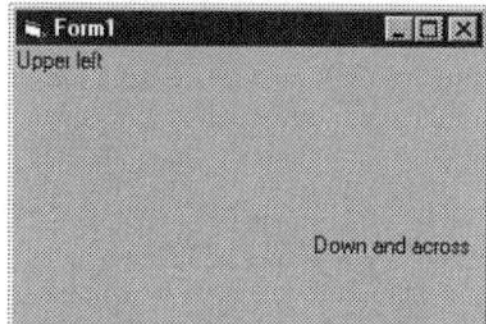

FIGURE 11.3.
Using `CurrentX` and `CurrentY` to position the `Print` method's text cursor.

Creating New Properties for Forms

You can create your own customized form properties. Although you'll not have to create form properties every time you write an application, you will, at times, find yourself making the same modifications to a form several times, and those times may lend themselves to customized form properties.

For example, suppose you want to include a title at the bottom of a form. If you were to create a form with a label at the bottom, not only would you have the label to deal with, but when you want to change the bottom title, you have to change the label. If the bottom title were just another form property, you could eliminate the use of the label control, because the bottom title will always be the text from the form's property you've designed.

11

The easiest way to learn how to create new form properties is to walk through a simple example. Create a new project with the controls and property values listed in Table 11.6. The application that you create demonstrates how you determine the `Print` method's coordinates.

TABLE 11.6. YOU CAN CHANGE THE `Print` METHOD'S COORDINATE MEASUREMENTS WITH `ScaleMode` VALUES.

Property	*Value*
Form `Name`	`frmTitle`
Form `Caption`	`Bottom Title`
Form `Height`	`3720`
Form `StartUpPosition`	`2-CenterScreen`
Form `Width`	`3975`
Command button `Name`	`cmdTitle`
Command button `Caption`	`&See Title`
Command button `Height`	`495`
Command button `Left`	`1320`
Command button `Top`	`1200`
Command button `Width`	`1215`

When the user clicks the command button, a title appears at the bottom of the form because of the following command button `Click` event procedure:

```
1:  Private Sub cmdTitle_Click()
2:    frmTitle.BottomTitle = "A new property"
3:  End Sub
```

Study line 2 well. Something probably seems wrong: There is no property called `BottomTitle`. However, after the next few steps, there will be! Follow these steps to add the new property called `BottomTitle` to your form's list of properties:

1. Click the Properties window's View Code button to enter the Code window.
2. Type the following line in the Declarations section that appears before the `cmdTitle_Click()` event procedure:

   ```
   Dim strTitle As String
   ```

   You now know that `strTitle` is a public variable available to the entire project. Public variables are frowned upon, so why declare `strTitle` as public? Remember that all controls are public to the entire application. There's no such thing as a private control or a private control property. The variable `strTitle` actually holds the value of the form's new property, the property that you'll eventually call `BottomTitle` by creating a special procedure in the next step. The `BottomTitle` property needs to have access to its placeholder variable `strTitle` at all times, thus, the requirement that `strTitle` be a public variable.
3. You'll now add a new kind of procedure to your project: a `Property Get` procedure. A `Property Get` procedure exists for all properties that you define. Visual Basic automatically executes the `Property Get` procedure when the program accesses the new property related to the `Property Get` procedure. In other words, once you create a `Property Get` procedure for the `BottomTitle` property, when the application uses the value of `BottomTitle`, Visual Basic automatically executes the `Property Get` procedure to return the current value of the property.

NEW TERM A *`Property Get` procedure* returns the value of a defined property.

Type the code in Listing 11.6 into the Code window.

LISTING 11.6. THE `Property Get` PROCEDURE RETURNS THE VALUE OF THE PROPERTY.

```
Public Property Get BottomTitle()
   ' This procedure supplies the value
   ' of the BottomTitle property
   ' which is actually held in the
   ' public strTitle variable
    BottomTitle = strTitle
End Property
```

Remember that forms do not come with a property called `BottomTitle`; you are defining this property. The true value for the `BottomTitle` property will remain in the public variable `strTitle`; however, the `Property Get` procedure makes the rest of the application think that the `BottomTitle` value is actually a property. In reality, the property value comes from a public variable.

4. You now need to supply the `Property Let` procedure for the new `BottomTitle` property. The `Property Let` procedure changes the value of the `BottomTitle` property. In reality, however, `Property Let` changes the public variable used as the code's placeholder for the `BottomTitle` property when the program assigns a value to the form's `BottomTitle` property.

NEW TERM A *`Property Let` procedure* assigns a value to the property you define.

Type the code in Listing 11.7 into the Code window.

LISTING 11.7. THE `Property Let` PROCEDURE SETS THE VALUE OF THE PROPERTY.

```
Public Property Let BottomTitle(strTitleEntered)
   ' This procedure assigns to the variable
   ' named strTitle whatever property value
   ' the program is putting into BottomTitle
   '
   ' The argument passed is the value that the
   ' program stores in BottomTitle
  strTitle = strTitleEntered
   '
   ' Place the next line to print on the bottom of the form
  frmTitle.CurrentY = (frmTitle.Height - 600)
   '
```

continues

Listing 11.7. continued

```
13:    ' If the form is so small that even a single line of
14:    ' characters cannot fit, do nothing
15:    If frmTitle.CurrentY < 600 Then
16:       Exit Property
17:    Else
18:       ' Print the property value on the form
19:       Print strTitle
20:    End If
21: End Property
```

Line 8 assigns the public variable the argument passed to the procedure. No matter where in the Visual Basic program the application assigns a value to the form's `BottomTitle` property, this procedure executes by sending that value as an argument.

Lines 11 and 15 set up the display of the title. Line 11 ensures that no matter how much the user has resized the form, the title position will appear 600 twips above the bottom of the window. If the user has resized the window too small so that even one line of text will not fit, line 16 exits the procedure without doing anything. As long as the title will fit, line 19 prints the value at the `CurrentY` position. (`CurrentX` is 0, the left edge of the window. The code never changed `CurrentX`.)

> **Tip**
>
> Once you type the `BottomTitle` property's `Property Get` and `Property Let` procedures, the `BottomTitle` property actually becomes part of the property list for the form! Although the Properties window will not ever include the new property, all property lists elsewhere will. For example, Figure 11.4 shows what happens if you were to assign one of the form's properties a value. The pop-up menu of properties will include the `BottomTitle` property. You've truly added the property to the form simply by coding the `Property Get` and `Property Let` procedures.

FIGURE 11.4.

The `BottomTitle` *property value appears in the list of properties that pop up as you enter code.*

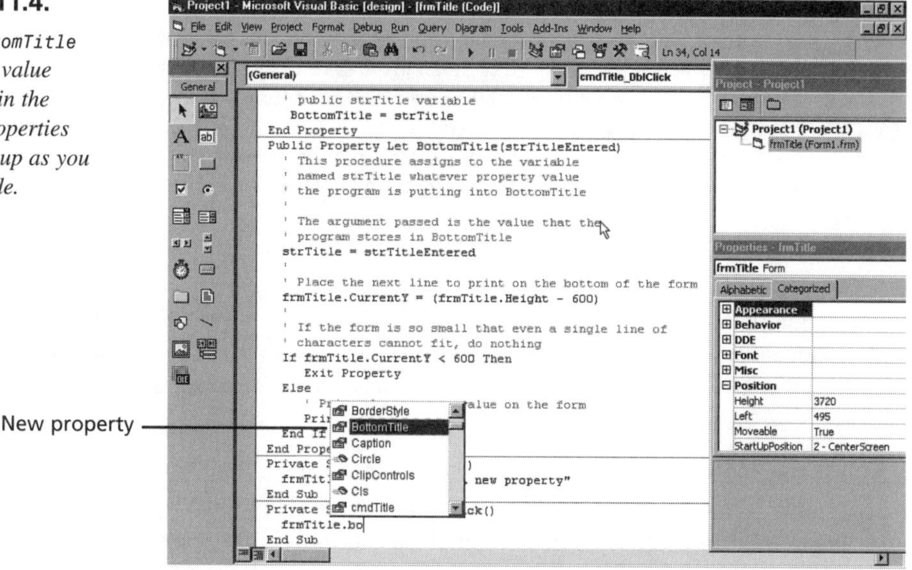

5. When you run the application and click the command button, the command button's `Click` event occurs and the `Click` event procedure that you entered earlier executes. The `Click` event procedure assigned the string literal `"A new property"` to the `BottomTitle` form property, and the `Property` procedures took care of the rest.

Multiple Forms

Until now, most of your applications have had a single form. Not much mention has been made of multiform applications because multiple forms are unnecessary for simple applications. When you need an added form, you can right-click over the Project window and add a form.

You're now ready to learn how to add additional forms to your applications. These forms will be special data forms. Therefore, you'll need to know how to distinguish and program SDI (Single Document Interface) and MDI (Multiple Document Interface) applications.

Using multiple forms generally requires that you keep track of two or more sets of forms. Because you assign each form a meaningful name, your programming burden shouldn't increase too much. The form name determines which set of controls you're working with at any given time, and you can hide and show forms as needed while the application runs (or users can switch between the forms).

Even when two or more forms appear on a user's screen, only one can be active. Users can activate an inactive form by clicking any part of it that shows from beneath the currently active form. Also, your application code can activate a form when the time is right. The `frmForm.Show` method activates the form window referenced by the name frmForm and hides other windows if the newly active form happens to consume more screen space than the other forms.

MDI development allows you to create applications that look very complex. Almost all major software applications contain multiple document interfaces. As this 21-day tutorial begins to describe more powerful programs that use files and additional controls, you'll see more need for an MDI application.

In addition to right-clicking the Project window to add a form, you can choose Add Form from the Project menu. Visual Basic displays the Add Form dialog box, as shown in Figure 11.5. You can select from several kinds of new forms to display, or you can select an existing form by clicking the Existing tab and then selecting from the list of forms.

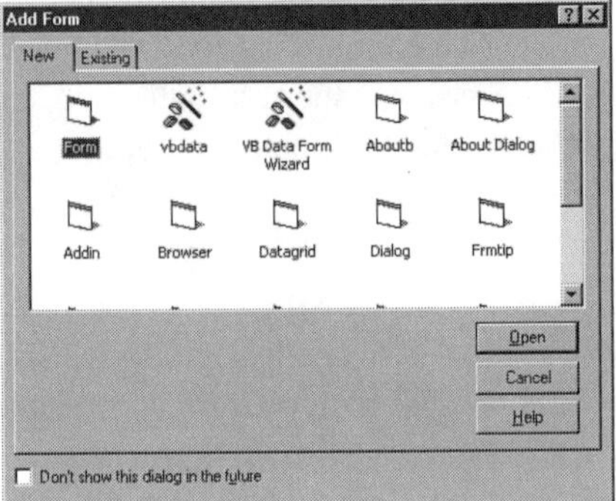

FIGURE 11.5.
Select the kind of form you want to add.

If you want to add another standard form, double-click Form to have Visual Basic open a new form. Visual Basic names your subsequent forms Form2, Form3, and so on. However, you should assign better names as soon as you add the forms.

Day 15, "Using Form Templates," explains how to incorporate the other kinds of forms offered in the Add Form dialog box.

The SDI and MDI Styles

Visual Basic supports the following interface styles:

- **Single Document Interface.** An SDI application contains a single data window. In Windows Notepad, for instance, you can open only one document at a time. An SDI application usually doesn't contain a Window menu on its menu bar because you can't move between data windows. When the user opens a new data file, the data replaces the data currently shown in the open window.
- **Multiple Document Interface.** An MDI application contains multiple data windows (often called *document windows*). Microsoft Word, for example, lets you open as many documents as you want; Word's MDI ensures that each document resides in its own window (see Figure 11.6). You can switch between windows by clicking the desired window with the mouse or by selecting choices from the Window menu. When users switch between document windows (which are forms, from the developer's point of view), the selected window becomes the active form and has the focus.

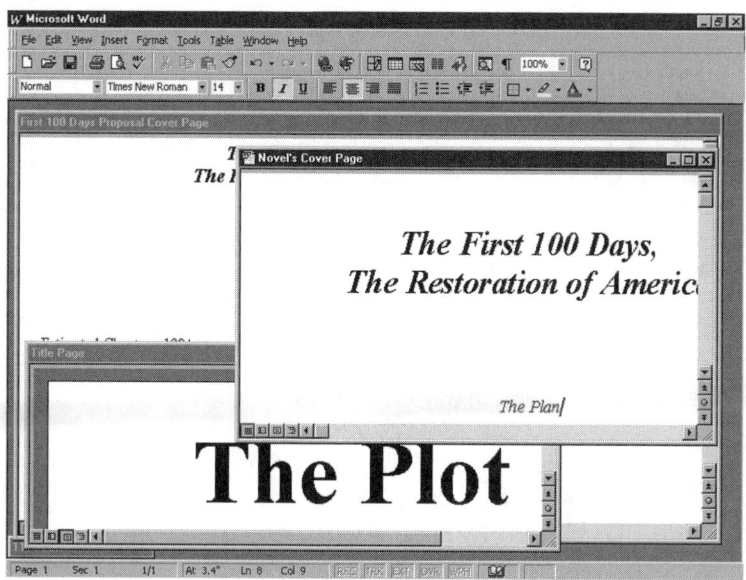

FIGURE 11.6.
MDI applications allow for multiple data windows.

- **Explorer-Style Interface.** This is the style used in Visual Basic's Help system and the Windows Explorer screens. An application that supports the Explorer-style interface has two windows: one on the left and one on the right. The left window displays a hierarchical view of the data detailed in the right window. Select an

Explorer-style interface when you're working with an application that manages data files and graphics. Such applications include TreeView and ListView controls, which help you traverse the Explorer-style windows. (These controls normally don't appear in the toolbox, but you can add them using the Project, Components menu option.)

Note

> An SDI application can have multiple forms. MDI simply means that your application might contain one or more child forms that hold data sets that are distinct from other data sets within the application. An MDI application uses a *controlling form* (also known as a *parent form* or *primary form*) to hold the other forms, and the other forms can't appear outside the controlling form's boundaries. If you create an SDI application—which most are—your application can have multiple forms, yet no form is considered the child of another. If your application works with only one set of data at a time (such as one customer file or one employee payroll file), or if your application doesn't work with any data except for program control information, the application should be an SDI application.

MDI Terminology

If you want to create an application that works with multiple data files, you must know the MDI terminology. The primary form used as the backdrop to hold the other forms is often called the *parent form* or *parent window*. The parent form acts like a form container that contains one or more child windows (also forms). In Microsoft Word, for example, the Word background with the menu bar, status bar, and toolbar is the parent window. As you open Word documents, they appear in child windows within the parent window, and the child windows never go outside the parent window's boundaries.

The parent window that provides boundaries for the child windows supports only the following types of controls:

- Controls that support the `Align` property.
- Controls without a visible interface (you'll learn more about such interfaces in Day 15).

Note

> If users minimize any of the child windows, these windows appear minimized at the bottom of the parent window, but not on the taskbar. Child windows are bound to their parent window and can't appear outside the parent window at all; the parent window defines the application's absolute boundaries.

The primary distinction of a child window form is that its `MDIChild` property is set to `True`. Also, an MDI application might contain non-child forms. For example, the application might contain an About dialog box (which users would reach by choosing About from the Help menu); this dialog box isn't an MDI child because the dialog box window doesn't hold program data.

When you want to create an MDI application, choose Add MDI Form from the Project menu and then add the child window forms with an `MDIChild` property of `True`.

Using the Application Wizard

Rather than build an MDI application from scratch, you can start with the Application Wizard. This wizard makes MDI applications much easier to produce than creating the forms and setting the `MDIChild` properties by hand.

When you create a new project and select the Visual Basic Application Wizard option, the second dialog box that appears lets you select the kind of interface style you prefer (see Figure 11.7).

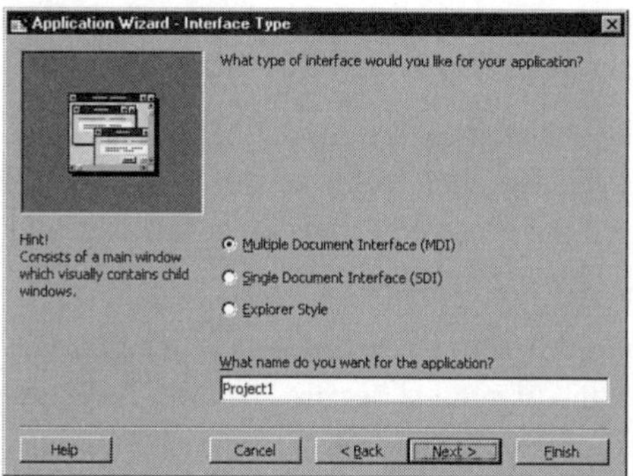

FIGURE 11.7.
Select the appropriate interface style from the Application Wizard.

The Application Wizard creates a project that supports the creation of multiple child windows through the File menu's New command. Listing 11.8 executes when you choose New from the File menu in the generated MDI application (the `mnuFileNew.Click()` event procedure executes this).

LISTING 11.8. CREATING A FORM DOCUMENT REFERENCE VARIABLE TO POINT TO THE CHILD WINDOW.

```
1:  Private Sub LoadNewDoc()
2:     Static lDocumentCount As Long
3:     Dim frmD As frmDocument
4:
5:     lDocumentCount = lDocumentCount + 1
6:     Set frmD = New frmDocument
7:     frmD.Caption = "Document " & lDocumentCount
8:     frmD.Show
9:  End Sub
```

The code in Listing 11.8 is tricky, but it contains nothing you can't figure out with the background you already have. Line 2's static variable named `lDocumentCount` is local to the procedure, yet it never goes out of scope. The first time this procedure executes, `lDocumentCount` is 0 (all static variables are 0 the first time they go into scope). If the procedure changes the value of `lDocumentCount` (which it does by adding 1 every time the procedure executes in line 5), Visual Basic remembers the new value. Although no other procedure can access `lDocumentCount`, its value remains intact inside this procedure. The value doesn't go away as it would if the variable were local and *automatic* (the opposite of static; all variables you've declared locally so far have been automatic).

NEW TERM A *static variable* holds its value even after the procedure it's defined within ends. Therefore, if a static variable holds a value of 7 when a procedure ends, this value will still be there if the procedure starts up again, as would happen if the procedure call were inside another procedure's loop.

Line 3 adds an interesting twist to the declaration statements you've seen before. Rather than declare a variable, this statement declares a form! The application contains, at startup, a child form named frmDocument that is specified at design time. Line 3's `Dim` statement declares a new variable named `frmD` to contain the same object as frmDocument; in other words, rather than refer to an Integer or String data type, `frmD` refers to a document that contains the same properties as frmDocument. `frmD` is an example of a control variable.

After updating the static variable that keeps track of all the newly created documents in line 5, the `Set` statement creates a new document and sets `frmD` as a reference to the document. For all intents, `frmD` is the new document. The next statement sets the new document's caption to `Document`, followed by the document number. Then, the last statement uses the `Show` method to display the new document on the parent window.

> The `Set` statement works almost like an assignment statement except that `Set` actually assigns a control variable to an actual control. In Listing 11.8, line 3 does *not* declare a new form! Rather, line 3 declares a form variable. The variable is empty until you associate the form variable with an actual form using the `Set` statement, as is done in line 6.

No matter how many times a user chooses New from the File menu, the `LoadNewDoc()` procedure is executed and creates another child window. The code for the File menu's Close command, if you run the Application Wizard and then execute the resulting MDI application, does nothing—the Application Wizard places no code there. You have to add code that will unload the active child window when the user chooses Close from the File menu.

> Child forms are useful for the dialog boxes you might want to add to your applications. Although the next lesson explains how to display common dialog boxes, such as the File Print dialog box, you also can create your own dialog boxes by displaying a child form with controls that make up a dialog box. You can set the default command button with the command button's `Default` property and initialize text box controls with default text if you want to help your users with common entries. If you set the command button's `Enabled` property to `False`, the command button can be grayed out and unavailable, depending on user action leading up to the dialog box's display.
>
> When a user needs to see the dialog box, you can display it with the `Show` method:
>
> ```
> frmDialog.Show vbModal, Me
> ```
>
> `vbModal` produces a modal dialog box that a user must respond to with OK or Cancel before he or she can do anything else in the application. The `Show` method's second option is the name of the parent form, but you can use `Me` if the parent form is the standard application form.

11

Placing Toolbars on Forms

Toolbars give your users a chance to perform pushbutton selections of common commands and menu options. To place a toolbar on your application, you need to add the toolbar control to your toolbox. Once you create the toolbar, you only have to write event procedure code for each toolbar button's `Click` event, just as you do for menu options.

If you write MDI applications, you can add a toolbar to the parent form or any combination of forms.

Adding the Toolbar Control to Your Toolbox

Toolbars, and the coolbars that you read about in the next section, are similar in the way they work and the way that you add them to applications. Although the toolbar is more common (almost every Windows application uses toolbars these days), the coolbar is slightly simpler to add due to its smaller collection of related property values that you must set. This section offers an overview of the steps necessary for adding toolbars. In the next section you see how to add coolbars using specific information about each of the coolbar controls. Once you master the somewhat simpler coolbars, you will be ready to add toolbars as well.

As you will learn in the next section, coolbars differ from toolbars because coolbars offer a way to slide controls on and off the screen.

Before adding a toolbar, you must add the toolbar control to your Toolbox. Select Project, Components to display the Components dialog box. Select the entry labeled Microsoft Windows Common Controls 6.0 and then click OK. Several new tools will appear in your toolbox window. You can run your mouse cursor over them to see which tools Visual Basic added.

The following steps describe the general procedure for adding toolbars to your applications:

1. After adding the toolbar control to your toolbox, double-click the toolbar control to add a toolbar to the top of your form window. (You must have the grid dots turned on to see the toolbar's outline.) The toolbar always spans the top of the form, automatically, no matter how wide your form is; therefore, you don't have to worry about width settings.
2. If you want your toolbar to include icons on its buttons, and not just text values, you'll have to add the image list control to your form. The image list control is one of the tools that appear on the toolbox window when you add the Microsoft Windows Custom Controls 6.0 tools. The image list control contains the images you'll place on the toolbar. You can drag the image list control out of the way

because its placement is trivial. Although the image list control is never actually seen on the form, its images will be placed on the appropriate toolbar buttons when you assign the icons to their respective buttons.

Although the standard location for a toolbar is at the top of the form (the default location for the toolbar control), you can change this location by setting the `Align` property value to `vbAlignBottom`. This causes the toolbar to appear at the bottom of the form.

3. Click the (Custom) entry in the image list's Properties window to display the Property Pages dialog box (see Figure 11.8).

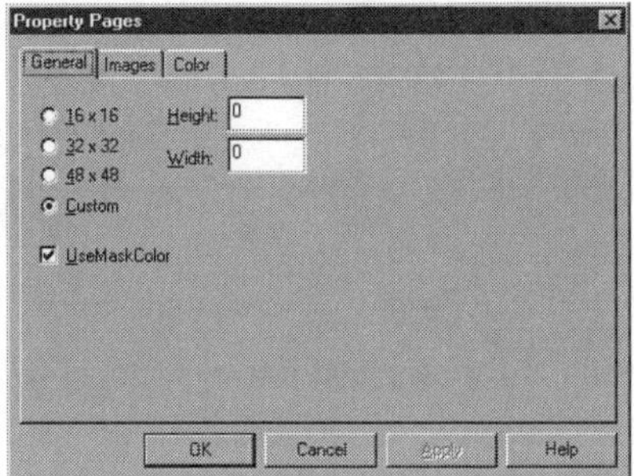

FIGURE 11.8.
The Property Pages dialog box makes entering image list control properties simple.

11

4. Click the Images tab.
5. Click the Insert Picture button and select the icon to add.
6. As you continue adding icons, Visual Basic updates each icon's `Index` value; the `Index` value is the value you'll use to link each icon to each toolbar button.
7. Close the image list's Property Pages dialog box.
8. Click the (Custom) entry in the toolbar's Properties window to display the toolbar control's Property Pages dialog box (see Figure 11.9). As with the image list control's Property Pages dialog box, the toolbar control's Property Pages dialog box allows you to enter property values easily.

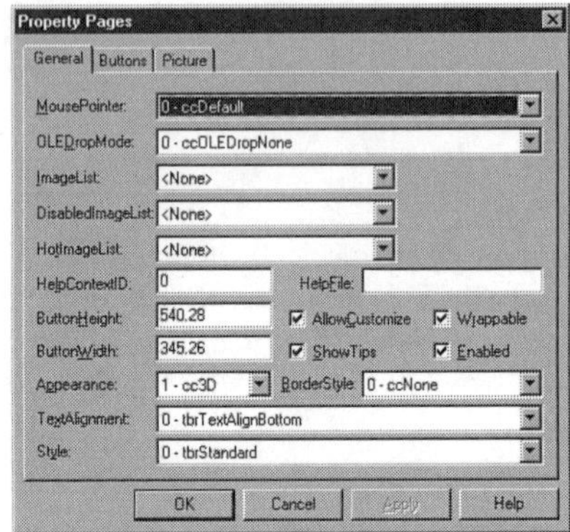

FIGURE 11.9.
The toolbar control also provides a Property Pages dialog box.

9. Change the property values and click the Apply button to see those changes appear on the form window's toolbar. Make sure you connect the image list control to the toolbar control in the toolbar Property Pages dialog box's ImageList option to assign images to each toolbar button. Be sure to add ToolTips in the `ToolTipText` option (located on the Buttons page) if you want to add pop-up descriptions for your users.
10. Click OK to close the toolbar's Property Pages dialog box.
11. Add `Click` event procedures for each toolbar button.

> The `Wrappable` property, when set to `True`, enables the toolbar to span more than one row across the screen if the toolbar contains more icons than will fit on a single row. Remember the `Wrappable` property when you need to create wide toolbars.

If you want to give your users something extra, let them customize the toolbar. When you set the toolbar's `AllowCustomize` property to `True`, the user, at runtime, will be able to double-click the toolbar to produce the Customize Toolbar dialog box shown in Figure 11.10.

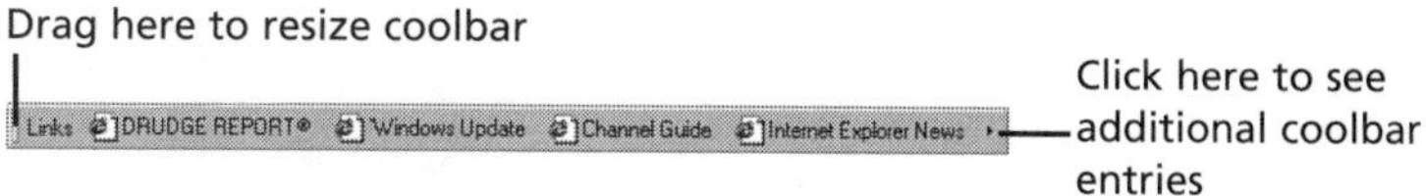

FIGURE 11.10.

You can let your users customize the application's toolbar.

Adding Coolbars

Starting with Visual Basic version 6, you can add *coolbars* to your applications. Figure 11.11 shows a coolbar from Internet Explorer. A user can move this sliding toolbar in or out of the way, as needed, by dragging its *sizing grippers* left or right. Coolbars enable you to add extra-wide toolbars to your application; your user can slide the coolbar left or right to see the coolbar options that reside off the screen.

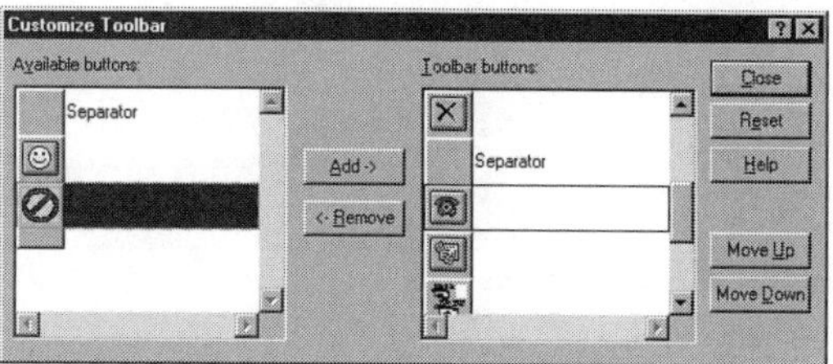

FIGURE 11.11.

The Coolbar control offers a sliding toolbar choice of icons.

> You must add the Microsoft Windows Custom Controls-3 6.0 control from the Project, Components dialog box before the coolbar appears on your toolbox window.

Adding a coolbar requires the same basic steps as adding a toolbar. You'll first add the and then connect each image to the coolbar via the image's `Key` value. Coolbars are actually simpler than toolbars because they require you to set fewer property values.

To add a coolbar, follow these steps:

1. Add the image list control to your toolbox by selecting Project, Components and checking the option Microsoft Windows Common Controls 6.0. You will also need the coolbar control; so while you're at the Components dialog box, check the option Microsoft Windows Common Controls-3 6.0 before pressing Enter. The image list and coolbar controls will now appear somewhere on your toolbox.

2. Double-click the image list control to add an image list to your application. Move the image list out of the way because it is not a control that will ever appear on the user's application window, but serves only to hold images used on the coolbar buttons.
3. Add Double-click the image list control's `Custom` property to display the image list's Property Pages dialog box.
4. Click the Images tab to display the Images page.
5. Click the Insert Pictures page to display the Select Picture dialog box from which you can locate a graphic file to use as the first image in the image list.
6. Select the image, such as a bitmap in Visual Basic's Graphics folder. When double-clicking a filename, the dialog box closes and the image appears as the first icon on the image list (see Figure 11.12).

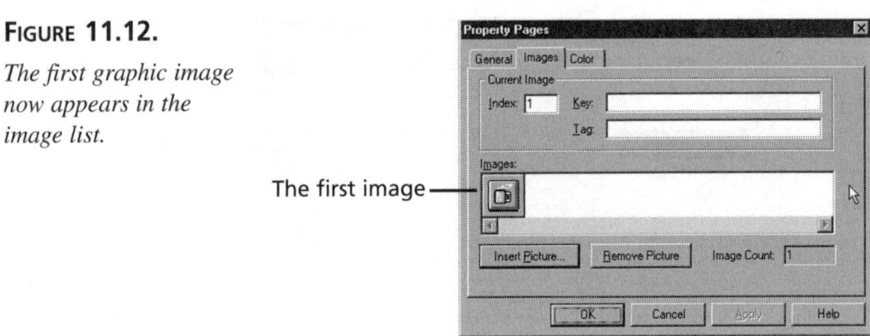

FIGURE 11.12.
The first graphic image now appears in the image list.

7. Continue adding the images to the image list on the coolbar.
8. Double-click the coolbar control to add a two-row (called *bands*) sliding coolbar to your Form window.
9. Double-click the `Custom` property to display the coolbar's Property Pages dialog box shown in Figure 11.13.

FIGURE 11.13.

Easily set coolbar properties from the Property Pages dialog box.

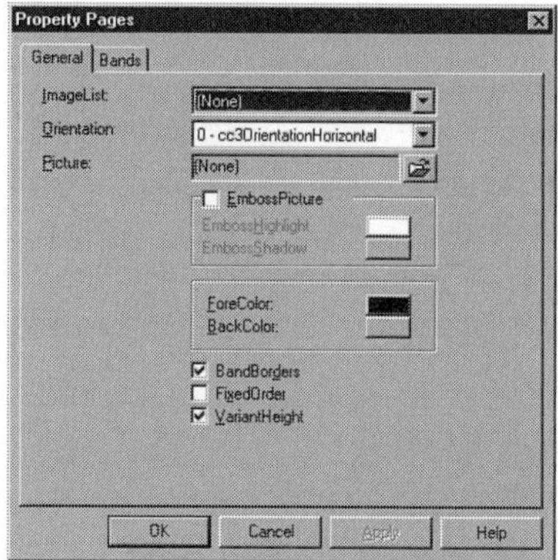

10. Select the image list in the ImageList listbox. Table 11.6 describes the other options you may want to set on the General page of the dialog box.

TABLE 11.6. THE DIALOG BOX'S GENERAL PAGE DESCRIBES THE OVERALL APPEARANCE OF THE COOLBAR.

Option	*Description*
Orientation	Places the coolbar vertically or horizontally (the default) on the form. Most coolbars are horizontal.
Picture	Determines the graphic image that appears on all the coolbar buttons. You will normally place a different image on each button with the image list as described in this section instead of placing the same picture on every button as you can do with the Picture option.
ForeColor	Specifies the color of the coolbar's foreground.
BackColor	Specifies the color of the coolbar's background.
BandBorders	Determines whether or not separating lines appear between the bands in a multi-banded coolbar.
FixedOrder	Determines if the user can change the order of the bands on the toolbar.
VariantHeight	Determines if each of the coolbar's bands are the same height or if each band is as high as the tallest button on that band.

The Picture option does give you access to special color modes and appearances available for the coolbar buttons such as what a button shows when the user presses it.

11

11. Click the Bands tab to add the individual coolbar images.
12. You can add or remove bands by clicking either the Insert Band or Remove Band buttons. Additional properties that you may want to adjust are described in Table 11.7. Of course, you will certainly want to add the images from your image list control.

TABLE 11.7. THE DIALOG BOX'S BANDS PAGE DESCRIBES THE BAND PROPERTIES, SUCH AS THE IMAGES THAT APPEAR.

Option	*Description*
Child	For advanced programming, this property determines if a child control, a control other than a command button, appears on the coolbar.
Style	Determines if the user can resize the coolbar. If set to `cc3BandNormal`, the user can resize the control with the sizing grippers that appear. If set to `cc3BandFixedSize`, the user cannot resize the coolbar and no sizing grippers appear.
UseCoolbarPicture	Determines if the coolbar displays the image from the Band page's Picture property or if the coolbar displays images from the image list control you've supplied.
Picture	Determines the picture that displays on the coolbar unless you've request, through the `UseCoolbarPicture` property, that the coolbar display images from the image list.
Caption	Determines the caption that appears under the image.
Width, MinWidth, MinHeight	Determines the size, in twips, of the coolbar.
Key	Available for coolbars that you use in collections so you can access the coolbar buttons in the collection by its index or by a unique `Key` value that you assign.
Tag	Specifies information that the coolbar does not use in any way. This information travels along with the toolbar in the application, as a property, so that subsequent programmers can learn about the coolbar that you've used.
EmbossPicture	If `True`, the coolbar picture appears in its original colors. If `False`, the coolbar image appears with foreground and background colors determined by the `EmbossHighlight` and `EmbossShadow` properties.
UseCoolbarColors	If `True`, the coolbar band uses the `Foreground` and `Background` colors. If `False`, the band displays using its own default colors.

13. The `Image` property is critical to use for adding your image list pictures to the coolbar buttons. Each `Image` value relates to each picture in the image list. Therefore, if your image list contains 10 pictures that you want on the coolbar, you will list 10 `Image` values in the coolbar's Property Pages dialog box.

> You will not see the images on the coolbar after you close the Property Pages dialog box. The images do not appear until runtime.

Summary

Today's lesson explained how to use forms and form properties, events, and methods. Being the background of your application, your form is an important part of your programming. You can reference multiple forms in a number of ways; however, as you learned today, the `Forms` collections is perhaps the easiest way to step through all the forms in an application.

Not only can you now work with form properties, but you can add your own properties to your forms. Once you add a property, you then can set the property and read the property value just as if the property were part of the form's original property set.

Although programming MDI windows can get tedious, by doing so you offer your users a chance to use multiple data windows with a different data set in each window. You can let the Application Wizard take care of generating the initial MDI application, and then you can complete the details.

The Toolbar and Coolbar controls add two more dimensions for your users. A toolbar gives your application's users one-button access to the most common commands. Before you can place icons on toolbar buttons, however, you must insert those icons inside the image list control. Coolbars are toolbars that the user can slide in and out of the way to make room for other items on the screen or other toolbars/coolbars you place in the application. You may want to offer coolbars and toolbars as View menu options so that your users can select what they want.

Tomorrow's lesson explores ways to use the disk as an external storage source for Visual Basic application data.

Q&A

Q Why must I mess with the ImageList control when I want to add icons to a toolbar or coolbar?

A Microsoft designed the toolbar control and the coolbar control to work with the ImageList control. It's that simple. Microsoft could have very easily let you place icons directly in the toolbar's or coolbar's property list, but instead chose to require that the ImageList control's icons match each toolbar or coolbar button. Microsoft actually did you a favor. You can set up several image list controls on a form and use them as templates for your toolbars or coolbars. For example, you can use one for the toolbar icons when they're active, and another image list control when you deactivate the toolbar because the user is performing a critical task onscreen that cannot use the toolbar. You only need to change the name of the image list control name inside the toolbar or coolbar `ImageList` property, and Visual Basic immediately uses the other image list control's set of icons.

Workshop

The Workshop provides quiz questions to help you solidify your understanding of the material covered and exercises to provide you with experience in using what you've learned. Try to understand the quiz and exercise answers before continuing to the next lesson. Answers are provided in Appendix A, "Answers to Exercises."

Quiz

1. How can the `Resize` event help you keep your form's controls centered?
2. What does the `ScaleMode` property control?
3. What is the value of the first subscript when working with predefined object collections?
4. True/False. An SDI application cannot support multiple forms.
5. What is the difference between an SDI and MDI application?
6. Where do toolbars most often appear on a form?
7. Which control stores the toolbar's icons?
8. Why does the location of the image list control make no difference when you use the control along with a coolbar?
9. What's the difference between `Spc()` and `Tab()`?
10. How do you use `Print` to output a blank line?

Exercises

1. Load these controls onto your toolbox window: Toolbar, Coolbar, and ImageList.
2. Write the output from the following two statements:

```
Form1.Print "Line 1";
Form1.Print "Line 2"
```

3. Run the Application Wizard to generate an Explorer-style application; then run the application's shell to see the result.
4. Write the code that outputs the numbers 1 to 100 on a form. Separate the numbers with one space. Don't use any controls for the output. Trigger the output in the form's `Click` event procedure.
5. Write a procedure that computes and prints the total number of controls in all forms within the current application.

WEEK 2

DAY 12

Interact with Files

Today's lesson explains the fundamentals of file *I/O* (*Input/Output*). Professional Visual Basic programmers use several different kinds of file I/O when working with Visual Basic. The types you'll learn in today's lesson are essential to understanding all other file-related techniques. Once you master today's fundamentals, you'll be ready to work with the more flexible data and database controls, such as the file controls and database tools, which you'll master later.

Three file types exist: *sequential*, *random*, and *binary*. Sequential access is the simplest file access, but it's prone to some drawbacks. Although sequential files are simple to create and read, they can be slow and cumbersome. Random access is a much faster and more useful method of access, but programs that use random-access files are often more complex than sequential-access programs. Binary files are special, compacted forms of random-access files.

Random-access files work with any kind of data you can declare. Once you learn how to declare user-defined data types today, you'll be able to use the `Put #` command to write (or read) an entire set of information to (or from) a data file in one statement.

Today, you learn the following:

- File types
- The difference between sequential and random files
- Why file numbers are important
- How to open files
- How to locate free file numbers
- About the `Print #`, `Write #`, `Read #`, `Get #`, and `Put #` file-related commands
- How to use the file-related controls

Working with Files

Many programs in existence today use files. At the very least, even if a program doesn't use files, the program itself is a file that executes when a user runs the program. Whether a program saves data into a database or just keeps information for its own use (such as a user's preferred color scheme or window position), most programs do rely on files.

Several Visual Basic commands are common to all forms of file input and output. These commands open files, specify file modes, close files, and check for free file numbers to be used as file associations. This section explains how fundamental file processing operates. One way you can better understand file concepts is to begin with the first statement of any file-based project: the `Open` statement.

The `Open` Statement

Sequential files and random-access files share common features. You use `Open` for both file types. The kind of file access you achieve with `Open` depends on the arguments you use in the `Open` statement. `Open` reserves a file handle, also called a *channel*, for reading from and writing to a file. The `Open` statement associates a number to the handle. When this file handle is open, the data stream can flow. The mode in which you open the file number—read, write, or both—dictates how the data stream can flow between the file and the computer.

A *file handle*, also called a *channel*, is a unique path to a file associated with a number from the `Open` statement. Once `Open` associates a file number to the file handle, the rest of the program uses the file number to access the file. The code never has to refer to the specific filename after the `Open` statement.

The following is the `Open` statement's format:

```
Open "strFileName" [For Mode] [AccessRestriction] [LockType] As
[#]intFileNum [Len = intRecordLength]
```

> Remember that when you open a program and assign a data file to a number, the program will use that file number to access the file. Your program never again has to use the filename to get to the file.

All `Open` statements must include the filename and file number arguments, but the other arguments are optional. A simple call to `Open` with only the required parameters might look like this:

```
Open "aFile.txt" As #1
```

This statement opens a file named aFile.txt as file number 1. To reference this file for input or output, you reference the file number. This file has been opened in random-access mode, because the default when you omit the `For Mode` portion is `Random`. All the commands in today's lesson work with text files. This lesson uses the filename extension .txt or .dat, two commonly used extensions for text files.

Learning the File Modes

Notice that the *`Mode`* value in the `Open` statement does not have a data type prefix before it. *`Mode`* must be a special keyword that indicates the file's mode of access. Table 12.1 explains the values you can supply for the *`Mode`* argument.

TABLE 12.1. USE ONE OF THESE `Open` STATEMENT *`Mode`* VALUES.

Mode	*Description*
`Append`	Opens a file number to a file for sequential output, beginning at the end of the file if the file exists. If the file doesn't exist, Visual Basic creates the file. `Append` never overwrites existing file data.
`Binary`	Opens a file number to a file for binary data access. In `Binary` mode, you can access a file at the byte level, meaning that you can write and read individual bytes to and from the file.
`Input`	Opens a file number to a file for sequential input, starting at the beginning of the file. Data is read in the same order it was sent to the file.

continues

TABLE 12.1. CONTINUED

Mode	*Description*
`Output`	Opens a file number to a file for sequential output, starting at the beginning of the file. If the file doesn't exist when you issue the `Open` statement, Visual Basic creates the file; otherwise, Visual Basic overwrites the file.
`Random`	Opens a file number to a file for random read and write access. This mode allows data to be read from and written to a file at any specific record boundary.

`For` *`Mode`* isn't required when using the `Open` statement. If you don't include the mode, Visual Basic assumes `Random` and inserts the `For Random` mode for you. The following statements demonstrate how to use various modes for opening a file:

```
Open "filInpdt.txt" For Input As #1

Open "Append.txt" For Append As #1

Open "Output.txt" For Output As #1

Open "Random.txt" For Random As #1
```

The last statement is equivalent to the following:

```
Open "Random.txt" As #1
```

Be sure to set up error-handling logic using the `On Error Goto` statement that you learned about in Day 9 "The Dialog Box Control." Anytime you open or access a file, an error might result. Good error-handling logic will help your application exit gracefully from the problem rather than burden your users with nasty runtime error messages.

Restricting Access

The optional `AccessRestriction` argument in an `Open` statement lets you restrict the access to `Read`, `Write`, or `Read Write`. This access restriction is often used when writing programs that will run across a network.

Specifying read-only access with `Read` lets users see the contents of the file but leaves them unable to modify the file. Specifying `Write` access lets users modify the file, and specifying `Read Write` lets users do both (read and modify).

Locking the File

Use a `LockType` argument value to specify the operations permitted on the open file by other processes. This parameter is useful when writing network applications. You can restrict access to a file so that only one user at a time has access to the file or can write to the file. This helps prevent two users from trying to make changes at the same time (which would inevitably result in losing the changes one of the users made).

The valid options for `LockType` are `Shared`, `Lock Read`, `Lock Write`, and `Lock Read Write`. `Shared` lets all users access the file simultaneously. `Lock Read` locks the file so that only the person with the file open for reading can access the file. `Lock Write` locks the file so that only the person who has the file open for write access can write to the file. `Lock Read Write` locks the file from all users except the one who has the file open for read and write access.

Managing the Record Length

The length specified by the `Len = intRecordLength` option is used by random-access files as the size of data records that will be passed from Visual Basic to the file. This size is necessary when accessing records from a file. The first record in a file begins at location 1, and all subsequent records are written at locations in increments of 1. The actual location in the file of any given record is *N* × `intRecordLength`, where *N* is the record number.

NEW TERM A *record* is one logical line from a file that holds a complete set of data. For example, if your file holds inventory data, one record would be one item's inventory information, such as the description, price, and quantity.

12

Accessing records operates quite like the way you access arrays. Whereas the first element in an array is stored in `Array(0)`, the first element in a file is stored at record number 1. To make index coordination between arrays and files easy, use `Option Base 1` in your `Declarations` section or define your arrays to begin with element 1 and ignore the 0 subscript.

Locating a Free File Number

Visual Basic lets you open multiple files at once, as long as you assign each file a different file number. You need to keep track of the next available number, especially if you open files in a function that has no way of knowing whether other functions have opened files. Visual Basic provides the `FreeFile()` function, which can be used to determine the next available file number. By using this function, you're guaranteed that the file number you use hasn't already been used by an open file. Here's the format of `FreeFile()`:

```
FreeFile[(intRangeNumber)]
```

The optional *`intRangeNumber`* parameter lets you specify that you want the returned file number to be in a specific range: 1–255 or 256–511. The default range, if you specify no *`intRangeNumber`* parameter, is 1–255. Almost all Visual Basic programmers keep the default because rarely, if ever, do programs need to open more than 256 files. Without the *`intRangeNumber`* parameter, you do not need to include the function's parentheses.

The following lines use `FreeFile()` to obtain a file number and then open a file with that number:

```
intFileNumber = FreeFile()
Open "AccPay.Dat" For Output As intFileNumber
```

Use `FreeFile()` whenever you want to ensure that a file number isn't already in use. This might not be necessary for small applications that use only a few files. However, even in small applications, it helps to use `FreeFile()` to ensure that you don't accidentally use the same file number for more than one file at a time.

> Avoid the shortcut of using `FreeFile` within the `Open` statement, as shown here:
>
> ```
> Open "strFileName" For Output As FreeFile()
> ```
>
> Although this works, you have no way of knowing the file number for later operations on the file.

Specifying the `Close` Statement

You need to close all the files that you've opened with the `Open` statement. The statement for closing a file is—not surprisingly—`Close`. This statement takes the open file number as its only parameter. Here's the complete format for `Close`:

```
Close [#] intFileNumber[, intFileNumber2][,...intFileNumberX]
```

You can specify any number of file numbers to close in a single `Close` statement. If you don't specify a file number, all opened files are closed. This can be useful for terminating your applications.

The code in Listing 12.1 opens two sequential files—one for reading and one for writing—using the next available file numbers and then closes both files.

LISTING 12.1. `FreeFile()` **CAN REQUEST A FILE NUMBER FROM VISUAL BASIC.**

```
1:  Dim intReadFile As Integer, intWriteFile As Integer
2:  ' Handle input file
3:  intReadFile = FreeFile   ' Get first file #
4:  Open "AccPay.Dat" For Input As intReadFile
5:  ' Handle output file
6:  intWriteFile = FreeFile   ' Get next file #
7:  Open "AccPayOut.Dat" For Output As intWriteFile
8:  '
9:  ' Code goes here to send the contents
10: ' of the input file to the output file
11: ' (You'll learn how to do this later in the lesson)
12: Close intReadFile
13: Close intWriteFile
```

You never have to use an actual file number in this example, because `FreeFile()` in lines 3 and 6 returns the available file numbers and the code stores those values as named integers.

If you don't close all open files, you run a risk, albeit a small one today due to improved hardware, that the file will incur damage. Generally, if power goes out when a file is open, the file's contents might be in jeopardy. Therefore, don't keep a file open longer than you need it to be open. If you don't close a file, the system closes it when your application terminates.

You can close as many files as you want with a single `Close` statement. The following simple line closes all open files:

```
Close
```

On the other hand, the following lines close only two files that might be open:

```
Close 3
Close 6
```

You may want to close certain files in the middle of a program when you're finished with them but still need to access other open files.

Working with Sequential-Access Files

Now that you've seen the basic statements required for opening files, closing files, and setting file access modes, this section looks at several examples that output to and input from sequential-access files. You'll see that a form of `Print`, which you used yesterday for sending text to the form, can also output text to a file.

Sequential file access means just that—you access the file sequentially. When you create a sequential-access file, you're creating a file that your application must read from and write to sequentially (that is, in order from the file's beginning to end). This sequential read and write limitation is the biggest weakness of a sequential file.

NEW TERM A *sequential file* is a file that you read and write in order from beginning to end.

To use the file, you must process the entire file from beginning to end. If you need to update only one byte of information in a 1,000-byte file, you must process 999 extra bytes every time you want to perform the update.

Sequential file access can be very useful when you need to process a text file such as a settings file or if you're storing small amounts of data where access speed isn't an issue. This section looks at the Visual Basic functions that handle sequential files.

The `Print #` Statement Outputs Sequentially

You must open files to use them in your program. After you open the files, you must put information into them. One common approach is to use the `Print #` statement. `Print #` writes only to a sequential-access file. Here's the format of `Print #`:

```
Print #intFileNumber, [OutputList]
```

`intFileNumber` is the open file number to which you want to write, and `OutputList` can consist of the following:

```
[Spc(intN1) ¦ Tab[(intN2)]] [Expression] [charPos]
```

Both `Spc()` and `Tab()` work with the `Print #` statement the same way they worked with `Print` in yesterday's lesson.

You can use either `Spc()` or `Tab()`, but not both together. Table 12.2 explains the components of *`OutputList`*.

Table 12.2. The `Print #` statement's contents describe the output of the method.

Component	*Description*
`Spc(`*`intN1`*`)`	Used to insert spaces in the output, where *`intN1`* is the number of spaces to insert.
`Tab(`*`intN2`*`)`	Used to position the insertion point to an absolute column number, where *`intN2`* is the column number. Use `Tab` with no argument to position the insertion point at the beginning of the next print zone (a *print zone* occurs every 14 spaces).
`Expression`	A numeric or string expression that contains the data you want to send to the file.
`charPos`	Specifies the insertion point for the next character to print. Use a semicolon to specify that the next character should appear immediately following the last printed character.

You can use `Tab()` in *charPos*; the functions that `Tab()` performs at the beginning of a `Print #` statement also apply here. If you omit *charPos*, the next character appears on the next line in the file.

The procedure in Listing 12.2 opens a file named Print.txt, writes the numbers 1 through 6 to the file, and then properly closes the file.

Listing 12.2. Using `Print #` to write to a sequential file.

```
Private Sub cmdFile_Click()
  Dim intCtr As Integer    ' Loop counter
  Dim intFNum As Integer   ' File number
  Dim intMsg As Integer    ' For MsgBox()
  intFNum = FreeFile
  ' Change the path if you want
  Open "C:\Print.txt" For Output As #intFNum

  ' Describe this proc
  intMsg = MsgBox("File Print.txt opened")

  For intCtr = 1 To 6
    Print # intFNum, intCtr     ' Write the loop counter
    intMsg = MsgBox("Writing a " & intCtr & " to Print.txt")
  Next intCtr

  Close # intFNum

  intMsg = MsgBox("File Print.txt closed")
End Sub
```

If you run this procedure, you see several message boxes that display the procedure's progress. The procedure tells you in line 10 that it has opened the file, and it then proceeds to write to the file in line 13 and show you what has been written in line 14. Finally, the procedure closes the file in line 17 and tells you that the file has been closed in line 19.

To verify that the procedure worked, open Notepad and look at the Print.txt file. You should see the numbers 1 through 5 printed inside the file, as shown here:

```
1
2
3
4
5
```

Listing 12.2 demonstrates a simple `Print #` statement (line 13). No statements existed to position the output, so the procedure defaulted to printing each number on a new line.

Creating and writing to a file won't do you much good if you can't retrieve the information when you want to. The following section covers retrieving information from a file.

Use `Input #` to Read What You've Written

After you write data to a file, you'll eventually need to retrieve that data. For sequential files, use the `Input #` statement to read sequential data. You must read the data in exactly the same order and format as you wrote it, due to the nature of sequential file processing. Here's the format of `Input #`:

```
Input # intFileNumber, Variable1[, Variable2][, ...VariableN]
```

`Input #` requires an open file number and variables to hold the data you're reading. The `Input #` statement and the `Print #` statement used to write the data to the file should use the same format. If you used delimiters to write the data, you should use the same delimiters for `Input #`.

> **Note**
>
> If you write a series of variables on one line and want to be able to read them reliably with `Input #`, you must either use `Write` instead of `Print #` or manually include comma delimiters. `Input #` reads up to the first space, comma, or end-of-line character if it reads into a numeric variable. It reads up to the first comma or end-of-line character when reading a string, unless the string contains quotation marks.

The following statement reads five variables from an open sequential file. The variables all reside on the same file line:

```
Input #intFileNumber V1, V2, V3, V4, V5
```

The `Print #` statement that created the file has to match the `Input #` statement's format and use the same variable data types; otherwise, `Input #` can't read the data.

`Input #` is fairly simple because it performs the mirror-image task of `Print #`. As the next section explains, `Write #` often outputs file data in a more general format than `Print #`, thus reducing your worry about matching the `Input #` statement to its original output code.

The `Write #` Statement Also Outputs to Files

`Write #` is another command that writes information to a sequential file. `Write #` and `Print #` vary only slightly. All data that `Write #` writes to a file is comma delimited. Also, `Write #` automatically encloses all string data inside quotation marks (the quotation marks appear in the file), encloses all date data within pound signs, writes Boolean data as `#TRUE#` or `#FALSE#`, and sends null data and error codes to the file as `#NULL#` and `#Error` *`errorcode`*`#`, respectively. *`errorcode#`* represents an error number that explains the output error that has occurred, such as a disk not found. You can search Visual Basic's Online Help for a list of error codes and their meanings.

NEW TERM A *comma-delimited file* is a file whose data is separated by commas.

12

Comma delimitation is required for files that certain mail merge and spreadsheet programs read. The commas also make reading the data less error prone, because subsequent `Input #` statements don't have to match the `Write #` statements exactly.

> To read data more easily, always write the data with `Write #` instead of `Print #`.

Here's the format for `Write #`:

```
Write # intFileNumber, [OutputList]
```

`OutputList` is the list of one or more variables you want to read from the file opened on the file number.

The earlier section "The `Print #` Statement Outputs Sequentially" that described `Print #` also showed how to output one value per line with the `Print #` statement. You can include the same formatting options in `Print #` that you can include in the regular `Print` method.

For example, if you want to print values one after another on the same line, you include a semicolon after the `intCtr` variable, as is done in Listing 12.3.

LISTING 12.3. USE THE SEMICOLON TO WRITE MULTIPLE VALUES ON A SINGLE LINE.

```
Private Sub cmdFile_Click()
  Dim intCtr As Integer    ' Loop counter
  Dim intFNum As Integer   ' File number
  Dim intMsg As Integer    ' MsgBox() return
  intFNum = FreeFile
  ' Change the path if you want
  Open "C:\Print.txt" For Output As #intFNum

  ' Describe this proc
  intMsg = MsgBox("File Print.txt opened")

  For intCtr = 1 To 6
  Print # intFNum, intCtr;     ' Notice semicolon!!
  intMsg = MsgBox("Writing a " & intCtr & " to Print.txt")
  Next intCtr

Close # intFNum

  intMsg = MsgBox("File Print.txt closed")
End Sub
```

When you run this procedure, the created file contains the following data:

```
1 2 3 4 5 6
```

Notice the spaces between the numbers when they're printed to the same line. `Print #` inserts these spaces because of the imaginary plus sign that appears before all positive numbers.

You should experiment with the different `Print #` parameters to see what results you get when creating a file.

After you write data to a file, reading back the data often takes place in another procedure, or perhaps even in another application. The procedures in Listing 12.4 provide examples of how you can write to a file and then read the information back into variables.

LISTING 12.4. YOU CAN READ FROM AND WRITE TO A FILE FROM WITHIN THE SAME PROCEDURE.

```
Private Sub cmdFileOut_Click ()
  ' Create the sequential file
  Dim intCtr As Integer   ' Loop counter
  Dim intFNum As Integer  ' File number
  intFNum = FreeFile

  Open "Print.txt" For Output As #intFNum

  For intCtr = 1 To 5
    Print # intFNum, intCtr;    ' Write the loop counter
  Next intCtr

  Close # intFNum
End Sub

Private Sub cmdFileIn_Click ()
  ' Read the sequential file
  Dim intCtr As Integer   ' Loop counter
  Dim intVal As Integer   ' Read value
  Dim intFNum As Integer  ' File number
  Dim intMsg As Integer   ' MsgBox()
  intFNum = FreeFile
  Open "Print.txt" For Input As #intFNum

  For intCtr = 1 To 6
    Input # intFNum, intVal
    ' Display the results in the Immediate window
    intMsg = MsgBox("Retrieved a " & intVal & " from Print.txt")
  Next intCtr

  Close # intFNum
  intMsg = MsgBox("The Print.txt file is now closed.")
End Sub
```


After the first procedure in Listing 12.4 writes the data to the file, the `cmdFileIn_Click()` procedure can read the data from the file.

Now look at the procedure in Listing 12.5, which creates a file named Write.txt.

LISTING 12.5. WRITING OUTPUT TO SEQUENTIAL FILES WITH `Write`.

```
Private cmdFile_Click ()
  Dim intCtr As Integer    ' Loop counter
  Dim intFNum As Integer   ' File number
  intFNum = FreeFile

  Open "c:\Write.txt" For Output As #intFNum

  For intCtr = 1 To 5
    Write # intFNum, intCtr;     ' Write the loop counter
  Next intCtr

  Close # intFNum
End Sub
```

If you run this procedure, you can use Notepad to look at the file created. You'll immediately notice the difference between the `Print #` and `Write #` statements. Here are the contents of Write.txt:

```
1,2,3,4,5,
```

If you don't use a semicolon after the data you write, each piece of data would be on its own line and no commas would separate the data, because the single value per line would make the commas unnecessary. (In this case, `Write #` and `Print #` behave identically.)

Tip

If you use sequential files often, you'll soon gain insight into ways you can improve your code. For example, you might want to write (as the first piece of data in the file) the number of values that appear in the file. This way, subsequent programs that read the data will know how many values exist and can loop accordingly.

Note

You've learned a lot so far today, but this may surprise you: Visual Basic programmers rarely use sequential file processing! You're not wasting your time with this lesson today, however, because all the common file access methods and controls use the fundamentals that sequential file processing teaches you.

Working with Random-Access Files

Whereas you must read and write sequential files in order, you can read and write *random-access files* (often just called *random files*) in any order. For example, you can write customer records to a random-access file and then read one or more customer records later in any order you want. If the customer file were sequential, you would have to read every record in the file that preceded the record you wanted.

NEW TERM A *random-access file* (or *random file*) is a file whose data you can read or write in any order without having to read or write all other data in the file.

As with sequential access, programmers don't use random access in its strictest form today as much as in the past because of the increased availability of data-access controls and advanced file-processing procedures. Nevertheless, most database-related file access is based on the concepts you'll learn here.

Random-access files offer a good opportunity to discuss a new programming technique called *user-defined data types*. Random-access files often read and write data records, and Visual Basic's user-defined data types let you define data items that look exactly like the records you need to write to (and read from) the random file.

NEW TERM A *user-defined data type* is one you define and use instead of one of the built-in data types (such as `Integer` and `String`).

Working with Random Access

Much of the work you perform with random files parallels sequential file processing. For example, the `Open` and `Close` statements work the same for both sequential- and random-access files. The only difference between the two is in the access mode.

Note

If you don't tell Visual Basic what mode to use to open a file, it assumes `For Random` and fills in the mode for you. For example, suppose you type the following:

```
Open "Random.txt" As #1
```

Visual Basic changes the line to this:

```
Open "Random.txt" For Random As #1
```

The following statement opens a file for random access:

```
Open "Random.txt" For Random As #1
```

You can open a file as a random-access file and then use it for sequential access. You sacrifice the benefits of a random-access file during the processing, but you may want to do this sometimes, especially if you've entered the records in a predefined order and you now want to print a report or display the file data in that exact order.

Consider an example of the difference between sequential and random access. Suppose you create a file that contains 10 lines of inventory totals. To read the sixth line (or *record*) of the file in sequential mode, you have to read the first five items to get to the sixth, and then you have to read the last four items. If you access the file in random mode, you can go straight to the sixth record, read the data, and then close the file.

The same holds true for writing to a file. If you have the same 10-line file and you want to change the eighth record with sequential access, you have to read all 10 records in the file, change the eighth record, and write all 10 records back to the file. In random mode, you can just write the changes to the eighth record.

When a file contains only 10 records, you don't benefit much from a random file, but when the file contains 10,000 records, you save a lot of time and decrease system overhead when you use random access.

Using `Get` and `Put`

Two statements are used for random-access files: `Put #` and `Get #`. These statements are similar to the `Print #` and `Input #` statements used for sequential file access. The major difference between these two sets of statements is that `Print #` and `Input #` handle one piece of data at a time and work all the way through the file. There's no way for these statements to position to a specific record and update only that record.

The format for `Put #` and `Get #` is a little different than those of `Print #` and `Input #`:

```
Put [#]intFileNum, [intRecNum,] Variable
```

```
Get [#]intFileNum, [intRecNum,] Variable
```

As you can see, these statements use a record number. By specifying the record number you want to work with, you can update or read certain data. Record numbers begin with 1. The variable you read or write can be of any data type—even an array or a user-defined variable (see the next section). The freedom to handle any type of variable as a single unit is one of the most powerful features of random-access files.

The examples that appear in the next section include procedures that read and write particular records in a random-access file.

Defining User-Defined Data Types

You've already learned about variables and arrays in this book. You'll now learn how to create your own data types consisting of other data types grouped together. These user-defined data types are sometimes called *structures* or *records*.

If you want to create a program that allows you to maintain an address book for all your contacts, you could use individual variables for each field you needed. For example, you could use a string named `strFName` for the first name, a string named `strLName` for the last name, and so on. These separate variables would work; however, such programming would become cumbersome when you had a large number of contacts to manage. It would be much easier to have one user-defined data type that contained all the same information and that you could handle as one entity just as you handle individual variables.

A user-defined data type is one that contains other existing data types grouped together to form a new data type. This grouping is referred to as a *composite declaration*.

> A user-defined data type is composed of preexisting data types (Visual Basic's built-in data types, other user-defined types, or both).

You use the `Type` statement to create your own data types. The format is as follows:

```
[Private ¦ Public] Type TypeName
  VarName1[(ArraySize)] As ExistingType [* StringLength]
  VarName2[(ArraySize)] As ExistingType [* StringLength]
      :
      :
End Type
```


Notice that the name of the user-defined data type you want to create follows the `Type` keyword. This name can be any word that isn't a reserved word, keyword, or declared variable name. If you've already declared a variable named `Client`, for instance, you can't create a user-defined data type named `Client`.

You must declare all user-defined types at the module level; it's invalid to declare them inside procedures. You can declare a type in a form module, but it must be declared as `Private`, and the data type will be private to the form's module code only.

Examine the code in Listing 12.6 to learn more about the `Type` statement.

LISTING 12.6. USE THE Type STATEMENT TO DECLARE YOUR OWN DATA TYPES.

```
1:  ' Module Page of the Project
2:  Type UserType
3:    strFName As String
4:    strLName As String
5:  End Type
6:  Public Names As UserType
```

This code creates a user-defined data type named `UserType`, beginning in line 2. The new data type contains two strings, `strFName` and `strLName`. Line 6 creates a variable named `Names` of type `UserType`.

Note

`UserType` isn't a variable but rather a type you've defined. `Names` is the variable name, and `strFName` and `strLName` are *members* (or *fields*) within the variable. You've added a new data type to the Visual Basic language for the duration of the program's execution. In addition to `Integer` and `Boolean`, you now can declare variables of the data type `UserType`.

Tip

To access the individual fields that make up the data type, use the variable name, a period, and then the field name.

The following statements initialize and work with the variable just declared:

```
Names.strFName = "John"
Names.strLName = "Doe"
lblFName.Caption = "First Name: " & Names.strFName
lblLName.Caption = "Last Name: " & Names.strLName
```

You can limit the size of string variables used in a structure by adding the `* StringLength` option to the declaration after an `As String` field type. The fixed-length string sets the absolute length of the string to `StringLength`. This usually is required when you're going to be randomly reading and writing your structures to a file. A fixed string length is needed to ensure that each record written to the file is the same size so that you can safely access records randomly.

To change Listing 12.6 to make the string sizes constant, you would enter the code in Listing 12.7.

LISTING 12.7. USE FIXED STRING SIZES TO DETERMINED THE LENGTH OF THE WRITTEN STRINGS.

```
' Module Page of the Project
Type UserType2
  strFName As String * 8
  strLName As String * 20
End Type
Public Names As UserType2
```

The fixed-length strings limit the string length to an inflexible maximum. Although the string data may not consume the entire string space you've reserved, Visual Basic pads the remaining length with spaces to ensure that any variables declared with `UserType2` and written to a random-access file will consume the same record length no matter what data the variable holds.

The procedure in Listing 12.8 demonstrates the basics of working with random files.

LISTING 12.8. YOU CAN WRITE TO ANY RECORD NUMBER.

```
Private Sub cmdCreate_Click()
  ' This procedure creates the file
  Dim intFile As Integer   ' Free file number
  Dim intCtr As Integer    ' Loop counter

  intFile = FreeFile
  Open "c:\Random.Txt" For Random As #intFile Len = 5

  ' Loop through numbers and write file
  For intCtr = 1 To 5
    Put # intFile, intCtr, intCtr  ' Record # same as data
  Next intCtr

  Close intFile
End Sub

Private Sub cmdChange_Click()
  ' This procedure changes 3rd record
  Dim intFile As Integer   ' Free file number

  intFile = FreeFile
  Open "c:\Random.Txt" For Random As #intFile Len = 5

  ' Write a new 3rd record
  Put #intFile, 3, 9   ' Record 3, value: 9
Close # intFile
End Sub
```


continues

LISTING 12.8. CONTINUED

```
28:
29: Private Sub cmdDisplay_Click()
30:   ' This procedure displays the file
31:   Dim intFile As Integer    ' Free file number
32:   Dim intVal As Integer     ' Read value
33:   Dim intCtr As Integer     ' Loop counter
34:   Dim intMsg As Integer     ' For MsgBox()
35:   intFile = FreeFile
36:   Open "c:\Random.Txt" For Random As #intFile Len = 5
37:
38:   intMsg = MsgBox("File Random.Txt opened...")
39:
40:   ' Loop through records and write file
41:   For intCtr = 1 To 5
42:     Get # intFile, intCtr, intVal
43:     intMsg = MsgBox(" Retrieved a " & intVal & " from Random.Txt")
44:   Next intCtr
45:   Close # intFile
46:
47:   intMsg = MsgBox("File Random.Txt is now closed")
48: End Sub
```

Notice that the random-access `Open` statement in line 7 uses the `Len` option. The procedure uses `Put #` in line 11 to create a random-access file with a record length of 5; the `Len` option specifies the record length. The record length is very important; if you don't know the record length, `Put #` and `Get #` won't know how far into the file to search for a particular record. (The formula for finding a record is *`RecordNumber * RecordLength`*.)

The application's form in Listing 12.8 has three buttons. One creates the file, another displays the file, and a third changes the file. Each of the buttons triggers one of the event procedures in Listing 12.8. You can easily create such an application and run it. Click the Create button and then click the Display button to see the message boxes pop up, telling you the data you have written. Click the Change button and then click the Display button again to see the results of the random change. After the file changes, the third record in the file holds 9 instead of 3. The subroutine that made this change, `cmdChange_Click()`, simply wrote the 9 to record number 3, using `Put #` to access the correct record.

Embedded User Types

You've seen how to create your first user-defined data type, but what if you want to include a user-defined data type inside another user-defined data type? One of the fields needs to be a user-defined data type rather than one of the built-in Visual Basic data types. Just be sure to declare the user-defined data type you want included *before* you declare the user-defined data type you want to include it in.

Listing 12.9 shows one example of a user-defined data type called `Address` that is embedded as a field inside another user-defined data type.

LISTING 12.9. USER-DEFINED DATA TYPES CAN BE USED INSIDE OTHER USER-DEFINED DATA TYPES.

```
' Entered into the Code module's Declaration section
Type Address
  strStreet As String
  strCity As String
  strZip As String
End Type

Type UserType3
  strFName As String * 10
  strLName As String * 25
  typAddr As Address  ' Another data type
End Type

Public Names As UserType3  ' Declare an application variable
```

Listing 12.10 contains code that initializes these fields and shows you how to get to the fields within fields.

LISTING 12.10. ONCE YOU DEFINE A PUBLIC DATA TYPE, ANY MODULE CAN USE THAT DATA TYPE FOR VARIABLE DECLARATIONS.

```
Names.strFName = "Jonathan"
Names.strLName = "Doe"

Names.typAddr.strStreet = "AnyStreet"
Names.typAddr.strCity = "AnyTown"
Names.typAddr.strZip "12345-9876"

' Work with the data
lblFName.Caption = "First Name: " & Names.strFName
lblLName.Caption = "Last Name: " & Names.strLName
lblAddr.Caption = "Street: " & Names.strAddr.strStreet
lblCty.Caption = "City: " & Names.strAddr.strCity
lblZip.Caption = "Zip: " & Names.strAddr.strZip
```


Using the File Controls

In Day 9, "The Dialog Box Control," you learned how to use the common dialog box control to display the File Open and File Save dialog boxes. Such dialog boxes work well for getting the user's file selections. These dialog boxes let the user search folders, disks, and even networked disk drives for data. Also, the File Save and File Open dialog boxes both follow the Windows standard.

When working with files, especially the sequential and random files you learned about in the previous sections, you may need to request a directory (called a *folder* starting in Windows 95), drive, or filename, without resorting to the complete File Save or File Open dialog box.

Visual Basic's three special list boxes help you manage directories, drives, and files. Here are descriptions of these special list boxes:

- **Directory list box**—Lets users select a directory.
- **Drive list box**—Lets users select a disk drive.
- **File list box**—Lets users select a file name.

Figure 12.1 shows a form window that contains all three kinds of special list boxes.

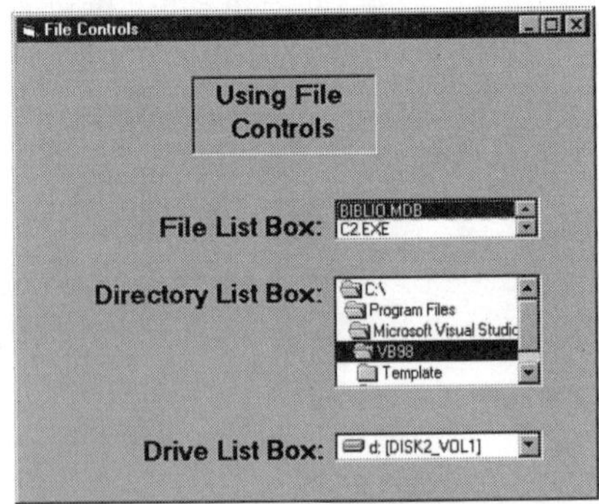

FIGURE 12.1.
You can work with these three special list boxes.

> **Note**
>
> You might wonder why Visual Basic supplies these file-related controls, because you've already seen the Common Dialog control, which supports the full use of these controls as a set without requiring you to place the controls individually on a form. Well, these special list controls let you place specific kinds of lists on a form whenever you need just one or two aspects of a file. For example, you might need to write data to a user's disk. Although your application will handle the filename and directory, you need to ask the user which disk drive should receive the application's data.

These lists don't work in tandem with each other unless you program them to do so. For example, if you place the three controls on one form and run the application, changing the disk drive doesn't change the directory or filename shown in the other two controls. If you really want to, of course, you can write event procedures to keep these controls in synch with each other.

The Drive List Box

Use the drive list box control to let users select a disk drive. This control is smart enough to search the host computer and determine which drives—local and remote, floppy, hard, and CD-ROM—exist on each user's system. The control then displays these choices graphically when users open the drive list box (see Figure 12.2).

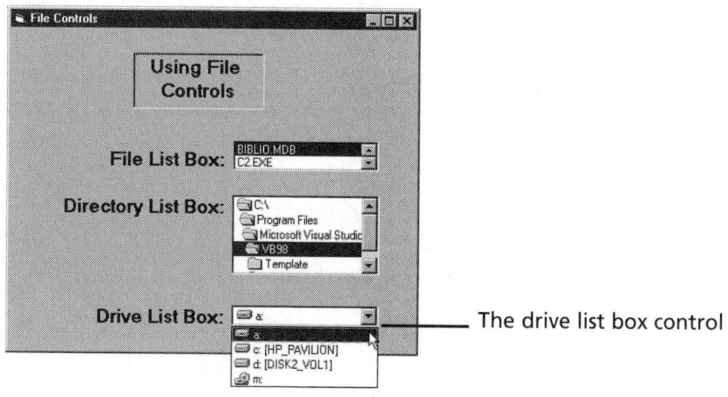

FIGURE 12.2. *Users can make a selection from the drive list box.*

The drive list box control first displays the drive from which the user launched the application, but you can override this default drive by using Visual Basic code to point the control to another drive.

The Directory List Box

Use the directory list box control to let users select a directory folder. This control is smart enough to search the host computer and determine which directories exist in the system. The directory list box displays these choices graphically by using the standard Windows format.

Remember that the directory list box control can't determine which drive is selected in the drive list box. You have to take care of linking the drive to the directory, as explained at the end of today's lesson.

12

The directory list box control first displays the directory from which the user launched the application, but you can override this default directory by using Visual Basic code to point the control to another directory.

The File List Box

Use the file list box control to let users select a file. This control is smart enough to search the host computer and determine which files exist in the file system. The file list box then displays these choices graphically by using the standard Windows format.

As with the directory list box control, the file list box control can't determine which drive (or directory) is selected in the drive (or directory) list box. You have to take care of linking the drive to the directory, as explained at the end of today's lesson.

The file list box control first displays the files from the directory in which the user launched the application, but you can override this default directory by using Visual Basic code to point the directory list box control to another directory before linking the file list box to the folder.

File-Related Commands

Visual Basic supports several drive and directory commands that prepare the file list controls, as described in Table 12.3.

Table 12.3. The Visual Basic language contains commands that work with drives and directories.

Command	*Description*
`ChDrive strDrive`	Changes the default drive to the drive in the string expression.
`ChDir strDirectory`	Changes the default directory to the directory in the string expression. If you specify no drive inside the string, Visual Basic selects the directory on the current drive.
`Kill strFileSpec`	Erases the file or files (represented by wildcards) specified by the string expression.
`MkDir strDirectory`	Creates the directory specified by the string expression.
`RmDir strDirectory`	Erases the directory specified by the string expression.

> `RmDir` produces an error if you try to remove a directory that still contains files.

In addition to the statements shown in Table 12.3, Visual Basic supports the `Dir()` function, which checks whether or not files exist, and the `CurDir()` function, which returns the name of the current directory.

Suppose that you want to point the drive list box and directory list box controls to the directory C:\MyFiles. You can insert the following code in the `Form_Load()` procedure:

```
ChDrive "C:"
ChDir "\MyFiles"
```

The drive list box, directory list box, and file list box controls now point to the C:\MyFiles directory when they appear on the form, rather than to the application's current directory.

The `Dir()` function requires a little more explanation. Suppose you want to know if a file named SALES98.DAT exists in the root directory on drive D. You can check for such a file like this:

```
If (Dir("c:\SALES98.DAT")) = "SALES98.DAT" Then
  intMsg = MsgBox ("The file exists")
Else
  intMsg = MsgBox ("The file does not exist")
End If
```


The `Dir()` function returns the filename you pass as an argument. The filename is returned only if that file resides inside the directory argument you provide. If `Dir()` doesn't return the filename, the file doesn't exist on the drive.

You can pass `Dir()` a wildcard file specification like this:

```
Dir("c:\Sales*.DAT")
```

`Dir()` will return the first file found that meets the wildcard specification—if any files meet the specification. After you pass the first file specification, you can make subsequent calls to `Dir()` by specifying `Dir` without parentheses or any argument. Visual Basic keeps returning files that match your wildcard file specification until the last file is found. When `Dir` returns a null string (`""`), you must include a file specification in the next call to `Dir()`; otherwise, `Dir` will return an error.

If you want to set the drive list box control's drive to a specific disk drive, set the control's `Drive` property this way:

```
drvDisk.Drive = "d:\"
```

The drive list box control will then display *D:* at the top of the list. If a user changes the drive list box to a different drive, the drive list box's `Change()` event occurs. You can set the user's selected drive to the default drive with the following statement inside `drvDisk_Change()`:

```
ChDrive drvDisk.Drive
```

Use the following code to set the `Drive` property of the directory list box control to the drive the control is to display:

```
dirDirect.Drive = drvDisk.Drive
```

This assignment statement sets the directory's drive to the directory selected by the user. You can add the directory list box control's disk assignment to the `drvDisk_Change()` event procedure.

After a user changes the directory list box control to a different directory, the control's `Change` event occurs. In the `Change` event procedure, you can set the current directory to the user's directory like this:

```
ChDir dirDirect.Path
```

The directory list box control supports a rather unusual access scheme—it supports a property named `ListIndex`. The value of `ListIndex` is `-1` for the selected directory, `-2` for the directory immediately above the selected one, `-3` for the directory immediately above that, and so on. The `ListIndex` property is `0` for the first subdirectory of the selected directory, `1` for the next subdirectory, and so on.

If you want to display only certain files in the file list box, assign a string file specification to the file list box control's `Pattern` property:

```
filFiles.Pattern = "*.vbp; *.frm"
```

You can include as many file specifications as you like, indicated with wildcards within the string's quotation marks. The file list box control immediately changes to reflect the new pattern by showing only those files. When a user selects a file, the file list box control's `Change` event occurs and the selected file appears in the `FileName` property. As with the drive list box control, the selected file also appears with the `ListIndex` value of `-1`.

After a user selects a path, you can change the file list box control to reflect files in that path:

```
filFiles.Path = dirDirect.Path
```

Summary

Today's lesson explained how you work with files from a fundamental level. Now that you've mastered the basics, you are better equipped to handle the more advanced file-related controls and commands, such as Visual Basic's database features.

Today you learned how to read and write sequential and random files. These files are useful for storing text values. Programming such files is relatively simple once you learn the Visual Basic commands. For example, the `Write #` statement parallels `Read #`, and `Get #` parallels `Put #`.

If you need them, the file controls on your toolbox window provide access to the user's disk drive, directory, and files. Although the common dialog box control works best for offering File Open and File Save dialog boxes, you can place the file controls on forms when you need specific information on a drive, directory, or file.

Tomorrow's lesson shows you how to write to another device, the printer.

Q&A

Q Why are user-defined data types called "user defined" when the user has nothing to do with defining them?

A Although the term includes the word *user*, you, the programmer, are the one who defines the data type and uses the data type in your programs. In a way, you *are* the user of the new data type because you use the new data type in your application.

Workshop

The Workshop provides quiz questions to help you solidify your understanding of the material covered as well as exercises to give you experience in using what you've learned. Try to understand the quiz and exercise answers before continuing to the next chapter. Answers are provided in Appendix A, "Answers to Exercises."

Quiz

1. How many open files can you close with one `Close` statement?
2. What function returns the next unused file number?
3. What happens if you open a file for sequential output access and the file already exists?
4. What happens if you open a file for sequential append access and the file already

exists?

5. What type of file does the following statement open?

```
Open "TestFile.dat" For Append As #1
```

6. Why do random `Open` statements need to know the record length of their data?
7. Why should you specify the absolute length of strings within a user-defined data type if you're going to read and write those strings to a random file?
8. What Visual Basic statement defines a new data type?
9. True/False. The following code declares a new user-defined variable named `CustRec`:

```
Type CustRec
   strFName As String * 10
   strLName As String * 15
   curBalance As Currency
  blnDiscount As Boolean
End Type
```

10. What is the difference between the `Dir()` function with an argument and the `Dir()` function without an argument?

Exercises

1. **Bug Buster:** Frannie has file problems. She gets an error when she runs an application with the following statement. Can you explain to her the most likely reason an error occurs? (Assume that the directory named Bills exists and resides in the root directory C.)

```
RmDir "C:\Bills"
```

2. Write a procedure that creates a sequential file that holds the following information: name, age, and favorite color. Fill this file with five records (each record should contain one name, one age, and one color). Use three `For` loops to write this information to the file. *Tip:* You should initialize three arrays, one for each kind of value you're writing.
3. Create a dialog box that mimics the File Open dialog box. Use only the drive, directory, and file selection lists as well as OK and Cancel command buttons. Write code so that an application that uses this dialog box will change the directory or file lists whenever a user selects a different drive or directory. (Although you'll use the standard common dialog box control for your applications, this exercise helps show you how the file controls relate to one another.)

WEEK 2

BONUS PROJECT 6

Reading and Writing Files

This Bonus Project's application demonstrates further how to read sequential files. The application also integrates the common dialog box control into the file-opening process to get a filename from the user. This Bonus Project builds on the file-based procedures you learned how to write in Day 12's lesson ("Interact with Files"). This Bonus Project is a file-viewing program. The user selects a file, and the file appears in a list box. The project performs the following tasks:

- Enables the user to select a file using the File Open dialog box.
- Enables the user to change the file's background color using the Color dialog box.
- Enables the user to resize the form. Once the form has been resized, the application adjusts the form's controls to the new form size.
- Performs error-handling in the File Open code so that the user can click the dialog box's Cancel button to keep the current file in view without selecting a different file.
- Enables the user to view either batch or text files (those with the .BAT and .TXT filename extensions, respectively) but limits the files that can be read to a maximum of 4,096 bytes.

Figure BP6.1 shows what the file viewer looks like after a file has been selected for viewing.

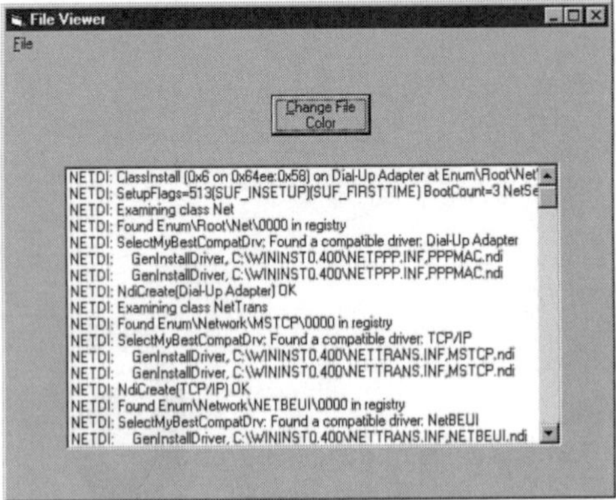

FIGURE BP6.1.
The user can view any text or batch file inside the list box.

First, you'll add the graphic elements to the form and then you'll add the code that responds to the user's actions.

Creating the Interface

Add the controls and their properties to the form according to Table BP6.1.

Indent all the menu items within the Menu Editor, except for the first item, File, which will appear on the application's menu bar. By indenting the subsequent menu items, they will appear in the File menu's drop-down list of options.

TABLE BP6.1. SET THESE CONTROLS AND PROPERTIES ON THE FORM.

Control Property Name	*Property Value*
Form `Name`	`frmFile`
Form `Caption`	`File Viewer`
Form `Height`	`4620`
Form `Width`	`6570`
List box `Name`	`lstFile`
List box `Height`	`2205`
List box `Left`	`720`

Control Property Name	*Property Value*
List box `Top`	`1320`
List box `Width`	`4815`
Command button `Name`	`cmdColor`
Command button `Caption`	`&Change the File Color`
Command button `Height`	`495`
Command button `Left`	`2760`
Command button `Top`	`480`
Command button `Width`	`1215`
Menu item #1 `Caption`	`&File`
Menu item #1 `Name`	`mnuFile`
Menu item #2 `Caption`	`&Open`
Menu item #2 `Name`	`mnuFileOpen`
Menu item #3 `Caption`	`-`
Menu item #3 `Name`	`mnuFileSep1`
Menu item #4 `Caption`	`E&xit`
Menu item #4 `Name`	`mnuFileExit`
Common dialog box `Name`	`comFile`
Common dialog box `DialogTitle`	`File Open`
Common dialog box `InitDir`	`c:\`
Common dialog box `Filter`	`Text (*.txt)¦*.txt¦Batch (*.bat)¦*.bat`
Common dialog box `CancelError`	`True`
Common dialog box `MaxFileSize`	`4096`

One of the easiest ways to set up the common dialog box control is to click the (Custom) entry in the Properties window and initialize the dialog box that appears, as shown in Figure BP6.2. Using the dialog box is simpler than entering the values from the Properties window.

FIGURE BP6.2.

Use the custom dialog box to enter common dialog box control properties.

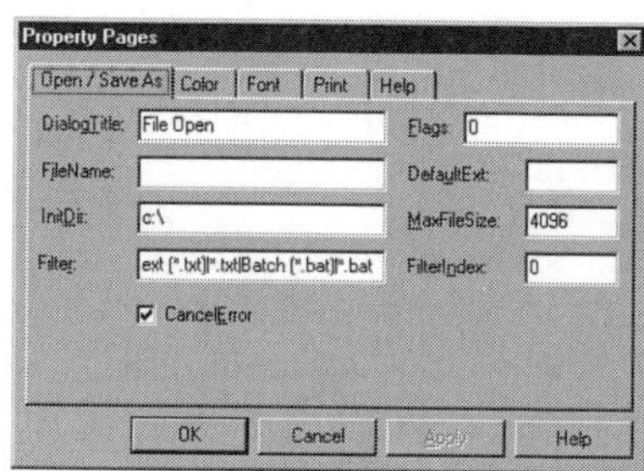

You do not need to set any color-related properties. The color selection dialog box needs no properties set before your program displays it. The user's color selection will not change any of the file-related properties that you set up for the common dialog box control.

Entering the Code

Listing BP6.1 provides the event code you need to enter for this project.

Instead of typing the code line by line, you can enter a new procedure inside the Code window easily by getting help from the editor. If you select Tools, Add Procedure, Visual Basic opens the dialog box you see in Figure BP6.3. Simply type the procedure name, its type, and its scope. Visual Basic automatically creates the wrapper lines for you so that you don't have to type the first and last procedure lines.

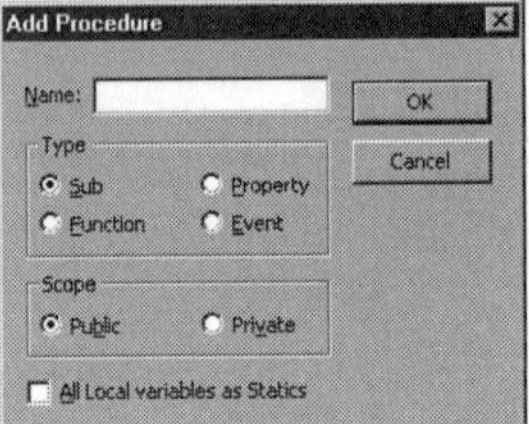

FIGURE BP6.3.
Let Visual Basic type the first and last procedure lines for you.

LISTING BP6.1. LOADING A FILE INTO A LIST BOX CONTROL.

```
Private Sub cmdColor_Click()
   ' Use the common dialog box to
   ' let the user change the background
   ' color of the list box.
   comFile.ShowColor
   lstFile.BackColor = comFile.Color
End Sub

Private Sub Form_Resize()
  Dim intMsg As Integer   ' For MsgBox()
  ' Change the size of the list box
  ' if the user resizes the form
  '
  ' This event procedure executes when the
  ' form first loads also
  '
```

```
    ' Make sure the form is not sized so small
    ' that the list box cannot display
      If (frmFile.Width < 4000) Or (frmFile.Height < 3500) Then
        ' Hide list box
        ' and warn user
        lstFile.Visible = False
        intMsg = MsgBox("The form is too small to display the file", _
        vbCritical)
      Else
        ' Turn on list box display in case it
        ' was turned off previously
        lstFile.Visible = True
        ' Adjust the size of the list box to the form
        ' Adjust the command button's location to the form
        lstFile.Width = frmFile.Width - 1440
        lstFile.Height = frmFile.Height - 2500
        cmdColor.Left = (frmFile.Width / 2) - 500
      End If
End Sub

Private Sub mnuFileExit_Click()
    ' Program termination option
    End
End Sub

Private Sub mnuFileOpen_Click()
     Dim strFileLine As String
     ' Set up for Cancel click
     On Error GoTo comErrorHandler
     '
     ' Display the File Open dialog box
     comFile.ShowOpen
     ' Code either continues if User clicks OK
     ' or skips to error handler if Cancel clicked
     '
     ' Open the file the user selected
     Open comFile.FileName For Input As #1
     ' Make room for new file
       lstFile.Clear
     '
     ' Read one complete line of the file
     Line Input #1, strFileLine
     lstFile.AddItem strFileLine
     '
     ' Keep reading and adding to the list
     ' box until the end of file is reached
     Do Until (EOF(1))
       Line Input #1, strFileLine
       lstFile.AddItem strFileLine
```

continues

Listing BP6.1. Continued

```
65:     Loop
66:     ' Close open file
67:     Close
68: comErrorHandler:
69:     ' Do nothing if the user clicks Cancel
70: End Sub
```

Analysis

The first event procedure in lines 1 through 7 displays the common dialog box control using the `ShowColor` method. When the user selects a color, line 6 sets the list box's background to that color, and whatever file the user is viewing is shown against that new background color. (If a file is not being viewed, the list box still shows the selected color in the background.) The list box retains the background color throughout the rest of the program unless the user once again clicks the command button to change the color.

Line 9 begins the second-longest event procedure in the program. When the user resizes the form, the `Form_Resize()` event procedure automatically executes. (The procedure also executes automatically when the form first loads.)

The resize procedure ensures that the form's command button and list box appear centered within the form's boundaries regardless of the size of the form. If the user shrinks the form too much for the list box to show up, line 19 ensures that the following events take place:

- The list box is hidden from view (otherwise, Visual Basic would issue an error because the list box could not appear in such a small form).
- The user is warned with a message box that the form is too small.

Assuming the resizing did not eliminate the list box, line 27 shows the list box, and the width and height of the list box are adjusted based on the form's `Width` and `Height` property values. In addition, the location of the command button changes depending on the form's `Width` property.

Line 41 begins the longest event procedure in the program. This procedure opens and reads the selected file. When the user selects File, Open, the common dialog box control opens to display the File Open dialog box, as shown in Figure BP6.4. The event procedure uses the `ShowOpen` method in line 47 to produce the File Open dialog box.

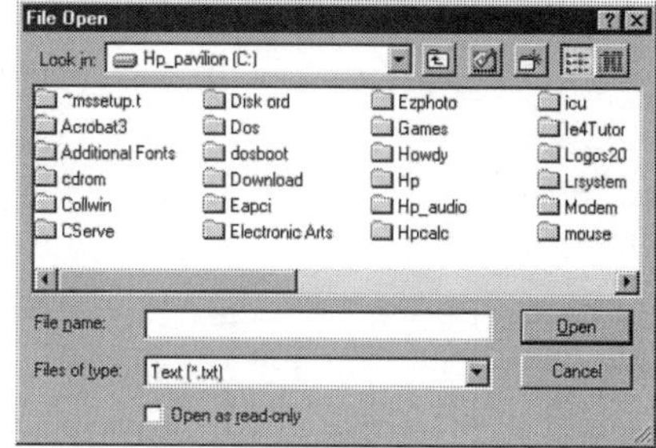

FIGURE BP6.4.

The user can select a batch or text file from the File Open dialog box.

Caution The user's File Open list of folders and files will differ from the list shown in Figure BP6.4, depending on the contents of the user's disk.

The user sees the File Open dialog box after selecting File, Open from the menu bar. The user can open the Files of type drop-down list box to display files with the extension .TXT or .BAT (all folders are always shown no matter which file type the user selects). The user can traverse folders to locate a file anywhere on the PC or even on a networked PC.

Line 44 sets up the error-handling code just in case the user clicks the File Open dialog box's Cancel button. The error-handler causes execution to jump to the end of the event procedure and leave everything on the form and inside the list box untouched.

When program execution reaches line 52, the user will have selected a file. Line 52 opens that file for input as a sequential file.

Note The file is opened for input only, not output; therefore, the program cannot harm the file's contents.

Line 54 clears the list box so that the contents of the newly selected file can replace the file whose contents were there previously. Lines 57 and 58 read the first line from the file and add that line to the list box using the `AddItem` method. Line 57 introduces a new command to you: `Line Input #`. After mastering `Input #` and `Get #`, you'll have no trouble with `Line Input #`. Here's the format of `Line Input #`:

```
Line Input #intFileNumber, strLineVar
```

Line input reads one complete line (or record) from the file into the string variable designated as `strLineVar`. If `Input #` were used instead of `Line Input #`, a full line might not be read because commas and spaces probably exist in the lines, and `Input #` stops reading when it hits a space or comma, even if the space or comma appears in the middle of the line.

Once the first line is read and sent to the list box, line 62 begins a loop to read the rest of the file. An internal function, `EOF()`, is then used to test for the end of file. The file can consist of one line or more, and the program does not know in advance how many lines reside in the file. Therefore, `EOF()` returns `True` when the end of the file is reached. If `True` is returned, the loop will no longer read a line and the program will continue starting in line 66.

Why didn't line 62 read like this?

```
Do Until (EOF(1) = True)
```

Line 62 could have tested the `EOF()` return value against the `True` value, but there was no reason to do so. Doing so would actually make the program less efficient. The `EOF()` function returns either a `True` or `False` result depending on the file's end-of-file condition. As you'll recall from the lessons you've already mastered, functions (the ones you write as well as internal functions) become their return values. Therefore, the call to `EOF()` becomes `True` or `False`, and no further testing is needed for the `Do Until` conditional phrase.

Line 67 closes the file, and the program then continues letting the user view the selected file or lets the user select another file.

DAY 13

Printing VB Output

Today's lesson shows you how to send output to the printer. Now that you've mastered Visual Basic's development environment, have learned a lot of the language, and can develop working applications, you should know how Visual Basic deals with printed output. Obviously, you'll want your applications to print things sometimes. Until now, you've had no way to send information to the printer.

Be forewarned—Visual Basic's printer interface isn't as simple as most of the other Visual Basic components you've mastered. Printing data from a VB program usually isn't a trivial task. This lesson explains how to work with the several printer interfaces available to Visual Basic programmers.

Today, you learn the following:

- About printer objects
- How to determine your user's printer settings
- About the `Is TypeOf` statement
- About printer-based methods
- How the printer methods mimic the form methods

- About proper printing techniques
- How to warn your users before printing begins
- How to print forms

Printer-Based Objects

Let's say you want to print a copy of the code in your Code window. To do this, you would select File, Print. Some PCs have multiple printers connected to them. Your applications have access to all the printers on the system. Also, internal faxes often act as printers. Therefore, you can print to any printer or fax from your application by selecting the appropriate printer as Visual Basic's default printer. After you set Visual Basic's default printer, Visual Basic will route all output to that printer and ignore the system's default printer until the application ends or you designate yet another default printer.

To set a different Windows default printer from the system's Printers window, click the Windows Start button and choose Settings, Printers.

Selecting a printer for your code listings is simple. Now, let's discuss producing printed output with your applications. Before getting to the specifics, you should take a moment to learn about a special set of objects—the `Printers` collection.

New Term The *`Printers` collection* is a list of all the printers on your application's PC, including internal modems that are set up to send faxes. The collection does not include the printers on the PC you create the application on necessarily, but the printers on the runtime PC.

The `Printers` collection is the list of all the printers on the system running your application. This collection obviously changes from system to system. A user might run your application one minute, add or remove a system printer, and then run your application again, causing the application's `Printers` collection to vary between the two runs. Today's lesson explains how to access the printers in the current collection.

The `Printers` collection is the same list of printers that appears in the system's Print dialog box when you open the Name drop-down list box.

Accessing the `Printers` Collection

As with most lists within Visual Basic, you can reference the `Printers` collection from your application by using an index value. The first printer (the system default printer) has an index value of 0, the second printer has an index value of 1, and so on. If you want to use a `For` loop to step through the printers, you can determine the number of printers now on the system by referencing `Printers.Count-1`. Alternatively, you can use the `For Each` statement to step through the printers without having to determine the number (as seen in an example that follows later in Listing 13.1).

Use the `Set Printer` statement to set Visual Basic's default printer to one of the printers on the system. The following statement sets Visual Basic's default printer to the second printer on the system:

```
Set Printer = Printers(1)   ' Change the default printer
```

Of course, determining the printer you want to print to at runtime isn't always easy. How can you even know what kind of printer you're testing for? You can test only for specific properties. For example, if you need to print to a printer that has a certain page size, you can loop through every printer on the system, looking for one that has that page size.

Testing for Printer Properties

Table 13.1 lists many important printer properties that you'll commonly use in determining which printer your application needs. Most of these properties have named constant values associated with them. Therefore, rather than test for property values of 1 or 2 for a page size, you can test by using named constants such as `vbPRPSLetter` and `vbPRPSLetterSmall`. These are easier to understand later when you maintain the program (but they take longer to type).

If you look up a property in the Online Help reference, you'll find a list of the named constants that Visual Basic supports for that property.

13

TABLE 13.1. YOU CAN DETERMINE IF THE USER'S PRINTER SUPPORTS THESE PROPERTIES.

Property	*Description*
`ColorMode`	Determines whether the printer can print in color or black-and-white.
`Copies`	Specifies the number of copies the user wants. (This is set at runtime by the user from the Print dialog box that your application displays or by your code setting this property.)

continues

TABLE 13.1. CONTINUED

Property	*Description*
`CurrentX`, `CurrentY`	Returns or sets the X and Y coordinates where the next character (or drawing) will appear.
`DeviceName`	Holds the name of the printer, such as Canon BubbleJet IIC.
`DriverName`	Holds the name of the printer. (Multiple printers from the same company may use the same printer driver.)
`Duplex`	Determines whether the printer can print on both sides of the paper or to only a single side.
`Height`	Returns the height of the printed page for the selected printer (in `ScaleMode` measurements).
`Orientation`	Determines or sets the printer's portrait or landscape orientation.
`Page`	Returns the current page number.
`PaperBin`	Returns or sets the paper bin used for printing. (Keep in mind, though, that not all printers support multiple bins.)
`PaperSize`	Returns or sets the paper size currently being used.
`Port`	Returns the name of the printer's port.
`PrintQuality`	Returns or sets the printer's resolution value.
`TrackDefault`	If `False`, `TrackDefault` keeps the current printer property settings when you change default printers; if `True`, it changes the printer property settings at runtime when a different default printer is selected.
`Width`	Returns the width of the printed page for the selected printer (in `ScaleMode` measurements).
`Zoom`	Returns or sets the percentage of scaling used for the printed output; for example, if you set the `Zoom` property to 75, subsequent output appears on the page at 75 percent of its regular size. (Not all printers support the `Zoom` property.)

When your application runs, the printer properties for the `Printer` object match those of the Windows system default printer. If you select a new default printer for Visual Basic, the properties change accordingly. At runtime, you can change many of these properties, as described in Table 13.1.

You'll use many of the properties from Table 13.1 to access the specific printer-output methods introduced in the next section.

The code in Listing 13.1 demonstrates how you might step through the system's current printers.

LISTING 13.1. YOU CAN LOCATE EACH OF THE USER'S PRINTERS.

```
Dim prnPrntr As Printer
For Each prnPrntr In Printers   ' Steps through each
  frmMyForm.Print prnPrntr.DeviceName
Next
```

The code simply prints each printer's name on the current form.

Notice the first line, which declares a variable with the data type `Printer`. As you learn more about Visual Basic, you'll notice that you can declare variables of virtually any data type, including `Printer` and `Form`. The `prnPrntr` variable lets you walk through each printer on the system. An equivalent `For` statement would be this:

```
For prnPrntr = 1 to (Printers.Count - 1)
```

Remember that `Printer` and `Form` are Visual Basic *objects*. You learn more about Visual Basic objects in Day 16, "Objects and Visual Basic."

Rarely, if ever, would you want to print every printer's name on a form. Nevertheless, the loop shown in this example will form the basis for much of your printer processing.

As an additional example, Listing 13.2 searches through all printers on the system, looking for a color printer to output a colorful chart.

LISTING 13.2. LOCATING A COLOR PRINTER ON THE USER'S SYSTEM.

```
Dim prnPrntr As Printer
For Each prnPrntr In Printers
  If prnPrntr.ColorMode = vbPRCMColor Then
    ' Set color printer as system default.
    Set Printer = prnPrntr
    Exit For  ' Don't look further
  End If
Next   ' Step through all of them if needed
```

Controlling the Output

The `Printer` object exists so that you can send data to the default printer without worrying about specific printer types and ports. You apply methods to the `Printer` object to route output—such as reports and graphics—to the printer. Although programming with the `Printer` object can be tedious, you'll develop general-purpose output procedures that can help you print more easily in subsequent programs.

Before sending output to the `Printer` object, set the default printer by using the previous section's `Set Printer` statement if you want the `Printer` object to point to a printer other than the system default printer.

After you select a default printer, use the `Printer` object to route text and graphics to the user's printer. This section explains how to control the `Printer` object and route text to the printer. In tomorrow's lesson, you'll learn graphics commands and methods that you can also apply to the `Printer` object.

With the `Printer` object, you *build* your output. This means that you send output to the `Printer` object, but nothing actually prints. When you've completed the output and are ready to send the completed output to the printer, you issue the `NewPage` or `EndDoc` method to start the actual printing. (Printing also begins when your application ends if you don't first issue the `EndDoc` method.)

Printing to the `Printer` Object

One of the easiest ways to route output to the `Printer` object is to use the `Print` method. The following lines send a message to the printer:

```
Printer.Print "This report shows sales figures for"
Printer.Print dteStart; " through "; dteFinish; "."
Printer.Print "If you need more information, call ext. 319."
```

Windows actually handles the printing details. Therefore, if the user runs out of paper or if the printer is turned off when the printing begins, Windows warns the user with an error message box, such as the one shown in Figure 13.1. Once the user corrects the problem, he or she can click Retry to continue the printing or click Cancel to completely discard the rest of the unprinted output.

FIGURE 13.1.

Windows lets the user correct printing error occurances.

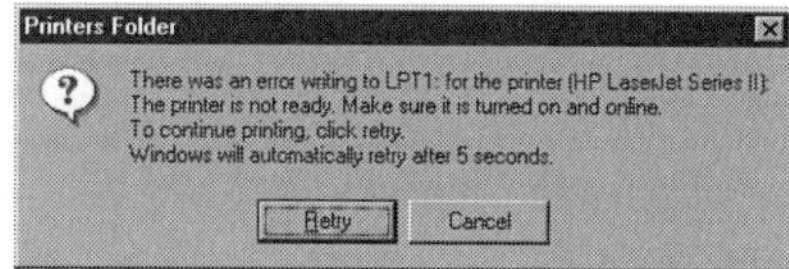

Of course, you can send literals, variables, and control values to the printer. Anything you can print to the form using `Print`, you can also print to the `Printer` object, as the following sample statements show:

```
sngTaxRate = .34
strTitle = "Sands on the Beach"
Printer.Print strTitle & " is the name of the book"
Printer.Print "Your tax rate is" & sngTaxRate
```

If you want to print blank lines, issue a `Print` method without any arguments:

```
Printer.Print      ' Prints a blank line
```

> Warn your users before printing occurs so that you don't surprise them. The last section in today's lesson discusses how you can alert your users to this.

You used the `Print` method to send output to a form in the lesson in Day 11, "Working with Forms," but as you can see here, `Print` is a general-purpose method that sends output to any valid object that can accept text.

You can move the print output to the top of the next page at any point by using the `NewPage` method:

```
Printer.NewPage  ' Go to top of next page
```

Scaling Output

When printing, you may want to scale the output to create margins on the page that subsequent printing-related methods will respect. Once you set the `ScaleMode` property to specify the measurement value your program will use, you can use other scaling-based properties to determine how your output will be positioned on the page.Table 13.2 lists the properties you can set to produce a scaling effect.

TABLE 13.2. SCALING PROPERTIES DETERMINE THE MEASUREMENT.

Property	*Description*
`ScaleLeft`	Defines the printable area's extreme left X coordinate. For example, a `ScaleLeft` value of 10 moves the subsequent left margin by 10 `ScaleMode` measurements.
`ScaleMode`	Determines the measurement value used for scaling. Generally, a `ScaleMode` of `vbPoints` (the value 2), `vbCharacters` (the printer's default character width), `vbInches`, or `vbCentimeters` is used for text printing.
`ScaleHeight`	Changes the `Printer` object's vertical coordinate system.
`ScaleTop`	Defines the printable area's extreme top Y coordinate. For example, a `ScaleTop` value of 5 moves the subsequent top margin by five `ScaleMode` measurements.
`ScaleWidth`	Changes the `Printer` object's horizontal coordinate system.

To set a top margin of five characters and a left margin of eight characters, you would issue the following methods:

```
Printer.ScaleMode = VbCharacters   ' Set scale to chars
Printer.ScaleTop = 5
Printer.ScaleLeft = 8
```

Subsequent `Print` methods will respect these boundaries.

`CurrentX` and `CurrentY` Positions

Unless you change the coordinate system from an upper-left page coordinate of 0,0 to another X,Y system with the `ScaleHeight` and `ScaleWidth` properties, the `Printer` object's `CurrentX` and `CurrentY` values begin at 0,0. (The coordinates always use the measurement set by `ScaleMode`.) You can change these values to different X and Y coordinate values if you want to print the next item at a specific location on the page.

> The `CurrentX` and `CurrentY` properties always respect the margins you've set with `ScaleLeft` and `ScaleTop`. Therefore, the coordinate pair `CurrentX`, `CurrentY` refers to the first character at the upper-left corner of the current page within any margins that you've defined.

To print a message 15 lines down the page and 25 characters to the right, you could use the following code:

```
Printer.ScaleMode = VbCharacters
Printer.CurrentY = 14   ' Remember the starting value = 0
Printer.CurrentX = 24
Printer.Print "Warning, warning, there's danger ahead."
```

Visual Basic's `Printer` object supports several methods that let you control the printing process. You can move the printing to the top of the next page at any time by using the `NewPage` method:

```
Printer.NewPage  ' Go to top of next page
```

At any point during the preparation for printing, the `KillDoc` method can be issued if the user wants to cancel the print job:

```
Printer.KillDoc  ' Don't send the output to the printer
```

`KillDoc` completely removes the output from the `Printer` object. If the user needs to reissue the printed document later, the output has to be re-created.

> `KillDoc` can't cancel anything that has already started printing. Also, `KillDoc` can't kill `PrintForm` jobs.

Microsoft recommends creating a general-purpose printing subroutine inside a standard module that you can call from subsequent applications—as long as you include the standard module in those applications. You can use this routine to print form graphics. The code in Listing 13.3 accepts two arguments of the `Object` data type. Because the subroutine receives the `Object` data type, you can pass it either a `Form` or `Printer` object.

Listing 13.3. You can use this procedure to print specific controls from a form.

```
Sub PrintAnywhere (Src As Object, Dest As Object)
  Dest.PaintPicture Src.Picture, Dest.Width / 2, Dest.Height / 2
  Is TypeOf Dest Is Printer Then
    Printer.EndDoc
  End If
End Sub
```

Suppose your application contains a form with a picture box or image that you want to display and also send to the printer. Perhaps you display a blank form in which users enter data and then send the completed form to the printer.

This subroutine requires source and destination arguments in line 1. The source will always be the form you want to print. The destination can be `Printer`. You can call the procedure whenever you're ready to print the form, like this:

```
Call PrintAnywhere (frmUserForm, Printer)  ' Print form
```

This subroutine uses the `PaintPicture` method to output the form. `PaintPicture` draws a form on the object to which you've applied `PaintPicture`. The `PaintPicture` method requires three values: the form to draw, the destination width, and the destination height. This code simply paints a form that's one-half the size of the destination area. To ensure that the form prints at the end of this method, the `If` statement immediately outputs the form with the `EndDoc` method if the destination is the `Printer` object and not another form. (You could pass a second form for the destination.)

The `Is TypeOf` statement demonstrates a kind of `If` you haven't seen before. The `Is TypeOf...Is` command lets you test objects for certain data types.

The `Is TypeOf...Is` statement does more than just test for specific objects, as you'll find out in Day 16.

Formatting with `Font`

Table 13.3 lists some font-related `Printer` object properties you can work with to set specific font properties before sending text to the printer.

TABLE 13.3. YOU CAN SET FONT-RELATED PROPERTIES BEFORE SENDING TEXT TO THE PRINTER.

Property	*Description*
`Font`	Returns a font you can use for setting font attributes.
`FontBold`	Holds either `True` or `False` to determine whether subsequent output will be boldfaced.
`FontCount`	Returns the number of fonts supported by the printer.
`FontItalic`	Holds either `True` or `False` to determine whether subsequent output will be italicized.
`FontName`	Holds the name of the current font used for output.
`Fonts`	Contains a list of values that holds the names of all installed fonts on the system. Access this list as if it were a control array so that `Fonts(0)` and `Fonts(FontCount - 1)` are the first and last subscripts, respectively.

Property	*Description*
`FontSize`	Determines the size, in points, of the font currently being used.
`FontStrikeThru`	Holds either `True` or `False` to determine whether subsequent output will be printed with a strikethrough line.
`FontTransparent`	Holds either `True` or `False` to determine whether subsequent output will be transparent.
`FontUnderline`	Holds either `True` or `False` to determine whether subsequent output will be underlined.

Use the font attributes when you want to add special effects to your printed output by changing the text font information. The following section of code produces the words *Visual Basic* in large letters on the printer:

```
Printer.FontItalic = True
Printer.FontBold = True
Printer.FontSize = 72      ' 1-inch letters
Printer.Print "Visual Basic"
```

Not only can you use these `Printer` methods for your printer, you can use them for forms as well. Study the code in Listing 13.4 and try to determine what will go to the form. (The identical output would go to the printer if you applied the `Print` methods to the `Printer` object, but by sending the output to the form, you can see on the screen what would otherwise appear on the printer.)

LISTING 13.4. YOU CAN USE THE SAME `Print` METHODS TO PRODUCE OUTPUT ON THE FORM OR THE PRINTER.

```
Private Sub cmdPrint_Click()
    ' Produces an interesting output on
    ' the form using the Print method
    Dim intCtr As Integer
    Dim intCurX As Integer
    Dim intCurY As Integer
    '
    ' First, set up the font
      frmPrint.FontItalic = True
      frmPrint.FontBold = True
      frmPrint.FontSize = 36      ' 1-inch letters
    '
    ' Set measurements to TWIPs
      frmPrint.ScaleMode = vbTwips
    '
    ' Save the current X and Y TWIP locations
```


continues

LISTING 13.4. CONTINUED

```
17:     ' each time the loop iterates
18:     For intCtr = 1 To 10
19:       intCurX = frmPrint.CurrentX
20:       intCurY = frmPrint.CurrentY
21:       ' Print either black or white
22:       If (intCtr Mod 2) = 1 Then   ' Even loop counter
23:          frmPrint.ForeColor = vbWhite
24:       Else
25:          frmPrint.ForeColor = vbBlack
26:       End If
27:       ' Output the text in the large font
28:       frmPrint.Print "Visual Basic"
29:       '
30:       ' Reposition the print location
31:       frmPrint.CurrentX = intCurX + 350
32:       frmPrint.CurrentY = intCurY% + 300
33:     Next intCtr
34:   End Sub
35:
36:   Private Sub cmdExit_Click()
37:     End
38:   End Sub
```

In lines 9 through 11, a large, italicized font is set up for the form using the various font-related methods. Line 14 then sets the measurement value to twips so that subsequent `CurrentX` and `CurrentY` properties are set to twips and not characters. Line 18 begins a loop that will, ultimately, produce 10 sets of *Visual Basic* on the form. The way the words appear is unusual, however.

> **Caution**
>
> If you reproduce this example for printer output, change the color named constant in line 23 to something other than `vbWhite`. As long as you have a color printer, you can use a color that will show up on paper, such as `vbBlue` or `vbRed`.

At the top of the loop, in lines 19 and 20, the code stores the current values of `CurrentX` and `CurrentY`. If the program did not save these values, each `Print` method would appear on a full line after the previous `Print` method. Remember that each `Print` automatically sends the text cursor down to the start of the next line unless you override the cursor movement by placing a semicolon at the end of the `Print` method or position the text another way (as was done here through the `CurrentX` and `CurrentY` values).

The `If` statement that begins in line 22 controls the color of the output. Every time through the 10 loop iterations, the output will be either white or black. The `Mod` operator in line 22 returns either 0 or 1, depending on the loop counter. If `intCtr` is even, line 22 computes a `Mod` value of 0, but if `intCtr` is odd, line 22 computes a `Mod` value of 1.

The simple printing of *Visual Basic* occurs on line 28. This `Print` method would normally place the text cursor down to the next line so that subsequent `Print` output would not overwrite the previous `Print` output, but lines 31 and 32 ensure that the text cursor goes right back up to the location of the previous `Print`—almost. Lines 31 and 32 add a partial line's worth of twips to the `CurrentX` and `CurrentY` measurements of the previous `Print` (saved back in lines 19 and 20). The end result is that the next time through the loop, the words *Visual Basic* will appear offset somewhat and in a different color than the previous `Print`. This printing continues through the loop's 10 iterations. Figure 13.2 shows the result on the form, and this result looks just as it would on the printer if you applied these `Print` methods to the `Printer` object.

FIGURE 13.2.

Using `Print` methods to modify the way the output looks.

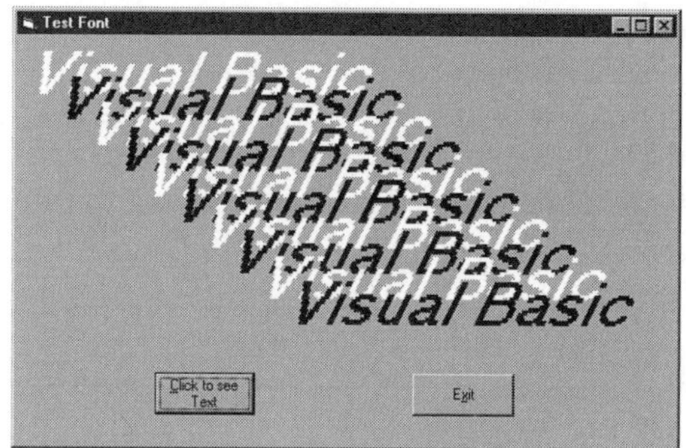

Printing Your Forms

One of the easiest ways to send output to your printer is to print a form. Visual Basic includes the `PrintForm` method, which applies to any form in your project. To get output to the printer, simply write to the form by using the standard controls with the `Print` method you've already mastered and then print the form.

This section explains the `PrintForm` method. Similar to the `Print` method, you apply `PrintForm` to your project's forms. When you issue a `PrintForm` method, Visual Basic begins printing the form immediately. Therefore, you must have the form ready for output before issuing `PrintForm`. This section explains how to use `PrintForm` to achieve the best results. You'll see that `PrintForm` won't suffice for much of your Visual Basic printing, but this method works well for outputting forms to the printer.

> Perhaps the biggest benefit of `PrintForm`, as well as Visual Basic's other printer-output capabilities, is that Visual Basic uses Windows `Printer` objects. Therefore, you never need to worry about specific printing instructions that are unique to a certain printer brand and model.

Here's the format for the `PrintForm` method:

```
[frmFormName.]PrintForm
```

Notice that *`frmFormName`* is optional; if you don't specify a form name, Visual Basic applies the `PrintForm` method to the current form.

To print a form named `frmAccPayable`, you would issue the following command at the event procedure or module procedure that requires the printing:

```
frmAccPayable.PrintForm      ' Print the Accounts Payable form
```

If `frmAccPayable` is the current form (the form with the focus whose title bar is highlighted), you can omit the form name:

```
PrintForm     ' Print the Accounts Payable form
```

`Me` always refers to the current form, so you can also issue the following statement to print the current form:

```
Me.PrintForm   ' Print the Accounts Payable form
```

> You can return to Day 11, "Working with Forms," to review the `Print` method. `Print` sends text output directly to the form. You can send output to a form with `Print` and then print the form with `PrintForm`. Remember, though, that all controls that appear on the form will also appear on the printed output.

`PrintForm` Warnings

The strength of `PrintForm` lies in its simplicity. `PrintForm` definitely provides the most useful—and simplest—printer output within Visual Basic. Unfortunately, along with its simplicity come a few problems you should know about.

No matter how high a resolution a user's printer can print, `PrintForm` prints the form at the screen's current resolution. This resolution generally goes no higher than 96 DPI (*DPI* means *dots per inch*). Printer resolutions often range as high as 600 DPI, so the form won't look as good on paper as it looks onscreen (96 DPI is quite adequate for screen resolution but isn't high enough for quality printout resolution).

You must always make sure the form's `AutoRedraw` property is set to `True` before you print any form that contains controls and other nontext graphic elements. By default, a form's `AutoRedraw` property is `False`, meaning that the `Print` method prints directly atop graphical controls. If you set `AutoRedraw` to `True`, the graphic stays in the foreground while `Print` does its thing behind the image and doesn't overwrite part or all of the graphic. You might use the `False` property of `AutoRedraw` to create background graphics first. You then can later write text on top of it, but then you must set the `AutoRedraw` property to `True` immediately before printing the form so that the output appears correctly at the printer.

Be careful, because `PrintForm` prints those objects placed on the form at design time (and their runtime control values for controls such as labels and text boxes) only if `AutoRedraw` is `False`. Therefore, if you add graphics and pictures to a form at runtime and then want to print the form with `PrintForm`, be sure to set the form's `AutoRedraw` property to `True` before adding the additional items. Otherwise, the runtime additions won't appear on the printed form.

Caution

Printing is sometimes the bane of the Windows programmer. Test your application on as many different printers as possible to make sure you're getting adequate results. You can't ensure that your printed output will look great on every printer, but you should have an idea of the results on a few common printer types if you distribute your applications to a wide range of users. Your application is dependent, of course, on your users' printer drivers being properly installed and set up. Your application also depends on users selecting an appropriate printer.

Your application can do only a certain amount of work toward good printing results, because the Windows printer interface takes over much of your printer interface job. Windows is only trying to help by putting this interface buffer between your application and the printer—and you certainly have to code much less than the MS-DOS programmers of old, who had to take into consideration every possible printer in existence (an impossible task because printers often came out after the code was written but before the application was distributed).

Listing 13.5 shows how you can print a text message to a blank form and then send that message to the printer.

LISTING 13.5. YOU CAN SEND MESSAGES FIRST TO THE FORM AND THEN TO THE PRINTER.

```
Dim blnAutoRedraw As Boolean   ' Holds value of AutoRedraw
'
frmBlank.Print "This is a Division Listing"
frmBlank.Print    ' Blank line
frmBlank.Print "Division"; Tab(20); "Location"
frmBlank.Print "--------"; Tab(20); "--------"
frmBlank.Print "North"; Tab(20); "Widgets"
frmBlank.Print "South"; Tab(20); "Presses"
frmBlank.Print "East"; Tab(20); "Dye Tools"
frmBlank.Print "West"; Tab(20); "Grinders"
'
' Save the form's AutoRedraw Property
'
blnAutoRedraw = frmBlank.AutoRedraw
'
' Now print the form
'
frmBlank.AutoRedraw = True
frmBlank.PrintForm
'
' Restore the AutoRedraw Property
'
frmBlank.AutoRedraw = blnAutoRedraw
```

This code demonstrates saving the form's `AutoRedraw` property before triggering the `PrintForm` method. Although, in this case, you're probably safe setting the `AutoRedraw` property to `True` at design time (assuming that you'll never send graphics to the form elsewhere in the application), you can use this property-saving feature before you print any form.

Create a standard module property that receives a form as its argument (you can send and receive forms just as you do variable data types), saves the `AutoRedraw` property, and prints the form with `PrintForm`. This general-purpose procedure will save you from having to code the `AutoRedraw`-saving property each time you print with `PrintForm`.

Any time you print, check for error conditions. The user's printer might not be turned on, might not be connected to the computer, or might not have paper. Use the `On Error Goto` command, as shown in Listing 13.6.

LISTING 13.6. THE `On Error Goto` COMMAND TRAPS ERRORS WHEN YOU PRINT.

```
Private Sub cmdPrintForm_Click ()
  Dim intBtnClicked As Integer
  On Error Goto ErrHandler     ' Set up error handler.
  frmAccPayable.PrintForm      ' Print form.
  Exit Sub
ErrHandler:
  intBtnClicked = MsgBox("A printer problem exists", vbExclamation, _
  "Print Error")
End Sub
```

When you need to print a fill-in-the-blank form from a Visual Basic application, there's no better way to do so than to create the form and then issue the `PrintForm` method.

You'll probably want to remove the form's title bar, control menu icon, and window buttons before printing most forms. You can temporarily hide a form and display another while your code removes these extras by setting the appropriate display property values to `False`.

Don't Surprise Your Users

Don't let your application begin printing until the user gives the go-ahead. The user typically has to prepare for your application's printing, perhaps by loading paper or by turning the printer on. Be sure that you offer the user a dialog box that lets him or her indicate when the printer is ready. Otherwise, a nasty error message will appear and make the user dislike and distrust your program.

Listing 13.7 contains an event procedure that you might want to modify for your own requirements. The procedure produces the message box shown in Figure 13.3. The message box is not fancy, but your users now have time to prepare the printer before your application prints anything.

LISTING 13.7. OFFERING YOUR USERS A MESSAGE BOX BEFORE PRINTING OCCURS.

```
1:  Public Function PrReady() As Boolean
2:  ' Make sure the user is ready to print
3:    Dim intIsReady As Integer
4:    '
5:    ' The user will respond to the following
6:    ' message box when ready for the printing
7:    intIsReady = MsgBox("Prepare the printer", vbOKCancel, "Print")
8:    '
9:    If (intIsReady = vbCancel) Then
10:      PrReady = False
11:   Else
12:      PrReady = True
13:   End If
14: End Function
```

Notice the function's declaration returns a `Boolean` data type. Therefore, you can place the function call for this procedure anywhere a valid `Boolean` data type can go. If the user clicks the message box's OK button, line 12 returns `True` for the function, meaning that the user is ready to print. If, however, the user clicks the Cancel button, line 10 returns a `False` value and the calling code must distinguish between the return values and then print or not print accordingly.

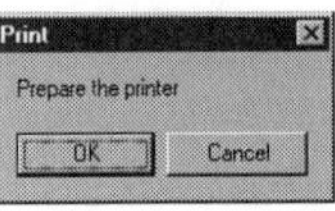

FIGURE 13.3.
The user responds to this message box when ready for the report.

Listing 13.8 shows a command button's event procedure that might be used to call the `PrReady()` function.

LISTING 13.8. CHECKING THE VALUE OF `PrReady()` BEFORE PRINTING.

```
1:  Private Sub cmdPrint_Click()
2:    ' Print when ready, but do nothing
3:    ' if the user clicks is not ready
4:    If PrReady() Then
5:       ' Call ReportPrint
6:    End If
7:  End Sub
```

Line 4 prints if and only if the user clicks the OK button from inside the `PrReady()` function.

Summary

Today's lesson explained how to output to the printer. Unlike much of Visual Basic, output to the printer can be tedious because no control exists to perform the output. Therefore, you must master several `Printer` methods to make the printing look the way you want. With that detail, however, comes power, because you can control exactly what gets to paper as well as how the output looks.

The `Printer` methods described here work for `Form` objects as well. Therefore, you can use the methods to send text in various font styles to the form or printer (or both, if you want to output to both devices). Nevertheless, if you want to print an application's forms, the `PrintForm` method is the easiest way to do it.

Tomorrow's lesson explores Visual Basic's graphics and multimedia capabilities.

Q&A

Q What if my application and another application send output to the printer at the same time?

A Fortunately, Windows takes care of queuing up printer output. Your PC actually cannot do two things at once, and even if two applications *seem* to send output to the printer at the same time, one will get there first. Windows queues up all printed output jobs so that they finish in the order applications send them.

Q Shouldn't I send all output to the form and then just print the form on the printer?

A The form prints at the screen's resolution and not the printer's resolution. You can get better printed output if you print directly to the printer. In addition, you may not want all of your application's printed output to appear on a form. For example, what if your application prints paycheck amounts onto checks? You certainly don't want to send each check to a form on the screen first and then send the form to the printer. You'll just want to print the checks directly to the printer where the check forms are. By the way, a check is just a page to your application and requires only that you position the output inside the check's fields.

Workshop

The Workshop provides quiz questions to help you solidify your understanding of the material covered and exercises to provide you with experience in using what you've learned. Try to understand the quiz and exercise answers before continuing to the next lesson. Answers are provided in Appendix A, "Answers to Exercises."

Quiz

1. How can your application determine the number of printers installed on the system?
2. True/False. The following declaration declares two variables:
   ```
   Dim intI As Integer, prnP As Printer
   ```
3. Which property determines the measurement scale of the `Printer` object's properties?
4. How can you force printing to begin on a new page?
5. Which form of `If` tests objects for specific data types?
6. True/False. You can pass objects, not just variables, to procedures.
7. True/False. `KillDoc` cancels all printed output, including `Printer.Print` commands and form `PrintForm` methods.
8. What shortcut reference can you use for the current form?
9. At what resolution does a `PrintForm` method usually print?
10. What value should you assign to the `AutoRedraw` property before you print forms?

Exercises

1. Create a line of code that writes your name beginning in column 32 on the printer.
2. **Bug Buster:** Patty the printer programmer is having trouble getting her reports to page properly. She learned how to program in BASIC years ago but has recently begun working in Visual Basic writing Windows applications. In the past, Patty assumed, correctly, that a normal page has exactly 66 lines of text in a text-based programming environment. Therefore, Patty would increment an integer counter variable every time she printed a line or blank line of text. When the counter got to 66, she would be at the top of the next page in her report. Now that Patty moved to Windows, her logic no longer works. Why do Patty's reports no longer have exactly 66 lines per page?
3. Change Listing 13.2, which searches for a color printer, by adding a Boolean variable that is set to `True` if and only if a color printer is found. As the code now operates, the default printer remains the same if no color printer is found. The new Boolean variable will inform subsequent code whether the loop has properly found a color printer. Make the code a function that returns a Boolean value.

WEEK 2

DAY 14

Introducing VB Graphics and Multimedia

Today's lesson shows you how to have fun with Visual Basic by drawing lines, ovals, and pictures on your form. You'll also learn how the image control compares with the picture box control. Once you finish with the graphics, you'll see how to include sound and video clips to make your applications come alive.

Today's computers are multimedia based. Multimedia is appearing in programs from all sectors—from business, education, and home applications. Several companies offer additional multimedia-based tools for Visual Basic, and if you find yourself writing very many multimedia applications, you may want to check out some of these tools. For most Visual Basic programmers, however, Visual Basic comes with a satisfactory assortment of multimedia controls. Today, you'll learn about the most common ones.

Today, you learn the following:

- About the picture box and image controls
- Why the picture box control is more flexible than the image control

- About the drawing methods
- How to draw points, lines, boxes, circles, and ellipses
- About the multimedia control
- Why the multimedia control is a multipurpose control, supporting several multimedia devices
- How to get the status of your multimedia device

Comparing the Picture Box and Image Controls

The picture box control and the image control both do basically the same thing. They allow you to place pictures, from graphics files, on a form. The two controls differ in these respects:

- The picture box control offers more flexibility by supporting additional methods and properties.
- The image control is more efficient and works best in sluggish applications on slower PCs.

As fast as computers are today, you'll rarely, if ever, be able to tell that the picture box control is less efficient than the image control. Therefore, unless you write for PCs that may be older (as are often found in companies and schools), stick with the picture box control to take advantage of its flexibility.

Both the image control and picture box control support the following graphics file formats:

- Bitmaps with the .BMP extension
- Cursors with the .CUR extension
- Graphics Interchange Format files with the .GIF extension
- Icons with the .ICO extension
- JPEG files with the .JPEG or .JPG extension
- Meta-files with the .WMF or .EMF (for enhanced meta-files) extension
- Run-length encoded files with the .RLE extension

Several files with these formats appear in the Graphics folder that you installed (or have the option of installing) with Visual Basic.

The most important property of both the image control and the picture box control is the `Picture` property, which holds the graphic. At design time, you can double-click the Properties window's `Picture` property to display a File Open dialog box and select a graphics file that has one of the required filename extensions. When you want to display an image at runtime, you must use the `LoadPicture()` internal function to associate a graphic file's location to the `Picture` property of the control.

The following assignment associates a graphic to a picture box's `Picture` property:

```
picPortrait.Picture = LoadPicture("c:\MyPhotos\Charlie.wmf")
```

Notice that you don't directly assign the path and file to the `Picture` property. The `LoadPicture()` function is the most important function to master when using the image and picture box controls. Here's the full format of the `LoadPicture()` internal function:

```
LoadPicture([GraphicFileName] [,varSize] [,varColorDepth], [varX, varY])
```

Notice that the graphics filename, the first argument of `LoadPicture()`, is optional. If you call the `LoadPicture()` function without specifying the filename, Visual Basic will erase the picture from the control.

Table 14.1 lists the named constants you can use for the *`varSize`* argument if you specify this argument. The *`varSize`* argument specifies the image's size for icons and cursors. The *`varSize`* argument is critical because users often use their Control Panel's display settings to determine the size of cursors and icons on their system. You can access these system values.

TABLE 14.1. SPECIFY ONE OF THESE *`varSize`* CONSTANTS TO CONTROL THE `LoadPicture()` IMAGE SIZE IF YOU LOAD AN ICON OR CURSOR FILE.

Named Constant	*Value*	*Description*
`vbLPSmall`	0	Small system icon as defined by your video resolution.
`vbLPLarge`	1	Large system icon as defined by your video resolution.
`vbLPSmallShell`	2	Determined by the Control Panel's Display Settings page. Click the Appearance tab to see the caption button size to locate the size of images you change with this *`varSize`* value.

continues

Table 14.1. Continued

Named Constant	Value	Description
`vbLPLargeShell`	3	Determined by the Control Panel's Display Settings page. Click the Appearance tab to see the icon size to locate the size of images you change with this *varSize* value.
`vbLPCustom`	4	The *varX* and *varY* arguments determine the size.

Table 14.2 lists the values you can use for the optional *varColorDepth* argument when you place icons and cursors.

Table 14.2. Specify one of these *varColorDepth* constants to control the `LoadPicture()` color depth if you load an icon or cursor file.

Named Constant	Value	Description
`vbLPDefault`	0	Best match
`vbLPMonochrome`	1	2 colors
`vbLPVGAColor`	2	16 colors
`vbLPColor`	3	256 colors

The *varX* and *varY* values are required if you use either the `vbLPSmallShell` or `vbLPLargeShell` size values.

When you place image and picture box controls on a form, they respond slightly differently, even if you place them at the same size measurements and point their respective `Picture` properties to the same graphics file. You must set an image control's `Stretch` property to `True` before you set the image control's `Width` and `Height` properties. If you do not, the width and height will shrink or expand to the size of the bitmap you place in the control and change the `Width` and `Height` settings automatically. When you place a picture box control on a form, the image automatically expands or shrinks to fill your size measurements for the control. Therefore, the picture box control will always change the size of its image to conform to your size property values, but the image control changes your size property values until you set its `Stretch` property to `True`.

Not only can you apply the `LoadPicture()` function to image and picture box controls, but you can apply it to forms as well! Therefore, you can place a graphic on your form's background instead of a solid color. The following statement assigns a check image to the form:

```
frmCheck.Picture = LoadPicture("Check.wmf")
```

Depending on your graphic files' location, you will have to insert the path to your graphics files. The path can get long. For example, you may have to write a line that looks like this:

```
frmCheck.Picture = LoadPicture("d:\program files\Microsoft Visual
Studio\Common\Graphics\metafile\business\Check.wmf")
```

Figure 14.1 shows the resulting form with command buttons and labels on the form. The picture becomes the form's background. (If you want to place a graphics file on the form's background at designtime, use the Properties window's `Picture` property.)

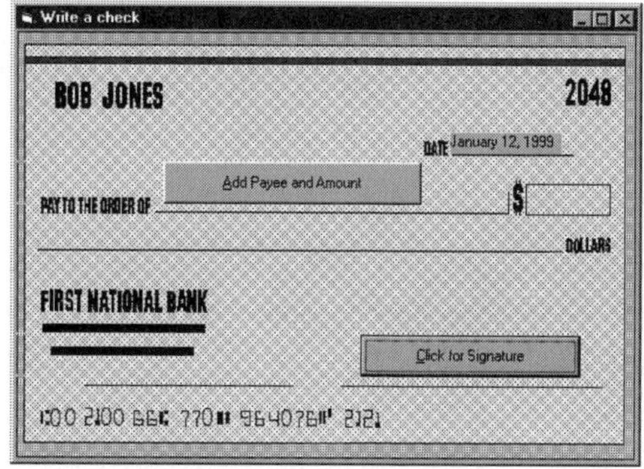

FIGURE 14.1.
You can place a graphics file as your form's background.

The Drawing Controls

The toolbox includes these two drawing tools:

- **Line control**—Draws straight lines between two points you specify.
- **Shape control**—Draws one of several shapes based on the criteria you specify in property values.

Drawing Lines

You'll find many uses for the line control, even if you don't need to work with multimedia graphics in the applications you write. The line control is useful for accenting form information by underlining and highlighting useful text. Figure 14.2 shows an application that uses the line control on a title form that appears for five seconds every time the user starts the application.

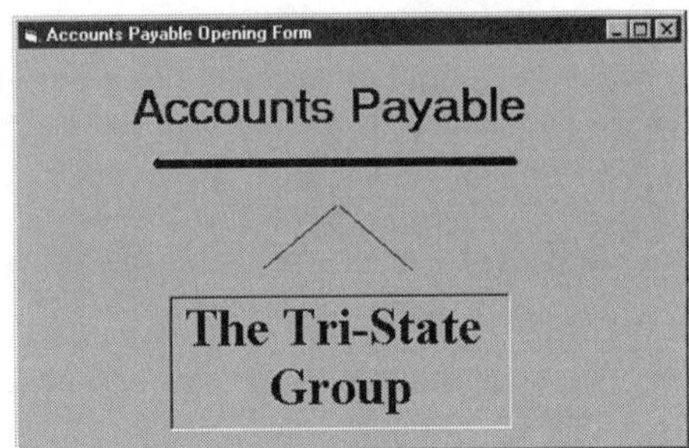

FIGURE 14.2.
Lines help accent and highlight important parts of this form.

When you double-click the line control, Visual Basic places a line in the center of your form with two sizing handles on the ends. You can drag the handles to lengthen or shrink the line, and you can move the handles up or down to change the line's direction. As you size and drag the handles, Visual Basic updates the appropriate property values that define the line.

The following properties are important to understand before placing lines on your form:

- `BorderColor` determines the line's color.
- `BorderStyle` determines the line's format, as specified by the values from Table 14.3 and shown in Figure 14.3.
- `BorderWidth` determines the line's width in points (1/72nds of an inch).
- `X1`, `Y1`, `X2`, `Y2` determine the line's starting and ending coordinate values. A point on your form is defined by two values, and a line is defined by two points (the line appears between the points).

The `BorderWidth` property must be `1` for the `BorderStyle` to show up on your line.

TABLE 14.3. THE `BorderStyle` PROPERTY DETERMINES HOW YOUR LINE APPEARS ON THE FORM.

Named Constant	*Description*
`0-Transparent`	The form's background color shows through the line.
`1-Solid`	Solid line.
`2-Dash`	Dashed line.
`3-Dot`	Dotted line.
`4-Dash-Dot`	Each dash is followed by a dot.
`5-Dash-Dot-Dot`	Each dash is followed by two dots.

FIGURE 14.3.

The `BorderStyle` property determines how Visual Basic draws the line.

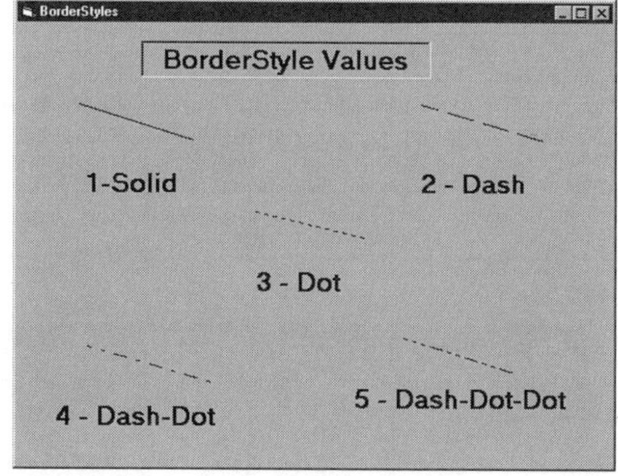

Drawing Shapes

Whereas the line control draws only lines, the shape control draws several shapes. The `Shape` property determines the shape, as described in the following list:

- `0-Rectangle` draws a rectangle.
- `1-Square` draws a square.
- `2-Oval` draws an oval.
- `3-Circle` draws a circle.
- `4-Rounded Rectangle` draws a rectangle with rounded corners.
- `5-Rounded Square` draws a square with rounded corners.

In addition to the `Shape` property values, Table 14.4 lists other important property values that affect the way the shape appears on the form.

TABLE 14.4. ADJUST THESE SHAPE CONTROL PROPERTIES TO DETERMINE HOW THE SHAPE APPEARS.

Property	*Description*
`BackStyle`	If `BackStyle` is set to `True`, the form's background shows through the shape as if the shape were transparent.
`BorderColor`	The shape's border color.
`BorderStyle`	Takes on one of the values from Table 14.3 to determine the style of the shape's bordering line.
`BorderWidth`	The width of the shape's border in twips.
`FillColor`	The color of the fill pattern (specified by the `FillStyle` property).

continues

TABLE 14.4. CONTINUED

Property	*Description*
`FillStyle`	Determines the shape's interior pattern. Figure 14.4 shows examples of the eight available fill patterns.
`Height`	The shape's height.
`Width`	The shape's widest axis.

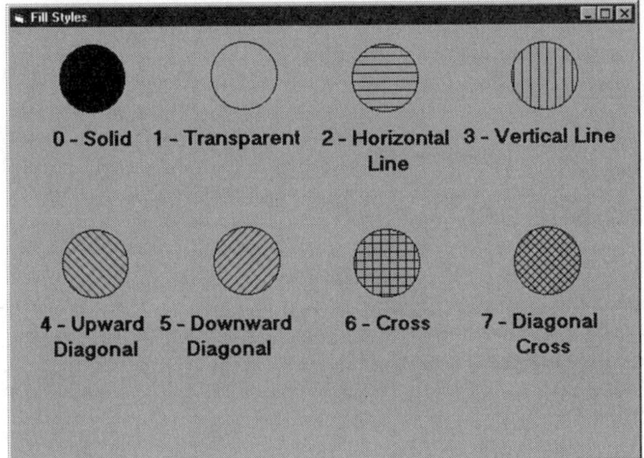

FIGURE 14.4.
These eight `FillStyle` patterns determine how Visual Basic draws the shape's interior.

By creating a simple application that changes a shape control's properties, you'll master the shape control quickly. Figure 14.5 shows the result of the application you'll create. By selecting from one of the two list boxes, you'll change the shape and pattern shown at the top of the form. The shape changes as soon as you select a new value from either list box.

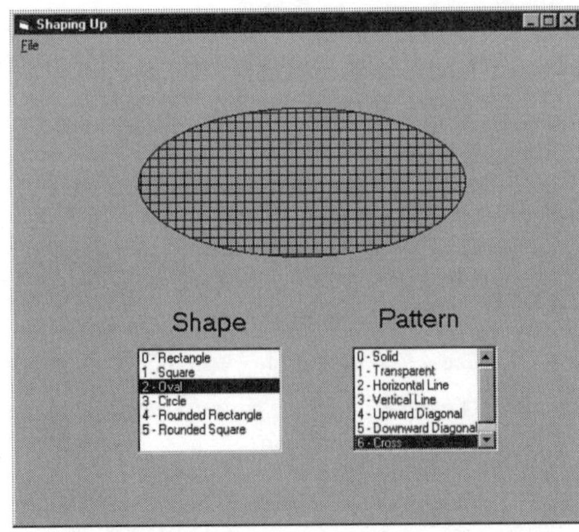

FIGURE 14.5.
Select a shape and pattern to see the result.

Follow these steps to create the sample application that uses the shape control:

1. Create a new application.
2. Place controls from Table 14.5 on the form.
3. Add the code in Listing 14.1 to initialize the two list boxes at runtime.
4. When you run the application, click any combination of shape and fill style values in the two list boxes to see the resulting object.

TABLE 14.5. USE THESE PROPERTIES AND VALUES ON THE SHAPE CONTROL FORM.

Control	*Description*
Form Name	frmShape
Form Height	7005
Form Left	105
Form Top	105
Form Width	7965
Menu option #1 Name	mnuFile
Menu option #1 Caption	&File
Menu option #2 Name	mnuFileExit (indented one level)
Menu option #2 Caption	E&xit
Shape Name	shpSample
Shape Height	2025
Shape Left	1710
Shape Top	720
Shape Width	4560
Label #1 Name	lblShape
Label #1 Caption	Shape
Label #1 Height	420
Label #1 Left	2160
Label #1 Top	3390
Label #1 Width	1215
Label #2 Name	lblPattern
Label #2 Caption	Pattern
Label #2 Height	420
Label #2 Left	5040

continues

TABLE 14.5. CONTINUED

Control	*Description*
Label #2 Top	3360
Label #2 Width	1215
List box #1 Name	lstShape
List box #1 Height	1425
List box #1 Left	1560
List box #1 Top	3960
List box #1 Width	2010
List box #2 Name	lstPattern
List box #2 Height	1425
List box #2 Left	4680
List box #2 Top	3960
List box #2 Width	2010

LISTING 14.1. CODE FOR INITIALIZING THE TWO LIST BOXES AND RESPONDING TO THE USER'S LIST BOX SELECTIONS.

```
Private Sub Form_Load()
  ' Initialize the shape drop-down list box
  lstShape.AddItem "0 - Rectangle"
  lstShape.AddItem "1 - Square"
  lstShape.AddItem "2 - Oval"
  lstShape.AddItem "3 - Circle"
  lstShape.AddItem "4 - Rounded Rectangle"
  lstShape.AddItem "5 - Rounded Square"

  ' Initialize the FillStyle pattern drop-down list box
  lstPattern.AddItem "0 - Solid"
  lstPattern.AddItem "1 - Transparent"
  lstPattern.AddItem "2 - Horizontal Line"
  lstPattern.AddItem "3 - Vertical Line"
  lstPattern.AddItem "4 - Upward Diagonal"
  lstPattern.AddItem "5 - Downward Diagonal"
  lstPattern.AddItem "6 - Cross"
  lstPattern.AddItem "7 - Diagonal Cross"

  ' Set the first value of each list as default
  lstShape.ListIndex = 0
  lstPattern.ListIndex = 0

End Sub
```

```
Private Sub lstPattern_Click()
  ' Change the pattern according to the selection
  shpSample.FillStyle = lstPattern.ListIndex
End Sub

Private Sub lstShape_Click()
  ' Change the shape according to the selection
  shpSample.Shape = lstShape.ListIndex
End Sub

Private Sub mnuFileExit_Click()
  End
End Sub
```

Neither the line control nor the shape control support event processing.

Drawing with Methods

Visual Basic does not limit your graphics to the line and shape controls. If you want, you can manipulate the individual graphic's pixels and draw a picture dot by dot. The `PSet` method, which you use with forms, exists so that you can draw lines, boxes, and circles without the use of controls. When you're drawing lines and shapes at runtime, the controls are somewhat cumbersome and do not lend themselves to precise drawing as the drawing methods do.

You can apply drawing methods to picture box controls that you place on the form as well as to the form itself.

The `PSet` method displays or hides individual pixels on a form. The following is the format of `PSet`:

```
frmName.PSet [Step] (intX, intY) [color]
```

Although you can change the scale used with the properties `ScaleX` and `ScaleY`, the pixel at row and column intersection 0, 0 (used in place of `(intX, intY)` in the `PSet` method's format) refers to the pixel in the upper-left corner of the form. The following statement turns on the pixel that resides 100 pixels to the right and 200 pixels down from the upper-left corner of the form:

```
frmDraw.PSet (100, 200)    ' Turns on a pixel
```

The color of the pixel is always the form's (or picture box control's) `ForeColor` value. You can change the color by specifying a new hexadecimal color value or by using one of these named constant colors: `vbBlack`, `vbRed`, `vbGreen`, `vbYellow`, `vbBlue`, `vbMagenta`, `vbCyan`, or `vbWhite`.

The following statement turns off the pixel at (100, 200) by changing the color used to the same color as the form's current background:

```
frmDraw.PSet (100, 200) frmDraw.BackColor   ' Turns off a pixel
```

If you followed this `PSet` method with the one that follows, another pixel appears at location (300, 350):

```
frmDraw.PSet (300, 350)    ' Turns on a pixel
```

The `PSet` method's `Step` option changes the location of subsequent pixel placements. After you call a `PSet` method the first time, the `Step` option makes the next `PSet` method's `intX` and `intY` pixel values relative. Therefore, if you were to add the `Step` option to the previous `PSet` method as done in the following statement, the pixel would appear 300 pixels to the right and 350 pixels down from the previously drawn pixel:

```
frmDraw.PSet Step (300, 350)    ' Relative pixel location
```

You can also use loops to draw lines with `PSet`. Here's an example:

```
For intX = 1 to 100
  frmDraw.PSet (intX, 250)
Next intX
```

Never go outside the pixel boundaries of the form on which you're drawing; otherwise, a runtime error will occur.

Instead of drawing lines one pixel at a time, you can use another method, the `Line` method, to draw lines more efficiently. Here's the format of the `Line` method:

```
frmName.Line [Step] (intX1, intY1) - [Step] (intX2, intY2), [Color] [B][F]
```

The two pairs of pixel coordinate values determine the starting and ending points of the line. The `Step` option, if you use it before either pair of coordinate values, turns the coordinates it precedes into relative coordinates from the most recently drawn line's endpoint.

The following method draws a line from pixel 100,100 to pixel 150,150:

```
frmDraw.Line (100, 100) - (150, 150)
```

As with the `PSet` method, the optional *`Color`* value lets you specify a hexadecimal color value or a named color constant. If you don't specify a color, Visual Basic uses the form's foreground color to draw the line.

To draw a box, use the `B` option with the `Line` method:

```
frmDraw.Line (100, 100) - (150, 150), , B
```

You have to include the extra comma even if you omit the color value so that Visual Basic knows that the `B` specifies the box-drawing option. The two coordinate pairs now specify the upper-left and lower-left corners of the box.

The coordinate pairs for lines and boxes specify opposing endpoints on the line or opposing diagonal corners of the box. Lines can slant up or down; the first coordinate pair may specify a point below or to the right of the second coordinate pair.

The interior of the box that you draw will be filled with the same color as the box's outline if you specify the `F` option:

```
frmForm.Line (35, 40) - (150, 175), vbGreen, BF  ' A green box
```

A solid box appears with its outline and interior filled with the same color. If you draw a box outside a form's boundaries, Visual Basic truncates the box to the form's edges. Even if you increase the size of the form after drawing a box that does not all fit on the form, the entire box never shows unless you redraw the box once again.

Listing 14.2 contains a command button's event procedure that draws a series of boxes on the form from the upper-left corner of the form to the lower-right corner. If you were to run this procedure, the lines shown in Figure 14.6 would appear on the form.

LISTING 14.2. USING A SERIES OF BOX-DRAWING `Line` METHODS TO CREATE PATTERNS.

```
Private Sub cmdBoxes_Click()
  Dim intStartX As Integer
  Dim intStartY As Integer
  Dim intLastX As Integer
  Dim intLastY As Integer
```

continues

LISTING 14.2. CONTINUED

```

    intStartX = 0
    intStartY = 0
    intLastX = 1000
    intLastY = 800

    For intCtr = 1 To 20
      frmBoxes.Line (intStartX, intStartY)-(intLastX, intLastY), , B

      ' Prepare for next set of boxes
      intStartX = intStartX + 400
      intStartY = intStartY + 400
      intLastX = intLastX + 400
      intLastY = intLastY + 400
    Next intCtr

End Sub
```

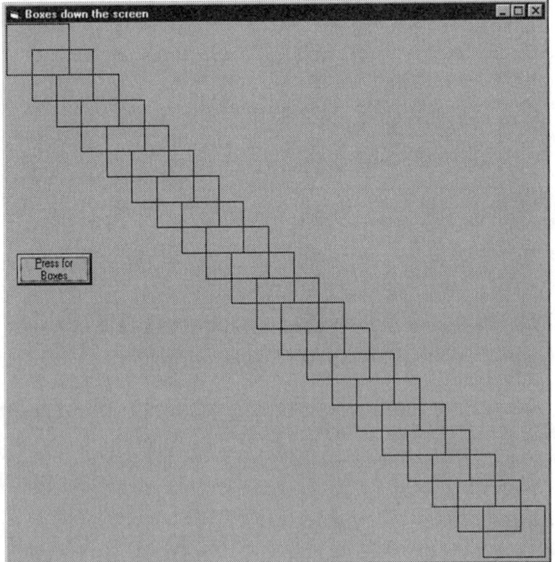

FIGURE 14.6.
Use the `Line` method to draw boxes on a form.

The drawing methods don't just work for straight lines, they work for circles and ellipses as well. Here's the format of the `Circle` method you can use to draw circles and ellipses:

```
frmDraw.Circle [Step] (intX, intY) sngRadius, [Color], , , , sngAspect
```

NEW TERM An *ellipse* is an elongated circle with an oval shape.

The commas are placeholders for advanced `Circle` arguments that this tutorial does not discuss. You must specify the commas if you use the *`sngAspect`* argument.

A circle has no endpoints, so the *`intX`* and *`intY`* coordinate values specify the circle's center point. *`sngRadius`* specifies the radius size, in pixels (unless you've changed the form's `ScaleMode` value). The optional `Step` keyword specifies whether the center coordinate pair is relative to a previously drawn object.

NEW TERM A circle's *radius* is the distance from the outside edge to the center point of the circle.

The following statement draws a circle with a center point at 300 pixels from the form's left edge and 200 pixels from the form's top edge, with a radius of 100 pixels:

```
frmDraw.Circle (300, 200), 100
```

The `Circle` method uses the foreground color of the form unless you specify a different *`Color`* value.

To draw an ellipse, you have to specify the shape of the ellipse with the *`sngAspect`* value to determine the ellipse's aspect ratio. The aspect value will either stretch the circle on its horizontal X-coordinate axis (if you specify a *`sngAspect`* value less than 1) or stretch the circle on its vertical Y-coordinate axis (if you specify a *`sngAspect`* value greater than 1). A *`sngAspect`* value of exactly 1 draws a perfect circle.

NEW TERM The *aspect ratio* determines how prominent the oval shape of the ellipse will be. The aspect ratio acts like a height and width measurement through the center of the ellipse. The ratio also acts as a multiplier of the radius in each direction. An aspect ratio of 4, for example, means that the ellipse is four times taller than its height. An aspect ratio of 4/10/2 (or .2) means that the ellipse is horizontally stretched five times its height.

The following statements draw the ellipses shown on the form in Figure 14.7:

```
frmDraw.Circle (1000, 1250), 400, , , , (4 / 10 / 2)
frmDraw.Circle (1750, 1250), 400, , , , 4
```

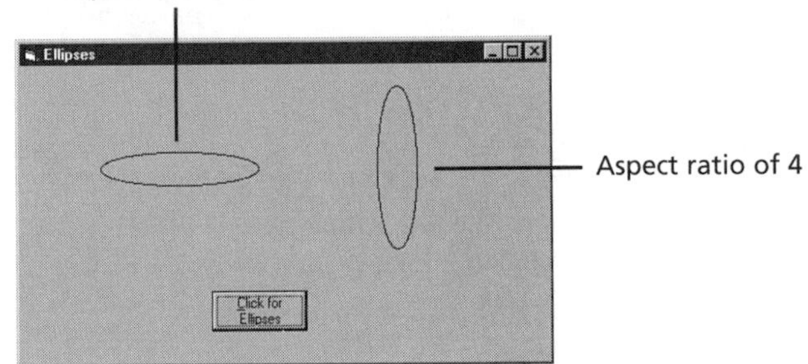

FIGURE 14.7.

The aspect ratio determines the shape of the ellipse.

The Multimedia Control

Despite its power, the multimedia control is extremely simple to use. You'll write only a small amount of code to use it. With the multimedia control, you'll be able to embed objects that represent the following simple multimedia devices:

- CD audio player (`CDAudio`)
- Digital audio tape player (`DAT`)
- Digital video files (`DigitalVideo`)
- Overlay (`Overlay`)
- Scanner (`Scanner`)
- Videotape player and recorder (`Vcr`)
- Videodisc player (`Videodisc`)
- Other devices not specified, supported by third-party drivers (`Other`)

> The values in parentheses are used in the multimedia control's `DeviceType` property, as described in the next section.

You can also embed objects that represent the following compound multimedia devices:

- The audio file player and recorder plays and records waveform files (files that have the .WAV extension).

- The MIDI sequencer plays Musical Instrument Digital Interface files (files that have the .MID extension).
- The video file player and recorder plays and records Audio Visual Interleave video files (files that have the .AVI extension).

NEW TERM A *simple multimedia device* requires no file associated with the control. For example, no file is associated with an audio CD you insert in your CD-ROM drive to listen to; the CD contains the music and no file is necessary. A *compound multimedia device* requires an extra file for the data, such as an audio file player that needs a WAV file to know which sounds to make.

Obviously, the PC on which your multimedia applications run must support standard multimedia devices, such as sound, graphics, and video, as well as have a CD-ROM drive (or a compatible device, such as a DVD drive).

Applying the Control

As with the common dialog box control, you must add the multimedia control to your toolbox window, because the standard toolbox does not list the multimedia control. To do this, press Ctrl+T to display the Components dialog box and select the control labeled Microsoft Multimedia Control 6.0. When you click OK, Visual Basic adds the control as the last tool on your toolbox window.

When you place the multimedia control on a form, a familiar set of buttons appears. These buttons mimic the ones that control your VCR or cassette tape player (see Figure 14.8).

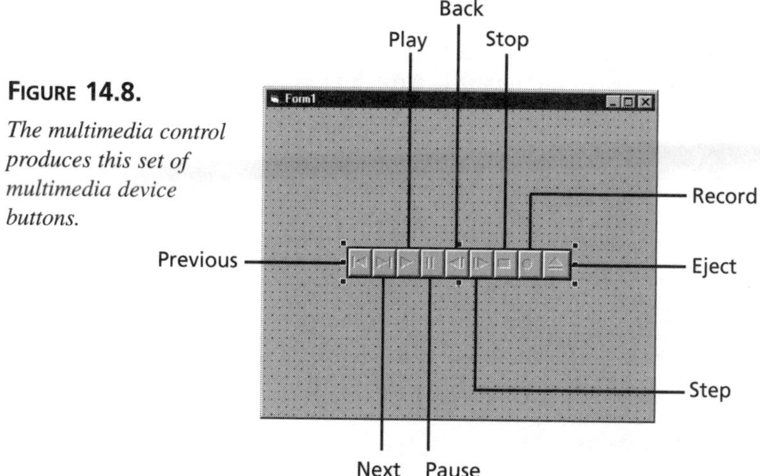

FIGURE 14.8.
The multimedia control produces this set of multimedia device buttons.

The multimedia control is an intelligent control that recognizes the capabilities of the devices you attach to it. Therefore, the Play button will not be active if you've ejected a CD from the CD-ROM drive. Of course, you have complete control, through various property value settings, over which buttons appear on the control. Instead of having an inactive Record button appear on the multimedia control when playing audio CDs (which cannot be recorded over), you'll want to completely hide the Record button.

The multimedia control provides information to your application about the device and its current settings. For example, your application can display the track numbers on an audio CD as the CD plays in the drive.

The multimedia control contains a list of devices with preselected buttons, so you don't have to specifically select individual buttons to appear on each control. The multimedia control supports a property called `DeviceType` that, when you initialize it with the device you want to use (such as the value of `CDAudio`, which specifies that you want the multimedia control to control an audio CD), the multimedia control automatically enables the correct buttons. The list of supported devices presented at the beginning of the previous section lists all the values allowed in the `DeviceType` property. Your job is to tell the application that the multimedia control is to be a CD audio player; then the multimedia control takes care of setting up the correct buttons.

As with many of the more involved controls, such as the common dialog box control, the multimedia control includes a (Custom) entry in the Properties window that you can select to display a dialog box that simplifies selecting properties. For example, if you click the Controls tab, the dialog box page shown in Figure 14.9 appears. From here, you can customize exactly which buttons appear on the control. You can also check if you want to display or enable any button on the control.

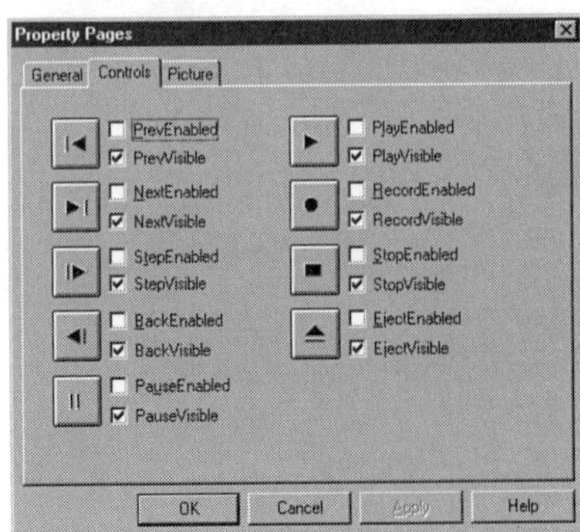

FIGURE 14.9.

The Properties window's (Custom) entry makes selecting properties, such as the visible buttons, simple.

The multimedia control automatically makes all buttons visible but disabled until you enable one or more of the buttons, or until you select a DeviceType value that determines the button collection the multimedia control is to enable and display.

An Audio CD Player

To control an audio CD from a Visual Basic application, you need to place the multimedia control on a form and adjust the DeviceType property to CDAudio to produce the correct combination of buttons that respond to audio CDs. You've almost done all you need to do to set up a basic audio CD player. However, if you want to follow the tracks being played, you might also want to add a label that displays the track number as the control plays the CDs.

The multimedia control updates its tracking information every time a StatusUpdate event occurs. The multimedia control updates its StatusUpdate event every time the track changes, as well as when the user begins playing the CD and stops playing the CD. Therefore, you'll update the tracking label in an event procedure you create for the StatusUpdate event.

The Multimedia Control's Command Language

The Multimedia control supports its own miniature command language (although this language is not nearly as robust as the Visual Basic language). The Multimedia control accepts, in its Command property, one word commands that control whatever device is currently playing. Table 14.6 describes each of the commands and their meanings.

TABLE 14.6. THESE COMMANDS FORM THE MULTIMEDIA CONTROL'S Command PROPERTY LANGUAGE.

Command	*Description*
Back	Steps backward through the device's tracks.
Close	Closes the device.
Eject	Ejects the CD from the CD-ROM drive.
Next	Goes to the beginning of the next track (or to the beginning of the final track if the last track is current).
Open	Opens the device.
Pause	Pauses the device.

continues

TABLE 14.6. CONTINUED

Command	*Description*
`Play`	Plays the device.
`Prev`	Returns to the beginning of the current track. If used within three seconds of the most recent `Prev` command, `Prev` returns to the beginning of the previous track (or to the start of the first track if the first track is current).
`Record`	Initializes recording on the device.
`Save`	Saves the open device file.
`Seek`	Seeks backward or forward a track (programmers typically use `Next` or `Prev` instead of `Seek` due to its directional ambiguity).
`Stop`	Stops the device.
`Step`	Steps forward through the device's tracks.

As your application runs, when your code changes the value in the `Command` property to a different value, the multimedia control responds accordingly.

Your users do not have to control the multimedia control's device. You can hide all the control's buttons and, through the `Command` property, control the device with your application's code.

Putting Together a CD Player

Now that you've been introduced to the multimedia control, you can use it to put together an application very quickly. Start a new project and assign properties shown in Table 14.7 to the application.

TABLE 14.7. USE THESE PROPERTIES AND VALUES ON THE MULTIMEDIA CONTROL FORM.

Control	*Description*
Form `Name`	`frmCD`
Form `Caption`	`CD Player`
Form `Height`	`3600`
Form `Width`	`4800`
Label #1 `Name`	`lblCD`
Label #1 `Alignment`	`2-Center`

Control	*Description*
Label #1 `BorderStyle`	`1-Fixed Single`
Label #1 `Caption`	`CD Player`
Label #1 `Font style`	`BoldUnderline`
Label #1 `Font size`	`18`
Label #1 `Height`	`495`
Label #1 `Left`	`1320`
Label #1 `Top`	`480`
Label #1 `Width`	`1935`
Label #2 `Name`	`lblTrack`
Label #2 `Alignment`	`1-Right Justify`
Label #2 `Caption`	`Track:`
Label #2 `Font style`	`Bold`
Label #2 `Font size`	`12`
Label #2 `Height`	`255`
Label #2 `Left`	`1200`
Label #2 `Top`	`2280`
Label #2 `Width`	`1215`
Label #3 `Name`	`lblTrackNum`
Label #3 `Caption`	(blank)
Label #3 `Font style`	`Bold`
Label #3 `Font size`	`12`
Label #3 `Height`	`375`
Label #3 `Left`	`2520`
Label #3 `Top`	`2280`
Label #3 `Width`	`615`
Multimedia control `Name`	`mmcCD`
Multimedia control `DeviceType`	`CDAudio`

Once you've placed these controls, enter the code you see in Listing 14.3 to complete the CD player application.

LISTING 14.3. THIS CODE HANDLES THE CD PLAYER.

```
1:  Private Sub Form_Load()
2:    ' Open the CD
3:    mmcCD.Command = "Open"
4:  End Sub
5:
6:  Private Sub Form_Unload(Cancel As Integer)
7:    ' Clean up the multimedia control when done
8:    mmcCD.Command = "Close"
9:  End Sub
10:
11: Private Sub mmcCD_StatusUpdate()
12:   ' Update the track number in the label
13:   lblTrackNum.Caption = mmcCD.Track
14: End Sub
```

The application opens the CD-playing multimedia control when the form first loads. Line 8 removes the CD player from memory right before the application ends (as with files, you should close any multimedia device you open). Line 13 updates the track number every time the CD's status changes. The value in the multimedia control's `UpdateInterval` property specifies the interval between updates of the status (the default is 1000).

Figure 14.10 shows the running CD player. The application is simple, but it works! You can hone the application so that the CD player has a way to exit the application through a File, Exit menu option. You can also add error-checking and notification, as described in the next section.

FIGURE 14.10.
This CD player application takes very little effort and time to create.

Obviously, some buttons that are disabled, such as the Record button, are not needed at all in this application. You can hide these buttons if you want to clean up the multimedia control a bit.

> You've not only mastered the multimedia control as a CD player, but you've almost mastered the control for all other multimedia devices as well! You'll see in subsequent sections that you'll deal with the multimedia control in almost the same way you did here, no matter which multimedia device you want the multimedia control to mimic.

Notification and Error-Handling

As the multimedia control performs its tasks, several notification and error-checking conditions are updated so that you can ensure smooth play of the device.

The `Notify` property generates a `Done` event every time the *next* multimedia control command completes properly. Therefore, if you want to issue a multimedia control command only after your previous command finishes, you can set the `Notify` property to `True`. The `Wait` property, when set to `True`, ensures that control will not return to your application until the previous multimedia control command executes properly.

If an error occurs after you've issued a multimedia control command, you can check for that error as follows:

```
If (frmCD.mmcCD.Error) then
  intMsg = MsgBox("CD Not working properly", vbCritical)
Else
   ' Code continues here to play the CD Player
```

It's best not to put an `On Error Goto` statement at the top of the CD player's procedure because you then would not know exactly which multimedia control command triggered the error condition. By following each command with an error-checking routine, you can better trace the meaning of an error.

Table 14.8 lists several `Mode` values. The `Mode` property lets you test various states, or *modes*, of the multimedia control during the application's execution to determine what is currently taking place.

TABLE 14.8. THESE `Mode` VALUES INDICATE THE CURRENT MODE OF THE MULTIMEDIA CONTROL.

Mode Named Constants	*Description*
`mciModeNotOpen`	Multimedia control device is not open.
`mciModeStop`	Multimedia control device is stopped.
`mciModePlay`	Multimedia control device is playing.
`mciModeRecord`	Multimedia control device is recording.

continues

TABLE 14.8. CONTINUED

Mode Named Constants	*Description*
`mcuModeSeek`	Multimedia control device is seeing past information.
`mciModePause`	Multimedia control device is paused.
`mciModeReady`	Multimedia control device is ready.

Putting Together a Wave Player

A wave file is an audio file stored on the computer. To play this file, you need a compound multimedia control device. Compound multimedia control devices get all their data from a file, not from an outside source such as an audio CD. Your computer comes with several wave files. The Windows Control Panel's Sound option uses these wave files to assign sounds to system events.

This section explains how to create a wave audio file multimedia player. You'll be able to use the `Mode` values in Table 14.8 to display status information about the file being played. You'll use the Windows wave file TADA.WAV, which is located in the Windows\Media folder.

Save your CD player project if you still have it open, and then use that project as the basis for this one. To keep both projects separate, save the project again under a new name (perhaps call this one Wave Player) and then modify the project according to these steps:

1. Change the top label's name to `lblWav` and change the `Caption` property to `Wave Player`. Increase the `Width` property to 2415.
2. Change the form's name to `frmWav` and the form `Caption` to `Wave Music Player`.
3. Change the multimedia control's name to `mmcWav` and change its `DeviceType` property to `WaveAudio`. You can change the property in the Properties window or from the Property Pages dialog box that appears when you click the (Custom) Property window's ellipses. Change `Filename` to the TADA.WAV file located in your \Windows\Media directory.
4. Wave files don't have tracks like CDs do, but you can still use the labels beneath the multimedia control buttons. Change the left label's name from `lblTrack` to `lblStatus` and change its `Caption` to `Status`.
5. Change the right label's name from `lblTrackNum` to `lblStatusValue` and blank out the caption. Change the `Width` property to `2565`.
6. Add another pair of labels beneath the two you just modified with the same width and font properties. (You could copy them to create a set of label arrays.) Name the

first label `lblFile` (unless you created a control array) and change the `Caption` property to `Filename:`. You'll have to extend the left edge to make room for the caption.

7. Change the right label's name to `lblFileValue` (unless you created a control array). Leave the label blank. After you center the labels beneath the buttons, your application should begin to take on the appearance of the running application shown in Figure 14.11.

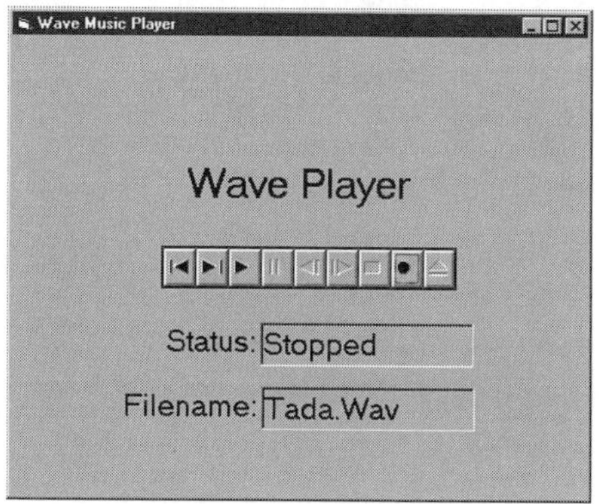

FIGURE 14.11.
The wave music player is almost complete.

Change the `Form_Load()` event procedure to the following:

```
Private Sub Form_Load ()
  ' Tell the Multimedia control to open the WAVE player
  mmcWAV.Command = "Open"
End Sub
```

You must also change the `Form_Unload()` event procedure as follows:

```
Private Sub Form_Unload(Cancel As Integer)
  ' Clean up the WAVE and form
  mmcWAV.Command = "Close"
  Unload Me  ' Unloads the form as well
End Sub
```

Run the application. When you click the Play button, you'll hear a sound. Click the rewind button and play the sound again.

The wave player isn't quite complete. The labels beneath the buttons don't display the status or filename information. You can supply these labels with their values in the `StatusUpdate()` event procedure (see Listing 14.4). You'll need to use the `Mode` values to determine the proper play mode.

LISTING 14.4. ADDING STATUS INFORMATION TO THE LABELS.

```
Private Sub mciWAV_StatusUpdate()
  ' Display the status
  If mmcWAV.Mode = mciModeNotOpen Then
    lblStatusValue(0).Caption = "Not Ready"
  ElseIf mmcWAV.Mode = mciModeStop Then
    lblStatusValue(0).Caption = "Stopped"
  ElseIf mmcWAV.Mode = mciModePlay Then
      lblStatusValue(0).Caption = "Play"
  ElseIf mmcWAV.Mode = mciModeRecord Then
    lblStatusValue(0).Caption = "Record"
  ElseIf mmcWAV.Mode = mciModePause Then
    lblStatusValue(0).Caption = "Paused"
  ElseIf mmcWAV.Mode = mciModeReady Then
    lblStatusValue(0).Caption = "Ready"
  End If
  ' Display the filename being played
  lblStatusValue(1).Caption = mmcWAV.FileName
End Sub
```

Caution

The `StatusUpdate` event procedure assumes you created control arrays for the labels. If you did not, change the label names to the actual names you used if you didn't create control arrays to hold the labels. Otherwise, your application won't run correctly.

Run the wave player to test the application. As you play the wave file, consider the following points:

- The wave player doesn't display a Stop button, except during the quick play of the audio file. The file stops playing when it comes to its end. If the wave file were longer, you would have more of a chance to stop the play.
- The file plays only once and then the player's position points to the end of the file. Click the Rewind button to return to the beginning of the audio file to replay the sound.
- The Record button is active. You can record at the beginning or end of the file and then rewind the file to play back the original sound plus your recording.
- Don't save your recorded audio in the file. You'll instead want to preserve this WAV file, which comes with Visual Basic. Also, before you can save the file, you would need to provide a way to enter a new filename with the Save dialog box. This application offers no provision for saving changes to protect the original file's integrity.

Playing Video Clips

You've already mastered the multimedia control! Believe it or not, playing a video clip isn't much different than playing a wave audio file, as you'll see in this section. You must supply the video filename to play (the multimedia control as a video player is a compound device, so the filename is critical). You must also set up the multimedia control to handle video playing, and then your application will be ready to show the latest in multimedia entertainment.

Your multimedia control requires a bit of help when playing video clips. Rather than use only a simple panel of buttons, you need a projection screen from which to show the video. The most common control to display videos with is the picture box control. Therefore, you'll add a picture box control to every application that needs to display a video file.

So far, you used the multimedia control `DeviceType` property value `CDAudio` to play compact discs and `WaveAudio` to play WAV audio files. Although you can enter these in the`Custom` property's Property Page dialog box, you may need to set these values at runtime with assignment statements if you need your multimedia control to perform double duty by playing different kinds of media files.

Your application might contain several picture box controls, so the multimedia control must know to which picture box control to send the video to. You tell the multimedia control the name of the picture box control in which to show the video in the multimedia control's `hWndDisplay` property.

`hWnd` is a common Windows programming prefix that represents a handle or, more accurately, a device context. Output from Visual Basic doesn't represent true screen output but rather windowed output. (Actually, you can send output to any Windows device with the same basic set of commands, so Windows devices are more virtual than real to your program. Windows performs all the complicated conversions to get output printed on a printer or color screen.) The bottom line is that your program doesn't send video clip output to your screen, but to a device context. That device context is almost always your screen, but the multimedia control needs to know the proper device context. This way, it knows which window to play the file inside, and it can manipulate the window's borders appropriately so that the video stays within the window.

Now, create a new application. Name the form `frmVideo` and specify `Video Player` for the form's `Caption` property. Add a multimedia control to the top center of the form. (You'll have to add the Microsoft Multimedia Control 6.0 once again to your toolbox window, if you haven't already.) Name the multimedia control `mmcVideo`.

Add a picture box control to the form. Place the picture box control below the multimedia control buttons and then size the picture box control to the approximate size you see in Figure 14.12. Name the picture box control `picVideo`.

FIGURE 14.12.

The picture box control will display the video.

Change the multimedia control's `DeviceType` property to `AVIVideo`. Select the AVI file named Count24.AVI for the `Filename` property. You'll find the file in Visual Basic's \Graphics\Videos directory. You're almost finished! As you can see, setting up a video player isn't any different than setting up an audio player. Now add the `Form_Load()` event procedure you see in Listing 14.5.

LISTING 14.5. YOU MUST CONNECT THE VIDEO TO THE PICTURE BOX CONTROL.

```
Private Sub Form_Load()
  ' Open the video player
  mmcVideo.Command = "Open"
  ' Connect the video player to the Picture Box
  mmcVideo.hWndDisplay = picVideo.hWnd
End Sub
```

Run your program to see the numbers in the video flash by (see Figure 14.13).

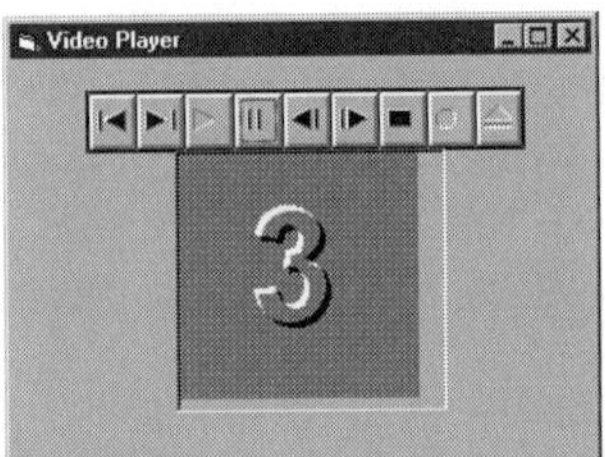

FIGURE 14.13.

The video plays flawlessly!

As you work with the multimedia control, you'll learn more shortcuts. For example, you don't have to specify the device type, such as `AVIVideo`, when programming compound devices, because Visual Basic will look at the compound device's file extension to determine the device type needed.

Also, you probably noticed that the status labels don't always update right on time. In other words, when you were running the previous section's video files: players:, the status label didn't always display *Play* until the clip was almost finished. The `StatusUpdate` event occurs every few milliseconds. If you want to update these labels more frequently to gain more accuracy, change the `UpdateInterval` property to a smaller value (`1000` is the default, so the status updates once each second).

Caution

Don't make the `UpdateInterval` property value too small, or your multimedia control application will consume too much time updating the label and slow down your system. Often, this slowdown results in shaky playback of multimedia control files.

Summary

Today's lesson explained how easy it is to spruce up your applications with graphics and multimedia. The line and shape controls enable you to accent your applications with lines and shapes that call attention to important elements on your form. You can add lines that separate controls and highlight important values.

Visual Basic also supplies drawing methods that enable you to draw anything you want using methods that turn on and off pixels, as well as draw lines, boxes, and ellipses. The methods are rather primitive, but they give you full control over the way the drawings you produce will look.

The last few sections described how to use the multimedia control. The multimedia control is one of the most comprehensive controls in Visual Basic, because it supports so many different kinds of multimedia devices. Your applications can easily control audio CDs and sound files, and even play video. The multimedia control comes with user command buttons that let the user operate the multimedia control, or you can control its operation through Visual Basic code.

Tomorrow's lesson describes how to add form templates to your projects so you can standardize the common forms your applications display.

Q&A

Q Can I use the multimedia control to display individual graphic images?

A The multimedia control is for multimedia devices only, and still photos stored in a graphics file do not qualify for multimedia. Nevertheless, you can display such pictures on the form by displaying them in an image control or a picture box control.

Q Should I use the drawing media control to display graphic images, such as photos stored on my disk?

A The drawing controls and the drawing methods are not mutually exclusive! You can use both. The line and shape controls take on specific forms that you can place on a form at design time and modify through property values at runtime. The drawing methods give you more drawing freedom in that you can even turn on and off single pixels, a chore that's possible, but too cumbersome, for the drawing controls. Therefore, although the drawing methods are more primitive than the drawing controls, these methods do provide more power for lines and such as long as you don't need to display graphic images.

Workshop

The Workshop provides quiz questions to help you solidify your understanding of the material covered and exercises to provide you with experience in using what you've learned. Try to understand the quiz and exercise answers before continuing to the next lesson. Answers are provided in Appendix A, "Answers to Exercises."

Quiz

1. What control draws circles on the form?
2. What method draws squares on the form?
3. Which of the following methods is used for drawing boxes?
    a. `PSet`
    b. `Line`
    c. `Box`
    d. `Draw`
4. True/False. The line and shape controls produce graphics that support properties but not events.
5. What `Line` method option adds a solid interior to boxes?
6. Why doesn't Visual Basic enable every button when you first place the multimedia control on a form?
7. What does the `Mode` property do?
8. How can you make the multimedia control device status update more frequently?
9. Why do you need to supply a picture box control for video clips?
10. How does the multimedia control know which picture box to send the video to?

Exercises

1. Add Fill Color and Border Color drop-down list boxes to Figure 14.5's application you created in today's lesson. You can now control not only the control's shape and fill pattern, but also its interior and border colors by selecting from the list boxes at the bottom of the form. Figure 14.14 shows what your form should look like after you add the two list boxes.

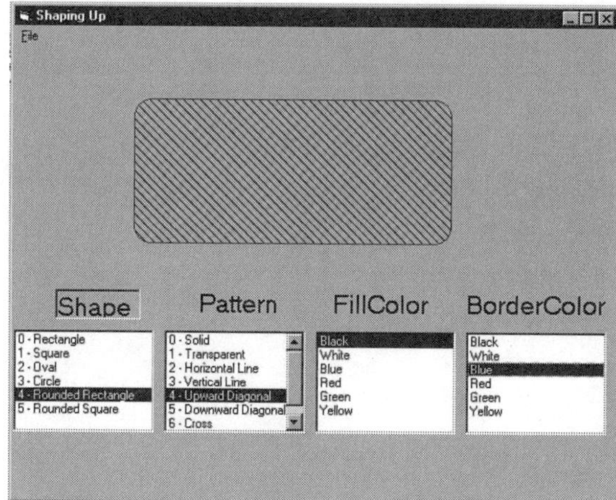

FIGURE 14.14.
You now have even more control over the shape.

Hint: Set the color to one of the named constant colors, such as `vbBlue`, when the user selects that color from either color list box. You don't have to offer all the named constant colors in the extra list boxes.

2. Practice drawing lines and circles with the drawing methods on a picture box control. As you can see, the picture box control accepts the same graphics methods the form does.

3. Change this lesson's wave player so that it displays a File Open dialog box that asks the user to select a wave file to play.

WEEK 2

BONUS PROJECT 7

Working with Scrollbars

This bonus project not only develops an application but also teaches you two new controls: the vertical and the horizontal scrollbars. You can easily master the vertical and the horizontal scrollbars because, as with the other controls, most of their behavior is controlled by the properties you set at designtime. You then write simple event procedures to respond to the user's actions.

Introducing Scrollbars

Often, your applications automatically come with scrollbars because controls, such as list boxes, require them. For example, a multiline text box that holds a lot of data, for example, will have scrollbars if you request them in the `ScrollBars` property. You would do this if the text box could not display a full line or all the entries in the text box. Figure BP7.1 shows such a list box. The figure points out the two kinds of scrollbars as well as the parts of each scrollbar.

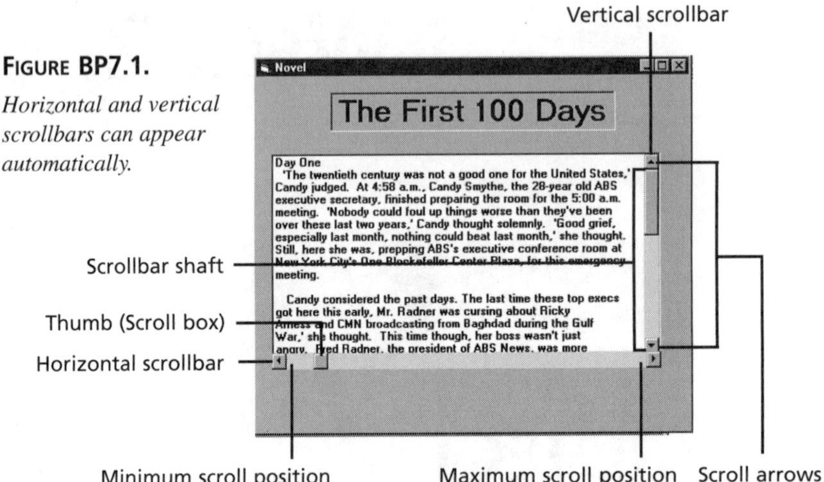

FIGURE BP7.1.
Horizontal and vertical scrollbars can appear automatically.

Multiline text boxes and list boxes are not the only reason for scrollbars. You can add scrollbars to your application to give the user flexible control over a changing scale of values, such as color depths, picture sizes, scrolling text displays, and numeric value ranges.

The toolbar contains both a horizontal scrollbar control and a vertical scrollbar control. Once you place these controls on a form, you then must set properties that define the scrollbar ranges.

Working with Scrollbars

Understanding the way scrollbars work goes a long way towards learning how to program with them, and the key to understanding scrollbars is learning the names of the parts of a scrollbar. Here are the actions users can take with scrollbars:

- Moving the horizontal scrollbar thumb to the leftmost (or highest for vertical scrollbars) position within the scrollbar shaft sets the scrollbar to its lowest setting.
- Dragging the horizontal scrollbar thumb left and right (or up and down for vertical scrollbars) decreases and increases the value the scrollbar is portraying.
- Moving the horizontal scrollbar thumb to the rightmost (or lowest for vertical scrollbars) position within the scrollbar shaft sets the scrollbar to its highest setting.

- Clicking either scroll arrow increases or decreases the scroll setting by a small amount.
- Clicking either side of the thumb, within the scrollbar shaft, increases or decreases the scroll setting by a large amount.

Scrollbar Properties

Table BP7.1 lists the most important scrollbar properties that you'll want to set at designtime (these are also available at runtime, although you'll almost always set them up completely at designtime). The properties coincide with the workings of scrollbars described in the previous section.

TABLE BP7.1. SCROLLBAR PROPERTIES HELP YOU DETERMINE THE SCROLLBAR'S RANGE AND MOVEMENT AMOUNT.

Property	*Description*
`LargeChange`	Specifies the amount the scrollbar changes when the user clicks within the scrollbar's shaft area (on either side of the thumb).
`Max`	Indicates the maximum number of units that the scrollbar value represents at its highest setting. The default value is 32,767.
`Min`	Indicates the minimum number of units that the scrollbar value represents at its lowest setting. The default value is 1.
`SmallChange`	Specifies the amount the scrollbar changes when the user clicks either scroll arrow.
`Value`	Specifies the unit of measurement currently represented by the scrollbar.

Knowing that the default range of all scrollbars is 1 to 32,767, you can adjust this range as your application requires. For example, suppose you're writing a loan calculation program that accepts a range of loans from $500 to $15,000. Your user could type the loan value into a text box, but you can also place a scrollbar on the form to let the user select a value by scrolling the scrollbar. Your scrollbar would take these property values:

```
Min: 500
Max: 15000
```

You could then decide on the change increments that you want the scrollbar to represent. Perhaps you calculate loans in $100 increments. The following property settings ensure that the loan amount (as indicated by the scrollbar's `Value` property) changes by $500 every time the user makes a large change by clicking within the scrollbar shaft, and changes by $100 every time the user makes a small change by clicking either scroll arrow:

```
LargeChange: 500
SmallChange: 100
```

You can resize the scrollbar's width and height. The physical size of your scrollbar does nothing to determine the range of the change values of the scrollbar.

Building an Application

This bonus project's application demonstrates the power and use of scrollbars. Figure BP7.2 shows the application's screen. As the user clicks the scrollbars, the image of the money increases or decreases in size. The code to make this happen is extremely light due to the scrollbars' properties that control the way they work.

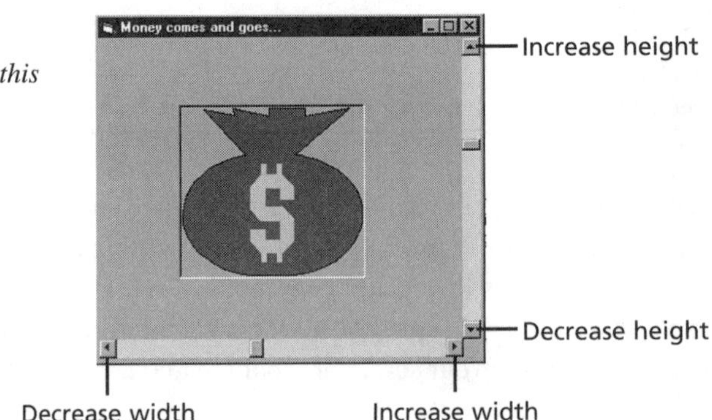

FIGURE BP7.2.
Scrollbars control this image's size.

Remember the direction of the scrollbars as you use this simple application. To increase the image's height, you must increase the value of the vertical scrollbar, which means moving the vertical scrollbar thumb *down*. The downward direction almost makes you feel, at first, as if the graphic image should get smaller. Although you could write the application to reverse the default direction by making the image's size respond in reverse, this application does not do that.

Do	**Don't**
DO insert your Visual Basic installation CD-ROM into your drive if you did not install the Graphics folder when you installed Visual Basic. You'll have to access a graphic file (or copy the image to your disk) in this application.	

Table BP7.2 contains the controls and properties you need to set when creating this application.

Table BP7.2. Set these controls and properties on the form.

Control Property Name	*Property Value*
Form `Name`	`frmScroll`
Form `Caption`	`Money comes and goes...`
Form `Height`	`4650`
Form `Width`	`5295`
Picture box `Name`	`picScroll`
Picture box `Height`	`1600`
Picture box `Left`	`1560`
Picture box `Picture`	`Common\Graphics\Metafile\Business\Moneybag`
Picture box `Top`	`1200`
Picture box `Width`	`1575`
Vertical scrollbar `Name`	`vscScroll`
Vertical scrollbar `Height`	`3975`
Vertical scrollbar `LargeChange`	`100`
Vertical scrollbar `Left`	`4920`
Vertical scrollbar `Max`	`3750`
Vertical scrollbar `Min`	`1600`
Vertical scrollbar `SmallChange`	`50`
Vertical scrollbar `Top`	`0`
Vertical scrollbar `Width`	`255`
Horizontal scrollbar `Name`	`hscScroll`
Horizontal scrollbar `Height`	`255`

continues

TABLE BP7.2. CONTINUED

Control Property Name	*Property Value*
Horizontal scrollbar `LargeChange`	100
Horizontal scrollbar `Left`	0
Horizontal scrollbar `Max`	3750
Horizontal scrollbar `Min`	1600
Horizontal scrollbar `SmallChange`	50
Horizontal scrollbar `Top`	3960
Horizontal scrollbar `Width`	4935

Every time the user clicks a scroll arrow, the size of the picture changes by 50 pixels, due to the `SmallChange` values for both scrollbars. Every time the user clicks on either side of the thumb, the size of the picture changes by 100 pixels, due to the `LargeChange` values for both scrollbars.

Entering the Code

Listing BP7.1 provides the event code you need to enter for this project.

Not only must the picture's size change when the user clicks the scrollbar, but the picture's location must also change so that the picture stays centered on the form.

LISTING BP7.1. CONTROLLING THE SIZE OF THE PICTURE USING SCROLLBARS.

```
Private Sub hscScroll_Change()
  ' Change the picture's horizontal size and location
  picScroll.Width = hscScroll.Value
  picScroll.Left = (frmScroll.Width / 2) - (picScroll.Width / 2) - 300
End Sub

Private Sub vscScroll_Change()
  ' Change the picture's vertical size and location
  picScroll.Height = vscScroll.Value
  picScroll.Top = (frmScroll.Height / 2) - (picScroll.Height / 2) _
  -300
End Sub

Private Sub vscScroll_Scroll()
  ' If the user drags the thumb, change during the drag
```

```
15:    Call vscScroll_Change
16: End Sub
17:
18: Private Sub hscScroll_Scroll()
19:    ' If the user drags the thumb, change during the drag
20:   Call hscScroll_Change
21: End Sub
```

Analysis

The code is repetitive because the two scrollbars do basically the same thing (controlling the width or height of the picture). The first procedure changes the picture's width in line 3 to match the value of the horizontal scrollbar. (Both scrollbars' `Min` and `Max` properties are set, at designtime, so that the picture always falls within a reasonable size range.) Line 4 determines the location of the newly sized picture. The location is adjusted according to the height of the picture compared to the height of the form. The form's midpoint is found (`frmScroll.Width / 2`) and from that, one-half the size of the picture is subtracted (`picScroll.Width / 2`) to place the midpoint of the picture halfway down the form. The extra 300 pixels are subtracted to adjust for the size of the scrollbar at the right of the form.

Lines 7 through 11 do exactly the same thing when the user changes the horizontal scrollbar value, except the width is adjusted instead of the height.

The last two procedures are interesting because they do nothing more than call the other procedures. The first procedures only execute if the user clicks somewhere on the scrollbar's arrows or shaft. However, what if the user *drags* the thumb? Without the event procedures for the `Change` events, the picture would not change until the user releases the mouse from dragging the scrollbar, thus completing the `Click` event. By calling the `Click` event's procedure from the `Change` event procedure, the picture changes *as the user drags the scrollbar thumb*. In other words, the `Click` event procedure is called during the drag for every value the user drags the scroll thumb.

A good case could be made for placing the `Click` events' code inside the `Change` procedure and doing away with the `Click` events. The event procedures would then execute every time the user did anything to change a scrollbar, whether by dragging or by clicking, because both actions produce a `Change` event. Nevertheless, you had yet to see one event procedure call another, so the example is a good one to use.

WEEK 2

In Review

You have moved from a beginning Visual Basic programmer to an advanced one. You have mastered most of the Visual Basic language and you are comfortable with Visual Basic's programming environment.

Much of your future learning will be honing the skills you now carry with you. As you study Visual Basic more thoroughly in the rest of this 21-day tutorial, in more advanced Visual Basic books, and through magazines and Internet Visual Basic sites, you'll feel comfortable picking up new skills because you now have the foundation necessary to understand more advanced concepts.

Your Week's Worth

In this week, you have mastered the following:

- **Procedural programming**—A Visual Basic program is more than just controls and event procedures. An application might consist of several forms and code modules that work together to do a job (Day 8).
- **Variable scope**—As you make your code more modular and easier to maintain, you must remember that variable scope plays a part in determining which procedures have access to an application's variables (Day 8).
- **Passing data**—Whether you write subroutine or function procedures, your procedures must be able to pass local data to other procedures (Day 8).
- **Passing controls**—You can pass any object, whether that object is a data variable or a control, between procedures (Day 8).

- **Internal functions**—Lighten your programming burden by letting Visual Basic handle common tasks such as calculating the square root and converting string data (Day 8).
- **Common dialog boxes**—Add standard dialog boxes to your applications so that your users will know how to load and save files, set colors, and print documents (Day 9).
- **Mouse control**—Your applications can monitor the user's mouse clicks and moves (Day 10).
- **List controls**—Visual Basic offers several kinds of list box controls so that you can determine the kind of list control that best suits your application's needs (Day 10).
- **Timer control**—The Timer is a control that checks the PC's clock and executes procedures that you write at preset time intervals (Day 10).
- **Arrays**—When your program must process a large amount of data, simple variables will not hold lists of data. For lists, you need to store data in special memory tables called arrays (Day 10).
- **Forms**—Forms, like other objects in Visual Basic, support a wide range of properties, events, and methods that you can use to hide and display forms at runtime (Day 11).
- **Text on forms**—Write directly to a form without using controls when you issue the `Print` method (Day 11).
- **Toolbars**—Give your users yet another way to specify choices in your applications with toolbars (Day 11).
- **Coolbars**—Although coolbars (sliding toolbars) are recent editions to Windows applications, thanks to Internet browsers and other programs that use them, coolbars add a cool flair to your applications (Day 11).
- **Working with files**—File processing is relative simple, but it does require programming (Day 12).
- **Sequential files**—Sequential files hold historical information and are easy to work with (Day 12).
- **Random files**—Random files enable you to read and write at any location in a file (Day 12).
- **File controls**—Although the file controls do not actually manipulate files, they do let the user zero-in to the file that the user wants your application to work with (Day 12).

- **Visual Basic printing**—As with file processing, printing data to the printer from a Visual Basic application requires some extra programming methods (Day 13).
- **Form output**—You can print your application's forms onto paper (Day 13).
- **Graphic files**—Visual Basic lets you display images from graphics files using the PictureBox and Image controls (Day 14).
- **Graphics controls**—Visual Basic supports the Line control and Shape control so that you can accent forms with graphics that you place on the forms (Day 14).
- **Graphics methods**—Apply drawings to both forms and picture boxes with the methods you learn here (Day 14).
- **Multimedia control**—The Multimedia control supports just about any multimedia device that you want your application to control (Day 14).

WEEK 3

At a Glance

You have come a long way from the point you were at two weeks ago when you first began learning how to write Visual Basic programs. Even though it's only been two weeks, you should now consider yourself past the beginning programmer stage. You can already make Visual Basic do about anything you need. Your job now is to improve upon the skills you have.

Where You're Going

The third and final week of this tutorial begins to examine some of the advanced aspects of Visual Basic programming. Just because they are advanced, however, does not mean that the features you learn this week are difficult. Almost everything you learn from this week forward is considered advanced. Nevertheless, you have such a strong foundation under you now that these additional skills should come quite easily.

As you begin to explore objects and ActiveX controls this week, you will see that such elements help you produce better code as well as write programs more quickly. You learn to reuse components that you create in the same way that you learned to reuse procedures last week. You will be developing your own tools for the Visual Basic Toolbox window by creating your own ActiveX controls.

As you will see, Visual Basic certainly lacks for little when it comes to supplying you with a broad range of controls. In this final week, you learn how to access files, manage data in popular database formats, and access the Internet using the tools that comes with Visual Basic. Rarely will you write an

15
16
17
18
19
20
21

application that requires more controls than the ones that you already have; but you'll rest easy knowing that you can obtain more and even write your own if you want to do so. Not only can you use those ActiveX controls in the Visual Basic programming environment, but you can also use the controls in other ways as well, such as embedding them in Web pages for Internet browsers that support the use of ActiveX.

After writing the application, you'll want to test it with Visual Basic's testing and debugging tools. Although some bugs are difficult to trace, Visual Basic goes a long way toward locating hard-to-find bugs. Once you develop an application, you must compile and distribute that application to others. At the end of this week, you learn how to package your applications with their own installation routines so that your users can install and run the applications that you write.

WEEK 3

DAY 15

Using Form Templates

Today's lesson shows you how to take advantage of template forms so that your forms will have a more uniform appearance when you create them for similar purposes. Visual Basic supplies several template forms that you can add, customize, and use in your own projects. So many forms in use today—such as the About dialog box that appears when Help, About is selected—have developed somewhat of a *de facto* standard appearance; therefore, you might as well follow the trend. The About box as well as several other standard forms all come with Visual Basic.

Once you know how to use the template forms, you can create your own. Suppose your company prefers each application's dialog box to take on a standard appearance, such as listing the company name, logo, time, and date at the top of the form. Once you create a template form that contains this information, all subsequent forms you use in your applications can have those same elements without you having to add them every time you add a new form to a project.

Today, you learn the following:

- About the purpose of template forms
- Why you should use the template forms

- How to implement template forms in your projects
- How to use the Application Wizard to add template forms
- How to create a "Tip of the Day" file
- How to add your own template forms to Visual Basic's supplied set of template forms

About Form Templates

A *template* is a model. A *template form* is a model form. When you start with a template form, as opposed to the blank form window, you'll save time, and your forms will take on a more uniform appearance.

NEW TERM A *template form* is a model for the forms you create.

Suppose you wanted to add a Tip of the Day screen to your application so that your users read a different tip every time they start your application. Perhaps the most common Tip of the Day screen people know about is the Windows 95 Tip of the Day screen. It appears when you start Windows 95. Other popular Windows applications also use a Tip of the Day screen, and they often have an appearance similar to the Windows 95 screen. For example, most of them include a check box at the bottom of the screen that lets you cancel the display of the tip screen upon subsequent application startups.

As you've already learned throughout this tutorial, creating standardized applications has many advantages: Your users will adapt to your applications more quickly, they will be more apt to like your applications, they will be prone to use the upgrades you write, they will learn the applications more quickly, and you will receive fewer support calls. As if these weren't reason enough to use standard screens and menus, you'll also find that you save time: You'll finish the applications more quickly, and you'll have fewer bugs to remove.

Figure 15.1 shows the Tip of the Day *template form* that Visual Basic provides. If you needed to add a Tip of the Day screen to an application, would you rather begin with the *template form* shown in Figure 15.1 or with a blank form window? Obviously, you'd rather start with the *template form*. The template provides a uniform appearance, and you have less work to do to complete the form.

15

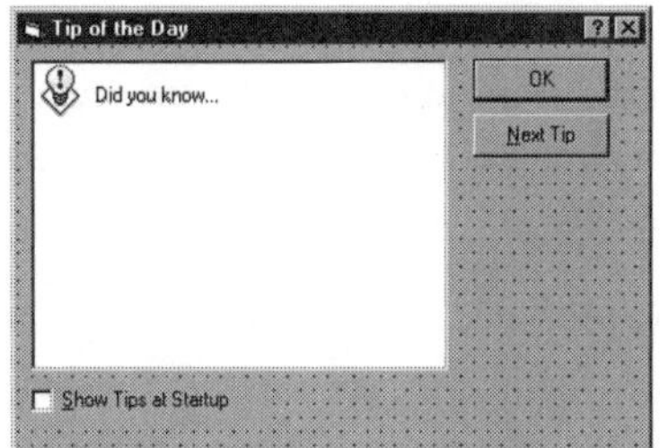

FIGURE 15.1.
Visual Basic supplies this Tip of the Day template form.

Note

As with the skeleton applications that the Application Wizard creates, a template form contains placeholders for the common elements, but you'll have to modify the template form quite a bit. You'll need to replace elements that you don't use and customize the form to your application's requirements. Nevertheless, despite the needed customization, you'll finish the form much more quickly if you start with the template form as opposed to a blank form window.

Form templates contain visual elements, such as icons and controls, as well as the code behind these elements to help you integrate the template form into your application.

A template form is nothing more than just a form with elements and code already placed in its module. The template forms are not special kinds of forms, rather they are a collection of predesigned forms. As you create forms that you want to use again, you can simply add them to the collection of template forms on your system, as explained in the section "Adding Your Own Form Templates."

The Supplied Form Templates

Visual Basic supplies the following template forms:

- **About box**—Usually produced from the Help, About menu option.
- **Web Browser**—Used for simple Internet Web browsing.
- **Data grid**—Used for managing tables of database-like data.
- **Dialog**—Used for creating dialog boxes.
- **Login**—Used for requesting name and password information.
- **ODBC**—Used for ODBC-related activities.

- **Option**—Used for multipaged dialog boxes and custom settings.
- **Splash**—Used for displaying an introductory startup screen when an application loads. (This startup screen typically appears for only one to five seconds.)
- **Tip of the Day**—Used for adding a startup tip.

NEW TERM *ODBC* stands for *Open Database Connectivity*. It provides a standard command set for accessing different kinds of data stored on different kinds of computers.

SQL stands for *Structured Query Language*. It defines a universal (in theory) programming language for accessing databases. You can issue SQL commands directly from a Visual Basic application.

> The rest of today's lesson describes how to implement many of these template forms in your own applications. Some of the template forms are too specific for today's lesson. For example, Day 19, "Adding Internet Access," covers Internet browsing in more detail using the Web Browser template form. Day 18, "Interacting with Data," describes how to link Visual Basic applications to database information as you might want to do with the Data grid or ODBC template.

The following sections review many of the more common template forms that you'll use. You'll learn how to use the Application Wizard to add template forms, and you'll see in detail how to add and customize the About dialog box for your applications. Once you've added and customized one template form, the others simply offer other options. After you've learned how to add the About box, subsequent sections will discuss some of the other template forms and their nuances.

Here are the general steps for adding a template form to your application:

1. Add the template form to your application's Project window.
2. Customize the template form with the details your application requires.
3. Connect the form to your project through code.

Using the Application Wizard

You can add one of the template forms to your application at any time. However, if you use the Application Wizard, you just let the wizard know that you want a specific template form and it takes care of all the details of adding the template form to your application.

Figure 15.2 shows the Application Wizard's dialog box in which you specify a template form. As you can see, the Application Wizard only offers four template form options: Splash screen, Login screen, Options dialog box, and About box.

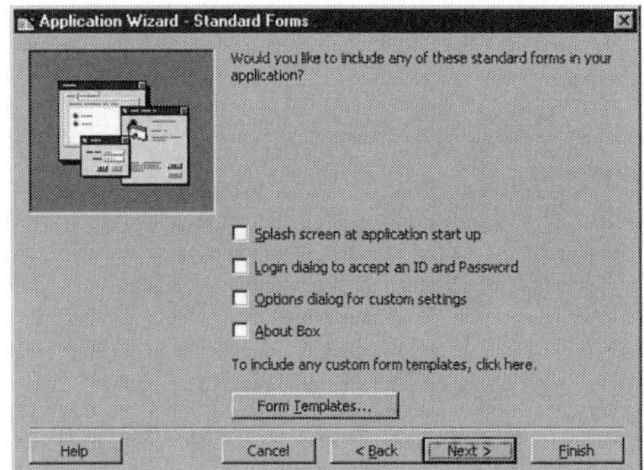

FIGURE 15.2.
The Application Wizard will add one or more forms to your application.

Although the dialog box lists only four template forms, when you click the Form Templates button, Visual Basic displays a list of the other template forms.

> The list that appears includes not only the supplied template forms described in the previous section but also the template forms that you've added to the library of template forms.

Adding Form Templates to an Application

To add a template form to an application, you simply add the form to your application the same way you normally add any other form:

- Select the Project, Add Form menu option and select a template form from the list of form icons that appear in the dialog box (Figure 15.3 shows such a dialog box).
- Right-click the Project window, select Add, Form, and then select the template form from the list of form icons that appear in the dialog box.

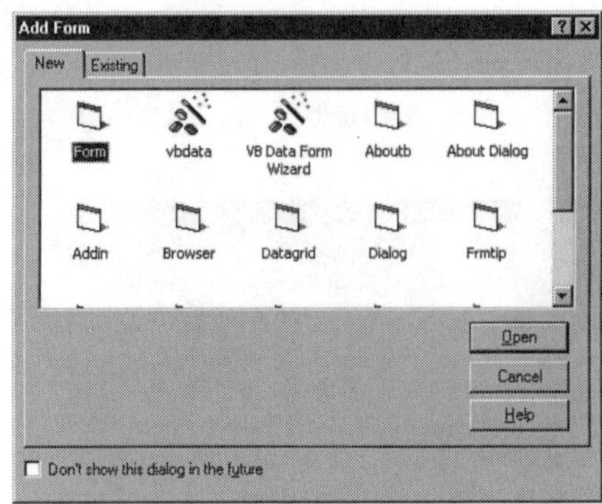

FIGURE 15.3.

Adding template forms is simple.

To add a new form, you select the dialog box's first icon (the one labeled Form). To add a template form, select the icon that matches the template form you want to add to your project.

Modifying the Templates

When you select Tools, Options and click the Environments tab, Visual Basic displays the Environments dialog box page shown in Figure 15.4. By checking or unchecking the Forms check box, you specify whether or not Visual Basic is to offer the list of template forms to you in the Application Wizard and in the Project, Add Form dialog box.

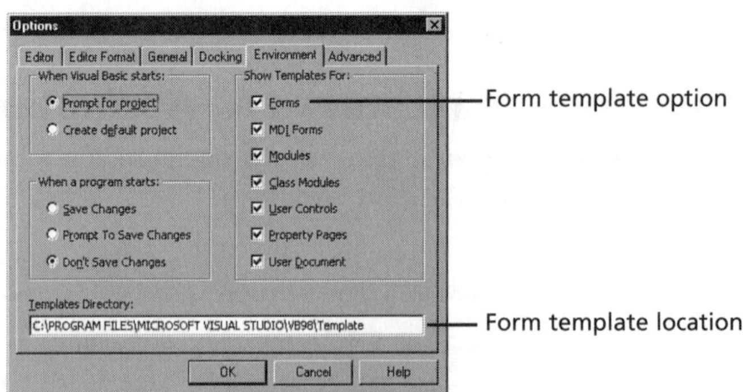

FIGURE 15.4.

You can control the templates that Visual Basic offers.

As you can see from the Options dialog box, Visual Basic supplies templates for many more objects than just forms. Visual Basic offers module templates, control templates, property page templates, as well as others. Although some of these non-template forms are used in fairly advanced applications, you can see that a model exists for just about any kind of object you want to create.

Note

If you uncheck the Forms option to hide the template forms from view, when you add a new project to an application, Visual Basic automatically creates and adds a new, blank form to your project without giving you any way to select a different kind of form.

The Options dialog box shows the folder where Visual Basic looks for template forms. Visual Basic expects all template forms to reside in this folder. If you set up various libraries of templates for different purposes (perhaps as a contract programmer might do when working for several different companies), you can store each of your different sets of templates in a different folder. When you want to work with one of the sets, enter its path into the Options dialog box.

Do	Don't
DO make permanent changes to the template so that it works better for your needs if you find yourself using the same template form often. Do save a copy of the form under a new name and make modifications to the copy. Do use the copy when you subsequently use the form.	**DON'T** make changes directly to the original template form itself.

Working with the About Form Template

The purpose for each of the template forms differs, but the general procedure for connecting a template form to your application is the same for all the template forms. In this section, you'll add a template form to an application to get familiar with the process. One of the most common dialog boxes that appears in almost all Windows applications is the About dialog box, which pops up when users choose About from the Help menu. Figure 15.5 shows what the About template form looks like in Visual Basic's form window.

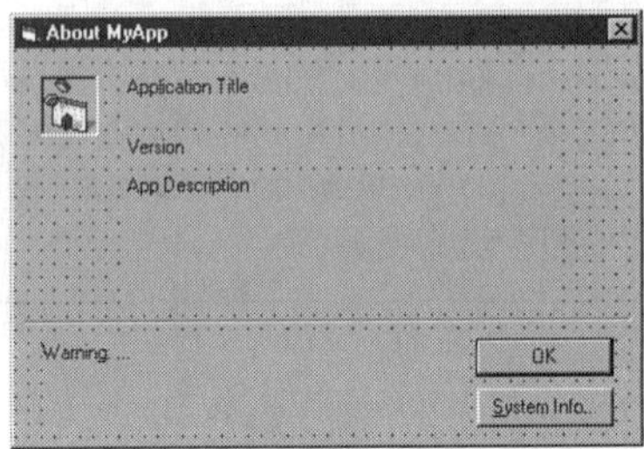

FIGURE 15.5.
The template form for the About dialog box, which appears in most Windows applications.

To give you an idea of how the template form differs from the actual form you'll eventually create, take a look at Figure 15.6. This figure shows Visual Basic's own About dialog box. As you can see, the template form provides placeholders for actual information you'll place in the template form in the final application.

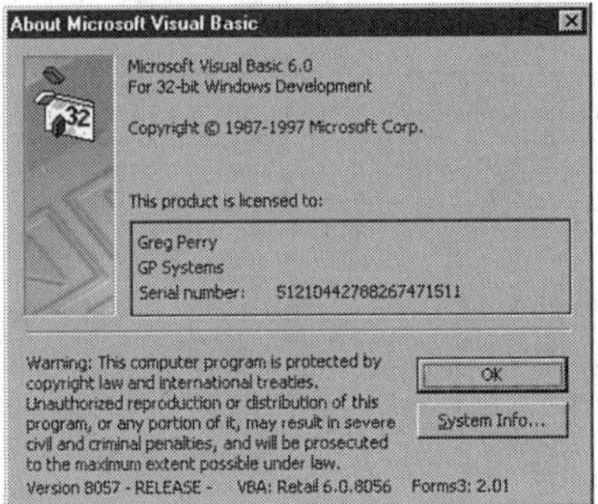

FIGURE 15.6.
Visual Basic's About dialog box matches the template form's format.

To practice adding the About template form, start a new application and follow these steps:

1. Open the Menu Editor, add Help to the menu bar, and list About as the only option on the Help menu. Name the About option `mnuHelpAbout`.
2. Name the project's form `frmTestAbout` and change the form caption to `Demonstrate the About Dialog Box`.
3. From the File menu choose Save Form As and then type `Form About Box` for the form's filename.
4. Choose Save Project As from the File menu and then type `About Proj` for the project's filename. (The About dialog box that you add will use the project name.)
5. From the Project menu choose Add Form to display the Add Form dialog box. Double-click About Dialog to add the About dialog box to your form. A dialog box is nothing more than a form with controls, and the About dialog box comes to your application as a new form named `frmAbout`.

6. Use the Window menu option to switch back to your original form (`frmTestAbout`). Add the following event procedure to the `mnuHelpAbout_Click()` procedure:

   ```
   Private Sub mnuHelpAbout_Click()
     frmAbout.Show
   End Sub
   ```

7. You can now run the application. When you choose About from the Help menu, the About dialog box appears. The About dialog box template form knows the name of the project and displays the name in its title area.
8. Click OK to close the About dialog box; then close the primary form's window to shut down the application.

The About dialog box template form knows the name of the project, and it displays this name in its title area. The About dialog box gets the name from a special location—the `App` object (tomorrow's lesson, "Objects and Visual Basic," discusses the `App` object and its properties).

Use the Window menu to display the About form in your form window editing area. The dialog box's `Form_Load()` event procedure contains the following code, which initializes the title from the `App` object:

```
1:  Private Sub Form_Load ()
2:      Me.Caption = "About " & App.Title
3:      lblVersion.Caption = "Version " & App.Major & "." & App.Minor & _
        "." & App.Revision
4:      lblTitle.Caption = App.Title
5:  End Sub
```

Line 3 sets the application's major, minor, and revision numbers at runtime in the primary form's `Form_Load()` event procedure. You can delete the About form module's reference to these values (and the labels that display the values) if you don't need version numbering.

The About dialog box's form module contains code that initializes these values (the title and version number) for you. The About dialog box, however, can't initialize certain labels, such as the application's description and warning area. You have to initialize the description yourself in the description label's (named `lblDescription`) `Caption` property. If you don't need a warning or copyright area, delete the About dialog box's warning label (named `lblDisclaimer`). You could, in its place, insert an icon or picture box control to grab your users' attention.

The About dialog box involves more code than just the application's name and version numbers. Obviously, the dialog box's form module contains the code to look for the application's name and version numbers. Also, the dialog box's form module contains code that unloads the dialog box if the user clicks OK. The real power of the About dialog box, however, lies in the System Info command button's event procedure:

```
Private Sub cmdSysInfo_Click()
  Call StartSysInfo
End Sub
```

`StartSysInfo` is a general procedure listed below the event procedures in the About dialog box's form module. The code in `StartSysInfo` runs a system program named MSINFO32.EXE, located in your Windows directory. Although you could override this program with your own code, why not stick with a standard system information program that users will see in other Windows programs?

If you were to rerun your application, display the About dialog box, and click the System Info button, the System Information application would start. (The application is known to be a *child process* of your application. Your application will continue when the user closes the System Information window.) Figure 15.7 shows the System Information window that the form module's code produces when you add the About dialog box to your application.

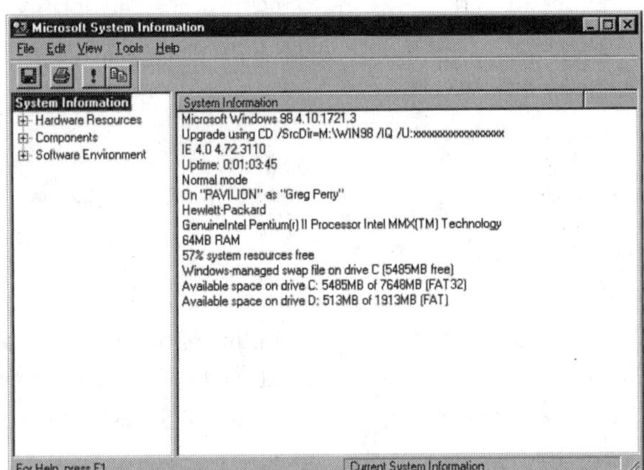

FIGURE 15.7.
The code that comes with the About dialog box displays the System Information dialog box.

Your System Information dialog box will differ from the one shown in Figure 15.7, depending on your system's configuration.

Other Form Templates

Now that you've built a project that uses the About dialog box, you'll have no trouble placing the other three primary template forms. When you choose Add Form from the Project menu, you have the chance to add several template forms to your current project.

This section looks at the following template forms in more detail:

- Splash screen
- Login dialog box
- Custom Options dialog box
- Tip of the Day dialog box
- ODBC Login dialog box

Not all applications should include all the template forms. However, most Windows applications do include the About dialog box, so you should make it a habit to include About in your applications. The remaining template forms may or may not fit into your application, depending on your application's goals and requirements. This section looks at these template forms in detail, so you can determine whether you need to add one or all of them to your projects.

Throughout this section, you'll learn how to connect the various template forms to your application. If you add one or more of these templates while using Visual Basic's Application Wizard, the wizard will take some of the work off your shoulders. This way, you won't have to do as much to integrate the templates into your project.

The Splash Screen

A *splash screen* is an opening screen that displays an introductory message and perhaps copyright and contact information about the project. (Although it's called a *screen*, the splash screen is actually another form window in your project's `Forms` collection.) The splash screen's primary purpose is to greet your users. Unlike the About dialog box, the splash screen isn't seen again until the application is run again.

The splash screen often displays a graphic image with introductory text. Figure 15.8 shows the splash screen that appears when Microsoft Excel is started. The splash screen contains an attention-getting image and information about the product.

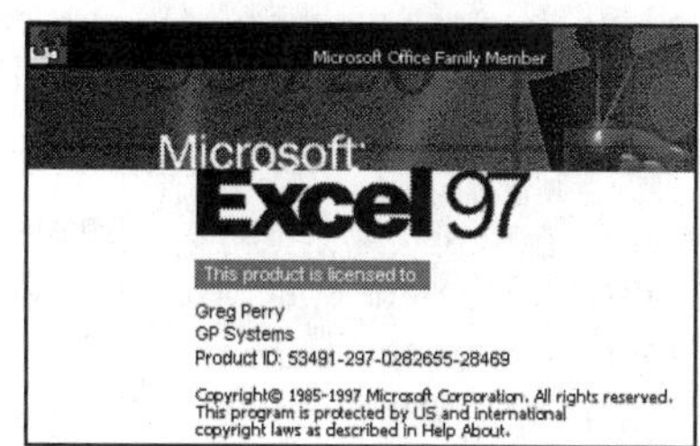

FIGURE 15.8.

Excel users see a splash screen similar to this one when Excel first loads.

A splash screen often goes away after a brief period of time. You can add a command button or write code that checks for a keypress to enable your users to get rid of the splash screen at their leisure. However, you'll generally use a timer control to display the splash screen for a fixed amount of time. Also, a splash screen is useful for masking a startup delay due to file and data initialization.

The splash screen does pose one requirement that the About dialog box does not. You must tell your application to display the splash screen *before* the normal form appears. You set the splash screen as the startup form in the Properties dialog box (which you access by choosing Properties from the Project menu). As soon as you add the splash screen's template form to your project, the Properties dialog box will include the splash screen form in your list of available startup forms. You also must add a command button or a timer control event to the splash screen to display the next window when it's time to do so.

Follow these steps to practice creating a project that contains a splash screen:

1. Create a new project. You won't do anything with the form named `Form1`.
2. From the Project menu, choose Add Form; then select the splash screen. Visual Basic displays the sample splash screen.
3. Change the labels to match those shown in Figure 15.9.

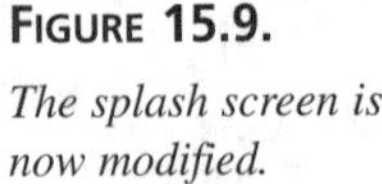

FIGURE 15.9.

The splash screen is now modified.

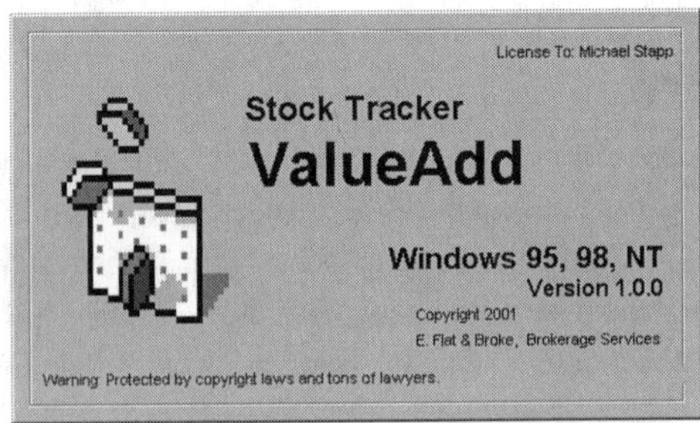

4. Choose Properties from the Project menu. Change the Startup Object to `frmSplash` (the name of the splash screen) and click OK.
5. Add the following line to both the `Form_Keypress()` event and the `Frame1_Click()` event (place the line after the `Unload Me` statement in both procedures):

```
Form1.Show    ' Display the regular form
```

6. Run the application. The first form that appears is your splash screen. When you press a key or click the mouse button, the splash screen will disappear and the normal form, named Form1, will appear. Close the form window to return to Visual Basic's development environment.

Caution

> The splash screen automatically gets the name of the program from the project name, no matter what you add in the center label. Therefore, you'll need to save the project under the name *ValueAdd* or edit the code to leave your original label alone.

The Login Dialog Box

As online computer use grows, the need for security grows with it. The Login dialog box is an interesting template form that you can add to your project. It asks for the user name and password and returns the values to your application for processing. Figure 15.10 shows the Login dialog box.

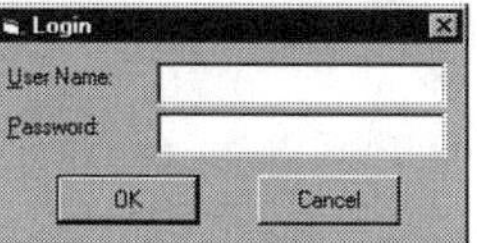

FIGURE 15.10.
Use the Login dialog box to request a user's name and password.

When a user enters his or her name and password, the actual user name appears, but the password displays as asterisks (thanks to the dialog box's `PasswordChar` property). Although asterisks display as the user enters the password (to protect the password from snooping eyes), your program will have access to the real password that's being typed. The initial password is *password*, and you can use it to test your program's Login dialog box. Listing 15.1 shows the form module's code behind the Login dialog box.

LISTING 15.1. THE LOGIN DIALOG BOX LETS USERS LOG IN TO YOUR APPLICATION.

```
Option Explicit
Public LoginSucceeded As Boolean

Private Sub cmdCancel_Click()
    'set the global var to false
    'to denote a failed login
    LoginSucceeded = False
    Me.Hide
End Sub

Private Sub cmdOK_Click()
    'check for correct password
    If txtPassword = "password" Then
        'place code to here to pass the
        'success to the calling sub
```

continues

LISTING 15.1. CONTINUED

```
16:         'setting a global var is the easiest
17:         LoginSucceeded = True
18:         Me.Hide
19:     Else
20:         MsgBox "Invalid Password, try again!", , "Login"
21:         txtPassword.SetFocus
22:         SendKeys "{Home}+{End}"
23: End If
24: End Sub
```

The form module uses a global variable named `LoginSucceeded` (declared in line 2) that your code can test for `True` or `False` on returning from the dialog box. If the user clicks the Cancel button, the `cmdCancel_Click()` event procedure sets `LoginSucceeded` to `False` in line 7 and hides the Login form.

To adapt the code for your own users, follow these steps:

1. Change the password string literal in the `cmdOK_Click()` event procedure to the password your application requires. Often the password will be stored in a file and encrypted. If you store the password in a random, binary, or database file, nobody will be able to detect the password by studying the password file with a text editor, as would be possible if you stored the password in a text file.
2. Change the message box text to the message you want to show if the user enters the wrong password.
3. For security reasons, consider putting the password-checking routine in a `For` loop to give the user a fixed number of tries before the application refuses to display the Login dialog box again. This will make it more difficult to break the password.

Just because Microsoft supplied the Login dialog box code with a global variable doesn't make the global good to use. As the `cmdOK_Click()` event procedure's remark explains, the global variable is the *easiest* way to inform the surrounding application of the success of the login, but good programming practice suggests that you replace the global variable with local variables. Perhaps the best way to modify this code to improve its maintainability is to turn the subroutine procedure into a function procedure and set the function's return data type to Boolean. The surrounding application can then test the function's return value for `True` or `False`.

The code at the end of the `cmdOK_Click()` routine might look confusing because it varies in style from what you're used to—plus you'll find a few new statements. Until now, `MsgBox()` has been a function, but this code contains the following `MsgBox` statement:

```
MsgBox "Invalid Password, try again!", , "Login"
```

Although Visual Basic 6 still supports this `MsgBox` statement format, Microsoft is trying to get programmers to use the `MsgBox()` function instead. To turn this statement into a function, you need to assign the function to a variable (a Variant will do) and add parentheses, like this:

```
varKeys = MsgBox("Invalid Password, try again!", "Login")
```

Note

The `MsgBox` statement can't determine which command button the user clicked to close the message box. On the other hand, the `MsgBox()` function returns the button clicked. If OK is the only `MsgBox()` button you choose to display, you don't need to test for a button click, because the user must click OK to close the message box.

The next statement returns the focus to the Password text box (this occurs only if the user enters an invalid password) with the `SetFocus` method. When you apply `SetFocus` to a control that can receive focus, the application sets the focus to that control. Although the focus might ordinarily move to another control, such as the OK button, the `SetFocus` method moves the focus back to the Password text box because the user has to reenter the password.

The final statement uses the `SendKeys` statement to highlight the text that appears in the Password text box. No matter what the user types as the incorrect password, the `SendKeys` statement moves the text cursor to the beginning of the text box and then to the end of the text box—in effect, highlighting the entire text box contents so the user's next keypress replaces the selected text.

Note

Day 7, "Advanced Keyboard and Screen Support," explained the `SendKeys` statement in detail.

The Options Dialog Box

Of all the template forms, the one for the Options dialog box does the least amount of work by itself but has the most potential uses. When you add an Options dialog box, you'll see the dialog box template shown in Figure 15.11. The dialog box contains four pages, with tabs at the top of each page and a frame on the body of each page. You can add pages and controls to the inside of the page frames for the options you require.

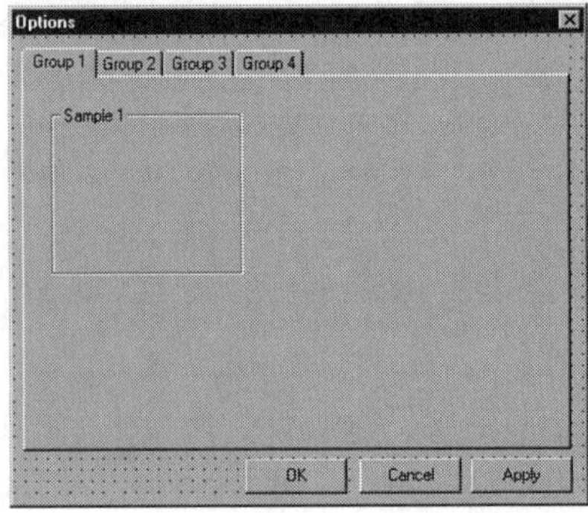

FIGURE 15.11.
The Options dialog box displays pages for various options.

Many Windows programs contain an Options dialog box (accessed from the Tools menu) that looks a lot like the Options dialog box this template form produces. Although it's just a dialog box shell, the Options template form is a starting point from which you can build a more complete dialog box.

The Options dialog box uses a special ActiveX control called *TabStrip*, which produces this multiple-page tabbed dialog box. If you want to add a TabStrip control to one of your applications—that is, if you don't want to use this template form—you'll have to add the control from the Project Properties dialog box's Microsoft Custom Controls 6.0 option (choose Properties from the Project menu).

When you want to use the Options dialog box, follow these general guidelines:

- Add as many pages to the Options dialog box as you need. The easiest way to modify the tabs and pages is to click one of the tabs and then click the ellipsis for the `Custom` property. The Property Pages dialog box that appears helps you set up the pages, tabs, and ToolTips you want to use in the Options dialog box (see Figure 15.12).

FIGURE 15.12.

Use the Property Pages dialog box to set up the dialog box pages.

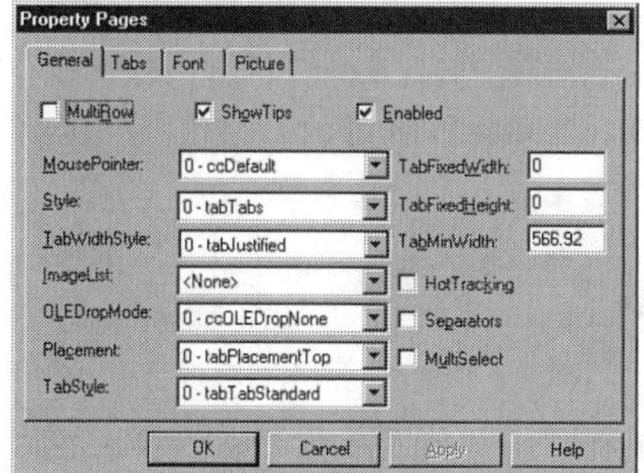

- Add a general procedure that reads all the controls in the Options dialog box and sets whatever options the dialog box contains.
- Call the options-setting procedure from the `cmdApply_Click()` procedure so that the options go into effect when the user clicks the Options dialog box's Apply button. (You can also remove the Apply button and its associated event procedure if you don't want your users to have the Apply feature.)
- Replace the following statement, which appears in the `cmdOK_Click()` event, with a procedure call to your own options-setting procedure:

  ```
  MsgBox "Place code here to set options and close dialog!"
  ```

- Modify the `Form_KeyDown()` event procedure to handle the focus order the dialog box supports as the user presses Ctrl+Tab. This code isn't trivial because you must determine exactly how the focus changes from control to control with programming statements.

Note

> The `tbsOptions_Click()` event procedure shows the appropriate page (and hides the other pages) in the TabStrip control as the program runs.

You can also practice adding template forms by using the Application Wizard to add a template form to an application. To do so, create a new project and run the Application Wizard. Accept the application's default values until you get to the Standard Forms dialog box. Click all four standard template forms (do not press the Form Templates button to add additional template forms), click Next twice, and then click Finish. Visual Basic builds the application shell while you wait. After the Application Wizard finishes, click OK to read the setup instructions before closing the dialog box.

As you might recall from Day 1, "Welcome to Visual Basic," the Application Wizard creates only a shell of an application. You must fill in the details. Nevertheless, this shell includes every one of the four standard template forms that the Application Wizard offers by default.

Test the application by running it to see how much of the application has already been created for you. Don't enter a password (the default password is blank until you add one to the code module), but you can see that the splash screen grabbed the user's name (*your name* in this case!) from the App object and displayed it automatically in the User Name text box.

The splash screen appears and then goes away quickly before the regular form appears. The About dialog box appears when you choose About from the Help menu, and the Options dialog box appears when you choose Options from the View menu. This project, although only a shell of an application, gives you a lot of good code to study when implementing your own applications that require one or more standard template forms.

The Application Wizard will list your applications among those of the supplied template forms (that is, if you add your own template forms), if you click the Form Templates button on the Application Wizard's screen.

Tip of the Day

Have you ever started software and were greeted with a tip on how to better use that software? Windows 95 offers just such a tip (that is, until you turn off the display option). Every time you start Windows 95, you'll see a different tip. To turn off the tip display, deselect the Show Tips at Startup check box. Figure 15.13 shows the Tip of the Day template form again.

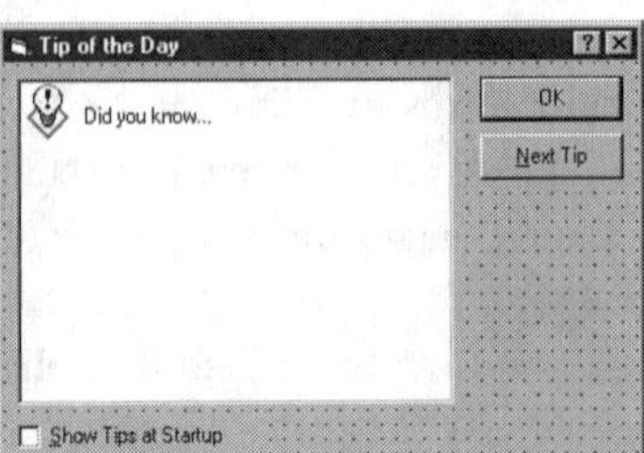

FIGURE 15.13.
A Tip of the Day dialog box can provide help for your program's newcomers.

When you add the Tip of the Day dialog box to a form window, Visual Basic adds the Tip of the Day form to your Forms collection. Depending on your screen size and default font settings, you may have to extend the label that holds the text Show Tips at Startup. Click under the Did You Know label to display the label named `lblTipText`. This text box holds the tips that you display.

The code inside the form module sets up the form to display a daily tip each time a user starts the application. The following guidelines help you understand the requirements of the Tip of the Day dialog box:

- The dialog box's code creates a new collection called `Tips`. The procedure grabs the startup tips from this collection.
- Obviously, the `Tips` collection needs to read the tips from a file you create and supply with the project. The file should hold one tip per line.
- The code loads the filename in the named constant `TIP_FILE` in the `LoadTips()` function. The procedure uses the `Add` method to add each tip to the collection as the file data is read. Your only real job is to create this tip file by using a text editor such as Windows Notepad.
- The `DoNextTip()` procedure randomly selects a tip from the collection and displays it by using a special method named `DisplayCurrentTip` (which is actually a subroutine procedure located at the bottom of the code).
- The most technical part of the code is the shortest. It's located in the procedure named `chkLoadTipsAtStartup()`. Fortunately, Microsoft supplies this code. The code uses the `SaveSetting` command to change your system Registry. The `SaveSetting` command, in this case, stores the value that determines whether the user wants to see startup tips. If the user deselects the check box labeled Show Tips At Startup, the Registry is updated accordingly and the code won't display tips in subsequent sessions.

The Tip of the Day template form is perhaps the most common of the remaining template forms described today. Follow these steps to practice setting up a Tip of the Day dialog box on your system:

1. Start the Windows Notepad editor. Create a file named Tipofday.txt (the default filename used by the tip's dialog box) and store this file in your application's directory. After you enter the following contents, save the file and exit Notepad:

```
Brush your teeth daily and your shoes weekly.
Save money for retirement (nobody else cares as much as you).
Plenty of sleep is a great cure for insomnia.
Read a good book before you see the movie.
Don't drive recklessly or carelessly; drive flawlessly.
Exercise more often than you eat desserts.
Don't gloss over you teeth, floss over them.
```

2. Create a new application and display the standard form window. Before doing anything else, save the form and project in the same application directory as you saved the tip file. If these files aren't in the same directory, the code won't be able to locate your tips.
3. From the Project menu choose Add Form; then select the Tip of the Day form.
4. Change the label's `Caption` property from `Did you know...` to `Be sure to....`
5. Run the application to see the results.

Where did the Tip of the Day dialog box go? Although you've set up the tip file and added the Tip of the Day dialog box to your application, you must remember that Visual Basic first displays your project's primary form (called Form1, unless you change it) at startup. You must set the Tip of the Day form for the initial form's startup and set up the code to display your regular form when the user closes the Tip of the Day dialog box.

From the Project menu choose Properties and then set the Startup Object to frmTip. Click OK to close the dialog box. The application is now set to display the Tip of the Day dialog box when the user runs the application.

You must connect the regular form (named Form1 still) to the Tip of the Day dialog box form module so that the regular form appears when the Tip of the Day dialog box disappears.Change the `cmdOK_Click()` procedure as follows:

```
Private Sub cmdOK_Click()
    Unload Me     ' Unloads the tip dialog box
    Form1.Show    ' Show the regular form
End Sub
```

You must attend to one more item. If the user decides not to see the tips in subsequent startup sessions, there's no way now for the tip's form module to display the regular form. Therefore, add the `Form1.Show` statement to the `Form_Load()` procedure as follows:

```
Private Sub Form_Load()
    Dim ShowAtStartup As Long

    ' See if we should be shown at startup
    ShowAtStartup = GetSetting(App.EXEName, "Options", _
    "Show Tips at Startup", 1)
    If ShowAtStartup = 0 Then
        Unload Me
        Form1.Show   ' Show the regular form   ** New statement
        Exit Sub
    End If     ' Rest of code is not shown here
```

You now can run the application and read the tips randomly by clicking the Next Tip command button. When you click OK, the regular form appears, although the form is blank and boring because you've added nothing to it. If a user decides not to see the tips in subsequent sessions, the application will show the regular Form1 form at startup.

You can set up the application to display the tip or the regular startup form in other ways, as well. For example, if you add proper `Show` methods to a subroutine procedure named `Main`, you can add this `Main` subroutine to the startup object.

The ODBC Logon Dialog Box

ODBC provides a standard command set for accessing different kinds of data stored on different kinds of computers. The ODBC standard enables your program to access data that it otherwise wouldn't be able to access. ODBC's goal is to let a number of different types of systems access data stored elsewhere.

Figure 15.14 shows the template form that appears when you insert the ODBC Logon form on your form window.

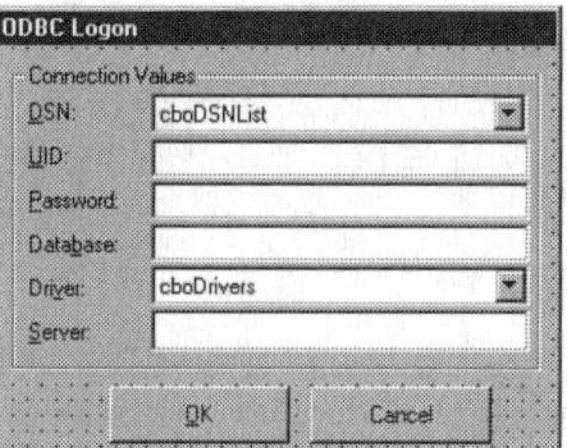

FIGURE 15.14.
The ODBC Logon template form lets you set up external database access.

The ODBC Logon dialog box can be added to your application so that users can select and access an ODBC database source. The source indicates the location and type of data the application is to access. Table 15.1 describes each ODBC field.

TABLE 15.1. THE ODBC LOGON DIALOG BOX'S TEXT BOXES SPECIFY ODBC OPTIONS.

Name	*Description*
DSN	The data source name. This option lists (in a drop-down list box) the currently registered ODBC sources in the user's system Registry.
UID	The user ID that supplies the connection with the user's identification so that the ODBC database can validate the user's access.
Password	The user's password to access the system.

continues

TABLE 15.1. CONTINUED

Name	*Description*
Database	The name of the database to connect to.
Driver	A drop-down list box that lists all the drivers on the system and lets the user register a new ODBC driver.
Server	The name of the server supplying the database if the DSN isn't available.

The code necessary to connect the ODBC Logon dialog box's values to the proper ODBC-compatible database is fairly extensive. You must understand the ODBC commands necessary to connect to the outside database. Such commands are beyond the scope of this book, because Visual Basic programmers rarely have to resort to such routines, except in system-related applications.

Adding Your Own Form Templates

Adding your own forms to Visual Basic's collection of template forms is easy to do. After you've created a form that you want to add to the template form collection, save the form in the \Templates\Forms folder. In all subsequent lists, including the Application Wizard's template form list, your form will appear along with the others.

Add forms to the template form folder that are general and do not have a lot of detail, unless you want that detail to appear in the forms you create from the template form.

To remove a form you've added to the template form folder, start Windows Explorer and traverse to the \Templates\Forms folder. Select and delete the form. The next time you display a list of template forms (from the Application Wizard's template form screen, for example), the form will no longer appear in the list.

Summary

Today's lesson explained how to use the template forms to standardize your applications and speed program development and accuracy. The template forms include several standard forms that programmers often add to Windows applications. Your users will appreciate seeing standardized forms in your applications.

Form templates are general-purpose forms that you can add to any project. The template forms contain placeholders for text and graphics that you can change once you load the template form into your project. Your application will control the display of the form and interact with the template form's code.

Tomorrow's lesson begins a two-day study of objects and how they relate to Visual Basic programming.

Q&A

Q Why should I make my template forms general?

A By making your template forms as general as possible (keeping only detail that won't change from application to application), you make generating new forms from these template forms easier. In today's lesson, you've seen several template forms that Visual Basic supplies. Most of the text on these template forms are text placeholders so that you know where to customize the form.

Workshop

The Workshop provides quiz questions to help you solidify your understanding of the material covered and exercises to provide you with experience in using what you've learned. Try to understand the quiz and exercise answers before continuing to the next chapter. Answers are provided at the end of today's lesson.

Quiz

1. What is the purpose of the template forms?
2. Describe two ways to add template forms to applications.
3. Describe the code needed to connect the About dialog box to your project.
4. True/False. You must write the code to display system information if a user clicks the About dialog box's System Info command button.
5. What's the difference between a splash screen and your regular form?
6. Would you consider the Tip of the Day dialog box to be a splash screen?
7. What's the purpose of the `SaveSetting` command?
8. What does ODBC stand for and what is its purpose?
9. What must you do in the Properties dialog box before your application can properly display a splash screen or a Tip of the Day dialog box?
10. Describe the format of the tip file required by the Tip of the Day dialog box.

Exercises

1. Follow the recommendation described earlier in the Login dialog box section that turns the Login dialog box's code into a better set of routines. Replace the global variable with local variables.
2. Create an application that displays a different PC tip every time the application starts. (You can modify the tip file described in today's lesson.) Add a menu option to the regular form to make the tips appear again at startup. *Hint:* Check out the `chkLoadTipsAtStartup_Click()` procedure and use the `SaveSetting` command to reset the tips. Although you haven't mastered `SaveSetting`, you have all the tools you need to complete this project quickly.

WEEK 3

DAY 16

Objects and Visual Basic

Today's lesson shows you how to work with objects in Visual Basic. You've already worked with some objects when you handled forms, controls, and the `Printer` object. Today's lesson extends that knowledge of objects. You'll learn a new control called the *OLE control*, which lets you use objects from outside Visual Basic's environment.

In addition, you'll learn more about Visual Basic's predefined objects, such as the `Screen` and `App` objects. These predefined objects send information to your applications that you can use to make decisions as well as to post titles and user information on the form. Once you learn how to use predefined objects, you'll learn how to work with collections of those objects.

Today, you learn the following:

- About the OLE control
- About the differences between object linking and object embedding
- How to place other applications' objects inside your own application
- About in-place activation

- How to use control arrays
- How to manage collections
- How to use the Object Browser

OLE for Outside Objects

OLE is a familiar term to Windows users and programmers. You can embed OLE objects into your applications to enhance the power of your program as well as reduce coding. By using OLE objects that are already defined by other applications, you take advantage of object reuse.

NEW TERM *OLE* stands for *object linking and embedding*. Many Windows applications offer their data as OLE objects, and you can embed such objects inside other Windows applications that support OLE.

> **Note** ActiveX technology is quickly replacing OLE technology. As a matter of fact, Microsoft calls ActiveX controls "former OLE controls." Nevertheless, OLE is still vital. Many Visual Basic applications still use the OLE control, as proven by Microsoft's decision to keep the OLE control among the default, intrinsic tools on the toolbox window. OLE makes a great introduction to ActiveX technology, so today's lesson is not only important on its own, it also offers an excellent introduction to tomorrow's lesson, "ActiveX Controls," which teaches about ActiveX-based objects.

The bottom-line reason for using OLE is that you can employ outside objects in the applications you write. The OLE control on your toolbox window maintains the OLE connection to your project's OLE object. Your users can take advantage of *in-place activation* when accessing embedded OLE objects.

NEW TERM *In-place activation* refers to the ability to edit an object inside a Visual Basic application using the object's parent application's menus and commands. Once you embed an OLE object in an application, you don't have to write menu options that guide the user in editing the OLE object—the original application's menus will automatically appear for the user.

Linking and Embedding

The OLE control either holds a link to an object or is an embedded object, depending on how you set up the control. When you link to another application, your OLE control (the *container control*) contains a link to another application's document. If the other application changes that document, your application will reflect the changes. The object is known as a *persistent object*, because you can keep the object's contents up-to-date via the link.

NEW TERM A *container control* is an OLE control that holds an outside application's data object.

NEW TERM A *persistent object* is an object outside your project that does not go away just because your application ends.

When you embed an OLE data object into your application, your OLE container control contains a copy of the object document that was created in the other OLE-compliant application. However, no links are maintained between your application and the original OLE object. Therefore, if the original application changes the object, your application won't reflect that change, because your application has a copy of the object.

Here's how the two kinds of OLE activities affect your project:

- If you link an object to your application's OLE control, Visual Basic actually starts the other object's application when the user attempts to use or change the object by double-clicking it. The user will choose the File, Close and Return to Visual Basic Application menu option when he or she finishes working with the object.
- If you embed an object into your application's OLE control, the object is part of your application, because it does reside inside your application.

Using the OLE Control

Open a new application and double-click the OLE control to add it to the form window. A large white box appears on the form for a moment and then the Insert Object dialog box, shown in Figure 16.1, appears. Other controls, such as the common dialog box control, produce dialog boxes when you click the Custom Properties window entry. The OLE control is the only control that pops up a dialog box as soon as you place the control on the form.

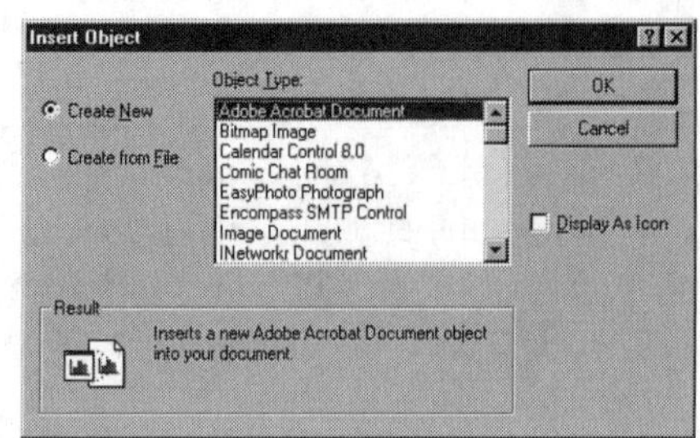

FIGURE 16.1.

The Insert Object dialog box contains all registered OLE applications on your system.

The Object Type list box contains the OLE-compliant application controls you have to select from. The list varies according to the software installed on your system. An application updates your Windows Registry database with its OLE objects when you install the application. Normally, one shrink-wrapped Windows application can yield two, three, or more custom controls. For example, if you have PowerPoint 97 installed, you'll find two PowerPoint controls in the list.

The Create New option lets you specify an application that can create the kind of object you want to embed. If, instead, the other application's data object already exists, you can click the Create from File option to display the Insert Object dialog box (see Figure 16.2). From the Insert Object dialog box, you can either embed the existing object or click the Link option to add a pointer to the object.

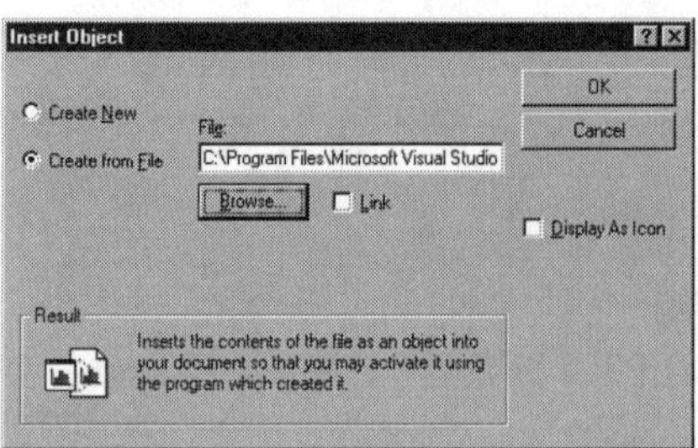

FIGURE 16.2.

You can embed or link an existing object into your OLE control.

Suppose you want to give your users a chance to create notes inside an application. The notes might relate to a customer record. You have a few options:

- Let the user enter the notes in a simple text box control.

- Improve upon the text box concept by writing a keystroke-capturing routine that analyzes the user's keystrokes and turns the simple text box into a full-fledged word processor that formats text and supports rulers and margins. (This would take quite a long time to write.)
- Embed an OLE-based WordPad document object.

Obviously, the last option sounds good, because you can give your users the power of a word processor and yet you don't have to write any code to handle word-processing commands: WordPad's already written. Not everybody has Microsoft Word on their system, but WordPad comes with all versions of Windows (starting with Windows 95). Therefore, your users will have access to WordPad, which allows them to perform in-place activation on the object.

To embed a WordPad document, follow these steps:

1. After inserting the OLE control on the form, select the Create New option (the default).
2. Scroll the Object Type list until you see WordPad Document.
3. Double-click the WordPad Document option to embed a WordPad document object in your application. You'll see part of the WordPad ruler above the OLE control, as shown in Figure 16.3.

FIGURE 16.3.

The OLE control now has a WordPad object.

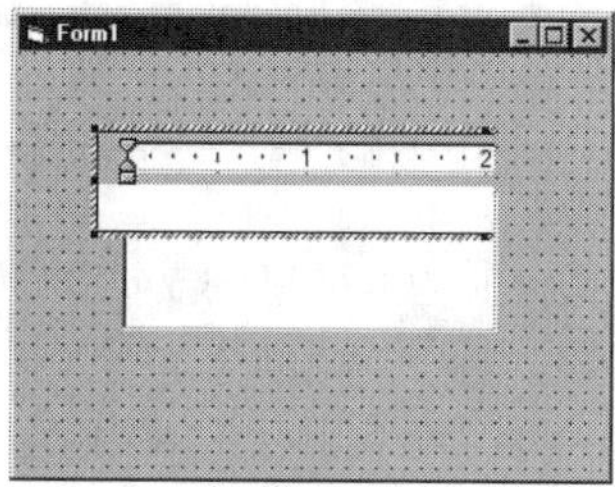

4. Change the OLE control's `SizeMode` property to `1-Stretch` to fit the WordPad object to the OLE control's size and width.
5. Increase the form's `Width` and `Height` to `6945` and `5670`, respectively.
6. Set the following properties for the OLE control:

```
Height: 3375
Left: 840
Top: 1080
Width: 5055
```

You could add extras to this project and provide a better name for the form, but don't worry about it right now.

7. Run the application. When the application starts, nothing special seems to happen except that the OLE control's outline appears in the center of the form.
8. Double-click the OLE control. Voilà! As Figure 16.4 shows, a lot happens when you double-click the control. A menu appears (due to the in-place activation of the embedded WordPad document) as well as a ruler.

FIGURE 16.4.
You've got a word processor in the middle of your Visual Basic application!

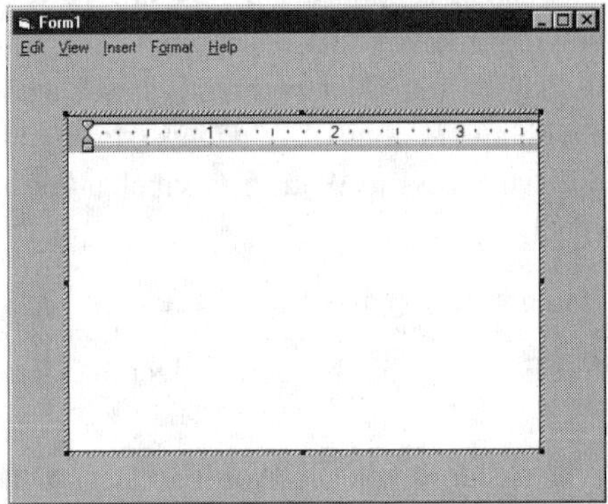

Note

Several other ways exist for activating the OLE object. For example, OLE activation could occur simply by the OLE object getting the focus. The `AutoActivate` property controls how the object activates. The default value for `AutoActivate` is `2-DoubleClick`.

9. Type something and use the menus to format what you type. All of WordPad's options are available within your Visual Basic application.
10. Close your application.

Caution

Nothing saves your WordPad typing! When you close the Visual Basic application, the WordPad document goes away and is never saved. Neither Visual Basic nor WordPad even warns you that your document hasn't been saved! Saving the document is one of *your* jobs as the programmer. Note that the WordPad in-place menus that appear do *not* include the usual File menu option.

Saving Object Contents

Microsoft recommends that you save and load changed embedded objects using one of several file-saving methods. Your application is responsible for holding the embedded object, so the source application really has no jurisdiction over saving the object's content inside your application.

Use the `SaveToFile` method when saving your OLE container control data. Suppose you want to offer a command button for saving changes made to an object. Listing 16.1 shows sample code that saves changes in a special binary file. A binary file is more limiting than the sequential or random-access files that you learned about in Day 12, "Interact with Files." Nevertheless, binary files provide a fast and efficient method for storing objects, as long as you later read objects in the same order you save them.

LISTING 16.1. SAVING YOUR OLE CONTAINER CONTROL OBJECT TO DISK.

```
Dim intFileNum as Integer

' Get next free file number
intFileNum = FreeFile

' Open output file
Open "TEST.OLE" For Binary As #intFileNum

' Save file
oleObj1.SaveToFile intFileNum

' Close the file
Close
```

During subsequent runs of your application, it should read the object's latest values (from the previous run) into the OLE container control by using the `ReadFromFile` method shown in Listing 16.2.

LISTING 16.2. READING THE OLE CONTAINER CONTROL'S OBJECT CONTENTS SAVED ON THE PREVIOUS RUN.

```
Dim intFileNum as Integer

' Get next free file number
intFileNum = FreeFile

' Open input file
```

continues

LISTING 16.2. CONTINUED

```
Open "TEST.OLE" For Binary As #intFileNum

' Read file into object
oleObj1.ReadFromFile intFileNum

' Close the file
Close
```

You can place the reading and saving code in event procedures linked to command buttons or menu items. Again, your application, not the OLE application, is responsible for saving and loading the data. The OLE application, however, takes care of all other tasks related to the object.

Working with Objects

Perhaps you've heard the term *object-oriented programming*, sometimes called *OOP*. Visual Basic is not a strict OOP language, although it does support objects in many ways. After today's lesson, you'll have a better understanding of Visual Basic objects, and you'll better understand how objects relate to arrays and collections.

NEW TERM *Object-oriented programming*, or *OOP*, is programming with data items that represent objects that have methods and properties not unlike Visual Basic objects. True OOP contains objects that can inherit from other objects. Visual Basic does not fully and accurately support the OOP model, although in practical use, Visual Basic does seem to fulfill the ultimate goals of OOP better than just about any true OOP language has done.

The following sections describe non-OLE objects. You'll learn how to hone your programming skills to take advantage of control arrays and object collections.

NEW TERM A *control array* is an array of controls you access via subscripts.

Programming with Objects

In Day 8's lesson, "The Nature of VB Programs," you learned how to use the `If TypeOf` statement to test for an object's form. Today's lesson further explains what `If TypeOf` does—it actually determines an object's *class*. If you're new to objects and classes (these terms are used in other programming languages, especially object-oriented languages), you'll learn all you need to know today.

An *object* can be just about anything in Visual Basic. You've already worked with objects such as controls, forms, and the `Printer` object. Also, you passed the Object data type to a procedure in Day 13 "Printing VB Output." You already know that *control objects* contain properties, methods, and events. The controls contain code and data items. In a way, an object—such as the command button control—is like a package handed to you by the Visual Basic developers. You don't have to write code to trigger a command button, declare variables that describe how a command button looks or what caption it has, or write code to perform work with a command button. The encapsulated command button methods do all the work for you.

16

NEW TERM Objects are *encapsulated*. Like a capsule that contains medicine or lunar astronauts, an object encapsulates methods, events, and properties. This encapsulation lets you work with objects from a higher perspective than if you had to write all the code needed to support the objects. A class defines the behavior and appearance of the objects it contains.

The Object Class

Objects not only bring encapsulation to your programming fingertips, but they are also part of an object hierarchy called an object *class*. The benefit of a class is that all objects in the class share the same features. (A single object is said to be an *instance* of the class.)

> **Note:** You can create your own objects. By making them part of an existing class, your objects automatically gain, or *inherit*, many properties, methods, and events from that class.

When you test an object with `If TypeOf`, Visual Basic returns the object's class. Therefore, the following line of code returns `True` or `False`, depending on whether the object named `myObj` is a part of the `CommandButton` class:

```
If TypeOf myObj Is CommandButton  ' Check the class
```

Visual Basic also supports the `TypeOf()` function, which returns the class name. For example, `TypeOf(myObj)` might return `CommandButton` or `Form`.

Classes make programming with objects more flexible than would be possible without the class structure. For example, the `With...End With` statement lets you easily assign multiple properties for a single object. Notice the following code's redundancy:

```
chkMaster.Caption = "Primary Source"
chkMaster.Alignment = vbLeftJustify
chkMaster.Enabled = True
chkMaster.Font.Bold = False
chkMaster.Left = 1000
chkMaster.RightToLeft = False
chkMaster.Top = 400
```

When you enclose an object inside a `With...End With` block, you can eliminate the repetition of the object name. The following code is identical to the previous code:

```
With chkMaster
  .Caption = "Primary Source"
  .Alignment = vbLeftJustify
  .Enabled = True
  .Font.Bold = False
  .Left = 1000
  .RightToLeft = False
  .Top = 400
End With
```

Note

Using `With...End With` for two or three property settings requires more typing than using straight assignments. When you need to assign more than three properties, however, the `With` clause is an appealing coding statement, because it requires less typing and is easier to maintain if you add properties and require more assignments later.

If you think you'll set additional properties in future versions of the program, you may want to go ahead and use the `With` clause with only one or two properties.

The System Objects

Unlike the objects you declare, *system objects* are the `Printer` and `App` objects you've already used in this book. Although you can't pass system objects (they're already global in nature), you can treat them much like the objects you create. System objects represent specific elements of your application.

Table 16.1 describes the system objects and lists some important methods you can apply to them.

TABLE 16.1. SYSTEM OBJECTS SUPPORT SEVERAL METHODS.

System Object	*Methods*	*Description*
`App`		The current application.
	`EXEName`	Returns the application's filename.
	`Path`	Returns the application's path.
	`Title`	Returns the primary startup form's title bar text.
	`PrevInstance`	Returns `True` or `False`, indicating whether another copy of the application is now running.
`Clipboard`		The Windows Clipboard region.
	`Clear`	Erases the Clipboard.
	`GetData`	Returns the graphic image stored on the Clipboard.
	`GetFormat`	Returns the format of the Clipboard object.
	`GetText`	Returns the text from the Clipboard.
	`SetData`	Copies a graphic image to the Clipboard.
	`SetText`	Copies text to the Clipboard.
	`SelStart`	Used for Clipboard selection operations.
	`SelLength`	Used for Clipboard selection operations.
	`SelText`	Used for Clipboard selection operations.
`Debug`		The Immediate window.
	`Print`	Copies information at runtime to the Immediate window (only possible in non-EXE Visual Basic programs that are run from the development environment).

continues

Table 16.1. continued

System Object	Methods	Description
`Err`		Holds information about current error status of an application.
		Key property `Number` holds an error code that corresponds to the most recent system error. (Holds zero if no error has occurred.)
`Printer`		The system printer. Day 13 introduced the methods of the `Printer` object and demonstrated how they provide printer support.
`Screen`		The user's screen.
	`FontCount`	Returns the number of fonts the current screen supports.
	`Fonts`	Contains a list of all the screen's possible font names.
	`Height`	Returns the height of the screen area in twips.
	`MousePointer`	Holds the shape of the mouse cursor or determines its shape if you specify a new mouse cursor.
	`TwipsPerPixelX`	Returns the number of possible horizontal twips.
	`TwipsPerPixelY`	Returns the number of possible vertical twips.
	`Width`	Returns the width of the screen in twips.

You've worked with most of the system objects—especially the `Printer` and `Screen` objects—before today's lesson. The `App` object is useful for determining runtime information about the program path and filename, and the `Clipboard` object provides some interesting functionality you may want to use. Also, the `Debug` object lets you interact with your program during testing to help get the bugs out.

Depending on your application's needs, the `Clipboard` object is relatively simple to program. The `Clipboard` object is the same Clipboard Windows uses; therefore, your application can copy or cut information to the `Clipboard` object, and users can paste that information in another Windows application. Also, your application can paste information that's contained in the Windows Clipboard into the `Clipboard` object.

You can use the `Clipboard` object and its properties to select text from within your program and to determine the text selected by users. For example, the `SelStart` property marks the starting position of the selection cursor in the text box (or whatever control receives the selection). A value of `0` for `SelStart` places the cursor before the first character. `SelLength` determines how many characters are selected for Clipboard work. If you select text by setting `SelStart` and `SelLength` values, that text goes to the `Clipboard` object when a user presses Ctrl+C (copy) or Ctrl+X (cut). `SelText` is a string that contains the selected text you've bounded with `SelStart` and `SelLength`.

If you've selected text in a text box control (or you've asked a user to select text), that text appears in the `SelText` string value. You can clear the `Clipboard` object of its current value (the `Clipboard` object can hold only one value at a time) and send the selected text to the Clipboard with the following code:

```
Clipboard.Clear    ' Erase current Clipboard
Clipboard.SetText txtName.SelText   ' Copy text
```

If you want to copy the Clipboard text into a variable, you can use `GetText()`, like this:

```
strInfo = Clipboard.GetText()
```

If you want to replace selected text in a control with the text in the `Clipboard` object, you can do so this way:

```
txtName.SelText = Clipboard.GetText()
```

The `GetText()` method sometimes uses arguments, and it requires parentheses even if you specify no arguments. For text-based Clipboard work, you don't need to supply any arguments.

Object and Control Arrays

One of the most interesting things you can do with objects is to declare an array of objects. For example, you can declare an array of command buttons or forms. Moreover, these objects don't even have to exist. For example, you don't have to declare all forms at design time, because you can still create an array of forms at runtime.

You already know about the `Forms` and `Printers` collections. Visual Basic also supports the `Controls` collection, which lets you step through all your controls as though they were array variables. For example, the following code hides all controls:

```
For intCtr = 0 to Controls.Count - 1
  Controls(intCtr).Visible = False
Next intCtr
```

If your application contains multiple forms, you can hide all controls on all forms by using a nested loop (notice that `For Each` eliminates the `Count - 1` requirement):

```
Dim frmAForm As Form
Dim ctlAControl As Control
For Each frmAForm In Forms    ' Step through all forms
  For Each ctlAControl In frmAForm.Controls
    ctlAControl.Visible = False
  Next ctlAControl
Next frmAForm
```

A menu is considered a control in the `Controls` collection. In many situations, you'll want to omit the menu controls in such a loop by testing with the `TypeOf()` function to determine whether the control is a `Menu` object before setting its visibility to `False`.

The `Controls` collection holds all controls on your current form; however, you can declare a control array to hold one specific type of control. You declare an array of controls as follows:

```
Dim ctlManyLabels(1 To 4) As Label
```

The next section discusses collections further. Collections work a lot like arrays in that you can access individual elements in the collections just as you can with arrays. You might want to create an array of objects, such as forms and controls. Rather than create the objects at design time, you can create the objects in an array as follows (notice the `New` keyword):

```
Dim frmArray(1 To 10) As New frmFirstForm
```

This `Dim` statement assumes that one form, `frmFirstForm`, exists. After the declaration, 10 new forms exist, subscripted from `frmArray(1)` to `frmArray(10)`. Subsequent code can then change the form properties of the forms in the array to make each form different from the base form, named `frmFirstForm`.

None of these forms will appear until you invoke their `Show` methods.

Suppose you want to decrease the font size of a form's controls if a user resizes a maximized form. You can use the `Controls` collection to decrease the font size of all controls:

```
Private Sub Form_Resize ()
  ' Decrease all the controls' font size
  Dim intCtr As Integer
  For intCtr = 0 to Controls.Count - 1
    Controls(intCtr).FontSize = Controls(intCtr).FontSize * .75
  Next intCtr
End Sub
```

Each control's font size will now be 25 percent smaller than it was before the user resized the form.

You won't see many Visual Basic programmers using control arrays when a collection exists for the same object (Visual Basic supplies a `Forms` predefined collection). If you want to use control arrays, however, you have to declare memory to hold the array contents and to initialize the arrays.

Visual Basic supports one technique for control arrays that you'll find yourself using a lot, even though collections are always available to you. When you copy a control and paste that control back onto the form, Visual Basic displays the message box shown in Figure 16.5.

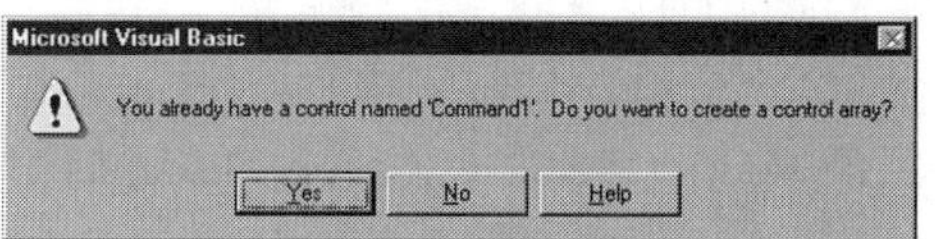

FIGURE 16.5.
Visual Basic will create a control array for you.

You might wonder why you'd ever copy and paste a control, but if you need to place several command buttons or labels that all have the same format—perhaps the same font size and caption alignment—it's a helpful technique. You just create one control, set all its properties, copy that control to the Clipboard, and then paste the Clipboard contents onto the form to add as many controls as you need.

As soon as you paste the copied control, Visual Basic displays the message box shown in Figure 16.5. If you answer Yes, Visual Basic automatically creates a control array with a name that matches the first control. For example, if the first control is a command button named Command1, the array is named `Command1`, and the elements begin at `Command1(0)` and increment as long as you keep pasting the control.

Your code then can step through all the control array elements from `Command1(0)` through `Command1(`*n*`)`, where *n* is the total number of `Command1` controls on the form, and set properties for them.

Collections

Collections play a vital role in Visual Basic programming, as you've seen in earlier lessons as well as in the preceding sections. Collections are always present, and Visual Basic updates them automatically; for example, if you add a form at runtime with the `New Form` declaration, Visual Basic updates the `Forms` collection's `Count` property accordingly.

Without a doubt, the predefined collections are helpful. So, why not create your own? Visual Basic lets you create your own collections. However, if you create a collection, you'll need to manage the collection yourself—this takes more effort than managing predefined collections.

As you learned in the previous sections, all objects belong to a class. If you know something about a class, you know something about all objects within that class. For example, if a control is a member of the `CommandButton` class, you know that the control supports the `Click` event, because all `CommandButton` class members support the `Click` event.

Your own collections must be objects of the `Collection` class. You define collections at the module level by using the `Private` or `Public` keyword, depending on the range of procedures that need access to your collection. The following statement declares a collection named `colMyCol`:

```
Private colMyCol As New Collection
```

A collection works like an empty bookcase. You can add objects (such as books), remove objects, count objects, and so on. Of course, a bookcase can hold more than just books. However, a collection can hold only one kind of item, but you can declare multiple collections that each hold different kinds of items. Here are the methods your collections can access:

- `Add`—Adds an item to your collection
- `Count`—Returns the number of items in your collection
- `Item`—Serves as an index number for the items in your collection
- `Remove`—Removes an item from your collection

As Listing 16.3 shows, Visual Basic takes care of updating `Count` as well as adding items to your collections. The code in Listing 16.3 creates a collection named `Cities` and adds four items (city names) to the collection.

LISTING 16.3. USING `Add` TO ADD ITEMS TO YOUR NEW COLLECTION.

```
Dim Cities As New Collection
Dim intCtr As Integer

' Add items
Cities.Add "Tulsa"
Cities.Add "Miami"
Cities.Add "New York"
Cities.Add "Seattle"

' Show that there are four cities
frmMyForm.Print "There are"; Cities.Count; " cities:"

' Print each city name
For intCtr = 1 To Cities.Count
  frmMyForm.Print "  "; Cities(intCtr)
Next
```

If you run this code, the following output appears on the form:

```
There are 4 cities:
  Tulsa
  Miami
  New York
  Seattle
```


This lesson only scratches the surface of the power of collections. Nevertheless, you should know that you can insert items into and remove items from your collections easily and in whatever order you prefer. Remember that each item in the collection contains a subscript, starting at `1`, that you use to reference a particular item. In the preceding example, `Cities(1)` is the first city listed in the collection named `Cities`. Remember that your collection index value begins at `1`, not `0` (as the control arrays require).

You can use a *named argument* (an argument in which you include the argument name followed by the named argument assignment operator, `:=`) named `Before` to add items to a collection at the exact location you want. The following line adds a city to the beginning of the `Cities` collection, no matter how many cities reside in the collection to begin with:

```
Cities.Add "St. Louis", Before:=1
```

A `Before` position of `1` adds the items to the front of the collection. In other words, Visual Basic inserts the new item *before* the specified indexed item in the collection. If you included this `Add` method statement at the end of the code shown earlier, the output would change to this:

```
There are 5 cities:
  St. Louis
  Tulsa
  Miami
  New York
  Seattle
```

If you added the code line without the `Before:=1` named argument, St. Louis would appear at the end of the collection.

You can remove specific items by using the `Remove` method. As you remove items, the remaining subscripts adjust so that they always begin at `1`. The following statement removes the second item (Tulsa) from the collection:

```
Cities.Remove 2
```

The Object Browser

As your Visual Basic knowledge improves, your need for better tools grows. Visual Basic includes a tool called the Object Browser, which lets you inspect variables, controls, and other objects throughout your application. Visual Basic programmers new to the Object Browser often use it much more than they think they will, because its features make programming with Visual Basic much simpler.

The *Object Browser* helps you locate and manage objects within your applications.

The Object Browser is a comprehensive online reference—but it's not online in the same sense as the Online Help reference. The Object Browser gives you a one-stop location to hunt for objects and object information. It also enables you to jump directly to the code you need to work with next.

The Object Browser describes your application's *type libraries*, which are the repositories of your class information. You can use the Object Browser to access all object properties, events, and methods for your application, including objects you've created.

The Object Browser Window

When you first choose Object Browser from the View menu or click the toolbar's Object Browser button, you'll see the Object Browser window (see Figure 16.6). You may have to expand your window as well as close the Properties window and toolbox to see the full Object Browser.

Table 16.2 describes the parts of the Object Browser window.

TABLE 16.2. THE OBJECT BROWSER WINDOW INCLUDES SEVERAL ITEMS YOU SHOULD BE FAMILIAR WITH.

Component	*Description*
Project/Library list box	Describes the source of the objects you want to browse. (You'll generally browse the <All Libraries> option, but you can browse, for example, the objects in a particular project by selecting your project's name.)
Search text	Lets you enter an object, event method, or property to search for.

Component	*Description*
Maneuver controls	Used to jump back and forth along a browsing path you've previously traveled.
Classes	Holds the class names from the project or library you've selected.
Members	Contains the members for the class you've selected.

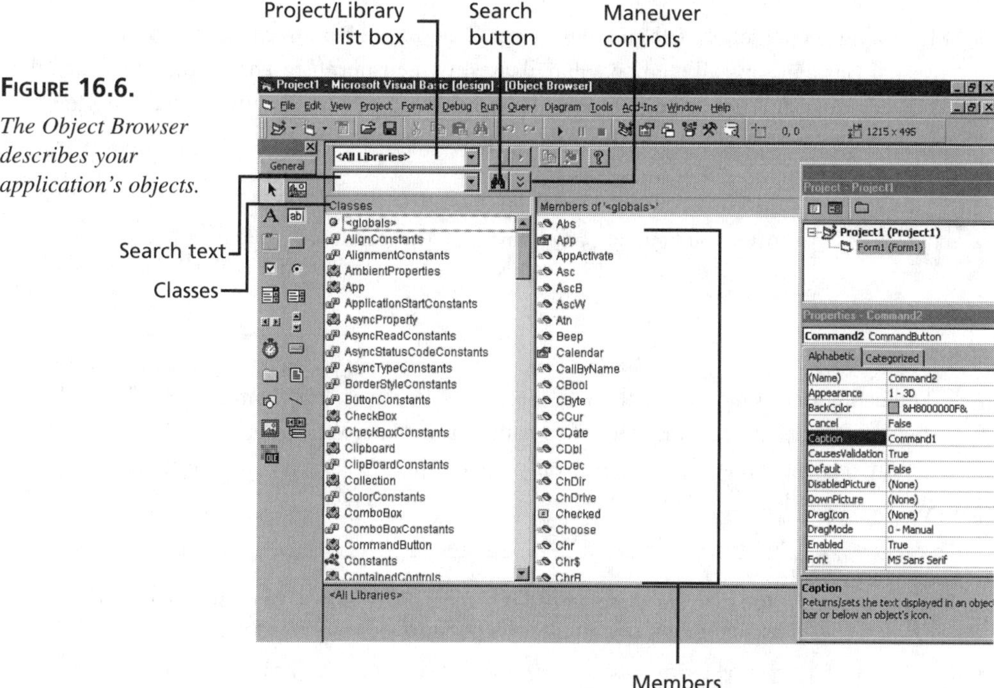

FIGURE 16.6.
The Object Browser describes your application's objects.

Traversing the Object Browser

The Object Browser contains much of the same information as the online Help system. The Object Browser, however, specifically targets you as a Visual Basic programmer and offers the information you need succinctly. For example, the <globals> entry in the Classes list describes all of Visual Basic's built-in functions. Scroll down to the Left entry to learn about the `Left()` function.

> **Note**
>
> As you learned in Day 8, the `Left()` function returns the left part of a string.

When you highlight the Left entry, Visual Basic describes the function at the bottom of the Object Browser window. The text not only describes the function's purpose but also shows the function's format. You can tell the nature of each object listed in the Members drop-down list by its icon. The small green icon indicates that the member is a function. You can spot collections (look at the Forms entry) and named constants by their respective icons. Scroll down to see the entire list of named constants that appears below the functions and collections in the Members scrolling list.

If you right-click either list and then select Group Members from the pop-up menu, Visual Basic groups all members and classes by their purpose. Therefore, rather than the named constants appearing in alphabetical order, the Object Browser displays all the named constants together, all the events together, and so on.

After you highlight any entry in an Object Browser window, click the toolbar's Help button (the icon is a question mark) to get Online Help information for that object.

You can get even more specific with the Object Browser. For example, the Classes list contains several entries that reference named constants. When you click the ColorConstants entry, for example, only Visual Basic's named color constants appear in the Members list (see Figure 16.7).

You may use these named constants anywhere in code you need a color. For example, you can set a form's background color like this:

```
frmMyForm.BackColor = vbRed   ' Set form to red
```

Notice that all the controls available in the toolbox also appear in the Classes list. If you click ComboBox, for example, the Object Browser displays all pertinent information for combo boxes, including properties, events, and methods. If you click one of the combo box entries in the Members list, you get a description of that method, event, or property.

Programmers use the Object Browser for many different purposes. Keep in mind that the Object Browser displays object information in an organized manner. In addition to objects, it coordinates all your programming specifics. For example, if you're writing code that takes advantage of the built-in date and time functions, click the Object Browser's Classes entry DateTime. As Figure 16.8 shows, the Members list is updated to show you only those built-in functions related to dates and times.

FIGURE 16.7.

The object search has been narrowed to particular constants.

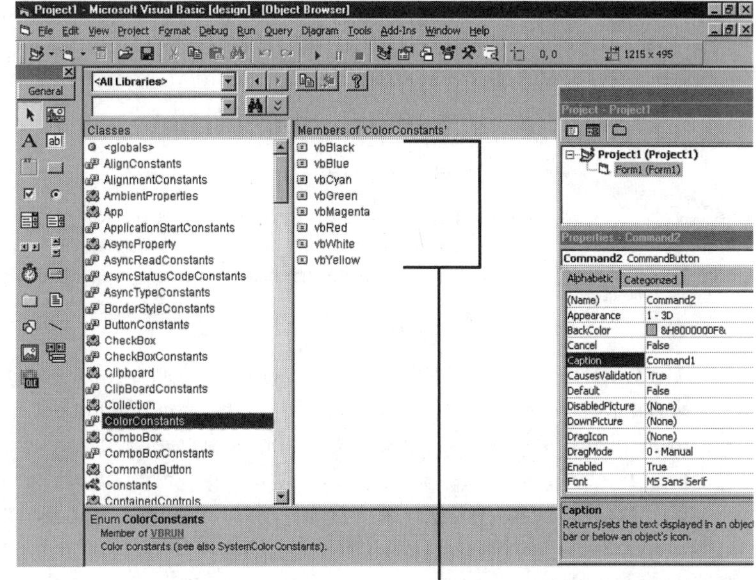

FIGURE 16.8.

Finding the built-in functions for a certain topic is easy.

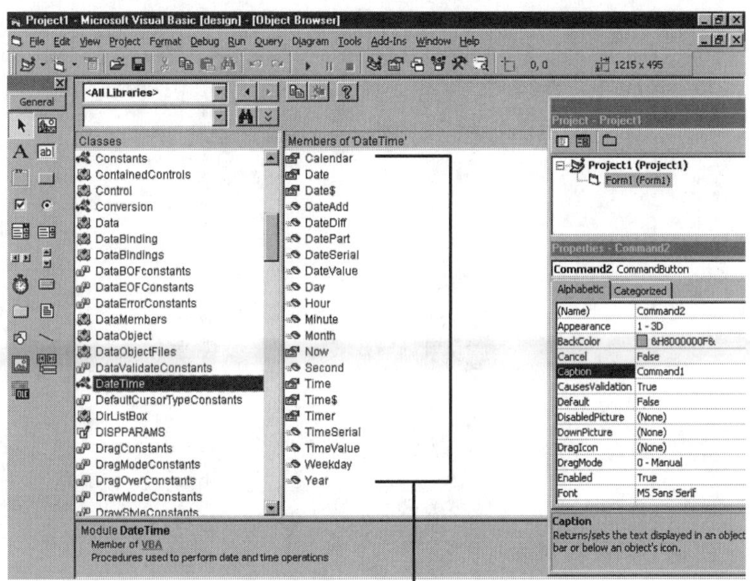

Although these functions are listed in the online Help guide and are also available from other locations in the Object Browser (such as in the <globals> Classes entry), reviewing the group of date and time functions makes programming with those functions simple, because all the functions are referenced in one location.

Remember that the Go Back maneuver button retraces your steps through the Object Browser, so it's easy to move back and forth with the mouse. This action mimics popular Internet browsers in use today.

The Object Browser is very useful for describing your own project. As you add objects, variables, and event procedures to your application, the Object Browser sits in the background filing everything. Figure 16.9 shows the Object Browser with Project1 selected in the Project/Library list. When Form1 (the only placed object in this project so far) is clicked, the Object Browser displays a list of all the event procedures, methods, and properties for that form. Only one entry, `Command1_Click`, is boldfaced, meaning that code has been added only to that event procedure so far.

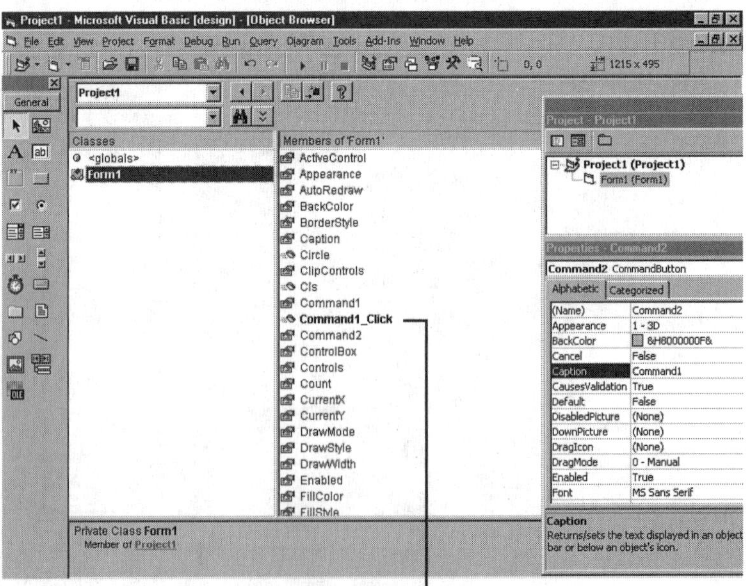

The only event procedure with code

FIGURE 16.9.

The Object Browser shows only active features of the application.

One of the most powerful aspects of the Object Browser is the View Definition option. If you highlight a member that's one of your own objects (such as an event procedure you've written or an object you've declared) and then right-click the object and choose View Definition, Visual Basic jumps directly to the code where you've defined that object! Therefore, you can use the Object Browser to locate specific code within a large application. You don't have to know which project an object was defined in, as long as you can locate the object in the Object Browser.

16

When you search for an item with the Object Browser, you get a list of every reference to that item within your entire application. For example, if you search for `Click`, Visual Basic displays an extra window (see Figure 16.10) that contains every relevant reference in the entire project (and in the entire Visual Basic repertoire, because the <All Libraries> option is selected in the Library/Project drop-down list).

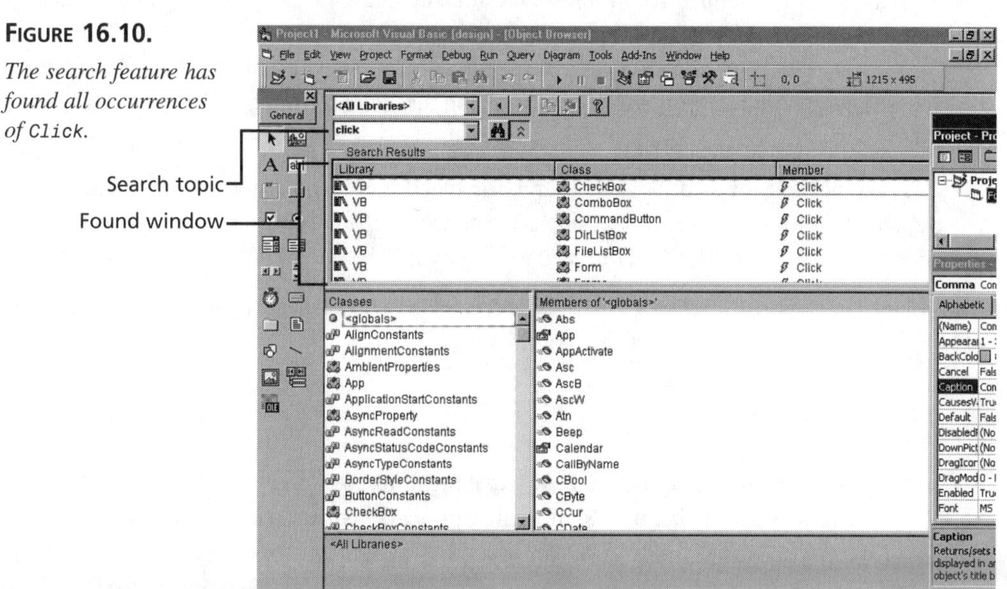

FIGURE 16.10.

The search feature has found all occurrences of `Click`*.*

The `Click` event occurs for several objects, so the Object Browser displays a window that contains every referenced object that supports `Click`. You then narrow the search by clicking the object or project that contains the `Click` event you're looking for.

Summary

Today's lesson was all about objects. You learned how OLE objects work in Visual Basic. The OLE control does nothing on its own except contain objects (or link to objects) from other applications. Once these objects are in place, the user of your application can edit and manipulate them from the other application inside your application. You don't have to write commands to access the other application. OLE objects are smart objects that bring all the editing tools, including menus, with them from the other application.

In addition to collections, Visual Basic allows you to declare control arrays, which often act like object arrays. You can replicate controls on a form so that they all share common features, leaving you the task of changing only the distinguishing features (such as captions or colors). The system objects provide common predefined objects through which your application can interact with resources outside the typical program environment. By accessing the `App` object, your application, at runtime, can determine the path from which the user started the application. The `Clipboard` object lets your application interact with the Windows Clipboard by copying and pasting text to and from the Clipboard area.

To organize things, Visual Basic supplies a tool called the Object Browser, which is basically a repository of data. You can search for specific events, properties, and methods, or you can look for a whole class of objects. The Object Browser even tracks your code for objects you initialize and event procedures you write.

Tomorrow's lesson, "ActiveX Controls," takes objects to their next generation by describing how to use and create ActiveX controls.

Q&A

Q Must my user have the OLE object's original application installed for the OLE object to work in Visual Basic applications that use them?

A Yes, given that in-place automation requires menus and all the features of the original application, your user must have the application installed; otherwise, he or she will be unable to edit the OLE object. Consider the fact that Microsoft Excel, a powerful worksheet system that consumes a lot of disk space and memory to do its job, is OLE compatible. Therefore, you can bring an Excel worksheet into an application that you write, and your user will have all the power of Excel in the middle of your application! Given Excel's size, as well as the menus and features of Excel, it could never come riding into your application on the object itself. Your user must have Excel installed in order to work with an Excel OLE object inside your application. You'll have to clearly state the requirements of your application, including auxiliary programs such as Microsoft Excel, for users to get full use out of your application.

Workshop

The Workshop provides quiz questions to help you solidify your understanding of the material covered and exercises to provide you with experience in using what you've learned. Try to understand the quiz and exercise answers before continuing to the next lesson. Answers are provided in Appendix A, "Answers to Exercises."

Quiz

1. What is the difference between linking and embedding?
2. Which kind of OLE technique, linking or embedding, do you think consumes the most disk space?
3. True/False. Visual Basic automatically saves your users' changes to the OLE embedded object.
4. Which method saves an OLE object to a disk file?
5. Which method loads an OLE object from a disk file?
6. Name two ways to test for an object's class.
7. True/False. You must pass system objects if you need to access them in multiple procedures.
8. Name three kinds of items that often appear in the Members list in the Object Browser.
9. What happens if you group the Members list in the Object Browser?
10. True/False. The Object Browser won't search for objects you've created.

Exercises

1. Why is `With...End With` probably a bad idea here?

```
With chkMaster
  .Caption = "Primary Source"
  .Alignment = vbLeftJustify
End With
```

2. Write a simple application that contains one OLE control. Embed a Windows Paint object in the control. Add a menu option for saving pictures and one for loading pictures. When you run the application, double-click the control and draw a picture. Save the drawing, exit the application, and then restart the application. Load the saved drawing to make sure your application's save and load procedures are accurate.

Week 3

Day 17

ActiveX Controls

Today's lesson shows you how to understand and use ActiveX controls. By adding ActiveX controls to your toolbox window, you add functionality to your Visual Basic environment and decrease the time required to develop subsequent applications.

Visual Basic's supported object technology lets you borrow functionality from other applications that support ActiveX and ActiveX automation. For example, your Visual Basic application can create a Word document or an Excel worksheet by borrowing ActiveX technology from the outside applications.

Once you understand how important ActiveX control technology is and the many ways you can benefit from ActiveX controls, you'll learn how to create your own ActiveX controls.

Today, you learn the following:

- About the history of ActiveX controls
- How VBX and OCX controls compare to ActiveX controls
- How to add ActiveX controls to your projects
- About automation of objects within your applications

- How to create an Excel worksheet from within a Visual Basic application
- How to create new ActiveX controls
- About subclassing of new ActiveX objects
- How to create your own property values for your controls

The Need for ActiveX

ActiveX technology is the current version of the set of add-in controls that began a few years ago as VBX controls. The filename extension .VBX meant that the control was a Visual Basic extended control. In other words, ActiveX controls began as Visual Basic controls that you could add to earlier versions of Visual Basic to expand upon the toolbox tools that came with Visual Basic.

Back then, Visual Basic controls were not compatible with browser technology, the Internet, and other Windows programming tools, such as Visual C++. Nevertheless, the Visual Basic controls in the early versions of Visual Basic were important for extending the Visual Basic programmer's ability to write code. The more controls the programmer had, the less work he had to do. As a result, an entire programming community and business developed that created Visual Basic controls that manipulated graphics, data, grids, multimedia, and so on. Due to the popularity of Visual Basic controls, Microsoft was forced to redesign them (given that they were compatible only with Visual Basic and not other Windows products).

Note

OLE is a cousin to VBX controls, but OLE is more universal among Windows applications—it was not designed to target Visual Basic programmers only. Nevertheless, as you saw yesterday, an OLE object is a data object (not a control) that you use as you would an added Visual Basic control.

Between Visual Basic controls and ActiveX controls, Microsoft designed special 32-bit OCX controls. These new Visual Basic controls extended Visual Basic as well as other programming languages, such as Visual C++. OCX controls had an .OCX filename extension. The older VBX controls supported only 16-bit applications.

Caution

If you've worked with previous editions of Visual Basic that supported 16-bit VBX controls, as versions before 5.0 supported, the current 32-bit Visual Basic system can't use these controls unless the system comes with 32-bit replacements for those old controls. For example, Visual Basic comes with a

32-bit version of the gauge control (16-bit VBX gauge controls were included with the early versions of Visual Basic). Therefore, if you load an older Visual Basic application that uses the VBX gauge control, Visual Basic will replace that control with the 32-bit version, and everything should work fine. If, however, a replacement doesn't exist and the VBX control's vendor can't supply you with a replacement, you'll have to eliminate that control from the application and substitute a similar one.

The OCX controls, although compatible with Visual C++, did not work easily over the Internet; therefore, Microsoft upgraded them to be ActiveX controls so that Internet browsers, as well as multiple applications and programming languages, work well with them.

Will there be a replacement for ActiveX? Probably some day, depending on new technology that requires something extra that ActiveX technology does not provide.

Note

Both the current versions of Internet Explorer and Netscape's Navigator (with an available plug-in from Netscape's support page) support ActiveX on Web pages. This means that users can interact with ActiveX controls in any Web pages that contain them.

Adding ActiveX Controls to a Project

Remember that ActiveX controls (to you as a Visual Basic programmer) are just additional controls you can add to the toolbox window and use for developing programs. All kinds of controls exist. Several come with Visual Basic, and you can find them by selecting Project, Components (or Ctrl+T), as you've done throughout the earlier days of this tutorial. In addition, you'll find ActiveX controls available on the Internet. Also, programming firms sell ActiveX controls that you can seamlessly integrate into the Visual Basic environment.

Do	Don't
DO look at Microsoft's Web site (`www.microsoft.com`) for a sample of ActiveX controls you can download to your PC.	

Do not add more ActiveX controls to your toolbox window than your application requires. Add as many as needed but no more. Every control you add is sent to your user's compiled application that you distribute. (You learn how to distribute applications in Day 21, "Distributing Your Applications.") The more controls the application contains, the larger the application will be, the slower the application will run, and the more resources the application will consume on the user's system. To remove unneeded ActiveX controls, display the Project, Components dialog box and uncheck any control that does not belong in your project.

Whether or not an application uses all the ActiveX controls loaded at the time of the compilation, you are required to distribute runtime ActiveX control files along with the project and its related files.

New Term A *runtime ActiveX control file* is an auxiliary file that you must supply with an application that uses the corresponding ActiveX control. The runtime file contains the instructions necessary to make the ActiveX control operate at runtime.

ActiveX controls exist for virtually any programming job you have. If you want more control over sound than the included multimedia control offers, you can find many kinds of sound-related ActiveX controls online. Also, 3D graphic controls, Internet controls, mathematical controls, printer controls, scanner controls, and a huge assortment of other controls are available. You'll have to decide what kind of programming you do the most and look for specific controls that can help you. For example, if you write publishing software, you'll want to find as many text editing and manipulation controls as possible.

When you add a new ActiveX control to your toolbox window, how do you go about using it? To start with, you can assume that the ActiveX control supports the following items:

- Properties
- Events
- Methods

In other words, you use the ActiveX control just as you would any other control, and the ActiveX control integrates into your Visual Basic application. You'll need to obtain a list of properties, events, and methods that the ActiveX control supports so that you can program it properly. Although many of the control's properties will appear in the Properties window, not all will (especially those available only at runtime). When you purchase

ActiveX controls or download them from Internet sites that provide them, you can also get instructions that list supported properties, events, and methods. For the ActiveX controls that come with Visual Basic, you can use the online Help as a reference.

Figure 17.1 shows the Components dialog box, which appears when you select Project, Components. You've already seen this dialog box several times throughout this 21-day tutorial, because you've added additional ActiveX controls to your toolbox before—for example, in Day 14, "Introducing VB Graphics and Multimedia," when you added the multimedia control.

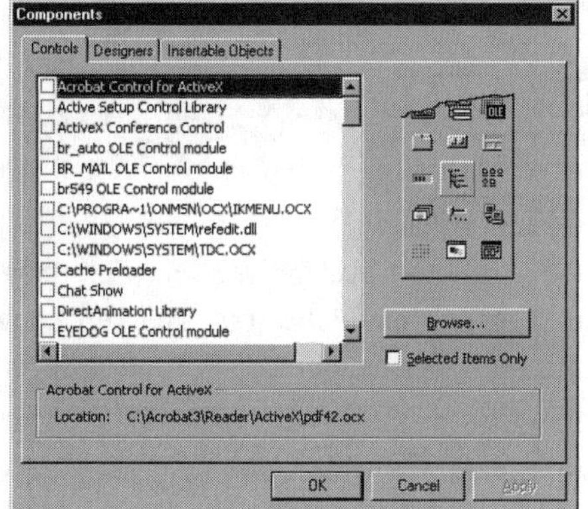

FIGURE 17.1.
Use the Components dialog box to add new ActiveX controls to your project.

When you install Visual Basic, it adds several ActiveX controls to your system that you, in turn, can add to a project through the Components dialog box. In addition, the Visual Basic installation routine searches your system for additional controls to add as well. Many of these controls will show up in your Components dialog box. Therefore, the same Visual Basic installation on two different computers may result in different sets of ActiveX controls listed in the Components dialog boxes on the two systems. Click the Components dialog box's Browse button to search your hard drive for ActiveX control files.

Tip

> The Components dialog box's list of ActiveX controls can get lengthy if you have several ActiveX controls on your system. After checking a few of the controls, you may want to click the option labeled Selected Items Only so that only your selected ActiveX controls appear in the list. If, however, you want to add more items, you'll have to uncheck the option so you can locate the controls you want to add.

As you add controls to your toolbox window, it can fill up quickly. Take a look at the General tab at the top of your toolbox. By right-clicking a blank area in the toolbox window, you can create new tabs for group-related ActiveX controls on the toolbox. To add controls to a new group, click the group's tab and then add the control. (The Components dialog box is available from the toolbox window's right-click pop-up menu.) Figure 17.2 shows a set of Internet-related controls added to a group designed just for them.

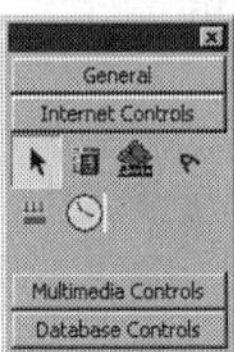

FIGURE 17.2.
Tabbed groups help you organize your toolbox window.

ActiveX Automation

At this point, you've added some controls, and you know all about setting properties, responding to events, and triggering methods. Some ActiveX controls, however, let you go a step further. You can actually use an embedded control inside your application and borrow that control's functionality for your own application's use.

Visual Basic supports such *automation* of controls between applications. For example, you can open Excel, load a worksheet, manipulate the worksheet's data with Excel-based commands, close Excel, and then embed the resulting worksheet in your application's form window without users ever knowing that you borrowed Excel's capabilities.

NEW TERM *Automation* is the process of one application using another application's data and manipulating that data with the help of the other application. Users will have no idea that the other application has started, helped, and then gone away.

You are somewhat limited to using automation only for ActiveX applications registered in your system's Registry. Generally, if you use an application that's ActiveX aware, that application registered its automation availability in your system Registry when you installed the application.

Normally, automation requires extensive knowledge of the other application's *object hierarchy*, and such a hierarchy can be complex. The example shown next teaches you automation through a demonstration using an ActiveX document. To fully understand automation, you must be well versed in the borrowed application's internals. This book cannot get into the specifics of non–Visual Basic applications. Fortunately, most automation concepts overlap applications, so the example's concepts you see here carry over to other applications in many ways.

To begin this example, you need to define a variable that represents the application you want to automate inside your own application. You'll use Visual Basic's `Object` data type to create a variable that references the automation application. First, you must define an application object, like this:

```
Dim obExcelApp As Object
```

Now, you must connect the application object variable to the application. If the application isn't running now, you must start the application in the background with the `CreateObject()` function. `CreateObject()` not only starts the application, but also connects your object variable to the application, like this:


```
Set obExcelApp = CreateObject("Excel.Application")
```

You'll substitute the application's name in place of the `CreateObject()` function's argument.

Do	Don't
DO use `Set` instead of a simple assignment to attach the automated application to your Visual Basic application. A variable can't hold an outside application; variables can only hold values such as numbers and strings. **DO** use `Set` to create a reference variable to the outside object. `Set` does not assign but rather points the variable to the object the variable represents.	

A problem can occur if the application is already running. In a multitasking, multiuser operating system, Excel can have more than one copy of itself running at the same time on the same computer. Therefore, you can use the `GetObject()` function in place of `CreateObject()` if the application is running:

```
Set obExcelApp = GetObject(, "Excel.Application")
```

Notice the comma at the beginning of the argument list. You can omit the first argument in most cases because the second argument describes the object you are getting. Without the second argument, you must supply an initial argument that lists a path to a file that describes the object you want to create.

If Excel is already running, you'll not want to start a new instance of Excel. Through error trapping, you can check to see if Excel is running. The `GetObject()` function will trigger an error if Excel is *not* running (because there's nothing to get). If you determine that Excel is not running, you then can use `CreateObject()` to start an instance of Excel.

The following code is an outline of the code you might use to check for a running instance of Excel:

```
1:  ' Trap errors
2:  On Error Resume Next
3:  '
4:  ' Set the Excel application reference
5:  Set obExcelApp = GetObject(, "Excel.Application")
6:  If Err.Number <> 0 Then
7:     Set obExcelApp = CreateObject("Excel.Application")
8:     blnRunning = False          ' Excel was not running
9:  Else
10:    blnRunning = True
11: End If
```

You've seen the `On Error Goto` statement in previous lessons, but this is the first time you've seen the `Next` option. In the past, a statement label has always been the location to which the `On Error` statement sends the code if an error occurs. The `Next` option simply tells Visual Basic, upon getting an error, to move down to the next statement and continue the program. Although a label could have been set up in this code, this situation provides an opportunity to mention that an error code is returned every time `On Error` traps an error. The error code is one of the properties of a predefined system object called `Err` (see Day 16,"Objects and Visual Basic").

Until an error occurs in a running program, the `Err.Number` is `0`. Therefore, if `Err.Number` ever contains any non-zero value, an error has occurred. In this case, line 6 will show an error code in `Err.Number` if the `GetObject()` function fails. Therefore, line 7, seeing that `GetObject()` could not work because Excel was not already running, starts an instance of Excel with the `CreateObject()` function. (If you want to trap additional errors later in the program, as you might do if you were displaying dialog boxes and needed to know if the user pressed Cancel, you can reset the error state by setting `Err.Number` to `0`.) The Boolean variable named `blnRunning` is set to `False` so that code later in the program will know how Excel was started.

Caution

> If Excel was already running, you *don't* want your code to stop that running instance.

> Automation application object variables are an exception to the general rule that you should only use local variables. The application is truly outside your application; therefore, you can safely use a global object variable so that your procedures don't have to pass the application variable around.

When you open another application and use automation, your application must intimately understand the other application's interface. In a way, your application is the user of the other application. Therefore, when you open the Excel application, you interact with Excel by using the normal row and column notation, except that you have to use some object property notation specific to Excel.

Now, you must declare a worksheet object so that the application can generate data:

```
Dim obWorkSheet As Object   ' Worksheet object
```

The following code adds data to some worksheet cells:

```
' Enter values in cells
obWorkSheet.Cells(1, 1).Value = "Sales"
obWorkSheet.Cells(1, 2).Value = "Month"
obWorkSheet.Cells(2, 1).Value = 21913.44
obWorkSheet.Cells(2, 2).Value = "April"
```

If you've put together everything in the preceding section and have added some cleanup code as well as code that saves the worksheet and closes the Excel object, you would come up with something like Listing 17.1.

LISTING 17.1. YOUR APPLICATION CAN USE EXCEL TO CREATE A WORKSHEET.

```
Private Sub cmdSendToExcel_Click()
  Dim obExcelApp As Object      ' Application object
  Dim obWorkSheet As Object     ' Worksheet object
  Dim blnRunning As Boolean     ' If Excel object exists is running

  ' Trap errors
  On Error Resume Next
  '
  ' Set the Excel application reference
  Set obExcelApp = GetObject(, "Excel.Application")
```

continues

LISTING 17.1. CONTINUED

```
11:     If Err.Number <> 0 Then
12:        Set obExcelApp = CreateObject("Excel.Application")
13:        blnRunning = False         ' Excel was not running
14:     Else
15:        blnRunning = True
16:     End If
17:
18:     ' Add a new workbook
19:     obExcelApp.Workbooks.Add
20:
21:     ' Reference the active sheet
22:     Set obWorkSheet = obExcelApp.ActiveSheet
23:
24:     ' Enter values in active sheet's cells
25:     obWorkSheet.Cells(1, 1).Value = "Sales"
26:     obWorkSheet.Cells(1, 2).Value = "Month"
27:     obWorkSheet.Cells(2, 1).Value = 21913.44
28:     obWorkSheet.Cells(2, 2).Value = "April"
29:
30:    ' Select the second row only to format
31:     obWorkSheet.Rows("2:2").Select
32:     obExcelApp.Selection.NumberFormat = "$##,###.##"
33:
34:     ' Save the workbook (change this name if already saved once)
35:     obExcelApp.Save ("c:\VBCreated.XLS")
36:
37:     ' Don't quit if Excel was already running!
38:     obExcelApp.ActiveWorkBook.Close False
39:
40:    If Not (blnRunning) Then ' If it was not running...
41:      obExcelApp.Quit         ' then quit Excel
42:    End If
43:
44: End Sub
```

If you tested to see that Excel wasn't already executing, you can close Excel (as is done in line 41). If, however, Excel was running (meaning that the `GetObject()` function did not return an error), then you don't want to quit Excel because it might be running a background process. The code shown in this quick example creates the simple worksheet shown in Figure 17.3.

FIGURE 17.3.

Your Visual Basic application can create Excel worksheets!

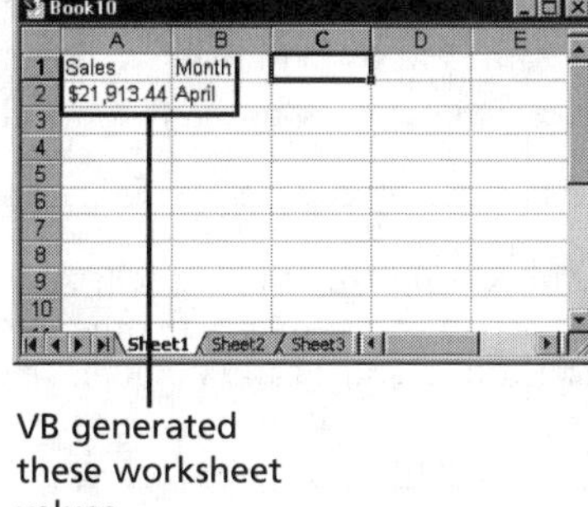

This worksheet is simple to make the example a reasonable size. Ordinarily, your Visual Basic application might adjust values and even trigger an Excel chart and print a report. The important thing to remember is that Visual Basic used Excel's brains to create a formatted worksheet without the user sitting at the keyboard knowing that Excel was involved.

Note

> Excel contains its own automation language, as does Word and all ActiveX-aware automation applications. Nevertheless, most of the applications support the opening and closing features used in this section to connect an application and its primary data object to Visual Basic object variables. Also, the applications support methods and properties such as the ones shown here, so you'll have little problem as long as you understand Visual Basic. You must have access to the application's internal language used for automation, however. Search the application's online Help for the application's object hierarchy, which shows the available objects you can work with.

After you use Excel or Word or some other ActiveX-compatible automation application, you then have to include that object in your Visual Basic application.

Creating Your Own ActiveX Controls

Although the thought of creating an ActiveX control may sound daunting, consider why you would want to do this. Not only could you distribute (that is, *sell*) your controls to other developers, but you can also reuse the controls you develop in your own applications. For example, if you find yourself making the same kinds of changes to Visual Basic controls to get them to operate the way you need, consider writing *new* controls that not only mimic the controls you already have but that also have built-in properties and methods that do what you need them to do! The next time you write an application that needs your control, add your own control to the toolbox and set the properties you want to set. Instead of writing the same old code to make the control behave a certain way, you just set its property values and get back to the real details of the application.

Another advantage to developing your own collection of ActiveX programming tools is that you can port those tools to other programming languages that support ActiveX, such as Visual C++ (although why would you use anything but Visual Basic?).

Designing the Control

Visual Basic contains tools that help you design your own ActiveX controls, although the process does require several steps to complete. To show you what is involved, the rest of today's lesson walks you through the design of a new kind of text box.

The New Text Box's Details

The new text box that you create will extend Visual Basic's generic text box control by offering the following features:

- The text box will support all the regular property values that the standard text box control supports.
- The text box will also contain a new property called `AutoTSize` that supports four possible values: `1-NA`, `2-Small`, `3-Medium`, and `4-Large`. These values will appear as an enumeration in a drop-down list box inside the Properties window. You can assign 1, 2, 3, or 4 to the text box in code to set the value. When set to `1-NA` (the default when you first place the control), the text box's font size will not change from its current size set in the `Font.Size` property value. When set to `2-Small`, the text box's text will be sized to 25% of the text box's `Height` value. When set to `3-Medium`, the text box's text will be sized to one half the text box's `Height` value. When set to `4-Large`, the text box's text will be sized to 75% of the `Height` value. (The `Font.Size` property will change to reflect the new size.) This gives you a simple way to set the text box's text to one of the three sizes.

NEW TERM An *enumeration* is a list of fixed values that a control can take, such as `True` and `False`. Enumerated values appear in a drop-down list box for that property value in the Properties window.

- The text box will also contain two new properties called `UCase` and `LCase`. These will be Boolean properties. When `UCase` is set to `True`, the text in the text box will be converted to uppercase letters. When `LCase` is set to `True`, the text in the text box will be converted to lowercase letters. Both `UCase` and `LCase` are set to `False`, by default, and neither can be `True` at the same time. Therefore, your control must make sure that when one of the case properties is set to `True`, the other is set to `False`.

The new ActiveX control that you create will look and act like other controls. You can insert it into the toolbox window, double-click the control to add it to the form window, and select its control properties from the Properties window. Although this new text box control that you create will be visible at runtime, if you want to create a background control that is not to appear on the running form window (as is the case with the timer control), you could set your control's `InvisibleAtRunTime` property to `True`. Such a control will work in the background when needed rather than appear on the end user's form. (The `Visible` property simply determines if the control can be seen, but the `InvisibleAtRunTime` property, when `True`, ensures that the control is never visible and cannot be displayed.)

> **Note:** The name of your new control will be `TextSizeUL`.

The Need for Classes

All Visual Basic objects, including variables and controls, are members of a *class*. The class grouping gives you a way to group like objects together. In addition, you can *subclass* a new object from an existing class to create new objects that have all the properties of the rest of the class as well as new properties unique to the object. By subclassing, you don't have to reinvent the wheel, because the object (in this case, the ActiveX control) automatically takes on the properties, methods, and supported events of its parent class; then you can add new properties, methods, and supported events as well.

New Term A *class* is a collection (or description, actually) of an object's properties, methods, and supported events. A control is nothing more than an actual instance of an object from a given class. A form that you add to a project, for example, is just another instance of the `Form` class that you've added. Being a member of the `Form` class makes the form take on properties, events, and methods that are distinct from other classes of objects, such as those from the `CommandButton` class.

To *subclass* means to create a new object from a class of existing objects. The new object will take on the properties, methods, and events of its parent class, and you can also add your own properties, methods, and events to the object.

Built-in data types, such as String, are not members of a Visual Basic class because they don't support events.

Let's say you want to create a control that somewhat mimics another control. By subclassing the new control, you automatically pull in all the parent control's properties, methods, and supported events. You don't necessarily have to subclass a new control, however, because you can create one without the help of subclassing.

Visual Basic offers these three ways to create new ActiveX controls:

- **Subclassed simple controls**—You can use an existing ActiveX control for the foundation of your new control. Your new control is *subclassed* from the original (*parent*) control. Your new control can receive all the functionality of the existing parent control and can extend that parent control's features by having additional features added to it. Subclassing a control is the easiest way to create an ActiveX control. You must modify the subclassed control's interface to support any new features you want your control to provide.
- **Subclassed aggregate controls**—You can subclass your new control from multiple controls that already exist. In other words, if your new control is a dialog box–like control that contains command buttons, text boxes, and labels, you can use existing command buttons, text boxes, and labels to reduce the effort you must put into your new control. Then you can concentrate on the added features that your control provides.
- **User-drawn controls**—If your control has nothing in common with existing controls, you can create it from scratch by defining all the control's properties, events, and methods and then drawing the control so that it looks exactly as you need. A user-drawn control requires quite an effort to create because you can't borrow functionality from any existing control.

Making the ActiveX Control

The following sections walk you through the creation of the new ActiveX control TextSizeUL.

Preparing Visual Basic

You will *not* follow the standard procedure for creating Visual Basic applications when you create an ActiveX control. When you select New, Project to see the New Project dialog box, instead of clicking the icon Standard EXE, you'll select the ActiveX Control icon. Visual Basic prepares for the new control, and your screen will look much like it does when you create new applications (except that the form window will seem to appear without its usual border, as shown in Figure 17.4). In reality, the window is not showing a form. Instead it's the backdrop for the ActiveX control that you'll create. Visual Basic assigns the default name `UserControl1` to this control. Of course, the word "User" in `UserControl1` is misleading, because you, the programmer, are creating this control to help with your programming efforts. Once you design the control, though, the end-user will actually interact with the control.

FIGURE 17.4.

You'll work from a familiar environment when creating an ActiveX control.

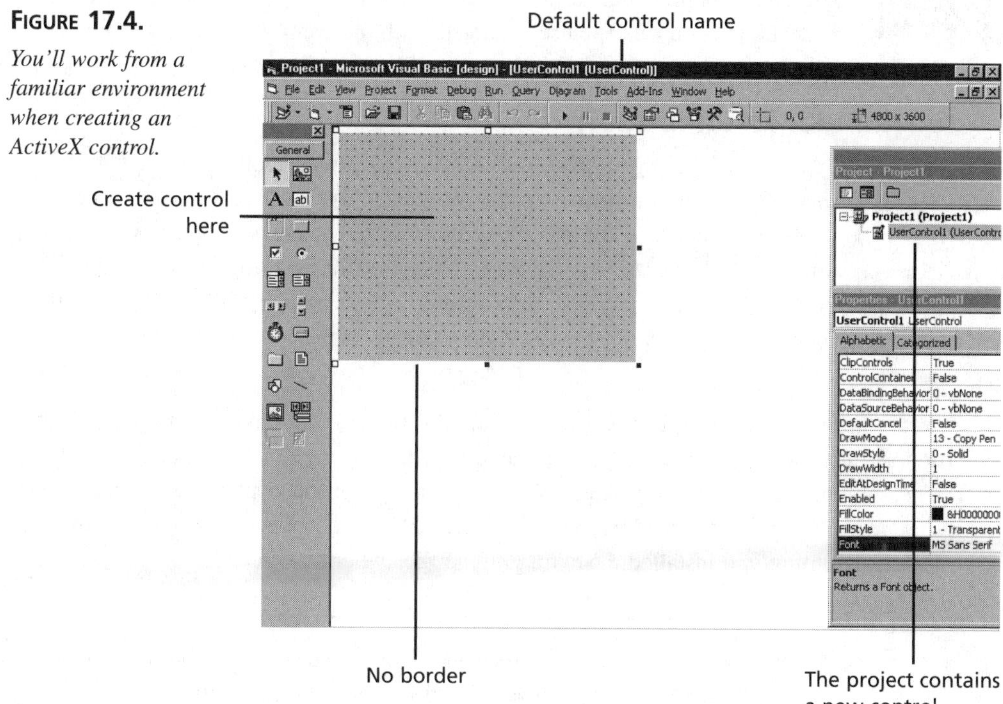

The terms *runtime* means something different when you create controls from when you create regular applications. Whereas a control's designtime occurs when you create and edit the control, a control's runtime occurs in either of these two situations:

- When a programmer inserts the control into an application at the application's designtime, the control is a compiled and executing control that responds to the programmer's setup instructions.
- When the programmer compiles and runs the application, the control is also running, except that it runs while responding to an end user.

Often, programmers distinguish these two kinds runtimes by calling them *designtime running* and *runtime running*, respectively. Generally, the context of the run mode is obvious as you create and work with the ActiveX control.

New Term *Designtime running* is the term applied to a control that you "run" to test when you create the control. The user interacts with the control. *Runtime running* is the term applied to a control that executes along with an application.

Beginning Customization

Remember that you can add your new ActiveX control to your toolbox window. Therefore, one of the first things to do, once you've decided on the goals of the control, is to pick an icon for your new control. The control's `ToolboxBitmap` property sets the icon you want to use. The gray box that looks somewhat like a form window in the upper-left corner of the editing area is your actual control, but the control is still blank. Therefore, when selected, the Properties window displays property values for your control.

Scroll through the Properties window to locate the `ToolboxBitmap` property. When you double-click the property, the Load Bitmap dialog box opens so that you can locate an icon on your disk to use as the ActiveX control's icon. For this control, select Plan.bmp from the \Graphics\Bitmaps\Assorted folder, which resides in Visual Basic's Common folder (assuming you installed the extra graphic files when you installed Visual Basic).

Tip

> You can create your own bitmap image in Windows Paint (or a similar drawing program). Keep the image at 15-by-16 screen pixels so that it appears in the same area as the other toolbox icons.

The Plan bitmap is an icon of a scroll, and a scroll icon would work well for this new text box's toolbox entry. The bitmap will appear in the control form's upper-left corner when you specify the `ToolboxBitmap` property.

Information about your control will appear in applications that use your control, so you'll want to document the control. Select Project, Properties and change the project name from `Project1` to `TextSizeUL`. Add a description in the text box labeled Project Description so that subsequent applications that use your control will be able to display this information. Type the following for the description:

```
A text box control that controls its own size and supports upper- and
lowercase conversion.
```

Change the control property's name to `NewControl`. Now that you've named the control and the project, save the control and save the project when prompted. Visual Basic saves the control under the name NewControl.ctl, although you'll eventually convert this control to an ActiveX file.

Subclassing the Control

You can now subclass your new control from the regular text box control so that it can take on the properties, events, and methods of the text box control. As you subclass the control, the ActiveX Control Interface Wizard will enable you to extend the functionality of the control.

The *ActiveX Control Interface Wizard* is a wizard that guides you through the process of subclassing of a new control.

The ActiveX Control Interface Wizard is not part of the default Visual Basic environment. You can add the wizard to your Visual Basic environment by following these steps:

1. Select the Add-Ins menu.
2. Select Add-In Manager to display the Add-In Manager dialog box shown in Figure 17.5.

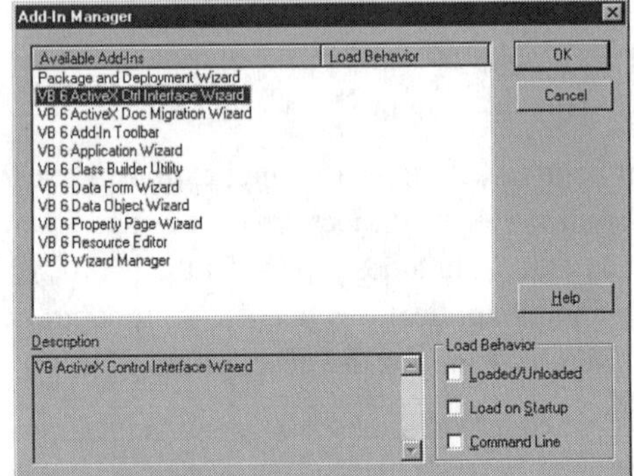

FIGURE 17.5.

Adding Visual Basic's ActiveX Control Interface Wizard to your environment.

3. Double-click the item labeled VB 6 ActiveX Ctrl Interface Wizard. The "Loaded" message that appears to the right of the entry informs you that the wizard is now part of the environment.

If you often find yourself creating ActiveX controls, you may want to click the Load on Startup option so that the ActiveX Control Interface Wizard always loads with your Visual Basic environment.

4. Click the OK button to close the dialog box.

Although you've loaded the wizard, you're not yet ready to start it because you must add an initial text box control to your blank ActiveX control to subclass from. However, you can see whether Visual Basic added the wizard to your environment by displaying the Add-Ins menu. The last option on the menu should read ActiveX Control Interface Wizard. Whenever you add components to your Visual Basic environment, they'll appear on the Add-Ins menu.

Before you start the wizard, you must add an intrinsic text box control to your project. Therefore, place a text box control on your control's background. Name the text box `txtParent`. This text box will be controlled by the new ActiveX control that you add, not by a programmer. The programmer who uses your ActiveX control will resize the new control and, in doing so, the event procedures of the new control will modify the internal text box. The text box control provides the functionality that you'll need to subclass.

In a way, the intrinsic text box will act like a hidden control (much like a local object of a public control) that other projects will use. Your control will use the intrinsic text box control, modify the behavior there, and then present that modified behavior to other applications.

Starting the Wizard

You're now ready to start the ActiveX Control Interface Wizard from the Add-Ins menu. The first wizard window that appears is an introductory screen that you can optionally hide upon subsequent runs by clicking the check box at the bottom of the window. After reading the introductory screen, click Next to see the Select Interface Members window, which is shown in Figure 17.6.

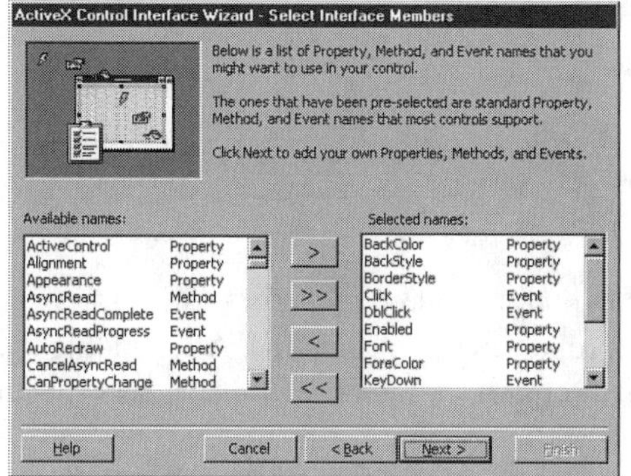

FIGURE 17.6.
You can select the items from the parent control that you want to include in your new ActiveX control.

The wizard displays two lists of information. The left list contains some or all the properties, events, and methods available that you can include with your new ActiveX control. The wizard generated the list by analyzing your current control and noticing that you placed an intrinsic text box control on the editing area.

The list on the right contains several properties, methods, and events that the wizard selected from the complete list on the left. You can select additional items if you want by clicking an item in the left window and then clicking the > command button to send that item to the right list of selected items. Additionally, you can select items in the right list and click < to remove that item.

Tip

The >> button sends *all* items to the right list from the left, and the << button erases all items in the right list so that you can start over.

Surprisingly, the wizard does not send several properties needed for subclassed text boxes to the right list; therefore, you need to select and send the following items to the right list:

- `Alignment`
- `Change`
- `FontBold`
- `FontItalic`
- `FontName`
- `FontSize`
- `FontStrikethru`
- `FontUnderline`
- `MultiLine`
- `PasswordChar`
- `ScrollBars`
- `Text`
- `ToolTipText`

You'll want to be able to apply all these properties to your new ActiveX-based text box control as well as new properties that you define. After adding the items, click Next to display the Create Custom Interface Members window, as shown in Figure 17.7.

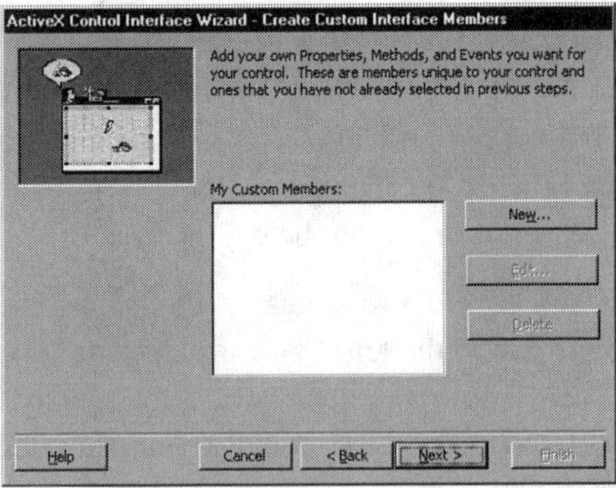

FIGURE 17.7.
You now can add your own properties, methods, and events.

The list box in the center of the window is blank because you have yet to add your own items to the control's set. You cannot just type the item, such as the property that automatically sets the new ActiveX-based text box's size. Instead, you must click the New button to describe the new property (or method or event) that you want to add.

When you click New, you'll see the dialog box shown in Figure 17.8 in which you enter the new item. As you enter an item's name, you must also select the item's type (whether it's a property, method, or event) by clicking one of the options at the bottom of the dialog box. As you enter a name and item type, click OK to send that item to the wizard's list box that shows your added items.

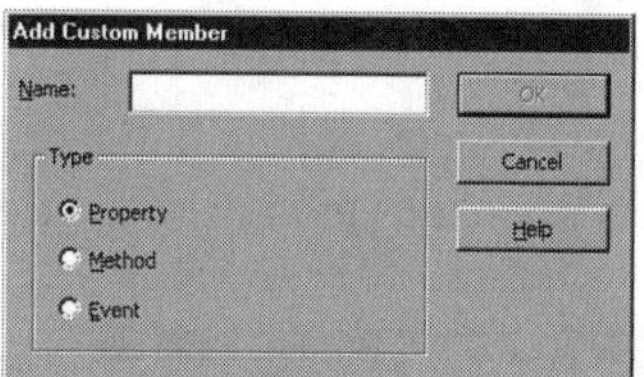

FIGURE 17.8.
Describing the new item's name and type.

For the ActiveX control you're now creating, enter the following two new items:

- `AutoTSize` (property)
- `ULText` (property)

Click Next to move to the next wizard window. This window, the Set Mapping window, is the place where you map, or *connect*, properties, events, and methods to the text box equivalents. In other words, the list you see in the list labeled Public Name is the list generated from the items selected earlier as well as the new items you added in the previous window.

You must tell the wizard how you want each of the properties, methods, and events to behave. In the case of the new text box you're creating, you want *all* properties, methods, and events to act the way they normally do for normal text boxes. (You could, however, change the mapping if you wanted. For example, you could map a `MouseDown` event to a `MouseClick` event; then, when the user clicks your control, a `MouseClick` event will be generated every place a `MouseDown` event would normally occur.)

The only two properties that you do not/ want to map to a normal text box control's behavior are the two new property items you added earlier: the `AutoTSize` and the `ULText` properties. Therefore, select all the items in the list except the `AutoTSize` and `ULText` properties.

> **Tip**
>
> The list supports multiple sections, so one quick way to select all but your two new properties is to click the top item in the list and then press Shift+End to highlight every item. Then, hold down the Ctrl key while clicking the `ULText` and `AutoTSize` properties to deselect them.

Select the item that you want to map all these items to. Open the Maps to Control drop-down list box and select `txtParent`. All these public items, except the two unselected items, are applied to the embedded text box control that you placed on the form. You want the internal text box to behave normally so that your ActiveX control can access that internal text box control as usual. The two new properties will certainly not apply to the internal text box—that's why you did not map those two properties to the internal control.

Click Next to display the Set Attributes window shown in Figure 17.9. The Set Attributes window is where you'll map the new properties to the new control.

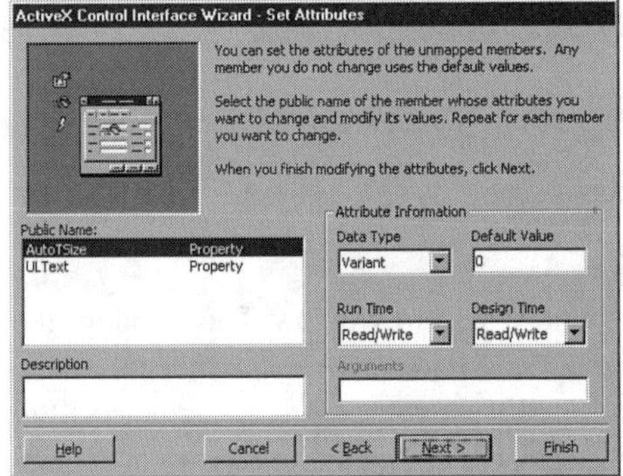

FIGURE 17.9.
You can now map the new properties to your control.

If you had added new methods and events to the new control, they, too, would appear in the Set Attributes window. You've already mapped the known properties, methods, and events to the internal control, and now you'll map the new properties to the new control. Follow these steps to prepare the new properties:

1. For the selected `AutoTSize` property, change the default value from `0` to `1`. (The rest of the fields are already correct.) If you'll recall, the `AutoTSize` property will take on one of four enumerated values, and those values range from `1` to `4`. The value `1` will be the default (that is, the initial startup property when you place the ActiveX control on a form), so you'll have to replace the `0` with `1`.
2. Type the following description for the `AutoTSize` property:
   ```
   Determines the percentage, 25%, 50%, or 75% of the text's font_
   size in relation to the Height property.
   ```
3. Select the `ULText` property. All of its fields are correct, but you must add this description:
   ```
   Sets the text to uppercase, lowercase, or no change.
   ```

4. Click Next to complete the wizard's task. The wizard can now build all its required information necessary to generate the control. You can click Finish to generate the control. If you leave the option labeled View Summary Report checked, the wizard displays a summary of what is left to be done.

Obviously, the ActiveX control is incomplete. You have not told it how to behave when the `AutoTSize` or `ULText` properties are selected. The wizard sets up the control's parameters, but you still have to add code and manually complete the ActiveX control to make it fully functional.

Completing the ActiveX Control's Body

The wizard could not add code to activate your `AutoTSize` or `ULText` properties because it has no way of knowing what you want done with those new properties. On the other hand, the wizard could map the existing properties, methods, and event properties to the parent control because those items are already defined.

To complete the ActiveX control, you must add code, and you do that, of course, from the code window. Select View, Code to look at the code window for the ActiveX control as it now stands. As you scan through the code, you'll notice that much of the code window is devoted to mapping the new control's properties, events, and methods to the underlying `txtParent` text box control's properties, events, and methods. In other words, when a programmer using this new control sets at designtime running (that is, when the completed control is used while another application is being designed) the `BackColor` property, the code actually sets the underlying text box's `BackColor` property. The code is complex in places, so don't expect to understand everything.

Do	Don't
DO look through the code to see all the `Let` and `Get` event procedures. As you may recall from Day 11, "Working with Forms," these two special function qualifiers are used to set and return property values for the properties you create. The wizard, in effect, created properties for the parent text box control when you mapped those properties to the new control.	

Although you'll edit this code directly, never make changes to code prefaced with the following remark:

```
'WARNING! DO NOT REMOVE OR MODIFY THE FOLLOWING COMMENTED
'LINES!
```

The code that follows those warning remarks are critical to your new control's operation and are to be left as is.

Do	Don't
DO complete any sections that contain remarks that begin with the words TO DO. You'll see such sections if you ever create new ActiveX controls based on any of the list controls. The wizard cannot handle lists properly, so you are expected to add the necessary code to process lists if you ever use a list control as the parent control.	

Listing 17.2 shows the first few lines from the code. These lines are devoted to the new properties you added to the project.

Listing 17.2. The wizard initialized the default values for your new properties.

```
1:  'Default Property Values:
2:  Const m_def_AutoTSize = 1
3:  Const m_def_ULText = 0
4:  'Property Variables:
5:  Dim m_AutoTSize As Variant
6:  Dim m_ULText As Variant
```

The `Const` keyword declares named constants, not variables. Therefore, in line 2, `m_def_AutoTSize` is not a variable but rather a named constant. Just as Visual Basic includes several named constants such as `vbWhite` and `vbInformation`, you can declare your own named constants, and they can be local or global. (Named constants are often global because they cannot change; therefore, they are in no danger of being inadvertently changed by a procedure that should not have access to them.)

Lines 2 and 3 declare named constants for the default values of your two new properties. You set these default values in the wizard's Set Attributes screen. These are the default values that will appear in the Properties window for these two properties when a programmer eventually places the ActiveX control on a form. Whenever the rest of the code refers to one of the named constants, the constant value of `1` or `0` is used, because these are the values that lines 2 and 3 in Listing 17.2 create for the named constants.

Lines 5 and 6 declare Variant variables that will represent the current value of the properties. When a programmer sets one of these property values at designtime running (or when the final application, through code, sets these values in assignment statements), the variables are the places where these values will be held.

You must define the enumerated values for the two properties that will appear in the Properties window. You define the enumerated list in an enumerated block of code that begins with the `Enum` statement. Directly below the General section of the code window, type the code in Listing 17.3.

LISTING 17.3. YOU MUST DEFINE THE ENUMERATED VALUES THAT WILL APPEAR IN THE PROPERTIES WINDOW.

```
Public Enum AutoTSizeEnum
  NA = 1
  Small = 2
  Medium = 3
  Large = 4
End Enum
Public Enum ULTextEnum
   AsIs = 0
   Uppercase = 1
   Lowercase = 2
End Enum
```

Declare all enumerated values as public so that all the code has access to them. The `Enum` statement begins the definition of enumerated values. Remember, these are the values that will appear in the drop-down list box for these two property values inside the Properties window. The `AutoTSize` values will appear in the following common format (which you've now seen for many other property values:

```
1 - NA
2 - Small
3 - Medium
4 - Large
```

To set an initial value, the programmer can select one of these values from within the Properties window when working with the ActiveX control. In addition, the code inside the application that uses this ActiveX control can assign `1`, `2`, `3`, `or` `4` to the property to set the control to one of those property values. Also, the assignment statement can assign the enumerated values, as done here:

```
NewControl.AutoTSize = Medium   ' Assigns 3
```

In the same way, the enumerated type `ULTextEnum` defines the `ULText` property's enumerated values, so assignments to that property work as expected.

The new control's sizing code is extremely simple, because the new control should size just as the parent text box would size. Often, a new ActiveX control needs to size differently than the control or controls that it subclasses from, especially for subclassed aggregate ActiveX controls (defined earlier in today's lesson). However, if a one-to-one correspondence occurs with the parent's size and the new control's size, you can add a `UserControl_Resize()` event procedure by typing the `Resize` event procedure shown in Listing 17.4 in the code window.

LISTING 17.4. THE NEW ACTIVEX CONTROL WILL BE LOCATED AND SCALED THE SAME AS THE INTERNAL TEXT BOX CONTROL.

```
1:  Private Sub UserControl_Resize()
2:      ' Set the height and scaling to the underlying control
3:      ' Stretch the control to the width and height
4:     If UserControl.Height <> txtParent.Height Then
5:        txtParent.Height = UserControl.Height
6:     End If
7:     txtParent.Move 0, 0, UserControl.ScaleWidth
8:  End Sub
```

Line 4 makes sure that, if the programmer using this control resizes the new control, the embedded text box control resizes also, because the internal text box control works as a holding area for the new control. Line 7 uses the `Move` method to move the parent's text box to the new control's upper-left coordinate (0, 0) and then sets the same scale for both properties. This ensures that the internal text box moves every time the programmer moves the new control. Again, the internal control is what the new control manages as the programmer moves and resizes the new ActiveX control. The `Move` method performs both the movement and the scale setting for the existing control to keep both controls equal. Therefore, the internal text box acts like a transparency over the ActiveX control and always stays right on top of the ActiveX control to accept and display text.

Now that the resizing is out of the way, your primary job is to set up the enumerated value display, write the code to handle selection of the `AutoTSize` property, and to convert the ActiveX control to uppercase or lowercase, depending on the `ULText` property. The wizard created placeholder code for the `AutoTSize` and `ULText` properties, but you must fill in the details.

You're now ready to set up `Get` and `Let` procedures for the new property values. When the user (that is, the programmer who ultimately uses this ActiveX control in an application) sets a property value, the `Let` procedure runs. When the user accesses a property value, the `Get` procedure runs.

The simplest of the two methods is the `Get` method. The wizard created sample `Get` function procedures for the two property values, but you'll have to change them. Instead of the Variant return data type, you'll need to use the enumerated data types, as shown in Listing 17.5.

LISTING 17.5. THE `Get` PROCEDURES FOR THE NEW PROPERTIES MUST RETURN THEIR CORRESPONDING ENUMERATED VALUES.


```
Public Property Get AutoTSize() As AutoTSizeEnum
    AutoTSize = m_AutoTSize
End Property

Public Property Get ULText() As ULTextEnum
   ULText = m_ULText
End Property
```

Listing 17.5 only assigns the current member's value to the state property. Converting the Variant to the enumeration for the return value is the only necessary change you must make.

You'll also have to change the two `Let` procedures' return data types. They require additional code as well. When a value is assigned to one of the two new properties, several things must take place, such as the sizing of the text or the conversion to uppercase or lowercase letters.

You now have two more procedures to complete: the corresponding `Let` procedures for the two properties. The wizard created shell code for these procedures. This code is shown in Listing 17.6.

LISTING 17.6. YOU MUST COMPLETE THE `Let` PROCEDURES FOR BOTH PROPERTIES.

```
Public Property Let AutoTSize(ByVal New_AutoTSize As AutoTSizeEnum)
    m_AutoTSize = New_AutoTSize
    ' Test the property's state and change the size
    ' according to the value of the property.
    '
    Select Case New_AutoTSize
       Case 1: ' No change necessary
```

continues

LISTING 17.6. CONTINUED

```
8:          Case 2: Font.Size = 72 * 0.25 * (Height / 1440)
9:          Case 3: Font.Size = 72 * 0.5 * (Height / 1440)
10:         Case 4: Font.Size = 72 * 0.75 * (Height / 1440)
11:      End Select
12:      PropertyChanged "AutoTSize"
13: End Property
14:
15: Public Property Let ULText(ByVal New_ULText As ULTextEnum)
16:      m_ULText = New_ULText
17:      ' Test the control's state
18:      ' and change the text box accordingly
19:      ' (ignore a ULText of 0 which means As Is)
20:      If New_ULText = 1 Then
21:        Text = UCase(txtParent.Text)
22:      ElseIf New_ULText = 2 Then
23:        Text = LCase(txtParent.Text)
24:      End If
25:      PropertyChanged "ULText"
26: End Property
```

Do	Don't
DO be sure that you change the passed data types in these `Get AutoTSize()` and `Get ULText()` procedures so that enumerated data is received instead of the Variant data types they receive by default.	

Lines 8, 9, and 10 adjust the internal text box control's font size to be a factor of the text box's `Height` property. Again, the programmer is working directly with the new ActiveX control, but the ActiveX control is actually just a go-between for the internal text box that appears on the form. The `UCase()` and `LCase()` internal functions in line 21 and 23 convert the text values to uppercase or lowercase, depending on the value assigned to the property. If the programmer who uses the ActiveX control assigns the `ULText` property at designtime or runtime, this procedure executes.

You're now finished designing and creating the ActiveX control. You must now prepare the control for insertion into another application and test it to be sure that it works as expected.

Implementing the ActiveX Control

Not only can you insert your new control into an application and place it on the form window just as you do other controls, but the new ActiveX control takes on every single benefit given to intrinsic controls. Therefore, the control's Properties window will act like other controls. Also, when a programmer who uses the ActiveX control inside a code window types an assignment to assign a property value, even the code window's Quick Info pops up to let him or her select a property. Also, the toolbox that holds the ActiveX control automatically displays a ToolTip describing the control's name. You'll be proud of your new ActiveX control when you begin using it, because the control will act as though it was supplied by Microsoft with Visual Basic!

When you compile the ActiveX control, Visual Basic compiles the control into an ActiveX file that you can then insert into a project just as you can other ActiveX controls. If you do not create the OCX file, you cannot use the control in an application.

You should save your control before compiling it. Choose File, Save Project to save both the control and the project. You can't run an ActiveX control by using the normal F5 keypress, because all ActiveX controls must be compiled before they can execute. Remember, of course, that the term *execute* actually means *work as the other controls work* when a programmer uses the ActiveX control inside an application.

To compile the ActiveX control, select File, Make. Visual Basic displays the Make Project dialog box shown in Figure 17.10. You can select the location of the compiled ActiveX control. You might want to place the control in your \Windows\System folder or in a Visual Basic work folder that you've created. (This is the folder you search when you want to load the ActiveX control into another Visual Basic application's toolbox from the Project Properties dialog box.) If the compiler notices errors, Visual Basic won't build the control and will highlight the error lines in the code. As soon as you eliminate the bugs, the compiler returns you to the development environment.

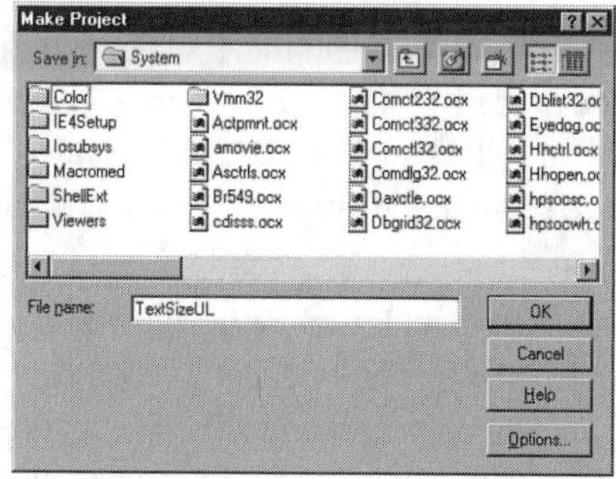

FIGURE 17.10.
Enter the filename of the ActiveX control and Visual Basic saves the control with the .OCX filename extension.

Visual Basic supports two ways to test the control:

- Open a new project and test the control from that project. A multiproject development environment is available only for testing ActiveX controls.
- Open a new Standard EXE project and drop the control into that new project.

You'll now test your new control by actually putting it to use. Select File, New Project and create a new Standard EXE file. Press Ctrl+T to open the Components dialog box. As Figure 17.11 shows, the TextSizeUL control appears at the top of the dialog box. The description you used for the control appears in the dialog box for easy selection.

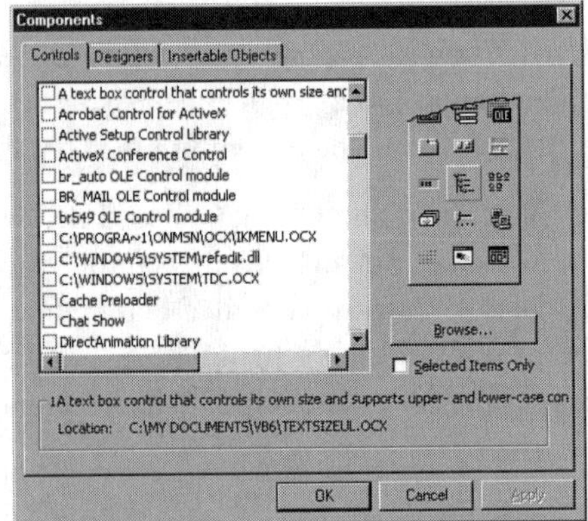

FIGURE 17.11.

Your ActiveX control's Project Description text appears in the Components dialog box.

Select the ActiveX control and close the dialog box. The control's bitmap image that you selected when you created the control appears in the toolbox. To use the control in a simple application, follow these steps:

1. Change the form name to `frmActiveX` and change the form's caption to `Test the ActiveX Control`. Expand the form's `Width` and `Height` properties to `7575` and `5775`, respectively.
2. Point to the TextSizeUL control and read the ToolTip that the ActiveX control wizard created for you. The name is rather boring: `NewControl` is not very fancy, but that's the name used because that's the project name under which you saved the control. For this practice session, the control's action is what we're concerned about more than its name.
3. Double-click the new control to add it to the form. (You could also drag and draw the control onto the form window.) Notice that the control looks like a normal text box control except for the two extra properties that it supports. Size the TextSizeUL control to approximately 4,815 twips (the `Width` property) by 1,215 twips (the `Height` property). Change the `FontSize` property to `18` and the `FontBold` property to `True`.

4. Click the `ULText` property's arrow to open the drop-down list box. You'll see the three enumerated values `AsIs`, `Uppercase`, and `Lowercase`, just the way you programmed them. For now, leave the control at its default `AsIs` state.
5. Click the `AutoTSize` property to see its enumerated values. Again, leave the default value in place.
6. Change the `Name` property to `MyFirstCtl` and blank out the `Text` property.
7. Add five command buttons to the form using the property values shown in Table 17.1.

TABLE 17.1. SET THESE COMMAND BUTTON CONTROLS AND PROPERTIES ON THE FORM.

Control	*Property Value*
Command button #1 `Name`	`cmdSmall`
Command button #1 `Caption`	`&Small text`
Command button #1 `Left`	`1320`
Command button #1 `Top`	`2640`
Command button #2 `Name`	`cmdMedium`
Command button #2 `Caption`	`&Medium text`
Command button #2 `Left`	`3120`
Command button #2 `Top`	`2640`
Command button #3 `Name`	`cmdLarge`
Command button #3 `Caption`	`&Large text`
Command button #3 `Left`	`4920`
Command button #3 `Top`	`2640`
Command button #4 `Name`	`cmdUpper`
Command button #4 `Caption`	`&Uppercase`
Command button #4 `Left`	`2160`
Command button #4 `Top`	`3600`
Command button #5 `Name`	`cmdLower`
Command button #5 `Caption`	`&Lowercase`
Command button #5 `Left`	`3960`
Command button #5 `Top`	`3600`

8. Add the event procedures shown in Listing 17.7.

LISTING 17.7. THESE EVENT PROCEDURES WILL TEST THE NEW ACTIVEX CONTROL.

```
Private Sub cmdSmall_Click()
  ' Test the Small text conversion
  MyFirstCtl.AutoTSize = Small
End Sub

Private Sub cmdMedium_Click()
  ' Test the Mediumtext conversion
  MyFirstCtl.AutoTSize = Medium
End Sub

Private Sub cmdLarge_Click()
  ' Test the Large text conversion
  MyFirstCtl.AutoTSize = Large
End Sub

Private Sub cmdUpper_Click()
  ' Test the uppercase conversion
  MyFirstCtl.ULText = Uppercase
End Sub

Private Sub cmdLower_Click()
  ' Test the lowercase conversion
  MyFirstCtl.ULText = Lowercase
End Sub
```

As you type the code, notice that Visual Basic helps you locate the new ActiveX control's property values when you type the equal (as shown in Figure 17.12) with a drop-down list box of choices. The choices offered are the only possible values that Visual Basic will let the control receive. Therefore, the selection list that appears when you type the equal sign is incredible, given that you did absolutely nothing to produce this feature.

FIGURE 17.12.

Your ActiveX control supports the pop-up list box Quick Info help.

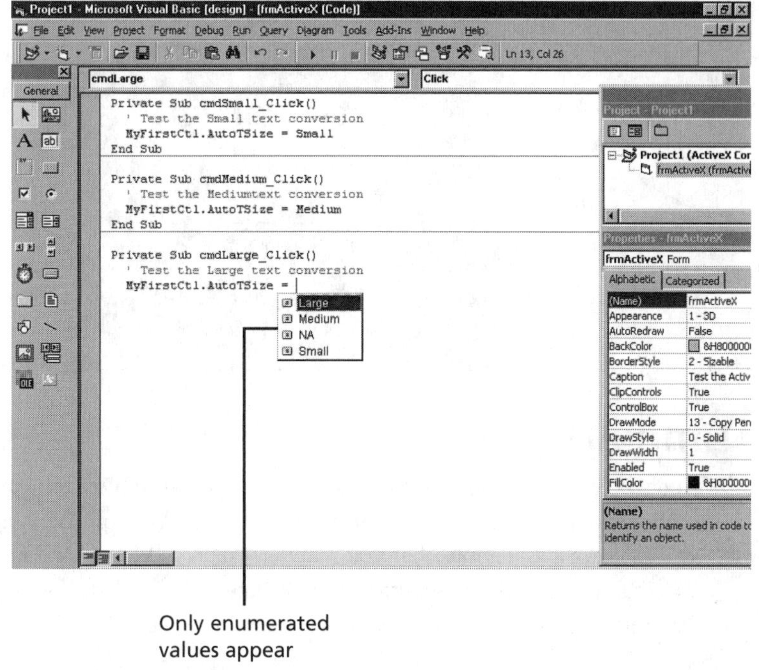

Compile and run the application. Type a value in the ActiveX control's text box area using a combination of uppercase and lowercase letters. Click the three sizing buttons to see the text change size. Remember that these buttons are linked *not* to a `Font.Size` property but to new the property values you've created for the control. In addition, click the case-conversion command buttons to see the text change case.

Note

> Once you convert the ActiveX control's text to uppercase or lowercase, the original case is lost until you type a new value in the control's Text field.

Figure 17.13 shows the running application. You didn't need a new control to perform these conversions; however, the new control supports built-in conversion properties that you can set at any time to control the text's size, based on the control's `Height` property, as well as the text's case.

17

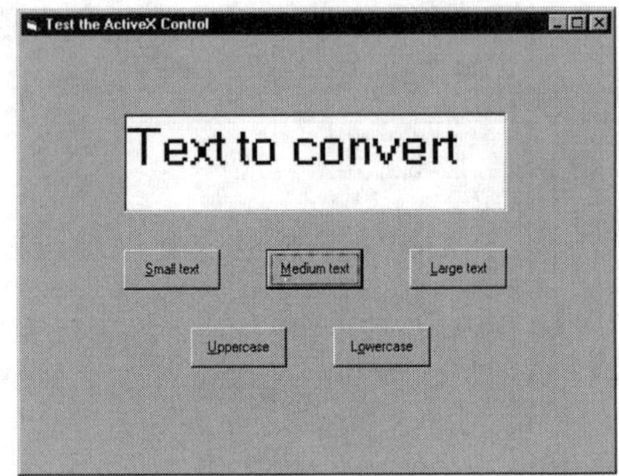

FIGURE 17.13.
The ActiveX control's properties now perform conversions.

Summary

Today's lesson explained how to work with special ActiveX objects. Not only do ActiveX objects add new controls to your toolbox window, but they work in other kinds of Windows applications that you may use, such as Visual C++ and Internet browsers. For this reason, ActiveX controls are available from a wide variety of sources. Once you learn how to use an ActiveX control, you then can use it in other applications.

You can even create your own ActiveX controls by taking advantage of the ActiveX Interface Control Wizard. You can subclass an ActiveX control from an existing control (even if that control is another ActiveX control that you or someone else has written). You'll eventually build a library of controls that help you create other controls and applications.

Tomorrow's lesson, "Interacting with Data," shows you how to integrate Visual Basic applications with databases so that your programs can access and manipulate large amounts of information.

Q&A

Q Why should I create new group tabs on my toolbox window?

A The tabs only exist to organize your controls. By grouping the controls together, you'll more easily locate the controls you need for a given purpose. For example, if you're creating a database-related Visual Basic application, you can group the set of database-related controls in their own tabbed group to access them more easily. You then do not have to search through all the controls in the General section to find one that you need. Despite the tabbed groups, all the controls on the toolbox window are always available for you to use.

Q Can I get rid of tabbed groups that I create?

A Certainly. Right-click any group name to display a pop-up menu that contains a Delete Tab option. In addition to deleting the tabs, you can also rename them from the right-click pop-up menu.

Workshop

The Workshop provides quiz questions to help you solidify your understanding of the material covered and exercises to provide you with experience in using what you've learned. Try to understand the quiz and exercise answers before continuing to the next lesson. Answers are provided in Appendix A, "Answers to Exercises."

Quiz

1. What does *automation* mean?
2. What happens if your application uses `CreateObject()` for a Word document and Word is already running?
3. Why can't you directly assign applications to object variables?
4. What is the purpose of the system object's `Err.Number`?
5. What are the three ways to create ActiveX controls?
6. Which method of ActiveX control creation is the easiest to use?
7. True/False. When you subclass a control, the new ActiveX control borrows properties, events, and methods from the parent.
8. What are enumeration blocks used for?
9. What extension does Visual Basic use for compiled ActiveX controls?
10. Which two procedures do ActiveX control properties require?

Exercises

1. Use the Components dialog box to search your disk for ActiveX controls. You'll probably find some that aren't in the Windows folder. For example, if you're a member of Microsoft Network's online service, you'll find several ActiveX controls in the Microsoft Network folder.

2. Change the ActiveX control and the application that you created at the end of this lesson. Modify the `AsIs` enumerated value so that it reads `AsEntered`. Change the ActiveX control so that, if a program changes the text from `AsEntered` to either `Uppercase` or `Lowercase`, the control remembers the text as it appeared before the conversion. Rewrite the final application in this lesson to add a sixth command button that reads As Entered. When the user clicks this command button, the text should revert back to its previous form.

WEEK 3

BONUS PROJECT 8

Elements That Spruce Up Apps

This Bonus Project describes how to create an application that includes the following items:

- An About box displayed from the Help, About menu option
- A sound file that automatically plays when the About box appears
- A picture box that moves to show simple animation
- A timer that controls the animation
- An array of picture box controls

This project contains nothing fancy. Despite the animated picture box, you'll see that the animation is rather dull. That's okay, though, because you'll understand the principle behind moving objects within picture boxes and you'll have hands-on experience with using an About box and adding a WAV file to your applications.

The Application's Goal

Figure BP8.1 shows the form as it will appear during the animation. (When you first run this application, the envelope is sealed and the letter is not on the screen.) The form is simple and large enough so that the letter can fly out of the open envelope when the user clicks the Animate button.

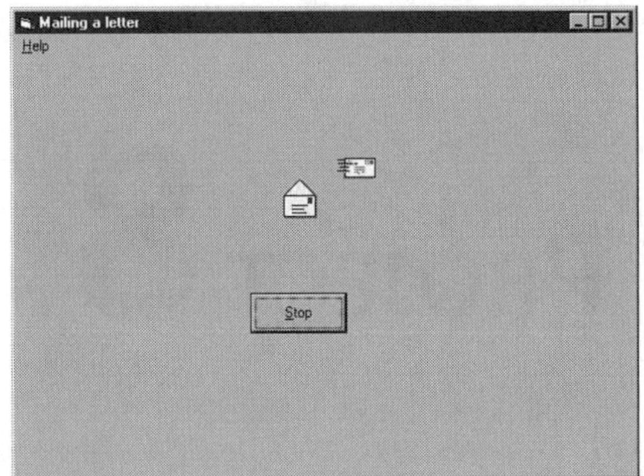

FIGURE BP8.1.
The application simply shows a letter flying out of the envelope.

Note

Once the user starts the animation, the letter keeps flying out of the envelope and the button caption changes to Stop.

Figure BP8.2 shows the About box that will appears when the user selects Help, About.

FIGURE BP8.2.
A WAV file plays when the user displays this About box.

Creating the Primary Form

Table BP8.1 contains the controls and properties you need to set to create the primary form that appears when the user starts the application. You must have installed the Graphics folder when you installed Visual Basic; otherwise, you'll have to insert your Visual Basic CD-ROM and point to its Graphics folder or you'll have to install the Graphics folder by running Visual Basic's Setup file once again. In addition, you must press Ctrl+T to add the multimedia control to the toolbox window before you can add the multimedia control to the form.

Note

Many of the controls in this project, such as the timer control and the picture boxes that you place during design time, are located along the outer edges of the form, just to keep them out of the way while you add the remaining controls. The timer control never appears to the user, so you can place it anywhere you want. The picture boxes will move to show animation, so their initial design time placement doesn't matter either.

Tip

This project contains three picture box controls that are part of a single control array. Although you could create three separate Picture box controls, making the array is good practice for projects that require numerous controls that are similar in appearance and purpose. To create the array, create the first array element's picture box control, `picAni2` (the Picture box control named `picAni1` is *not* part of an array but is a single standalone control). Once you place `picAni2` and assign its properties, copy `picAni2` to the Clipboard with Edit, Copy. When you select Edit, Paste, answer Yes to the dialog box that asks if you want to create a control array. Visual Basic turns the original nonarrayed `picAni2` into `picAni2(0)`, the first element in the control array. Paste once again for the third item in the `picAni2` control array when you're ready to place that control on the form.

To give you a better idea of your form window's appearance, Figure BP8.3 shows the form window as it will look after you place all the controls from Table BP8.1. The executing program will make some of the controls invisible and will animate others to take on the appearance of a letter flying out of an envelope.

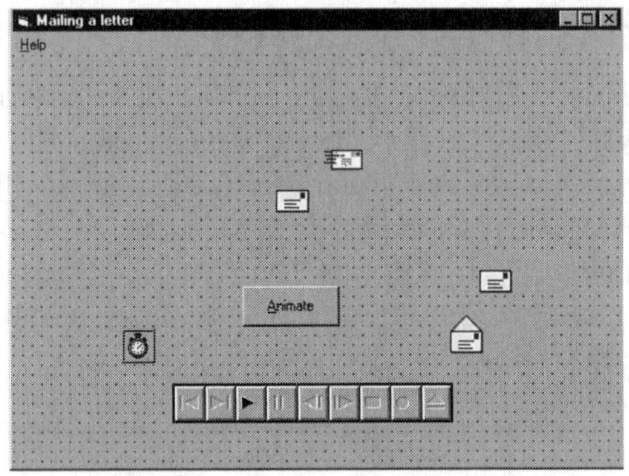

FIGURE BP8.3.
Your form window will look like this after you place the controls on it.

TABLE BP8.1. SET THESE CONTROLS AND PROPERTIES ON THE FORM.

Control Property Name	*Property Value*
Form `Name`	`frmEnvelope`
Form `Caption`	`Mailing a Letter`
Form `Height`	`5790`
Form `Width`	`7845`
Menu option #1 `Caption`	`&Help`
Menu option #1 `Name`	`mnuHelp`
Menu option #2 `Caption`	`&About`
Menu option #2 `Name`	`mnuHelpAbout`
Command button `Name`	`cmdAni`
Command button `Caption`	`&Animate`
Command button `Left`	`2940`
Command button `Top`	`2880`
Timer `Name`	`tmrAni`
Timer `Enabled`	`False`
Timer `Interval`	`300`
Timer `Left`	`1410`
Timer `Top`	`3405`
Picture box #1 `Name`	`picAni1`
Picture box #1 `Height`	`495`
Picture box #1 `Left`	`3330`
Picture box #1 `Picture`	`Common\Graphics\Icons\Mail\Mail01a`

Control Property Name	*Property Value*
Picture box #1 `Top`	`1485`
Picture box #1 `Width`	`1215`
Picture box #2 `Name`	`picAni2(0)`
Picture box #2 `Height`	`495`
Picture box #2 `Left`	`5895`
Picture box #2 `Picture`	`Common\Graphics\Icons\Mail\Mail01a`
Picture box #2 `Top`	`2520`
Picture box #2 `Width`	`1215`
Picture box #3 `Name`	`picAni2(1)`
Picture box #3 `Height`	`495`
Picture box #3 `Left`	`5520`
Picture box #3 `Picture`	`Common\Graphics\Icons\Mail\Mail01b`
Picture box #3 `Top`	`3240`
Picture box #3 `Visible`	`False`
Picture box #3 `Width`	`1215`
Picture box #4 `Name`	`picAni2(2)`
Picture box #4 `Height`	`495`
Picture box #4 `Left`	`3960`
Picture box #4 `Picture`	`Common\Graphics\Icons\Mail\Mail03`
Picture box #4 `Top`	`1080`
Picture box #4 `Visible`	`False`
Picture box #4 `Width`	`1215`
Multimedia control `Name`	`mmcEnv`
Multimedia control `DeviceType`	`WaveAudio`
Multimedia control `PlayEnabled`	`True`
Multimedia control `Filename`	`\Windows\Media\Chimes.wav`
Multimedia control `Left`	`2520`
Multimedia control `Top`	`4080`
Multimedia control `Visible`	`False`
Multimedia control `Width`	`3540`

The sound, Chimes.wav, that plays when the user selects Help, About is a standard sound file that comes with Windows.

Adding the Opening Form's Code

Listing BP8.1 contains the code you need to add to the opening form. The code activates the form and controls the animation that takes place. The animation is simple. It results from moving a picture box control to and from only three locations on the form.

LISTING BP8.1. ANIMATION CODE CAN BE SIMPLE.

```
Private Sub cmdAni_Click()
  ' Use the command button to control the animation
  If cmdAni.Caption = "&Animate" Then
    cmdAni.Caption = "&Stop"
    tmrAni.Enabled = True
  Else
    cmdAni.Caption = "&Animate"
    tmrAni.Enabled = False
  End If
End Sub

Private Sub mnuHelpAbout_Click()
    mmcEnv.Command = "Open"
    mmcEnv.Command = "Play"
    frmAbout.Show
End Sub

Private Sub tmrAni_Timer()
  ' Determine the correct picture
  ' location to display
  '
  ' The following variable begins at zero
  ' and retains its value every time the
  ' procedure executes.
  Static intCounter As Integer

  Select Case intCounter
    Case 0:
      picAni1.Picture = picAni2(1).Picture
      picAni2(2).Visible = True
      picAni2(2).Left = 3840
      picAni2(2).Top = 1220
      intCounter = 1
    Case 1:
      picAni1.Picture = picAni2(1).Picture
```

```
36:        picAni2(2).Visible = True
37:        picAni2(2).Left = 4040
38:        picAni2(2).Top = 1120
39:        intCounter = 2
40:      Case 2:
41:        picAni1.Picture = picAni2(1).Picture
42:        picAni2(2).Visible = True
43:        picAni2(2).Left = 4240
44:        picAni2(2).Top = 1220
45:        intCounter = 3
46:      Case 3:
47:        picAni1.Picture = picAni2(0).Picture
48:        picAni2(2).Left = 4440
49:        picAni2(2).Top = 1320
50:        intCounter = 4
51:      Case 4:
52:        ' Stop the animation
53:        picAni1.Visible = True
54:        intCounter = 0
55:        picAni2(2).Visible = False
56:      End Select
57: End Sub
```

Analysis

The `cmdAni_Click()` event procedure toggles the command button's caption from Animate to Stop. If the button shows the Animate caption, line 4 changes the caption to Stop and enables the timer control in line 5. By enabling the timer, the command button's `Click` event begins triggering line 18's `tmrAni_Timer()` event. The timer's `Interval` property value of `300` means that the `tmrAni_Timer()` event procedure executes every 300 milliseconds, thus producing the animation. The animation continues until the user clicks the Stop button. Then line 7 changes the button's caption back once again and line 8 disables the timer.

Moving on the `tmrAni_Timer()` event procedure that begins in line 18, remember that the `Timer` event causes this procedure to execute every 300 milliseconds. The procedure performs one of four actions, controlled by the `Select Case` statement in line 27. The variable that determines which of the five actions takes place is a static variable. The static variable, declared in line 25, begins with a value of `0` (as all static variables begin). Once assigned a value, subsequent executions on `tmrAni_Timer()` will retain the value that `intCounter` had in it the previous procedure's run. Therefore, `intCounter` has one of five values, from `0` to `4`, updated each time through the procedure.

Each of the first three cases performs the following actions:

- Assigns the closed envelope the open envelope icon (see lines 29 and 35).
- Makes the letter icon visible (see lines 30 and 36).
- "Moves" the letter icon by changing its `Left` and `Top` properties (see lines 31 and 32).
- Increments the `intCounter` static variable so that the next time `tmrAni_Timer()` executes, a different set of `Case` statements execute.

This process continues until the `Case` value is `4`. At this time, in line 53, the procedure shows the closed envelope once again and once again hides the letter icon (line 55). Unless the user clicks the Stop button at this time, the letter will once again fly out of the envelope after another 300 milliseconds go by, because line 54 assigns `0` to the static variable to force the first `Case` to execute once again.

The remaining event procedure, `mnuHelpAbout_Click()`, controls the display of the About box in line 15 after lines 13 and 14 open the WAV device and play the WAV file. The About form's properties are described in the next section.

Although the About box does contain code, the code comes from the form template that you use for the About box (described in the next section). You don't need to add to or edit this code. The code ensures that the system information routine begins when the user clicks the command button to request the system information.

Creating the About Box

Use the About Box form template for the About box. After creating the first form, right-click the Project window and select Add, Form. Select About Dialog to add the About dialog box to your Form window. (This adds both the form and its code to your project.)

Table BP8.2 contains the control values you'll use for the About box. These controls are already on the form, and Table BP8.2 contains only those properties you need to change.

Table BP8.2. Set these controls and properties on the About box form.

Control Property Name	*Property Value*
`lblDescription Caption`	`Seeing simple animation and hearing a sound`
`lblDescription Font size`	`14`
`lblDescription Font style`	`Bold`
`lblDisclaimer Caption`	`Warning: Programmer on board!`

The code that comes with the About box adds the About box title and version number from the system objects `App.Title`, `App.Major` (for the major version), `App.Minor`, and `App.Revision` to produce the 1.0.0 version number.

WEEK 3

DAY 18

Interacting with Data

Today's lesson shows you how to access databases through your Visual Basic applications. A *database* is a collection of files that work together to form a complete data-management system. A database system, such as Microsoft Access, creates the database your Visual Basic applications might need to connect to. By using the special database controls and methods, your applications can communicate with the database itself.

Today, you learn the following:

- Which databases Visual Basic interacts with
- About database terminology
- About the importance of index fields
- About the Visual Data Manager's capability to analyze database structures
- About the data control
- How the ADO controls compare to the data control
- How the Visual Basic Application Wizard can analyze tables and generate forms

Database Data and Visual Basic

By offering you the ability to interact with databases, Visual Basic gives you the power to access and manipulate large data resources from a Visual Basic program. The databases that Visual Basic can access take on many forms and formats. Visual Basic supports the following popular database formats:

- Microsoft Access
- Excel
- dBASE
- FoxPro
- Lotus spreadsheet-based databases
- ODBC-compliant databases
- Paradox
- Text files formatted with comma-delimited data

New Term A *database* is an organized collection of data. The data is not usually text based, as word processing data is, but rather it's based on groups of items that you must track, whether those items are personnel, customers, vendors, inventory, books, or software (in other words, any kind of data you must keep track of, report on, and change). Often, you use a *database system*, such as Microsoft Access, to create and manage the database structure. Visual Basic can access the database you create from within the database system.

Visual Basic can access and manage data from many different versions of these database systems. As long as you use a version that has been around as long as Windows 95, you can be sure that Visual Basic supports the data format (although Visual Basic supports some versions of the listed database systems that go back further than Windows 95).

To understand how Visual Basic supports database use, you must understand terms related to database technology. Today's lesson only scratches the surface! You're reading this book to learn Visual Basic, not database technology. If you want more of an in-depth look at databases and Visual Basic's advanced access to database systems, check out *Sams Teach Yourself Database Programming with Visual Basic in 21 Days* and *Database Developer's Guide with Visual Basic*.

You don't have to be a database expert, however, to get to know Visual Basic's database access techniques. Visual Basic includes numerous controls that support database access in a structured environment. The rest of today's lesson will introduce you to those tools and to database processing in general.

Learn the Terms

Historically, one usually begins learning about a database by starting with data files in general. You have an advantage already because you learned about records and fields in Day 12, "Interact with Files." Figure 18.1 illustrates a typical scenario that clearly shows the concept of records and fields. A record is thought to be one row of information in a data file, even though one logical record could extend into two or three actual physical lines in the file. Each record is broken into fields, or *columns*, that help distinguish each record's piece of data.

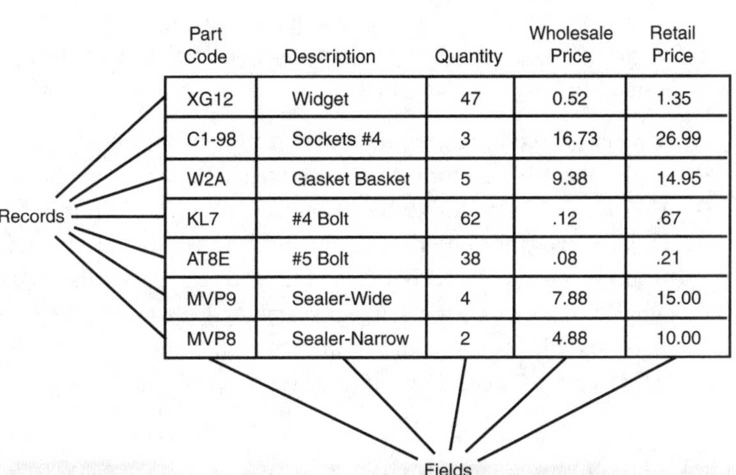

Part Code	Description	Quantity	Wholesale Price	Retail Price
XG12	Widget	47	0.52	1.35
C1-98	Sockets #4	3	16.73	26.99
W2A	Gasket Basket	5	9.38	14.95
KL7	#4 Bolt	62	.12	.67
AT8E	#5 Bolt	38	.08	.21
MVP9	Sealer-Wide	4	7.88	15.00
MVP8	Sealer-Narrow	2	4.88	10.00

FIGURE 18.1.
A typical data file is broken into records and fields.

Note

> The data file in Figure 18.1 shows seven records and five fields. If more items were added to the inventory, the number of records would increase, but the number of fields would remain the same. Your data files are not necessarily fixed, however, in that you can expand the number of fields. You must change the file's design to do this, though, and adding fields is not normally the same process as adding and removing records. Most often, you add and remove items to and from the inventory, which adds and removes records from the database.

> **Caution:** The field names are never part of the data. They serve only to label the fields, just as a variable name labels the contents of the variable.

The file shown in Figure 18.1 is known as a *flat-file database* because the file stands on its own, and a program can access the information simply—either sequentially or randomly. The records don't have to appear in any particular order, although usually the database designer will keep the file sorted by some access field, such as the part number, because such a file is often easier to use when you're locating sorted data. Today's database systems go far beyond the single flat-file data concept shown in this figure.

In today's database terminology, a *table* is one data file, and the database is the collection of those tables. Therefore, your database might consist of a customer data table, a vendor data table, an employee data table, and an inventory data table. By putting these tables into a single database, programs that can access the database have access to all the tables at the same time. Therefore, the program could determine which vendor sold a part wholesale to you or which employee sold a particular product. In other words, a database system can take these separate tables and produce consolidated information from them.

A *query* is used to retrieve information from a database. In other words, a program queries the database for data when a certain record or combined record of data is needed. Also, a database table usually has at least one index defined. An *index* is a key field with unique values for every record. The index works just like a book's index: When you need to access a particular record in a table, you can specify the index value, and the database jumps directly to the row without searching the entire table (as would be done in typical sequential file access routines). In Figure 18.1, the best field for the index would be the Part Code field, because every part has a unique part number.

> **Note:** Do you sometimes feel as though you're just a number? Are you tired of all those account numbers you have (checking account, savings account, loans, car tags, drivers license, social security number, and so on)? You now have a better idea why the numbers are so important: The computer can more quickly identify you. If a company stored information by name, that information would often be difficult to find. For example, several people in a national credit card file would probably have your same name. If your name

were MacDonald and you called for your current balance, the receptionist might search for McDonald or Mac Donald or MAC DONALD, and the computer would probably not match the name. (Computers are *so* literal!) The unique identification number used for index fields means fewer mistakes will occur. Also, companies can automate to save time, and their saved time ultimately is reflected in better prices and interest rates for you.

When working with databases (instead of just single data files), programmers prefer the term *table* to *file*, as you read earlier. However, in addition, they also use *columns* and *rows* to refer to *fields* and *records*. That makes sense, because the files, or *tables*, are rectangular in theory (though not in reality; they are stored physically quite differently) and are made up of rows and columns, as shown in Figure 18.1. Also, multiple files inside a single database file could get confusing, thus the term *table* for one occurrence of one data set (one data file) inside the database. In addition, most of today's database systems are *relational*, meaning that no two tables contain exactly the same data so that file redundancy is eliminated as much as possible. Microsoft Access is such a relational database. For database files that are not relational, such as pre-dBASE 4.0 files, you have to add fairly complex Visual Basic code to make the database file mimic relational access before performing I/O with Visual Basic's database tools.

Most databases inherently support the user's interface, as well. For example, database files can contain predefined reports that produce output based on the data, screen forms to display and receive new data from users, stored queries so the user does not have to create a new query every time information is needed, and database definitions so that programs can analyze the database and read the format using standard procedures. These procedures let programmers know how many tables exist and how their structures look.

Obtaining Sample Data

Visual Basic comes with the following two sample database files, both in the Microsoft Access format:

- BIBLIO.MDB—Contains a database of computer book dealers and titles.
- NWIND.MDB—Contains an imaginary company's complete database system, including inventory, customers, vendors, employees, marketing statistics, and more. The company's name is Northwind Traders, Inc.

All Access database files end in the extension .MDB (for *Microsoft database*). An Access database file can be huge—one file contains all the tables, reports, forms, screens, and stored queries in the database. The advantage of a single file is that you can more easily back up your entire database (that is, you don't have to keep track of multiple files every time you perform a backup).

To make today's introduction of databases easy, this lesson uses the supplied NWIND.MDB database to demonstrate some of the data-related controls and commands. However, not every Visual Basic programmer has access to an outside database system. Fortunately, Visual Basic does include a special add-in tool called the *Visual Data Manager* with which you can create and modify database files.

NEW TERM The *Visual Data Manager* is an add-in program available from within the Visual Basic environment that you can use to create databases, enter and edit data, and modify and report on the data structure. The files you create and analyze from the Visual Data Manager help you write and test Visual Basic programs that must work with similar data.

Caution

If you use the Standard edition of Visual Basic, you don't have the Visual Data Manager. Your version of Visual Basic still comes with the NWIND.MDB database file, however, so you can still work with some of the following examples. Unfortunately, though, you'll be unable to use the Visual Data Manager.

The Visual Data Manager is the only default add-in tool in the Add-Ins menu. Select Add-Ins, Visual Data Manager, and Visual Basic starts the Visual Data Manager by opening the VisData window (see Figure 18.2).

With the Visual Data Manager, you can perform the following tasks:

- Create new database files
- Enter new data into data files
- Edit existing database file structures
- Edit existing database data
- Search for database fields, queries, and recordsets

FIGURE 18.2.

The Visual Data Manager helps you create and analyze database files.

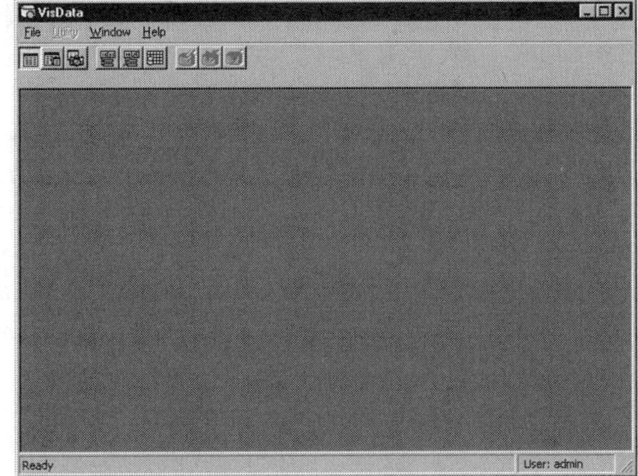

NEW TERM A *recordset* is just a collection of records. Several kinds of recordsets exist. The default recordset is simply all the records (*rows*) in a table. You might create a new recordset by retrieving only records that meet a specific criteria (such as "All records that contain a Balance field greater than $500"). A *dynaset* is a changing recordset that continues to meet a certain criteria when you request the recordset. A *snapshot* is a recordset from a specific point in time, such as all records that meet a specific criteria on the last day of the month.

18

In other words, the Visual Data Manager acts like a database system, not unlike Microsoft Access. Remember, though, that the Visual Data Manager is extremely limited and is more of an administrative tool for analyzing database files than it is an actual database system. You cannot, for example, create data reports and forms for the user of the data.

> **Caution**
>
> Again, this lesson provides only a cursory overview of database technology and terminology. Mastering a complete database system, such as Microsoft Access, takes almost as long as mastering the Visual Basic development system.

Here are the general steps you would follow to create a new database using the Visual Data Manager:

1. Create the database file by selecting File, New and then choosing the type of database you want to create by picking vendor from the list. The Visual Data Manager can create and edit all the database formats listed in the first section of today's lesson.
2. Create each table in the database by right-clicking the database window and selecting New Table from the pop-up menu. The Visual Data Manager displays the Table Structure form, shown in Figure 18.3, into which you can enter the name of the table, each field in the table, the field types (each database field supports a unique data type, just as each variable does in Visual Basic), security and validation requirements (such as password-protected fields), and the indexed fields (a table may have multiple indexes depending on how the application is to access the data).

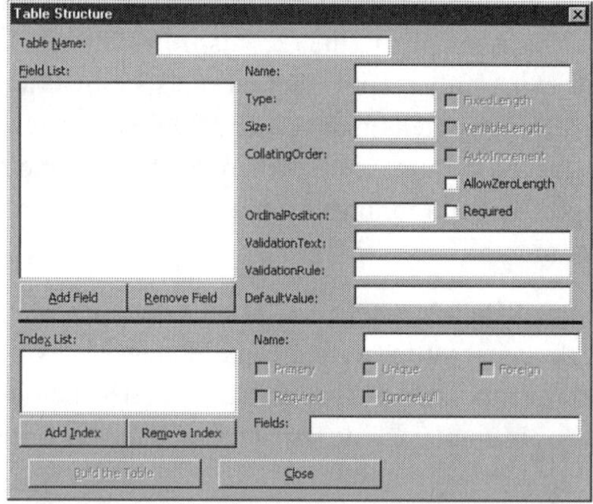

FIGURE 18.3.

You can design each table and its field structure from the Table Structure form.

3. Click the Build the Table button to build the table structure and to add additional tables.
4. Click the toolbar button whose ToolTip text reads "Use Data Control on New Form" so that Visual Data Manager has a tool (called the *data control*) to use for entering the database table data.
5. Double-click one of the table names in the database window and enter each record of data using the data entry form shown in Figure 18.4.

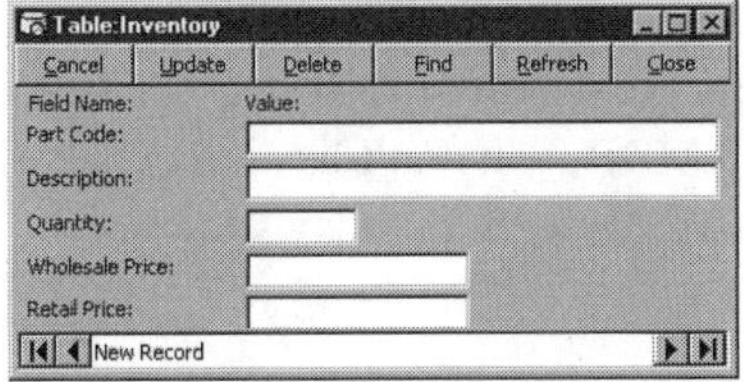

FIGURE 18.4.
Enter each table's data so you have a database to work from.

If you first clicked the toolbar's dynaset-type recordset button or snapshot-type recordset button, the data you enter would take the form of one of these advanced recordset types.

6. Select File, Close to close and save the new database.

Although creating a database requires much more detail than described here, you now have a general idea of the steps needed to create a database using only the tools Visual Basic provides.

18

If your programming eventually requires extensive database work, you'll not want to rely on the Visual Data Manager to produce and edit your database files. Although the Visual Data Manager is helpful for deciphering database formats and for creating simple databases for the testing and debugging of programs, its capabilities do not come close to those of Microsoft Access, FoxPro, or the other database systems on the market. For example, you would not want to use the Visual Data Manager to design and create a company's complete database. The Visual Data Manager is not flexible or simple enough to work with on a regular basis when you're managing a live database file. For serious database programming, you'll want to add a database system to your collection of programs.

Although the Visual Data Manager offers several query tools that let you search for data and create complex queries for locating records, the Visual Data Manager is limited to database administration only. You've got Visual Basic waiting patiently along the sidelines ready to wrap a complete end-user application around a database file when you want to *really* work with the database. Now that you've had an overview of the Visual Data Manager, you're ready to see how Visual Basic can access the database files that you create, whether you create them with the Visual Data Manager or with a standalone database system such as dBASE. Remember that because Visual Basic comes with the complete database file NWIND.MDB, you don't have to create a database to begin learning how Visual Basic's database tools work in today's lesson.

The Data Control

The data control, the final intrinsic toolbox window control you have to learn, is often considered by many to be a slow, cumbersome tool for managing data. Nevertheless, in its defense, the data control is still useful for the following reasons:

- The data control is simple, which makes learning how Visual Basic interacts with database files easier.
- The data control is always on the toolbox window because it's an intrinsic control. Therefore, you don't have to locate and add an ActiveX control to use it.
- Visual Basic's Standard edition does not come with all the advanced database tools that the Professional and Enterprise editions come with. (In today's final sections, you'll learn how some of these advanced database tools and techniques help the Visual Basic programmer access a database in more ways than the data control allows.) However, not everyone has the Professional or Enterprise edition. Therefore, these more advanced techniques simply are not available to all, whereas the data control is.

The following sections describe how to use the data control to access the NWIND.MDB database. Once you've mastered the data control, the more advanced controls will not seem nearly as daunting.

Setting Up the Data Control

When you want to access a database, the simplest way to do so is to use the data control. When you place the data control on a form, it looks somewhat like the multimedia control you learned about in Day 14, "Introducing VB Graphics and Multimedia." After extending the data control's width somewhat, you'll see that the control looks like the one shown in Figure 18.5.

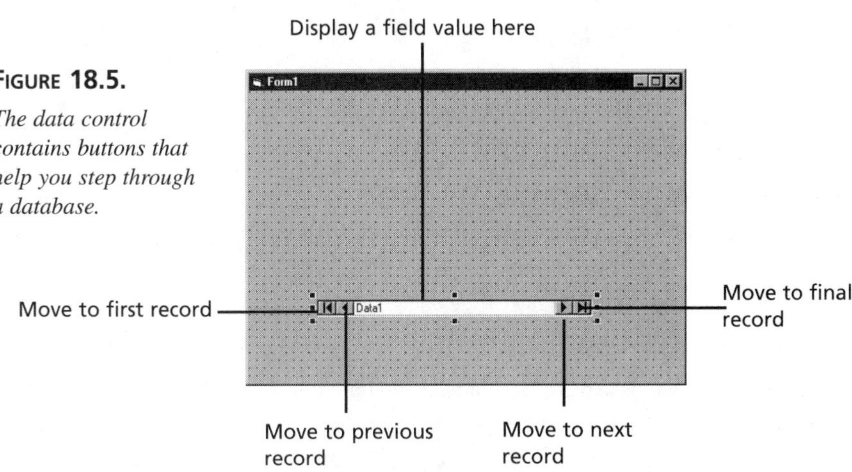

FIGURE 18.5.
The data control contains buttons that help you step through a database.

A data control has these parts:

- Two inner arrows that let you move forward and backward through a database table one record at a time.
- Outer arrows that move you to the first and last records in a database table.
- A middle area that displays whatever information from the database that you want to display.

18

The data control is a *bound control*. You can bind many Visual Basic controls, such as a text box control, to a database. When a user steps through a database, the text box displays the field you've set up. When you bind the control to the database, you don't have to worry about displaying the field data, because Visual Basic does all the work.

NEW TERM A *bound control* is a control that is bound to your database data in a way that makes traversing the database simple for a Visual Basic program.

If you want to display one record at a time from a recordset that you've defined in the database, use a bound control. Bound controls usually display only the current record or a field within the current record. As a user traverses the database, clicking the buttons on the data control, the current record changes to reflect the user's position in the database table.

Using the Data Control

To see the data control in action, take a moment to create an application that displays records from one of the NWIND.MDB database tables. The following steps describe how to create the application:

1. Create a new application and add the data control to the form. Change the data control's `Width` to `4620` to make room for the text that will appear on the control's middle field display section. Move the control toward the bottom of the window so that its `Top` property value is `3240`.
2. Name the data control `dtaBooks`.
3. Use the `DatabaseName` property to connect the data control to the database. Double-click the `DatabaseName` property to select the file named NWIND.MDB from your Visual Basic folder. The data control is an intelligent control that can distinguish between multiple tables in a single database. The data control will only be able to access one table's records at a time (or, more accurately, one recordset at a time), and after you specify the `DatabaseName` property, the data control can decipher the tables within the database.
4. Double-click the `RecordSource` property and select the Customers table from the list (Customers is the name of one of the database tables). The `RecordSource` property specifies which recordset the data control will report from when the application accesses the database.
5. Change the data control's caption to `Click to change customers`. The caption appears in the center of the data control.
6. Add a label control to the form with these properties:
   ```
   Name: lblCust
   Alignment: 2-Center
   FontSize: 18
   Height: 915
   Left: 1680
   Top: 1440
   Width: 4320
   ```
7. Open the label's `DataSource` property. This is a property you've never had to set before. You're going to bind the label to the data control. (A label is one of several controls that can be bound controls.) The label's `DataSource` property will enable you to select the value of `dtaBooks`, because `dtaBooks` is the database table the data control is attached to. If multiple data controls resided on the form and were attached to databases already, the `DataSource` property would list each of those databases so that you could select the source for this label's data.

8. Now that you've bound the label to the correct table, you must bind the label to the correct column (*field*) in the table. Open the `DataField` property and select `ContactName` as the column in the table whose data is to appear in the label.
9. You're ready to run the application. Press F5 to run the application: The first customer name will appear automatically in the label. Remember that the label is bound to the data control, which is bound

FIGURE 18.6.
You can now step through the database, one record at a time, either forward or backward.

10. Click the application window's Close button to terminate the program and save your project.

You're certainly not limited to one column in the table. You can add as many labels as you want to display multiple columns. Figure 18.7 shows a complete customer record displayed. The extra labels simply have their `DataField` values bound to specific columns in the table. In addition, extra labels help describe the data being displayed. (You'll have the chance to modify this database program by adding these extra columns in the first exercise at the end of today's lesson.)

> **Tip:** If you want to display columns from multiple tables, you'll have to create a recordset, such as a dynaset, from within your database system that pulls the columns out of the appropriate tables. More advanced Visual Basic controls and commands let you perform advanced database selection, as you'll see throughout the final sections of today's lessons.

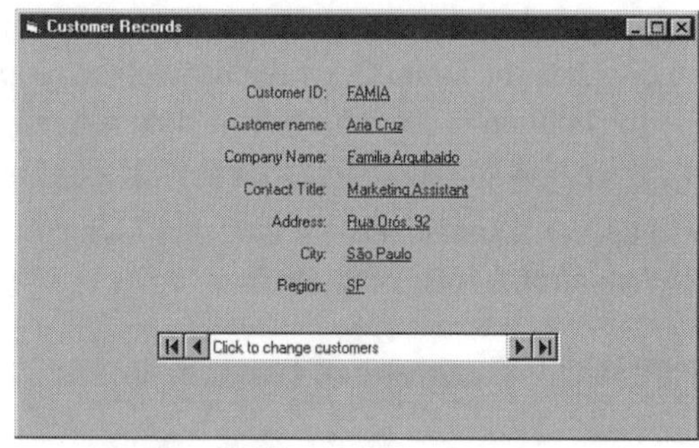

FIGURE 18.7.
Displaying multiple table columns requires only additional labels.

To display data formatted with the Boolean data type, use a check box or an option button to indicate the `True` or `False` value of the Boolean field. The option can indicate the Yes or No and True or False data values that often appear in database tables.

Advanced Data Control Usage

Your database applications certainly don't have to be read-only. You'll want to be able to let users change the database. Several ways exist to do this. The simplest approach is to display the data control's table data in text boxes instead of in labels. Your users will see the information just as they do with labels, but they can also edit the information inside the text boxes to update the database.

Caution

Keep security in mind at all times. You may need to issue a password dialog box to limit the database update to certain people (see Day 15, "Using Form Templates"). In addition, the database itself might limit what kinds of updates can occur. The data control's `Exclusive` property determines whether a user can have exclusive rights to a database and be the only user with access to it (for networked systems), but the data control itself offers little in the way of security. You'll have to master more advanced controls and commands (some of which are discussed in the rest of today's lesson) to incorporate true database security in your applications

As your programming skills improve, you'll learn ways to use the data control for more advanced database access. For example, the data control supports several `Move`-related methods you can use to move the current record pointer to the same locations the data control's buttons do. The following methods move the record pointer to the first, last, next, and previous records in the database pointed to by the data control's `DataSource` property:

```
dtaCust.Recordset.MoveFirst      ' Moves to the first record
dtaCust.Recordset.MoveLast       ' Moves to the last record
dtaCust.Recordset.MoveNext       ' Moves to the next record
dtaCust.Recordset.MovePrevious   ' Moves to the previous record
```

New Term The *record pointer* keeps track of the current record in an open database's table. When you first open a database table, the record pointer points to the first record. As you read through the table sequentially, the record pointer moves forward in the table. The `Move`-related methods manipulate the record pointer so that you can access various records in the table.

The data control's default recordset is defined by the property values you set. For example, if you add a command button that includes a `Click` event procedure which, in turn, contains one of these methods, the label displays the record selected by the method every time the user clicks the command button. In addition to the record-movement controls, methods exist that add and delete records to and from the database.

Use the `BOF` and `EOF` Boolean properties to see whether the record pointer is at the beginning or the end of a table. Visual Basic programmers often use a `Do...While` loop to step through every table record. The loop terminates when `dtaCust.Recordset.EOF` is equal to `True`.

Advanced Database Controls

The Professional, Enterprise, and Visual Studio editions of Visual Basic support an advanced set of controls, properties, methods, and events you can use if you have to write major database-access applications. The texts listed in this lesson's first section provide in-depth training for these controls. Although this 21-day course cannot explore all the advanced database concepts, this lesson does introduce you to these advanced concepts. If you have to add more database coverage to your applications, you'll at least know what Visual Basic is capable of and you'll better understand some of the terminology.

Note

Bonus Project 9, "ADO Controls," walks you through the creation of an ADO-based database project.

Starting with version 6, Visual Basic supports a wide range of *ADO* objects (ADO stands for *ActiveX Data Objects*). Because these objects are ActiveX-based, they work across different platforms and programming languages (unlike the data control, which works strictly in the Visual Basic environment). The ADO objects support database access both for local as well as remote data objects (known as *RDO*). Remote data can come from across a network or a communications line.

Mastering the ADO controls is important because they offer several advantages over the data control. Despite the background necessary to work with the ADO controls (you still have more to learn in order to use them fully), they are the current choice among Visual Basic database programmers due to their power and flexibility.

ADO technology supports faster database access than the data control does. Although today's computers run quickly, you'll notice speed degradation when you use the data control for large database tables, especially ODBC-based databases.

When you use ADO, you'll generally write more program code than you would with the data control. Although you can write code that accesses the various data control methods, straightforward database access is less involved with the data control. ADO enables you to control data access in a much stricter way than the data control. The ease of the data control reflects its inability to be flexible. Also, the overhead of the data control doesn't burden ADO-based programs.

Perhaps the most important advantage of ADO is its capability to access many kinds of data. Not limited to just relational and nonrelational database information, ADO controls can access, through advanced programming, Internet browsers, email text, and even graphics.

Multiple ADO controls placed on the same form can begin to degrade the application's performance, because each control works independently of the other and consumes its own set of resources.

The ADO technology supports (in all editions to some extent, but fully in the Professional, Enterprise, and Visual Studio editions) the following data controls:

- **ADO Data control**—Works like the data control by connecting to a database and letting the user step through the records
- **ADO DataCombo control**—Resembles a standard list box but gives your users access to a column showing multiple records for that column
- **ADO DataList control**—Resembles a standard combo box but gives your users access to a column showing multiple records for that column

Non-ADO versions are available for these controls.

Using the VB Application Wizard

Visual Basic can do much of your database work if you use the Visual Basic Application Wizard to generate an application that contains database access. Although the wizard provides more limited access than you could otherwise obtain throughout ADO programming, you can create an initial application and then modify it to produce a more complete application through programming.

The code that results from the wizard's application generation is fairly complete and forms the basis for a true database application. Figure 18.8 shows the wizard window that first offers database access.

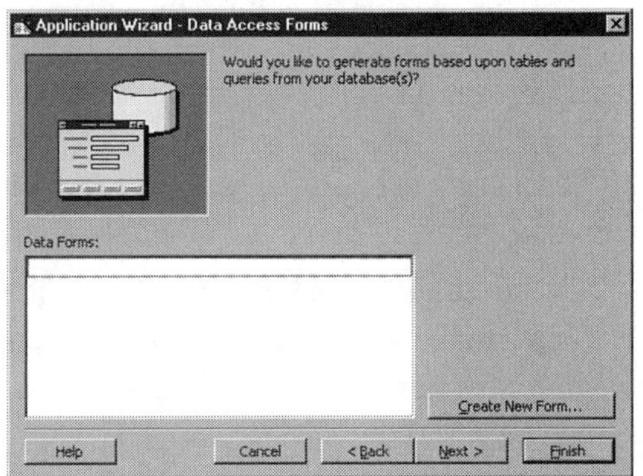

FIGURE 18.8.
The Visual Basic Application Wizard lets you create database programs.

18

Suppose you wanted an application that provides database access for the BIBLIO.MDB file so that your users could view and update this sample database that comes with Visual Basic. After starting the Visual Basic Application Wizard and running through the initial windows, you'll see the window shown in Figure 18.8. Here, you let the wizard know that you need it to generate forms that access database data. Although you can create these forms yourself (select the SDI option), you can let the wizard do the initial work and then you can customize the forms yourself.

Once you click the Create New Form button to generate a form, the wizard will ask you for a profile setting in case you've use customized profiles. For this example, click Next to select a database type for the application to access. The BIBLIO.MDB database that comes with Visual Basic is a Microsoft Access database, so select Access and click Next.

Next, the wizard requests a database name in the window shown in Figure 18.9. Specify the path and filename for the database. (You can click the Browse button to locate the file.)

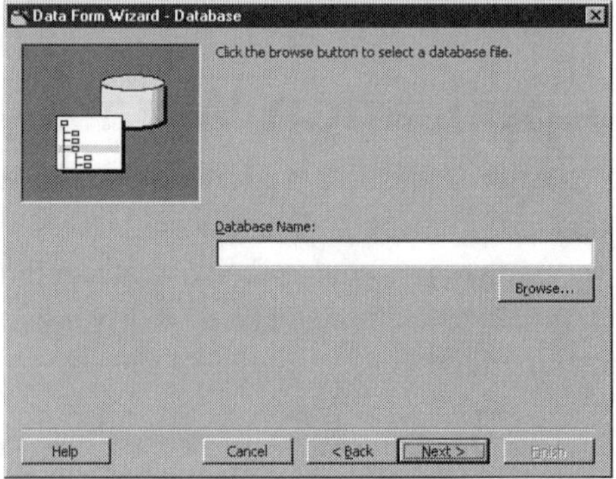

FIGURE 18.9.
The wizard requests the database to use.

After you've specified the database and clicked Next, the wizard asks for the name of the main form (enter frmADO for this example) and for the layout of the form you desire. You have these five choices for the layout:

- **Single record**—Lets users access, display, and edit one record at a time
- **Grid (datasheet)**—Lets users access, display, and edit multiple records at a time in a table-like view
- **Master/Detail**—Lets users access, display, and edit detail records related to a single master record; for example, all products (the detail record) that a vendor (the master record) bought in the past through a *one-to-many relationship*
- **MS HFlexGrid**—Lets users access, display, and edit multiple records in a tabular format
- **MS Chart**—Lets users access, display, and edit multiple records in a chart format

NEW TERM A *one-to-many relationship* exists among some records throughout the tables in most databases. One record might contain a column value that resides in several records of another file. For example, an author database would contain a table of authors, and a book table might exist with multiple books written by the same author. The author would appear as the master record, and the books would appear as the detail records in this author-to-books, one-to-many relationship.

You must also specify the *binding* (the way Visual Basic binds the database information to the controls). The wizard offers these three data bindings:

- **ADO Data control**—Uses the ADO Data control to bind controls to the data
- **ADO code**—Uses ADO code to bind controls to the data
- **Data class**—Creates a special data class for the database and binds data to controls through that class

For this example, select ADO Data Control and click Next. At the next window, the wizard needs to know which table (or which recordset) you want to access in the database. Open the Record Source drop-down list box to select from the Publishers table. Immediately, as Figure 18.10 shows, the Available Fields list updates to show all fields, or *columns*, from the Publishers table.

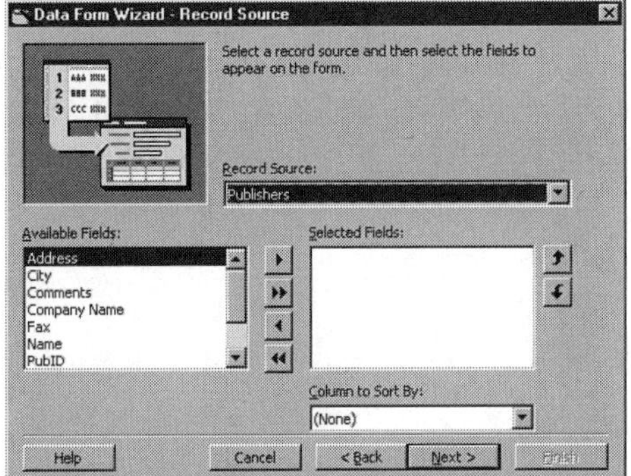

FIGURE 18.10.

Visual Basic analyzes the table and locates the fields for you to select.

The fields you select determine the fields the wizard places on the ADO-based form it generates. You can select one of the fields in the left list and click the .button to send that field to the right list. The wizard uses the right list to generate matching fields on the resulting form. For this example, send all the fields to the right list.

Rearrange the field order so that the Company Name field appears first in the list. Click the Company Name field and then click the up arrow three times to move this field to the top of the list. To ensure that the form displays the records in alphabetical order by company name, select Company Name from the Column to Sort By list.

Click the Next button to display the Control Selection window shown in Figure 18.11. This window lets you specify the buttons that will appear on the form that accesses the data. The buttons reflect the abilities you give the user. If you want to keep your users from deleting records from the table, uncheck the Delete button option. For this example, keep all the buttons checked.

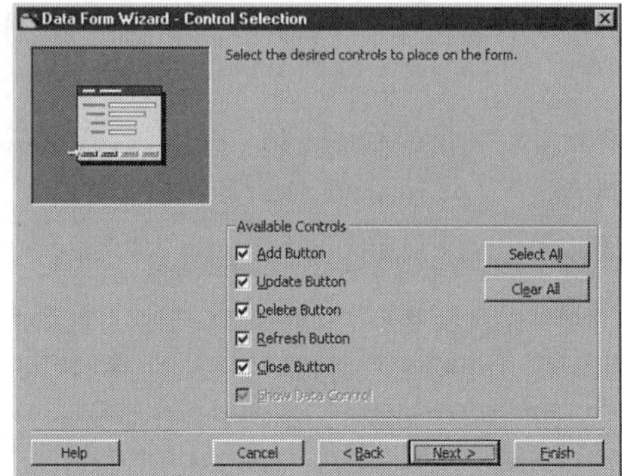

FIGURE 18.11.
You can control the user's ability to add, change, and delete fields from the database table.

When you click the Finish button, Visual Basic generates the application.

The Finish button does *not* complete the wizard, just the database form-creation portion of the wizard. You must complete the wizard in the normal manner. For this example, when you return from the form-generation windows, you can click the wizard's Finish button to complete this section's application.

Once you run the application, the Publishers form displays, as shown in Figure 18.12. The wizard placed all the necessary text boxes and buttons on the form so that the fields of the data could be accessed properly. You can add to the form, perhaps customizing it to make it fancier, once you see that the generated application works correctly.

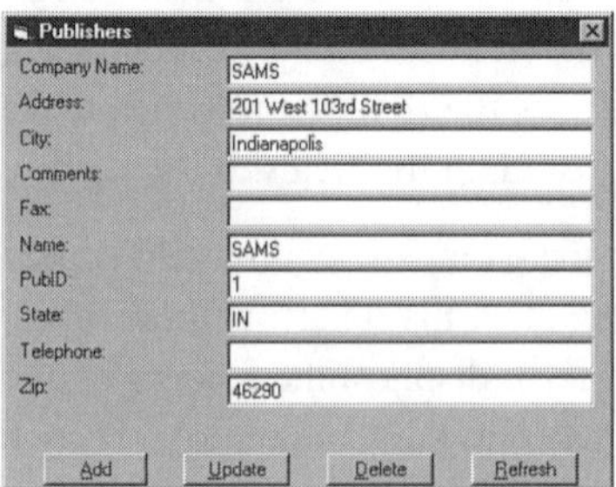

FIGURE 18.12.
The wizard generated the form with all the necessary fields and database buttons.

Summary

Today's lesson explained database access with Visual Basic. The simplest way to access a database (assuming that you don't use the Application Wizard) is to add the data control to your form. The data control takes care of updating the underlying database and changing the bound controls as you move between records. Methods can be used to extend the functionality of the data control.

The ADO interface can require extensive programming, but you get much more control and flexibility when accessing your database. Although your application must update controls and move between records as its events are triggered, the overall database application is faster.

Tomorrow's lesson explores ways to integrate the Internet with Visual Basic. The computer world is quickly becoming an online world, and your applications often need to be able to offer Internet capabilities.

Q&A

Q Do one-to-many relationships always exist in database tables?

A Several kinds of relationships exist among data, and some or all of these may appear in a database at any one time, depending on the database structure. Again, it's not the goal of today's lesson to delve deeply into database theory. However, the one-to-many relationship is required for many Visual Basic applications, so understanding something about it at this point is good. Often, you'll need to display all the records related to a particular key value, and the one-to-many relationship provides this.

The wizard's Master/Detail view is a great way to create applications that provide this relationship among data. At least one field must match in both tables for a one-to-many relationship to exist. A *one-to-one* relationship sometimes appears in data when one column in a table relates to another column in another table. This might be the case if the same part is sold by two vendors. *Many-to-many* relationships also exist. All these relationships are part of the relational database design, and they form the basis for understanding how relational databases work. The key to these relationships is not how you access them. These relationships are designed and developed when the database is developed. Your job as the Visual Basic programmer is to access these relationships, but you won't be reconstructing them in the data unless you're also the author and designer of the database itself.

Workshop

The Workshop provides quiz questions to help you solidify your understanding of the material covered and exercises to provide you with experience in using what you've learned. Try to understand the quiz and exercise answers before continuing to the next lesson. Answers are provided in Appendix A, "Answers to Exercises."

Quiz

1. What tool does Visual Basic supply that lets you edit and look at database files?
2. What is the difference between a file and a table?
3. True/False. As you add records to a table, the number of columns in the table grows as well.
4. True/False. A table is a subset of a recordset.
5. What is a bound control?
6. What are the differences between a recordset, a dynaset, and a snapshot?
7. Name two advantages of ADO over the data control.
8. What do the `EOF` and `BOF` values determine?
9. What's the difference between a Master view and a Detail view?
10. What tool does Visual Basic offer that generates database forms directly from your database structure?

Exercises

1. Change the database access application you created (shown in Figure 18.6) so that it displays all the fields from the Customer table. Your form should mimic the form shown in Figure 18.7. (Be sure to add the descriptive labels so the user knows what each column contains.)
2. Use the Application Wizard to generate a Master/Detail view of the BIBLIO.MDB database that presents the author's name in the Master view and all his or her books' ISBNs in the Detail view.

WEEK 3

BONUS PROJECT 9

ADO Controls

This Bonus Project describes how to create an ADO-based database application. You'll use the sample `BIBLIO.MDB` database that comes with Visual Basic as data for this project. The ADO database controls support extra programming statements (as you'll see in this Bonus Project), but the ADO control as described and used here is easy to understand.

The Application's Goal

Figure BP9.1 shows the form that you'll create. The form contains several lines and controls and may take some time to create. The form offers a complete database-management system for the `BIBLIO.MDB` database that comes with Visual Basic. Although this Bonus Project cannot describe every action of the ADO control, it does describe how to begin manipulating the `BIBLIO.MDB` database with the ADO control. After working through this project, you'll understand some of what is involved when working with ADO applications.

FIGURE BP9.1.
Your ADO-based application will manage this book database system.

Although this application somewhat mimics what the Visual Basic Application Wizard can produce, by completing this bonus project, you'll gain an insight into the requirements of ADO controls. You'll learn how to incorporate ADO control-based programming statements that can access and change database tables without the user's intervention.

Caution

This bonus project will *not* fully teach you how to master the ADO control or the programming language behind the control. However, you will learn the fundamentals of ADO programming. Fortunately, many Visual Basic programmers never have to program the ADO control using the in-depth language that you'll read about here. This bonus project is intended to provide an introduction to the skills needed to use the ADO control effectively.

Creating the Initial Form

To begin, create the initial form by placing the controls and setting their respective values as described in Table BP9.1. Press Ctrl+T to open the Components dialog box and select the Microsoft Active Data Control 6.0 to place the ADO control on the Toolbox. You'll add more properties to these controls before you've completed this bonus project.

TABLE BP9.1. SET THESE CONTROLS AND PROPERTIES ON THE FORM.

Control Property Name	*Property Value*
Form `Name`	`frmBookTitle`
Form `Caption`	`Book Titles - ADO Application`
Form `Height`	`4590`
Form `Width`	`7740`

Control Property Name	*Property Value*
ADO `Name`	`adoBooks`
ADO `Height`	`735`
ADO `Left`	`5400`
ADO `Top`	`0`
ADO `Width`	`2055`
Label #1 `Name`	`lblApp`
Label #1 `Alignment`	`Center`
Label #1 `BorderStyle`	`Fixed Single`
Label #1 `Caption`	`Book Titles`
Label #1 `FontStyle`	`Bold`
Label #1 `FontSize`	`18`
Label #1 `Left`	`2520`
Label #1 `Height`	`495`
Label #1 `Top`	`240`
Label #1 `Width`	`2535`
Label #2 `Name`	`lblTitle`
Label #2 `Alignment`	`Right Justify`
Label #2 `Caption`	`Title:`
Label #2 `FontSize`	`10`
Label #2 `Left`	`720`
Label #2 `Height`	`255`
Label #2 `Top`	`840`
Label #2 `Width`	`495`
Label #3 `Name`	`lblYear`
Label #3 `Alignment`	`Right Justify`
Label #3 `Caption`	`Year Published:`
Label #3 `FontSize`	`10`
Label #3 `Left`	`120`
Label #3 `Height`	`255`
Label #3 `Top`	`2400`
Label #3 `Width`	`1455`
Label #4 `Name`	`lblISBN`

continues

TABLE BP9.1. CONTINUED

Control Property Name	*Property Value*
Label #4 `Alignment`	`Right Justify`
Label #4 `Caption`	`ISBN:`
Label #4 `FontSize`	`10`
Label #4 `Left`	`2880`
Label #4 `Height`	`255`
Label #4 `Top`	`2400`
Label #4 `Width`	`495`
Label #5 `Name`	`lblPubID`
Label #5 `Alignment`	`Right Justify`
Label #5 `Caption`	`Publisher's ID:`
Label #5 `FontSize`	`10`
Label #5 `Left`	`120`
Label #5 `Height`	`255`
Label #5 `Top`	`3000`
Label #5 `Width`	`1455`
Label #6 `Name`	`lblSubject`
Label #6 `Alignment`	`Right Justify`
Label #6 `Caption`	`Subject:`
Label #6 `FontSize`	`10`
Label #6 `Left`	`3480`
Label #6 `Height`	`255`
Label #6 `Top`	`3000`
Label #6 `Width`	`855`
Text box #1 `Name`	`txtTitle`
Text box #1 `DataField`	`Title`
Text box #1 `DataSource`	`adoBooks`
Text box #1 `Height`	`1095`
Text box #1 `Left`	`1320`
Text box #1 `Top`	`840`
Text box #1 `Width`	`5535`
Text box #2 `Name`	`txtPub`
Text box #2 `DataField`	`Year Published`

Control Property Name	*Property Value*
Text box #2 `DataSource`	`adoBooks`
Text box #2 `Height`	`345`
Text box #2 `Left`	`1680`
Text box #2 `Top`	`2400`
Text box #2 `Width`	`975`
Text box #3 `Name`	`txtTitle`
Text box #3 `DataField`	`Title`
Text box #3 `DataSource`	`adoBooks`
Text box #3 `Height`	`345`
Text box #3 `Left`	`1680`
Text box #3 `Top`	`2400`
Text box #3 `Width`	`975`
Text box #4 `Name`	`txtISBN`
Text box #4 `DataField`	`ISBN`
Text box #4 `DataSource`	`adoBooks`
Text box #4 `Height`	`345`
Text box #4 `Left`	`3480`
Text box #4 `Top`	`2400`
Text box #4 `Width`	`3495`
Text box #5 `Name`	`txtPubID`
Text box #5 `DataField`	`PubID`
Text box #5 `DataSource`	`adoBooks`
Text box #5 `Height`	`345`
Text box #5 `Left`	`1680`
Text box #5 `Top`	`3000`
Text box #5 `Width`	`1575`
Text box #6 `Name`	`txtSubject`
Text box #6 `DataField`	`Subject`
Text box #6 `DataSource`	`adoBooks`
Text box #6 `Height`	`345`
Text box #6 `Left`	`4440`
Text box #6 `Top`	`3000`

continues

TABLE BP9.1. CONTINUED

Control Property Name	*Property Value*
Text box #6 `Width`	`1575`
Command button #1 `Name`	`cmdSave`
Command button #1 `Caption`	`&Save`
Command button #1 `Left`	`240`
Command button #1 `Top`	`3600`
Command button #1 `Width`	`735`
Command button #2 `Name`	`cmdAdd`
Command button #2 `Caption`	`&Add`
Command button #2 `Left`	`1200`
Command button #2 `Top`	`3600`
Command button #2 `Width`	`735`
Command button #3 `Name`	`cmdNew`
Command button #3 `Caption`	`&New`
Command button #3 `Left`	`2160`
Command button #3 `Top`	`3600`
Command button #3 `Width`	`735`
Command button #4 `Name`	`cmdDelete`
Command button #4 `Caption`	`&Delete`
Command button #4 `Left`	`3120`
Command button #4 `Top`	`3600`
Command button #4 `Width`	`735`
Command button #5 `Name`	`cmdCancel`
Command button #5 `Caption`	`&Cancel`
Command button #5 `Left`	`4080`
Command button #5 `Top`	`3600`
Command button #5 `Width`	`735`
Command button #6 `Name`	`cmdPrec`
Command button #6 `Caption`	`&<`
Command button #6 `Left`	`5160`
Command button #6 `Top`	`3600`
Command button #6 `Width`	`495`
Command button #7 `Name`	`cmdNext`

Control Property Name	*Property Value*
Command button #7 `Caption`	`&>`
Command button #7 `Left`	`5760`
Command button #7 `Top`	`3600`
Command button #7 `Width`	`495`
Command button #8 `Name`	`cmdExit`
Command button #8 `Caption`	`E&xit`
Command button #8 `Left`	`6600`
Command button #8 `Top`	`3600`
Command button #8 `Width`	`855`
Line #1 `Name`	`Line1`
Line #1 `X1`	`120`
Line #1 `X2`	`7440`
Line #1 `Y1`	`2160`
Line #1 `Y2`	`2160`
Line #2 `Name`	`Line2`
Line #2 `X1`	`0`
Line #2 `X2`	`7800`
Line #2 `Y1`	`3480`
Line #2 `Y2`	`3480`
Line #3 `Name`	`Line3`
Line #3 `X1`	`5040`
Line #3 `X2`	`5040`
Line #3 `Y1`	`3480`
Line #3 `Y2`	`4280`
Line #4 `Name`	`Line4`
Line #4 `X1`	`6480`
Line #4 `X2`	`6480`
Line #4 `Y1`	`3480`
Line #4 `Y2`	`4280`

As you place these controls, notice that the text boxes are bound to their respective fields from the `BIBLIO.MDB` table, which is pointed to by the ADO control named `adoBooks`. You learned to do this same kind of binding with the simple Data control in Day 18,

"Interacting with Data." Unlike the Data control, however, the ADO control has more potential, as you'll see before you finish this bonus project.

Connecting the ADO Control to the Data

When you use an ADO control, you must connect the control to the data the control will access. Of course, you also do something similar with the data control; however, the ADO control can, you'll recall, connect to data that's not necessarily in a database table. The ADO control can access e-mail, graphics, and virtually any data source that might reside outside your application.

Most of the time, a programmer will connect to databases, either a local database on the current PC or on a networked database connected to the user's machine. Therefore, your first step in making the ADO control work is to connect the control to the data source. In this project, that source will be the `BIBLIO.MDB` Access 97 database that comes with Visual Basic.

The ADO control is much more difficult to connect to a simple database than the Data control is. Nevertheless, the benefits far outweigh the complications due to the greater efficiency of the ADO control and its capability to connect to virtually any kind of data.

You can connect a data source to the ADO control in two ways:

- Set the `ConnectionString` property
- Use code to connect the control to the data

When you use the Properties window to connect to data, you can use the dialog boxes that help simplify setting up the connection. If you use code, you'll have to write some rather cryptic code. (This section will demonstrate both ways.)

Making the connection in the Properties window is not as simple as doing so with the data control. For example, when you click the `ConnectionString` property, the dialog box shown in Figure BP9.2 appears. You must determine which option meets your data source's type.

For this example, as with many of the applications you'll create with the ADO control, you're going to create a simple connection string that points to your database file. The first two options, a Data Link file option (used for passing data between two locations) and an ODBC file option (used for ODBC-compliant databases), are not needed for this project's simple database access. Click the third option to specify a connection string.

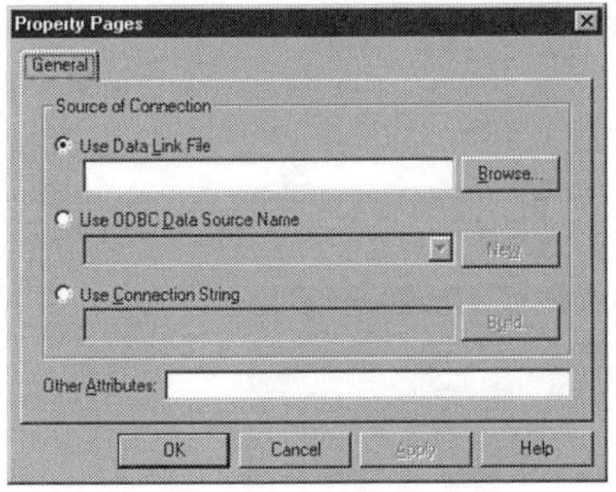

FIGURE BP9.2.

The ADO control's Property Pages dialog box helps you specify a connection string.

Connection strings can get rather lengthy, but Visual Basic can help you build the string. To specify the string, follow these steps:

1. Click the Build button to display the Data Link Properties dialog box.
2. Double-click the first option labeled Microsoft Jet 3.51 OLE DB Provider. Access 97 databases have as their underlying database access system the Jet technology that Microsoft uses for fast database access. After selecting Jet access, the Data Link Properties dialog box appears so that you can select the database.
3. Click the ellipses button to the right of the first text box and locate the `BIBLIO.MDB` database on your disk.
4. Click the Open button to attach the database to your ADO control.

Tip

> To ensure that you've connected properly to the database, click the Test Connection button. If you've specified the correct connection string properties, Visual Basic displays a message box that lets you know you've connected properly. If you don't get a proper connection, the message box will let you know. You can then go back to the other dialog box's tabbed pages and fix the problem.

5. To see what you've specified, click the All tab to see the connection string summary dialog box page shown in Figure BP9.3. The other items listed in the dialog box are available for you to modify from the other dialog box pages if you want to (for example, you can set the security access).
6. Click the OK button to return to the first Property Pages dialog box page; then click OK to close the dialog box and return to your form.

Instead of selecting from the dialog box, you can use code to create a connection string anywhere in the application. For example, you may want to build the connection string when the form loads or perhaps not until the user needs access to a database table. The longer you wait to connect to data, the less likely that a power outage or a system hang-up will adversely affect your data. Your application will start faster if you wait to build the connection string at the time the database access is required.

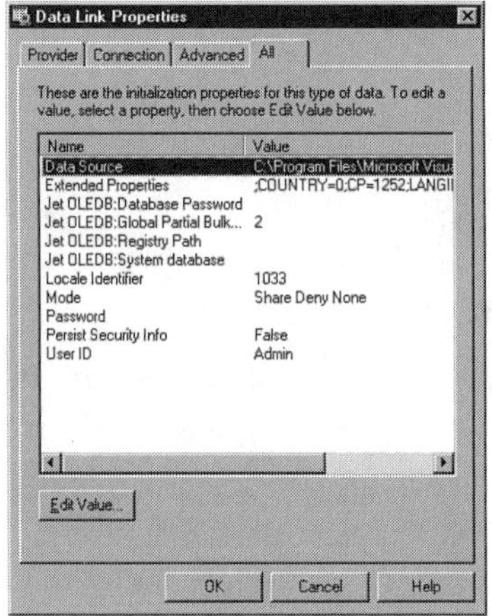

FIGURE BP9.3.

Visual Basic reviews your connection string settings.

Caution

Even if you use code to access the data, you need to place the ADO control on your form. You'll set its `Visible` property to `False` if you don't want to give your users access to the control but you still want to use the control, along with code, to access data. You cannot use *both* code and the Properties window to set the connection string, however, so be sure to keep the `ConnectionString` value blank if you use program code to set the connection string.

To set the ADO control to the database with code, you could place the following statement in the `Form_Load()` event procedure:

```
adoBooks.ConnectionString = "Provider=Microsoft.Jet.OLEDB.3.51;" & _
"Persist Security Info=False;" & _
"Data Source=C:\Program Files\Microsoft Visual" & _
"Studio\VB98\Biblio.mdb"
```

The statement assigns the very same connection string created at the beginning of this section when you set the connection string with the dialog box. As you can see, the format can get tricky, but all the information from the dialog box goes into the `ConnectionString` property.

The control is not quite ready to display data from the database, however. You'll need to specify exactly which rows from which table in the database are to be available to the rest of the application. You must use SQL (a database programming language that Visual Basic supports as a `RecordSource` property) to tell Visual Basic to access all the records (indicated by the wildcard character, `*`) from the Titles table in the `BIBLIO.MDB` database with this statement:

```
adoBooks.RecordSource = "Select * From Titles"
```

Table BP9.1 listed the data fields for each text control on the form. Therefore, by setting the ADO control's `Visible` property to `False`, erasing any `ConnectionString` property value you may have assigned with the dialog box that appears when you double-click the `ConnectionString` property in the Properties window, and by assigning the `DataSource` and `DataField` properties described for each text control in Table BP9.1, you can set up the form with an invisible ADO control that accesses the data. Of course, without the control being visible, your program's code must step through the data as needed. For this example, the command buttons at the bottom of the form require code to step through the data, and that's what you'll do in the next section.

Note

When you run the application with the code-based `ConnectionString` and `RecordSource` properties (set as described here) but leave the rest of the fields as you entered them from Table BP9.1, no database data will yet appear in the text fields. Even though the text fields all point to the ADO control, the control isn't connected to the database until it loads, and by then the text controls have failed to locate any data because their `DataSource` property, the ADO control, is not connected to a database. Once you link the first text field to the newly connected data source, however (as described in the next section), all the fields linked to the ADO control will display their data.

Code or Control?

Should you let your users control the ADO control by clicking the control's buttons or by hiding the control and using code to step through the connected table? In this project, you're learning both ways. A user can click the ADO control buttons to see data bound to the control or he or she can click the buttons at the bottom of the form to step through the database.

The choice of offering the control or performing the database traversal using code depends on the application you're writing. Often, the application is to update or display a single record or a record that meets specific criteria. Your application needs to be able to retrieve a specific record, or perhaps step through all records, computing totals and averages. Such data processing of a table requires code, because the code will step through the data in the background.

Finding Data

To make sure that the Title field displays the titles for the books, you must connect the title's `DataSource` property to the ADO control and the title's `DataField` property to the Title field in the table. To do so with code instead of setting the properties from the Properties window, you could use these two statements:

```
Set txtTitle.DataSource = adoBooks
txtTitle.DataField = "Title"
```

Remember that you cannot assign this field in the Properties window if you connect the ADO control to the database with code at runtime, as described in the previous section.

Once you link one text box to the ADO control, you can either do the same for the rest of the text boxes or you can use the `DataSource` and `DataField` properties described in Table BP9.1, because they will work once you set one text control on the form to the newly connected database table.

Traversing the Data

When you run the application after assigning the first text box to the ADO control, as described in the previous two sections, the first record and its related fields appear as shown in Figure BP9.4.

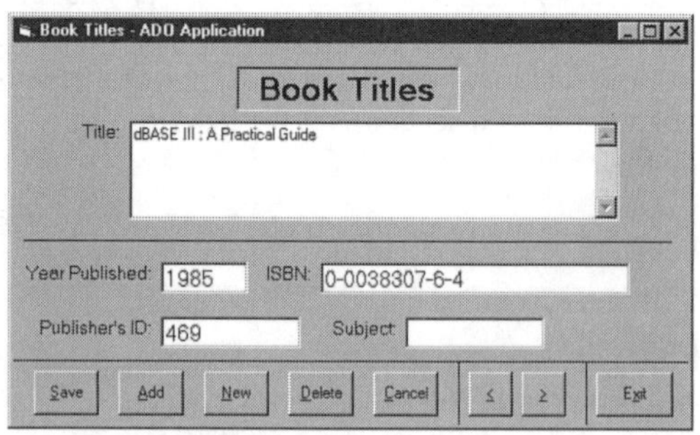

FIGURE BP9.4.
The first record can now appear.

The table's fields do not all contain accurate or complete data. For example, the first record in the `BIBLIO.MDB` database shows nothing in the Subject field, and some subjects contain strange values such as `2nd`, which is perhaps the edition number but not the book's subject.

Only the first record will appear because the user has no access to the invisible ADO control and the command buttons are not connected to code. You can double-click the Next button (the button with the `Caption` property `&>`) to add code to activate this button. The following code moves the table pointer to the next record in the table so that the bound controls can access the data:

```
1:  Private Sub cmdNext_Click()
2:     ' Move forward one record in the data
3:     If Not adoBooks.Recordset.EOF Then
4:        adoBooks.Recordset.MoveNext
5:        If adoBooks.Recordset.EOF Then
6:          adoBooks.Recordset.MovePrevious
7:        End If
8:     End If
9:  End Sub
```

The *recordset*, used in lines 3 through 6, is the list of records that you're currently working with. You specified the recordset earlier with the SQL statement that limited the records to the Titles table only. The recordset's method called `MoveNext` moves the pointer in the database forward one record in line 4. All other controls bound to the table move as well.

A problem can arise in the following situations if you do not check for them:

- If no records exist in the final record database table, an error will occur if you attempt to move forward.
- If the current record is the final record in the database table, an error will occur if you attempt to move forward.

Therefore, the `If` statement in line 3 ensures that the table is not already at the end of file by checking the recordset's `EOF` property using a `Not` operator. In effect, line 3 says "if the recordset is not at the end of file, then continue." Line 5 ensures that, if the `MoveNext` method moves to the end of file, the `MovePrevious` method backs up once again, always keeping the pointer from moving past the end of the table. `MovePrevious` is the recordset method that moves backward through the table one record at a time.

You can use the `MovePrevious` method to add an event procedure to the Previous button (the button with the `Caption` property `&<`) that moves backward through the table:

```
Private Sub cmdPrev_Click()
   ' Move backward one record in the data
   If Not adoBooks.Recordset.BOF Then
     adoBooks.Recordset.MovePrevious
     If adoBooks.Recordset.BOF Then
       adoBooks.Recordset.MoveNext
     End If
   End If
End Sub
```

The BOF recordset property checks for the beginning of the file, so you must ensure that you do not let the user attempt to back up to a previous record when the table is already at the beginning.

> You can place an End statement inside the Exit command button's Click event procedure so that the user can easily exit the program.

Table Updates

The ADO control automatically updates the underlying table record if a user makes a change in a bound text box control. Therefore, if you change a title or subject, that change stays with the table. Then, when you later run the application once again, the modified data appears in the form.

Nevertheless, you, yourself, must be able to save data to a database using code, as well. Such code writing can get lengthy and tedious and is far beyond the scope of this project. For example, you may want to keep unique values in a certain field and issue an error message if the user enters a bad value. Also, you may get data from another source and want to assign that data to the database.

To give you an idea of what's involved in updating database data using the ADO control, the record-saving procedure in Listing BP9.1 writes data from the text boxes on the control to the database. (Of course, this is redundant for this application because the text boxes are already bound to the table. However, when the text boxes or outside data are not bound to the table, you'll use code similar to the code found in this listing.)

LISTING BP9.1. YOU CAN USE METHODS TO WRITE DATA TO THE TABLE THROUGH CODE.

```
Private Sub cmdSave_Click()
  ' Assign all the text boxes to the fields.
  ' Assign only non-null data
  ' (long lines are continued)
  adoBooks.Recordset!Title = _
    IIf(txtTitle = "", "N/A", txtTitle)
  adoBooks.Recordset![Year Published] = _
    IIf(txtPub = "", "N/A", txtPub)
  adoBooks.Recordset!ISBN = _
    IIf(txtISBN = "", "N/A", txtISBN)
  adoBooks.Recordset!PubID = _
    IIf(txtPubID = "", "N/A", txtPubID)
  adoBooks.Recordset!Subject = _
    IIf(txtSubject = "", "N/A", txtSubject)
```

```
15:
16:     ' Make the actual update to the recordset
17:    adoBooks.Recordset.Update
18:
19: End Sub
```

The `IIf()` function is used throughout Listing BP9.1 so that the value `N/A` (for *not applicable*) is written to any saved fields that have no data in them. The `IIf()` ensures that each value written is non-null. The bracketed field name in line 7 is required because the field contains a space. Visual Basic treats `[Year Published]` as a single field name, but without the brackets it would not be able to recognize the embedded space.

Listing BP9.1 adds only changed data from this project's form at this time, but you can easily adapt the code to retrieve the data to save to the table from other sources. For example, in line 14, you would now look at the external data, such as a user's input into an input box, instead of going to the form's text box for data to write to the table. Line 17 is required to make the actual update, because the table will not accept the new data without the `Update` method.

The code in Listing BP9.1, therefore, actually writes the edits the user makes to the form's data to the table, even though those values would be written anyway due to the bound text box controls in this example. If you want completely new data to be written to the table (added at the end of the table), you must first clear the form's fields so that the user can enter the data. (You could connect this code to the New command button, but this application does not take the time to do that.)

Before the new record can be written, the table pointer needs to be moved to the end of the file to accept the new data (instead of overwriting the data at the current record pointer) with this code:

```
adoBooks.Recordset.AddNew    ' Prepare for new record
```

The data you subsequently save to the table will appear as a new record in the table.

Concluding with the ADO Control

As you can see, programming the ADO control is not as simple as the Data control, but the ADO control's power and speed is its advantage. You've been working on this bonus project for awhile now, but its functionality—although getting closer to being finalized—is still incomplete. Consider the following issues required to complete the task:

- When writing the Add or New command buttons' code, you must clear the fields on the form as well as reset the focus to the first field so that the user can save the current record or add a new one.

- The `AddNew` and `Update` methods always update the table with new or updated bound field data.
- Use the `MoveLast` method to move the table pointer to the very end of the table before you ever add a new record.
- Program the Cancel button so that the user can click it in order to *not* save his or her edits or new record data. The Cancel button's event procedure needs to call the form-displaying procedure once again to return the record to its prior settings.

To really master the ADO control and its related programming, consider getting Sams Publishing's *Sams Teach Yourself Database Programming with Visual Basic 6 in 21 Days*, which explains ADO in detail and completes your study of the subject.

DAY 19

Adding Internet Access

Today's lesson shows you how to access the Internet from Visual Basic applications. No Visual Basic tutorial worth its price would be complete without some mention of Visual Basic's ties to the Internet. Visual Basic is one of the easiest programming tools available today to use for Internet access. Bear in mind, however, that even with Visual Basic, programming for Internet access is challenging. Today's short lesson only scratches the surface, offering a glimpse of how Visual Basic views and works with the Internet.

Today, you learn the following:

- About Visual Basic's Internet connection
- How to add a Web browser to an application
- About the Visual Basic Internet controls
- How to work with encapsulation
- About ActiveX documents
- How to turn virtually *any* Visual Basic application into an Internet application

The Internet Wizard

The Visual Basic Application Wizard does some of the work for you when you want your application to access the Internet. Simply by you selecting the appropriate choices, the wizard can add Internet access to your application, giving it worldwide communications capabilities.

The Internet tools described in this lesson work equally well for Internet and intranet applications. Both the Internet and intranet technologies support a common protocol, so they both can run the same kinds of applications.

NEW TERM An *intranet* is a local networked system (perhaps a network inside a single building or even a small area on the same floor) that provides the same features as the Internet.

NEW TERM A *protocol* enables two computers to communicate. Internet and intranet connections use a common protocol called *TCP/IP*, which stands for *Transfer Control Protocol/Internet Protocol*. It's used for universal Internet connections.

This section explains what the Visual Basic Application Wizard does when you use it to add Internet access to your application. Although the wizard supports access, it specifically gives your application the capability to browse World Wide Web (WWW) pages.

Your application's users must already have an Internet service provider, or they can't access the Web with your application. Also, you must have Internet Explorer 4 or later installed on your own development system to work with Visual Basic's full Internet support. Visual Basic offers Internet Explorer 4 as an installation option when you install Visual Basic.

NEW TERM An *Internet service provider*, also known as an *ISP*, is an organization that offers accounts that connect to the Internet. Company-provided Internet services wired directly to the PCs need no ISP.

When you create an application shell with the Visual Basic Application Wizard, the sixth dialog box you see (shown in Figure 19.1) is the Internet Connectivity dialog box, which sets up Internet Web access for the application you're building.

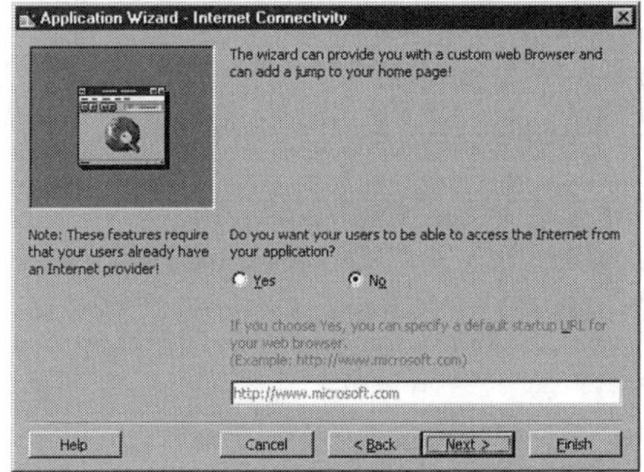

FIGURE 19.1.
You can select Web access from the wizard's Internet Connectivity dialog box.

The wizard supplies a default URL—Microsoft's home page. You need to change this default URL if you want your users to see something else. When a user triggers the browser inside the application, the browser logs on (using the user's own Internet service provider) and connects to the URL you specify in the wizard. You might, for example, want to insert the URL of your company's home page in the default URL text box. When you select the Yes option button, the wizard actually inserts the engine for a Web browser in the application you're producing.

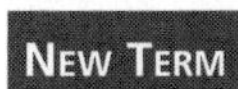

An *URL* (uniform resource locator) is a Web site address. Every Web site has a unique URL.

Always begin the URL with `http://`. (The letters *http* stand for *Hypertext Transfer Protocol* and designate the standard communications procedure used to access Web pages.) Although most modern browsers do not require the `http://` prefix, the wizard does require the prefix.

You can quickly build a test application that accesses the Internet. Follow these steps to add an Internet-browsing feature to the wizard's generated application:

1. Create a new project and double-click the icon labeled VB Application Wizard.
2. Click Next to bypass the first dialog box.
3. Select Single Document Interface (SDI) to keep the generated application simple.
4. Click Next to move through the next four dialog boxes and to accept the default menu options.

5. At the Internet Connectivity dialog box, click Yes. For this example, leave the Microsoft Web site's URL address in the text box.
6. Click Finish to finalize and generate the application.

If this is the first time the Internet controls have been used since your Visual Basic environment was installed, you'll see the dialog box shown in Figure 19.2. Click OK to unpack these controls to prepare them for loading into your Visual Basic environment.

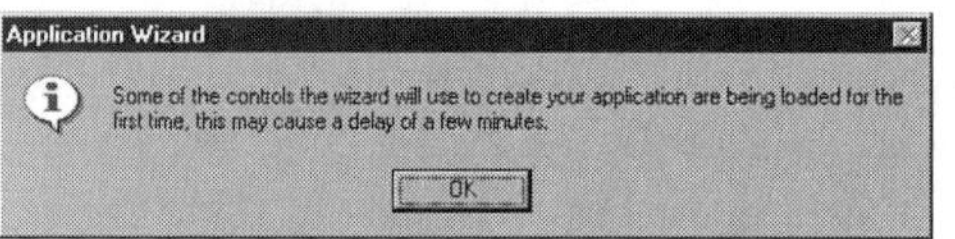

FIGURE 19.2.
Visual Basic will have to prepare the Internet controls the first time you use them.

When you return to Visual Basic's development environment, notice the toolbox. Figure 19.3 shows the tools the wizard has added to the usual collection of intrinsic controls. You've used some of these added controls before in this tutorial: the common dialog box, the toolbar, the image list, and the slider. (Note that the toolbox window in Figure 19.3 is resized to distinguish the tools better.)

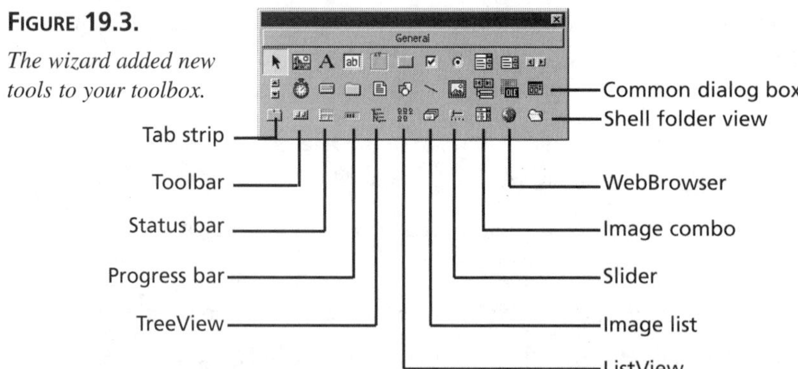

FIGURE 19.3.
The wizard added new tools to your toolbox.

The extra tools give the application's Web-browsing portions the control they need to do their job. Obviously, the Web browser control is the primary tool this lesson is concerned with.

To get a feel for the application's shell, press F5 to run the application. The screen you see looks no different than the other screens for wizard-generated applications you've seen before. The default menu and toolbar display on the form. The Internet feature appears, however, when you choose Web Browser from the View menu. In the middle of the application's screen, a Web-browsing dialog box appears and requests that you log on with your typical provider's logon dialog box (unless you are already logged on or have automatic logon capabilities). After you enter your user name and password, an Internet Explorer–like window appears in the center of the application screen and displays Microsoft's Web site (see Figure 19.4).

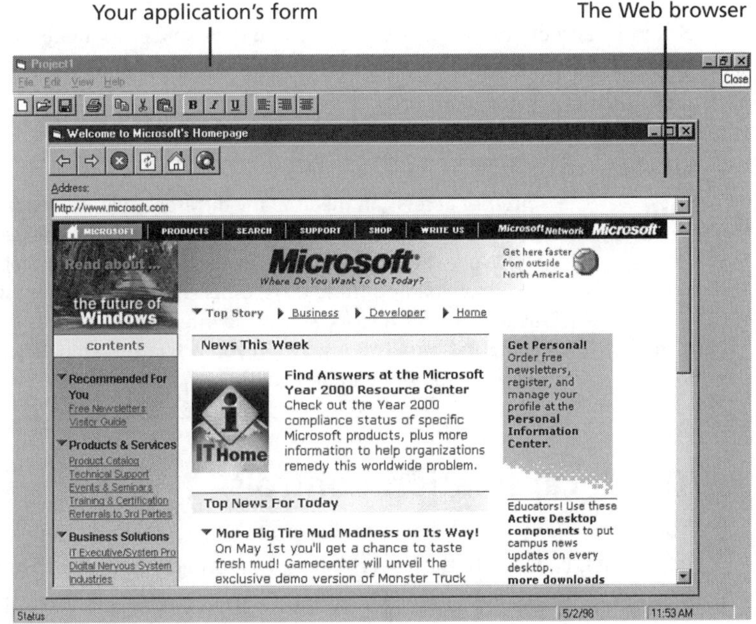

FIGURE 19.4.

Your wizard-generated application is now hooked into Microsoft's Web site.

Tip

The Internet Explorer window you see is actually a small application wrapped around a huge ActiveX control. The Web browser that Visual Basic's wizard inserted is an example of such an ActiveX control. Although the application's Web browser is simpler than the full-blown version of Internet Explorer (fewer toolbar buttons appear and no menus exist), the embedded browser supplies all the common browser features needed, such as a Previous button, Next button, Home button, and so on. If you click the toolbar's Search button, Internet Explorer uses Microsoft's search site to launch the search request.

If you want to log off the Internet, you must close the Web browser, double-click your service provider's taskbar icon, and then select the logoff option. Although the Web browser doesn't include a logoff feature, you could add one through programming.

Looking at Some Internet Controls

If you use Visual Basic's Professional or Enterprise edition, you can use several advanced Internet-based ActiveX controls to add and control Internet access from within your applications. The previous section's example demonstrated the power of one single control—the WebBrowser control. This section explains more about these controls.

Several Internet controls appear when you choose Components from the Project menu. This section reviews those controls and explains how and when you can use them in projects that access the Internet.

Internet access can mean many different things in today's world—for example, it can refer to a complete application that a user accesses and runs from the Web. The Internet provides more services than Web page viewing and file downloading these days, especially with all the new ActiveX controls available, which work across the Internet as easily as they work inside single-computer applications. When you activate Web pages with programs, Visual Basic can be the engine you use.

The Encapsulation Controls

The term *encapsulation* refers to different things, depending on whether you're encapsulating data, code, or both. Nevertheless, in a broad sense, encapsulation always refers to *packaging*. Visual Basic includes some Internet controls that encapsulate, or *package*, your existing applications and code into Internet-aware applications. These controls encapsulate your applications so that they work with Internet technology.

Encapsulation refers to the packaging of components, as occurs with Visual Basic objects that support properties, methods, and events.

Here's a list of the encapsulation controls:

- Internet transfer control—Encapsulates the three most popular Internet protocols: HTTP, FTP (File Transfer Protocol), and Gopher (a searching protocol to help you locate information on the Internet). You can download files directly from within your Visual Basic applications by using FTP.

- WebBrowser control— Encapsulates a Web browser directly inside your application.
- WinSock control— Gives you a Windows common connection and data-exchange control that provides two protocols: UDP (User Datagram Protocol) and TCP (Transmission Control Protocol).

You saw one of these encapsulation controls—the WebBrowser control—in the previous section. The Visual Basic Application Wizard uses the WebBrowser control to insert a browser in the generated application. As you saw, the WebBrowser control isn't as full functioned as Internet Explorer, but it does provide simple and direct Internet access for any user who subscribes to an Internet service.

Internet Explorer Controls

Visual Basic comes with several controls you can add to a project so that it can interact with the Web using Internet Explorer technology. These controls begin with the *IE* abbreviation in the Components dialog box. This section describes those controls.

Table 19.1 helps you locate the controls described in this section. Often, the control names don't describe their capabilities. Table 19.1 describes the control you select from the Components dialog box to get the functionality you need. (To access the Components dialog box, choose Components from the Project menu.)

TABLE 19.1. SEVERAL COMPONENTS INCLUDE INTERNET EXPLORER–RELATED CAPABILITIES AS WELL AS OTHER INTERNET CONTROLS.

Component Name	*Description*
IE Animated Button	Animated display showing Internet Explorer's connection
IE Popup Menu	A menu control that appears on the Web page
IE Preloader	Preloads a page from a site before the visible Internet access begins
IE Super Label	A Web page label
IE Timer	Provides timing operations for Internet services
Microsoft Internet Controls	Web browser control
Microsoft Internet Transfer Control 6.0	The Transfer Protocol control
Microsoft Winsock Control 6.0	The Windows connection to common Internet protocols

If you use The Microsoft Network online service, a set of controls comes with Visual Basic 6 that offers Microsoft Network–related services from the applications you write, such as the MSN mail control. These controls begin with the MSN abbreviation in the Components dialog box.

Preview of Advanced Issues

Assuming you want to use Visual Basic to interact with the Internet when building your applications, you've already seen a start of what's in store. The simplest way to add Internet capabilities to your applications is to use the Visual Basic Application Wizard, as you did earlier in this lesson. If you want to go further than that, you have somewhat of a steep learning curve ahead of you.

This section discusses some of the terms and concepts you'll first face as you dive into the Visual Basic–to-Internet foray. By learning what's in store now, you won't be faced with a completely new environment if and when you learn the details needed to provide comprehensive Internet interaction from your applications.

ActiveX Documents

If you want to develop an Internet-only Visual Basic application, you can use ActiveX documents to get started. An *ActiveX document* acts and looks just like a regular Visual Basic application on a form window, except that an ActiveX document sends ActiveX controls to the end user's computer if the computer doesn't contain the ActiveX controls used by the document. The document comes to the user looking like a regular HTML-based Web page. For example, the ActiveX document can contain hypertext links (ActiveX controls that are downloaded or used, depending on the end user's machine contents). Also, the ActiveX document's menus can be automatically merged with its parent application (like OLE servers).

NEW TERM *HTML*, or *Hypertext Markup Language*, is the primary language for Web page formatting. A Web browser can decipher all HTML codes to format and display the Web page and application the HTML code describes. The final section of today's lesson shows an example of HTML code. An HTML file is strictly a text file that contains

HTML codes. Although you can create an HTML file using a text editor, numerous visual tools exist to let you create and design Web pages without typing any HTML code. Even Visual Basic can help you design Web pages when you select the DHTML Application Wizard. All HTML files contain the .HTM filename extension.

Visual Basic 6's Professional and Enterprise editions support *DHTML* (*Dynamic Hypertext Markup Language*), which responds to actions on a Web page. The ActiveX document links to an HTML page that you create or use. When the end user clicks the link to your ActiveX document, your ActiveX document activates, the controls get to the user's computer, and the Web page's ActiveX document code executes as the user views the page. The content is dynamic, meaning that settings such as text color and style might differ on each user's machine depending on the user's settings.

Note

The ActiveX document isn't static. The *document* in *ActiveX document* is, in every respect, a running application. Using a document concept helps programmers see how Web pages use the embedded ActiveX document.

Perhaps the most important reason for creating an ActiveX document is that Internet Explorer can run it as though it were a control program or operating system program launcher. The ActiveX document's menus merge with those of Internet Explorer (and override functionality when needed), and you don't have to learn a new language, such as Java, to activate the Web pages.

NEW TERM *Java* is an Internet programming language, based on C++, used to activate Web pages and interact with users by sending small Java programs, called *applets*, along with a Web page. The applets run on the user's PC when the user views a Web page that contains Java applets.

Note

The New Project dialog box contains two icons—ActiveX Document EXE and ActiveX Document DLL—that create ActiveX document shells. (Figure 19.5 shows these icons.) After you start creating the ActiveX document, you can add whatever features you like to the form window, just as you do for regular applications.

FIGURE 19.5.

Start the New Project Wizard to locate the ActiveX Document Wizards.

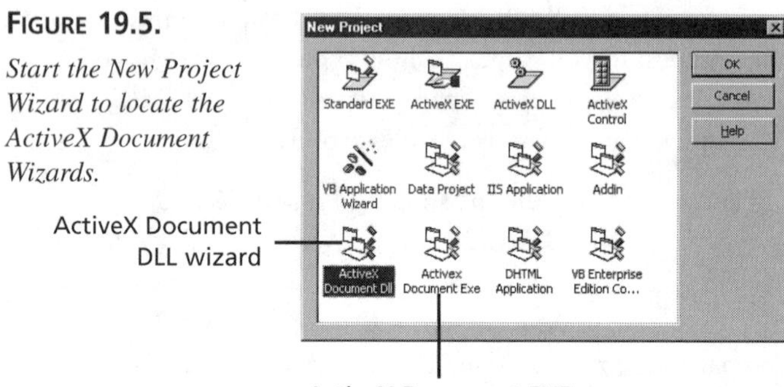

The ActiveX Document Migration Wizard

One of the easiest ways to port your applications to the Internet is to let Visual Basic do it for you! When you add the ActiveX Document Migration Wizard to the Add-In Manager menu option, you add a powerful tool that will turn virtually *any* Visual Basic application into an Internet-ready application. You can place your converted ActiveX document applications on a Web server, and users can interact with your applications through a Web browser, just as they can interact with Web pages that contain HTML, VBScript, and Java code.

To see how easy it is to convert an application into an Internet-ready application, follow these steps to use the ActiveX Document Migration Wizard:

1. Select Add-Ins, Add-In Manager and double-click the entry VB 6 ActiveX Doc Migration Wizard to add the wizard to your list of add-ins.
2. Click OK to close the Add-In Manager dialog box.
3. Open the sample Calc.vbp project that comes with Visual Basic. You will have to locate your Samples folder on the installation CD-ROM or on your hard disk if you installed the samples when you installed Visual Basic.
4. Press F5 to run the application. As Figure 19.6 shows, the application simulates a pocket calculator on your screen.

FIGURE 19.6.

The Calculator application mimics the features of a pocket calculator.

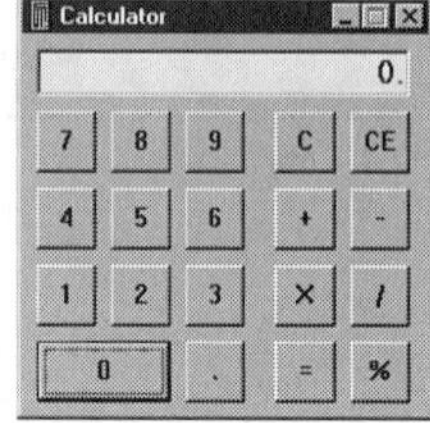

5. Stop the running application.
6. Select Add-Ins, ActiveX Document Migration Wizard to start the Migration Wizard.
7. Click the Next button to bypass the introductory window.
8. The second window appears, as shown in Figure 19.7, which lists all the current project's forms in a checked list. Of course, the simple Calc.vbp project contains only a single form, so that's the only form you'll see listed here. Click the Calculator entry to select it.

> If several forms resided in your project, you could elect to send only some of the forms to Web-compatible ActiveX documents. Each form will become its own ActiveX document.

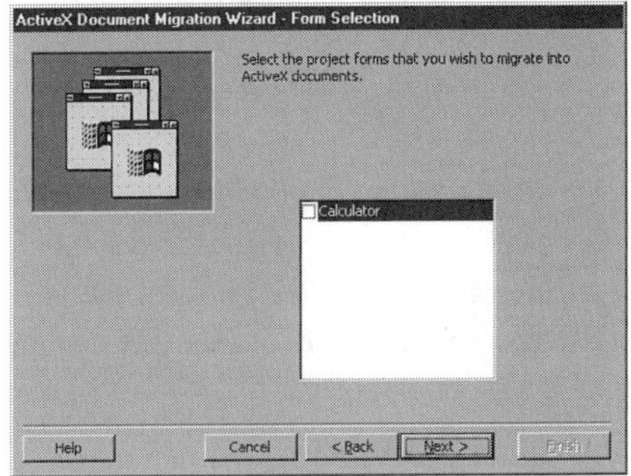

FIGURE 19.7.
Select the application's form that will ultimately appear on the Web page in an ActiveX document.

9. The Options window, shown in Figure 19.8, determines how the wizard handles the elements that it cannot convert. Some kinds of advanced communications code cannot work inside an ActiveX document, although most Visual Basic code will run smoothly. If you check the first option, Visual Basic will place remarks before all code that the wizard cannot convert. Although the resulting application may not be complete, you can search for the remarks and fix the code, or remove it if it's not vital to the application. No invalid code exists in the Calc.vbp application, so you'll not have to choose this option.

In addition, you may want to remove the forms that you convert from the project, because those forms will reside in an ActiveX document after the wizard completes. Leave the ActiveX EXE option checked so that the wizard creates an executable module as opposed to a DLL.

A *DLL*, or *dynamic link library*, is a compiled routine that more than one compiled application can share.

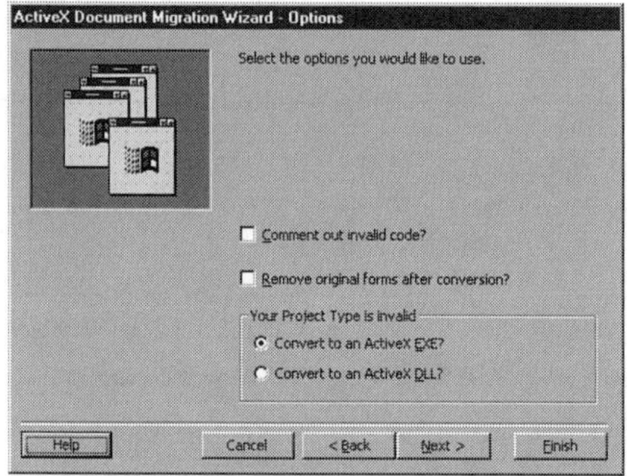

FIGURE 19.8.
Set the options for the ActiveX document that will appear.

For this example, leave the Options dialog box with its default settings and click Next to continue the wizard.

10. Leave the default settings alone and click Finish at the Finished window to start the migration of the Calc.vbp application to an ActiveX document. Once the migration is completed, a final dialog box appears.
11. Click OK to close the final dialog box.

After each migration, a Summary Report window appears, such as the one shown in Figure 19.9. The Summary Report window is important, because the instructions within the window let you know what you're to do next to test the migration. After you read through this report, you can click the Save button to save the text and close the window. For this example, you can close the window without saving the report.

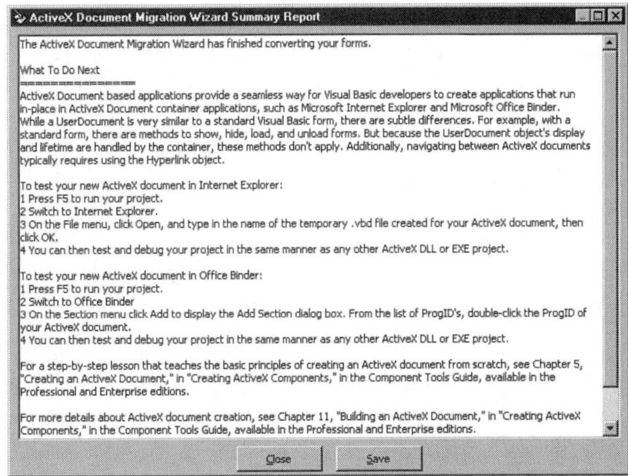

FIGURE 19.9.

The Summary Report window describes your next and final actions necessary to complete the migration.

Now that you've completed the migration, you must run the application once more inside the Visual Basic environment to prepare an executable ActiveX document object. In a way, Visual Basic compiles the application, but unlike the typical program compilation (Day 21, "Distributing Your Applications," explains more about Visual Basic compilation), running the migrated application creates an ActiveX document with the filename extension .VBD (for *Visual Basic Document*). (You will still have to compile the ActiveX document into its EXE format if you want to use the ActiveX document without the Visual Basic environment running.)

As soon as you run the application, Visual Basic displays the Project Properties dialog box shown in Figure 19.10. The Project Properties dialog box determines how the ActiveX document will behave when you run the program. Look at the Project window and you'll see two components—the usual `Calc` form and a second object named `docCalculator`. The `docCalculator` object is the ActiveX document component you created when you pressed F5 to run the application.

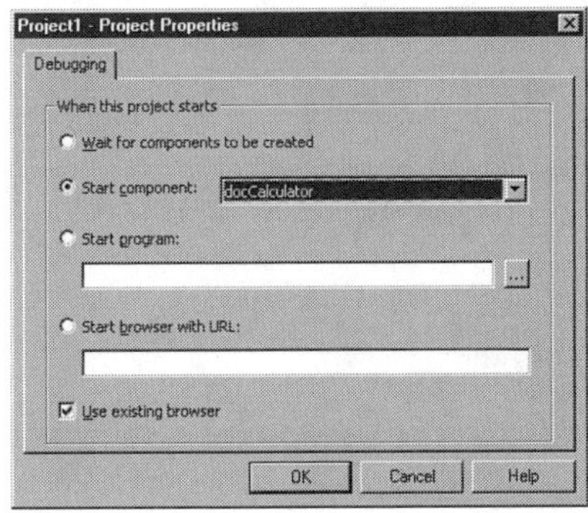

FIGURE 19.10.

Specifying the ActiveX document's project properties.

When you click OK, Visual Basic will start the ActiveX document inside your Internet Browser. Figure 19.11 shows the result. Notice what has happened:

- The Internet browser, itself, is executing your Visual Basic application.
- You wrote no messy HTML code to produce the Web page.
- The Calculator application is successfully migrated to a Web application.
- If you close the project, you can, at any time, restart the Internet browser, select File, Open, locate the docCalculator.vbd file, and execute the compiled ActiveX document-based application from inside the browser without starting Visual Basic.
- If you place the application on your Web server (assuming you have access to a Web server from where you can offer Web pages to those on the Internet), any Internet user in the world who owns a Web browser that is ActiveX compatible will be able to run your application. The application will execute on the user's machine after downloading along with the Web page. (This simulates the action of a Java applet as well.)

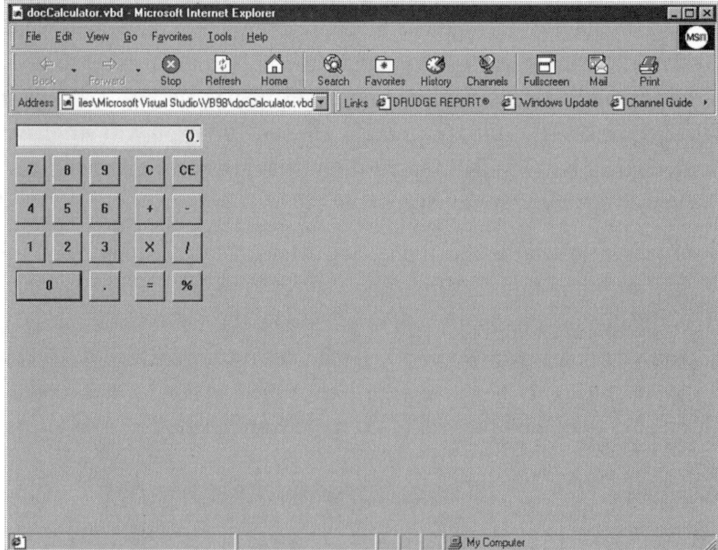

FIGURE 19.11.
Internet Explorer is the platform from which the Calculator application now runs.

After you close your Internet browser, you can select Run, End to stop Visual Basic's execution.

Tip

Any container that can hold an ActiveX control can hold an ActiveX document. That's important to understand, because you can see how universal an ActiveX document can become. In other words, if you use an application, such as a drawing application or another programming language, that lets you embed ActiveX controls inside that application, you'll be able to add your ActiveX documents to those applications as well. An ActiveX document is just a fancy term for an ActiveX control that you migrated from a Visual Basic application. Today's second exercise shows you how to use this drop-in feature if you have Microsoft Office Professional installed on your computer.

HTML and VBScript

Although you only need to know the Visual Basic programming language to access all the Internet connectivity features found in Visual Basic 6, you need to master two auxiliary languages to tie things together well. HTML is the formatting language behind Web pages. The HTML language is designed to achieve the following goals:

- Format Web pages in columns, with graphics, and appropriate titles
- Allow the integration of additional Internet service programs, such as VB ActiveX documents and Java (a small programming language that activates Web pages)

HTML is known as a *scripting* language. The language doesn't compile and become executable as Visual Basic programs do. Instead, HTML formats Web pages, specifies where graphics and dividing frames go, and allows for embedded activated applications such as ActiveX documents and Java programs.

VBScript, as the name implies, is another scripting language, but Microsoft designed VBScript based on the Visual Basic programming language. Therefore, you'll feel right at home with VBScript. VBScript is useful when you want to add key Visual Basic features to a Web page, such as pop-up messages, input boxes, loop-through calculations, and so on. VBScript, despite its foundation in Visual Basic, doesn't replace Visual Basic's ActiveX documents but instead loads the ActiveX documents into an HTML page for execution. Therefore, VBScript is the medium through which HTML documents locate and execute Visual Basic ActiveX document applications.

Note

VBScript wasn't originally designed to be used solely as a launcher for ActiveX documents—in fact, VBScript was around before ActiveX. The loading of ActiveX documents into HTML pages is one of VBScript's many jobs, but for a VB6 programmer, the ActiveX document is perhaps VBScript's most important job.

Listing 19.1 shows an example of the first few lines of HTML code for Microsoft's Web site.

LISTING 19.1. A FEW LINES OF HTML CODE CAN REVEAL TO YOU HOW THE FORMATTING CODES WORK TO FORMAT WEB PAGES.

```
<HTML>
<HEAD>
<TITLE>MSN.COM</TITLE>
<meta http-equiv="Content-Type" content="text/html;
  charset=iso-8859-1">
<META http-equiv="PICS-Label" content=
 '(PICS-1.0 "http://www.rsac.org/ratingsv01.html"
 l comment "RSACi North America Server" by
 "Microsoft Network"'>
</HEAD>
<FRAMESET rows="20,*" frameborder="0"
 framespacing="0" border="0">
<FRAME src="/pilot.htm" name="pilot"
 NORESIZE scrolling="no" marginwidth="0"
 marginheight="0" frameborder="0" framespacing="0">
</FRAMESET>
</html>
```

Log on to the Internet and point your Web browser to Microsoft's home page at `http://www.microsoft.com`. Although the page might vary slightly from the page that Listing 19.1 describes, the page looks *nothing* like Listing 19.1! HTML is a formatting page description language. Listing 19.1's commands tell your Web browser how to display the informational text and graphics that come to your computer when you point your Web browser to that page.

Listing 19.2 shows a section of a VBScript example. Notice how much of the VBScript listing you can understand because you know the Visual Basic language.

LISTING 19.2. A SAMPLE OF A VBSCRIPT LISTING SHOWS YOU HOW CLOSE TO VISUAL BASIC THE VBSCRIPT LANGUAGE IS.

```
<SCRIPT Language="VBScript">
        Call PrintWelcome
        Call ModMessage

Sub PrintWelcome
               If Date() = "2/2/98" Then
                      document.write ". . . .Kathy's Birthday!"
               End If
               If Date() = "2/5/98" Then
```

```
                document.write ". . . .Eric's Birthday!"
            End If
            If Date() = "5/17/98" Then
                document.write ". . . .Michael's Birthday!"
            End If
            If Date() = "7/25/98" Then
                document.write ". . . .My Birthday!"
            End If
        End Sub
Sub ModMessage
        Document.Write "<BR>This page was last modified:
"+Document.lastModified +"</FONT><BR>"
End Sub
</SCRIPT>
```

VB to Java?

One technology you can look for shortly is Visual Basic–to-Java conversion programs. Some vendors already sell such tools, and others have announced their intent to do so. The big advantage of these conversion tools is that you do not have to worry much with Internet-based controls. If you can write an application that uses any VB controls, the conversion program translates the Visual Basic project into a Java-based project. In Java, you can embed the application inside your intranet or Internet Web pages, and the application automatically ends up on the end user's screen over the intranet or Internet as soon as the he or she displays the Web page.

These Java conversion tools don't necessarily replace the ActiveX Document Migration Wizard you read about earlier. However, some non-Windows systems support Java, but not ActiveX, so active Java applications can be more universally accepted than ActiveX-based applications.

19

Note

If Java is new to you, note that Java provided true active content on Web pages long before ActiveX controls appeared on the scene. Java works through Web pages and executes on the end user's machine, even if that user's machine and operating system vary from the developer's. If you want additional information on Java, check out Sams Publishing's *Sams Teach Yourself Java in 21 Days* for one of the best well-rounded introductory texts on the Java technology.

> *Visual J++* is Microsoft's Java-like implementation. Visual J++ contains a programming interface that looks and acts a lot like Visual Basic's programming interface. (Both environments support the Visual Studio style.) Therefore, you'll already understand the programming environment if you use Visual J++ as your Java language.

Visual Basic Internet Application Types

Visual Basic can create the following two kinds of Internet applications:

- **IIS applications**—The simplest way to incorporate the Internet into Visual Basic applications is to do so as an Internet Information Server (IIS) application. The Web browser that you embedded in the application you created earlier from the Visual Basic Application Wizard was an IIS application. The server handles all the processing of the Visual Basic commands.
- **DHTML applications**—Enables you to write code that responds to events on an HTML Web page. The end user's Web browser interprets and carries out these commands so that the remote server has little to do but respond to special requests when they arise, such as fetching additional Web pages.

Do	Don't
DO remember that today's lesson provides only a high-level overview of creating Visual Basic applications. No matter how strong a programmer you are, the world of an Internet programmer, not unlike that of a database developer, requires training in online protocol management, scripting languages, communications-based ActiveX controls, and client/server computing.	

New Term In online terminology, the *client* is the application that accesses the Internet, and the *server* is the computer that holds the Web pages the end user (the client) views and interacts with. The entire online world is transaction based; that is, the user issues a request in the Web browser, for example, and the service processes that request and sends a resulting transaction back to the user in the form of a Web page or ActiveX control applet.

Visual Basic supports these two Internet development application types so that you can develop the applications inside Visual Basic as well as test them with the debugging tools that you'll master in Day 21's lesson. For a more in-depth study of Internet programming with Visual Basic, check out Sams Publishing's Web site for some of the best books on the subject (`www.mcp.com`).

Summary

Today's lesson previewed Visual Basic's role as an Internet player. Obviously, this lesson can't cover even a small fraction of the details needed to truly turn Visual Basic into an Internet programming tool. A huge background is needed in just about every aspect of Internet technology before you tackle Visual Basic's interface. Several good books and online references exist, but your first and best bet is to study the online references that come with Visual Basic 6. There you'll find step-by-step descriptions that detail your role as an Internet programmer.

Don't be scared away from learning to write applications that interact with the Internet. Please realize that the promised goal of keeping every lesson a reasonable day's length could not be met if today's lesson were to teach many of the Internet specifics needed to write Internet programs. Nevertheless, Internet programmers are well rewarded for their abilities due to the in-depth study required and the rapid pace they must maintain to keep up with the technology.

Tomorrow's lesson describes how you create Help pages for your Visual Basic applications. You'll gain insight into the way HTML works when you create an interactive Help system using HTML-like pages.

Q&A

Q I have an application that contains three forms. Does the ActiveX Document Migration Wizard compile these three forms into a single ActiveX document?

A The ActiveX Document Migration Wizard converts forms but not complete applications to ActiveX documents. In other words, if your application contains four forms, each of those forms will result in a separate ActiveX document (assuming the forms contain no code that violates the ActiveX document requirements). You'll be able to link the documents together with hypertext links by using HTML code, but each form does become its own ActiveX document. Therefore, the migration wizard does not actually convert a whole application to a single ActiveX document if the application contains numerous forms.

Q What kinds of applications does the ActiveX Document Migration Wizard *not* migrate?

A The Migration Wizard converts most Visual Basic applications, except those with embedded OLE objects, because OLE is an older technology that Internet browsers do not support. In addition, certain advanced communications commands and controls may not work as expected in the migrated ActiveX document. Nevertheless, most Visual Basic applications should convert with little problem.

The limitation of one ActiveX document per form, discussed in the previous question, does pose a problem if any form in the application uses the `Hide`, `Show`, `Load`, or `Unload` methods to hide or display another form. The Migration Wizard comments out these methods, as well as the `End` command, because an ActiveX document's application does not end in the usual sense that an application does—the ActiveX document's application stays active until the user displays another page or closes the Internet browser.

Workshop

The Workshop provides quiz questions to help you solidify your understanding of the material covered and exercises to provide you with experience in using what you've learned. Try to understand the quiz and exercise answers before continuing to the next lesson. Answers are provided at the end of today's lesson.

Quiz

1. What does the Web-browsing application you generate with Visual Basic's Application Wizard do with the URL you supply?
2. True/False. Your application's end users must use the Internet Explorer Web browser before your Visual Basic Web-browsing control will work.
3. True/False. You must use the Internet Explorer Web browser before your Visual Basic Web-browsing control will work.
4. What is *encapsulation*?
5. Which online service do some of the Visual Basic controls support?
6. What's the difference between an *intranet* and the *Internet*?
7. What's the difference between an ActiveX document and a regular Visual Basic application?
8. What does Java do?

9. Which scripting language works with HTML to load and execute ActiveX documents?
10. How can you convert existing applications into an ActiveX document?

Exercises

1. If you have Microsoft Office Professional, you can use the Office Binder to hold ActiveX documents! Try it using the calculator's ActiveX document you created in today's lesson.
2. Select an application that contains multiple forms, such as the sample project named Controls. Convert that application to an ActiveX document.

WEEK 3

DAY 20

Providing Help

Today's lesson explains how to help your users. By the time you finish this lesson, you'll know how to add a Help system to an application so that your users can read online documentation to help them better understand your application. The online Help system is online *not* because you send users to the Internet but because the information is available instantly when the user requests the help—instead of the user having to refer to a printed manual. The help that you provide is nice because it mimics the online Help found in virtually all other Windows programs. Therefore, your users won't have a startup learning curve ahead of them when learning how to use your application's online Help system.

To prepare you for the online Help, this lesson first teaches you how to add ToolTips to controls. The all-important What's This? Help can also add after you've mastered the creation of Help files.

Today, you learn the following:

- About ToolTips and What's This? Help
- Preparing HTML help files
- How to decide between offering HTML help or the traditional WinHelp-based Help

- How to create and format the text in Help files
- About the RTF file format's requirements
- How to link Help messages to controls
- How to use the common dialog box control for controlling Help screens
- How Help context IDs point to specific Help topics

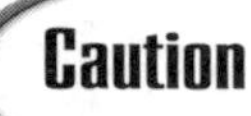

Several ways exist for you to add online Help to Visual Basic applications. Today's lesson teaches you about two of the most fundamental ways to add Help to your applications. This lesson describes how to add the online Help that you still see in most of today's Windows applications called *WinHelp*. Starting with Visual Basic version 6, you can also add HTML-based Help to your applications. Some of today's lesson explains what you must do to add HTML help to your applications. Not all users will have Web browsers capable of displaying the HTML-based Help, so you cannot ensure that your application will be compatible with such systems unless you add Help using the standard online Help described today.

ToolTip and What's This? Help

ToolTips are simple to add to various objects, and the special *What's This?* Help relies heavily on your Help file. You can add ToolTips to a control when you add the control to the form. The Properties window's `ToolTips` property value holds text that you can enter. When a user rests the mouse pointer over any control with a `ToolTips` property, the ToolTip appears after a brief pause. Also, as long as you've created a detailed Help file, adding eye-catching What's This? Help is simple.

New Term *ToolTips* are the pop-up Help descriptions that appears when you rest your mouse cursor over a control.

New Term The *What's This?* Help is a *context-sensitive* Help (meaning the Help that appears depends on where the user requests the Help) that describes controls on the screen. The user clicks the What's This? question mark in the window's upper-right corner or selects Help, What's This?, and the cursor changes to a pointing question mark. Then whatever control the user clicks produces Help about that control.

Offer What's This? Help when your application's screen contains many elements that might confuse new users. They can click the What's This? title bar button or select Help, What's This? (depending on the link to the What's This? Help you provide) and then click with the pointing question mark on whatever screen object they want to know more about.

In addition to ToolTips, you can provide What's This? Help to give your users additional information for your applications. What's This? lets the user see the Help text for any object that supports What's This? Help. Figure 20.1 shows one program's What's This? Help box that appears after the user selects Help, What's This? and clicks the Browse button. (The pointing question mark turns into a regular pointing cursor as soon as the What's This? Help box appears.)

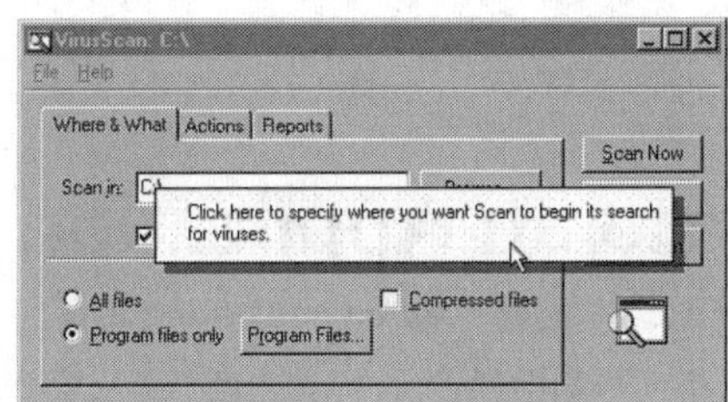

FIGURE 20.1.
The user can ask, "What's this?"

Make your What's This? Help match the objects. Figure 20.1 uses the closest Help page available for the Browse button from the Help pages set up. (This process is described throughout the rest of this lesson.)

One of the reasons you're learning about ToolTips along with What's This? Help is their similarity to the user. The user either needs to rest the mouse over a control to read a ToolTip or click the What's This? trigger to get Help on the control. Despite these similarities for the user, you might be surprised at how much more difficult it is to add What's This? Help to applications than it is to add ToolTips (which is extremely simple). Therefore, the rest of this section describes how to add ToolTips, and the final section of today's lesson describes how to add What's This? Help (after you learn how to create Help files that you can integrate into What's This? online Help).

You may be surprised at how easy it is to add ToolTips-based Help to any control that you place on the form. To add ToolTips to any object, you only need to enter the ToolTips text in the object's `ToolTipText` property. Visual Basic does the rest of the work. Look through the Sample folder for the MDI Notepad application named Mdinote. When Microsoft's programmers created this application, they added ToolTips to almost every control on every form. You can select almost any control and read its `ToolTipText` property to see what will pop up when you rest the mouse pointer over that control.

Do	Don't
DO get in the habit of adding ToolTips text as you add controls to your applications' form windows, given how easy ToolTips are to add. You're less likely to add ToolTips later, so add them when the purpose for the control is fresh in your mind.	

How Help Fits into an Application

Although writing an online Help system can be a daunting task, you can borrow the Windows Help system for your applications. All you really have to do is write the text that becomes the Help text and then use the Windows Help system to display that Help text at the right time and place in the application. Your users won't have a learning curve, because they already know how to use the Windows Help system.

Don't wait until your application is completely finished before designing the online Help system. The best time to write the Help text is when you design and create the application. At design time, you have a better working knowledge of the application than at any subsequent time, and you'll be better equipped to write the kind of help your users need.

HTML-Based Help Systems

If you use Visual Basic's Help system, you will see the Help based on *HTML* help files. In other words, the Help appears in a Web browser-like format with hyperlinks. You can click the Back button to display previous Help screens you've visited. The left pane contains the summary topics and, when you double-click a topic, the right pane shows the details for that topic.

New Term *HTML* stands for *HyperText Markup Language* and is the language that formats Web pages to look the way they do.

You can add such HTML-based Help files to your Visual Basic applications. This kind of help is new because before Web browsers appeared, all Windows applications used the same Help engine called *WinHelp*. This displays online help and also utilizes hyperlinks but not in a browser-like format (see Figure 20.2). The WinHelp version of the online help system in Windows applications has been the same for several years. Programmers predict that HTML help will become the standard online Help system for Windows applications within a few years, but WinHelp still maintains a strong lead.

WinHelp is the online Help system used in most Windows applications that may someday be replaced by the browser-based HTML Help system.

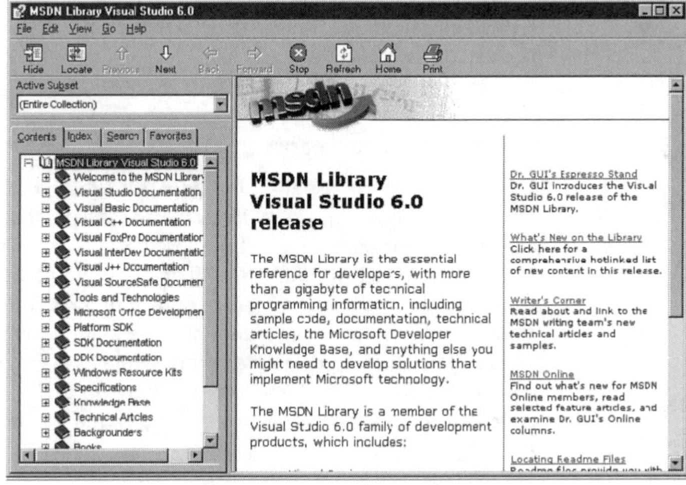

Figure 20.2.

WinHelp uses an Explorer-like two-pane window.

> **Caution**
>
> Despite the modern look and feel of the HTML-based Help, the users who use your application will be unable to obtain online Help if those users have no Web browser installed on their system or have a Web browser that appeared before Internet Explorer 4.0. Therefore, you limit your audience base considerably if you require Internet Explorer 4 for all your application's users. Until a Web browser is guaranteed on the user's system, you must stick with the standard WinHelp online Help described in the next section. In the meantime, this section explains what is in your future as the computing world continues to move toward a browser-based PC interface.

The way that you connect an HTML help file to a Visual Basic application is identical to that of the WinHelp Help file: Specify the HTML help file name in the `HelpFile` property. In addition, you can set the `HelpContextID` property for any object on the form so that a specific context-sensitive Help topic appears when the object is selected on the screen when the user requests help.

The big deal is not connecting the Help file to your application and the application's objects, but creating the Help file. Beginning in the next section, you walk through a rather tedious example that creates a WinHelp-based Help file and, despite the length, the file is still rather incomplete. Help screens for even simple applications can be numerous and the more you provide complete hyperlinks, the more tedious your job as a Help file designer will be.

Note

HTML help files have the filename extension .CHM and WinHelp files have the extension .HLP.

Tip

Creating a Help file, whether it is an HTML file or a WinHelp file, takes more effort than it is often worth. Nevertheless, the practice you get beginning in the next section serves a good purpose because you will better understand how a Help file's text interacts with an application. Do yourself a favor as soon as you complete this lesson: Go to your local software retailer and look for a more automated Help-creation tool. Many software utilities are available that make authoring much simpler than creating a Help file from scratch. In addition, the newer Help-authoring tools produce both WinHelp and HTML help from the same instructions that you provide.

Several tools exist—in addition to the Help authoring programs available now—with which you can create HTML pages to use for the Help files. Even many of today's word processors, such as Microsoft Word 97, saves and reads HTML files. Instead of a word processor, however, if you don't have access to an HTML-based Help-authoring program, use a Web page designer to create the HTML files. Microsoft provides a version of its HTML Web page designer program called *FrontPage Express* with Internet Explorer 4. FrontPage Express is also available for download from Microsoft's Web site.

Complete texts exist that explain how to create HTML pages, including Web and Help page elements such as hyperlinks and embedded graphics. For a more complete description of using HTML help with a Visual Basic application, pick up *Sams Teach Yourself More Visual Basic 6*.

Using RTF Help

The following sections explain how to build and link the Help topic file to your application using the traditional WinHelp method. Not only must you write the Help topic file, but you must also build a Help project that you then compile into a Help system that links to the application. The text that goes in your Help topic file must be in the special RTF (Rich Text Format) format, which the application can use to embed hypertext jumps from topic to topic when appropriate.

A *hypertext jump* is a link to another topic in the Help system.

You must have access to a word processor or text editor that creates RTF files. In addition, your word processor must support footnotes. Microsoft Word is perhaps the most popular word processor used for Help files. If you do not use Word, see if your word processor supports RTF file formats and footnotes.

Remember that a good reason to build WinHelp-based Help files is that every user who uses your application is going to be able to access your Help files. Every copy of Windows comes with a special Help-producing system called the *Windows Help Viewer* that is capable of managing the WinHelp-based RTF source files that you compile as described here. (The Windows Help Viewer cannot display HTML-based Help files; your users must have a Web browser available for that.)

NEW TERM The *Windows Help Viewer* is a Windows-supplied tool that all users will have. The Windows Help Viewer displays WinHelp-based files.

The compiling that you perform for Help files is not related to the compilation of your actual application. In tomorrow's lesson, "Distributing Your Applications," you'll learn how to compile your application for distribution. In order for your application, compiled or not, to access a Help file, you must compile that file into a file that has the standard .HLP file extension, as the next section explains.

Preparing for the Topic File

When you use Word to create the Help file, you should turn on the hidden formatting codes. Although most people write documents without the codes showing, the hypertext jumps require hidden text, which you need to be able to see even though that text will be hidden from all eyes but yours. Click the Show/Hide button (the paragraph symbol) on Word's toolbar to display hidden codes.

Creating Hypertext Jumps

Most of your Help file will consist of regular text that describes the Help topics. Regular Help text requires no special formatting, but you can vary the font size and style as much as you want. The hypertext jumps require some special formatting, however, so that the Help system can recognize hypertext jump keywords and know where the linked topics reside.

The more you cross-link your Help file topics with hypertext jumps, the more useful your Help system will be to your users. When you add hypertext jumps, your users don't have to use a menu to select every topic that might benefit them; instead, they can "jump" directly to the topic they want to read.

The requirements for creating hypertext jumps are as follows:

- Double-underline all hypertext jump phrases. Hypertext jump phrases appear in green text when users see the jump phrases in the Help window. You can double-underline in Word by highlighting the word or phrase, choosing Font from the Format menu, and selecting Double from the Underline drop-down list box. You can also press Ctrl+Shift+D to double-underline selected text as well as customize Word by putting a double-underline icon on the toolbar.
- Follow the hypertext jump phrase with a unique tag called the *context string*, which holds the jump target topic and is formatted as hidden text. Don't add a space between the hypertext jump and the context string. Be sure to format only the context string as hidden text and nothing else (not even punctuation or paragraph marks). You can hide text by choosing Format, Font and clicking the Hidden check box. You can also press Ctrl+Shift+H to hide selected text as well as customize Word by placing a hidden text icon on the toolbar.

A *context string* is a string that follows a hypertext jump phrase that appears when the user requests context-sensitive Help.

- Separate the topic page that contains the hypertext jump from the target jump page with a page break. You can insert a page break from the Insert menu when you choose Break, Page Break (or press Ctrl+Enter).
- Connect the text for the hypertext jump to the jump page with at least one of three custom footnote symbols

Symbol	*Description*
#	Used to connect to the jump page via the context string
$	Used to place the jump page title in the Help system's Locate text box and to connect the hypertext to the jump page's title
K	Used to connect to a topic search on one or more particular keywords

Many Help topics link to their jump pages with all three footnote symbols. In other words, users can jump from topic to topic, the topic titles appear in the Help system's Locate text box, and users can find topics by searching with multiple keywords.

- Display pop-up Help descriptions and definitions by underlining the topic to define with a single underline. You can underline text from the Format menu by choosing Font and then choosing Single from the Underline drop-down list box. You can also press Ctrl+U or click the toolbar's underline button to underline selected text.

Describing the Help file is much more involved than showing you an example. Therefore, the next section illustrates the different ways you can set up hypertext jumps and jump targets.

Tip

If you use the K footnote symbol to designate a topic search, add as many search topics as you can. As you'll see in the example, K footnotes often contain multiple entries separated by semicolons. The following footnote entry tells the Help system that the Help topic should appear in four entries in the Help index:

```
KChange Options;Menu commands;Change;Changing text
```

Practice Creating a Help File

Earlier in today's lesson, you loaded the sample MDI Notepad (Mdinote.vbp) project to see how the ToolTips Help worked. This example begins to create an auxiliary Help system for that MDI sample program. The application uses MDI forms to manage a tiny multiwindowed text editor. Although the application's text editor is fairly complete and extends past the Windows Notepad editor (because MDI Notepad supports multiple windows and Windows Notepad does not), the MDI Notepad application supports no online Help beyond that of the ToolTips.

Note

This example uses Microsoft Word to create the Help file. You might need to use a different word processor, depending on the contents of your system.

Figure 20.3 shows a sample opening Help screen in Word for the MDI Notepad application. Remember that the double-underlined phrases are the hypertext jump phrases that will appear in green on the user's Help system. All hidden text is turned on, so the dotted-underlined text represents the hidden text that holds the context strings.

FIGURE 20.3.

MDI Notepad's opening Help screen contains hypertext jumps.

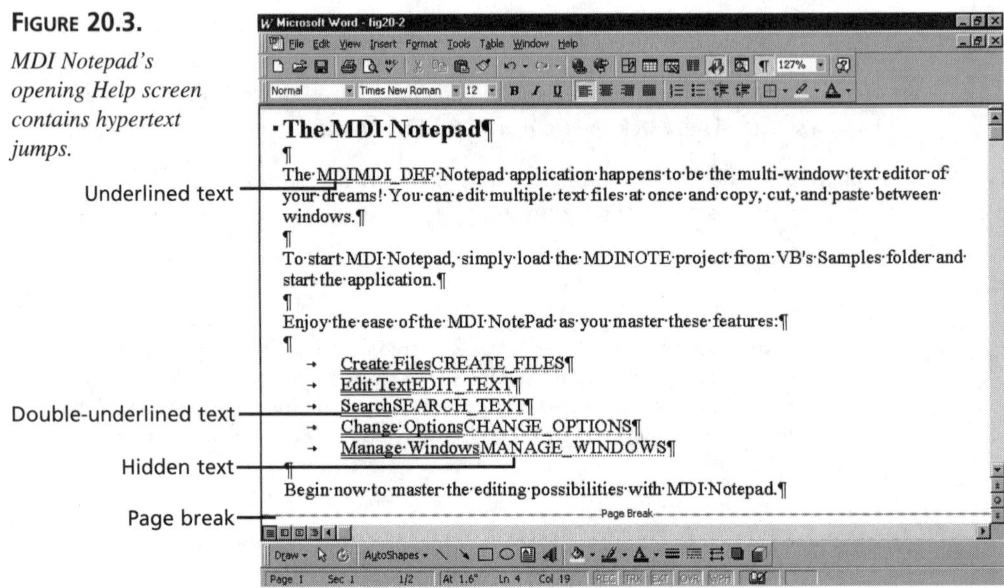

Figure 20.2 shows six jump phrase context strings: `MDI_DEF`, `CREATE_FILES`, `EDIT_TEXT`, `SEARCH_TEXT`, `CHANGE_OPTIONS`, and `MANAGE_WINDOWS`. Therefore, at least six more Word pages must appear below the opening Help screen. You connect these pages to their original hypertext jump links with one or more of the special footnote symbols. The first jump, `MDI_DEF`, will be a pop-up definition box for the term *MDI*.

The entire Help file needs a Help context ID value so that the underlying application can reference this opening Help screen when needed. Figure 20.4 shows two footnotes created for the opening Help text. To add a footnote, you would move the text cursor before the first character in the title, choose Footnote from the Insert menu, and type `#` for the custom symbol that indicates the hypertext jump page location. Repeat these steps to enter the `$` footnote for the hypertext jump link's title. The two footnote symbols appear to the left of the opening text as well as next to their respective footnote text in the bottom window. The application can use the Help context ID to reference this Help screen, and the Help engine's search tools can display the title that appears next to the `$` footnote symbol.

Caution

> Don't use the `K` footnote symbol for the opening Help window. Remember that `K` is reserved for those times when you want a pop-up Help box to appear if the user clicks an underlined Help topic. Also, you'll use a `K` footnote along with `#` and `$` so that every topic appears on the Help dialog box's indexed list of topics.

FIGURE 20.4.

The entire opening Help window now appears when its context ID or title is called for.

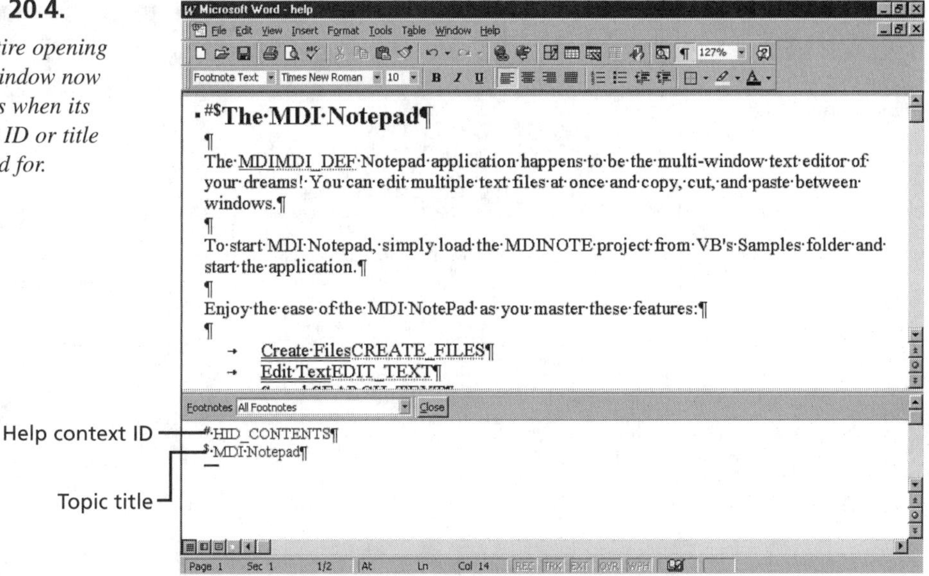

In the next few paragraphs, you'll learn that the RTF document contains a different kind of Help context ID than the type Visual Basic wants to use. As a result, you'll have to map the RTF file's textual context ID values to numeric values before an application can use context-sensitive Help.

The remaining Help hypertext jumps now need corresponding Help pages as well as footnotes to connect the pages to the opening screen. The first Help topic to create is the pop-up definition for MDI. The page below the opening Help screen must contain the following information:

- The MDI title on the first line
- A separating blank line
- The definition of MDI

20

The footnote in Figure 20.5 completes the connection between this page and the opening page's MDI location by adding a Help context ID to the definition. In addition, the K footnote symbol indicates that the connected page is a pop-up definition and not a hypertext jump.

Note

> The Help file in today's lesson typically uses the same Help context ID (in uppercase) as the topic title that the context ID links to, but these values don't have to be the same.

FIGURE 20.5.

The definition will now pop up thanks to the K footnote symbol.

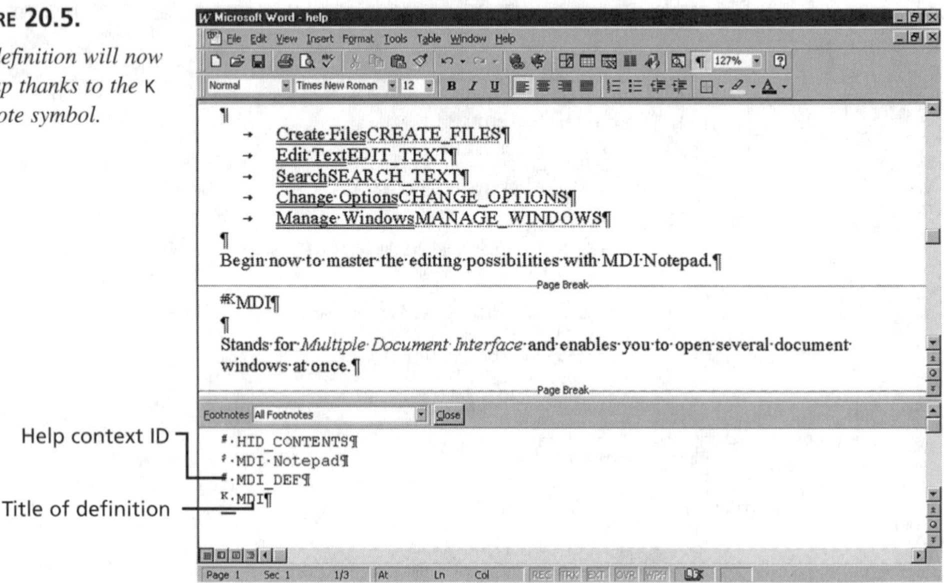

Finally, Figure 20.6 shows the first part of the remaining Help hypertext jump topics. The # footnote connects the opening page's hypertext jump topics to the subsequent jump pages.

FIGURE 20.6.

Subsequent jump pages are now linked to the opening Help page.

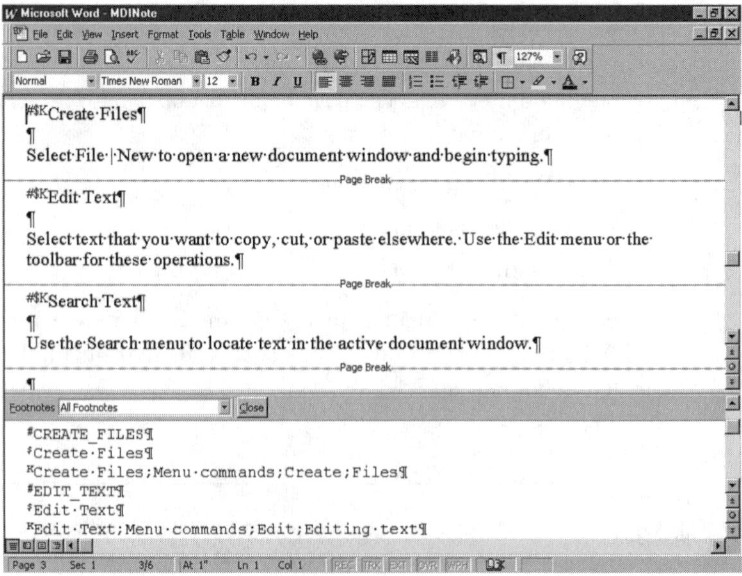

Any of these subtopics can contain additional links to additional pages (and to each other) as well as pop-up Help definitions.

As soon as you finish your RTF Help file, you must save the document. Be sure to select the Rich Text Format file type when saving the file. Now you must create the Help project file by using yet another file type—the ASCII text file type. Word can save ASCII text files, and you can even use the MDI Notepad sample application to create this file. The following project file was used for the Help file just described:

```
[OPTIONS]
contents=HID_CONTENTS
title=MDI Notepad Help

[FILES]
MDINote.rtf
```

The `[OPTIONS]` section describes the opening Help page context ID and the title bar text. The `[FILES]` section describes the Help file being compiled (you might need to specify a path name if the file resides in a special location). Enter the name of the RTF Help file you created and saved earlier. You can set other Help project file options from within the Help compiler.

Save the project file under any filename (the name of the application file is perhaps the best project filename). Use the .HPJ extension, however.

You need to run the Help compiler from your Visual Basic installation CD-ROM, because the Help compiler doesn't install with the normal Visual Basic installation. At this writing, you must run the Help system by following these steps:

1. Insert the Visual Basic Installation CD-ROM in your CD-ROM drive.
2. Select the Start menu's Run option.
3. Execute the HCW.EXE program located in the CD-ROM's \Common\Tools folder. Figure 20.7 shows the program window that appears, along with a helpful tip.

After starting the Microsoft Help Workshop program, load your Help project file when you want to compile the project. After you click the Compile toolbar button and accept all the default values, the compilation will begin. Read the warnings and errors that the compiler might display after the compilation finishes. Often, warnings occur that won't affect your Help system, but you should attempt to eliminate all warnings completely to perfect your Help file under all conditions. If errors exist, the compiler will be unable to compile the file.

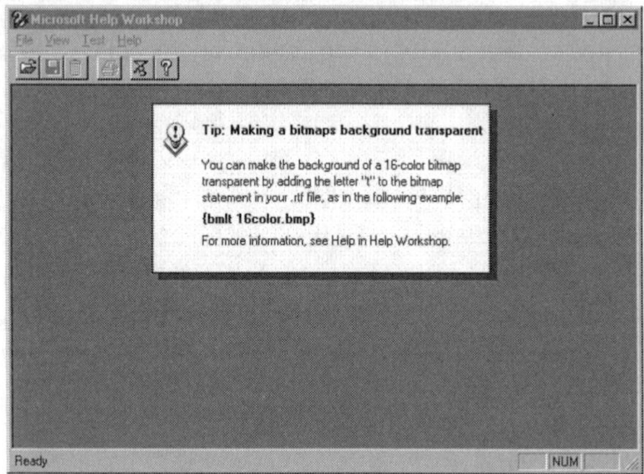

FIGURE 20.7.

The Help compiler window offers a tip to get you started.

After you compile the Help system, you can run it to test your Help entries. You won't learn how to connect the system to the application until the next section, but you can follow these steps to test the Help file:

1. Start the Windows Explorer.
2. Locate the Help file's folder. You'll see the Help file in the list of files with a Help icon.
3. Right-click the Help file and choose Open. The Windows online Help system begins, and you can check out your Help file.

The first Help window that appears (which you can return to by clicking the Contents button at any time) displays the opening Help page. The Index page shows a complete listing of all K footnote values that cross-reference Help topics.

Displaying the Help File

After you generate the Help file, you need to connect the application to the file. The Help context IDs associate the various Help topics to controls and parts of the application. Also remember to add a Help menu option so that users can request help at any time on any subject in the Help file.

The number of Help connections varies dramatically from application to application. You can use the depth of the Help file as well as the complexity of the application to predict how much help users will need. The rest of this section explains some of the ways you can connect the Help file to the application. (Visual Basic supports a number of Help file connections, but this section describes the most common ones.)

The Project Properties Dialog Box

The Project Properties dialog box, shown in Figure 20.8, is the primary link between your project and the Help file. The Project Properties dialog box ensures that the Help file connects to the user's F1 keypress.

FIGURE 20.8.

Connect the Help file to your project.

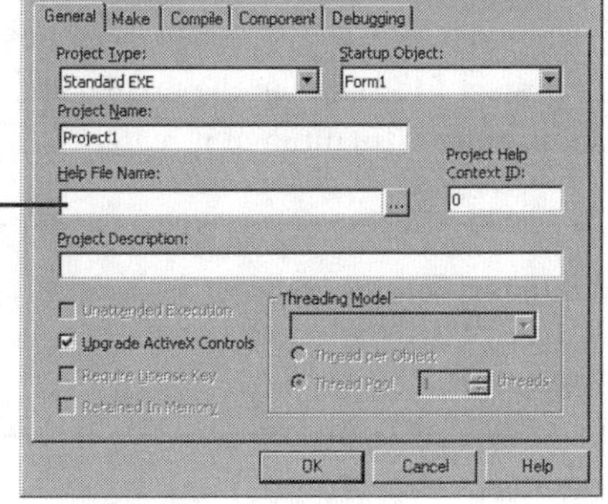

Note

You don't need to worry about changing the text box labeled Project Help Context ID. Any Help context ID you enter there determines the type of Help that appears when you click this application's Help toolbar button from within the Object Browser.

The Common Dialog Box Control

You've taken care of the easiest part of the Help system connection now that you've gotten the F1 key to generate the complete Help window. The window will contain your Help file because your project's properties point to that file. If you want to add context-sensitive Help to your application so that users can press F1 to get help when a control has the focus or during a menu selection, you must complete a few more steps.

20

Day 9, "The Dialog Box Control," showed you how to use the common dialog box control to produce various dialog boxes such as the File Open and Print dialog boxes. Now that you've created a Help file, you can use the common dialog box control to display the interactive Help screens as well.

When you place the common dialog box control on a form, set the `:HelpFile` property and then set the `ShowHelp` method. Visual Basic runs the Windows Help engine that interprets your Help file and provides the usual Contents, Index, and Find pages that other Windows applications support.

You can limit the Help engine's ability to show just the Contents, the Index, or the Find tab by modifying the `HelpContext` property (see the online Help for values). However, you'll usually offer all three tabs.

If you offer context-sensitive Help, you must describe to the Help engine exactly which Help window page to display when the user selects context-sensitive Help. Doing so requires that you edit the Help project file and map the textual context IDs to unique numeric context IDs. This sounds more difficult than it really is.

If you fail to add context-sensitive Help to all controls, but the user selects context-sensitive Help, Visual Basic displays the Help file's Contents page (the opening Help page).

You now must reedit the project file and map the textual context IDs to numeric ones. To do so, you'll add a `[MAP]` section to the project file. Given the MDINote.rtf Help file and the associated project file described earlier, the following code provides such an edit of the project file:

```
[OPTIONS]
contents=HID_CONTENTS
title=MDI Notepad Help

[FILES]
MDINote.rtf

[MAP]
HID_CONTENTS 1
MDI_DEF 2
CREATE_FILES 3
EDIT_TEXT 4
SEARCH_TEXT 5
CHANGE_OPTIONS 6
MANAGE_WINDOWS 7
```

Make sure that no two context ID numbers are the same. The mapping can begin at 1, but many Visual Basic programmers reserve series of numbers to represent different kinds of Help topics. For example, all command button Help topics might range from 1000 to 1050. The numbers, therefore, don't have to be sequential. Recompile the project file to embed the new map information in the Help file.

Tip

> If you play around with the Help Workshop, reading the Help screens and familiarizing yourself with their operation, you'll learn how the Help Workshop program makes mapping unique context IDs even faster than editing them with a text editor.

Your sleuthing now begins. You must locate every control and form to which you want to add context-sensitive Help. For example, in the MDI Notepad application, you could display the `frmFind` form (the form that supports the Find menu option that locates data in the document) and change the Find command button's `HelpContextID` property to `5`. If that were the only change you made, users would always see the standard opening Help Contents screen when they run the application and press F1, except when the Find button has the focus; users would then see the Help topic for the Search page. Of course, you would want to add additional context-sensitive Help displays to other controls, including some forms, for your users' benefit.

Note

> As you add the context-sensitive Help to controls, you'll likely find other areas of the application that need explanation. Therefore, you might add to your RTF Help file many times before you've provided ample Help support to the application.

Tip

> When you add Help pages, try your best to locate every place in the application from which users might need specific help. Every time you add context-sensitive Help, your users won't have to search through the Help Index or Contents page that otherwise would appear.

Listing 20.1 shows code that displays the Help topic supplied by a specific context ID. You can incorporate code such as this into a command button or Help menu option if you want to offer specific Help topics from your Help file.

LISTING 20.1. YOU CAN DISPLAY CONTEXT-SENSITIVE HELP.

```
cdbHelp.HelpFile = "MDINote.hlp"  ' Point to the help file
'
' You can now provide specific help for a particular
' topic by pointing to the number in the .HPJ's [MAP]
' section (your textual context IDs)
cdbHelp.HelpContext = 3  ' Point to the section
cdbHelp.HelpCommand = cdlHelpContext  ' Request context-sensitive
cdbHelp.ShowHelp      ' Display the context-sensitive help
```

Adding What's This? Help

Now that you better understand how to create a Help file, you can create What's This? Help. You must add a Help page for every What's This? Help feature that you want to support. After you add the pages and connect them to the other Help pages in the system through the custom footnotes described earlier in today's lesson, you must map the pages to the numeric context ID. The What's This? Help engine uses those context ID numbers to determine the proper Help box to display when the user requests the What's This? Help.

The secret to What's This? Help is twofold:

- Make sure that the form supports What's This? Help by setting the form's `WhatsThisButton` property to `True` and the `WhatsThisHelp` property to `True`.
- Enter the Help page's context ID in the object's `WhatsThisHelpID` property.

The What's This? Help from the MDINotepad application (if you've followed the earlier sections and created a Help file with Help pages that you can use) requires only that you perform these steps:

1. Open the Project window and double-click the form named `frmFind` to display the Find dialog box's form.
2. Assign `True` to the `WhatsThisButton` and `WhatsThisHelp` properties. When you subsequently display this form when the application executes, you'll see the What's This? question mark button on the form.
3. Repeat the assignment for the other two forms in the application.
4. Look through the Help project file's `[MAP]` section for context ID numbers and assign these context ID values to various menu options (use the Menu Editor) and form objects that might need the description. Although the Help file is far from complete, several of the Help pages work well for the objects, especially the menu bar items.

Summary

Today's lesson explained how to incorporate Help in your Visual Basic applications. Several forms of Help are available to Visual Basic developers. By using the HTML help or the WinHelp Windows Help engine, you can build a complete hypertext jump system with interconnected Help pages and pop-up definitions. Your user can get context-sensitive, access-specific Help pages by pressing F1. The common dialog box control assists in providing this Help, enabling users receive help at the push of a button.

Adding context-sensitive Help allows your users to locate the help they need. You can assign context-sensitive Help to various objects so that specific Help text appears when a users selects an object and press F1. The context-sensitive Help feature keeps your users from having to search through the index every time they require help.

Two simple Help features that you can add quickly are the ToolTips and What's This? Help elements. ToolTips are extremely simple and require only that you add the ToolTips text in the Properties window. Before you can assign What's This? Help, you must build a comprehensive Help file and assign various numeric context IDs to objects.

Tomorrow's lesson concludes your 21-day training by showing you how to test, debug, and distribute your applications to others.

Q&A

Q Why can't I create my application's Help file after I complete the whole application?

A You can. That's what you did today for the MDI Notepad application. Nevertheless, you understand the ins and outs of your application the best at the time you write the application. Therefore, you'll provide better help if you create ToolTips, What's This? Help, and Help files as you create your project. You can keep your word processor open in a second window and switch to the it (by using Alt+Tab) when you're ready to add more to the Help file.

Q Why is adding Help in the Help file so tedious?

A The tedium arises from the fact that you must ensure that all the hypertext jumps connect to appropriate topics, that all topics are covered that need to be covered, and that you use proper formatting in the RTF Help file. Of course, the Help compiler will catch improperly formatted Help files, so you'll debug your Help file when you compile it. Actually, as you build and test your application, you may want to compile the Help file as well so that it stays accurate as you build the project. Creating a Help file incrementally like this makes the overall process less tedious.

Many Help-authoring tools exist that you use to add help to your Visual Basic programs that assist you in building Help files without using the tedium of creating RTF or HTML files. Do not use HTML-based Help unless you assume that your user has an Internet browser active that is ready to display the HTML files.

Using these visual Help designer programs will make your Help file creation go smoothly. In addition, you'll not inadvertently type as many Help file errors as naturally happens when you use the RTF approach. In addition, these programs let you create Help diagrams that show visually how hypertext jumps connect, thereby further reducing the amount of RTF coding you have to do to build your Help file.

Q Why not use these tools and forego today's lesson entirely?

A Visual Basic supports the online Help described today as well as other kinds—such as HTML-based Help. You can use third-party tools to make creating Help much easier, and if you develop many applications, you'll certainly want to look into these tools. Nevertheless, you've started with Visual Basic, and Visual Basic does contain all the tools needed, except for an RTF editor, to create the Help support described today. In addition, not all your users will have Web browsers to view HTML help, so this is not for universal applications unless you require that a Web browser be installed before your application runs. By creating Help files using today's lesson's "old-fashioned method," you learn more about how the Help system works and you appreciate the complexities of a hypertext system. Despite today's lesson's RTF file approach, most of the tedium does *not* come from the approach, actually, but from the design of the Help system. The more complex and complete you make your Help system, the better your users will appreciate your application. Such complex Help systems, however, are not trivial to produce. That's why you should create the system along with the application to ensure that you've offered the appropriate Help that your application deserves.

Workshop

The Workshop provides quiz questions to help you solidify your understanding of the material covered and exercises to provide you with experience in using what you've learned. Try to understand the quiz and exercise answers before continuing to the next lesson. Answers are provided in Appendix A, "Answers to Exercises."

Quiz

1. What file format must you use to create an online Help file?
2. How can hypertext jumps improve a Help system?
3. Which custom footnote symbol creates pop-up Help definitions for underlined Help page text?
4. What are some of the features of the Help project file?
5. After you compile a Help file, how can you attach such a file to an application so that the Help file appears when a user presses F1?
6. How do you connect context-sensitive Help to the Help file topics?

7. True/False. The context-sensitive Help uses the textual context IDs in your Help file.
8. What's the difference between the What's This? Help and ToolTips?
9. How can you add the What's This? button on forms?
10. True/False. You can offer What's This? Help for forms as well as for objects on the form. (*Hint:* Check the form's properties.)

Exercise

Add What's This? Help to every object in MDI Notepad. This task might seem tedious (and it is somewhat), but you'll quickly get the hang of working with What's This? Help, context IDs, and Help pages.

WEEK 3

DAY 21

Distributing Your Applications

Today's lesson shows you how to test, debug, and distribute your Visual Basic applications. No application is ever complete. You always can add more features, and many times errors appear long after you think you've removed all of them. Therefore, long-term maintenance is part of the programming process. You can take steps to eliminate some of the maintenance headaches, however. Throughout the previous lessons, this 21-day tutorial has offered tips to help you better document your code and reduce maintenance problems.

One of the best ways to reduce maintenance problems is to thoroughly debug and test your application before you distribute it to your users. This lesson describes some of the debugging tools Visual Basic supplies, as well as some testing procedures you might want to run your application through before you distribute it.

You've reached the final day of this 21-day tutorial. After you finish this lesson, you can consider yourself graduated from the University of Visual Basic 6 with a degree in Programming Arts and, more important, consider yourself primed for the rank of Visual Basic guru. Your next step is to develop as much as you can with Visual Basic to hone the skills you've gained throughout this tutorial.

Today, you learn the following:

- About the types of bugs a program can generate
- How to locate bugs while writing code
- About the debugger's many windows
- How to use the debugger's single-step mode to locate specific areas of the program during execution
- About multiple breakpoints
- How to create an installation routine for your application
- How to use the Package and Deployment Wizard
- The importance of supporting application installation

Debugging and Testing

All applications need testing. Too many bugs can find their way into an application during the programming stages. When you test an application, you run it through a series of test-case executions. During the testing, you enter random and extreme values in all the user-entry controls to ensure that the application can handle values outside the typical range. You'll find that bugs almost always appear during the testing phase.

Debugging is a three-step routine:

1. Determine the problem bugs and their locations
2. Correct the bugs
3. Retest the application to ensure that you eliminated the bugs

Bugs range from mild errors, such as misspellings or text-alignment mistakes, to serious errors, such as when an application terminates the entire Windows session and loses data. To your users, a *bug* is anything that doesn't match expected program results or prevents the application from running.

Programmers face many debugging problems when looking for bugs. You must decide that you've found as many bugs as you can possibly find, and you must test and retest to ensure that the bugs are gone and don't reappear. Careful planning before, during, and after the coding process helps you reduce the time it takes to debug your application.

> You should develop and test your application from within the Visual Basic development environment. The development environment contains debugging tools that help you track and locate errors. Only after you're satisfied with your test results should you then compile and distribute your application to users.

Windows and the powerful Visual Basic development environment help you locate errors. When you run a Visual Basic application, Visual Basic might find an error during the compilation or preparation for the program's execution (such as a misspelled keyword) and display an error message, such as the one shown in Figure 21.1.

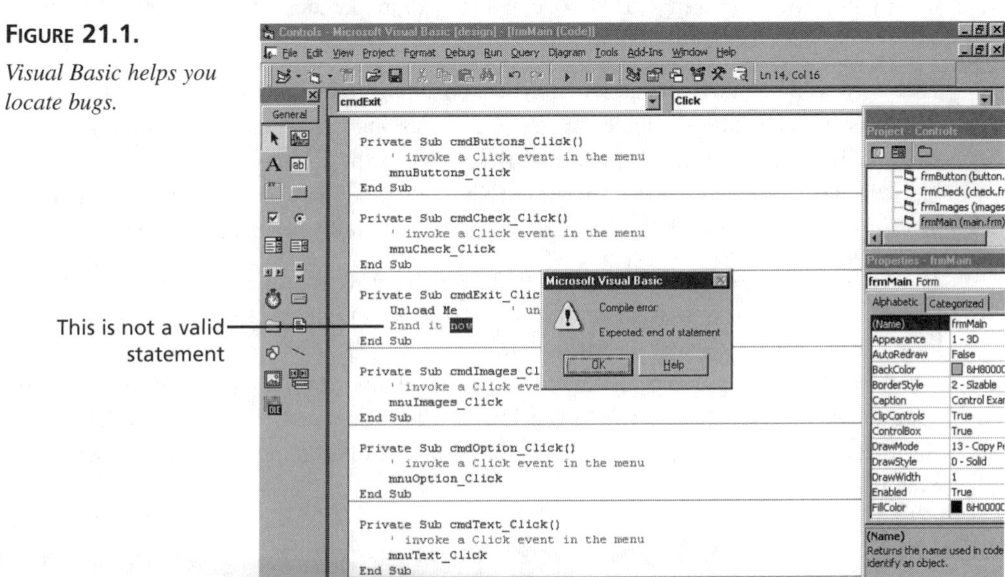

FIGURE 21.1.
Visual Basic helps you locate bugs.

If, when you run an application, you see such an error message before the first form appears onscreen, you probably typed a syntax error in your code. The error in Figure 21.1 is a syntax error. The error message rarely reads `Syntax Error`, but if an error occurs due to a spelling or grammar mistake, the error was a result of a syntax problem.

NEW TERM A *syntax error* is an error in a programming language's grammar or spelling.

21

Notice that Visual Basic not only told you about the error in Figure 21.1, but it also located the error inside the code window. Even if the code window is closed when you try to run the program, Visual Basic highlights the error. The problem is that a proper `End` statement was not used. After you fix the syntax error, you then can click the Run toolbar button to start the program from the corrected error.

If you have the Auto Syntax Check box selected on the Tools, Options dialog box's Editor page, Visual Basic checks for syntax errors as you type program code into the code window. Some programmers, however, like to have more freedom at design time to sprinkle partial statements here and there that they will repair later in the programming process. However, such incomplete code can lead to errors later if you're not careful; you may forget to correct a statement that you've left undone. Nevertheless, there are times when you'll want to fill in gaps of code at a later time, perhaps after checking with the users to answer a design question.

Therefore, you can turn off automatic syntax checking. When the option is off, Visual Basic doesn't check for coding errors, such as a missing parenthesis, until you run or compile the program. Either way, Visual Basic locates these kinds of bugs for you with message boxes, such as the one shown in Figure 21.1, but the Auto Syntax Check option gives you the choice of when you want Visual Basic to tell you about the code problem.

More difficult errors appear during the runtime of your application. A syntax error is easy to spot, because Visual Basic finds it for you. A runtime error is more difficult to locate and correct. Consider the error shown in Figure 21.2. The error involves program logic. No error message appears, but the field that should show a name shows an address instead. Obviously, an address field was loaded where a name field should appear. Visual Basic does not know this is unusual because it just follows the programmer's orders, even if logic errors result.

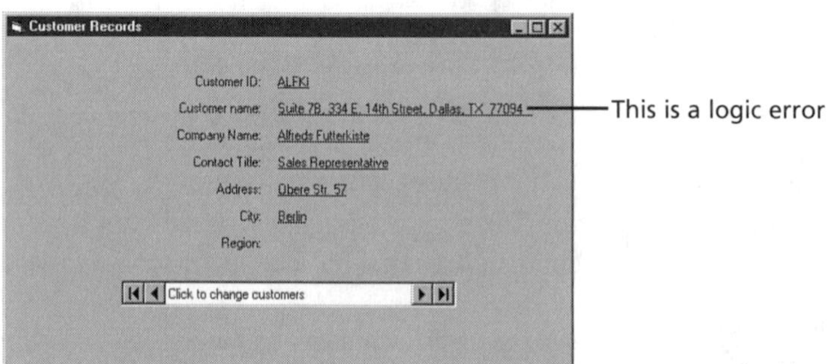

FIGURE 21.2.

Visual Basic cannot catch logic errors.

Logic errors that you catch require that you stop the program. (Visual Basic doesn't recognize the error and stop the program as it does with syntax errors.) You then must track down the problem.

To track the problem, you must search through the program code looking for traces where such a runtime logic error might reside and then fix the problem. If the problem involves the form's or a control's appearance onscreen, you have to trace all references to that part of the object. Often, but not always, the Object Browser can help you find the specific code that goes with an object.

Visual Basic can locate *some* logic errors if the logic error results in a request for Visual Basic to do something impossible. For example, Figure 21.3 shows what happens when a program asks Visual Basic to divide a number by zero. Division by zero isn't defined mathematically, so Visual Basic cannot accomplish this calculation, even if no syntax errors appear in the calculation. Visual Basic halts the program's execution and describes the error in a message box.

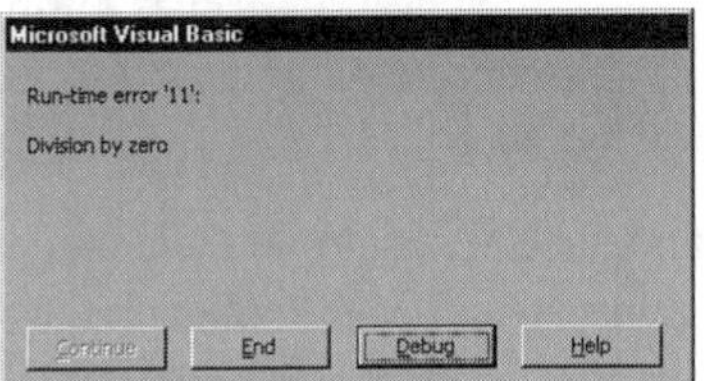

FIGURE 21.3.
Some logic errors request that Visual Basic attempt something impossible.

The application runs smoothly without the code window showing. However, as soon as Visual Basic realizes that the program is requesting an impossible task, it displays the code window and locates the approximate place in the code where the division by zero occurs. You can click the error dialog box's Help button to get more help with the error message, click End to terminate the program's execution, or click Debug to enter Visual Basic debugging mode.

Tip

> Notice that a division by zero error produces the error code 11 (see the error message in Figure 21.3). You can test for errors in the `Err.Number` system object. Therefore, if you suspect that a calculation may result in a division by zero error, due to missing data, you can trap the error with an `On Error Goto` statement. If the offending `Err.Number` is 11, you can inform the user that a value is not filled in on the form instead of the user having to deal with an error message box.

Using the Debugger

Visual Basic's development environment includes a debugging tool that becomes part of the development environment when you request debugging help. The debug tool lets you do all the following tasks:

- Analyze variable contents at runtime.
- Stop the program at any statement and restart when ready.
- Set *breakpoints* throughout the code that automatically stop the program execution when one is reached.
- Change variables during the execution of a program to different values from their current state to test the application.
- Set *watch variables* that halt the program's execution when one receives a specific value or range of values.
- Skip statements you don't want to execute during a test.
- Use the `Debug` object's output window to print values during a program's execution. The debug window lets you capture output, such as variable values, without disturbing the normal form window.

You can enter debugging mode and have access to all the debugger's features (primarily found on the Debug menu) when you do any of the following:

- Press Ctrl+Break to stop the program's execution in midstream.
- Receive a runtime error message box.
- Set a breakpoint, and execution reaches that breakpoint.
- Click a statement in the program and then, from the Debug menu, choose Run To Cursor to execute the program as usual. Visual Basic halts the program and enters debugging mode as soon as execution reaches the cursor.

Setting Breakpoints

One of the easiest breakpoints to set is the run-to-cursor breakpoint. To test breakpoints, load the Controls application found in your Samples folder. The Test Buttons form, `frmButton`, changes a stop signal as the user clicks command buttons. Suppose you suspect that the Controls application's code doesn't change the signal properly. You can click the first executable statement in the standard module's `ChangeSignal()` function and select Run To Cursor from the Debug menu. (Do not select a remark because a remark cannot be set for any kind of breakpoint or halt.) The program starts up as usual, but it halts at the breakpoint and highlights the line.

The program isn't halted permanently. Up to this point, all the program variables have been initialized, the code has run, and its effects are available. If output occurs before the cursor's location is reached (as done here when the initial form appears), you see the output appear onscreen as usual. The program, as indicated by Visual Basic's title bar, is in its *break* state, which is reached due to the breakpoint. The yellow highlight is the line where the cursor rests when you chose Run To Cursor from the Debug menu.

Listing 21.1 shows the procedure where this particular example stops.

LISTING 21.1. YOU CAN ANALYZE INDIVIDUAL PROCEDURES AT A BREAKPOINT.

```
Private Sub ChangeSignal()
    ' Check to see what color the light is, and then change
    ' it to the next color. The order is green, yellow,
    ' and then red.
    If imgGreen.Visible = True Then
        imgGreen.Visible = False
        imgYellow.Visible = True
    ElseIf imgYellow.Visible = True Then
        imgYellow.Visible = False
        imgRed.Visible = True
   Else
        imgRed.Visible = False
        imgGreen.Visible = True
    End If
End Sub
```

Perhaps the signal doesn't work because more than one color is visible at a time. Therefore, you can look at the current value of the `Visible` properties for the three possible signals (named `imgGreen`, `imgYellow`, and `imgRed`) to ensure that one and only one contains a `True` value when this procedure begins.

Looking at a control's (or even a variable's) contents has never been easier. As Figure 21.4 shows, all you need to do to see the value of any variable or object's property value is rest your mouse pointer over the control.

Suppose you check all three values and find that only one has `True` in it, which is correct. You've just determined that the problem does not lie in the `ChangeSignal()` procedure, and you have to search back further in the code to see where the signals got messed up. Then again, depending on when the problem shows itself during the program's execution, you might want to run the program a little further. Either way, by stopping the execution and analyzing controls and variables, you can determine if values are where they should be at runtime.

FIGURE 21.4.

Visual Basic displays all control and variable values when the program halts using the debugger.

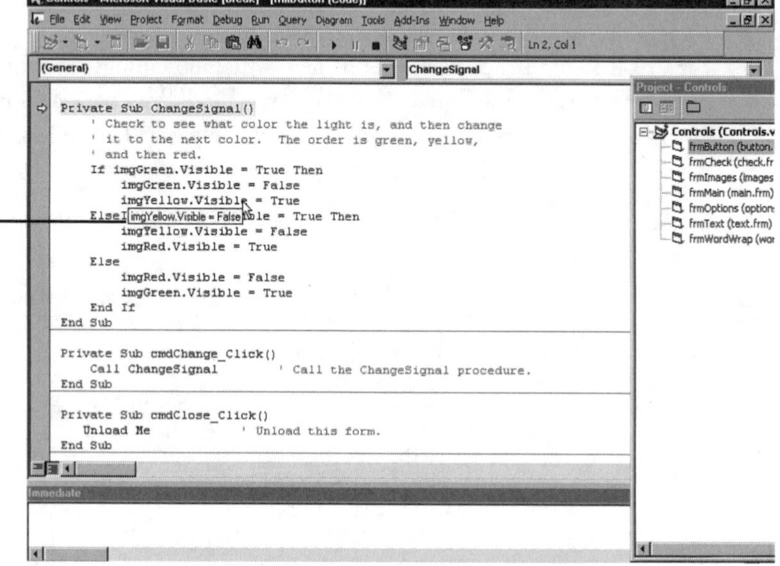

`imgYellow.Visible` is `False`

Retracing Your Steps

Before going further, display the Debug toolbar. From the View menu, choose Toolbars and then Debug to display the Debug toolbar. (As you debug, the toolbar can float, or you can dock it to the upper toolbar area.) When you need to see where the program's execution has been up to a breakpoint, you can use one of the most useful debugging features—the *call stack*. Click the toolbar's Call Stack button. As Figure 21.5 shows, the Call Stack dialog box appears and shows your program's execution, procedure by procedure, until its current position.

If you see a call stack entry labeled `[<Non-Basic Code>]`, execution occurred from another source, as happens when code calls the Windows API.

NEW TERM The *Windows API* (for *application programming interface*) is a set of internal Windows procedures that you can call from languages such as Visual Basic and Visual C++ when you need to borrow a routine or trigger a function from Windows itself. The Visual Basic debugger does not have the capability or authority (due to Windows' system protection) to trace through operating system procedures.

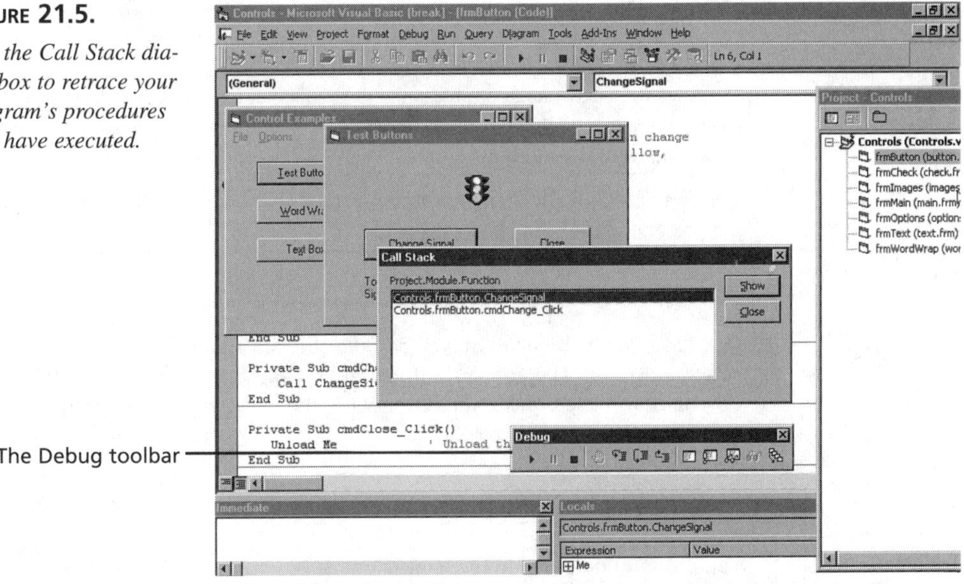

FIGURE 21.5.
Use the Call Stack dialog box to retrace your program's procedures that have executed.

If you want to show one of the Call Stack dialog box's procedures, double-click that entry to move to the procedure. From there, you not just look at code—you're actually looking at live values as well. Keep in mind that the application is in a breakpoint stage still, so you can view the values of any control, variable, or named constant within that previous procedure.

Single-Stepping Through Code

At any breakpoint, you can click the Debug toolbar's Step Into button to execute the next statement in the program. Whatever statement normally comes next executes when you click Step Into (even if that statement is a call to another procedure).

The Debug toolbar contains three step-related buttons. Table 21.1 describes how to use them. You might not want to single-step through *every* statement in an application; the step buttons give you some freedom to determine how you want the program to continue.

TABLE 21.1. THE STEP MODES DETERMINE HOW YOUR APPLICATION IS TO CONTINUE.

Step Mode	*Description*
Step Into	Executes only the next statement. Even if the statement is in another procedure (or a return to a previous procedure), the next statement executes and the cursor is placed at that statement. Therefore, you can single-step through an entire application by pressing F8 continually.

continues

Table 21.1. continued

Step Mode	*Description*
Step Over	Executes the next statement unless the next statement is a call to a different procedure. The new procedure executes in its entirety, and execution halts at the statement following the procedure call.
Step Out	Finishes executing the current procedure and then, at the next statement outside the procedure, execution halts again.

Of course, at any breakpoint, you can click the Start button to continue execution in its normal manner. If subsequent breakpoints are set, the execution halts at those breakpoints. Otherwise, the program behaves normally, as if you'd never stopped it.

You can terminate debug mode at any time by clicking the Visual Basic toolbar's End button or by choosing End from the Run menu.

Multiple Breakpoints

As your application executes, you might want to set breakpoints along the way. The breakpoints halt the program's execution so that you can study variables and controls during mid-execution. For example, if you see runtime problems that you want to analyze on the next program run, you can add a breakpoint by clicking the Debug toolbar's Toggle Breakpoint button at the highlighted statement. You can set multiple breakpoints on additional lines by clicking the Toggle Breakpoint button throughout the code. If you reach a breakpoint (indicated by a red highlight) that you set in a previous session but no longer need, use Toggle Breakpoint again on that line to remove the breakpoint from that location. You can also click to the left of any statement to add or remove a breakpoint.

You can set breakpoints only for lines that execute. You can't set a breakpoint on lines that declare user data types or contain only remarks.

The Debug Window

At any breakpoint, you can display the Debug window to work outside the program's environment. The Debug window is often called the *Immediate window.* When you click the Debug toolbar's Immediate Window button, the Immediate window opens at the bottom of your code window (that is, in its docked position) or in a free-floating location if the Immediate window isn't docked to the edge of the screen.

NEW TERM The *Immediate window* (another name for the Debug window) is a window inside the Visual Basic environment in which you can view program values and print messages during the program's execution. By sending a message to the Immediate window, you can read progress messages as your application executes by using the `Debug.Print` method. Those messages will not interfere with the program's normal output.

You can type any Visual Basic statement in the Immediate window and see the results of that statement's execution immediately. One of the most common Debug window methods used is `Print`, which prints variable values and control properties. `Print` sends output to different objects (not just to the printer or form), including the Immediate window. Figure 21.6 shows an object's value displayed to show that the values you work with in the Immediate window are live values set by the part of the application that's executed to that breakpoint. Also, you can print the results of any expression, If you need to, you can change variable values during execution. After you do that, the rest of the program works with the new value instead of the one assigned originally in the code; that way, you can see the results of the variable's change.

FIGURE 21.6.

Using the Immediate window to print values and change results.

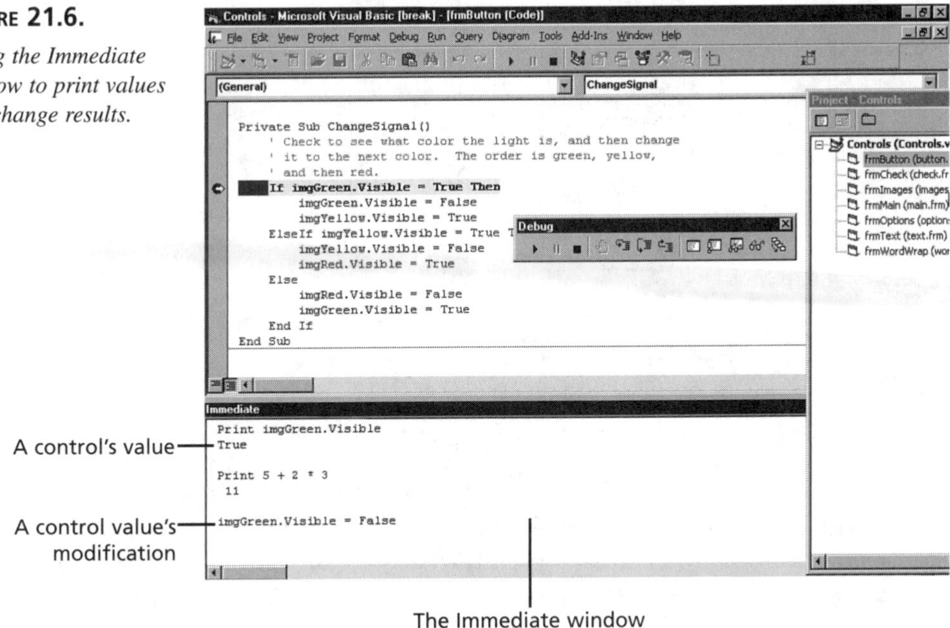

21

Although the interactive nature of Visual Basic's development environment makes such output less important than it used to be in text environments, your program can write directly to the Immediate window by using the `Debug` object's `Print` method. Therefore, if your program includes a statement such as `Debug.Print cmdN6xt.Caption`, the output goes to the Immediate window, where you can view the output without having to interfere with the normal application's output in the form window.

The Locals Window

When you click the Locals Window button on the Debug toolbar, Visual Basic displays the Locals window (see Figure 21.7). The Locals window shows the current value of all variables local to the current procedure (the procedure holding the current breakpoint) as well as global constants and variables. Perhaps the most helpful aspect of the Locals window is its display of all the values for the form's controls. You can expand and shrink the Explorer-like view to see as much detail as you want.

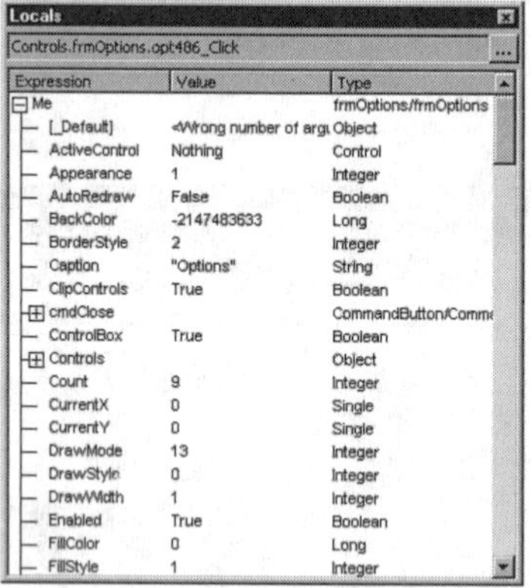

FIGURE 21.7.
The Locals window shows all variables that are local to the current procedure as well as globals.

If you modify a local variable from within the Immediate window, its value changes in the Locals window as well.

In addition to the variable name and value, the Locals window displays the variable's or control's data type. Click the ellipsis button to the right of the Locals window's current procedure name to view a call stack list. When you click one of the call stack procedure names, the Locals window updates to show that procedure's local variables.

The Watch Window

As your debugging process continues, you might find that a bug occurs only when a variable has a certain value. Sometimes problems can't be traced to a single statement, so you have to watch a variable or expression throughout an entire procedure. For this reason, Visual Basic provides the Watch window, in which you can enter values for variables or expressions. You can set up the Watch window with values to watch for at design time or runtime by clicking the Debug toolbar's Watch Window button. You can use either of the following two methods to add values to the Watch window:

- From the Debug menu, choose Add Watch to display the Add Watch dialog box (see Figure 21.8).
- Right-click the Watch window (you must first display the Watch window by clicking its Debug toolbar button) and choose Add Watch to display the Add Watch window.

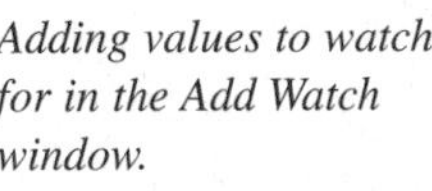

FIGURE 21.8.

Adding values to watch for in the Add Watch window.

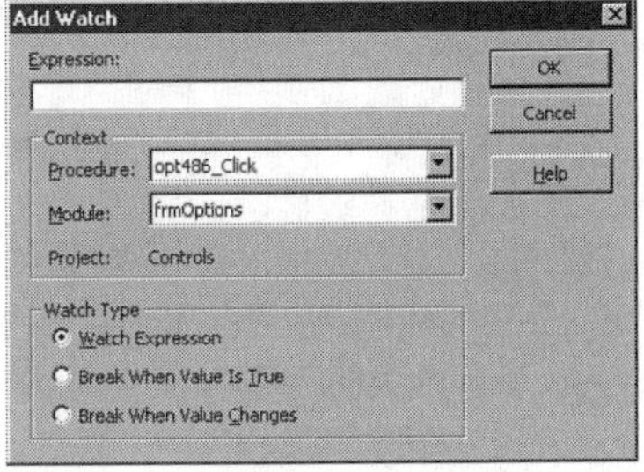

When you're adding a watch expression, the context of the watch tells Visual Basic the scope of the watch (where it should monitor the expression). Visual Basic can watch a single procedure, a form, a module, or the entire project.

The Watch Type area lets you specify how you want Visual Basic to respond to the watch value. Visual Basic can display the data in the expression as the value changes at runtime, break the execution when the value is reached, or break every time the watched value changes. During subsequent execution, Visual Basic updates the Watch window according to your watched values.

Tip

> Visual Basic includes the Quick Watch window, which lets you add watch values on the fly during any breakpoint. Highlight a variable, expression, or control property and then click the Quick Watch button on the Debug toolbar. You can add this expression to the regular Watch window by clicking Add.

Many programmers find that using Quick Watch during a program's debugging breakpoint is easier to do than trying to collect all the values to watch at design time through the Add Watch dialog box.

Distributing Your Application

You've created, tested, and debugged your application. The final step is packaging it for distribution to others. If you're creating the application for yourself, you'll probably just want to compile the application and then copy the compiled application and its support files to the folder from where you want to run the program. You can use the Start menu's Settings, Taskbar option to hook the application to your Start menu's structure.

If you want others to use your application, you need to automate the installation so that all the project's files get to their proper location and the Windows Start menu gets the program. This section explains how to distribute an application by using one of the sample applications that come with Visual Basic as a guide.

Compiling an Application

Visual Basic makes compiling your application simple. The compiled file is a final executable file with the .EXE filename extension. All the related modules and forms work together to form the executable file. Although auxiliary files might still be necessary—such as a Microsoft Access database file used for initial data—most of your project's files combine into the executable to make distribution easier.

The compiled application is more secure than a distributed source project. If you distribute the source code (the project and its related files), anyone with Visual Basic can modify your work. However, most users couldn't even run the source code for your program, because they don't have Visual Basic to load and run the program. Therefore, a compiled file is necessary so that all can use your application.

Your compiled application runs much faster than the application running within Visual Basic's development environment. You want your application to run as quickly and smoothly as possible without your users doing more than necessary. The compiled executable file makes the application's execution simple.

Before you compile your application, make sure you've debugged the application as much as feasibly possible. You can't debug compiled applications with the Visual Basic debugger, because you run compiled applications from outside the Visual Basic development environment.

When you're satisfied that you have your program running as accurately as possible, choose File, Make. Visual Basic displays the Make Project dialog box (see Figure 21.9). Select the folder where you want to store the compiled application. (Visual Basic uses the project name as the default executable name.)

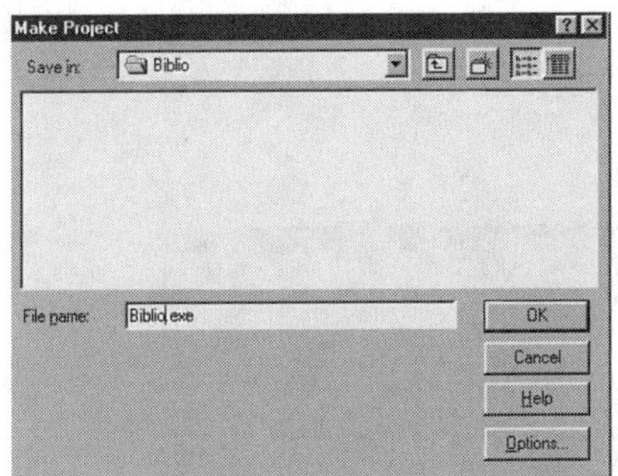

FIGURE 21.9.
Compiling the application from the Make Project dialog box.

Before clicking OK to start the compilation, click the Options button to display the Project Properties dialog box (see Figure 21.10). (You also can access this dialog box by choosing Properties from the Project menu.) The dialog box lets you specify version information for the compiled application. If you plan to release several versions of the software, the version numbers let you determine the order of versions. You can specify the version information from the development environment's Project Properties dialog box so that you don't have to specify versions just at compile time. The version numbers and description information stay with the project's source code.

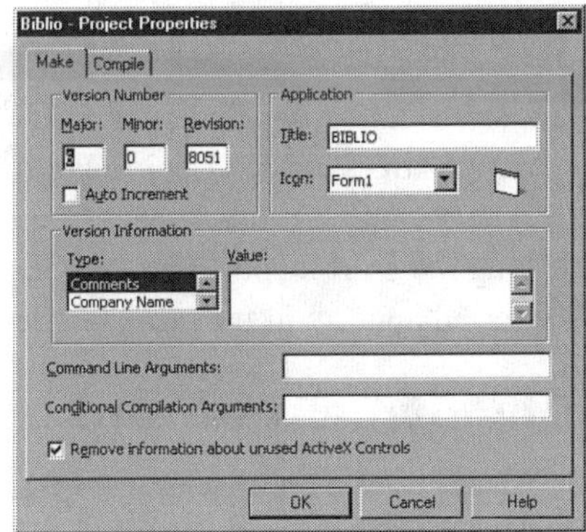

FIGURE 21.10.
Setting the compiled project's options in the Project Properties dialog box.

The Icon entry designates the application's icon that appears on the Windows Start menu and on a taskbar button. Generally, you'll leave the primary form name in the Icon field. The form's Properties window also contains an Icon entry from which you can select an icon for the form and, therefore, for the compiled application.

Click the Compile tab to display the Compile options page (see Figure 21.11). To optimize the compiled project to make it run as quickly as possible, select the Compile to Native Code option. (If you compile to *p-code*, or *pseudocode,* the application requires that your users keep a runtime Visual Basic–based DLL file in their Systems folder. Native code runs faster and requires fewer files, but does still require the services of a DLL file.)

FIGURE 21.11.

The Compile page holds the project's compilation options.

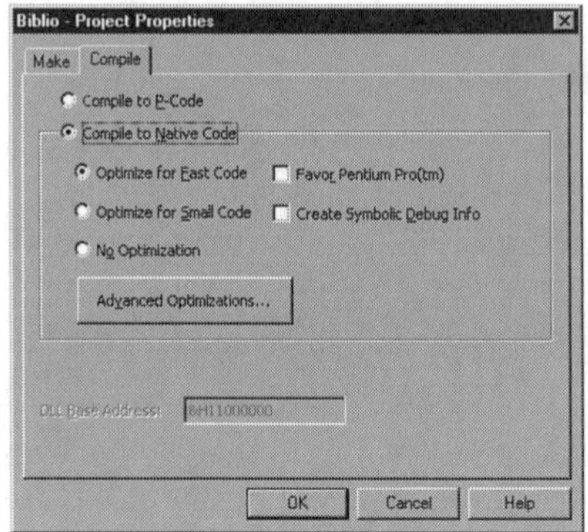

Note

If you select any of the options that appear when you click the Advanced Optimizations button, you forsake some of the runtime error checking but gain execution speed.

When you close the Project Properties dialog box and click OK, Visual Basic compiles your code. Assuming that no compile errors exist, Visual Basic creates the .EXE file (you'll see the compilation status in the upper-right corner). You can exit Visual Basic and run the application by selecting the Start menu's Run option after locating the .EXE file. The form's icon that you selected appears in the taskbar when you run the program.

The Package and Deployment Wizard

The Package and Deployment Wizard does a lot of work for you, including the following tasks:

- Compiles the application and compresses the files.
- Creates a setup program that can be used to install the application.
- Determines the best fit for installation floppy disks, creates the numerous setup disks, and splits extra-large files across multiple floppy disks. The Package and Deployment Wizard tells you in advance how many floppy disks the setup requires.
- Copies your compiled application to a hard disk so that you can install the application over a network or onto a CD-ROM creator.
- Sets up your application for distribution across the Internet for Internet Explorer users.

The Package and Deployment Wizard generates a list of several files needed for the setup. A single Setup.exe file is not the only thing to come out of the setup routine. Often, a Visual Basic application requires DLL and OCX files, and those files must reside in the targeted setup area (floppy disks or a hard disk) with the compiled program and the Setup.exe program.

Before you can run the Package and Deployment Wizard, you must load your application's project. After you've debugged and compiled your project, you're ready to create the installation module. The Package and Deployment Wizard will compile your code one final time just in case you've made an edit since your most recent compilation.

The Package and Deployment Wizard isn't part of Visual Basic's development environment. You need to select the Package and Deployment Wizard from the Add-Ins, Add-In Manager. This loads the Package and Deployment Wizard to the Add-Ins menu, where you can start the wizard. Figure 21.12 shows the opening window for the Package and Deployment Wizard.

The first Package and Deployment Wizard option (which is the option you'll probably

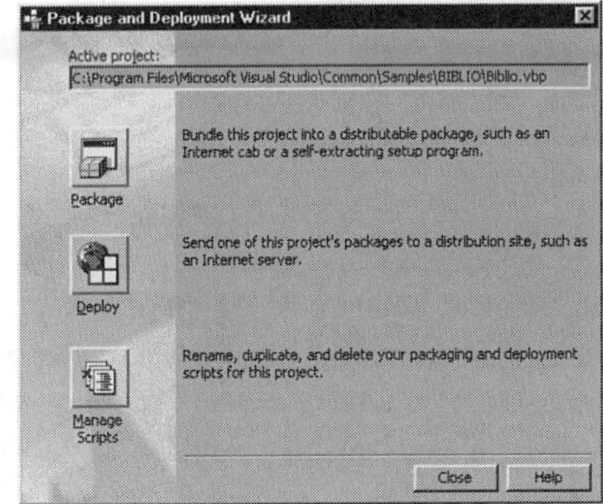

FIGURE 21.12.
The Package and Deployment Wizard prepares your application for distribution.

select most of the time) creates a standard Setup.exe routine that your users can install. The Package and Deployment Wizard can prepare this installation routine on a hard disk, floppy disks, CD-ROM writer, or in special CAB files that you can send out over the Internet for online distribution. The second option sends the installation routine to an Internet server that can install the application remotely. During the installation creation routine, the Package and Deployment Wizard creates a script file that describes the setup routine. In subsequent sessions, you can either modify a setup script that you've already created, or you can create the setup from the original project. The third option on the Package and Deployment Wizard's opening window lets you manage your installation scripts.

The first option generates the most common forms of an installation routine for most applications. After you click the first option, you'll see the window shown in Figure 21.13. Unless your application requires external ActiveX controls or database files, you can keep the first option selected.

If you want to set up an ActiveX control, be sure to select the Dependency

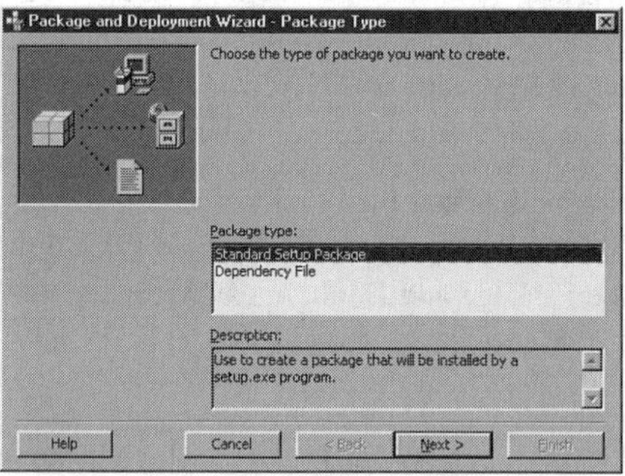

FIGURE 21.13.
Determining the kind of setup package to create.

File option so that the wizard can collect the proper files in the order the application needs them.

Click Next to show the Build Folder dialog box, which requests distribution information. The Package and Deployment Wizard needs to know where your final setup application should go. The directory you select should be empty. Therefore, when the wizard finishes, you'll know that all the files in that directory are there as the result of the wizard. When you click Next, the wizard scans your project file to determine which program files your application needs. The wizard can't determine which database drivers are needed if your application contains any data-related controls. You'll see the dialog box shown in Figure 21.14 if your application requires database access. Copy the application's required database driver to the right-hand window.

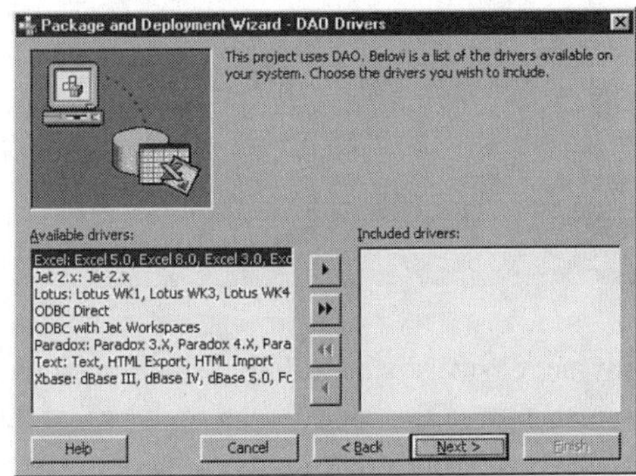

FIGURE 21.14.
You may have to select the data access files manually if your application requires data access.

> **Caution**
> Your dialog box may differ depending on the type of data access (ADO, DAO, and so on) your application uses.

After clicking Next, you might see the DAO ODBC Access dialog box if your application requires ODBC support. If so, you'll have to specify the kind of ODBC your application requires. If you didn't use a database with ODBC access, you won't need to worry with this dialog box.

When you click Next again, the wizard collects all the application's files you've specified and displays the dialog box shown in Figure 21.15. Make sure you look through the files to determine that every file is listed that your application requires. You might need to add (by clicking Add) more files, such as Readme.txt or a database file. Additional database support files might be needed. If so, you need to add those database files to the file list so that the installation routine stores these database files along with the installation files in the setup package.

> **Caution**
> Make sure you have proper access to any ActiveX control you distribute with your application. You might not always have the proper license authority to distribute ActiveX controls, unless you created those controls yourself. Therefore, consult your ActiveX control vendor to learn the rules under which you can distribute the controls.

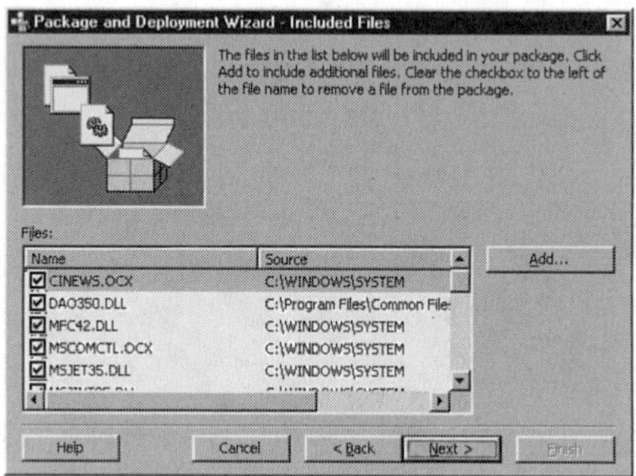

FIGURE 21.15.

Looking through the files to make sure the Package and Deployment Wizard collected all the files your project needs.

The Package and Deployment Wizard's next dialog box requests distribution information. You can create a single distribution file, or you can request that the setup routine be placed across multiple floppy disks or other kinds of media. After you determine how you want the Package and Deployment Wizard to divide your installation routine, click Next to display the Installation Title screen. Here, you'll type your installation project's title and then click Next to move to the Icons dialog box.

From the Icons dialog box, you create the submenu that will appear on the PC's Start menu. By clicking the New button and displaying the Start Menu Items dialog box shown in Figure 21.16, you can add submenu items to the Start menu's entry for this application. The submenu items might include a Readme file or an auxiliary program (such as a system utility).

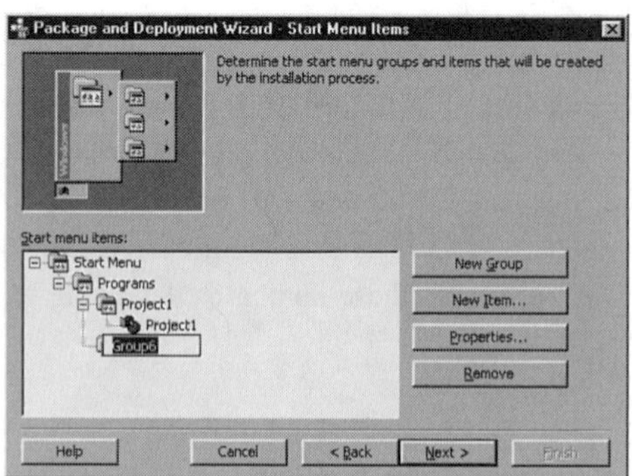

FIGURE 21.16.

You can determine the way the application will appear on the end-user's Start menu.

The next screen you see, called the Install Locations screen, determines the locations of each of the installed files. Although you'll want the majority of the files installed in the folder that the user selects during the installation procedure, as specified by the system variable `AppPath`, you can select individual files in the Package and Deployment Wizard's list and send those files to an alternate folder, such as the user's Program Files folder (specified by the system variable `ProgramFiles`).

Note

> As you can see, the Package and Deployment Wizard requires numerous decisions. With those decisions, however, comes complete control over how and where your application arrives on the user's system.

Click Next to select any files you want to designate as shared files. A file may be shared not only by other users (as would be the case for a database file the application might access) but also by other programs on the computer, as might be the case with ActiveX controls your project contains. Designate which files are shared by clicking next to each shared file (that is, by placing a check mark in the box next to that file).

After clicking Next, you'll see the final Package and Deployment Wizard screen, which asks what you want to call this installation's script file. By creating a script file, you won't have to answer the long list of wizard queries you've had to answer to this point the next time you create the installation routine. In addition, you can modify the script without having to redo the installation screens if something changes in the installation process, such as the removal of a shared file.

When you click Finish, the Package and Deployment Wizard will build the installation script, create the installation routine, and place that routine in one or several files, depending on the options you selected. When this is finished, a setup file (or files) will reside on your PC that you can distribute to install and re-create your application on other computers.

After Generating the Setup

After the wizard generates the setup routine, you should test it. To test the routine, run the generated setup program to make sure that no bugs appear and that the final application runs smoothly on the computer.

Tip

> If you really want to test the setup routine, run the setup program on a computer that has never contained your application. Even better, make sure that the computer doesn't even have a copy of Visual Basic installed. By testing your application on such a clean machine, you help ensure that your application installs properly on other computers.

The Package and Deployment Wizard creates the setup file (or files) in the location you specified during the setup process. If you generated the setup file in a single test directory, you'll find the Setup.exe file, the Setup.lst file (which contains a list of all the install-related files), and possibly several other files whose filename extensions end with an underscore (_). The files with the shortened extension are compressed; the Setup.exe routine expands those compressed files onto the target machine or location.

The simplest way to test the generated setup routine is to choose Run from the Start menu and then find the Setup.exe file. Click the Run button to start the application's setup. A typical setup installation will occur. The setup program will analyze the target computer to ensure that no programs are running that may conflict with a file that is about to be installed. Figure 21.17 shows a warning dialog box that greets your user if he or she runs the setup routine while running other programs that use any of the routine's shared files.

FIGURE 21.17.

Setup takes over and begins the installation process.

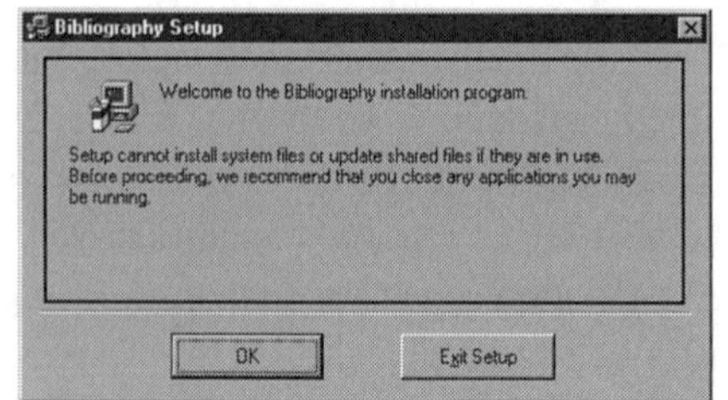

If you cancel the setup program at any time before it completes, it closes after removing any files copied to that point. Therefore, if you cancel the process at any time, setup removes all traces of the application's setup.

Uninstalling the Application

The Package and Deployment Wizard not only generates the installable setup routine, it also generates an application uninstaller. This enables users to uninstall all the application's files at any time. The Package and Deployment Wizard hooks to the system Control Panel's Add/Remove Programs icon. Therefore, if a user wants to remove the application from the system, he or she only has to follow these steps:

1. From the Start menu, choose Settings and then Control Panel.
2. Double-click the Add/Remove Programs icon.
3. Select the application from the list of installed applications. After getting verification that the user wants to remove the application, the uninstall routine takes over and removes the program and all its related files from the user's computer.

The Package and Deployment Wizard stores the uninstall information in the same directory as the application. The file that contains the removal instructions is named ST6UNST.LOG, and it holds the necessary details for the Add/Remove Programs system utility to do its job. Not all files should be removed, especially system files that might be shared by other programs. Before removing such potentially needed files (such as ActiveX controls), the removal utility displays a warning dialog box that lets the user decide how to remove such files.

Summary

Today's lesson explained how to use Visual Basic's powerful debugging tools. Learning how to debug an application pays dividends when you need to track bugs. Although Visual Basic's debugging tools can't locate logic errors, the debugger makes it easier for you to locate them. You can trace a program's execution, set breakpoints, and retrace a program's execution from where it came.

One of the most powerful aspects of the debugger is its interaction with the program during a breakpoint session. When your program reaches a breakpoint, all the values initialized and computed to that point are still live. Therefore, you can view variables to see whether their intermediate results contain the same values you expect. Also, you can change a variable's or control's value in the middle of the program's execution and watch how the rest of the execution reflects on that change.

After you debug your application, you're ready to distribute the application to your users. Application distribution is more involved than simply compiling your application. You must consider the installation routine and ensure that your users have all the necessary files related to the application.

Q&A

Q Can I catch all my application's errors as I write the code if the Auto Syntax check box is checked?

A As you type your program, this checked option will certainly catch many mistakes. The problem is that the option catches only syntax errors. You can still make runtime errors, such as dividing a value by zero. The code window cannot catch those kinds of errors.

Q Which errors are the easiest to locate?

A Sadly, syntax errors are the easiest to locate. (It's sad because not only are they easy to catch, but Visual Basic locates them for you.) If you've turned on the Auto Syntax Check box option (or even if you haven't), Visual Basic will locate all syntax errors either as you write your program or as soon as you attempt to run your program. The logic errors are the hard ones to locate because Visual Basic will have no idea that something is wrong. Even you won't always realize there's a problem at first. For example, suppose a general ledger total is off by a dollar or two each day. The user might not notice the error for a few days, and then other data will be affected by the problem. That's why you should test your applications extensively.

Q How long should I test my application before distributing it?

A The answer depends on the application's complexity. Certainly, if the application generates critical details used for decision making, such as payroll reporting and accounting systems, one of the best ways to test the application is to run a *parallel test*. That is, run your application along side the current system, whether that system is manual or an older computerized application you're replacing. Check the results against the current system and have your users do the same. Only after running the parallel test for a few cycles of the system (which may be a month or two if accounting cycles are involved), should you have the needed confidence to replace the original system with your application.

Workshop

The Workshop provides quiz questions to help you solidify your understanding of the material covered and exercises to provide you with experience in using what you've learned. Try to understand the quiz and exercise answers before continuing to the next bonus lesson. Answers are provided in Appendix A, "Answers to Exercises."

Quiz

1. What is a syntax error?
2. What's the difference between a syntax error and a logic error?
3. True/False. Some runtime errors can cause the running program to stop executing.
4. True/False. Some syntax errors can cause the running program to stop executing.
5. How can you analyze variables during a program's execution?
6. How can the single-step mode help you debug a program?
7. True/False. You can change the values of variables and controls *during* the execution of an application.
8. Which runs faster: a compiled program or a Visual Basic program that you run from inside the Visual Basic environment?

9. What tools does Visual Basic provide that let you create an installation routine for your application?
10. What happens if your installation routine is larger than a disk can hold, but you need to offer your application on disks?

Exercises

1. What kind of error does the following statement contain?

```
If (a < b) Therefore
   lblTitle.Caption = "Too small"
End If
```

2. True/False. The following sentence contains two kinds of errors (this one takes some thought):

```
This sentence has two mistaks.
```

WEEK 3

In Review

Congratulations, you have completed the most important 21 days of your Visual Basic programming career! You now understand virtually every area of the Visual Basic system. You have the ability to produce just about any Visual Basic program that you'll ever want to code.

All you need now is more practice.

Through this tutorial's daily lessons and Bonus Projects, you learned what the days of a Visual Basic programmer are like. Visual Basic programming is richly rewarding. Of course, programming jobs are in high demand in this high-tech world, but satisfaction from programming comes from more than just an income. When programming with Visual Basic, you not only have the power to create any Windows application needed, but you'll have fun doing so. Most importantly, Visual Basic never forgets its roots so Visual Basic will be there to help you debug your programs, add flair to the programs you've written, and create compiled executables that you can distribute so that others will benefit from the job you did.

Your Week's Worth

In this week, you have mastered the following:

- **Form templates**—Why reinvent the wheel? Use form templates to simply the adding of standard forms to your applications (Day 15).
- **Creating your own form templates**—Although Visual Basic supplies several form templates, you'll create your own as well and add these new form templates to the collection that Visual Basic supplies (Day 15).

- **Application Wizard form templates**—Although the Application Wizard can add form templates to your projects, you still have to modify the code and customize the form templates to conform to your application's requirements (Day 15).
- **OLE control**—Object linking and embedding is a concept that has been around almost as long as Windows has been in existence. Although other tools, such as ActiveX, have taken over the spotlight, many programmers still work with the OLE control to embed objects in their applications (Day 16).
- **Objects**—Although some programming purists would cringe upon hearing that Visual Basic is an object-oriented language, Visual Basic does support many object-like programming constructs (Day 16).
- **Pre-defined objects**—Visual Basic defines several objects for you, such as the `Screen`, `Printer`, and `App` objects. As your application runs, you can use these pre-defined objects to learn more about the application's environment (Day 16).
- **Outside objects**—You have insight into the requirements to access objects outside Visual Basic's scope, such as Excel worksheet values, from within your Visual Basic program.
- **Object collections**—Object collections let you work with several object items as a single group (Day 16).
- **ActiveX controls**—An ActiveX control can operate on many levels, from a new Visual Basic Toolbox window control to an Internet Web page program (Day 17).
- **Creating your own ActiveX controls**—You are not limited by the ActiveX controls that come with Visual Basic or those you get from others, because you can write your own ActiveX controls and use those controls in future projects that you build (Day 17).
- **Data control**—By adding the Data control to your application, you ensure that your user can not only access a database file but even navigate through the file and make changes along the way (Day 18).
- **Programming datasets**—After learning some simple concepts, you understand what it takes to manage complete database applications through a Visual Basic interface (Day 18).
- **Internet access**—Add a browser to your applications (Day 19).
- **Internet programming**—Control Internet processes through your Visual Basic application (Day 19).
- **Adding Help**—Give your users the access they need for help by installing a complete Help database inside your application (Day 20).

- **Help options**—Visual Basic offers the choice of several means for adding help to your applications (Day 20).
- **ToolTip help**—On a small scale, ToolTips can benefit a user who uses your application's toolbars and controls (Day 20).
- **Debugging code**—Visual Basic's interactive debugger makes testing for and eliminating program bugs painless (Day 21).
- **Application compiles**—Before you distribute your applications, you'll want to compile the code so that your code cannot be easily viewed or changed and so that your applications run faster (Day 21).
- **Code distribution**—You can make it easy or you can make it hard on your users. Use Visual Basic's tools for packaging your application into a distributable, installable, bulletproof application (Day 21).

Bonus Chapters

Day 22

Multidimensional Arrays

Day 10, "Adding Power with the Mouse and Controls," explained how to declare and use arrays. Arrays hold lists of data values. If you must keep track of and process several items, you have the choice of putting those items in separate variables with different names or storing those items in a single array with only one name. The advantage of an array is that you can step through all the variables with a loop statement, such as a `For` loop. The `For` loop's counter variable can increment through the array subscripts.

Visual Basic supports several different kinds of arrays. Although you can declare an array of any data type to hold a list of variables, you can also declare control arrays that work like variable arrays but offer the advantage of multiple form objects using one name and a similar set of property values. (Each control in the array does not have to have the same property values, however.) You can step through the control array as easily as a variable array when you want to work with the controls.

This bonus lesson takes the concept of variables one step further. The arrays you have learned about so far have been called *single-dimensional arrays*, because they have one subscript. In this lesson, you are going to learn how to expand on the array concept to produce arrays with more than one dimension, called *multidimensional arrays*. These multidimensional arrays are sometimes called *tables*. They let you store values in a row and column format. They can also expand the number of dimensions past two dimensions to create some useful data-storage areas.

Once you learn about multidimensional arrays in this bonus lesson, you'll learn about the grid control. The grid control contains the functionality to present two-dimensional data efficiently; the most common multidimensional table you create will contain two dimensions so the grid control will come in handy.

Today, you learn the following

- What multidimensional arrays are
- How to declare multidimensional arrays
- About the various ways to initialize multidimensional arrays
- How loops help you process multidimensional arrays
- About the limits that Visual Basic sets on multidimensional arrays
- About the grid control
- How the grid control's properties determine the number of rows and columns in the final grid
- About the methods used for assigning data to grids
- About the `FormstString` property
- How to display pictures in the grid's cells

Introduction to Multidimensional Arrays

Some data fits into single-dimensional arrays (the types of arrays you've seen so far throughout this 21-day tutorial). Other data is better suited for table format. The arrays you've seen so far, single-dimensional arrays, are arrays that have only one subscript. Single-dimensional arrays represent a list of values. Figure 22.1 shows that an array with a single dimension has a sense of length and direction, just as a line has.

> **Note**
>
> Keep in mind that arrays are stored inside your computer's memory without any sense of the direction that Figure 22.1 illustrates. The sense of a single direction, however, works well to demonstrate the linear nature of a group of array elements that go together as a single array. As you add a dimension, you also add an additional sense of direction, as you'll see in a moment when you learn about two-dimensional arrays.

FIGURE 22.1.

A one-dimensional array has length and direction.

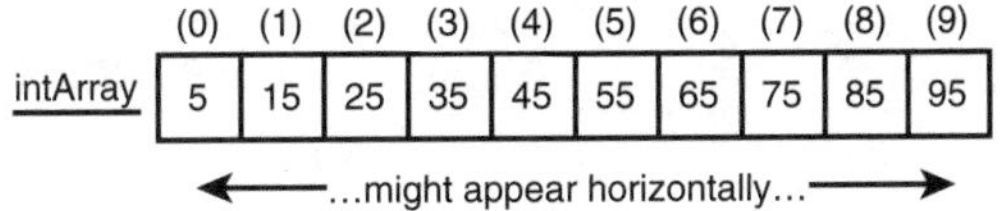

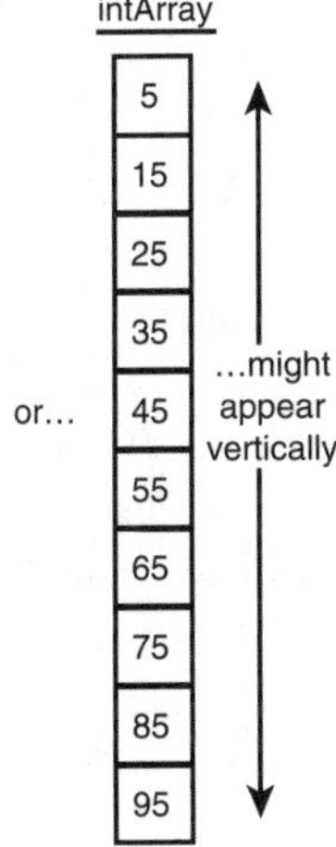

The rest of this bonus lesson explains how to use arrays of more than one dimension, called *multidimensional arrays*. Multidimensional arrays, sometimes called *tables* or *matrices*, have rows and columns.

NEW TERM A *multidimensional array* has more than one subscript and, therefore, more than one dimension. The number of dimensions relates to the number of directions the table has. Therefore, a single-dimensional array has a sense of one direction, but a three-dimensional array has three directions, just as an object in 3D space has width, length, and height.

Suppose that a softball team wants to keep track of its players' hits. The team played eight games, and 10 players are on the team. Table 22.1 shows the team's hit record.

TABLE 22.1. A SOFTBALL TEAM'S HIT RECORD WORKS WELL AS A TABLE.

Player	*Game1*	*Game2*	*Game3*	*Game4*	*Game5*	*Game6*	*Game7*	*Game8*
Adams	2	1	0	0	2	3	3	1
Berryhill	1	0	3	2	5	1	2	2
Edwards	0	3	6	4	6	4	5	3
Grady	1	3	2	0	1	5	2	1
Howard	3	1	1	1	2	0	1	0

continues

TABLE 22.1. CONTINUED

Player	*Game1*	*Game2*	*Game3*	*Game4*	*Game5*	*Game6*	*Game7*	*Game8*
Powers	2	2	3	1	0	2	1	3
Smith	1	1	2	1	3	4	1	0
Townsend	0	0	0	0	0	0	1	0
Ulmer	2	2	1	1	2	1	1	2
Williams	2	3	1	0	1	2	1	1

Do you see that the softball table is a two-dimensional table? It has rows (the first dimension) and columns (the second dimension). Therefore, you call it a two-dimensional table with 10 rows and eight columns. (Generally, the number of rows is specified first.) The table with two dimensions, therefore, it has two directions—a horizontal direction and a vertical direction. The single-dimensional array has only one sense of direction at any one time. As with single-dimensional arrays, multidimensional arrays are not literally stored in this table-like manner in memory, but the Visual Basic language lets you manipulate the data as if it were stored in rows and columns.

A matrix, just like a single-dimensional array, has only one name. In addition, a matrix can hold only one data type—the data type with which you declare the matrix. If you declare the matrix to hold the Variant data type, the cells can hold any kind of data that the Variant data type can represent.

NEW TERM A *cell* is one element from an array of any dimension. In a single-dimensional array, a cell is one element from the array list, but in a two-dimensional array (such as the softball team's hit record in Table 22.1), a cell is comprised of a row and column intersection.

In Table 22.1, each row has a player's name, and each column has a game number associated with it, but these headings aren't part of the data. The data consists of only 80 values (10 rows times eight columns). In this case, every value is an integer. If the table contains names, it's a string table, and so on.

The number of dimensions—in this case, two—corresponds to the dimensions in the physical world. The first dimension represents a line, and a single-dimensional array is a line, or list, of values. Two dimensions represent both length and width. You write on a piece of paper in two dimensions—two dimensions represent a flat surface. Three dimensions represent width, length, and depth. You may have seen three-dimensional movies; not only do the images have width and height, but they also (appear to) have depth.

Tip

> The reason so much emphasis is placed on the way people view dimensions is that your job as a programmer is made easier when you view, mentally, multidimensional data in space with its row and column (and possibly more) dimensions.

Although Visual Basic lets you work with up to 60 dimensions, it is difficult to visualize more than three dimensions. You can, however, think of each dimension after three as another occurrence. In other words, you can store a list of one player's hit record for the season in an array. The team's hit record (as shown in Table 22.1) is two dimensional. The league, made up of several teams' hit records, represents a three-dimensional table. Each team (the depth of the table) has rows and columns of hit data. If more than one league exists, you can consider multiple leagues another dimension.

Note

> Despite Visual Basic's generous allowance of up to 60 dimensions, you'll rarely write programs that require more than three or four dimensions at the maximum. Most of the time, you'll work with one- and two-dimensional arrays.

Declaring Multidimensional Arrays

As you do with single-dimensional arrays, you'll use the `Dim` or `Public` statement to reserve storage for multidimensional arrays. Rather than put one value in the parentheses, you put a value for each dimension in the table in the parentheses. The basic formats for reserving multidimensional arrays are as follows:

```
Public taName(intSub) [As dataType][, taName(intSub) [As dataType]]...
```

```
Dim taName (intSub) [As dataType][, taName (intSub) [As dataType]]...
```

The table's *`intSub`* values can take on this general format:

```
[intLow To] intHighRow[, [intLow To] intHighColumn][, [intLow To]
intHighDepth][,...]
```

As is the case with single dimensions, actually reserving storage for tables is easier than the formats lead you to believe. To declare the team data from Table 22.1, for example, you can use the following `Dim` statement:

```
Dim intTeams(1 To 10, 1 To 8) As Integer
```

This statement reserves a two-dimensional table in memory with 80 elements. The elements' subscripts are shown in Figure 22.2.

FIGURE 22.2.
The softball team table requires two sets of subscripts.

intTeams(1, 1)	intTeams(1, 2)	intTeams(1, 3)	•••	intTeams(1, 7)	intTeams(1, 8)
intTeams(2, 1)	intTeams(2, 2)	intTeams(2, 3)	•••	intTeams(2, 7)	intTeams(2, 8)
intTeams(3, 1)	intTeams(3, 2)	intTeams(3, 3)	•••	intTeams(3, 7)	intTeams(3, 8)
•	•	•		•	•
intTeams(9, 1)	intTeams(9, 2)	intTeams(9, 3)	•••	intTeams(9, 7)	intTeams(9, 8)
intTeams(10, 1)	intTeams(10, 2)	intTeams(10, 3)	•••	intTeams(10, 7)	intTeams(10, 8)

If you have an entire league of 15 teams to track, you add yet another subscript:

```
Dim intTeams(1 To 15, 1 To 10, 1 To 8) As Integer
```

The first subscript indicates each team in the league, the second subscript indicates the number of players in each team, and the third subscript indicates the number of games each player played.

Think of a three-dimensional table as you would a three-dimensional chessboard, with layer upon layer of boards. A four-dimensional representation would then be several three-dimensional chess sets. The fourth dimension would be the number that corresponds to each of the 3D chess sets.

How do you know the order of subscripts, such as the subscripts in a three-dimensional table? How do you know that the far-right subscript represents columns? You do not know that the far-right subscript represents columns. You can make the subscripts represent anything you want. However, the standard for a two-dimensional table is to consider the left subscript the row and the right subscript the column. By taking a two-dimensional table to a three-dimensional table, the added subscript is almost always the first subscript to ensure that the last two represent rows and columns in a table. By keeping the table-level subscripts as the final two subscripts, you help keep the subscripts straight.

The following statement reserves enough memory elements for a television station's shows for one week:

```
Dim strShows(1 To 7, 1 To 48) As String
```

This statement reserves seven days (the rows) of 30-minute shows (because there are 24 hours in a day, and this table holds up to 48 30-minute shows).

As you know, every element in a table must always be the same data type. In this case, each element is a string variable. You can initialize some of the elements with the following assignment statements:

```
strShows(3, 12) = "As the Hospital Turns"
strShows(1, 5) = "Guessing-Game Show"
strShows(7, 20) = "Raspberry Iced Tea Infomercial"
```

Reserving space for several multidimensional arrays quickly consumes memory space. The following statements reserve a lot of space:

```
Public ara1(10, 20) As Single
Dim ara2(4, 5, 5) As Double
Public ara3(6, 10, 20, 30) As Integer
```

`ara1` consumes 200 single-precision memory locations, `ara2` consumes 100 double-precision memory locations, and `ara3` consumes 36,000 memory locations. As you can see, the number of elements adds up quickly. Be careful that you don't reserve so many array elements that you run out of memory in which to store them.

By reading table data into multidimensional arrays and working with the data in the arrays instead of in database tables, you can speed your program's running times. Anything you can do in memory is faster than reading and writing to disk every time you access values. However, you have much more disk space than memory space. When you're working with large files, you have to forsake the efficiency of memory for the disk capacity.

Using Tables and `For` Loops

As you'll see in some of the next few program examples, nested `For` loops are good candidates for looping through every element of a multidimensional table. For instance, Listing 22.1 prints all six possible subscript values from a multidimensional array in successive message boxes.

LISTING 22.1. NESTED LOOPS ENABLE YOU TO STEP THROUGH TABLES QUICKLY.

```
For intRow = 1 To 2
  For intCol = 1 To 3
    MsgBox("Row: " & intRow & ", Col: " & intCol)
  Next intCol
Next intRow
```

If you run the code in Listing 22.1, you would see the following output in the message boxes:

```
Row: 1, Col: 1
Row: 1, Col: 2
Row: 1, Col: 3
Row: 2, Col: 1
Row: 2, Col: 2
Row: 2, Col: 3
```

Instead of message boxes, you could change the code to use `Print` methods to print directly on the form. `Print` is probably a good method to use when practicing using multidimensional array subscripts because you can place a lot of output on a single form easily. For example, Listing 22.2 uses the `Print` method to print directly to a form. Figure 22.3 shows what the form would look like.

LISTING 22.2. NESTED LOOPS PROVIDE SUBSCRIPTS THAT STEP THROUGH YOUR ENTIRE TABLE.

```
For intRow = 1 To 2
  For intCol = 1 To 3
    Form1.Print "Row: " & intRow & ", Col: " & intCol
  Next intCol
  Form1.Print
Next intRow
```

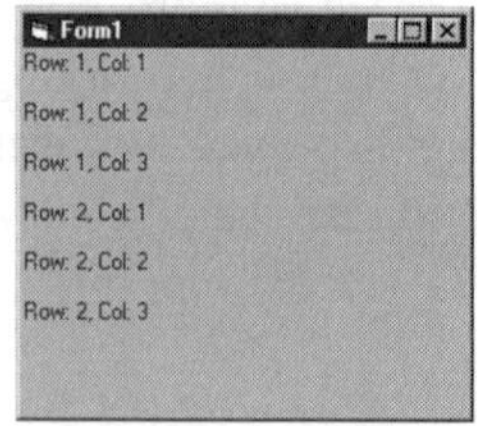

FIGURE 22.3.
You can practice printing table values with `Print` so that you can see all your output on a single form.

> Be careful when studying Figure 22.3. Remember that the goal of Listing 22.2 is to show you how a nested `For` loop provides values that can step through a table a row and column at a time. The printed values in Figure 22.3 are *not* array values but rather subscripts for an array that you declare with two rows and three columns.

If you were to print the subscripts, in row order, for a two-row-by-three-column table dimensioned with the following `Dim` statement, you'd see the subscript numbers shown by the nested loops in Listing 22.2.

```
Dim intTable(1 To 2, 1 To 3)
```

Notice that there are as many `For...Next` statements as there are subscripts in the `Dim` statement (two). The outside loop represents the first subscript (the rows), and the inside loop represents the second subscript (the columns). The nested loop is perhaps the most common way to step through a table; therefore, mastering nested loops is critical to programming with multidimensional arrays efficiently.

Initializing Arrays

You can initialize the elements of a multidimensional array in several ways. Here are just a few:

- Assign values to the table elements
- Use `InputBox` to fill the elements, one at a time, from a message box
- Read the values, one at a time, from a disk or database file
- Calculate the values from other values

If you think about this list of ways to initialize tables, you'll realize that you initialize tables and all other multidimensional arrays just as you do any other variable. This method, however, allows you to think about your data in tabular form, which helps speed your programming and maintenance.

Most multidimensional array data comes from forms or—more often—from disk file data. Regardless of what you actually use to store values in multidimensional arrays, nested `For` loops are excellent control statements for stepping through subscripts. The following example further illustrates how nested `For` loops can work with multidimensional arrays.

Suppose that a computer company sells two disk sizes: 3 1/2 inch and 5 1/4 inch. Each disk comes in one of four capacities: single-sided, low-density; double-sided, low-density; single-sided, high-density; and double-sided, high-density. The disk inventory is well suited for a two-dimensional table. The disks have the following retail prices:

	Single-Sided Low-Density	*Double-Sided Low-Density*	*Single-Sided High-Density*	*Double-Sided High-Density*
3 1/2″	$2.30	2.75	3.20	3.50
5 1/4″	$1.75	2.10	2.60	2.95

The procedure in Listing 22.3 stores the price of each disk in a table and prints the values to the form by using a nested `For` loop. You can put this procedure in a standard module or event procedure to trigger its execution.

LISTING 22.3. INVENTORY ITEMS OFTEN APPEAR IN A TABLE.

```
Private Sub disks ()
' Assigns and prints diskette prices
  Dim curDisks(1 To 2, 1 To 4) As Currency
  Dim intRow As Integer, intCol As Integer
  ' Assign each element the price
```

continues

LISTING 22.3. CONTINUED

```
6:     curDisks(1, 1) = 2.30     ' Row 1, Column 1
7:     curDisks(1, 2) = 2.75     ' Row 1, Column 2
8:     curDisks(1, 3) = 3.20     ' Row 1, Column 3
9:     curDisks(1, 4) = 3.50     ' Row 1, Column 4
10:    curDisks(2, 1) = 1.75     ' Row 2, Column 1
11:    curDisks(2, 2) = 2.10     ' Row 2, Column 2
12:    curDisks(2, 3) = 2.60     ' Row 2, Column 3
13:    curDisks(2, 4) = 2.95     ' Row 2, Column 4
14:    ' Print the prices in table format
15:    Form1.Print
16:    Form1.Print Tab(12); "Single-sided,  Double-sided,   ";
17:    Form1.Print "Single-sided,  Double-sided"
18:    Form1.Print Tab(12); "Low-density    Low-density    ";
19:    Form1.Print "High-density   High-density"
20:    For intRow = 1 To 2
21:      If (intRow = 1) Then
22:         Form1.Print "3-1/2 inch"; Tab(15);
23:      Else
24:         Form1.Print "5-1/4 inch"; Tab(15);
25:      End If
26:      For intCol = 1 To 4
27:        Form1.Print curDisks(intRow, intCol); Spc(8);
28:
29:      Next intCol
30:      Form1.Print   ' Moves the cursor to the next line
31:    Next intRow
32: End Sub
```

This procedure produces the output shown in Figure 22.4 after you resize the window to show the entire table. Although the table is small, the 2-by-4 multidimensional array demonstrates how your data sometimes makes a good match for table storage. The two rows and four columns of the disk pricing data works well as a multidimensional array. The code does seem rather long for a table that has only 8 values. Keep in mind, however, that you rarely initialize tables as done here in lines 6 through 13. For this small example, and as an early exposure to tables, the assignments are probably the best way to begin.

In Day 10's lesson, you learned about the `Array()` function, which assigns a complete array a set of values in one statement. Don't use `Array()` for multidimensional arrays. `Array()` only works for single-dimensional arrays. You cannot initialize multidimensional arrays with the `Array()` function.

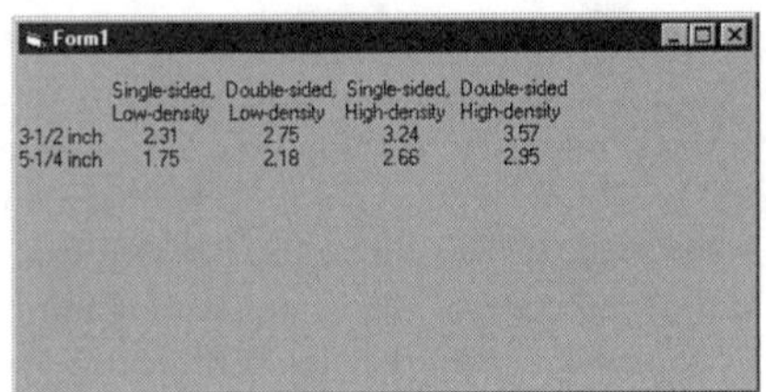

FIGURE 22.4.

The table of disk prices appears in a table form.

Using the Grid Control

The most common two-dimensional array, a table, is best presented to your users in row and column format. The grid control offers a convenient way for you to display table data to your users. The users can navigate the table's values using scrollbars. Therefore, the grid control does not have to be as large as the table, because the grid control automatically displays scrollbars.

Preparing for the Grid Control

The grid control is not part of the standard toolbox window. Therefore, follow these steps to add the grid control:

1. Press Ctrl+T to open the Components dialog box.
2. Select Microsoft FlexGrid Control 6.0.
3. Click OK. The FlexGrid control (usually just called the *grid control*) appears in your toolbox window, as shown in Figure 22.5.

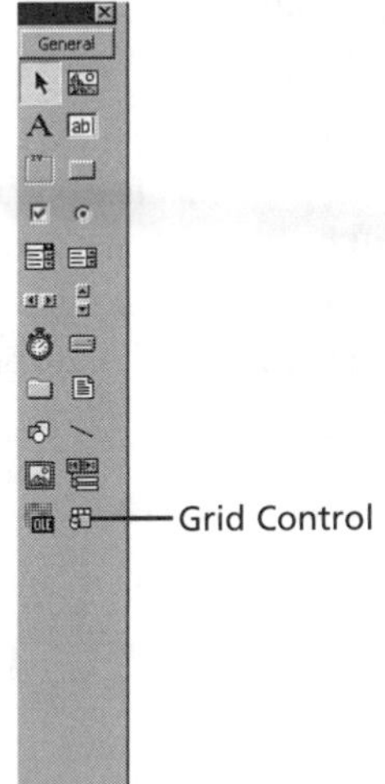

FIGURE 22.5.

The grid control enables you to display tabular data.

Visual Basic includes several kinds of grid controls. You will see them if you scroll through the Components dialog box. Some are bound controls that, as you learned in Day 18, "Interacting with Data," are linked to database data so that a user can look at the underlying database values that the table displays. (The bound grid control allows only the reading of database data.) Depending on your Visual Basic edition (Enterprise, Professional, or Learning), you'll have a different set of available grids to choose from when you display the Components dialog box.

Understanding the Grid Control's Use

When you place the grid control on a form, you'll have to resize it before the control takes on a tabular appearance. As you expand the size of the control, it doesn't look too much more like a table (as you can see in Figure 22.6). The problem is that the table's default number of rows and columns are both two. As you add to the table's row and columns, the grid control looks more like a table.

FIGURE 22.6.

The grid control doesn't look too much more like a table when you first place it on a form.

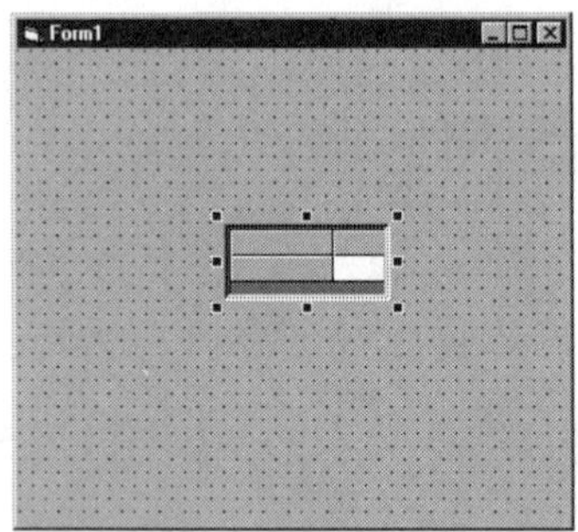

As you can see, one of the first tasks you must perform after adding the grid control is to expand its number of rows and columns until the grid contains a reasonable number. Keep in mind that the grid control doesn't need to show the same number of rows and columns as your multidimensional array, because the control displays scrollbars with which the user can navigate through the grid's data.

The grid control supports fixed rows and columns, as Figure 22.7 illustrates. You can control the number of fixed rows and columns that appear. If you increase the number of fixed rows and columns, the shaded area increases as well.

NEW TERM *Fixed rows* and *columns* refer to the rows and columns in a grid control that do not scroll when the user clicks the scrollbars. The fixed rows and columns provide labels that describe the data in the grid, not unlike worksheet cell row and column numbers and names.

The fixed rows and columns are often called *row* and *column headers*.

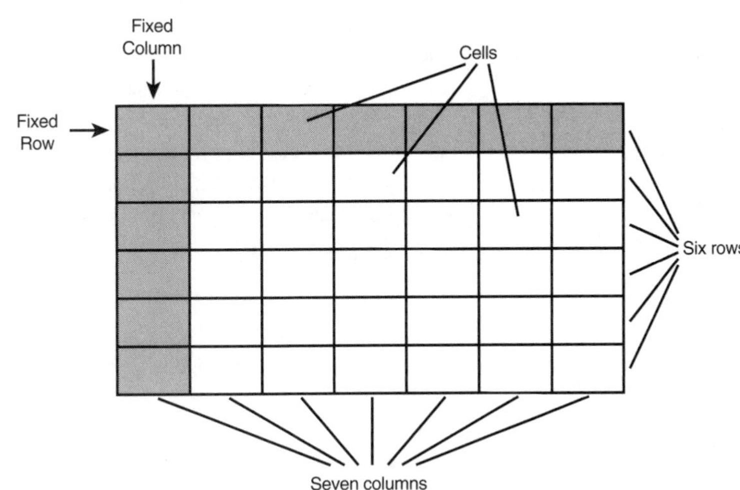

FIGURE 22.7. *The fixed rows and columns provide a place for labels.*

Once you fill the grid control with data, your users can scroll through the data and select one or more cells in the grid. Through programming, you can update or copy selected cell values to or from other cells, variables, or controls.

The grid control holds all kinds of information, including text, numbers, and even pictures.

Table 22.2 contains several properties unique or important to the grid control. (The table does not describe several properties that you already know, such as `Height` and `Width`, as well as more obscure properties.) By studying these properties, you can learn much about how to use this control. Many of the properties relate to cell selections within the grid control's tabular data.

TABLE 22.2. THE GRID CONTROL SUPPORTS SEVERAL IMPORTANT DESIGN-TIME PROPERTIES.

Property	*Description*
`AllowBigSelection`	Enables users to select an entire row or column with a single mouse click. If set to `True`, this property allows the user to click a fixed row or column header to select the entire row or column.
`AllowUserResizing`	Determines how much control you give users to change the width and height of columns and rows. If this property is set to `flexResizeNone`, the user cannot change the width or height of the columns or rows. If it's set to `flexResizeColumns`, the user can change the width of columns. If it's set to `flexResizeRows`, the user can change the height of the rows. If it's set to `flexResizeBoth`, the user can change the width and height of the columns and rows. Depending on the data, your user may need the ability to resize the rows and columns to read the data in the grid control.
`Cols`	Determines the number of columns in the grid control.
`Custom`	Opens the grid control's Property Pages dialog box (see Figure 22.8). The dialog box enables you to set various properties easily.
`FillStyle`	Specifies how a cell or range of cells receives formatting. If this property is set to `flexFillSingle`, the current cell is formatted. If this property is set to `flexFillRepeat`, all selected cells (if any are selected) will be formatted.
`FixedCols`	Specifies the number of fixed (nonscrolling) columns used for headers.
`FixedRows`	Specifies the number of fixed (nonscrolling) rows used for headers.
`FocusRect`	Determines how the user's selection of the current cell appears on the screen. If this property is set to `flexFocusNone`, the current cell does not appear with special highlighting. If it's set to `flexFocusLight`, a light outline appears around the current cell. If it's set to `flexFocusHeavy`, the current cell appears with blue highlighting.

Note

If you set the `FocusRect` property to `flexFocusHeavy`, the cell will not stand out in a group of selected cells.

`FormatString`	Contains a string that determines how a cell or selected cells are to be formatted. See the section "Using the `FormatString` Property."
`GridLines`	Specifies how the grid's nonfixed lines are to look. If this property is set to `flexGridNone`, no lines separate the cells. If it's set to `flexGridFlat`, gray lines separate the cells from one another. If it's set to `flexGridInset`, dark lines separate the cells. If it's set to `flexGridRaised`, the cells appear raised in a 3D style.

`GridLinesFixed`	Specifies how the grid's fixed lines are to look. If this property is set to `flexGridNone`, no lines separate the cells. If it's set to `flexGridFlat`, gray lines separate the cells from one another. If it's set to `flexGridInset`, dark lines separate the cells. If it's set to `flexGridRaised`, the cells appear raised in a 3D style.
`HighLight`	Determines how selected cells appear. If this property is set to `flexHighlightNever`, the selection of cells never appears on the screen. If it's set to `flexHighlightAlways`, selected cells appear highlighted (with the background darkened). If it's set to `flexHighlightWithFocus`, the highlighted cells appear only when the grid control has the focus.
`RowHeightMin`	Specifies the minimum number of twips a row can be so that the user cannot shrink a row to smaller than the set value.
`Rows`	Specifies the number of rows that appear in the grid control.
`SelectionMode`	Determines how cell selection occurs. If this property is set to `flexSelectionFree`, the user can select any rectangular section of cells. If it's set to `flexSelectionByRow`, the selected cells always span the entire row. If it's set to `flexSelectionByColumn`, the selected cells always span the entire column.
`WordWrap`	Determines whether or not the cell contents wrap within a cell when the user increases the width or height of a column or row.

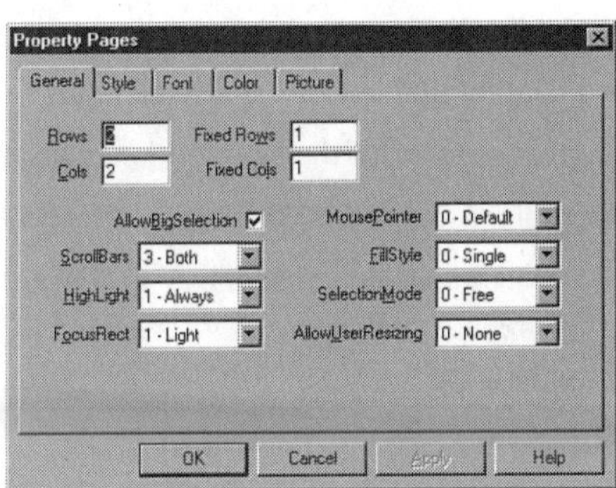

FIGURE 22.8.

The Property Pages dialog box enables you to set common grid control properties easily.

The grid control is unusual in that it supports several runtime properties that *must* be set; otherwise, the control will not be functional. Table 22.3 contains many runtime properties, some of which your code will have to set to use the grid control properly.

Note

> Some of the formatting properties, such as `CelAlignment`, exist to let you control formatting at runtime. To format a cell at designtime, use the `FormatString` property in Table 22.2.

TABLE 22.3. YOUR VISUAL BASIC CODE MUST SET SEVERAL RUNTIME PROPERTIES.

Property	*Description*
`CellAlignment`	Determines the alignment of values within cells. If this property is set to `flexAlignLeftTop` (`0`), the cell contents align in the upper-left corner. If it's set to `flexAlignLeftCenter` (`1`), the cell contents align left and centered. In a similar manner, the other named constant values that align the cell in other ways are `flexAlignLeftBottom` (`2`), `flexAlignCenterTop` (`3`), `flexAlignCenterCenter` (`4`), `flexAlignCenterBottom` (`5`), `flexAlignRightTop` (`6`), `flexAlignRightCenter` (`7`), `flexAlignRightBottom` (`8`), and `flexAlignGeneral` (`9`) to default to normal behavior of left-centered strings and right-centered numbers.
`Col`	Sets the column number of the cell whose value you want to change. A current cell is tracked, starting at the cell at row and column intersection 0,0. The value that you assign to the grid control's `Text` property goes into the cell in the column defined by the `Col` value.
`ColAlignment`	Determines the alignment of values within a specific column using the same named constants as `CelAlignment`.
`ColWidth`	Determines the width, in twips, of a column.
`Row`	Sets the row number of the cell whose value you want to change. A current cell is tracked, starting at the cell at row and column intersection 0,0. The value that you assign to the grid control's `Text` property goes into the cell in the row defined by the `Row` value.
`SelEndCol`	Specifies the column number of the selected range's far-right column.
`SelEndRow`	Specifies the row number of the selected range's lowest row.
`SelStartCol`	Specifies the column number of the selected range's far-left column.
`Text`	Specifies the contents of the given cell. You can assign the current cell (made current by the `Row` and `Col` intersection) a new value by assigning that value to the `Text` property.

Many other designtime and runtime properties exist, but Tables 22.2 and 22.3 list the most important ones for new users of the grid control.

Although the cell's content is set or read by the `Text` property, the data itself does not have to be string data. You can assign numeric values to the `Text` property, and Visual Basic converts the numbers to a string before making the assignment. In a similar manner, you can assign a cell to a numeric variable, and Visual Basic converts the number within the text cell to a number before making the assignment. If, however, Visual Basic cannot convert the value to a number, a runtime error will occur if you assign the value to a numeric variable.

Using the Grid Control in an Application

One of the best ways to understand the grid control is to create an application that utilizes it. Therefore, you might want to follow along with the next several sections, which create an application that includes both multidimensional arrays and a grid control. The application requires the grid control to manage selected cells within the control so that you can see how to work with ranges of cells.

Setting Up the Project

Figure 22.9 shows the screen from the application that you will now create. The grid control displays sales commissions for particular products and sales staff. The salespeople's names will appear across the row headers, and the product names will appear down the left side of the grid.

All the data is stored in a two-dimensional table and transferred to the grid control. This application does not load the initial table from the disk or store the table to disk upon exiting. Therefore, the source of the table's values is a series of assignment statements. In a real application, you would want to load and store the table to disk or, more likely, to a database table somewhere. If this application included disk I/O, the project's scope would be expanded too much to focus just on tables and the grid control. Therefore, this application keeps things simple by staying away from disk files.

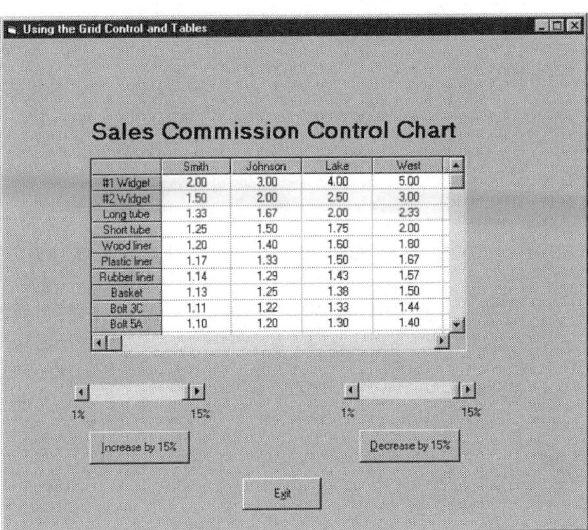

FIGURE 22.9.

The grid control easily enables you to manage sales commissions.

The following points highlight the use of this application:

- The scrollbars can be used to increase or decrease the sales revenue for any salesperson's commission on any product.
- The increment or decrement amount can change via the use of the scrollbars, thus dynamically changing the command button's caption.
- The current cell is the only cell that changes when the user increases or decreases the commission percentage, unless the user first selects a range of cells, in which case the entire range of commissions will increase or decrease by the given percentage.
- Most of the grid control's default property values will work for this project. As usual, Microsoft selected the most common property values for the control's default values. You'll certainly have to set property values at runtime (as described in the previous section), but at design time you only need to modify the name, number of columns, and number of rows in the control.
- The number of sales people or products tracked can easily be expanded by changing the number of rows and columns of both the table and the grid control. No visual change is necessary because of the grid control's scrolling capabilities.

Once you create and run this application, you'll have a better feel for the grid control's use. Also, you'll be able to see how you might adapt this simple example to use in other applications.

Create a new project and add the controls and property values listed in Table 22.4.

Remember to add the grid control to your toolbox before you start working with the form. Add the control Microsoft FlexGrid Control 6.0, as described earlier in the section "Preparing for the Grid Control."

TABLE 22.4. PLACE THESE CONTROLS AND PROPERTY VALUES TO CREATE THE SALES COMMISSION FORM.

Property	*Value*
Form `Name`	`frmSales`
Form `Caption`	`Using the Grid Control and Tables`
Form `Height`	`7920`
Form `Width`	`9180`
Label #1 `Name`	`lblSales`
Label #1 `Alignment`	`Center`

Property	*Value*
Label #1 Caption	Sales Commission Control Chart
Label #1 Font size	18
Label #1 Font style	Bold
Label #1 Height	495
Label #1 Left	1200
Label #1 Top	1200
Label #1 Width	6015
Label #2 Name	lblInMin
Label #2 Alignment	Center
Label #2 Caption	1%
Label #2 Font Size	8
Label #2 Height	255
Label #2 Left	960
Label #2 Top	5640
Label #2 Width	375
Label #3 Name	lblInMax
Label #3 Alignment	Center
Label #3 Caption	15%
Label #3 Font Size	8
Label #3 Height	255
Label #3 Left	2880
Label #3 Top	5640
Label #3 Width	375
Label #4 Name	lblDeMin
Label #4 Alignment	Center
Label #4 Caption	1%
Label #4 Font Size	8
Label #4 Height	255
Label #4 Left	5160
Label #4 Top	5640
Label #4 Width	375
Label #5 Name	lblDeMax
Label #5 Alignment	Center

continues

TABLE 22.4. CONTINUED

Property	*Value*
Label #5 `Caption`	`15%`
Label #5 `Font Size`	`8`
Label #5 `Height`	`255`
Label #5 `Left`	`7080`
Label #5 `Top`	`5640`
Label #5 `Width`	`375`
Grid control `Name`	`grdSales`
Grid control `Cols`	`8`
Grid control `FocusRect`	`flexFocusNone`
Grid control `Height`	`3015`
Grid control `Left`	`1320`
Grid control `Rows`	`20`
Grid control `Top`	`1800`
Grid control `Width`	`5895`
Horizontal scrollbar #1 `Name`	`hscIncrease`
Horizontal scrollbar #1 `Left`	`1080`
Horizontal scrollbar #1 `Max`	`15`
Horizontal scrollbar #1 `Min`	`1`
Horizontal scrollbar #1 `Top`	`5280`
Horizontal scrollbar #1 `Width`	2055
Horizontal scrollbar #2 `Name`	`hscDecrease`
Horizontal scrollbar #2 `Left`	`5280`
Horizontal scrollbar #2 `Max`	`15`
Horizontal scrollbar #2 `Min`	`1`
Horizontal scrollbar #2 `Top`	`5280`
Horizontal scrollbar #2 `Width`	`2055`
Command button #1 `Name`	`cmdIncrease`
Command button #1 `Caption`	`&Increase by 15%`
Command button #1 `Height`	`495`
Command button #1 `Left`	`1320`
Command button #1 `Top`	`6000`

Property	*Value*
Command button #1 `Width`	`1575`
Command button #2 `Name`	`cmdDecrease`
Command button #2 `Caption`	`&Decrease by 15%`
Command button #2 `Height`	`495`
Command button #2 `Left`	`5520`
Command button #2 `Top`	`6000`
Command button #2 `Width`	`1575`
Command button #3 `Name`	`cmdExit`
Command button #3 `Caption`	`E&xit`
Command button #3 `Height`	`495`
Command button #3 `Left`	`3720`
Command button #3 `Top`	`6720`
Command button #3 `Width`	`1215`

Once you place these controls and set their values, you're ready to enter the code. Remember that the original data will reside in an array whose rows and column numbers match, by design, the number of rows and columns in the grid control. From Table 22.4, therefore, you already know that the grid control receives its data from a two-dimensional table with eight columns and 20 rows.

Understanding the Code

Listing 22.4 contains code that initializes the overall program values. The code is a controlling procedure because, when the form loads, several `Call` statements execute other subroutine procedures. Keep in mind that much of this procedure performs the initializing of the grid's headers with salespeople's last names across the top of the grid and products listed down the side.

Listing 22.4 shows a good example of *modular programming*. When you must make a change to the program later, you won't have to wade through several pages of code within a single procedure. Instead, the called procedures each have one purpose. You can more easily modify a procedure's action without interfering with unrelated code.

NEW TERM *Modular programming* refers to the practice of placing code with a single purpose in a general subroutine procedure and then calling that code from a controlling procedure.

LISTING 22.4. THE `Form_Load()` PROCEDURE INITIALIZES SEVERAL VALUES THROUGH SUBROUTINES.

```
1:  Private Sub Form_Load()
2:     ' Define the justification of the grid cells and
3:     ' assign cell titles to the fixed row and column
4:     ' headers. Additionally, initialize the table of
5:     ' values and send that table to the grid control.
6:     '
7:     Call InitScrolls       ' Initialize scrollbars
8:     Call CenterCells       ' Center cell alignments
9:     Call SizeCells         ' Specify cell widths
10:    Call Titles            ' Place column and row titles
11:    Call FillCells         ' Fill cells with values
12: End Sub
```

At a glance, you can determine what `Form_Load()` does by looking through the called routines in lines 7 through 11. If the called code were not in separate procedures but were embedded within `Form_Load()`, you would have a more difficult time finding the code you want to study or change later.

Listing 22.5 contains the code for the first three called procedures: `InitScrolls()`, `CenterCells()`, and `SizeCells()`. These, as well as all the general subroutine procedures, must appear before `Form_Load()`, so they reside in the module's General section of the code window.

LISTING 22.5. THE FIRST THREE PROCEDURES THAT `Form_Load()` CALLS ARE USED TO SET UP THE GRID.

```
Private Sub InitScrolls()
   ' Set both scrollbars to their maximum values
   ' Although you set these values in the Properties
   ' window, this proc enables you to more easily change
   ' the scrollbar maximum values if the program's
   ' requirements change.
   '
   hscIncrease.Value = 15
   hscDecrease.Value = 15
End Sub

Private Sub CenterCells()
   ' Sets the justification of the grid's cells
   ' to a centered alignment. Be sure to center
   ' the header rows and columns.
   '
   Dim Column As Integer
   '
```

```
19: ' First center the header cells
20: For Column = 0 To 7
21:     grdSales.Col = Column    ' Sets current column
22:     ' Center the fixed cells in this column
23:     grdSales.ColAlignment(Column) = flexAlignCenterCenter
24:   Next Column
25: End Sub
26:
27: Private Sub SizeCells()
28:   ' Specify the width of each cell
29:   Dim Column As Integer
30:   For Column = 0 To 7
31:     grdSales.ColWidth(Column) = 1100   ' In twips
32:   Next Column
33: End Sub
```

The `InitScrolls()` procedure is not actually necessary, because you set the scrollbar maximum positions in the Properties window when you placed the scrollbars on the form. Nevertheless, this application changes the maximum scrollbar value at the user's request, so you can easily change the initial position of the scrollbar from code without bothering to locate the `Max` property of the scrollbar if your application's initial scrollbar values are to change.

The `CenterCells()` procedure centers all cell values in the grid. The `ColAlignment` property requires a column number to center as its index. Line 23 provides this index. Finally, the `SizeCells()` procedure in line 27 sets all cell widths at 1,100 twips by stepping through the grid and applying the `ColWidth` property to each column (line 31).

Listing 22.6 shows the tedious code that initializes the grid. Actually, the majority of the code initializes the titles in the grid and then fills a table with values and copies those values to the grid itself. The two-dimensional table is a go-between storage area that's not actually required in this particular application. Nevertheless, by studying the code, you'll see how easy it is to display table information stored in a multidimensional array with a grid.

LISTING 22.6. YOU SHOULD INITIALIZE THE GRID HEADINGS AND DATA CELLS.

```
Private Sub Titles()
  ' Fill in the column titles
  ' Typically, this data would come from a database table
  grdSales.Row = 0  ' All sales people's names are in row 0
  grdSales.Col = 1
  grdSales.Text = "Smith"
  grdSales.Col = 2
  grdSales.Text = "Johnson"
```

LISTING 22.6. CONTINUED

```
grdSales.Col = 3
grdSales.Text = "Lake"
grdSales.Col = 4
grdSales.Text = "West"
grdSales.Col = 5
grdSales.Text = "Gates"
grdSales.Col = 6
grdSales.Text = "Kirk"
grdSales.Col = 7
grdSales.Text = "Taylor"
' Now fill products
grdSales.Col = 0  ' All product names are in column 0
grdSales.Row = 1
grdSales.Text = "#1 Widget"
grdSales.Row = 2
grdSales.Text = "#2 Widget"
grdSales.Row = 3
grdSales.Text = "Long tube"
grdSales.Row = 4
grdSales.Text = "Short tube"
grdSales.Row = 5
grdSales.Text = "Metal liner"
grdSales.Row = 5
grdSales.Text = "Wood liner"
grdSales.Row = 6
grdSales.Text = "Plastic liner"
grdSales.Row = 7
grdSales.Text = "Rubber liner"
grdSales.Row = 8
grdSales.Text = "Basket"
grdSales.Row = 9
grdSales.Text = "Bolt 3C"
grdSales.Row = 10
grdSales.Text = "Bolt 5A"
grdSales.Row = 11
grdSales.Text = "Hex nut 3C"
grdSales.Row = 12
grdSales.Text = "Hex nut 5A"
grdSales.Row = 13
grdSales.Text = "#12 Nail"
grdSales.Row = 14
grdSales.Text = "#15 Nail"
grdSales.Row = 15
grdSales.Text = "#16 Nail"
grdSales.Row = 16
grdSales.Text = "Eye bolt #4"
grdSales.Row = 17
grdSales.Text = "Eye bolt #6"
```

```
57:    grdSales.Row = 18
58:    grdSales.Text = "Eye bolt #8"
59:    grdSales.Row = 19
60:    grdSales.Text = "Gasket"
61: End Sub
62:
63: Private Sub FillCells()
64:    ' Fill in all 160 cells with values
65:    ' calculated just from the row and column
66:    ' values. Although this data is meaningless,
67:    ' it quickly puts data in the table and grid.
68:    '
69:    ' Normally, this data would come from a database.
70:    '
71:    ' Declare a 20-row and 7-column table that
72:    ' matches the grid on the form. Keep zero-based
73:    ' subscripts because the grid uses them also.
74:    Dim curData(19, 7) As Currency
75:    Dim Row As Integer
76:    Dim Column As Integer
77:    '
78:    ' Fill the table with data
79:    For Row = 1 To 19
80:      For Column = 1 To 7
81:        curData(Row, Column) = ((Row + Column) / Row)
82:      Next Column
83:    Next Row
84:    ' Copy table contents to grid
85:    For Row = 1 To 19
86:      For Column = 1 To 7
87:        grdSales.Row = Row
88:        grdSales.Col = Column
89:        grdSales.Text = Format(curData(Row, Column), "###.00")
90:      Next Column
91:    Next Row
92: End Sub
```

The huge list of assignments in lines 4 though 60 serve only to place salespeople names across the top headers and the product names down the column headers at the left of the grid. When you work with a grid, there's little else you can do to initialize the headers. Many times, however, this information comes from a database, and you'll load the column and row headers from a list in a database table. For this simple application, the assignments were necessary.

Lines 79 through 83 fill the table, whose row and columns match that of the grid control, with data values. The values are comprised of a calculation based on row and column numbers just to place different values in the various table elements. The table acts as an intermediate storage area for the grid's values and is not necessary for this application. Nevertheless, you can study the initialization of a table with a nested loop here. As earlier sections of this bonus lesson explained, nested loops work well for stepping through tables and other multidimensional arrays. Of course, being that a grid works so much like a table, lines 85 though 91 use nested loops for copying the data to the grid control.

Note that line 89 uses the internal `Format()` function to format the data so that it's displayed in the grid displays in dollars and cents. Later, in the section "Using the `FormatString` Property," you'll learn how to use a grid-based property to set the format of cells.

The rest of the code works to control the application's reaction to the user's clicking of the command buttons and scrollbars that appear beneath the grid. These control the various commission price increases and decreases the user wants to implement. For example, if the commission for a particular salesperson's product is to rise or fall, the user can select that cell and click the scrollbar to change that commission only. In addition, the Increase by 15% and Decrease by 15% command buttons serve to implement the fixed 15 percent change of the selected commission when the user clicks the command button. Listing 22.7 shows the code that makes these commission changes.

LISTING 22.7. THE COMMISSIONS ARE AFFECTED BY THE USER'S SELECTION OF CONTROLS.

```
Private Sub hscDecrease_Change()
  ' Change the command button's Caption
  cmdDecrease.Caption = "&Decrease by" & Str(hscDecrease.Value) & "%"
End Sub

Private Sub hscIncrease_Change()
  ' Change the command button's Caption
  cmdIncrease.Caption = "&Increase by" & Str(hscIncrease.Value) & "%"
End Sub

Private Sub cmdIncrease_Click()
  ' Increase selected cell values by
  ' increasing the scrollbar percentage
  Dim SelRows As Integer
  Dim SelCols As Integer
  Dim SelStartRow As Integer
  Dim SelStartCol As Integer
  Dim RowBeg As Integer
  Dim ColBeg As Integer

```

```
  If (grdSales.HighLight) Then  ' If selected...
    ' Save the selected cell values
    SelStartRow = grdSales.RowSel
    SelStartCol = grdSales.ColSel
    RowBeg = grdSales.Row
    ColBeg = grdSales.Col
    ' Step through all selected cells
    For SelRows = RowBeg To SelStartRow
      For SelCols = ColBeg To SelStartCol
        grdSales.Row = SelRows
        grdSales.Col = SelCols
        ' Increase the cell by scrollbar amount
      grdSales.Text = grdSales.Text + (hscIncrease.Value / 100 * _
      grdSales.Text)
      grdSales.Text = Format(grdSales.Text, "####.00")
     Next SelCols
   Next SelRows
   ' Reset selection highlight
   grdSales.Row = RowBeg
   grdSales.Col = ColBeg
   grdSales.RowSel = SelStartRow
   grdSales.ColSel = SelStartCol
  End If
End Sub

Private Sub cmdDecrease_Click()
  ' Decrease selected cell values by
  ' decreasing the scrollbar percentage
  Dim SelRows As Integer
  Dim SelCols As Integer
  Dim SelStartRow As Integer
  Dim SelStartCol As Integer
  Dim RowBeg As Integer
  Dim ColBeg As Integer

  If (grdSales.HighLight) Then  ' If selected...
    ' Save the selected cell values
    SelStartRow = grdSales.RowSel
    SelStartCol = grdSales.ColSel
    RowBeg = grdSales.Row
    ColBeg = grdSales.Col
    ' Step through all selected cells
    For SelRows = RowBeg To SelStartRow
       For SelCols = ColBeg To SelStartCol
         grdSales.Row = SelRows
         grdSales.Col = SelCols
         ' Decrease the cell by scrollbar amount
         grdSales.Text = grdSales.Text - (hscDecrease.Value / 100 * _
         grdSales.Text)
         grdSales.Text = Format(grdSales.Text, "####.00")
       Next SelCols
```

continues

LISTING 22.7. CONTINUED

```
70:      Next SelRows
71:      ' Reset selection highlight
72:      grdSales.Row = RowBeg
73:      grdSales.Col = ColBeg
74:      grdSales.RowSel = SelStartRow
75:      grdSales.ColSel = SelStartCol
76:    End If
77: End Sub
78:
79: Private Sub cmdExit_Click()
80:    ' Terminate application
81:    End
82: End Sub
```

The `hscDecrease_Change()` and `hscIncrease_Change()` functions serve only to change the `Caption` property for either command button as the user clicks the scrollbar. The scrollbars determine the amount by which the command button increases or decreases in value.

Although the rest of the code beginning in line 11 is rather lengthy, the two large procedures in the code, `cmdIncrease_Click()` and `cmdDecrease_Click()`, do basically the same thing, except that one increases the value stored in whatever cells are selected and the other decreases the values stored in the selected cells.

> If the user only selects a single cell before clicking a command button, only that cell will change when the command button's `Click` procedure executes.

Given the similarities of the two large procedures, this analysis looks at only one, the `cmdIncrease_Click()` procedure. Line 21 ensures that the user has selected at least one cell before the increase of the cell values is performed. If no cell is selected, the procedure does nothing. Lines 23 through 26 save the rectangular area of the selected range. This range is determined by the current cell's row and column (the cell in the upper-left corner of the selection) and the end of the selection's row and column.

Lines 28 and 29 then use a nested `For` loop to step through every cell in the selection. Each cell is increased by the value of the scrollbar. (Remember, the value of the scrollbar determines what percentage the command button changes.) Lines 38 through 41 reset the selection, because if you ever change the grid's `Row` and `Col` values, any selection goes away and the `Row` and `Col` values determine the current cell by replacing the selected area. Lines 40 and 41 use `RowSel` and `ColSel` to put the selection back in its original location.

Using the Application

Now that you've created the application and have added the code, you can run the program. At first, you may not see the significance of the scrollbars and how they tie in with the command button, but once you perform these program tasks, you'll quickly learn how the program works:

1. Click the left scrollbar to decrease its position (move its position to the left). Notice that the `Caption` property of the command button beneath the scrollbar changes.
2. Click a cell to highlight it in the grid.
3. Click the right command button to see the value in that cell decrease by 15%.
4. Select a range of cells, such as the range shown in Figure 22.10.

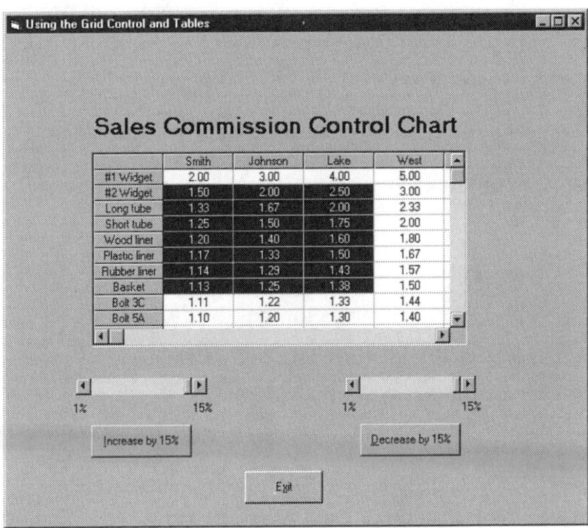

FIGURE 22.10.
No matter how many cells you select, you can increase or decrease the values within that selection by clicking a button.

5. Click the left command button to change the selected cells by the value shown on the command button. Notice that the selection remains in case you want to keep increasing the commission for a range of cells.
6. Select another range and decrease these values.
7. Click the Exit button to terminate the program.

Using the `FormatString` Property

Instead of using the internal `Format()` function to format data as you place it in a grid, you can set the format of a cell or range of cells so that any data you subsequently place in the cell is formatted according to the format you supply. The grid control's `FormatString` property requires a string value that determines the appearance of the cell's contents. Although `FormatString` is slightly cryptic at first, once you master it, you'll be able to format grid data more quickly than you could before.

> You can enter a `FormatString` value in the Custom dialog box, which appears when you click the `Custom` property value of the grid control. Enter the `FormatString` property in the Format text box when you click the dialog box's Style tab. In addition, you can assign the `FormatString` property's value directly, as this section shows.

One of the best features of `FormatString` is that you can use it to set row and column header titles so that you don't have to assign values as you did in the previous section's application.

The following guidelines determine the contents of the `FormatString` property:

- The pipe symbol (¦) separates `FormatString` segments from one another.
- Each segment between pipes defines a column.
- Text in each segment acts as the header values for row 0.
- Text in each segment defines the width of that grid's column.
- The character < left-justifies text in that segment, ^ centers text in that segment, and > right-justifies text in that segment.
- Text following a semicolon (;) defines the column 0 headings that appear to the left of each row.
- The longest row heading text value determines the width of the headings for column 0.
- The number of segments determines the minimum number of columns in the grid.

Although the `FormatString` property defines the rows and columns, as well as the headers and their widths, you must still size the grid control on your form window so that the user sees all the rows and columns. `FormatString` does not resize the grid in any way.

The following example produces the grid shown in Figure 22.11:

```
Dim strCol As String
Dim strRow As String
' Set the grid's column headers
' The ^ symbol causes all subsequent header values
' to appear centered. The pipe symbol defines each
' column.
strCol = "^|Smith|Johnson|Lake|West|Gates|Kirk|Taylor"
' Set the grid's row headers by building a string.
' the semi-colon tells Visual Basic to define these
' values as row headers.
strRow = ";|#1 Widget|#2 Widget|Long tube|Short tube|"
strRow = strRow & "Metal liner|Wood liner|Plastic liner|"
strRow = strRow & "Rubber liner|Basket|Bolt3C|Bolt 5A|"
strRow = strRow & "Hex nut 3C|Hex nut 5A|#12 Nail|#15 Nail|"
strRow = strRow & "#16 Nail|Eye bolt #4|Eye bolt #6|"
strRow = strRow & "Eye bolt #8|Gasket"
' Format the grid by assigning the two strings
grdSales.FormatString = strCol & strRow
```

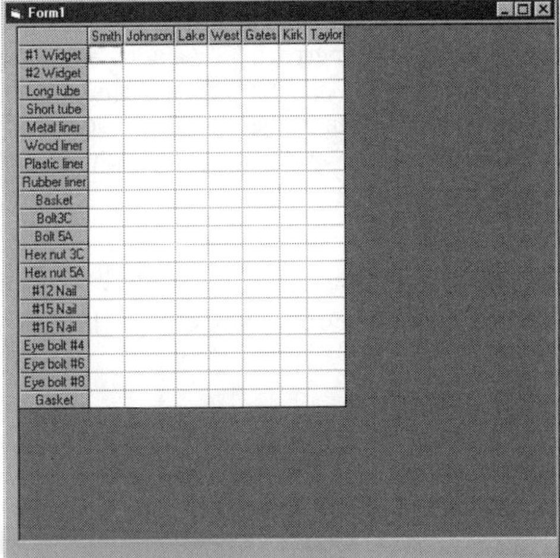

FIGURE 22.11.
Use the `FormatString` property to set up row and column headers.

Notice that the grid is basically identical to the one you created in the earlier application, except that the grid in Figure 22.11 has column widths that are equal the widths of the column header.

> **Tip**
>
> Obviously, using `FormatString` eliminates many tedious lines of code from the previous application. Listing 22.6 contains multiple assignment statements to assign column and row headers. The `FormatString` property can take care of the headers much more efficiently.

Storing Pictures in the Grid Control

The grid control enables you to store bitmap and icon pictures in the grid cells using the `CellPicture` property. To place a picture in any cell, follow these steps:

1. Assign the `Row` and `Col` properties to the cell you want the picture to appear in.
2. Assign the `ColWidth` and `ColHeight` properties to the same width and height of the picture if you want to control the picture size.
3. Assign the picture to the `CellPicture` property.

Caution You cannot assign a picture at designtime.

Tip If you first place your image in an image control on the form and then set the image's `Visible` property to `False`, you can assign the image control to the cell instead of using `LoadPicture()` to specify the exact filename of the picture you want to place in the cell. The image control enables you to more easily set the cell's width and height to match the picture.

Suppose you wanted to place a picture in the upper-left cell of the grid control. This cell normally contains no header text. The following code will place an image control's picture in that cell:

```
' make the upper-left hand cell current
grdSales.Row = 0
grdSales.Col = 0
' Set the cell's width and height to match the picture
grdSales.ColWidth(0) = Image1.Width
grdSales.RowHeight(0) = Image1.Height
' Assign the picture to the cell
Set grdSales.CellPicture = Image1.Picture
```

Notice that you must use a `Set` statement to assign the picture to the cell. A regular assignment statement will not suffice for the picture, because only the picture's pathname would then be assigned to the cell instead of the image itself. Figure 22.12 shows what this would look like with a bitmap picture of a beanie cap.

FIGURE 22.12.

Pictures can spruce up a grid control.

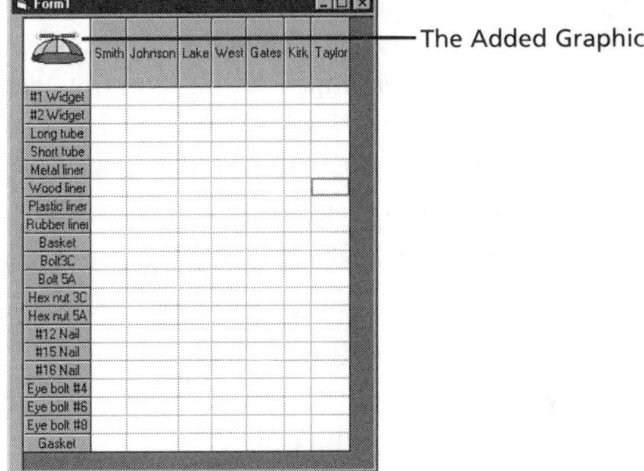

Summary

This bonus lesson explained how to set up multidimensional arrays so that you can more easily manage data. The most common multidimensional array, the two-dimensional table, appears in many kinds of situations where you must track rows and columns of data, as you might have to manage in a price inventory system, for example. Visual Basic enables you to track up to 60 dimensions of data, although three or four dimensions are all you normally must manage.

One of the easiest ways to present table data is with a grid control. Several kinds of grid controls exist, and you'll find them in the Components dialog box that appears when you select Project, Components. The FlexGrid is one of the most typical examples of a grid control. This bonus lesson explained how to set up and manage the FlexGrid control.

Q&A

Q How do I know what the subscripts are supposed to represent if I declare a multidimensional array with four or five dimensions?

A Each subscript can represent whatever you want them to represent. For example, in a two-dimensional table, the first subscript does not have to represent rows and the second does not have to represent columns; you can reverse them and use them the other way around. It's just the most common approach to make the far-right subscript the columns, the subscript to the left of it the rows, and the subscript to the left of it the layers of the table (as you would have in a cube of blocks). It is because the standard approach is to let the far-right column represent columns, that you should follow that standard. If someone else ever maintains your code, you help simplify the job if you've followed the standard way of using table values.

Although people do not visualize more than three dimensions well, a fourth subscript would simply keep track of the number of three-dimensional tables you have reserved in the three right subscripts. A fifth subscript, then, would represent the number of groups of the three-dimensional tables, and so on. If you increase the number of dimensions more than three, your programming does not get a lot harder, but remembering what each subscript represents can be.

Q Will I often use a multidimensional array with more than three or four dimensions?

A Probably rarely, if ever.

Q If I probably won't use multidimensional arrays with more than three or four dimensions, why learn about them?

A Actually, by the time you understand multidimensional arrays (and by the time you see that adding another dimensional subscript, in terms of computer storage, simply gives you additional occurrences of the array that the other dimensions declare), you haven't added that much complexity to your understanding. Just because you don't use multidimensional arrays past the fourth dimension very much doesn't mean you shouldn't learn how simple it is to add a subsequent dimension. Just remember, however, that every dimension increases the factor of the amount of memory you're using, so don't declare too big of a table with too many elements without considering the memory of the target computer on which your application will run. Some scientific and mathematical modeling applications do require several dimensions, so if you write applications for technical areas, you're more likely to find a use for five or more dimensions than if you write strictly business applications.

Q Can I use `FormatString` to add data to my grid control?

A No, `FormatString` serves only to add row and column header values to your grid. You must assign the data values that appear beneath and to the right of the grid's headers.

Workshop

The Workshop provides quiz questions to help you solidify your understanding of the material covered and exercises to provide you with experience in using what you've learned. Try to understand the quiz and exercise answers before continuing to the next bonus lesson. Answers are provided in Appendix A, "Answers to Exercises."

Quiz

1. True/False. All elements in a multidimensional table's row must be the same data type, but the different rows can be different data types.
2. Given the following multidimensional declaration, which subscript—the first, second, or third—usually specifies the rows?

   ```
   Dim sngArray(8, 9, 10)
   ```

3. Given the table of integers (called `intAra`) that follows, what values do the following elements represent, assuming that an `Option Base 1` statement appears in the program?

   a. `intAra(1, 1)`

   b. `intAra(3, 2)`

   c. `intAra(2, 3)`

   ```
    4   1   3   5   9
   10   2  12   1   6
   25  43   2  91   8
   14   7  28  71  14
   ```

4. True/False. Visual Basic supports up to 60 dimensions.
5. True/False. You can use the `Array()` function to initialize a multidimensional array in one statement.
6. What kind of control works well for the display of table data?
7. What are the fixed rows and columns used for in a grid control?
8. How can you assign a table to a grid's cells?
9. True/False. To assign a picture in a cell, you can use the `CellPicture` property at design time, just as you do for other controls.
10. Which is more efficient? Using `FormatString` or assignment statements to set up a grid's headers?

Exercises

1. Calculate the number of elements are reserved with the following statements?

   ```
   Option Base 1
   Dim intAra(4, 7) As Integer
   ```

2. If you were to omit the `Option Base` statement in the procedure's declarations module, calculate the number of elements reserved with the following statement?

   ```
   Dim intAra(4, 7) As Integer
   ```

3. Change the salesperson grid application from earlier in this lesson so that the grid's values are written back to the table before the program ends. Although nothing is

done with the table, this practice is good to show the one-to-one relationship between grids and tables. It also provides the place where you would write such values back to a database file if you needed to save the commission changes made by the user.

Bonus Chapters

Day 23

The Windows API

This bonus lesson describes how to access internal Windows routines. Although Visual Basic can do just about anything you need, some applications require features that Visual Basic cannot perform without tedious programming on your part. Fortunately, you can use routines that are already available elsewhere in Windows—such as those you write in C or C++ and store in DLLs—for your Visual Basic application.

By utilizing these Windows routines, you can extend the power of Visual Basic and make it perform some functions that only Windows has the true authority to perform. This bonus lesson describes not only how to access these Windows routines, it also describes many of the routines you can work with. If your application needs to manage a window's cursor, for example, the internal routines inside Windows already manage window cursors; therefore, you may find it easier to call one of these routines from your Visual Basic application.

Today, you learn the following:

- What the Windows API is
- Why your applications may require Windows routines not found in Visual Basic

- About dynamic link libraries (DLLs)
- How Visual Basic connects to the Windows API routines with the `Declare` statement
- About several new procedures available for use with API routines
- About ways to avoid problems when specifying API routines
- How to interpret and use new argument data types required by the Windows API routines
- How to create wrappers for common API routines so your Visual Basic applications will more easily access the procedures

The Windows API

The *Windows API* is a collection of routines available to you, the Visual Basic programmer. In a way, these API routines work just like Visual Basic's own internal functions. When you need to use the code in an API routine, your Visual Basic program calls that routine. When the Windows API finishes, control returns to your program so that it can continue.

So many Windows API routines exist that just about anything you can do from Windows, you can do from a Visual Basic application by calling the appropriate Windows API routine. For example, you can even force a system reboot by calling the appropriate Windows API routine.

NEW TERM The *Windows API*, or *Application Programming Interface*, is a set of internal Windows routines you can call from Visual Basic.

All the Windows API routines are stored in special files called *DLLs*. Several thousand API routines are available for use. These API routines appear in files stored in your Windows and Windows\System folders. When you install Windows, the DLL files install as well; therefore, you have access to these libraries automatically.

NEW TERM A *DLL*, or *dynamic link library*, is a set of API-based routines available for applications written in Visual Basic and other languages that support DLLs to use.

Most DLL files have the .DLL filename extension or the .EXE filename extension. Any program you write has access to the Windows DLLs. These same DLLs were part of older Windows versions as well (before Windows 95), except that these files didn't have "32" in their names, designating them as 32-bit compatible. Pre–Windows 95 versions were 16-bit compatible, meaning that data traveled through the system 16 bits (two bytes) at a time. Programming in a 32-bit environment adds much more flexibility, speed, and efficiency over the older 16-bit environment.

Here are the three most common DLLs:

- **USER32.DLL**—Contains functions that control the Windows environment and the user's interface, such as cursors, menus, and windows.
- **GDI32.DLL**—Contains functions that control output to the screen and other devices.
- **KERNEL32.DLL**—Contains functions that control the internal Windows hardware and software interface. Most of the memory, file, and directory service routines are located in KERNEL32.DLL.

Note

The GDI32.DLL library gets its name from the graphics device interface.

Windows is an operating system of several layers, starting with the layer the user sees (the *graphical user interface*) and ending with the layer closest to the hardware that controls the data flow between programs and hardware. This lowest level of the operating system is called the *kernel*. Hence, the name KERNEL32.DLL for the dynamic link library that contains the kernel-based routines.

These three files hold most of the API routines, or functions, that you'll call from your Visual Basic applications. As you glance through your Windows and Windows\System folders, you'll see other dynamic link libraries, as well, with names such as COMDLG.DLL, MAPI32.DLL, NETAPI32.DLL, and WINMM.DLL. As Microsoft adds features to the operating system, new DLL files appear.

DLLs are not just part of Windows. When you add a new application to your system, that application often supplies its own DLL. Therefore, over time, many DLL files begin to appear in your system.

Caution

DLLs give you much more power over your system than Visual Basic normally provides. When using a Windows API function, you're working with the internals of the operating system. As always, with power comes responsibility. Visual Basic's environment and debugger recognize normal internal Visual Basic functions. However, API functions are far outside Visual Basic's scope. Therefore, you can cause a system to crash, losing all your work, just by specifying improper arguments when running a Visual Basic application that calls a Windows API function.

Save your project often when calling API functions. This way, if you inadvertently call an API function that causes a system crash, you'll not lose all your work.

Figure 23.1 shows how an API routine appears to your Visual Basic application. Notice that the API routines come from the operating system and are completely separate from Visual Basic.

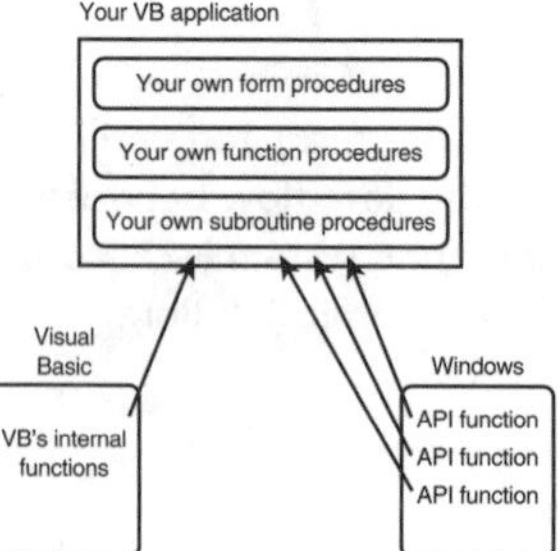

FIGURE 23.1.
API routines reside in the operating system.

The Nature of DLLs

The term *dynamic link* has special implications for programmers. When a routine is said to be *linked dynamically to a program*, it means that the routine, whether a subroutine or function, is not connected to the program until after the program is compiled. The function is available at runtime only. The functions that you write in the code window are *statically linked*, meaning that the functions combine with the rest of your source code when you compile the program. The DLL files, however, do not merge with your program. Your program has runtime access to these routines, but your program's EXE file does not contain the physical DLL routines at any time.

This difference is critical when it comes to using functions found in such places as dynamic link libraries, because neither the library nor the functions that your application calls are ever considered to be part of your program. The API functions never add to the size of your application's files. During program execution, these routines are loaded just long enough to run; then, if they are no longer needed, the Windows operating system can free up their resources so that more memory and CPU time is left for new routines that might start up.

The big advantage to such dynamic linking is not, however, its efficient use of resources. If Windows changes, the DLLs are replaced with new DLLs. Therefore, your applications will be able to support new Windows features without you needing to recompile every application that uses a Windows API. For example, you may recall that Windows 95 changed the look of windows. The icons in the upper-right corner of a window are different than the Windows 3.11 icons. Every Visual Basic program that calls a Windows API to display a window works in either Windows environment. Such a program, when run in a Windows 3.11 environment, would show the old icons. The same program, when run in a Windows 95 environment, shows the new icons, even though the program itself did not change. Therefore, in most cases, your programs that access the Windows API require no change when you move between Windows versions.

Note

Windows is not just one big program. Instead, Windows is actually a collection of many programs, several of which reside in DLL files. Windows, itself, is probably the biggest user of DLL files.

Tip

Anadvantage of using DLL routines is that several executing Windows programs can access the same DLL file's routines. In addition, all your users should have standard DLL routines. Windows is required to run a Visual Basic application, so needed DLLs will be available.

Using the `Declare` Statement

Calling Windows API routines requires a special statement called `Declare`. Normal internal Visual Basic functions need no `Declare` statement because Visual Basic understands how its own functions work and knows the arguments required by its own functions. API routines, however, are outside of Visual Basic's entire scope, so you must use `Declare` to give Visual Basic information about the API function you're calling.

The `Declare` statement performs the following tasks:

- Specifies where the API function is located
- Identifies arguments needed by the API function by number and data type
- Specifies whether or not the API function returns a value

The location of the `Declare` statement also impacts the way your Visual Basic application manages the function. Your `Declare` statement's location determines how much of your application can call the Windows API function described by the `Declare` statement. The `Declare` statement describes one of two Windows API function scopes, depending on these two conditions:

- If you declare the Windows API routine in the form module, outside of the form module's general declaration section (such as inside an event procedure), only the code in the form module can call the API routine. The `Declare` statement must designate the API routine as a private routine with the `Private` keyword.
- If you declare the Windows API routine in the general declarations section of a module or form, that API routine is available to the entire application, and the routine is said to have *public scope* across all the application's modules. Use the `Public` keyword to indicate the public scope.

As with all procedures, a Windows API routine can either be a subroutine or function, depending on whether the routine returns a value. The following format describes the subroutine procedure version of the `Declare` statement:

```
Declare Sub procName Lib "libName" [Alias "alias"] [([[ByVal] var1 [As _
dataType][,[ByVal] var2 [As dataType]] ... [,[ByVal] varN [As dataType])]
```

The `Declare` statement tells Visual Basic of the type of API procedure (subroutine or function), the name of the routine, the DLL library filename the routine is stored in (such as KERNEL32.DLL), and the arguments and data type of those arguments. If the routine is a function, the `Declare` statement also describes the return data type.

> As with most statements, the format of `Declare` looks foreboding, but its actual use is slightly simpler than its format seems. However, you must still be very careful to match all arguments and required values perfectly to the API routine you call so that the routine executes properly.

The following format describes the function procedure version of the `Declare` statement. Notice that the format differs from that of a subroutine procedure only by the `Function` keyword and the return data type at the end of the statement:

```
Declare Function procName Lib "libName" [Alias "alias"] [([[ByVal] var1 _
[As dataType] _
[,[ByVal] var2 [As dataType]] ... [,[ByVal] varN [As dataType])] As _
dataType
```

The following statements illustrate `Declare` (you'll find these statements in the general module named Module1 of the CallDlls.VBP sample project that comes with Visual Basic):

```
Declare Function GetWindowsDirectory Lib "kernel32" Alias
"GetWindowsDirectoryA"_
(ByVal lpBuffer As String, ByVal nSize As Long) As Long
Declare Sub GetSystemInfo Lib "kernel32" (lpSystemInfo As SystemInfo)
```


Notice that some DLL declarations are lengthy and some are small. Just as different internal functions require different numbers of arguments, so do Windows DLL declarations and calls.

Caution

You *must* match the Windows API routine name with the exact uppercase and lowercase letters used by the original Windows API function. These API functions are actually C routines and Visual Basic needs to use syntax that C recognizes for the functions to operate properly from a Visual Basic application. Visual Basic will unsuccessfully match the routine's call with the API routine if the letters differ in case or if you use a different format.

Understanding API Data Types

One of the reasons the API routines are difficult to call is that Windows uses a slightly different set of data types than Visual Basic. Although the Windows API uses the String and Long data types, it also uses other data types such as RECT and MSG. Therefore, getting the format exact can be difficult.

Note

Not only must your arguments match the required API argument list in number and data type, you must also pass the arguments in the proper way—either by value or by reference. (Day 8, "The Nature of VB Programs," explains the difference in the two methods of argument passing.) Therefore, use the `ByVal` keyword when needed, because without `ByVal`, `ByRef` is assumed. Some arguments in the same API routine require different methods of passing.

The `Alias` keyword is used in a `Declare` statement to convert some string values that contain illegal characters to legal Visual Basic equivalents. The `Alias` keyword also serves to convert Windows API routine names that aren't allowed, such as `_lopen` (a valid Windows API name but an invalid Visual Basic procedure name) to the Visual Basic naming standard.

You'll run across strange data types that you may not recognize. Table 23.1 describes some of these data types that you'll run across when working with API routines. This table lists the data types that differ from Visual Basic's own data types.

TABLE 23.1. SPECIAL DATA TYPES USED BY THE API ROUTINES.

Data Type	*Description*
ANY	A Windows API routine that accepts different kinds of data types will list ANY for those data types. All ANY arguments are passed by reference, so you won't use the `ByVal` keyword.
ATOM	Integer data. Always passed by value and described in an API routine's declaration as `ByVal` *`argument%`* or `ByVal` *`argument`* `As Integer.`
BOOL	Long integer data. Always passed by value and described in an API routine's declaration as `ByVal` *`argument%`* or `ByVal` *`argument`* `As Long.`
CHAR	Byte data. Always passed by value and described in an API routine's declaration as `ByVal` *`argument`* `As Byte.`
COLOREF	Long integer data used for specifying color values. Always passed by value and described in an API routine's declaration as `ByVal` *`argument%`* or `ByVal` *`argument`* `As Long.`
DWORD	Long integer data. Always passed by value and described in an API routine's declaration as `ByVal` *`argument%`* or `ByVal` *`argument`* `As Long.`
NULL	Long integer data types used for uninitialized values. Described in an API routine's declaration as `ByVal` *`argument&`* and `ByVal` *`argument`* `As Long.`
LPSTR, LPCSTR	Matches the String data type. Described in an API routine's declaration as `ByVal` *`argument$`* or `ByVal` *`argument`* `As String.`
STRUCTURE	Sometimes, you'll run across a strange API data type such as RECT, MSG, and UDT. These define complex data types that may be a collection of several other data types. Each structure-based API routine requires a special structure, and you'll have to look at the API routine's required arguments to know how to format them.

Remember that Table 23.1 contains only a few of the data types you'll find in the Windows API `Declare` statements. Given these special API routines and their numerous arguments, how are you possibly supposed to know which to use? The next section shows you how to use a special tool that comes with Visual Basic that lets you manage API routines.

> If the API routine requires a String data type, you should pass a string that you've defined as a fixed-length string with much padding in the string. For example, double the length of the longest string you ever expect the API routine to return and then declare the fixed string argument with that much space before passing the string to the API routine. (You don't need to worry about the string length if the routine does not modify the string in any way.)

Using the API Viewer

Windows contains thousands of API routines you can call. Knowing the format of even a small number of the routines would be difficult. Therefore, Visual Basic includes a special tool called the *API Viewer* you can use to get help with the format of the API routines.

NEW TERM The *API Viewer* displays API procedures and groups them together by subject so that you can locate the routines you need to use.

The API Viewer enables you to locate API routines and arguments and then copy and paste that information into your code window. Depending on your Visual Basic installation, you start the API Viewer in one of two ways.

> The API Viewer's Copy button copies the selected declaration information to the Windows Clipboard. In addition, if you click the API Viewer's Public or Private option before clicking Copy, the API Viewer designates the appropriate `Public` or `Private` qualifying keyword in the `Declare` statement so that you don't have to change the declaration's qualifier manually.

Some installations put the API Viewer on the Start menu. To see if you have the API Viewer on your Start menu, select Start, Programs, Microsoft Visual Basic 6.0, Microsoft Visual Studio 6.0 Tools, API Text Viewer. If you don't locate the API Viewer program in your Start menu, you may be able to start it from within the Visual Basic environment. To do so, select the Add-Ins, Add-In Manager to display the Add-In Manager dialog box. Double-click the API Viewer entry, if it exists, to add the API Viewer to your Add-Ins menu. You can start the program by selecting Add-Ins, API Viewer.

Figure 23.2 shows the API Viewer window that appears.

FIGURE 23.2.

The API Viewer enables you to more easily determine the format of API routines.

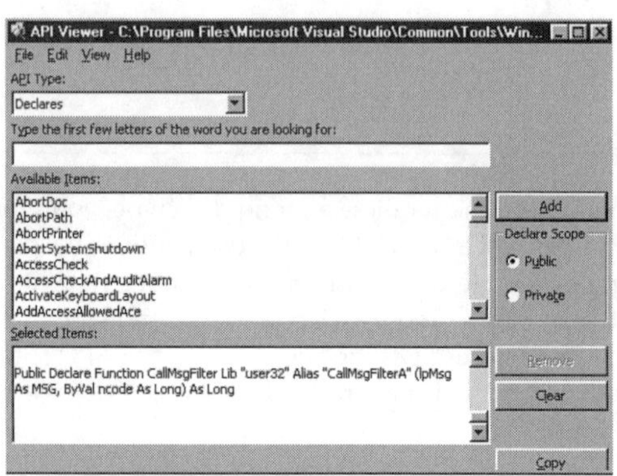

Caution

You may still not be able to start the API Viewer. If not, perhaps the it's not installed on your system. You will have to start the Control Panel and select the Add/Remove Programs icon. Locate the Visual Basic entry and install the API Viewer from the Tools entry in the list. You may have to locate your original Visual Basic installation CD-ROM to complete the installation of the API Viewer.

Note

The API Viewer locates its underlying information from text files Apiload.txt, Mapi32.txt, and Win32api.txt that install on your system along with the API Viewer.

Given that most of the API routines you'll be interested in are located in the Win32api.txt file, select File, Load Text File from the API Viewer and select Win32api.txt. The API Viewer can convert the text file to an Access database (with the .MDB filename extension) if you select Yes from the message box that appears and then choose the Win32api.txt file (see Figure 23.3). After you convert the text file to a database, the loading menu option becomes File, Load Database File.

Notice that the top list box in the dialog box is labeled API Type. When you open this list box, you'll see these three values:

- **Constants**—Lists all the named constants that the loaded Windows API file recognizes
- **Declares**—Lists all the declarations that appear in the loaded API file
- **Types**—Lists all the data types recognized by the loaded Windows API file

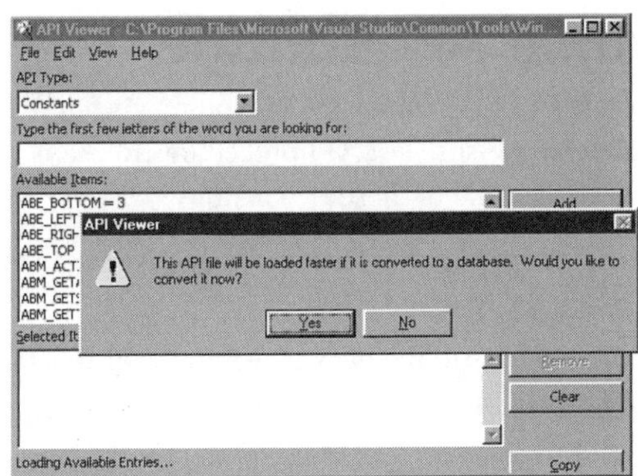

FIGURE 23.3.

The API Viewer can store its underlying information in a database for quicker access.

The Available Items list box contains all the Windows API routines for the file you loaded and the type of value you want to see. For example, if you want to locate the `Declare` statement needed for the `GetWindowsDirectory` API routine shown earlier, follow these steps:

1. Select Declares from the API Type list box. Numerous `Declare` candidates appear in the Available Items list box.
2. You can quickly locate a specific `Declare` by typing the first few letters in the text box. Type `getw` and all items that begin with those letters appear in the Available Items list box.
3. Scroll down to the `GetWindowsDirectory` entry.
4. Double-click the `GetWindowsDirectory` entry to display the `Declare` statement needed for that function, as shown in Figure 23.4.

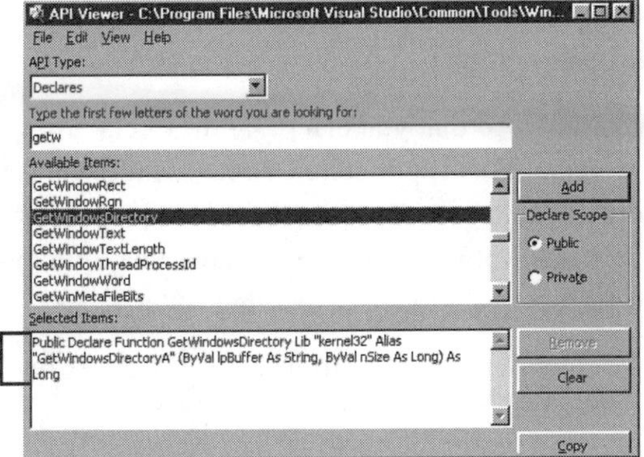

The function's `Declare` statement

FIGURE 23.4.

The API Viewer displays the `Declare` statement required by the statement you select.

You can now select and copy the entire `Declare` statement and paste it into your code window.

Calling a Simple API Routine

Before learning more about the Windows API, you may want to see one of the API routines in action. One of the simplest API procedures to use is the `MessageBeep` function. The function does one of these two actions:

- If the argument you pass to the `MessageBeep()` API function is positive, a beep sounds through the PC's *sound card.*
- If the argument you pass to the `MessageBeep()` API function is negative, a beep sounds through the PC's *speaker*.

Sure, you can more simply use the Visual Basic Beep command to sound a beep, but this small application that you build will offer quick insight into the process of calling API routines. Actually, many Visual Basic functions and commands map directly to API calls, because Microsoft internally calls the needed routine when you issue the corresponding function or command that happens to be mapped to an API routine.

Create a project with a single command button in the center of the form window. Set the command button's name to cmdBeep and change the caption to `&Beep`. Double-click the command button to open a new `Click` event procedure.

Now, start your API Viewer (if you do not still have the API Viewer running from earlier in this lesson). Load the win32api.txt file (or the database file, if you converted the file earlier in this lesson) and change the API Type to Declares. In the second list box, type `message`, and a list of API procedures will appear in the Available Items list box. The first function is `MessageBeep`. Double-click this entry to display the procedure's declaration in the Selected Items text box.

Select the entire declaration so that you can paste the declaration into your code window. Switch back to your Visual Basic application's code window. Insert a line before the `Click` event procedure so that you can paste the declaration in the general declarations section of your code window. (You can insert a blank line by moving your cursor to the upper-left corner of the code window and pressing Enter.)

Paste the Clipboard contents you copied from the API Viewer into your code window. Change the `Public` statement to `Private`.

You must change the `Public` qualifier to `Private` because the function declaration is local to the form's module and is not stored in a general declarations section.

Then, add the following code to the middle of the command button's `Click` event procedure:

```
Dim Beeper As Variant
Beeper = MessageBeep(1)
```

Listing 23.1 shows the whole procedure.

LISTING 23.1. YOU CAN USE THE WINDOWS API TO SOUND THE SPEAKER.

```
Private Declare Function MessageBeep Lib "user32" (ByVal wType As Long) _
As Long

Private Sub cmdBeep_Click()
  Dim Beeper As Variant
  Beeper = MessageBeep(1)
End Sub
```

The `Declare` statement tells Visual Basic exactly how to find the `MessageBeep()` function. If the function were an internal Visual Basic function, such as `Abs()`, Visual Basic wouldn't need a `Declare` statement because it would have no trouble finding the function. The `MessageBeep()` function, however, is completely outside of the Visual Basic environment. Therefore, the `Declare` statement tells Visual Basic exactly how to execute the function and how to pass values. In addition, the `Declare` statement tells Visual Basic that the function resides in the USER32.DLL file.

Notice that `MessageBeep()` is a function and not a subroutine procedure. Therefore, `MessageBeep()` returns a value, and the value is a Long data type. Your application does not need to do anything with this return value, however. The Variant variable named `Beeper` simply stores the return value instead of leaving it hanging at the return of the function.

When you run the program, the command button appears in the middle of the form. If you click the command button, you'll hear a beep from your sound card. If you don't hear the beep, you can change the argument to `-1` so that the sound comes from your PC's speaker. Even without a sound card or with your sound card's speakers turned off, the PC's internal speaker will still sound.

As with the Beep statement, many Visual Basic statements duplicate Windows API routines. That is fortunate, because you don't have to call nearly as many API routines as you would otherwise have to call. In addition, many hundreds of Windows API routines exist that you'll never need because they don't perform useful tasks for an application program.

Calling a Different API

You can create another simple application to test the calling of a Windows API routine. Consider Listing 23.2, which sends to a label the kind of disk drive found.

LISTING 23.2. USING THE WINDOWS API TO LEARN MORE ABOUT A DISK DRIVE FROM INSIDE YOUR APPLICATION.

```
Private Declare Function GetDriveType Lib "kernel32.dll" Alias _
"GetDriveTypeA"(ByVal nDrive As String) As Long

Private Sub cmdDrive_Click()
  Dim lngDriveType As Long

  ' Pass the drive name that you are interested in
  ' to the GetDriveType() function
  lngType = GetDriveType("c:\")
  '
  ' Use the return value to determine
  ' the kind of drive tested
  Select Case lngType
    Case 2
      txtDrive.Text = "Removable drive"
    Case 3
      txtDrive.Text = "Fixed hard disk"
    Case 4
      txtDrive.Text = "Remote (network) drive"
    Case Else
      txtDrive.Text = "Unknown"
  End Select
End Sub
```

If you want to enter and test the code in Listing 23.2, locate the `GetDriveType()` declaration in the API Viewer and copy the declaration to your Clipboard. Replace the `Declare` statement in the code window with the copied text and then change the `Public` keyword to `Private`. Fill in the rest of the code window to match Listing 23.2.

Next, add a command button named `cmdDrive` to the bottom of the form window and then add a text box control named `txtDrive` to the top of the form. You can adjust the font and size of these controls if you wish, but doing so is not critical for this simple example. Change line 8 to another drive, such as the disk drive, if you want to test for another type of drive. Run the program to see the drive description message appear, as shown in Figure 23.5.

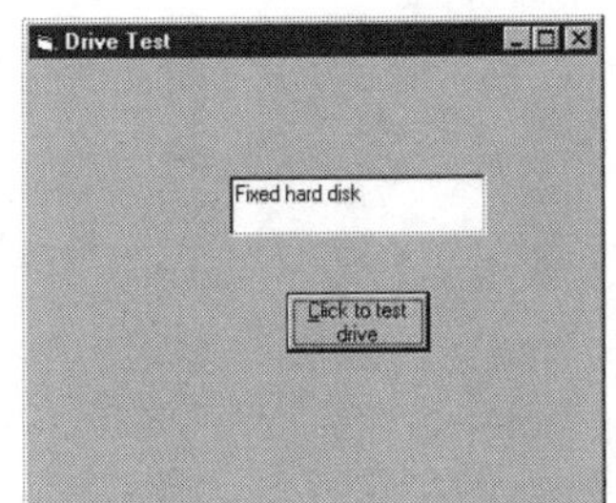

FIGURE 23.5.
The API routine returned information about your disk drive.

Locating the Windows Folder

Sometimes, when writing programs that access system files or that store files in the Windows directory, Visual Basic programmers use the Windows API routines to locate the Windows folder (the directory where Windows is installed). Other folders you might want to locate are the System and Temp folders. Windows API routines exist to give you both sets of information. You might, for instance, want to store temporary files used by your application in your user's Temp folder. (The term *folder* is synonymous with *directory*.)

Always delete files you store in the Temp folder during your application's execution. Many users routinely delete files that appear in Temp that are more than a day or two old to clean it out and retrieve needed disk space. You don't want your application to be one of those applications that stores old files in Temp without deleting them; otherwise, your users will not favor your program for long. Also, for those users who do not routinely clean their Temp folders (most of them fail to clean the Temp folder and many don't even know the folder exists), you don't want to store temporary files in the folder and leave them there. You'll waste disk space, and your users won't even know why they have less disk space every time one of your applications finishes.

The following steps describe how to create a small application that gives you practice in retrieving Windows folder information:

1. Create a new application.
2. Place the controls from Table 23.2 on the form. Figure 23.6 shows the form window that you'll create using the values in Table 23.2.

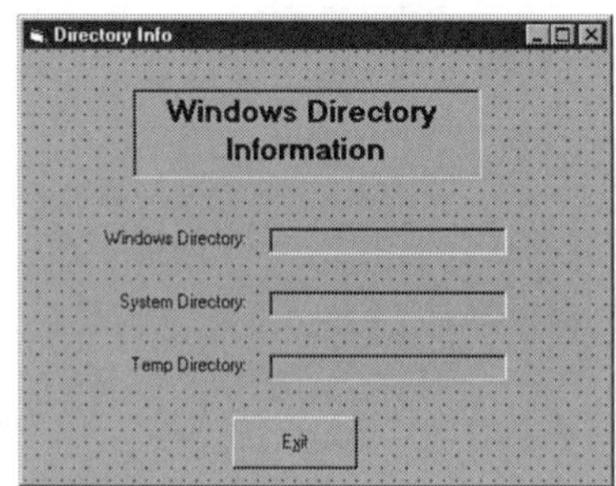

FIGURE 23.6.
This form window will display the user's Windows directory folder information.

3. Double-click the form to produce the `Form_Load()` event procedure. Insert a few blank lines before the `Form_Load()` procedure so that you can include the `Declare` statements that will produce the three directories.
4. Start the API Viewer if you closed it in the previous section. Open the Win32api text or database file.
5. Select the Declares entry from the API Type list box.
6. Locate the `GetWindowsDirectory` declaration entry in the Available Items list box and double-click the entry to display the declaration for the `GetWindowsDirectory()` routine.
7. Copy the `GetWindowsDirectory()` function from the API Viewer and paste it at the top of your code window.
8. Change the `Public` keyword to `Private` because the declaration resides in your form module, not in a general code module.
9. Repeat steps 6 through 8 for the `GetSystemDirectory()` and `GetTempPath()` function declarations.
10. Enter the rest of the coded needed as described in Listing 23.3.
11. Run the application to see successful retrieval of the directory information. Figure 23.7 shows the resulting execution on one machine.

TABLE 23.2. PLACE THESE CONTROLS ON YOUR APPLICATION'S FORM TO PRACTICE LOCATING WINDOWS FOLDERS.

Control Property	*Property Value*
Form Name	frmFolder
Form Caption	Directory Info
Form Height	4500
Form Width	5790
Label Name	lblTitle
Label #1 Alignment	2-Center
Label #1 BorderStyle	1-Fixed Single
Label #1 Caption	Windows Directory Information
Label #1 Font Size	14
Label #1 Font Style	Bold
Label #1 Height	855
Label #1 Left	1080
Label #1 Top	360
Label #1 Width	3375
Label #2 Name	lblWD
Label #2 Alignment	1-Right Justify
Label #2 Caption	Windows Directory:
Label #2 Height	255
Label #2 Left	720
Label #2 Top	1680
Label #2 Width	1455
Label #3 Name	lblSD
Label #3 Alignment	1-Right Justify
Label #3 Caption	System Directory:
Label #3 Height	255
Label #3 Left	720
Label #3 Top	2280
Label #3 Width	1455
Label #4 Name	lblTD
Label #4 Alignment	1-Right Justify
Label #4 Caption	Temp Directory:

continues

TABLE 23.2. CONTINUED

Control Property	*Property Value*
Label #4 Height	255
Label #4 Left	720
Label #4 Top	2880
Label #4 Width	1455
Label #5 Name	lblWinD
Label #5 Alignment	0-Left Justify
Label #5 BorderStyle	1-Fixed Single
Label #5 Height	255
Label #5 Left	2400
Label #5 Top	1680
Label #5 Width	2295
Label #6 Name	lblWinS
Label #6 Alignment	0-Left Justify
Label #6 BorderStyle	1-Fixed Single
Label #6 Height	255
Label #6 Left	2400
Label #6 Top	2280
Label #6 Width	2295
Label #7 Name	lblWinT
Label #7 Alignment	0-Left Justify
Label #7 BorderStyle	1-Fixed Single
Label #7 Height	255
Label #7 Left	2400
Label #7 Top	2880
Label #7 Width	2295
Command button Name	cmdExit
Command button Caption	E&xit
Command button Left	2040
Command button Top	3480
Command button Width	1215

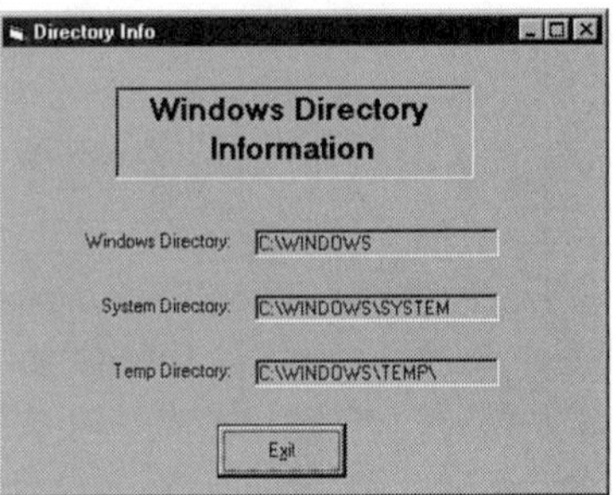

FIGURE 23.7.

The directory information will change depending on the user's machine's setup.

LISTING 23.3. THE API FUNCTIONS THAT RETRIEVE FOLDER INFORMATION REQUIRE SLIGHTLY MORE WORK THAN EARLIER API ROUTINES THAT YOU SAW.

```
Private Declare Function GetWindowsDirectory Lib "kernel32" Alias _
"GetWindowsDirectoryA" (ByVal lpBuffer As String, ByVal nSize As Long) _
As Long
Private Declare Function GetSystemDirectory Lib "kernel32" Alias _
"GetSystemDirectoryA" (ByVal lpBuffer As String, ByVal nSize As Long) _
As Long
Private Declare Function GetTempPath Lib "kernel32" Alias _
"GetTempPathA"_
(ByVal nBufferLength As Long, ByVal lpBuffer As String) As Long

Private Sub Form_Load()
  ' Initialize the system folder labels when the form loads
  ' Declare a fixed-length string long enough to hold information
  Dim strFolder As String * 255
  Dim intLength As Integer

  '
   ' Get the Windows directory information
   intLength = GetWindowsDirectory(strFolder, 255)
   lblWinD.Caption = Left(strFolder, intLength)
   '
   ' Get the System directory information
   intLength = GetSystemDirectory(strFolder, 255)
   lblWinS.Caption = Left(strFolder, intLength)
   '
   ' Get the Temp directory information
   intLength = GetTempPath(255, strFolder)
   lblWinT.Caption = Left(strFolder, intLength)
 End Sub

 Private Sub cmdExit_Click()
   End
 End Sub
```

The code you must use to retrieve the folder names is interesting because it takes more work than previous API-based code you've seen. These routines do retrieve the needed folder information, but you must pick off that information from a long string that the functions return.

Line 7 reserves space for a fixed-length string that is 255 characters. Although systems will not require nearly that much string space for the folders, more space is better than not enough space. Line 8 then declares an integer variable that will be used as each function's return value. That return value, stored in `intLength` (as done in line 12), will contain the number of valid characters of that 255-character string that contains the folder path information. Different computers will return longer or shorter paths, depending on where the folders are stored. Therefore, the 255-character string gives your application plenty of room to hold any PC's path to these folders, except in the extremely rare that the path to one of these directories is longer than 255 characters.

When line 12 gets the folder, notice that the `GetWindowsDirectory()` API function requires both the string to store the pathname in as well as the length of that string. Therefore, `GetWindowsDirectory()` will not attempt to store more than 255 characters in the string named `strFolder`.

Once the function returns, line 13 then picks off its left portion, which contains the pathname information. The API function's return value determines how many characters from the string hold the actual path. The characters in the 255-character fixed string that appear to the right of the path contain meaningless information, so you don't want to display that data in the label.

Line 20 shows one anomaly that you'll often find with the API routines: Even though the `GetTempPath()` function is extremely similar to the `GetWindowsDirectory()` and `GetTempPath()` functions, the string and integer arguments are reversed in `GetTempPath()` from their positions in the other two functions. Pay close attention to the `Declare` statements when you work with system API routines so that you don't inadvertently confuse arguments.

Note

> The uniqueness of these three functions shown in this application are not, it turns out, all that unique. Many of the Windows API routines require such manipulation before and after the function call. Sometimes, similar functions reverse their arguments (as is done here with the `GetTempPath()` function and the other two API functions called). The beauty of Visual Basic's own internal functions is that they offer more uniformity, they mate perfectly with Visual Basic's built-in data types, and they do not pose the danger that the Windows API, if used incorrectly, can produce (such as an unexpected system reboot).

Summary

This bonus lesson explained how to use the API routines that come with Windows. Windows is, itself, just a collection of dynamic link libraries that contain thousands of routines you can access from a Visual Basic program. Although you'll not use many of the available API procedures, many of them do come in handy when you need to work with system information or perform a system-related function, such as the reading of the user's system Registry or rebooting the user's PC.

Mastering the Windows API takes time, and many programmers never learn all the API procedures—many procedures are necessary for proper operating system flow but do nothing for applications run by users. Nevertheless, by having access to these Windows API procedures (both subroutine and function procedures), you can tap into a rich assortment of procedures that return and manage the user's system.

Using the Windows API is somewhat tedious. Fortunately, Visual Basic includes a tool called the *API Viewer*. You can use it to view every possible Windows API routine on your system and grab the procedures' declaration statements, which you can paste directly into your own code. Once you paste a declaration into your Visual Basic application (using a `Declare` statement), you can call the Windows API from your program. At runtime, Windows will make the procedure available to your running program.

Q&A

Q Why do the Windows API routine declarations and calling procedures seem so complex?

A The complexity comes from the connection between your Visual Basic application and the routine itself. Remember that the API routines were not written with Visual Basic in mind. The original API routines were designed and written to be called by the C language, which uses a slightly different set of data types than Visual Basic and calls routines differently as well. The declaration is Visual Basic's way of understanding these routines that lie outside of its environment.

Q What are some other examples of Windows API routines that I might want to look for?

A The routines are too numerous to mention. Nevertheless, the following list, although far from exhaustive, gives you a starting point for knowing what is available to you:

- Retrieving System Registry values
- Determining free and used system resources, such as memory and disk space
- Accessing the current Windows version
- Working with a window
- Low-level graphics
- Managing values in an INI file (INI files were used by pre–Windows 95 versions to store system values and are still in use by some Windows programs)

Sometimes, locating a routine is guesswork. Generally, however, if you find an API routine that you think you want to use, you should locate that routine in Visual Basic's online Help to see if the routine does what you need. You cannot always tell what an API routine does from its name. For example, to retrieve and save a value from an INI file, you use the `GetSetting()` and `SaveSetting()` functions.

Q How can I find out which Windows API routines are available?

A Several sources are available, including your Visual Basic Online Help system, Microsoft's Web site, and the following excellent titles:

- *Visual Basic 6 Unleashed*
- *Dan Appleman's Visual Basic 5 Programmer's Guide to the Win32 API*

Q Is there any way to make the API routines easier to use?

A If you find yourself using one or more of the Windows API routines often, you can make these routines somewhat easier to use. Instead of starting the API Viewer each time your application needs to use an API routine and pasting the `Declare` statement and calling the routine, you can add common API routines you frequently use to a standard code module with the .BAS filename extension. The module will hold all the `Declare` statements for each API routine you think you'll use. You can also write a Visual Basic function or subroutine procedure that calls the API routine. Use an argument list for the Visual Basic procedure that matches, in data type, the arguments of the API routine. Such a Visual Basic procedure is called a *wrapper* procedure, because you've wrapped Visual Basic's calling conventions and argument data types around a nonstandard Windows API procedure.

Subsequently, when a Visual Basic application requires one or more of these routines, you need to add that API-based code module to your application, and your application then only needs to make a call to the Visual Basic wrapper you've placed in the code module to execute the API routine. In other words, to your application, the Windows API is called and returned from just like all the other

Visual Basic procedures you write. Once you debug your Visual Basic library of API routines, you'll have a safer way of calling the API procedures you need the most.

Workshop

The Workshop provides quiz questions to help you solidify your understanding of the material covered and exercises to provide you with experience in using what you've learned. Answers are provided in Appendix A, "Answers to Exercises."

Quiz

1. What does *API* stand for?
2. Given Visual Basic's rich collection of internal functions, why would you ever want to call a Windows API routine?
3. Why do the DLLs your applications use not add to the size of those Visual Basic applications?
4. Why have the names of the standard DLLs changed over time as Windows has changed?
5. What tool lets you more easily view the API routine formats?
6. Which statement declares Windows API routines?
7. True/False. The Windows API routines have a uniform appearance and calling mechanism.
8. What does the `Declare` statement do?
9. Which qualifier, `Public` or `Private`, is required for Windows API procedures that you declare inside a form module?
10. What is the purpose of a wrapper procedure?

Exercise

Which file, GDI32.DLL or KERNEL32.DLL, contains the `GetSystemTime` API function? How can you determine this for any API routine you run across?

APPENDIX A

Answers to Exercises

Day 1, "Welcome to Visual Basic"

Quiz Answers

1. BASIC is the language Visual Basic is based on.
2. Visual Basic is visual and uses a simple BASIC-like programming language, yet Visual Basic enables you to create powerful Windows programs.
3. Visual Basic's visual nature is more important than its programming language in many ways. The visual interface provides your program's character and interacts with the user. The programming language works behind the scenes to connect the visual elements.
4. A form window *can be* the application's window, but an application can also contain several form windows. The form window is the window your user is looking at when the user runs your program.
5. A *bug* is any kind of error in a program, and *debug* refers to the process of removing program bugs.

6. A program written in a compiled language runs much faster than one written in an interpreted language.
7. A program written in an interpreted language is easier to debug than one written in a compiled language.
8. A Splash screen always looks the same and appears every time a program begins. A Tip of the Day screen is different on different days, and the user can control whether the screen continues to appear.
9. A control is an element, such as a text label, command button, or option button, on a form. A control property value helps distinguish one control from another.
10. False. Controls do not hold code. Most controls are visual objects on the form window with which the user interacts. The code is stored separately (in something called a module), as you'll see throughout the next 20 lessons.

Exercise Answer

Run the Application wizard and select Yes when the wizard asks if you want to add Internet access to the application. If you have Internet access, select View, Web Browser when you run the program, and a web browser will open from which you can access the Internet.

Day 2, "Working with Visual Basic"

Quiz Answers

1. The toolbar gives you quick, one-button access to common commands and menu options. The toolbox is a collection of controls that you can place on your form.
2. MSDN is Microsoft's subscription-based online service.
3. False; the Form window holds as many forms as the application requires, although only one form can be selected at any one time.
4. The mouse cursor changes to a crosshair when you move the mouse over the form so that you can draw the control on your Form window.
5. Visual Basic places the control in the center of the Form window so that you can then move and resize the control.
6. False. You set control properties from the Properties window (you can also set properties in code).
7. The Properties window displays the properties for the selected object.
8. An ellipsis, as on the `Font` property, indicates that a dialog box will appear after you click the ellipsis so that you can specify multiple values for that property.

9. The command button's `Caption` property determines the title that appears on the button.
10. The default names are cryptic. When you rename the controls to a more descriptive name, especially when you add a prefix to the control name, you can better tell the purpose for a control from its name alone, which is useful when you are working with numerous controls in a project.

Exercise Answer

To add a blue background, click the form's `BackColor` property. (The property description for the selected property at the bottom of the Properties window lets you know that the `BackColor` property controls the background color.) A drop-down list box appears. When you open the list box, a tabbed dialog box appears. The Palette tab offers numerous colors from which you can choose to set the form's background, and the System tab offers more conventional Windows colors. Click the Palette tab and select a blue color.

Add a command button somewhere on the form, perhaps in the lower-right hand corner of the Form window. Change its `Name` property to `cmdExit`. Change its `Caption` property to `Exit`. To add the one line of code required, double-click the command button and type `End` in the center of the procedure that appears. When you run the program, you'll see the blue background and the new command button. After you display the graphic image, click the Exit command button to terminate the program.

Day 3, "Managing Controls"

Quiz Answers

1. An accelerator key is a shortcut key on a menu option or control that lets the user select that control with a keystroke, such as Alt+R.
2. False. Controls support events.
3. The `Cancel` event enables the user to select the command button by pressing Esc.
4. The control in focus is outlined by a dashed line.
5. The user presses Tab and Shift+Tab (and sometimes the arrow keys, depending on the application) to move the focus from control to control.
6. The `TabIndex` property determines focus order.
7. You know that `LoadPicture ()` is some kind of procedure because of the parentheses. `LoadPicture ()` was the procedure that displayed the happy face image in yesterday's image control. `LoadPicture ()` is a function, but it's a special function that is internal to the Visual Basic programming language. You don't write the code for `LoadPicture ()` because the code already exists inside Visual Basic. These

internal functions save you time because you don't have to write common code that you use over and over. You'll learn all about such internal functions in Day 5, "Analyzing VB Data."

8. False. Visual Basic often generates a `Click` event procedure, but not always. Visual Basic guesses at the most common event procedure for the control you double-click. In some cases, such as a text box control, Visual Basic generates a `Change` event procedure's first and last line inside the Code window.
9. True.
10. The `PasswordChar` property lets you hide a user's input when sensitive information is requested that you want to keep private from someone who may be looking over the user's shoulder during data entry.

Exercise Answers

1. `1: Private Sub frmMyApp_Load ()`
2. Lines 1 and 5 indicate that the procedure is a function, and event procedures must be subroutines. Replace `Function` with `Sub` to correct the problem.
3. The three text boxes must have different `Style` properties set for the three different scrollbars. You'll supply the default text in the `Text` property when you write the program. You won't be able to specify multiple lines in the `Text` property, so just put a short word or phrase for the default text.

   Be sure to use `E&xit` for the command button's `Caption` property so that the user can use an accelerator key to end the program.

Day 4, "Creating Menus"

Quiz Answers

1. The Menu Editor helps you create menus.
2. True.
3. Menu options generate the `Click` event only.
4. A shortcut key is a command that triggers a menu option without the user needing to display the menu first.
5. Users can select menu options quickly by using shortcut keys.
6. Shortcut keys mimic mouse clicks on the menu, so they generate `Click` events.
7. False. The Menu Editor helps only with a menu's design, not the code behind the menu.
8. The Checked option lets you display a check mark to the left of a menu option.

9. True. Multiple menu options might be checked, but you can control how many are checked with code if you need to.
10. These lines are remarks and offer program description information, in plain language, to those who maintain the program. The first Bonus Project, "Controls, Properties, and Events," that appeared before today's lesson explains what remarks are and how to use them.

Exercise Answers

1. The Menu Editor contains a set of arrow buttons. When you click the right arrow to produce an ellipsis, the Menu Editor will use the option there at the ellipsis as a drop-down menu option.
2. Manuel needs to understand that he is responsible for unchecking a menu option, within the code, before a check mark goes away. Checked menu options don't have to be mutually exclusive on a menu as they were in today's lesson, so the programmer must specify the exact behavior of the check marks.
3. Open the Code window and click each drop-down menu option in the lower half of the window. Select a shortcut key from the list provided in the Menu Editor. When you run the program again, the shortcut keys will appear next to their corresponding menu options. Test a shortcut key by typing the shortcut key without first displaying the menu that the shortcut key goes to.

Day 5, "Analyzing VB Data"

Quiz Answers

1. Data declaration code goes in the declarations section of a program.
2. You can share local variables between two or more procedures; you'll learn how to do that as you learn more about the Visual Basic language in these 21 days.
3. True.
4. False. A variable can hold different values as the program executes.
5. One division operator performs regular, floating-point division, whereas the other performs integer division.
6. An overloaded operator is an operator that performs two different operations depending on its context in the program.
7. The ampersand is preferred because the plus sign is more commonly used (and understood) as an addition operator.
8. The `Variant` data type can hold any other data type.

9. False. Although Visual Basic does not require the prefixes, you should use them to help document your code.
10. You can put an `Option Explicit` statement at the beginning of a declarations section or check the appropriate option in the Options dialog box. The dialog box acts globally, whereas the `Option Explicit` statement ensures only that its own code module's variables are declared.

Exercise Answers

1. If you said that Visual Basic would issue an error for the middle variable `abc`, that's a good guess but incorrect. Remember that Visual Basic assumes that all declared variables are of the `Variant` data type unless you specify otherwise. Therefore, Visual Basic will declare `abc` as the variable with the `Variant` data type.
2. Visual Basic is computing the division before the addition, but for a true average, Sally must first total the grades as done here:

   ```
   sngAvg = (sngGrade1 + sngGrade2 + sngGrade3) / 3
   ```
3. a. 5

   b. 6

   c. 5

   d. 5

   e. 7
4. a. `a = (3 + 3) / (4 + 4)`

   b. `x = (a - b) * (a - 2) ^ 2`

   c. `f = a ^ (1/2) / b ^ (1/2)`
5. The ampersands concatenate the string literals so that Visual Basic treats them as one continuous literal as the line is continued.

Day 6, "Controlling Programs"

Quiz Answers

1. The `Or` operator returns a `True` result if either value is true.
2. A conditional operator compares two values. A logical operator combines conditional expressions.
3. A loop is one or more statements that can execute more than once.
4. The integer variable will, after the assignment, hold 10 less than it did before the assignment.

5. The loop never executes because `intN` is equal to zero at the top of the loop.
6. If `Exit For` appears without being part of an `If` statement, the `For` loop always executes only once because the `Exit For` terminates the loop the first time through the loop.
7. False. Only one block of an `If...Else` statement ever executes. The `If` block executes if the condition is true, and the `Else` executes if the condition is false.
8. True. If the ending value is already greater than the starting value when the `For` loop first begins, the loop does not execute at all, but the program flow continues at the statement following the `For`.
9. Nest loops when you want to execute a loop more than once.
10. A decision statement may or may not execute its body of code once and only once depending on the decision's result. A looping statement may execute its body of code many times.

Exercise Answers

1. `If (a = b) And (b = c) Then   ' The If's body would follow`
2. Larry's loop never ends because the controlling variable never changes in the body of the loop, so the loop has no way to exit.
3. The clock in a football game perfectly mimics a nested `For` loop. Consider the following code:

```
For Qtr = 1 to 4
  For Minutes = 15 to 0 Step -1
    ' Ball in play
  Next Minutes
Next Qtr
```

   The inner loop counts down from 15 to zero four times, just as the minutes do in a football game, before the quarter increments to two. As long as the quarter variable (`Qtr`) has yet to reach zero, the minutes keep counting down again.

4. The following code uses all three kinds of `Case` statements inside one `Select Case`:

```
Select Case intHours
  Case 1 To 40
    curOverTime = 0.0
  Case 41 To 49
    curOverTime = (intHours - 40) * 1.5 * sngRate
  Case Is >= 50
    curOverTime = ((intHours - 50) * 2 + (10 *  1.5)) * sngRate
End Select
```

Day 7, "Advanced Keyboard and Screen Support"

Quiz Answers

1. An internal function uses an argument value that you send to it and returns a new value based on that argument.
2. True.
3. `Empty` is the keyword equivalent to an empty string.
4. False. Actually, the tables all describe *one* argument, the `MsgBox()` function's second argument referred to in today's lesson with the *`intStyle`* placeholder.
5. Visual Basic uses the application's name for the title if you don't specify a window title.
6. The user can select as many check boxes as necessary but the user can select at most one option button on a form or frame at any one time.
7. True—if you assign all their values to `False` when the form first loads (such as in the `Form_Load()` event procedure).
8. A `Value` property of 1 or 0 indicates that a check box is checked or unchecked.
9. A `Value` property of `True` or `False` indicates that an option button is selected or not.
10. If you want to place groups of option buttons on a form so that the user can select one option button from any group at the same time, you must place the groups on a frame.

Exercise Answers

1. Check to see if the `InputBox()` function returns an empty string. You can test against the empty string literal, `""`. If the function returns anything other than a match against `""`, the return value is the user's valid answer.
2. Use the following statement to produce the message box shown:

```
strAns = MsgBox("You are out of paper", vbExclamation + _
vbDefaultButton2 +
 vbAbortRetryIgnore, "For Printer")
```

3. The following event procedure merges the user's city and state and displays the merged string in a message box:

```
Private Sub cmdGetLocation_Click()
' Get the user's city and state in 2 separate input boxes.
' Concatenate them together.
```

```
4:  ' Display the merged string.
5:     Dim strCity As String
6:     Dim strState As String
7:     Dim strBoth As String
8:     ' Placeholder for MsgBox() return
9:     Dim intAnswer As Integer
10:
11:      ' Ask user for city and state
12:      strCity = InputBox("What is your city?", "Get city")
13:      strState = InputBox("What is your state?", "Get state")
14:
15:      ' Concatenate the strings
16:      strBoth = strCity & ", " & strState
17:
18:      ' Display the merged string
19:      intAnswer = MsgBox("You live in " & strBoth, "Location")
20: End Sub
```


Note

Notice that line 9 declares a placeholder integer variable for the `MsgBox()` function. The user's selection of OK or Cancel really doesn't matter when line 19 displays the message but you still must provide a place for the return value to go.

4. Your option button procedures will all be `Click` event procedures because `Click` is the event procedure that triggers when the user clicks any of the option buttons. You do not have to concern yourself with clearing one option button when the user selects another because Visual Basic takes care of that.

Day 8, "The Nature of VB Programs"

Quiz Answers

1. Public variables have the broadest scope.
2. Local variables have the narrowest scope.
3. True. All arguments are passed by reference unless you specify `ByVal`.
4. Subroutine procedures cannot return values.
5. `IIf()` and `Choose()` as shortcuts to the `If` statement.
6. `Choose()` returns Null if its first argument is less than 1.
7. `Abs()` returns the absolute value of its argument.
8. a. `74135-`

b. `12 2 pm` (the answer depends on the day and time the statement executes)

c. 12345.67

9. `intN` will hold 192.

10. `Now` returns both the date and time where `Time` returns only the time.

Exercise Answers

1. The code that follows contains the `SalesTax()` function.

```
Private Sub GetTotal()
' This procedure collects totals from a form
' and sends the grand total and a discount
' percentage to a sales tax procedure
  Dim curTotal As Currency
  Dim sngDisc As Single   ' Special tax discount
  '
  ' Collect the totals from the form's text boxes
  curTotal = txtSale1.Text + txtSale2.Text + txtSale3.txt
  '
  ' Send the total to a sales tax procedure
  intMsg = MsgBox("The sales tax is " & SalesTax(curTotal, _
  sngDisc))
End Sub

Public Function SalesTax(curTotal As Currency, sngRateDisc As _
Single) As Currency
' Compute sales tax and deduct percentage discount
  Dim curSalesTax As Currency
  '
  ' This code appears in the lesson as a subrouutine
  ' The following computes a tax based
  ' on 3% plus a millage of 1/2 percent
  curSalesTax = (curTotal * .03) + (curTotal * .005)
  '
  ' Now, deduct percentage discount
  curSalesTax = curSalesTax - (sngRateDisc * curTotal)
  '
  ' Set up the return value
  SalesTax = curSalesTax
  '
  ' Procedures automatically return to their
  ' calling procedure when finished
End Function
```

2. The following `IIf()` function does the same work as the `If` statement:

```
strTitle = IIf(intTotal > 1000, "Good job!", "Didn't meet goal")
```

3. The following `Choose()` function does the same work as the `If` statement:

```
Choose(ID, intBonus = 50, intBonus = 75, intBonus = 100)
```

4. `intN` holds –6, `intO` holds –5, and `intP` holds – 6.

Day 9, "The Dialog Box Control"

Quiz Answers

1. You must add the control to your Toolbox window from the Project, Components menu option.
2. The Common Dialog Box control displays the Color selection, File Open, File Save, Font selection, Print, and Windows Help dialog boxes.
3. The Common Dialog Box control produces one of six standard dialog boxes.
4. The form's Common Dialog Box control is there just for placement and not for looks because the Common Dialog Box control does not show up on the running application. The Common Dialog Box control appears only when the user triggers one of the Common Dialog Box control methods that displays the dialog box in the middle of the screen.
5. True.
6. The `Filter` property determines which file types display in the File-related dialog boxes.
7. The `Flags` property sets up a common dialog box before you display the dialog box with a method.
8. True.
9. False. The Print dialog box requires no preset `Flags` values, although you'll almost always assign values to `Flags`, such as the `DialogTitle` property, before displaying the dialog box.
10. False; you must further qualify the method, such as `ShowFont` and `ShowPrinter`.

Exercise Answers

1. The following code sets up the Font dialog box with error-handling for the Cancel command button click:

```
' Assumes CancelError is True
On Error Goto dbErrHandler
' Set the Font Flags property.
CdbFont.Flags = cdlCFBoth Or cdlCFEffects
CdbFont.ShowFont  ' Display the Font DB
' Set a label's properties to the
' user's selected font information
LblMessage.Font.Name = CdbFont.FontName
LblMessage.Font.Size = CdbFont.FontSize
LblMessage.Font.Bold = CdbFont.FontBold
```

```
  LblMessage.Font.Italic = CdbFont.FontItalic
  LblMessage.Font.Underline = CdbFont.FontUnderline
  LblMessage.FontStrikethru = CdbFont.FontStrikethru
  LblMessage.ForeColor = CdbFont.Color
  Exit Sub  ' Don't fall through

dbErrHandler:
  ' User clicked the Cancel button
  Exit Sub  ' Don't change the font
```

2. The following code produces the Print dialog box shown in Figure 9.10:

```
Private Sub mnuFileOpen_Click ()
' Assumes CancelError is True
  On Error Goto dbErrHandler
  ' Determine what appears in
  ' the Files of type text box
  cdbFile.Filter = "Text Files (*.txt) | *.txt"
  ' Specify default filter
  cdbFile.FilterIndex = 1
  cdbFile.DialogTitle = "Open"
  ' Display the Open dialog box.
  cdbFile.ShowOpen

  '**********************************
  ' You must place code here or call *
  ' a procedure to open the file     *
  ' selected by the user             *
  '**********************************
  Exit Sub  ' Don't fall through

dbErrHandler:
  ' User clicked the Cancel button
  Exit Sub  ' Don't open a file
End Sub
```

Day 10, "Adding Power with the Mouse and Controls"

Quiz Answers

1. The `MouseDown` event responds to specific mouse buttons and lets you know which button the user clicked through the arguments the events pass to their procedures. The `Click`, `DblClick`, and `MouseUp` events don't keep track of which button the user clicked to generate them.
2. Check the intButton argument to determine the button clicked.

3. Select the icon's path in the control's `DragIcon` property value.
4. Ignore some timer events that occur and respond only when a certain amount of time has passed.
5. You can initialize the control at design time by putting items in the `List` property, or you can set them at runtime (the more common method) by adding them with the `AddItem` method.
6. The list control's `Value` property determines which index item the user has selected.
7. You can remove the items one at a time using the `RemoveItem` method, or you can use the `Clear` method to remove all the items at once.
8. When the focus moves, the triggered event procedure can then add the new item to the list.
9. Set the `Sorted` property to `True`.
10. Twenty-three elements are reserved by the statement.

Exercise Answers

1. You can create a form with a list box control and initialize it with the following code in the `Form_Load()` event procedure:

```
Private Sub Form_Load()
   lstFamily.AddItem ("Martha")
   lstFamily.AddItem ("William")
   lstFamily.AddItem ("Clyde")
   lstFamily.AddItem ("Larry")
   lstFamily.AddItem ("Sandy")
   lstFamily.AddItem ("Pauline")
   lstFamily.AddItem ("Paul")
   lstFamily.AddItem ("Eddie")
   lstFamily.AddItem ("Carlton")
   lstFamily.AddItem ("Charlie")
   lstFamily.AddItem ("Robert")
End Sub
```

2. No answer is necessary for this exercise.
3. Once you add the three combo boxes, you must write a `Change` event procedure for each one. When one combo box changes, you have to assign the item at the value index (the selected item just added) to the *end* of the other combo box lists by using the `AddItem` method and putting the item at the `ListCount` index of those controls.

Day 11, "Working with Forms"

Quiz Answers

1. When the `Resize` event occurs, you can center your controls within the new form's size measurements.
2. The `ScaleMode` property determines which unit of measurement subsequent `Print` methods use for the `CurrentX` and `CurrentY` coordinate location.
3. The first subscript is 0.
4. False. SDI applications *can* support multiple forms, but not when each form window holds a different data set.
5. An MDI application may have multiple form windows with different sets of data.
6. Toolbars most often appear across the top of forms.
7. The image list control holds the toolbar's icons.
8. The image list control does nothing but hold the icons for the coolbar control. The image list control will not appear on the form at runtime, so its location does not matter.
9. `Spc()` inserts a fixed number of spaces on a line of output, and `Tab()` sends the text cursor to a specific column.
10. Use the `Print` method but don't place anything to the right of the method to print.

Exercise Answers

1. No answer or help is necessary for this exercise. If you can locate the control, you've added the control properly from the Project, Components menu option.
2. The output of the two `Print` methods appear next to each other due to the trailing semicolon at the end of the first `Print` method:

   ```
   Line 1Line 2
   ```

3. No answer is necessary for this practice exercise.
4. In the `Click` event procedure, you should have a `For` statement that looks something like this:

   ```
   For intCtr = 1 To 100
      Form1.Print intCtr; " ";
   Next intCtr
   ```

5. The following code counts the number of controls in all forms within an application:

   ```
   ' Set the count to zero before you count
   ```

```
intCount = 0
' Step through each form
For intCtr = 1 to Forms.Count
   ' Add the number of controls in each form
   intCount = intCount + Forms(intCtr).Count
Next intCtr
```

Day 12, "Interact with Files"

Quiz Answers

1. You can close all open files with one `Close` statement.
2. The `FreeFile()` function returns the next unused file number.
3. Visual Basic overwrites a file, if one exists, that you attempt to open for sequential output.
4. Visual Basic adds to the end of the sequential file at the next file output statement.
5. The statement opens a sequential file and lets subsequent output statements write to the end of the file.
6. Random files must be able to calculate the location of any given record number; therefore, the records must be of uniform length for the calculation to work.
7. The fixed-length strings allows for fixed-length records, whereas variable-length strings would produce records of different lengths.
8. The `Type` statement defines new data types.
9. False. The statement defines a new data type but declares no variables of that type.
10. `Dir()`, with an argument, returns the first file found that matches your wildcard characters. `Dir()`, without an argument, returns the next file in the folder that matches your wildcard characters.

Exercise Answers

1. Frannie probably is attempting to remove the Bills folder while it contains files. The `RmDir` command refuses to remove folders that contain files.
2. The following procedure fills the arrays in lines 10 through 14 and writes the arrays to the open disk file in lines 21 through 23:

```
1:  Private Sub output ()
2:    Dim strNames(5) As String
3:    Dim intAges(5) As Integer
4:    Dim strColors(5) As String
5:
6:    Dim intCtr As Integer    ' Loop counter
```

```
    Dim intFNum As Integer  ' File number

    ' Get array info
    For intCtr = 0 To 4
       strNames(intCtr) = InputBox("What is next name?", "Get _
       names")
       intAges(intCtr) = InputBox("What is next age?", "Get ages")
       strColors(intCtr) = InputBox("What is next color?", "Get _
       colors")
     Next intCtr

     intFNum = FreeFile

     ' Write output
     ' Change the path if you want
    Open "C:\Stuff.txt" For Output As #intFNum
     For intCtr = 0 To 4
       Write #intFNum, strNames(intCtr), intAges(intCtr), _
       strColors(intCtr)
     Next intCtr

     Close #intFNum
  End Sub
```

3. Create a dialog box similar to the one in Figure 12.1. For each of the three file-related list boxes, you need to write an event procedure that updates the other two. The event that triggers the event procedure depends on the control. The directory list box supports a `Change` event, so in that control's `Change` event procedure, you must also change the files displayed, because the directory will now be different. Here's an example:

```
Private Sub Direct_Change()
  ' The user changed the directory list box
  filFile.Path = dirList.Path  ' Change the file control
  '
  ' Ensure that only one file is selected
  If (filFile.ListCount > 0) Then
    ' Select the first file from list
    filFile.ListIndex = 0
  End If
End Sub
```

When the user selects a different drive, you must change the path to that drive (which, in turn, will trigger the previous event procedure), like this:

```
Private Sub Drive_Change()
  ' Sets the default path to the drive
  dirList.Path = drvList.Drive
End Sub
```

Day 13, "Printing VB Output"

Quiz Answers

1. Reference the value in `Printers.Count-1` to determine the number of printers on the system.
2. True.
3. The `ScaleMode` property determines the measurement Visual Basic uses.
4. Use the `NewPage` method to send printed output to a new page.
5. The `Is TypeOf` statement tests objects for data types.
6. True.
7. False. `KillDoc` cancels only the application's printed output.
8. Use `Me` as a shortcut reference to the current form.
9. `PrintForm` uses the screen's resolution for output.
10. Set the `AutoRedraw` property to `True` before you print forms.

Exercise Answers

1. The following line writes *Printing Peter* to the printer starting at column 32:

   ```
   Printer.Print Tab(32); "Printing Peter"
   ```

2. Patty needs to realize that Windows supports various fonts and font sizes so her calculations for page length (determining when a page fills up) has to take into account the size of the fonts she uses.
3. The following code completes Listing 13.2:

```
Public Function IsColor() As Boolean
  Dim blnIsColor As Boolean
  Dim prnPrntr As Printer
  '
  ' Assume no color printer is found yet
  blnIsColor = False
  '
  ' Look through all the printers
  For Each prnPrntr In Printers
    If prnPrntr.ColorMode = vbPRCMColor Then
      ' Set color printer as system default.
      Set Printer = prnPrntr
      blnIsColor = True
      Exit For  ' Don't look further
    End If
  Next   ' Step through all of them if needed
  '
```

```
    ' blnIsColor will still be false if no color
    ' printer is present and true if one is present
    ' Set the function's return value accordingly
    IsColor = blnIsColor
End Function
```

Day 14, "Introducing VB Graphics and Multimedia"

Quiz Answers

1. The shape control draws circles.
2. The shape control draws squares (and rectangles).
3. The `PSet` and `Line` methods draw boxes on the form.
4. True.
5. The `B` option adds a solid interior to boxes.
6. Not all buttons are required by all multimedia control devices.
7. Returns the state of the multimedia control's device.
8. Decrease the value in the `UpdateInterval` property to increase the frequency that the multimedia control device updates.
9. The picture box control holds the video's output.
10. Your code must set the Windows device context to the picture box control so that the multimedia control will know where to send its video output.

Exercise Answers

1. The Code window to support the extra list boxes should contain code that works like the following:

```
Private Sub Form_Load()
   ' Initialize the shape drop-down list box
   lstShape.AddItem "0 - Rectangle"
   lstShape.AddItem "1 - Square"
   lstShape.AddItem "2 - Oval"
   lstShape.AddItem "3 - Circle"
   lstShape.AddItem "4 - Rounded Rectangle"
   lstShape.AddItem "5 - Rounded Square"

   ' Initialize the FillStyle pattern drop-down list box
   lstPattern.AddItem "0 - Solid"
   lstPattern.AddItem "1 - Transparent"
   lstPattern.AddItem "2 - Horizontal Line"
```

```
  lstPattern.AddItem "3 - Vertical Line"
  lstPattern.AddItem "4 - Upward Diagonal"
  lstPattern.AddItem "5 - Downward Diagonal"
  lstPattern.AddItem "6 - Cross"
  lstPattern.AddItem "7 - Diagonal Cross"

  ' Initialize the FillColor pattern drop-down list box
  ' (not all colors represented)
  lstFillColor.AddItem "Black"
  lstFillColor.AddItem "White"
  lstFillColor.AddItem "Blue"
  lstFillColor.AddItem "Red"
  lstFillColor.AddItem "Green"
  lstFillColor.AddItem "Yellow"

  ' Initialize the BorderColor drop-down list box
  lstBorderColor.AddItem "Black"
  lstBorderColor.AddItem "White"
  lstBorderColor.AddItem "Blue"
  lstBorderColor.AddItem "Red"
  lstBorderColor.AddItem "Green"
  lstBorderColor.AddItem "Yellow"

  ' Set the first value of each list as default
  lstShape.ListIndex = 0
  lstPattern.ListIndex = 0
  lstFillColor.ListIndex = 0
  lstBorderColor.ListIndex = 0
End Sub

Private Sub lstPattern_Click()
  ' Change the pattern according to the selection
  shpSample.FillStyle = lstPattern.ListIndex
End Sub

Private Sub lstShape_Click()
  ' Change the shape according to the selection
  shpSample.Shape = lstShape.ListIndex
End Sub

Private Sub lstFillColor_Click()
  ' Change the fill color according to the selection
  Select Case lstFillColor.ListIndex
    Case 0:
       shpSample.FillColor = vbBlack
    Case 1:
       shpSample.FillColor = vbWhite
    Case 2:
       shpSample.FillColor = vbBlue
    Case 3:
       shpSample.FillColor = vbRed
```

```
    Case 4:
        shpSample.FillColor = vbGreen
    Case 5:
        shpSample.FillColor = vbYellow
    End Select
End Sub

Private Sub lstBorderColor_Click()
  ' Change the border color according to the selection
  Select Case lstBorderColor.ListIndex
  Case 0:
     shpSample.BorderColor = vbBlack
  Case 1:
     shpSample.BorderColor = vbWhite
  Case 2:
    shpSample.BorderColor = vbBlue
  Case 3:
     shpSample.BorderColor = vbRed
  Case 4:
      shpSample.BorderColor = vbGreen
  Case 5:
      shpSample.BorderColor = vbYellow
  End Select
End Sub

Private Sub mnuFileExit_Click()
  End
End Sub
```

2. No answer is necessary for this practice exercise.
3. You must use the common dialog box control to set up the File Open dialog box. Add a File, Open menu option to allow for the display of the dialog box. Be sure to set the filter to WAV files only. Once the user selects the file, that filename should be assigned to the `Filename` property and then the audio clip can be played.

Day 15, "Using Form Templates"

Quiz Answers

1. Form templates enable you to add standard forms to your applications and to speed up your program development.
2. You can add form templates from within the Application Wizard, from the Project, Add dialog box, and by right-clicking the Project window and selecting Add, Form from the pop-up menu.
3. Simply apply the `Show` method to the About box's form when the user selects Help, About from your application's menu.

4. False. The About box already contains the necessary code for displaying the System Information dialog box.
5. A splash screen should stay onscreen for a limited period of time during the program's startup.
6. The Tip of the Day dialog box stays onscreen as long as the user wants it to, whereas the splash screen appears only briefly as an introduction. In addition, the Tip of the Day screen keeps displaying additional tips as the user clicks the Next Tip button. The user can also turn off the Tip of the Day screen so that it does not appear the next time the application begins. On the other hand, the Splash screen always appears when the application starts.
7. The SaveSettings entry, when used in conjunction with a Tip of the Day dialog box, specifies whether or not the user wants to see a Tip of the Day screen.
8. *ODBC* stands for *Open Database Connectivity.* It provides a standard way to access databases from different computer systems.
9. You must make the Tip of the Day dialog box or the splash screen the startup form.
10. The tip file is a text file that you create with a text editor such as Notepad. The file contains one line for each tip. You must store the tip file in the same folder as the application that uses it.

Exercise Answers

1. The chapter's text describes how to make this change.
2. No answer is necessary for this project. The most complicated requirement is creating the set of tips in Notepad.

Day 16, "Objects and Visual Basic"

Quiz Answers

1. When you link an OLE object, the object stays with its parent application. When you embed an OLE object, your application gets a copy of the object. If an embedded object is modified within the parent application, your application will not know about the change.
2. Embedding takes the most disk space because a copy of the object must appear with your application.
3. False. You must write code that saves and loads any changes to the OLE object.
4. The `SaveToFile` method saves objects to disk.

5. The `ReadFromFile` method loads objects from disk.
6. The `If TypeOf` statement and the `TypeOf()` function test for object classes.
7. False. System objects are global already, so you don't ever pass them between procedures.
8. Functions, named constants, internal functions, procedures, and classes often appear in the Members list.
9. Visual Basic groups all members and classes by their purpose instead of alphabetically when you group the Members list.
10. False. One of the Object Browser's most rewarding features is its capability to locate your own application's objects.

Exercise Answers

1. The `With` clause saves no programming effort when only two properties are being set.
2. Follow this lesson's instructions for adding a WordPad object to an application (but add the Paint object instead). You must use the save and load OLE data code listings shown in this lesson to save and load your drawings. Although this exercise requires little in the way of an answer, by performing this exercise, you'll gather experience using OLE objects inside other applications.

Day 17, "ActiveX Controls"

Quiz Answers

1. *Automation* is the process of borrowing another application's functionality to create that application's data object.
2. Another instance of Word will start and many system resources will be eaten up by the two redundant processes.
3. You cannot store applications in variables, so you must create a reference to an application through the `Set` command.
4. If you trap an error with the `On Error` statement, you can determine the error that occurred by testing the `Err.Number` value.
5. You can create ActiveX controls by subclassing simple controls, by subclassing aggregate controls, and by creating user-drawn controls.
6. The simplest ActiveX control to create is one you subclass as a simple control.
7. True.

8. Enumeration blocks are used to define enumerated constant lists.
9. Visual Basic uses the .OCX extension for ActiveX controls you create.
10. ActiveX controls require at least a `Get` and a `Let` procedure so that you can assign and read property values.

Exercise Answers

1. No answer is necessary.
2. You must first declare a variable that will hold the original text. You then can save the text in the variable before converting the text to uppercase or lowercase. You could create a public variable that retains its value when the procedure that converts the case terminates. The variable could hold the original contents of the text box.

   Given that local variables are better than public variables, the public variable option leaves a lot to be desired. Although there are several ways to save the original text box value, perhaps the simplest would be to place a hidden text box on the form (keep the text box's `Enabled` property `True` but its `Visible` property `False`). As soon as the user enters text in the ActiveX control, the ActiveX control's `Text` property should be saved in the hidden text box's `Text` property. When the user clicks the As Entered command button, the ActiveX control's `Text` property needs to be assigned the hidden text box's text value. *Hint:* Be sure to update the hidden text box's `Text` property every time the user types a new value in the ActiveX control (as you would do in the `Change` event procedure).

Day 18, "Interacting with Data"

Quiz Answers

1. The Visual Data Manager lets you analyze databases.
2. A table is a data file located inside a database.
3. False. The number of columns does not grow unless you expand the fields in your database.
4. True. A table is one form of a recordset.
5. A *bound control* is a control bound to a database control, such as the data control, that displays records as the user steps through the database.
6. A *recordset* is a collection of records, including (but not limited to) the records in a table. A *dynaset* is a collection of records that differs from the default order, perhaps a set of records that meet a specific criteria. The dynaset changes as the

database changes. A *snapshot* is a dynaset from a specific location in time. In other words, a snapshot is a recordset that does not change but that contains certain records with database values as they appeared at the time the snapshot was created.

7. The ADO is quicker, more powerful, and more flexible than the data control.
8. EOF determines the end of a table, and BOF represents the beginning of a table.
9. A Master view is one record, and a Detail view is a set of records that go with the master record. A one-to-many relationship exists in the Master/Detail view; for example, one vendor may have sold multiple products to your company over time.
10. The Visual Basic Application Wizard will generate forms directly from your database table structure.

Exercise Answers

1. Don't add additional data controls to the form. You only need to add additional text box controls and link them to the data control already there. Set the `DataSource` property in each text box control to the data control and set the `DataField` property in each text box control to its corresponding column (field) in the table.
2. To form a one-to-many relationship, you must select two tables that have at least one field in common. When you select the Master/Detail form type, the next window gives you the chance to select the table you want to use for the master record source. Select the Authors table from the list and send the Author field to the right list so that only the author's name appears for the Master view side of the form. After you click Next, the Detail Source Record window appears. From it you can select the Title Author table. Send the ISBN field to the right list and click Next to display the window shown in Figure A.1. Highlight both the fields named `Au_ID` (the only common field) to connect the records. When you run the application, the author's name will appear at the top of the form, and the ISBNs for each book the author wrote will follow in the lower section of the form.

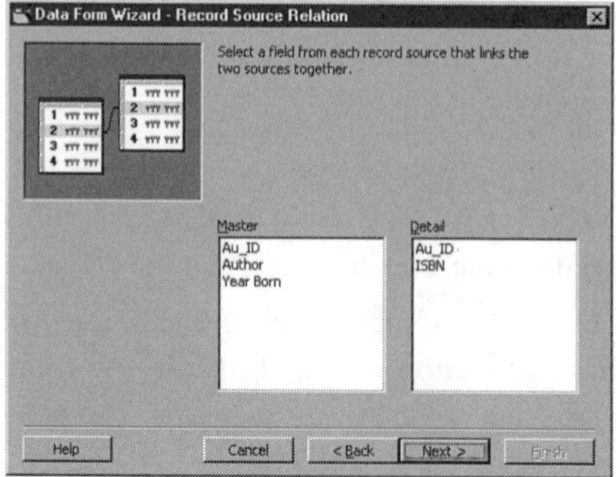

FIGURE A.1.

You must tell the wizard how to link the two sets of fields.

Day 19, "Adding Internet Access"

Quiz Answers

1. The generated application's Web browser will display the Web page at the URL you supply when the application's user logs onto the Internet.
2. False. Your applications will contain an embedded Web browser that the user can use no matter what Web browser your users have installed on their system.
3. True. You must have the Internet Explorer 4 Web browser installed on your system to use Visual Basic's full Web programming features. This browser comes with Visual Basic (if you do not have it already installed). You do not have to make Internet Explorer your default Web browser, but it is the browser that Visual Basic requires for development.
4. Encapsulation, in its most elementary form, refers to the packaging together of code and properties so that an object carries with it its own behaviors and descriptions.
5. Some of the Visual Basic 6 controls provide direct access to the Microsoft Network online service. Of course, if your end users do not have access to Microsoft Network, the controls will not allow the user to log onto the Microsoft Network.
6. An intranet is an internal Internet-like connection made between networked computers.
7. An ActiveX document is a Web page that contains a full-featured Visual Basic application.
8. Java is a C++-like programming language that enables its authors to write small programs, called applets, that travel the Web pages and execute on an end user's PC when the he or she views the applet's Web page.
9. The VBScript language works with HTML to load ActiveX documents.
10. Use the ActiveX Document Migration Wizard to convert existing applications into ActiveX documents.

Exercise Answers

1. After converting an application to an ActiveX document, you can add that ActiveX document to the Office Binder application. The Office Binder is nothing more than an ActiveX control container. Until you learn how to compile to EXE files in Day 21's lesson, you'll have to experiment with the Office shortcut bar while keeping Visual Basic running. After converting to an ActiveX document, start the Office Binder program, display the Section menu, and click Add to display the Add

Selection dialog box. Locate and double-click your ActiveX document, and the document will appear on your Office Binder collection of tools. Therefore, in an Office project, you could integrate non-Office applications in a project alongside Office documents to complement an entire presentation of programs.

2. With the multiple forms, the Migration Wizard will have to create several ActiveX documents. You must test each one individually by start your Web browser and selecting File, Open for each ActiveX document created from each form in the project.

Day 20, "Providing Help"

Quiz Answers

1. You must use RTF (Rich Text Format) files for the Help text and an HPJ project file, unless you use HTML help in which case your Help file ends in the extension CHM.
2. The user can move from Help topic to Help topic without returning to an index.
3. The `K` footnote label is used to connect Help to underlined topics.
4. The Help project file identifies the Help file, Help page context IDs, and the Help engine's title bar text. The Help compiler uses the project file during the Help file's compilation.
5. Use the Project Properties dialog box to attach Help to the F1 key.
6. Use context ID values to target specific Help topics to context-sensitive Help objects.
7. False. The context-sensitive IDs use the numeric Help context IDs.
8. The ToolTips pop up when the user rests the mouse cursor over an item, and the What's This? Help appears only when requested from the Help menu or from the user's click of the What's This? title bar button.
9. Set the form's `WhatsThisButton` property to `True` to turn on the What's This? button on a form's title bar.
10. True.

Exercise Answer

Expand on this lesson's example. Adding the other Help topics will be simple. Follow these guidelines:

1. Make sure that each object's `ToolTips` property has a value.

2. Create a context-sensitive Help message for each object on the form.
3. Assign context ID values in the project file for each Help topic.
4. Compile the Help file.

Day 21, "Distributing Your Applications"

Quiz Answers

1. A syntax error is a mistake in spelling or a language misuse.
2. The computer catches syntax errors but people must catch logic errors.
3. True.
4. False. If an application has a syntax error, Visual Basic will not let the application execute until you fix the bug.
5. The Visual Basic debugger lets you halt a program at any point by placing breakpoints in the code. You then can rest your mouse cursor over a variable to read its runtime value or place that variable in the Watch window.
6. By executing a program one line at a time, you can analyze variable and control values at your pace as well as check your logic and the program flow.
7. True. You can place assignment statements inside the Immediate window.
8. A compiled Visual Basic program runs much faster than one you run from inside the Visual Basic environment.
9. The Package and Deployment Wizard creates installation routines for your applications.
10. The Package and Deployment Wizard can create a multiple-disk installation set of files.

Exercise Answers

1. The statement includes a syntax error because `Therefore` replaces `Then` in the `If` statement's first line.
2. True. Not only does the sentence have a syntax error due to the misspelling, but the sentence also has a logic error. Instead of two errors, the sentence only has one error. Therefore, the sentence's logic is incorrect!

A

Day 22, "Multidimensional Arrays"

Quiz Answers

1. False. All elements in every row and column of an array with any number of subscripts must be the same data type.
2. The second subscript (9) generally determines the number of rows in the multidimensional array.
3. a. 4

   b. 43

   c. 12
4. True.
5. False. `Array()` works only for one-dimensional arrays.
6. The grid control displays table data effectively.
7. The fixed rows and columns act as title cells in the grid.
8. You should use a nested loop to assign the elements of a table to a grid.
9. False. You must assign the `CellPicture` property at runtime using the `LoadPicture()` internal function or assign an image control to the cell's `CellPicture` property.
10. `FormatString` is easier to use and is more efficient than assignment statements for setting up a grid's header titles.

Exercise Answers

1. Twenty-eight elements are reserved.
2. Thirty elements are reserved (remember the zero subscript).
3. Perhaps the best place to store the grid values in the table is in the `cmdExit_Click()` procedure, as shown here:

```
Private Sub cmdExit_Click()
  ' Terminate application and save values
  Dim curData(19, 7) As Currency
  ' Fill the table from the grid data
  For Row = 1 To 19
    For Column = 1 To 7
      grdSales.Row = Row
      grdSales.Col = Column
      curData(Row, Column) = grdSales(Row, Column)
    Next Column
  Next Row
```

```
   ' Quit the program
   End
End Sub
```

Day 23, "The Windows API"

Quiz Answers

1. *API* stands for *Application Programming Interface.*
2. Although Visual Basic includes many functions, it does not do everything. For example, Visual Basic does not include a function that reboots your system. The Windows API routines provide system-level functions you can access from your Visual Basic application.
3. DLLs are dynamically linked to your application at runtime, not at compilation time. This means that the resources for the DLLs are not set aside by the operating system for the full execution of your program.
4. When Windows 95 moved to a 32-bit operating environment, the names of the standard DLL files changed as well. To distinguish the new files from the old, Microsoft added "32" to the name (for example, GDI32.DLL).
5. The API Viewer is a tool you can add to your Visual Basic environment (through the Add-Ins menu) that lets you select from lists of API routines and view the declarations for those routines. You then can copy and paste those declarations into your own applications.
6. The `Declare` statement declares Windows API routines.
7. False. Virtually nothing about the Windows API routines are standard. Even among families of similar routines, the argument lists can differ greatly as well as the return data types for the function-based routines.
8. The `Declare` statement informs Visual Basic of the external Windows API routine's location and argument list. Visual Basic does not recognize such external routines because it includes its own set of internal functions, which are different from the Windows set of procedures. The `Declare` statement enables Visual Basic to locate and properly connect to the Windows API routine you need to call from your application.
9. Use the `Private` qualifier when declaring Windows API routines from inside a form module.
10. A *wrapper* is Visual Basic code you place around a Windows API call. Such wrappers can appear in a general Visual Basic code module that you write and maintain for subsequent applications that require API routines. Instead of requiring the API

Viewer and looking up exact argument data types and requirements, you only need to call the Visual Basic procedures that you've placed around the API routines. Debugging will be easier, and you'll complete applications that require API Windows routines faster.

Exercise Answer

The KERNEL32.DLL file contains the `GetSystemTime()` function. You can tell by selecting the `GetSystemTime()` function from the API Viewer and looking at the argument that names the file that contains the function.

APPENDIX B

Operator Precedence

Table B.1 lists the operator preference order. The table includes the operators grouped by their type of operation.

TABLE B.1. VISUAL BASIC'S ORDER OF OPERATORS.

Arithmetic	*Comparison*	*Logical*
Exponentiation (^)	Equality (=)	`Not`
Negation (-)	Inequality (<>)	`And`
Multiplication and division (*, /)	Less than (<)	`Or`
Integer division (\)	Greater than (>)	`Xor`
Modulus arithmetic (`Mod`)	Less than or equal to (<=)	`Eqv`
Addition and subtraction (+, -)	Greater than or equal to (>=)	`Imp`
String concatenation (&)	`Like`, `Is`	

APPENDIX C

ASCII Table

Dec X_{10}	*Hex* X_{16}	*Binary* X_2	*ASCII Character*
000	00	0000 0000	null
001	01	0000 0001	☺
002	02	0000 0010	☻
003	03	0000 0011	♥
004	04	0000 0100	♦
005	05	0000 0101	♣
006	06	0000 0110	♠
007	07	0000 0111	•
008	08	0000 1000	◘
009	09	0000 1001	○
010	0A	0000 1010	◙
011	0B	0000 1011	♂
012	0C	0000 1100	♀
013	0D	0000 1101	♪
014	0E	0000 1110	♫
015	0F	0000 1111	☼
016	10	0001 0000	►
017	11	0001 0001	◄
018	12	0001 0010	↕
019	13	0001 0011	‼
020	14	0001 0100	¶
021	15	0001 0101	§
022	16	0001 0110	▬
023	17	0001 0111	↨
024	18	0001 1000	↑
025	19	0001 1001	↓
026	1A	0001 1010	→
027	1B	0001 1011	←
028	1C	0001 1100	∟
029	1D	0001 1101	↔
030	1E	0001 1110	▲

Dec X_{10}	*Hex* X_{16}	*Binary* X_{2}	*ASCII Character*
031	1F	0001 1111	▼
032	20	0010 0000	space
033	21	0010 0001	!
034	22	0010 0010	"
035	23	0010 0011	#
036	24	0010 0100	$
037	25	0010 0101	%
038	26	0010 0110	&
039	27	0010 0111	'
040	28	0010 1000	(
041	29	0010 1001	)
042	2A	0010 1010	*
043	2B	0010 1011	+
044	2C	0010 1100	´
045	2D	0010 1101	-
046	2E	0010 1110	.
047	2F	0010 1111	/
048	30	0011 0000	0
049	31	0011 0001	1
050	32	0011 0010	2
051	33	0011 0011	3
052	34	0011 0100	4
053	35	0011 0101	5
054	36	0011 0110	6
055	37	0011 0111	7
056	38	0011 1000	8
057	39	0011 1001	9
058	3A	0011 1010	:
059	3B	0011 1011	;
060	3C	0011 1100	<
061	3D	0011 1101	=

Dec X_{10}	Hex X_{16}	Binary X_2	ASCII Character
062	3E	0011 1110	>
063	3F	0011 1111	?
064	40	0100 0000	@
065	41	0100 0001	A
066	42	0100 0010	B
067	43	0100 0011	C
068	44	0100 0100	D
069	45	0100 0101	E
070	46	0100 0110	F
071	47	0100 0111	G
072	48	0100 1000	H
073	49	0100 1001	I
074	4A	0100 1010	J
075	4B	0100 1011	K
076	4C	0100 1100	L
077	4D	0100 1101	M
078	4E	0100 1110	N
079	4F	0100 1111	O
080	50	0101 0000	P
081	51	0101 0001	Q
082	52	0101 0010	R
083	53	0101 0011	S
084	54	0101 0100	T
085	55	0101 0101	U
086	56	0101 0110	V
087	57	0101 0111	W
088	58	0101 1000	X
089	59	0101 1001	Y
090	5A	0101 1010	Z
091	5B	0101 1011	[
092	5C	0101 1100	\

Dec X_{10}	*Hex* X_{16}	*Binary* X_2	*ASCII Character*
093	5D	0101 1101	]
094	5E	0101 1110	^
095	5F	0101 1111	_
096	60	0110 0000	`
097	61	0110 0001	a
098	62	0110 0010	b
099	63	0110 0011	c
100	64	0110 0100	d
101	65	0110 0101	e
102	66	0110 0110	f
103	67	0110 0111	g
104	68	0110 1000	h
105	69	0110 1001	i
106	6A	0110 1010	j
107	6B	0110 1011	k
108	6C	0110 1100	l
109	6D	0110 1101	m
110	6E	0110 1110	n
111	6F	0110 1111	o
112	70	0111 0000	p
113	71	0111 0001	q
114	72	0111 0010	r
115	73	0111 0011	s
116	74	0111 0100	t
117	75	0111 0101	u
118	76	0111 0110	v
119	77	0111 0111	w
120	78	0111 1000	x
121	79	0111 1001	y
122	7A	0111 1010	z
123	7B	0111 1011	{

Dec X_{10}	*Hex* X_{16}	*Binary* X_2	*ASCII Character*
124	7C	0111 1100	¦
125	7D	0111 1101	}
126	7E	0111 1110	~
127	7F	0111 1111	Δ
128	80	1000 0000	Ç
129	81	1000 0001	ü
130	82	1000 0010	é
131	83	1000 0011	â
132	84	1000 0100	ä
133	85	1000 0101	à
134	86	1000 0110	å
135	87	1000 0111	ç
136	88	1000 1000	ê
137	89	1000 1001	ë
138	8A	1000 1010	è
139	8B	1000 1011	ï
140	8C	1000 1100	î
141	8D	1000 1101	ì
142	8E	1000 1110	Ä
143	8F	1000 1111	Å
144	90	1001 0000	É
145	91	1001 0001	æ
146	92	1001 0010	Æ
147	93	1001 0011	ô
148	94	1001 0100	ö
149	95	1001 0101	ò
150	96	1001 0110	û
151	97	1001 0111	ù
152	98	1001 1000	ÿ
153	99	1001 1001	Ö
154	9A	1001 1010	Ü

Dec X_{10}	*Hex* X_{16}	*Binary* X_2	*ASCII Character*
155	9B	1001 1011	¢
156	9C	1001 1100	£
157	9D	1001 1101	¥
158	9E	1001 1110	₧
159	9F	1001 1111	ƒ
160	A0	1010 0000	á
161	A1	1010 0001	í
162	A2	1010 0010	ó
163	A3	1010 0011	ú
164	A4	1010 0100	ñ
165	A5	1010 0101	Ñ
166	A6	1010 0110	ª
167	A7	1010 0111	º
168	A8	1010 1000	º
169	A9	1010 1001	¿
170	AA	1010 1010	⌐
171	AB	1010 1011	¬
172	AC	1010 1100	½
173	AD	1010 1101	¼
174	AE	1010 1110	¡
175	AF	1010 1111	«
176	B0	1011 0000	»
177	B1	1011 0001	░
178	B2	1011 0010	▒
179	B3	1011 0011	█
180	B4	1011 0100	│
181	B5	1011 0101	┤
182	B6	1011 0110	╡
183	B7	1011 0111	╢
184	B8	1011 1000	╖
185	B9	1011 1001	╕

Dec X_{10}	*Hex* X_{16}	*Binary* X_2	*ASCII Character*
186	BA	1011 1010	╣
187	BB	1011 1011	║
188	BC	1011 1100	╗
189	BD	1011 1101	╝
190	BE	1011 1110	╜
191	BF	1011 1111	╛
192	C0	1100 0000	┐
193	C1	1100 0001	└
194	C2	1100 0010	┴
195	C3	1100 0011	┬
196	C4	1100 0100	├
197	C5	1100 0101	─
198	C6	1100 0110	┼
199	C7	1100 0111	╞
200	C8	1100 1000	╟
201	C9	1100 1001	╚
202	CA	1100 1010	╔
203	CB	1100 1011	╩
204	CC	1100 1100	╦
205	CD	1100 1101	╠
206	CE	1100 1110	═
207	CF	1100 1111	╬
208	D0	1101 0000	╧
209	D1	1101 0001	╨
210	D2	1101 0010	╤
211	D3	1101 0011	╥
212	D4	1101 0100	╙
213	D5	1101 0101	╘
214	D6	1101 0110	╒
215	D7	1101 0111	╓
216	D8	1101 1000	╫

Dec X_{10}	*Hex* X_{16}	*Binary* X_2	*ASCII Character*
217	D9	1101 1001	╪
218	DA	1101 1010	┘
219	DB	1101 1011	┌
220	DC	1101 1100	█
221	DD	1101 1101	▄
222	DE	1101 1110	▌
223	DF	1101 1111	▐
224	E0	1110 0000	▀
225	E1	1110 0001	α
226	E2	1110 0010	β
227	E3	1110 0011	Γ
228	E4	1110 0100	π
229	E5	1110 0101	Σ
230	E6	1110 0110	σ
231	E7	1110 0111	μ
232	E8	1110 1000	γ
233	E9	1110 1001	Φ
234	EA	1110 1010	θ
235	EB	1110 1011	Ω
236	EC	1110 1100	δ
237	ED	1110 1101	∞
238	EE	1110 1110	ø
239	EF	1110 1111	∈
240	F0	1110 0000	∩
241	F1	1111 0001	≡
242	F2	1111 0010	±
243	F3	1111 0011	≥
244	F4	1111 0100	≤
245	F5	1111 0101	⌠
246	F6	1111 0110	⌡
247	F7	1111 0111	÷

Dec X_{10}	*Hex* X_{16}	*Binary* X_2	*ASCII Character*
248	F8	1111 1000	≈
249	F9	1111 1001	∘
250	FA	1111 1010	•
251	FB	1111 1011	·
252	FC	1111 1100	√
253	FD	1111 1101	^{n}
254	FE	1111 1110	^{2}
255	FF	1111 1111	■

INDEX

Symbols

A

B

C

D

E

F

G

H

I

J–K

L

M

N

O

P

Q–R

S

T

W

X-Z

Sams Teach Yourself Database Programming with Visual Basic 6 in 21 Days

Curtis Smith

Sams Teach Yourself Database Programming with Visual Basic 6 in 21 Days is a tutorial that allows the reader to learn about working with databases in a set amount of time. The book presents the reader with a step-by-step approach to learning what can be a critical topic for developing applications. Each week will focus on a different aspect of database programming with Visual Basic. Week 1—Data Controls and Microsoft Access Databases. Learn about issues related to building simple database applications using the extensive collection of data controls available with VB. Week 2—Programming with the Microsoft Jet Engine. Concentrate on techniques for creating database applications using Visual Basic code. Week Three—Programming with the ODBC Interface and SQL. Study advanced topics such as SQL data definition and manipulation language, and issues for multiuser applications such as locking schemes, database integrity, and application-level security.

$45.00 US/$64.95 CDN *900 pp.*
ISBN: 0-672-31308-1

Sams Teach Yourself More Visual Basic 6 in 21 Days

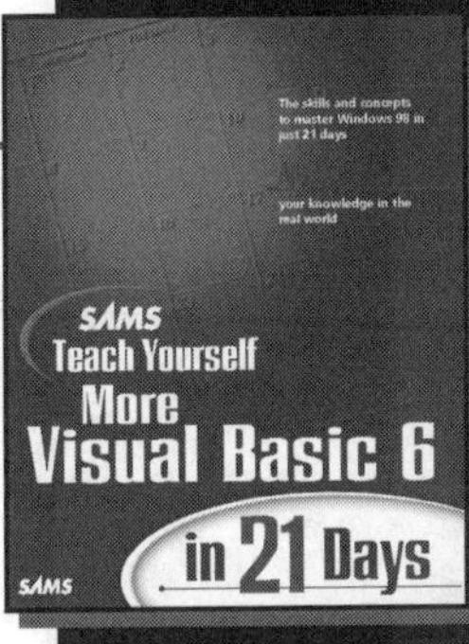

Lowell Mauer

Provides comprehensive, self-taught coverage of the most sought after topics in Visual Basic programming. This book uses the step-by-step approach of the best-selling *Sams Teach Yourself* series to continue more detailed coverage of the latest version of Visual Basic. Not only will this book cover a wide array of topics, but it will also go into each topic to a level that the reader will be able to apply to his own programs. In addition, this book will include various tips and tricks of Visual Basic programming that will help the more inexperienced programmer. Topics include: enhanced controls, collections, loops, and other things; procedures, functions, and logic; MDI and SDI window types; database processing and designing a database application; data-bound controls, Data Form Wizard, and OLE drag and drop; Internet programming and ActiveX documents; building online help; and using Crystal Reports. Includes complete coverage of database applications. Uses real-world applications to demonstrate specialized programming.

$29.99 US/$42.95 CDN *700 pp.*
ISBN: 0-672-31307-3

Sams Teach Yourself Object-Oriented Programming with Visual Basic in 21 Days

John Conley

In just 21 days, you'll have all the skills you need to get up and running efficiently. With this complete tutorial, you'll master the basics and then move on to the more advanced features and concepts. Understand the fundamentals of object-oriented programming with Visual Basic. Master all of the new and advanced features that object-oriented programming with Visual Basic offers. Learn how to effectively use the latest tools and features of topic, by following practical, real-world examples. Get expert tips from a leading authority on implementing object-oriented programming with Visual Basic in the corporate environment. This book is designed for the way you learn. Go chapter by chapter through the step-by-step lessons, or just choose those lessons that interest you the most.

$39.99 US/$57.95 CDN *600 pp.*
ISBN: 0-672-31299-9

Sams Teach Yourself Visual InterDev 6 in 21 Days

Michael Van Hoozer

This book is organized in the familiar day-by-day format of the *Sams Teach Yourself* series. Each lesson provides an overview of the topic being presented as well as hands-on examples. Each chapter ends with a summary as well as quiz questions and exercises to verify the reader's learning. The book will cover a number of key topics related to Visual InterDev, including: designing and developing dynamic Web sites; editing Web pages; working with images and multimedia; client-side scripting; working with databases; using the visual data tool; understanding database component; and more! In addition to an overall revision of the book for the new version, the following specific changes have been made: exercises added to all the chapters; the weeks in review expanded to include hardcore example applications incorporating the elements of the previous week; coverage of new Visual InterDev features added including Dynamic HTML, scriptlets; and more. After only a year in release, the first version of Microsoft Visual InterDev is used by over 225,000 professional developers worldwide, making it the leading Web application development tool, with nearly twice as many users as its nearest competitor. Visual InterDev is Microsoft's primary development tool for creating dynamic Internet, intranet, and Web-based applications. The reader will learn about existing Active Desktop features such as advanced HTML, ActiveX, and ADO as well as new features such as Dynamic HTML and scriptlets.

$34.99 US/$50.95 CDN *750 pp.*
ISBN: 0-672-31251-4

Add to Your Sams Library Today with the Best Books for Programming, Operating Systems, and New Technologies

To order, visit our Web site at www.mcp.com or fax us at

1-800-835-3202

ISBN	Quantity	Description of Item	Unit Cost	Total Cost
0-672-31308-1		Sams Teach Yourself Database Programming with Visual Basic 6 in 21 Days	$45.00	
0-672-31307-3		Sams Teach Yourself More Visual Basic 6 in 21 Days	$29.99	
0-672-31299-9		Sams Teach Yourself OOP With Visual Basic in 21 Days	$39.99	
0-672-31251-4		Sams Teach Yourself Visual InterDev 6 in 21 Days	$34.99	
		Shipping and Handling: See information below.		
		TOTAL		

Shipping and Handling

Standard	$5.00
2nd Day	$10.00
Next Day	$17.50
International	$40.00

201 W. 103rd Street, Indianapolis, Indiana 46290 1-800-835-3202 — FAX

Book ISBN 0-672-31310-3

Order Your VB Program Disk Today!